THE SEXUAL DEAD-END

by
Stephen Green

LONDON

© Stephen Green 1992

The right of Stephen Green to be identified as the Author of the Work has been asserted by him in accordance with the Copyright, Designs and Patents Act 1988

First published in 1992 by
Broadview Books
PO Box 782 London SW16 2YT

All rights reserved. No part of this publication may be reproduced, in any form or by any means, without the prior written permission of the publishers, with the exception of short attributed passages of text in context for criticism.

ISBN 0 9519934 0 2   Paperback

British Library Cataloguing in Publication Data:

Green, Stephen
The Sexual Dead-End

A catalogue record for this book is available from the British Library

Notice

Nothing is implied in this publication about any person living or dead which is not herein explicitly stated.

Nothing is therefore to be inferred from this publication that is not distinctly stated in the text.

The reader is warned that this publication contains written and visual material of a nature which could cause offence or shock.

Printed in Great Britain by BPCC Wheatons Ltd, Exeter

Contents:

			Page
Chapter	1:	An introduction to gay politics	1
Chapter	2:	Homosexual behaviour and the law	12
Chapter	3:	The effects of the Sexual Offences Act 1967	22
Chapter	4:	The homosexual subculture	33
Chapter	5:	The battle for Clause 28	46
Chapter	6:	How many and how promiscuous?	58
Chapter	7:	The inner drive to make sexual contact	69
Chapter	8:	Homosexual activity	80
Chapter	9:	Disease and the active homosexual	90
Chapter	10:	The prejudiced virus	103
Chapter	11:	The politics of AIDS	116
Chapter	12:	The myth of the gentle gay	130
Chapter	13:	The origins of a homosexual orientation	144
Chapter	14:	Recruitment into the homosexual lifestyle	158
Chapter	15:	Deceiving the young	172
Chapter	16:	Paedophilia	186
Chapter	17:	Paedophile groups and their supporters	204
Chapter	18:	The invention of children's rights	217
Chapter	19:	Assault on the family	231
Chapter	20:	Lesbianism	244
Chapter	21:	Lesbian religion	257
Chapter	22:	The myth of a Christian homosexual theology	269
Chapter	23:	The Lesbian & Gay Christian Movement	281
Chapter	24:	Homosexual marriages and emotional orphans	295
Chapter	25:	Change of scenes: healing the homosexual	309
Chapter	26:	Iron John or Jesus Christ?	322
Chapter	27:	Homosexuality and the parties of the left	334
Chapter	28:	Gay rights and the victimless crime	344
Chapter	29:	Homosexuality and Conservatism	358
Chapter	30:	Gay rights v liberal democracy	365
Chapter	31:	The sexual marketplace	374
Chapter	32:	Gay materialism or family values?	383
Chapter	33:	Pressure groups, AIDS, and the myth of pluralism	389
Chapter	34:	Homosexuality, decline and fall	398
Chapter	35:	Filling the spiritual vacuum	407
Chapter	36:	Back to normality	420
Appendix	1:	The signatories to the Independent 1/2/88	434
Appendix	2:	D of H figures for AIDS deaths, cases, HIV+	447
Appendix	3:	The Blaze article by Michael Swift	450
References			453
Index			469

1
An introduction to gay politics

Over the last twenty-five years, a "gay mythology" has been carefully built up. Through soft-left newspapers and periodicals, sympathetic radio and television programmes and letters to national press and local free sheets, gay activists have attempted to convince the outside world that active homosexuals are gentle, caring, normal, faithful, family-minded individuals who would never pose any threat to children, nor any problem for the moral or physical health of society and whose "sexual orientation" is unchangeable. Gay politics depends on an uncritical acceptance of the mythology to argue that the sexual activities of homosexuals should be the moral and legal equivalent of normal heterosexual love and marriage. In fact, although "the gays" claim a desire for less public ignorance of homosexuality, a dispassionate investigation is the last thing they want.

Any objection to homosexuality "prejudiced"

In the "gay mythology" it is irrational to have one age of consent for "heterosexuals" and another for "homosexuals," what people do in the privacy of their bedrooms is up to them, and it has been most unlucky that the disease AIDS has affected people involved in homosexual activity, considering that in Africa AIDS is spread "heterosexually."

With great diligence, liberal commentators, media presenters and researchers and indeed all the chattering bien pensants have assisted the building-up of this mythology, adjusting the facts, some through ignorance, some through mendacity and some through a process of psychological denial, to fit their preconceptions, to the extent that it is considered politically incorrect in the extreme to voice any objection to any part of it. To take just one example, the head of a local human rights agency was asked on American television, just before a gay rights measure was to be debated, whether she thought there really was no moral difference between giving special protection to people who happened to be born black and giving special protection to those who had made a voluntary choice to commit sodomy with other men. "Why," she announced, "gays would never do that!"[1]

Liberal myths about homosexuality

The mythology was readily available. It was most painstakingly raised to an art-form in the old GLC's glossy "Changing the World - a London Charter for GAY and LESBIAN rights," which we shall examine. But the truth was contained in published research and in the many books "written by gays to be read by gays,"[2] which I took the trouble to read, in newspapers and periodicals written for the same market, in medical books and articles in learned journals and of course in various news items. I really did come to the study with an open mind and with no preconceptions about the reality of homosexual behaviour and lifestyles, or for that matter about the psychology and healing of homosexuality, so it was as much a learning process for me as it will be for the reader. As we embark together on this educational voyage, the liberal myths about homosexuality will evaporate one by one.

At the same time, I am very conscious that what is to me and to the majority of my readers in part an intellectual exercise touches the very being of the people whom this study concerns, namely people with homosexual personalities and those locked into homosexual lifestyles. This book challenges the authenticity of their sexual desires, and although I might declare that I care about them and want the best for them, still I do not expect them to be much impressed. Indeed, many homosexuals and their liberal apologists - I cannot use the word friends, because I do not believe them to be true friends in the sense of wanting the objective best for them - will be so challenged by what has been for me a simple research project that they will not be able to bear the logical conclusions that arise from what I hope has been dispassionate study, careful respect for context and a search for the truth.

The ideology of the homosexual movement

The emergence of homosexuality as a "movement" started in June 1969 in America. A routine raid was carried out by police on the Stonewall gay bar in Christopher Street, New York, well known for illegal sexual behaviour.[3] The police saw what they expected and began making arrests. The "camp queens" - as homosexual activist Roy Burns puts it - fought back and a riot ensued. Militant "gays" decided that they should use the same language as black civil rights workers and invented homosexual rights.[4] The day of the Stonewall riot has become "Gay Pride" day, and is "celebrated throughout the United States, often with the blessing of local city councils."[5] In the UK, the latest homosexual lobby group is named after the Stonewall riot. An Australian group has similarly adopted the Stonewall name.

According to Roy Burns, the early American homosexual rights campaigns were witnessed by two British visitors, Bob Mellor, a student at the London School of Economics, and Aubrey Walter when on a visit to New York in 1970. On their return to the UK they resolved to start a British campaign on the same lines, and the Gay Liberation Front was formed. Roy Burns writes:

> Gay Liberation Front was to build on the preceding decade's overthrow of convention. Indeed, the theme "proud to be gay" was revolutionary. It transferred the stigma from the individual homosexual to the bigoted opposition. This was a brilliant strategy. Homosexuals were not now sick or perverted: what was sick was the prejudice existing within society against homosexuals and homosexuality. If one was not sick or perverted then one could be proud to be gay.[6]

Those who write to newspapers from time to time complaining that a nice old word has been robbed of its meaning miss the point. "Gay" applied to homosexuality is a masterpiece of marketing. The word contains just the right flavour of liberated, happy-go-lucky, debonair, bon-viveur rejection of all that is seen by its users as out-moded, restrictive, staid and circumscribed morality. Some activists now want to be "queer and proud of it" again but whilst I admire their honesty, I believe they will lose support.

"Gay" - a good piece of marketing

As American lawyer Roger Magnuson says:

> "Gay" is used to suggest a cheerful, free, and sunny approach to life. "Lesbian" suggests something more assertive and masculine. Both project a consciously chosen identity, putting a more positive face on the respective groups than the taunting language of the street.[7]

Therefore, "Gay" is being open about a homosexual orientation and feeling good about it. It is pride in the achievements of allegedly homosexual authors and artists. It is walking hand-in-hand with a "gay" lover and daring the decent to censure you. And in case the man in the street *is* tempted to disapprove, "gay" needs "rights." Again,

Roger Magnuson explains:

> Its goal was, and is, total acceptance of homosexuality. In seeking that end result, the movement ran up against two significant social impediments: laws that made homosexual conduct illegal (eg laws against sodomy) and language that made homosexual conduct unattractive (eg "sodomy"). A movement aggressively seeking full social acceptance had to clear both hurdles. Laws could be changed only if public perception were changed; public perception could be changed only if language were changed. Imagine a group calling for "bugger's rights" or speaking of "bugger's pride."[8]

The sort of language used in American gay rights legislation, as Roger Magnuson explains, speaks of forbidding "discrimination" based on a person's "affectional or sexual preference," and again prejudges the issue:

> To be affectionate is an unqualified good. ... We like to receive affection and give it. To interrupt the affection two people have for one another comes off as a Scrooge-like interference in wholesome and humane relationships. The same is true of "preference" in tolerant society; a gentleman always recognises another's preferences.[9]

A polite term for buggery invented

Apologists for homosexual behaviour and their allies in the media and medical profession have predictably tried to encourage use of the term "anal intercourse" instead of "buggery."[10] We already had "social intercourse" and "sexual intercourse" and now we have "anal intercourse." It is hoped that by use of this expression, pseudo-sexual acts involving the part of the body used for the excretion of human waste will be regarded as another sort of normal sexual activity, and by implication that those performing such acts will be regarded as sexually normal.

Nevertheless, if we keep to definition, the expression "sexual intercourse" only applies to the genital sexual union of male and female, and that is how I shall use the term in this book. Homosexuals need to invent other practices to achieve orgasmic satisfaction, and we shall consider these in chapter 8 and the health risks involved in chapter 9.

The rage with which homosexual activists greet the terms "sodomy" or "buggery" is an indication of how seriously the distortion of language referred to needs to be taken. I was told after one discussion

An introduction to gay politics

programme that I had "insulted every gay man in the studio" simply by the very use of the term "buggery."[11]

"Gay" better than "homosexual"

Homosexual activists argue that being "gay" is better than being just "homosexual." "Homosexual," so the argument runs, means "self-oppression:" being ashamed of what you are and concealing it. Sir Maurice Oldfield, with his secret hordes of homosexual pornography and furtive assignations with "rent-boys," his hiding his homosexuality from vetting committees, possibly denying it to himself, so that it would not damage his career, was homosexual, not gay. He was "self-oppressed," in the sense that he censured his own homosexuality. Homosexuals are "in the closet," whereas "gays" are "out and we're staying out."[12] If "gay is good," that is if homosexuality is as "good" as heterosexuality, then a number of things follow inevitably:

Firstly, it will be right to "come out" and tell others about your "gayness." The "gay movement" depends on individuals "coming out," and by this is meant an acceptance and even celebration of their homosexuality. It means announcing to other homosexuals, to teachers, pupils, family, Miriam Stoppard, in fact to anyone who will listen, that a discovery of "gay orientation" has been made. The coming out process is of course very difficult to undo, and once having made the statement and become part of the "gay community," the impression will be the stronger that homosexuality is not arrived at by choice.

Homosexuality is "unchangeable"

Secondly, it must never be suggested that it would be possible to be anything other than "gay." Gay rights activists, like Peter Campbell of the Conservative Group for Homosexual Equality, are especially keen to foster an acceptance of the myth:

> that homosexuality, like left-handedness, is a fact of life about some people who do not differ in other respects from the majority; that it is not a matter of seduction, corruption, perversion or whim.[13]

Lord Gifford said more or less the same thing in the House of Lords debate on clause 28 of the 1988 Local Government Bill,[14] knowing that if homosexuality is a matter of choice, or a learned pattern of behaviour, then the demands of homosexual rights activists for special beneficial treatment for those who choose to follow a homosexual lifestyle cannot be treated with the same respect as if homosexuals were a "third sex," with their sexual persuasion immutable. Before 1970, as we shall see later, virtually all psychotherapeutic and psychological opinion treated homosexuality as a psychological condition; as a "pathology" in other words. Charles Socarides for instance attributes it to "severe disturbances in the early child-parent relationship when critical maturational changes are taking place"[15]

Clearly homosexuality as a psychological condition does not square with "gay is good," and a campaign was mounted by militant homosexuals in the USA and the UK to persuade psychiatrists that a homosexual condition was not something about which they should be concerned. They had a great deal of success, and their results are documented in chapter 13.

Gay writers and homosexual activists are dismissive of any attempts to change from homosexuality to heterosexuality. This willingness to belittle the attempts of men and women to be free from homosexual actions and tendencies should come as no surprise; it harms the political needs of the "gay rights" proponents if homosexuals can change. "Gay rights" is based on the assumption that homosexuals are deeply analogous to racial civil rights groups, and if a single homosexual becomes heterosexual, the argument falls as surely as if a black man were to become white. We shall discover whether it is possible for a homosexual to become heterosexual in chapter 25.

Language of the market-place appropriated

At the same time as arguing that homosexuals cannot change their orientation, activists claim that it is valid to *choose* to be homosexual. This cynical adoption of the language of the market-place enabled the GLC to claim that "many of us never consider we have a choice of sexuality as that "choice" is so clearly an unequal one."[16] It was evidently thought that, in "Thatcher's New Britain," anything that widened "choice" would be seen as a Good Thing. So:

> throughout this [GLC Lesbian & Gay] Charter the use of the words "lesbian," "gay" and "homosexual" shall include those who choose to define themselves as bisexual and anyone who chooses to express or acknowledge the homosexual part of themselves.[17]

The evidence seems to show that the use of the word "choose" in connection with bisexual behaviour was extremely apt. In a piece about changing sexual habits, a young woman illustrated the point that sexual behaviour is heavily influenced by the cultural environment in which people move. She was reported as saying:

> "Friends of mine are very worried because lots of them have had encounters with bisexual men. A couple of them have even taken

An introduction to gay politics

the (AIDS) test. At art college everybody tried bisexuality. There wasn't one straight man there."[18]

The decision to "try" bisexuality just because everyone else is trying it illustrates how fashionable homosexual behaviour has become amongst those who wish to believe themselves liberated.

Homosexuality "may be chosen"

The homosexual activist can claim that a homosexual choice is revolutionary, because it challenges the accepted order. Activists will skip from arguing homosexuality as an immutable orientation to seeing homosexuality as a valid sexual choice just according to political expediency.

It takes some getting used to, to recognise that the pragmatic homosexual apologist is quite prepared to make with the same breath the claim that sexual orientation is unchangeable, and also the contradictory statement that people should be able to choose to be homosexual. Both statements ignore the truth, yet each is useful at different times to the libertarian view that homosexuality is as good and as valid as heterosexuality.

Far-left homosexuals are angered by the arguments of political expediency and by those of their number who are "self-oppressed" - that is, apologetic - enough about homosexuality to discuss the origins of a homosexual condition, even though this might only be to claim that "cures" for the condition do not work. The possibility of changing from homosexual to heterosexual is embarrassing to the born-like-it activist view, whilst origins and cures are irrelevant to the radical.

Labour MP caught in a time-warp

When the openly homosexual Labour MP Chris Smith told the House of Commons in a debate on Clause 28 that homosexuality cannot be promoted, that Labour councils did not want to promote it, that "We are what we are, it is impossible to force or to encourage someone into a different sexuality from that which pertains to them," he was using the arguments of political expediency. Radical activist Peter Kent-Baguley of the Labour Campaign for Lesbian and Gay Rights quite rightly took him to task for perpetuating myths, "like sexuality being concretely pre-set during conception (or immediately afterwards)" and thus for using "the ideology of the biological determinists."

It was, according to Mr Kent-Baguley, "as though the gay liberation movement of the early 70s had never happened; as though ideas about the *social* rather than the *biological* construction of sexuality had never been discussed; as though the notion and *reality* of *choice* had never been recognised." Chris Smith was caught "in a Wolfenden time-warp," and his argument that "what is important is to enable people to understand the sexuality that they have, and that cannot be changed," was dismissed on the good ground that "it perpetuates the archaic theory of innate genetically determined sexuality."[19]

Freedom of sinful choice

We should be grateful to Mr Kent-Baguley for his honesty and clarity of argument. There is indeed an element of choice in sexual activity and type of lifestyle, and it is interesting to recognise that this is exactly the position taken by St Paul, and maintained up to the beginning of the nineteenth century, that homosexual activity is a matter of sinful choice. Although I do not suppose that Mr Kent-Baguley would recognise the worth of the word "sinful," I should expect him to agree that even with all the advances in understanding the origins of homosexual orientation (which he would find irrelevant) people in the end make up their own minds whether to begin homosexual practice, or not.

Indeed it is argued that it may be politically necessary to choose homosexuality, especially for women. Some women choose to follow a homosexual pattern of behaviour after years of heterosexuality, a pattern that is rare for male homosexuals. Again, the activists oversimplify this procedure, as we shall see when we examine the psychological background to lesbianism. London Lesbian Line, to whom "agony aunts" Gill Cox, Marjorie Proops and Anna Raeburn refer correspondents,[20] claims in a leaflet:

> *Being a lesbian can be fun. Being a lesbian need not be a problem ... Any woman can be a lesbian but we are constantly divided from one another by expectations of heterosexuality. Who you relate to should be your choice.*[21]

The slogan "Every woman can be a lesbian" appeared on a Gay Liberation Front badge, whilst the American National Organisation for Women states "The simple fact is that every woman must be willing to be identified as a lesbian to be fully feminist."[22]

Essential to proselytise

Thirdly, it must be essential to tell others about the goodness of being "gay." We shall look in chapters 14 and 15 at the way homosexuality is promoted amongst the young, but readers who wish to follow up the indoctrination of school-children could also look at the booklet "Gay Lessons."[23]

The cynicism of "helping all pupils to see that they are not necessarily heterosexual, but that their sexuality can be a matter of active and positive choice"[24] is very much part of the "gay agenda." Children often pass through some sort of homosexual phase at school, typified by crushes on teachers or older pupils, and sometimes involving actual sexual activity. But if gay is good, why bother to progress to heterosexuality? In an atmosphere of benevolence towards homosexuality, these children will be encouraged to see a "homosexual orientation" as their proper leaning, and to take "pride" in it, believing that it is a good thing to have.

Fourthly, it would be oppressive for society in its laws and morality to treat "gay" persons differently from "straight" persons in any respect. "Gays," like black people and women, so the argument runs, are oppressed. It is better for this argument if homosexuality is innate than if it is adopted by choice.

In fifth place, any "non-gay" person discriminating against a person on account of their "gayness" is said to be behaving irrationally, psychotically even. A person exhibiting this condition is termed "homophobic," as a claimed result partly of a fear of their own latent homosexuality and partly of their conditioning in a "heterosexist" society. Some Christians who should know better have taken up this word from the homosexual activists' lexicon without really knowing what it means to the activist and have urged fellow Christians not to be "homophobic." Being uneasy about "gay rights" whilst treating individual homosexuals with charity and praying that they will be drawn to healing is the position of one or two groups claiming to be "pro-family" and is thought to assure homosexuals of the sincerity and lack of homophobia of these Christian groups. Such a stance is still rank "homophobia" to the activist. Homophobia is anything less than full acceptance of homosexuality as an equal and valid lifestyle. Furthermore, for the activist, the law must establish that a "homophobic" person is also behaving unlawfully.

Talking up the numbers and practices of homosexuals

Next, it becomes essential to claim that homosexuals exist in large and growing numbers. In the 1970s the Campaign for Homosexual Equality spoke of 1 in 20 people being homosexual. In the mid 1980s it rose to 1 in 10. Recently one activist claimed 26% of London's population to be homosexual,[25] and Richard Kirker, of the "Lesbian and Gay Christian Movement" has claimed that one third of the Anglican Clergy is homosexual.[26] We shall investigate the true figures in Chapter 6, observing that it is always in the interests of activists to claim the biggest possible numbers in their client group.

Finally, activists seem driven to lower society to their level and regularly mock and caricature what is noble and good about human relations and sexuality. They appear to hate the mere existence of decency, morality, and Godliness. If the behaviour, which we shall record, of the male homosexual transvestite "nuns" known as the "Sisters of Perpetual Indulgence" or of homosexual activists and abortionists outside St Patrick's Cathedral in New York, or of "Outrage" at St Michael's Belgravia was and is not satanic, then the word has lost all meaning. A report to the Tasmanian State Legislature concluded:

> *If all sex can be made tawdry, then gay sex is no worse; if all use the anus for sexual pleasure then homosexual sex is OK. Where parents wish to shield children from the worst and to gradually introduce them to their sexuality, gay activists want even the youngest to be as sexually driven as they. Gays revel in scandal and the warping of social convention. In the guise of "realism" homosexuals promote a society with only one standard - that of the lowest common denominator - themselves. The reason gays dress like clowns and act so silly in their demonstrations? - to show their contempt for society as a whole.*[27]

"Coming out"

The fundamental plank of the gay structure remains the practice of "coming out." According to one book "Written by gays to be read by gays":

> *The phrase "coming out," as used by the gays, has three meanings: to acknowledge one's homosexuality to oneself; to reveal oneself as homosexual to other gay people; and lastly to declare one's homosexuality to everyone and anyone.*[28]

Roy Burns explains the significance of coming out like this:

> *The importance to the individual of coming out is now central to the entire gay movement, and terms such as "coming out" and "out of the closet" have passed from being the jargon of a subculture to being a part of the general vernacular.*
>
> *The crucial legacy of Gay Liberation Front was the concept of telling other people that you were gay. It is very difficult if someone*

An introduction to gay politics

you know and like comes out to you to retain homophobic attitudes. Coming out was to have an immense effect on public opinion.[29]

It also, as Mr Burns goes on to say, encourages yet more people to come out and the visibility of those coming out together with the fury with which liberals shout down any opposition gradually changes public perception. In the end, activists hope that every homosexual will have come out as gay, and if they won't, then activists claim them as homosexuals anyway and force then to confirm or deny it - a process known as "outing" the person involved. How very different, as we shall see in chapter 2, from the reign of King Henry VIII.

2
Homosexual behaviour and the law

It is appropriate in the face of the language of gay politics to look at what the law says about homosexual activity, and to see how the law has developed. We shall see that sexual acts committed against or with members of one's own sex have been totally proscribed in British Law until very recently, and that even the limited freedom from prosecution that practitioners of homosexual acts now enjoy still leaves such acts immoral in the eyes of the law. Even in circumstances where homosexual activity is not illegal, the law still describes it as grossly indecent.

The first Act of Law in 1533

Prior to the reign of King Henry VIII, homosexual activity, and indeed other indecent and immoral conduct, was dealt with under the common law, that is, the law which has come into being through precedent, and also by ecclesiastical courts under Canon Law. However, when the King limited the sphere of church involvement, he brought certain offences into the realm of the secular courts.

Buggery was one of them, and an Act for the Punishment of the Vice of Buggery became law in 1533, with a maximum sentence of death. The Act calls it "a detestable and abominable vice ... committed with mankind or beast." It "pleased the King's Highness" that "no person offending in any such Offence shall be admitted to his Clergy,"[1] so he would not have been pleased by the American Episcopal Church, but more of that later.

The Offences Against The Person Act 1861

The last execution for buggery was in 1836, although the death penalty itself was not abolished until 1861.[2] The 1861 Act which abolished the death penalty for buggery was passed to consolidate and amend the law relating to Offences against the Person.

Under a heading of "unnatural offences," virtually the same wording as in 1533 is employed in connection with sodomy and bestiality, which are named as such. Buggery was an "abominable crime" and was punished by life imprisonment or by a minimum of ten years penal servitude. The standard became adopted that it is not necessary for there to be "the actual emission of seed" for carnal knowledge to be established; proof of penetration suffices. Attempted buggery on a male or a female also became an offence under the Offences against the Person Act as did indecent assault on males and females.[3]

An indication of the greater severity with which Parliament viewed such offences when committed between men is given by the relative terms of imprisonment stated. An indecent assault on a woman was liable to two years' imprisonment, and whilst the same assault on a man could be punished in the same way, the courts had discretion to impose ten years penal servitude.

Despite the relative severity of offences against men, it is clear from a careful reading of the 1861 Act that the common preconception,[4] that lesbianism was not outlawed in Queen Victoria's time because her ministers did not want to admit to the Queen that such behaviour existed, may be misplaced and is certainly irrelevant.

In the first place, the Act contains a quite detailed enough catalogue of depraved human behaviour which it might have been thought good to spare the Queen by the same argument. Secondly, the Act does not actually specify the sex of the person sexually assaulting a man, the person who participates passively in buggery, the human partner in bestiality, or the person sexually assaulting a woman.

Although men are clearly the more likely to commit an indecent assault on a woman, the crime could equally well be committed by a woman even if the woman assaulted were a willing participant. It is not necessary to put the label "lesbian" on two women committing such an offence any more than it is necessary to label two men committing the equivalent offence "queers" or "gays." The law here categorises offences, not people.

The Criminal Law Amendment act 1885

Twenty-four years passed before acts of indecency between males other than buggery and indecent assault were specifically made illegal in the statute book. The Criminal Law Amendment Act 1885 is probably best known for Josephine Butler's courageous and unremitting efforts to stamp out child prostitution, which at the time was endemic. It raised the age at which a girl could give her consent to sexual intercourse from twelve, under the Offences against the Person Act, to sixteen.[5]

It should be noted that the last two decades of the nineteenth century were a time of appalling vice, drunkenness, drug abuse and crime against the person. One of the factors, or symptoms perhaps, was the fashion for compartmentalising public houses. This reached its height around 1890, when some pubs had as many as 15 "boxes." As one historian of drinks and drinking observes:

> Small and enclosed bars invited crime the length and breadth of the country, according to magistrates of the day. Snugs were especially singled out for attack: there had been robberies in snugs in Hull, and a prostitute of 19 had robbed a man of 70 in a snug at the "Lion Hotel," Lincoln, in 1894.
>
> Among the upper classes, only "bohemians" went into pubs during the late 1800s. A 96-year-old matriarch named Rosie who was still patronising a snug in Islington, London, during the late 1960s, used to entertain drinkers with a story about one such Bohemian, Oscar Wilde. She claimed she had once given Wilde sexual satisfaction when she was a teenage flower-girl. She was not a whore, she explained; she had done the deed by hand, for two pence. Most of the girls did it for "gents," and the practice was known as "twopenny nutting." Subsequently the term, "I don't give a twopenny toss" found its way into common usage.[6]

It may be that homosexual activity short of buggery between males was also beginning to be recognised as a problem in the 1880s, for at the committee stage of the 1885 Bill, Henry Labouchere put down an amendment to make guilty of a crime and an offence any male person who "in public or private, commits ... or procures or attempts to procure the commission by any male person of any act of gross indecency with another male person." This amendment became section 11 of the 1885 Act.[7]

The Vagrancy Act 1898

The Vagrancy Act may well have been intended, as some homosexual writers maintain, primarily to cover importuning by pimps for prostitution,[8] but the Act also covers the approach of a male for homosexual acts when it deems "a rogue and a vagabond" every male person who "in any public place persistently solicits or importunes for immoral purposes."[9]

Homosexual behaviour and the law

It is all very well for gay activists to complain that:

> there was no intention by the legislators that it should be used against homosexuals. It is an interesting comment on contemporary attitudes that the police and the courts interpreted the clause as covering homosexual soliciting, and it was soon applied almost exclusively in this context, a practice which has persisted to this day,[10]

but the truth is that the courts have always had the responsibility of the interpretation of terms used in Acts of Parliament. These three Acts dating from the late nineteenth century that deal with sexual offences, including the Vagrancy Act, are not at all exceptional. Buggery is the introduction of the male organ into the human rectum, except in bestiality, where it refers to penetration of the rectum or vagina, with the animal active or passive. Acts of gross indecency have customarily been interpreted as all other homosexual activity and an immoral purpose covers homosexual activity of all kinds, prostitution and extra-marital sexual activity.

The Criminal Law Amendment Act 1921

There was now an anomaly inasmuch as an offence existed of gross indecency between males, with no comparable offence between women. In 1921 there was an attempt to put this right, and an amendment was accepted by the Commons to the 1921 Criminal Law Amendment Bill. When the Bill reached the Lords the amendment was withdrawn without a vote on the grounds that if there were to be a prosecution, "it would make public to thousands of people that there was this offence, that there was such a horror."[11]

> Lord Desart, in pointing to the dangers of "spreading" lesbian sexual conduct by making it a criminal offence, drew support for his argument from the aftermath of the Oscar Wilde trials. These had "attracted very great public attention" and were followed by "a perfect outburst of that offence all through the country"[12]

What is more probably true is that the police had been waiting for clarification from the courts before taking action against known offenders.

The Public Health Act 1936

Since a great many homosexual acts take place in public conveniences, the Public Health Act of 1936, which contains a section referring to "loitering without reasonable excuse in a public sanitary convenience" is relevant to this examination, and may well have been included in the 1936 Act to cope with situations where a specific offence of importuning or indecency could not be proven.[13] It would have been, and remains, difficult to see why someone would wish to loiter in a public convenience except for the purpose of procuring a homosexual act. We shall investigate "Cottaging," as the practice is known within the homosexual network, in Chapter 7.

The Sexual Offences Act 1956

The Sexual Offences Act 1956 consolidated a number of Acts of Parliament including the Offences against the Person Act 1861, the Criminal Law Amendment Act 1885 and the Vagrancy Act 1898, and repealed the relevant parts of those Acts of Parliament, which in the case of the 1885 and 1898 Acts was the whole Act. The Sexual Offences Act 1956 is more or less the last word in law on such crimes with the exception of the Indecency with Children Act 1960, and the Sexual Offences Act 1967, which we shall consider presently.

Under a heading of "Unnatural Offences" the 1956 Act prohibits buggery and gross indecency, whilst under "Assaults" are prohibited both indecent assault and assault with intent to commit buggery. It is an offence under another section for a man "persistently to solicit or importune in a public place for immoral purposes."[14] Now as in the nineteenth century, this section is most often applied in connection with "cottaging" and "cruising." A homosexual act most certainly remains in British law "immoral," and we shall see that nothing in the 1967 Act removes this immorality from such activities.

Homosexual scandals of the "50's"

The 1950s were of course plagued by scandals of homosexual behaviour involving politicians, civil servants, diplomats and spies. A sympathetic account of the disgrace of one politician is provided by an obituary in the journal of the Conservative Group for Homosexual Equality. The incident dates from the late fifties, but it is typical of the sort of thing that influenced "informed" opinion:

> Ian [Harvey] ... had a prolonged homosexual relationship which started when he and his partner were at school .... In 1949 he got married for the sake of companionship and having children; the marriage was his sole heterosexual relationship. He was devoted to his family but did not suppress his true nature. ... Towards midnight one day in November 1958 a soldier and Ian were detected in St. James Park. They were charged with breaking park regulations,

convicted and fined £5.00 each - Ian paid for both. The real penalty for Ian was paid out of court, like the penalties paid by a Labour M.P. [W T Field] in 1953 and by very many other men in and out of politics; the immediate ruin of his career and the subsequent wreck of his marriage. He resigned his office and his seat at once.[15]

Wolfenden and the BMA report

Some of these men had been subject to blackmail on account of their behaviour and this was a major factor in the appointment of a committee under Sir John Wolfenden to consider the law and practice relating to homosexual offences. Some of the evidence presented to the Wolfenden Committee now looks extremely dated. For example, one gay activist bases his claim that Wolfenden's "assessment of the facts was generally good"[16] on the committee's rejection of:

> many of the traditional myths, for instance that homosexuality is a disease, a threat to the stability of the nation, the so-called "seduction theory," the supposed dangers of anal intercourse ...[17]

The British Medical Association produced a report, entitled "Homosexuality and Prostitution," which we shall consider in chapter 25. Briefly, the report:

> distinguished between two types of homosexuality, essential and acquired, which was broadly similar to the invert/pervert distinction. Essential homosexuality was defined as either genetically determined or caused by early environmental influences such as an exaggerated emotional attachment to one parent. Acquired homosexuality included a range of casual homosexual behaviour which was not indicative of a basic predisposition.[18]

The genetic connection remains completely unsubstantiated, and it is significant that the activist who wrote the above piece failed to mention the famous appendix to the BMA report, which catalogued the release from both "essential" and "acquired" homosexual behaviour by religious conversion in all of the 14 cases it considered.

Be that as it may, Wolfenden finally proposed a limited decriminalisation of homosexual offences, although the report makes clear that any change in the law should "not be taken as saying that society should condone or approve homosexual behaviour."[19]

Arts and media propaganda

The Wolfenden Committee was sitting at the time the 1956 Act was discussed and given Royal Assent, but Parliament moves slowly, and a considerable softening-up exercise had to be undertaken by the media before a Bill could be brought before Parliament, with young men being interviewed in silhouette or with their backs to the camera:

> They would haltingly vouch for the irrevocability of their condition, the blackmail to which it exposed them, and their utter wretchedness.[20]

In 1958 The Homosexual Law Reform Society was formed, with A E Dyson and Andrew Hallidie Smith its driving forces. Two letters were written in its support to The Times, the first signed by Lords Annan and Attlee, A J Ayer, Robert Boothby MP, Dr Alex Comfort, Dyson, Trevor Huddleston, Julian Huxley, C Day Lewis, J B Priestley and his wife Jacquetta Hawkes, Bertrand Russell, Donald Soper, Stephen Spender, Angus Wilson and Barbara Wooton, amongst others. It must be noted that militant anti-Christian humanists were represented by at least Freddie Ayer, Baroness Wooton and Bertrand Russell, Julian Huxley was a philanderer and Lord Boothby and Angus Wilson were homosexual. Dyson is now a Stonewall group volunteer. Six weeks later appeared a letter from fifteen married women of the country house set, not owning up to their titles, but in fact led by Lady Adrian, the Countess of Albemarle, Lady Longford and Lady Rothschild, with Iris Murdoch giving literary weight.[21]

The film world joined in, with "The Killing Of Sister George" and especially, in 1961, "Victim," which stared Dirk Bogarde. As a homosexual activist admits, writing in a "gay campaign manual":

> the film delineated a wide range of male homosexuals: young, middle-aged, elderly; professional, labourer, artist; used car salesman, politician, hairdresser; butch, effeminate, normal. Behind every line of dialogue lay out-and-out propaganda for a change in what its makers, like the Wolfenden committee, regarded as a cruel and unjust law. Backed by the Rank Organisation, "Victim" was an effective tool in helping to modify so-called informed public opinion.[22]

The propaganda did its stuff, and homosexual acts were decriminalised more or less as Wolfenden recommended. The private member's bill that did the job was brought in by Leo Abse, MP, but piloted through by Antony Grey of the Albany Trust and the Homosexual Law Reform Society (which later dropped the "homo" prefix) Curiously, the Bill's sponsor was nearly Sir David Steel, who told Scottish homosexuals afterwards that when he was drawn in the ballot, he considered bills to liberalise either divorce or homosexuality as vehicles with which to make his name. His constituents threw a fright at these, particularly so far as homosexuality was concerned, and the Liberal MP, who has scarcely missed an opportunity to support a permissive or sexually immoral cause over the past 25 years, finally opted for abortion.

The 1967 Sexual Offences Bill debate

In the debates on the 1967 Sexual Offences Bill, it was made clear that Parliament was refusing to do anything more than permit homosexual acts in certain circumstances. This was emphasised again and again by, for example, Lord Arran:

> in all the discussions we have had, and in all the speeches, no single noble Lord or noble Lady has ever said that homosexuality is right or a good thing. It has been universally condemned from start to finish, and by every single member of the House.[23]

According to Lord Henderson, speaking in the recent House of Lords Clause 28 debate, the Earl of Arran "asked the homosexual people of the future to comport themselves quietly and with dignity and to eschew any form of ostentatious behaviour or public flouting."[24]

Lord Arran actually used the word "flaunting," saying that any evidence of it would "make the sponsors of this Bill regret that they have done what they have done."

One homosexual activist sums up the arguments of the Bill's supporters like this:

> The protection afforded by the Sexual Offences Bill, particularly for young people, was stressed repeatedly; homosexuality was a lesser evil than the blackmail which its prohibition encouraged; relaxing the law would make it easier for homosexuals who wished to be free of their practices to seek help from the caring ministries.[25]

One sponsor of the Bill was Norman St. John Stevas, now Lord St. John, who said:

> This Bill would create no recognised status for homosexuality. It would remain contrary to public policy. Homosexual relations would give rise neither to rights nor duties.[26]

Gross indecency and buggery decriminalised in private

A look at the Sexual Offences Act 1967 shows that this intention did actually pass into law. In the section of the Act which decriminalises homosexual activities, a "homosexual act" is defined thus:

> For the purposes of this section a man shall be treated as doing a homosexual act if, and only if, he commits buggery with another man or commits an act of gross indecency with another man or is a party to the commission by a man of such an act.[27]

Homosexual behaviour is therefore a matter of "gross indecency" in British law, and by virtue of the 1956 consolidation of the 1898 Vagrancy Act, "immoral." It remains illegal in prison, where it violates the privacy requirements of the 1967 Act, in the Merchant Navy, where the Seamen's Union actively lobbied for it to remain an offence in law,[28] and in the Armed Forces, as the Minister, Sir Philip Goodhart, explained in 1981:

> Members of the Armed Forces are often required to serve in conditions where, both off and on duty, they are unavoidably living in closed communities, sometimes under stress. Such conditions, and the need for absolute trust and confidence both within and between all ranks, require that the potentially disruptive influence of homosexual practices should be excluded. It is above all necessary to ensure that those in authority over younger or junior men do not use their position to coerce or persuade those in their charge to perform acts in which they would otherwise not engage.[29]

Such arguments failed to sway the Armed Services Select Committee in 1991. In a muddled bit of thinking, it voted that although active homosexuals should not be recruited, homosexual activity should not be cause for dismissal. Armed Forces Minister Archie Hamilton immediately restated the Government's opposition to the Committee's point of view, but as we shall see in chapter 29, the homosexual lobby ultimately won the day.

"Permissive" legislation

The Sexual Offences Act 1967 is termed "permissive" legislation. This does not mean in law that it forms part of Roy, now Lord, Jenkins' permissive society, although of course on one level it does. Rather does it mean in law that, like the Abortion Act 1967, it removes the threat of prosecution from persons who commit certain illegal actions under certain circumstances, which in all other circumstances remain illegal and open to prosecution. Neither of these two 1967 Acts of Parliament confers "rights."

Sexual "progressives" had been beavering away at nullifying traditional Christian-based sexual morality since the "enlightenment." They asserted that the drive an individual feels to carry out certain deeds should never be resisted. The path was already well-trodden when "Do what thou wilt shall be the whole of the law" became the motto of the dissolute self-styled "beast" Aleister Crowley, and "rumours of abominable rites and orgies, some of them well-founded," emanated from his "abbey" at Cefalu in Sicily in 1920.[30]

Crowley and his perversions seem a world away from Britain seventy years later, but the only major difference seems to be that whereas Crowley used the excuse of ritual magic for his sexual excesses, nowadays no excuse is even offered, and sexual freedom is carried on for its own sake. There are plenty of examples of the "Do as thou wilt" type of sexual proselytisation in our own age.

It flourished in the soft-porn pseudo intellectual "journals of human relations" of the seventies, where articles by academic luminaries would appear on the liberating effects of legalising pornography,[31] using a vibrator in masturbation,[32] orgiastic group sex,[33] teenage sex[34] and of course the pill, which was approved in no uncertain terms, amid claims that: "there is still no evidence to show, or even hint, that long-term administration is harmful. It may now be seriously doubted whether any such effects will ever be found."[35]

The five examples given are in fact taken from just one issue alone of a seventies sex journal, "Forum," by name, and came respectively from John Trevelyan, Professor John Taylor, Dr Robert Chartham, the Reverend Chad Varah and abortionist Dr Philip Cauthery. Did they think we would be happier carrying on like a nation of libertines and tarts? They are certainly all of a piece with the flavour of the nineteen-sixties, when it became politically possible for a Labour Home Secretary, fired with a curious belief that permissiveness was civilised, to allow time for legislation that would commend the morality of the gutter to everyone.

Decriminalisation of homosexuality dovetails perfectly in the anti-Christian agenda with liberalisation of divorce, relaxation of restrictions on the publication of pornography, legalisation of abortion and the abolition of capital punishment. Empirically, the evidence shows that these measures have failed to help those who they were intended to help, have to varying degrees brought misery in their wake, and have had the opposite effect to that intended by their advocates. In the case of the 1967 Sexual Offences Act, the disparity between intention and outcome is dramatic.

3
The effects of the Sexual Offences Act 1967

It is quite untrue to say, as did Viscount Falkland in the House of Lords debate on Clause 28 of the Local Government Bill 1988, that: "Homosexuality is legal in this country."[1] It is not, and he was evidently misinformed by "Democrats for Lesbian and Gay Action" (DELGA) of which he is president. Similarly the statement made by the actor Simon Callow on BBC2's "Newsnight" that "homosexuality is legal except in certain circumstances"[2] is the exact opposite of the truth. Homosexual acts are *illegal* except in certain circumstances. The 1967 Act, according to one gay activist, legalised what men were rarely if ever prosecuted for, that is, committing a homosexual act in private. However, that is not to say that a homosexual act in private was a thing prominent men had not been blackmailed over, or that other men, persuasive and articulate men with the ear of highly-placed civil servants and ministers, were not afraid that blackmail in such circumstances might happen to them.

Conviction rate for indecency doubles

That the passage of the Act led to a doubling of the conviction rate for offences of gross indecency bears the activist's view out. Police Authorities had waited for the Sexual Offences Act 1967 to clarify the law, and had adopted a low profile over prosecutions for public homosexual behaviour in the meantime of the late sixties. When the clarification occurred, they were able to prosecute activity which had been going on all the time, but prosecute it now with greater confidence. Exactly the same thing happened after the 1885 Act.

The 1967 Act did not and was not intended then to legalise homosexuality or to define it as anything less than an indecent, immoral and corrupting activity. These interpretations were reinforced by the "IT" case in 1973.

Conspiracy to corrupt public morals

International Times magazine published contact advertisements for homosexual activity and those responsible were prosecuted for the common law offence of "Conspiracy to Corrupt Public Morals." In rejecting IT's appeal, one of the judges said:

> There is a material difference between merely exempting certain conduct from criminal penalties and making it lawful in the full sense. Prostitution and gaming provide examples of this difference. So we must examine the provisions of the Sexual Offences Act 1967 to see just how far it altered the law. It enacts subject to limitation that a homosexual act in private shall not be an offence, but it goes no further than that ... I find nothing in the Act to indicate that Parliament thought or intended to lay down that indulgence in these practices is not corrupting.
>
> I read the Act as saying that, even though it may be corrupting, if people choose to corrupt themselves in this way, that is their affair and the law will not intervene. But no licence is given to others to encourage the practice.[3]

Those responsible for the magazine had in law conspired to corrupt public morals, since homosexual conduct remains in law corrupting. Interestingly, Tom McGrath, the first editor of International Times, was a former features editor of the pro-homosexual libertarian-left magazine, Peace News, qv.[4] Two other recent applications of the same common law charge as that under which IT was convicted resulted, firstly, in the exposure and subsequent break-up of the Paedophile Information Exchange in 1981 and 1984, and secondly in the prosecution in 1985 and conviction of those behind another "gay" contact paper.

In the second case, "Rendezvous and Gay Amie" was held to have acted outside the law. The prosecutor said that people with deviant practices used a code to disguise their activities, which included sex with animals and children. The two defendants, Betty Hartley and Lewis Brown, received only suspended sentences, and the company was simply fined £5,000, although Judge Ferrer told them:

> "I thought I had seen everything until this trial. I hope I am as broadminded and as tolerant as most right-thinking members of society but I am bound to say I have been shocked by what I have seen and read during the course of this trial."[5]

The Paedophile Information Exchange

We shall look at the whole paedophile movement later, but here we should note that in 1981 Tom O'Carroll, the then chairman of PIE, was jailed for two years for publishing a list of paedophile contacts for PIE members and thus "conspiring to corrupt public morals."[6]

In 1984 three members of PIE, chairman Steven Smith, newsletter editor Peter Bremner and a member of the editorial collective, David Joy, were remanded on bail on four counts, under the 1956 Sexual Offences Act, the Indecency with Children Act, the Obscene Publications Act 1969 and the Post Office Act 1953. Finally, in November, Joy and Bremner were jailed for six months for sending indecent articles through the post, whilst Smith fled to Holland.[7] More about this later, as promised.

Robin Cook extends the 1967 Act to Scotland

Meanwhile the Sexual Offences Act 1967 did not apply to Scotland or to Northern Ireland. Co-operating with the Scottish Minorities Group, and the Scottish Council for Civil Liberties, Labour MP Robin Cook tabled an amendment to the 1980 Criminal Justice (Scotland) Bill, extending the provisions of the 1967 Act to Scotland. The amendment was passed by a large majority in the Commons but only scraped through the Lords by 11 votes.[8]

The Northern Ireland question

In May 1976 a member of the Northern Ireland Gay Rights Association began proceedings against the Government under the European Convention of Human Rights. Northern Ireland MPs unanimously opposed the extension of the Act to the province, and the case finally came before the European Court of Human Rights which ruled in October 1981 that the law in Northern Ireland was in breach of article 8 of the Convention, but that it was not necessary to examine it under Article 14.[9]

Article 8 of the convention says: "Everyone has the right to respect for his private and family life..." and this Article, as Lord Gifford explained in the House of Lords Clause 28 debate, is subject to the following qualifications:

> There shall be no interference by a public authority with the exercise of this right except such as in accordance with the law and is necessary in a democratic society in the interests of: and various matters follow, including the protection of morals. Finally, Article 14 of the convention says: "The enjoyment of the rights and

freedoms set forth in this Convention shall be secured without discrimination on any ground such as sex, race, colour, language, religion, political or other opinion ... or other status.[10]

The Dudgeon Case

Clearly, and as we shall see later, homosexual rights activists maintain that their homosexual activity gives them "other status" within Article 14, but the court did not consider this Article at all, confining its ruling to Article 8. Lord Gifford also refrained from reminding their Lordships that the protection of health is another matter in which exceptions to Article 8 are allowed. As far as the Court's ruling in the case of "Dudgeon v United Kingdom":

> In that case the court declared that it was a violation of the rights of the applicant, Mr Dudgeon, for the law in Northern Ireland to prohibit homosexual acts. As a result of that decision, the Government had to change the law. The court, whose interpretation of the convention binds this country, had some very interesting things to say about Article 8, in particular. It said: "The present case concerns a most intimate aspect of private life. Accordingly, there must exist particularly serious reasons before interferences on the part of the public authorities can be legitimate for the purposes of Article 8(2)."[11]

So was the Court able to see protection of morals as a reason serious enough to uphold the UK's prohibition of homosexual acts in Northern Ireland? No. Although the Court allowed that different requirements might arise in Northern Ireland, the Government was still in the wrong, and did indeed have to change the law, by an order in council in October 1982 which extended the 1967 Act to Northern Ireland.[12]

"Save Ulster from sodomy"

What is odd is that the UK had wanted to extend the 1967 Act to Ulster in the first place, and had published in July 1978 a draft order. However, in the face of public opinion, a fierce year-long "Save Ulster from Sodomy" campaign from the Protestant churches, the opposition of the Roman Catholic church and Ulster MPs, the Government had reluctantly withdrawn the draft order. Some suspected that the reasons of the UK Government were subtle, and somewhat unscrupulous; that it was hoped that extending the 1967 Act to Northern Ireland would place an obstacle in the way of union with Catholic Ireland, as if there were not enough obstacles already. Ulster politics seem never to be straightforward, and Jeffrey Dudgeon, a left-winger but from the Protestant community, lost support from British homosexual left-wingers because he failed to campaign for a united Ireland and troops out.

When the case reached the European Court, the European Commission, which had taken on Mr Dudgeon's case, fielded the National Council for Civil Liberty's veteran gay campaigners Terry Munyard, a barrister, and solicitor Paul Crane, their team being headed by Lord Gifford himself, then a junior counsel. The Government was represented by Nicholas Bratza and Brian Kerr, and their case relied entirely on the different moral perceptions in Northern Ireland from those in the rest of the United Kingdom.

As to the case itself, the Court accepted that between 1972 and 1980, not one person had been prosecuted in Northern Ireland for behaviour that would not have been an offence in England and Wales. Following a drugs raid at his address, Mr Dudgeon's diaries and correspondence had been seized, and he had then been questioned by police about the sexual life his diaries revealed. He was not charged, and his case was that homosexual acts he *might* commit would be unlawful in Northern Ireland. One of the dissenting judges was surprised that the UK had failed to argue that Mr Dudgeon was not actually a victim at all. The UK failed also to argue that the 1967 Act was necessary to protect health under Article 8.

The European Court disallows "Gay Charter"

Jeffrey Dudgeon did not have it all his own way. He had asked that he be allowed sexual activity with young men under twenty-one, that the existence in law of certain common-law offences was in breach of the Convention, and that he had suffered discrimination within the meaning of Article 14 on grounds of sex, sexuality and residence, to add to his complaints under Article 8. In other words, as one of the judges pointed out, he and his backers were seeking "a "charter" declaring homosexuality to be an alternative equivalent to heterosexuality, with all the consequences that that would entail."[13] Mr Dudgeon and his backers in the "gay lobby" and the NCCL failed to win this "charter" and all these points were lost.

The judgment was in part self-contradictory, maintaining in one place that the Court "is not concerned with making any value-judgment as to the morality of homosexual relations between adult males,"[14] and claiming in another that compared with the 1960s, "there is now a better understanding, and in consequence an increased tolerance, of homosexual behaviour."[15] One dissenting judge argued

The effects of the sexual offences act 1967

that the court should have been bound by a judgment of 1976, that "There is no uniform European conception of morals. State authorities of each country are in a better position than an international judge to give an opinion as to the prevailing standards of morals in their country."[16] What is apparent from the dissenting opinions is that the judgment of the Court depended not on an interpretation of law but on the moral standpoint of each of the 19 judges. Morality was decided by a vote, and the conclusion of the Court was ultimately the highly subjective value-judgment, that the immorality of homosexual acts, in the law of the United Kingdom, is not sufficient to allow the proscription of such acts in a part of the United Kingdom.

Extend sodomy to Jersey and the Isle of Man

The parliaments of the Isle of Man, Gibraltar and Jersey have been under increasing pressure to abolish their own laws that forbid homosexual practice.[17]

On the Isle of Man there is great opposition to decriminalisation, and to the Government of the UK legislating over the head of the House of Keys. Demonstrations by mainland gay activists on the Island have hardened opinion, and imported activist Alan Shea secured only 54 votes in the Island's November 1991 elections. Such legislation would be of grave constitutional significance on the Isle of Man, where the UK has promised to help the Island to full independence. The Isle of Man does not recognise the right of individual petition of Islanders to the European Court, and contends both that the UK Government, as a contacting party, may not decide the issue itself, and furthermore and correctly, that the issue of health was never considered by the European Court. There is no case of AIDS on the Isle of Man. Be all that as it may, the Home Office in London threatened to legislate over their heads should Tynwald persist in maintaining its anti-sodomy law, and in March 1992 the House of Keys passed 1967-style clauses by 13 votes to 11.

In Jersey there was little choice. Jersey recognises the right of individual petition to the European Court, and the States, the Jersey parliament, felt obliged to legislate to repeal the island's 1932 anti-sodomy law.

Amnesty International is under intense pressure from the International Lesbian and Gay Association and its national affiliates to regard people imprisoned for homosexual activity as prisoners of conscience. Reports coming out of its conference in Japan in September 1991 seemed to indicate that it will now adopt people imprisoned for homosexual activity as prisoners of conscience, so transforming it from respected international authority into left-wing anti-religious pressure group. Pressure is also continually brought to bear upon the United Nations, and the European Commission. An attempt by ILGA activists Lisa Power and John Clark in 1991 to secure consultative status at the UN for ILGA was only defeated because of the opposition of Muslim countries.

The 1980 Policy Advisory Committee

Although the actual statute law has not changed since 1967, in 1979 Roy Jenkins tried to make the law concerning homosexual acts more permissive still. There had been a Criminal Law Revision Committee in 1975, to which sexual libertarians had sent papers. Following pressure from the Campaign for Homosexual Equality and from its allies, the Sexual Law Reform Society (originally the Homosexual Law Reform Society, and operated out of the premises of the British Humanist Association), and the National Council for Civil Liberties, Roy Jenkins established a "Policy Advisory Committee." As homosexual activist Nigel Warner says:

> The clearest indication of their general thinking comes in the PAC's discussion of the male age of consent. It acknowledges that "the law has a part to play in bringing about acceptance of homosexuals by not discriminating unnecessarily."[18]

As Mr Warner goes on to say, though not in these terms, using the law to achieve the acceptance of the activities of those whose actions are in British law morally unacceptable "is indeed an advance from the position of the 1960s."[19] The Committee ended up by recommending that the age at which a girl can consent to sexual intercourse should remain at 16, but that the minimum age for homosexual acts should be reduced to 18. Its reasons for not going the whole distance and advocating the lowering of the minimum age for homosexual activity to 16 were that it "was not convinced that there does not exist a vulnerable minority of young men aged 16 - 18 who may be in need of protection."[20]

Unhappiness takes over from immorality

The committee was trying to reflect the majority view in society that: "Most people feel that the natural and proper fulfilment of human sexuality is heterosexuality."[21] The second premise on which its conclusions were based is in the eyes of Nigel Warner, flawed:

The effects of the sexual offences act 1967

"*in the vast majority of cases the homosexual way of life is less likely to be satisfactory and more likely to lead to unhappiness,*" thus did the supposed *relative* unhappiness *of homosexual lifestyles take over from their supposed* immorality *as a ground for discrimination.*²²

It is significant that Mr Warner does not trouble to argue that the committee was actually *wrong* in its understanding that homosexual relationships lead to unhappiness. In the rest of his argument, that "unhappiness" is not as good a reason for proscribing certain behaviour as is "immorality," he has touched upon a key flaw in what passes for modern thinking. In the debate on the 2nd reading of David Alton's Abortion Amendment Bill, Mrs Audrey Wise, opposing it, claimed that: "People also have a right to happiness."²³

This is nonsense. In the first place, the argument in its context assumes that happiness flows from the killing of a child in the womb, and unhappiness from letting the child live, a line of argument that is highly suspect. But secondly, and more relevant to the argument, although it is good if people are happy and whilst people have the right other things being equal to pursue happiness, happiness itself is not a human right. Homosexual acts are not proscribed because they lead to a lifestyle that can make practitioners unhappy, but because they are immoral and corrupting.

The Gay News blasphemy trial

Two other events from the late seventies are worth mentioning in connection with the legal position of homosexuality. The first is the 1977 Gay News blasphemy trial, a private prosecution initially brought by Mrs Mary Whitehouse over a poem "The love that dares to speak its name," which appeared in Gay News and in which it is proclaimed that a homosexual relationship existed between Saint John and Jesus Christ. The newspaper's editor (and publishers) were convicted, after Mrs Whitehouse had been subjected to what can only be described as a campaign of intimidation and hatred against her, her home and her family by homosexual activists.²⁴ Despite the glee at the publicity given to Gay News expressed by liberal commentators subsequently, it remains that no publication has repeated such a blasphemy.

The prosecution and conviction were a blow to libertarian progress, and organisations like the National Secular Society were furious. Mary Whitehouse achieved an important statement of the way in which the law exists to uphold public morality. God, so the liberal Bishop of Manchester said, does not need the law to come to His aid.

On the other hand, it is clear that the public good did. The fact that Gay News also published a contact address for the Paedophile Information Exchange and ran regular articles sympathetic to paedophilia did not help its case.[25]

The Child Pornography Act 1978

This leads to the second achievement of Mary Whitehouse in the late seventies, and one which I should not have mentioned were it not for the extraordinary way in which it seems to get gay activists like Stephen Gee of "Gay Left" hot under the collar, and that is the 1978 Child Pornography Act, introduced as a private member's Bill by Cyril Townsend MP, and enacted after an unopposed passage through Parliament. This Act makes trafficking in indecent representations of children an offence. Section 160 of the Criminal Amendment Act 1988 now makes mere possession an offence. Children are defined as under 16 and it is easier to ask a jury to agree on what is indecent than on what is obscene.

Pornography of any sort is important to homosexual men, and representations of children and adolescents do not even have to be indecent to be exciting to their voyeurs. As the head of Scotland Yard's Porn Squad pointed out, a paedophile can spend years amassing a collection of titillating material. These Acts of Parliament are therefore seen in homosexual circles as an attack on homosexuality itself.[26]

Homosexual activity remains immoral in law

In an Appeal case in November 1990, it was upheld that to ask a female stranger to come to bed was importuning for an immoral purpose. The phrase "immoral purposes" concerned sexual conduct. Furthermore, an immoral purpose did not have to be equated with a criminal offence. For instance, where one adult male importuned another in a public lavatory, although the sexual activity proposed might if carried out to the letter of the 1967 Sexual Offences Act no longer constitute a criminal offence, the activity "could still constitute an 'immoral purpose' within s32 of the 1956 Act."[27]

Sadists and masochists jailed

In Operation Spanner, investigations by the Obscene Publications Squad into the circulation of home-made videos depicting acts which bordered on torture led to the conviction of the leaders of a group of homosexual sadists, bestialists and masochists. The charges included possessing isoamyl nitrite drugs, causing actual bodily harm, assault, taking, publishing, sending through the post or possessing indecent or

The effects of the sexual offences act 1967

obscene photographs, including child pornography, and keeping or aiding and abetting a disorderly house. Eight of the men were jailed, four more received suspended sentences, and others were fined, put on probation or conditionally discharged.

The group advertised in the homosexual press for "slaves," and recruited "scores, perhaps hundreds" of men, including teenagers, whom they corrupted, between 1979 and 1987. The masochists in the group were convicted largely of aiding and abetting assault or actual bodily harm on themselves. The convictions were upheld on Appeal.

Judge James Rant told the Old Bailey: "Much has been said about individual liberty, and the rights people have to do what they want with their own bodies, but the courts must draw the line between what is acceptable in a civilised society and what is not." The practices were "degrading and vicious" and no-one who had heard what had happened would say that men "should be free to practise this kind of thing on one another."[28]

Inevitably, the libertarian left promptly said exactly that. Andrew Puddephat, Director General of the National Council for Civil Liberties, now called "Liberty," condemned the jailings, as did the Haldane Society of Socialist Lawyers, homosexual pressure groups and the "gay press," on the grounds that morality was not for judges to decide and that all parties consented to the activities. The judge had accepted this latter point, but "had to consider the injuries inflicted, the extent to which younger men were corrupted, the use of drugs and the involvement of child pornography and sex with animals."

The Sexual Offences Act 1967 - a failure

A judge and leading member of the Bar Council was recently blackmailed after letters were stolen from his homosexual lover, a Loughborough shop owner. He immediately offered his resignation, just as men in public life and caught in similar circumstances have done before.[29] What does all this say about the 1967 Sexual Offences Act, and what should be our assessment of that particular piece of legislation in its third decade?

The conclusion must be that the 1967 Act was by its own standards a failure. It did not remove the fear of blackmail from discrete active homosexuals. It did not result in more homosexually inclined men and women coming forward for psychiatric treatment or for Christian or other counselling and it did not enable the community to take, as Leo Abse himself put it, "the preventive action which might possibly save a little boy from the terrible fate of growing up homosexual."[30]

Neither did it succeed, as was the intention of those who spoke in its favour, in condemning homosexuality in the public mind "as utterly wrongful."[31] So what did it do? We already know the answer, but it was never better expressed than by a homosexual activist by the name of Roy Burns, whose summary opens Chapter 4.

4
The homosexual subculture

The consequences of the passage of the 1967 Sexual Offences Act, which made male homosexuality partially lawful, were not only unexpected but were to be condemned by the proponents of this modest act.

Within five years a social revolution which had been simmering behind closed doors had exploded on to the streets. There were openly gay bars, gay clubs, gay social organisations, gay newspapers and even gay demonstrations. Homosexual men and women in Britain were publicly identifying themselves as gay, and were demanding to be recognised on their own, gay, terms. This had not been the intention of Parliament.[1]

Thus wrote homosexual activist Roy Burns in a "gay" campaign manual and as an objective analysis it is hard to fault. Mr Burns goes on to ask why Parliament so misjudged things and to agree that the Wolfenden report and the 1967 Sexual Offences Act were a response by the establishment to a number of politically embarrassing homosexual cases, some of which had involved blackmail. He also writes correctly that it was not the intention of the 1967 act to make homosexual behaviour lawful, and that indeed it did not. We have seen that importuning for an immoral purpose, gross indecency, conspiracy to corrupt public morals (a common-law offence mainly invoked until recently against homosexual dating agencies and contact groups), all remain offences indicating that homosexual acts are immoral in British Law and also that this is acknowledged in the 1967 Act. Nevertheless, the "gays" have worked hard to blur morality and now support the major service industry to which Roy Burns refers.

The gay leisure industry

It is the market for this service industry that is now known as the "pink pound." There had always been a homosexual subculture, but it was on a very much smaller and quieter scale. Donald West, a leading Cambridge criminologist whom we shall meet again, recorded way back in the 50s, in his sympathetic review of homosexual life:

> Entry into the camaraderie is a matter of visiting the right places in the right clothes and knowing the right conversational gambits and doubles entendres. A newcomer puts on just the shadow of a meaning look, remarks with just a tinge of the accepted inflection, "Isn't it gay in here?" and, if he is a presentable young man, he is lonely no more.[2]

Homosexual customs are still today just as much to do with behaviour and dress. In reality they become so conforming that popular newspapers are able periodically to run a piece vouchsafing "ten ways to spot one." I really am trying to avoid this approach, and yet the stereotypical leather-jacketed, bushy moustached, short-haired or prematurely receding, VW Golf-driving, tight-trousered, cat-loving, whole-foodie, politically-liberal-leftish, non-judgmental "gays" doing the week's shopping a deux before returning to their grey silk-emulsion flat hung with black and white stylish photographs of movie stars in the sitting room, naked male torsos and backsides on the landing, and something a little more explicit by Philip Core in the bedrooms rather does the tabloids' job for them.

There is now a "gay businessmen's" association, whose members represent various different aspects of the "gay" leisure industry. The sort of quiet discrete club that Professor West described has been overtaken by the gay disco. Today, in the 1990s, the sub-culture is a multi-million pound network. It boasts "gay" pubs and clubs, escort and dating agencies, telephone sleaze lines, restaurants, hotels and travel agencies, often with names indicating their homosexual leanings, magazines and newspapers. Those who are active and involved in the "scene" have their own customs and jargon, if not traditions. The argot has moved on from "Julian and Sandy" of "Round the Horne" with "How bona to varda your jolly old eke, Mr 'orne," but remains not least in euphemistic descriptions of sexual practices and encounters, and locations for sexual activity. The "H" aspirant is dropped by certain homosexuals as routinely as their trousers, as in "Do be'ave!" The bookshops are not now called "Bona Books" but "Gays the Word" and there are other specialist shops, discotheques like "Heaven" with its Terrence Higgins Trust stall, specialist travel firms like" Uranian Travel"[3] and hotels in Amsterdam advertising striptease, gay movies, "escort boys," and "private relax rooms" in which to sodomise them.[4]

The gay pubs

Many of the gay pubs provide entertainment or cabaret. As a "Gay Guide To London" explains:

> For years a night of dancing and cruising was enough for most people, but times change, and venues are ... finding a corner somewhere for the singer, the drag act or the male stripper.[5]

One drag act is said by the guide to "range from the depths of bad taste and foul language"[6] whilst one stripper is remembered "mainly for his size - and I don't just mean his height!"[7] The pubs have different clientele on different nights, with one night for men only, another for the "disco crowd" and one pub at least kept Thursday night for "women but organised by Chain Reactions, for 'proud women perverts' into leather, rubber etc.," in other words, for lesbian practitioners of sadism and masochism (S & M).[8]

Many pubs involve their clientele in "competitions" usually involving the male organ in some way, for instance in "wet jockey shorts" or male strips. "Body beautiful" competitions are regularly held, whilst one pub runs what the gay guide describes in inverted commas as "sports days."[9] The Terrence Higgins Trust has raised funds by "Slave Markets" where sadistic homosexuals bid for men who gain sexual satisfaction from being abused.

The Gay Clubs

The clubs are slightly higher up the market, and expect a higher standard of dress, but the male clubs are apparently very careful to discriminate against women and against heterosexuals. As activist writer John Hart explains:

> Clive, who at 21 sees himself as gay, developed a sexual relationship with a girlfriend which went along fine on a physical level, but he was reminded of the separation of social worlds when they went to a gay club he knew, and were at first refused admission. Clive had to describe a number of clubs he had been to before they were allowed in, having persuaded the person on the door that they were not "just a straight couple."[10]

Some clubs cater for specific sexual tastes, and again sadism & masochism features highly. The latest is the "Clit Club" which opened in April 1991 for S & M lesbians. It replaced "Chain Reactions." Actual sexual activity reportedly occurs in the Clit Club, and according to "Capital Gay," weekly circulation 18,000, money was raised in April

1992 for AIDS charity "Positively Women" by volunteers paying to have their pubic hair publicly shaved in the club. Reports of this enterprise make it clear that a strict dress code and a highly-charged sexual atmosphere are what lesbian S & M clubs are about. It is clear that the same is true of the equivalent in the male "scene:"

> If, on the other hand, you like your clubs murky, your men macho and "collar and cuffs" means something totally different to you, then the denim/leather crowd is possibly what you're looking for.[11]

Kennedy's Gay Guide explains that the leather and rubber "scene" is growing, and this trend was spotted as long ago as 1980 by an eminence gris of the homosexual network, Dennis Altman. Writing in a Gay Left book, Altman complains:

> Homosexuality is now signified by theatrically "macho" clothing (denim, leather and the ubiquitous key rings) rather than by feminine style drag; the new "masculine" homosexual is likely to be non-apologetic about his sexuality, self-assertive, highly consumerist and not at all revolutionary, though prepared to demonstrate for gay rights. This, one might note, is far removed from the hope of the early seventies liberationists who believed in a style that was androgynous, non-consumerist and revolutionary.[12]

Sadism and masochism as a way of life

In other words, the hedonistic macho gays have kicked the feminism of the early gay idealists into touch. They exhibit a relentless misogynism, and women, whom they despise, are banned from male leather clubs. A columnist from Gay Times told its 45,000 readers about a club called "The Block." Living, he said, in a nuclear-free, vegetarian household, the sight of a man apparently pulling a dog along on a lead in the dark, heavily-atmosphered leather club - it boasts a dressing-room at the back where members can "change" - was made the more menacing when he realised that the "dog" was another man on all fours clad in a harness. The very next month, Gay Times printed a letter from just such a leather practitioner. The following is an extract:

> To some of us the SM scene is a way of life. I wear a chain and padlock all the time of which I am proud. It shows other people I am somebody's boy. I have also been taken to the club by my Master on a collar and lead and have felt very proud and privileged to have done so.[13]

This element of pride in humiliation is a central element in masochistic thought; it is present in the French S & M fantasy "The Story of O," in which O comes to be proud of the marks of her subjection and is progressively dehumanised. It is no wonder that John Hart, doing his best to shed the "perverts" image, has trouble with S & M in his twee apologia for homosexuality written for young people. He inevitably tries, if the expression does not fall too awkwardly, to rope the rest of us into the perversion:

> *one is very wary of stating the obvious fact that, like hetero- and bisexuals, and lone masturbators, homosexual men and women are sometimes into sexual variations. This includes sado-masochism - the deliberate integration of pain and suffering into sexual experiences. This may be mild - biting and scratching, spanking - or it may be heavier. Male gays in Britain and the US especially have recently featured such role-playing - slave/master - in leather bars. Recently, some lesbians have also taken on this interest and caused controversy about its "political correctness."*[14]

The clone clothes shops

The "clone," as the macho look is called, is served by specific clothes shops. These exist for the total homosexual market, but it will come as no surprise to learn that most of them target the leather and rubber niche. Advertisements for them in the homosexual press feature the "macho" look or depict models partly and provocatively clothed. The advertisement for one such shop depicts leather jock straps and pouches, leather whips and long gloves, and a pair of leather briefs with a zipper up the backside.[15] A shop called "Zipper" is run downstairs from the publishers of "Gay Times" and the homosexual pin-up magazines "Zipper," "Him" and "Vulcan."

Another leather and rubber shop, Clone Zone, saw dramatically increased turnover to substantially more than a quarter of a million pounds in its financial year ended in June 1986, with the contribution from "men's fashion wear" more than doubling to £220,000. "Greetings cards" provide a good contribution to profits, and the indecent nature of these has led to trouble with the law. But in strict retailing terms, this is target marketing at its best. Clone Zone in particular appears to be what Londoners call a nice little earner, with the year's gross profit nudging £124,000, out of which the homosexual directors were able to make a contribution to an unnamed charity of a more than generous ninety-nine pounds.

Some shops have cafes attached, and this is especially true of the various "gay" bookstores, which are a fundamental part of the "gay scene."

Misogynism amongst male homosexuals

Homosexuals cultivate an impression that they are gentle and non-threatening to women. At the same time, as Roy Kerridge has pointed out, transvestism and misogynism combine in the way homosexuals admire, and dress up as, "dyed blonde-and-lipsticky women." He observes that ageing female popsingers can have a second career on the homosexual circuit, and that when a homosexual man dresses up as a woman, it is as a tart, not as a wife and mother:

> With the tart as ideal woman, and a rough uneducated boy the ideal partner for a cultured man, the homosexual cannot understand heterosexual love and marriage at all.[16]

We shall find out why the sort of boy described appeals to an adult male homosexual as we go along. Homosexual men are rarely genuinely complementary about women and a cabaret act called "The Trollettes" - which is incidentally a pun on the homosexual practice of "trolling" or having promiscuous anonymous sexual encounters; the word comes from "trawling" - is even described in a gay guide as "confusing gayness with disgust for women."[17] The clash between the more hedonistic men and the politically motivated women always creates tensions. According to John Hart:

> The gay movement itself is divided, without a common programme for action. The Campaign for Homosexual Equality (CHE) reflects this in that it currently has a low membership, a history of internal fighting and a division between men and women[18]

It is true that at the 1976 CHE conference in Southampton, only 35 women turned up out of a total attendance of 600.[19] The female presence on the CHE committee was severely curtailed when a leading lesbian activist resigned, and the CHE has since become unashamedly male, with most lesbians, as homosexual Jeffrey Weeks reports: "seeing their focus of concern within the women's (feminist) movement."[20]

Further divisions exist at the London Lesbian and Gay Centre in Islington between Sadism & Masochism gays, who now hold regular discos, and the rest. Kennedy's Guide comments: "Born into controversy, this continued internally with squabblings over who should and shouldn't use the centre, for a time threatening the success of the whole project."[21] The squabblings have continued, with a motion of censure being proposed on the management committee, who ran up a deficit of £48,000 in 1987/88 despite being supported first by the GLC and then by its successor, the London Borough Grants Committee, to the tune in that year alone, of £144,596.[22]

Gyms, bodybuilders and narcissism

Two further areas of the "gay scene" are those of the saunas and gyms. Saunas are often simply brothels, and many have been prosecuted as "disorderly houses." Bodybuilding in the gym is tremendously popular amongst male homosexuals, and it is claimed that this is simply part of a general fitness drive. "Some wish to build their bodies to some self-image of a muscled Greek God, but most are just concerned with keeping in shape," claims Kennedy's Guide.[23]

Unfortunately for this argument, the emphasis in the photographs in Gay Times, Zipper, Mister, and Kennedy's Guide itself, is on virile young men doing their best impersonation of a "muscled Greek God." Videos abound of well-proportioned men performing obscene acts, and even the cover of Kennedy's Guide shows a popular male stripper, renowned for his body-built shoulders, and the size of his penis. Parades and competitions to find Mr Gay UK or Mr Gay Britain, in which young men parade in the briefest possible underwear, are very popular indeed on the homosexual circuit.[24]

So why is there this emphasis on bodybuilding amongst male homosexuals? The reason seems to be that male homosexuality is based on looks and appearance. It is then no coincidence that it is allied to bodybuilding, which is dedicated to perfecting those same looks and appearance. But there is another, psychological, dimension.

Psychological problems in narcissism

John McVicar investigated the bodybuilding phenomenon for a Sunday magazine in the context of a possible connection with psychopathic crime:

> Lifting weights as a competitive sport or doing it as a training aid for other sports is OK, but using weights just to build the body is suspect. An instructor at one gym I visited - Battersea's Club on the Park - caught the general attitude well: "I don't like bodybuilders. There is no ultimate purpose to what they're doing except posing."[25]

John McVicar spoke to Dr Maurice White, a consultant psychiatrist:

> The cases you're talking about are where there is a compulsion to get bigger and bigger. They have a macho swagger and use their physique to throw their weight around. They want to be admired, respected, feared. But underneath the muscle is an empty shell, a hollow life, a sense of impotence. Often these guys are sexually insecure. Their narcissism speaks of a hollow relationship with the world.[26]

Another consultant, Professor Laurie Taylor, agrees, although I suspect he may be embarrassed to see his remarks quoted in connection with homosexuality:

> "I always think that the bodybuilder has affinities with the obsessive masturbator who meticulously chronicles the steps of his own orgasm," he said. "There is the same assiduous concentration upon the body, the same precision, the same claustrophobic self-regard, the same fascination with chronicling performance. And there is the mirror: a crucial factor in all exercises in narcissism. ... Narcissistic fantasies have nothing to do with the real world - they have nothing to do with constructive, enjoyable or even plausible relationships with other human beings."[27]

The destructive effects of the subculture

This is a brief sketch of the subculture which services the homosexual network. It exists, not out of community spirit, although obviously a camaraderie does exist, but out of the primary need to make sexual contacts and the secondary need for reassurance in a lifestyle that its practitioners know deep down to be utterly wrong. The following bleak picture is painted by activist John Shiers:

> I have never resolved my basic self-disgust; consequently I have never let anyone relate sexually to me for more than a few weeks. My sexual and emotional responses are totally disconnected from each other. I have friends, women and men whom I care a lot for and feel close to, and casual sexual encounters with people who then get to be defined as "friends" (and therefore not sexual partners) or who disappear altogether from my life.
>
> Sex becomes a means of affirming to myself that other people can find me attractive, physically can like my body. If I go for more than a month without any sexual encounter, I just feel permanently depressed. I get deep feelings of self-worthlessness. That is how I

The homosexual subculture

have come to dabble with cottaging (which is counter-productive because the guilt after the encounter is worse than the depression which leads me to go in the first place) and gay saunas (which are at least in physically comfortable surroundings).[28]

The GLC and homosexual culture

The GLC in its heyday had an entirely cynical view of the homosexual network as at the same time a destabilising influence on society, and as fodder for the polling booth. Its leader Ken Livingstone clearly regarded men and women locked into homosexual behaviour as a sort of primitive island race:

> The Council is in a unique position to pursue policies that counteract discrimination (of homosexuals) and enable the gay community to develop its own range of services and establish itself as a viable section of the population....[29]

Leaving aside the misuse of ratepayers money implicit in this statement, the picture conjured up is quite extraordinary. It even begins to sound reasonable to encourage this underprivileged community to maintain its own buses and sewers and to trade with the outside world. They could sell the "heterosexual community" studded leather manacles, which would balance their imports of high-tensile condoms. In time their financial base might grow to the point where they would be able to offer their own enlightened life assurance policies that would not regard the periodic takers of AIDS tests as a bad risk.[30]

Unfortunately for the argument, homosexual men are in general quite well off, and even homosexual women seem to be better off than ordinary families. Reviewing a new selection of magazines for the American homosexual market, Markie Robson-Scott reports:

> Gays and lesbians, without kids to put through college, have the highest disposable incomes in the US, as well as the best education of any group. More than 90% of gay men and 82% of lesbians read magazines; their combined total annual household incomes amount to more than $394 billion. Of their spending, 73% is in response to gay media advertising, and Armani, Brooks Brothers, Reebok, Remy Martin, Coke, Sony and Pioneer (favourites among gays) are just beginning to put their [advertising] money where it counts.[31]

It is unnecessary for us to join battle with the GLC when the mighty pen of Bernard Levin has been put to paper, in reply to author Larry Kramer. Mr Kramer, an American homosexual, claims:

> I belong to a culture that includes Proust, Henry James, Tchaikovsky, Cole Porter, Plato, Socrates, Aristotle, Alexander the Great, Michelangelo, Leonardo da Vinci, Christopher Marlowe, Walt Whitman, Herman Melville, Tennessee Williams, Byron, E.M. Forster, Lorca, Auden, Francis Bacon, James Baldwin, John Maynard Keynes, Dag Hammarskjold ... Why don't they teach any of this in the schools? ... the only way we'll have real pride is when we demand recognition of a culture that isn't just sexual ... All through history we've been there, but we have to claim it, and identify who was in it, and articulate what's in our minds and hearts and all our creative contributions to this earth.[32]

Bernard Levin accepts that "it is true that there have been great artists, scientists, administrators and teachers who were homosexual. But that does not seem to me to add up to 'a world elsewhere.'" And in answer to Mr Kramer's claim:

> The eloquence of that plea must not be allowed to disguise the boldness of his demand, which is for a recognition of a special, separate role, function and position for homosexuals in a heterosexual world. I have to say - and I write as one who has repeatedly come to the defence of homosexuals suffering discrimination, injustice and contempt (and now fear) - that it cannot be accepted. Either a homosexual is like the rest of us except in the matter of sexual orientation (which is what I believe), or the very fact of his homosexuality sets him apart from - even, it seems, above - the rest of us. The names in that list of homosexuals (which itself needs thoroughly glossing) have nothing in common other than their sexual nature, and with one or two obvious exceptions, I do not believe that their homosexuality could be deduced from their contribution to "a culture that isn't just sexual."[33]

Homosexual artists used as positive images

Of course the reasoning behind the playing up of the alleged homosexuality of great artists is to do with positive images. Homosexuality does not lead necessarily to artistic excellence, and may actually stultify the artistic search. But it is thought by the left that children in particular will be happier to choose to be homosexual if they have such a thing in common with important figures in history. Naturally this aim is dressed up in the clothes of a search for knowledge and background to assist the appreciation of artistic works. For example:

The homosexual subculture 43

In the study of music or art the sexuality of the composer or artist may have an important and direct influence on their work. Knowing that Tchaikovsky, Ravel, Michelangelo and Hockney were/are homosexual is important in fully appreciating their lives and works.[34]

Scraping around for "Gay forebears"

Bernard Levin mentioned the "glossing" necessary to claim vast numbers of public figures as "gay." Ravel and Michelangelo were claimed as homosexual above on the scantiest of evidence. Just as it is in the interests of homosexual activists to "talk up" the percentage of the population who are homosexually active, so it is important to have a good number of artists, writers, philosophers, to whom the activist can point when presenting a "positive image" of homosexuality.

For example, in trying to claim Edward Lear as a homosexual, Gay Times says: "throughout his life, Lear formed passionate - but probably unfulfilled - attachments to young men." If this is the best Gay Times can do, it seems far from conclusive evidence of homosexual inclination, let alone activity.[35]

The same issue of Gay Times printed a "Day-by-day listing of births, deaths, anniversaries and events with a gay connection,"[36] and named some 37 individuals. The "Pink Plaque Guide" listed addresses where famous people lived who were alleged to be homosexual - "our gay forebears."[37] Bernard Levin refers to "the risk of exchanging one kind of ghetto for another," and using a racial simile that is perhaps only appropriate in its context, says:

> If it is wrong, as I believe it is, to define a black man by his blackness, it must be no less wrong to define a homosexual by his homosexuality, whether the definition (in either case) is made by his enemies or his friends.[38]

In this artistic homosexual ghetto, artists are appreciated for their homosexuality, rather than for any artistic worth. As an example, a book called "Teleny" has been reprinted by Gay Men's Press. Oscar Wilde is supposed to have had a hand in writing it, but as even the reviewer for "Gays the Word" observes:

> That ... does not make it literature; indeed, if he had foreseen that it would hang round his neck like a millstone for years after his death, he might have had second thoughts about handing the manuscript on to whoever was his next collaborator. As an incidental look at late-Victorian sexuality, an indication of how some gay men of the period saw themselves and each other, and merely for its

existence as an early gay novel, Teleny has its merits. As a work of art it has none.⁣[39]

"Photography and the dirty word"

Perhaps the nadir of homosexuality as art is in the works of Gilbert and George. This self-proclaimed homosexual pair made a name in the eighties by producing collages of boys, whom they found in Spitalfields. They would take them home to photograph them in various poses and states of undress, put Gilbert, George, or both into the picture, and give the resulting photo-piece a random name like "cry," "hope," "we are," "worlds." One art critic summarised the process as "Got some kneeling boys left over, Gilbert." "Better use them up then, George."[40]

Gilbert and George are feted to the skies in the homosexual and liberal press, but are they, by any reasonable standard, any good? The art critic Brian Sewell is not known for a prudish taste in art, but even he was disenchanted with G & G. Commenting on the sheer volume of their output, he asked:

> How can they produce one a week? They have to take the photographs, develop them, enlarge them, cut them up, stick them together in a collage, re-photograph, re-stick, silhouette and colour them, put them in their thin black frames, jig-saw them into the right order - the amount of sheer drudgery is appalling and there can be no time left for art.[41]

Brian Sewell has rarely written as withering an attack as on the contribution of Gilbert and George to art:

> G & G have never been able to paint or draw or sculpt, but I do not blame them for taking the charlatan's way out when they so desperately wanted to be taken for artists after such long apprenticeships at public expense. They drew attention to themselves by painting their faces and turning to photography and the dirty word.
>
> Subsequent developments have made them cult figures - a pathetically weak and puerile art establishment is to blame for that - and the cult is now self-generating so that even G & G have advanced from pretence to belief in their repellent sanctity.
>
> If, as they proclaim, "the true function of art is to bring about new understanding, progress and advancement," then their failure is wretched, for their "accessible modern art form" recognises no distinction between spiritual lift and prurient titillation, between art and advertisement, or between the National Gallery and the public lavatory.[42]

Homosexual art synonymous with pornography

Excluding some of the more incomprehensible and risible lesbian literature, homosexual art often seems indistinguishable from pornography. The reader only has to pick up a homosexual work of fiction or view any homosexual visible art if this seems far-fetched. Early in 1990, a collection of photographs including a whip sticking out of a man's anus, various plants depicted as phalli, and other unpleasant images by the late homosexual "artist" Robert Mapplethorpe, who died of AIDS, emerged as "a travelling barometer of the shift in America's social climate."[43]

The National Endowment for the Arts first put on the collection at the Corcoran Gallery in Washington, but the directors cancelled the show of "homoerotic art" and were then denounced by the "arts" world. Then the main art gallery in Cincinatti displayed the photographs. When the director of this gallery, Dennis Barrie, refused to cancel the exhibition at the local prosecutor's request, a grand jury charged Mr Barrie with obscenity and using minors in pornography, and the police ordered about 500 viewers out.

This has been a brief look at the homosexual sub-culture. If we can assess a group of people by their art we see homosexuals as people obsessed by sex, lacking restraints and for whom no image is too pornographic. The homosexual movement simply measures all things by the standard of whether or not they promote homosexuality to the homosexual. In the 1980s some local authorities thought that they should use ratepayer's money to do the same, and we shall look at this phenomenon next.

5

The battle for Clause 28

The politics of homosexuality and the politics of the left are so intertwined, that it came as no surprise to find local authorities actively promoting the cause of homosexuality in the 1980s. The average working class Labour voter does not want homosexual rights preached in public, so nor does the Labour Party leadership, except when it is necessary to appear "right-on" at Conference, or in the Marxist or homosexual press. Local Labour activists, of the sort that become councillors and hard-left MPs, are a different matter entirely.

Greater London Council

Local Councils had started promoting homosexuality in the 80s, in their "equal opportunities" policies, and by grants to homosexual contact groups. The Greater London Council was the most active, with Ken Livingstone announcing its "positive images" policy in May 1984.[1] This became the starting point. The GLC stacked up its foyer with homosexual literature[2] and Lambeth planned the first-ever "Gay Games,"[3] and then sent top Council officers on a course to "challenge their own heterosexism.[4] Heterosexism, according to the GLC Women's Committee, is "an oppression:"

> Like other oppressions, it is perpetrated by a dominant and powerful group, in this case heterosexuals. Like other oppressions it works both on an institutionalised level, and through individuals ... it stinks and makes plenty of people's lives a misery ... Unless you see that heterosexuality is the propagandised sexuality, and that other possibilities were forbidden to you, you have heterosexist attitudes.[5]

"Changing the world"

The promotion of homosexuality really got into gear with the publication in October 1985 of "Changing the World - a charter for lesbian and gay rights" by the GLC. And a charter for homosexual rights is exactly

The battle for Clause 28   47

what it was. It proposed sweeping away all laws and practices by which homosexuals, and homosexual couples, are treated differently in any way to heterosexual people and married couples. We shall look at homosexual rights in chapter 28, but as an example, churches would be forbidden under the charter to preach that homosexuality is contrary to the Bible. Homosexual couples would have exactly the same rights to council housing, and to inheritance, as married couples. The GLC had already given around £1 million to homosexual groups and projects in three-and-a-half years.[6]

Islington Council promptly proposed to draw 100 flats from the hat to let out to young couples, including homosexuals,[7] and the next day it was reported that a conference for homosexuals was held in Lambeth Town Hall to discuss, amongst other things, "fostering and adoption by homosexuals - and gays working in children's homes."[8] This conference led to the setting up of a "gay and lesbian working party," a forerunner of the Council's lesbian and gay subcommittee. Councillor Graham Norwood said that Social Services should encourage lesbians and gay men to register as child-minders, and Amenity Services would include films showing lesbians and gays in a positive light in a series of films in the borough. This was actually done during "Gay Pride Week" the next year. The same Directorate started immediately to purchase books for and about lesbians and gays for the Borough's libraries.[9]

Homosexual literature promoted by local authorities

In the libraries of Labour-controlled local authorities, lists became available of literature supposedly of interest to homosexuals. Lambeth for instance now produces two glossy booklets, one entitled "Creative writing by and about gay men," and the other "Stories and poems by and about lesbian women," to replace their earlier "Gay men's fiction" and "Lesbian fiction." Camden libraries indicate books that "gay men" will wish to read by a large pink triangle, and books avidly sought by "lesbians" by two intertwined symbols of the female sex.

The purpose of the lists is rather complicated. Libertarian-left councils want firstly to politicise homosexual users of libraries, secondly to convince other users that homosexuality is larger and more visible than it really is, thirdly to convert some waverers and young people to homosexuality itself, and fourthly to gain votes amongst minorities and credence amongst far-left allies.

As its abolition present to London's women, the GLC's women's committee published a handbook giving information on "Chinese

48 THE SEXUAL DEAD-END

lesbians, Irish lesbians, anti-sexist bookshops, "gay bereavement" and the Catholic Lesbian Sisterhood," and how to contact "The English Collective of Prostitutes, the Gay Sweatshop and the Lesbian Herpes Sufferers."[10]

Positive images after May 1986 council elections

The Inner London Education Authority immediately took up the baton. Its magazine ILEA Contact advertised a "lesbians and gays in education conference" run by the Gay Teachers Group,[11] a "gay teacher's group open meeting" at London Lesbian & Gay Centre to discuss sex education with Jill Clay, its Inspector for Health Education,[12] and a "Lesbian and gay summer arts festival" at the Oval House Theatre in Kennington.[13] The ILEA also caused a storm by recommending the use of the book "Jenny lives with Eric and Martin." qv

Hackney Lesbian Strength and Gay Pride festival was held in June 1986[14] and in neighbouring Haringey, the council's Lesbian and Gay Unit wrote to school and college heads "telling them it is now council policy in education 'to promote positive images of lesbians and gays ... from nursery through to further education.'"[15] These plans of Haringey, which were exactly in line with the Labour group's 1986 Election Manifesto, led eventually to a question in Parliament from Lord Monson, with support from Labour peers Lords Molloy and Mellish and Lord Elwyn Jones. Lord Molloy drew the appropriate reaction from Lord Swinton, who "deplored" Haringey's plans, and said he needed more details.[16]

"Gay" officers appointed by councils

Ealing Council, which had come under Labour control in May 1986, decided to "promote positive attitudes towards homosexuality, removing any sexist or heterosexual practices and materials." This led to a protest by parents,[17] which was taken up in the House of Commons by Kenneth Hind. In reply, Labour's front bench education spokesman supported the employment of homosexuals as teachers and "positive images" teaching as a means "to try and end discrimination against gay and lesbians." By this stage, according to Andrew Lumsden and Denis Campbell writing in the New Statesman:

> Out of 12 London boroughs held by Labour six intend to appoint or have already appointed "out" lesbian/gay officers (as do or have eg Nottingham, Leicester and Manchester) and all have pro-gay commitments. The forum for Labour-held London boroughs, the

Association of London Authorities, is advertising a £17,000 job-share lesbian/gay post now.[18]

In the meantime, the details of which Lord Swinton was in need concerning Haringey Council were collected into a dossier at the request of Education Secretary Kenneth Baker.[19] The powerlessness of the Education Secretary in this matter of sex education was illustrated when Kenneth Baker appealed to ILEA to withdraw "Jenny"[20] and in reply ILEA issued a "resources guide" of 150 books and videos including sexually explicit books promoting homosexuality.[21]

The 1986 Education Act

That there was a possibility that schools might include positive images sex education was illustrated when Michael Marland, head of North Westminster Community School, told the Secondary Heads Association that "the positive features of homosexuality have to be mentioned."[22] Parents as much wanted the "positive features" of homosexuality mentioned as the positive features of heroin use, but parents have always been regarded by "progressives" as a bit of an irrelevance. This time, however, they achieved limited success. During this time, the Education Bill was going through Parliament, and in June 1986 the Government introduced Lord Buckmaster's sex education amendment in a diluted form to encourage pupils "to have due regard to moral considerations and the value of family life."

The Government had dropped Viscount Buckmaster's word "stable" and had added "whenever reasonably practicable," which was immediately seen as a get-out clause.[23] However, the whole clause aroused the ire of the left. Giles Radice, Labour's education spokesman, said "the Government has given way to the moral right, the Lord Buckmasters of this world and those who believe that moral standards are flying away like straws in the wind, and that the sins of Sodom and Gomorrah are rampant in the land."[24] There was a barrage of pressure in the media, ill-willing the Government to drop the clause.

There was increased pressure on the Government to accept amendments to its clause when the Bill returned to the Commons in the autumn. Two sponsors of Conservative Family Campaign, Ivor Stanbrook and Peter Bruinvels, tabled amendments respectively to add "stable family life" and "fidelity within marriage," and to give parents the absolute right to withdraw children from sex education in any case. In the end, on 22nd October 1986, the Government rewrote its clause to give school governors power over sex education, the Bruinvels amendment was defeated with 46 Conservative MPs supporting it in a vote against a three-line whip, and Ivor Stanbrook's amendment was not called.

"Gay lessons"

A book published in October 1986 took the argument on a stage further. In "Gay lessons," Rachel Tingle detailed ways in which local authorities and especially local education authorities had been promoting homosexual lifestyles using ratepayers' money. She explained that if "Gay is Good," which gay rights activists claim, and many local authority politicians accept, then homosexuality would be promoted amongst children in particular as a valid lifestyle and as an alternative to normal heterosexual marriage and family life.

Miss Tingle detailed in her book ways in which the GLC, the ILEA, many London local authorities and education authorities, and boroughs such as Southampton, Liverpool and Manchester had actively encouraged and promoted homosexual lifestyles.[25]

A cross-bench peer, Lord Halsbury, then introduced a private member's Bill into the House of Lords, "to restrain local authorities from promoting homosexuality." The Bill passed through the Lords unopposed, and was being introduced into the House of Commons by Dame Jill Knight when it was buried by the General Election of June 1987.

Halsbury clause added to Local Government Bill

Mrs Thatcher declared herself sorry to lose the Bill, and after the election there was continuing concern at the way sexual liberals and their local government allies were promoting homosexuality. There was a debate in the General Synod of the Church of England in November, which was fudged by John Yates, then Bishop of Gloucester, but which eventually called practising homosexuals to repentance. The Bishop of Ripon announced that he would not ordain a practising homosexual. In December 1987, during the committee stage of the Local Government Bill, David Wilshire MP introduced a version of the Halsbury Bill as an amendment. He was supported by the Government and also by Dr Jack Cunningham, the Labour Party environment spokesman, and his colleagues on the committee, with the single exception of Bernie Grant. However, Labour support for this new Clause 28 lasted only a few hours, and by the Report stage, the Labour Party front bench had decided to oppose it. Neil Kinnock became concerned to display his credentials to homosexual activists, and in Edinburgh described Clause 28 as a "pink triangle clause" (the Nazis made homosexuals in their prison and death camps wear pink triangles) "produced and supported by a bunch of bigots."

"Arts loophole" proposed for Clause 28

Clause 28 still went unchanged to the Lords. The House of Lords debated its committee stage in a committee of all its members, and it was here that an amendment was proposed by Viscount Falkland to exempt from the provisions of Clause 28, "any material which is published in the bona fide belief that such material serves or may serve a literary, artistic, scientific or educational purpose."[26] This transparent amendment, so reminiscent of the get-out clauses of the Obscene Publications Act, became known as the "arts loophole."

A great deal of media pressure came into play, with articles by Simon Callow, Robert Kilroy-Silk and Ben Pimlott, lobbying by David Hockney, Luke Ritner and the Arts Council, and idiotic claims by Peter Jonas, director of the English National Opera, and Matthew Evans of Faber and Faber, that Clause 28 would ban respectively the opera "Billy Budd" and John Betjeman's poem "The Arrest of Oscar Wilde." An editorial in The Observer expanded the list of future proscribed works, and in full Roy-Jenkinsite flow described Clause 28 as "An assault on the civilised society."

Advertisement in "The Independent"

Most superficially impressive of all, a full-page advertisement was taken in the Independent on 1st February 1988, where Members of Parliament were supported by luminaries from the worlds of academia, journalism and entertainment in expressing "a sense of alarm" over Clause 28. On closer inspection well over half of the signatories were people pushing a left-wing world-view, if not the full gay rights agenda. The MPs were overwhelmingly from the Labour front bench, and amongst their supporters, the militant homosexuals and even the odd paedophile were in the main very careful to conceal their true campaigning credentials.

Appendix 1 analyses the Independent signatories, finding correlations between the "Indy" list and Charter 88, the AIDS lobby, the British Humanist Association, the National Secular Society and the "Rationalist" Press, promoters of euthanasia, Streetwise Youth, Brook Advisory, the June 20th group, CND, ANC supporters from the anti-apartheid movement, the Haldane Society, the National Council for Civil Liberties, known homosexual activists and many more.

Conservative Family Campaign report

It was against this backdrop that Conservative Family Campaign sent a report to selected members of the House of Lords, cataloguing what had happened in the fifteen months since the publication of "Gay Lessons." In straight contradiction of the claims of the arts lobby and the left, the report observed that promotion of homosexuality by local authorities in London and elsewhere as a valid alternative to family life had not abated in the slightest. After all, if there were no promotion being attempted, gay activists would not be campaigning so hard against a Clause which sought to end promotion.

The report recorded that many London Boroughs had organised yearly "Gay Pride" marches and events, and Peers were reminded that the London Borough of Lambeth financed and promoted a Lambeth "Gay Pride Week," which culminated in a rally at Kennington Park in July 1986 and 1987. At the 1986 rally, as on previous occasions, dangerous nitrite drugs, "poppers," were on sale, tiny tots paraded "gay" badges and a local newspaper recorded that: "An outrageous minority with bare bottoms hanging out the back of torn jeans" had "forced families out of the park."[27]

"Outrageous decisions" by local authorities

Towards the end of 1986, the leader of the SDP group slammed an Islington council policy whereby "any job shall be offered first to a disadvantaged group on the basis of race, sex, disability and sexuality."[28] Parents opposing Haringey Council's plans to teach "gay awareness" to children were beaten up[29] and a novel detailing the seduction and buggery of a 16-year-old boy by a teacher, "The Milkman's On His Way," was first put on an ILEA book list and recommended to teachers and then placed in Haringey libraries where it was actually borrowed by children.[30]

Camden Council's £100,000 lesbian and gay unit advertised four £15,000 a year posts, its women's committee approved a £15,000 grant to establish a Camden lesbian centre and a "lesbian day" was organised for December 6, at a cost of £2,000, to discuss "lesbian mothers' rights, fostering and adoption and other lesbian issues."[31] Islington Council's housing committee proposed to let men with AIDS have priority over families,[32] whilst Haringey Council's plan to introduce "positive images" of lesbians and gays was denounced by black parents on the very day that the London Borough of Newham's equality subcommittee recommended that gay men and women be allowed to foster children. Newham area Dean, the Rev. Martin

Continued promotion in New Year 1987

In the New Year 1987, the homosexual activist mayor of Islington withdrew "personal courtesies" from SDP members of the council after they criticised the involvement of his "companion" at a remembrance day ceremony in which a "pink triangle" wreath was laid as a "gay rights" publicity stunt.[34] Lambeth Council mounted an extraordinary £100,000 AIDS campaign, and recruited staff to persuade people *not* to cut down on their numbers of sexual partners,[35] whilst Mr. Ken Livingstone attempted to convince the British public that they were all bisexual.[36] Lambeth Council also advertised in the homosexual magazine "Gay Times" for groups to apply for grants towards "community projects."[37]

In only a three-month period in 1987, Southwark Council tried to block a training grant for a Christian Fellowship because they stated what they regarded as the biblical prohibition on homosexual acts,[38] Lambeth Council promoted a "gay community play,"[39] Lewisham proposed to spend £250,000 capital and contribute £200,000 for the first-year running costs of a gay and lesbian centre,[40] whilst considering gay and lesbian fostering.[41] Haringey spent £10,000 alone on putting up posters advertising its "Lesbian Strength and Gay Pride Week" outside schools and in local museums,[42] promoted the sex manual "Young Gay and Proud" for 13-year-olds,[43] and showed the video "A Different Story - How to be a Lesbian in 35 minutes" to teenagers,[44] whilst Brent Council was criticised for its "positive images" programme in the school curriculum.[45]

"Fairy Dykemother"

The SDP member for Greenwich then revealed that "women town hall workers had received a letter from their "Fairy Dykemother" inviting them to a lesbian meeting."[46] Camden, which employed four full-time workers in its £124,000 lesbian and gay unit, offered a weekend away for gay and lesbian employees to discuss "heterosexism," regarded as a serious problem because it "promotes only heterosexuality and heterosexual family life as normal and natural,"[47] and then redefined "ladies first" to recommend that "the word lesbian should always precede gay" to "emphasise the existence of lesbians."[48]

Teachers at a primary school in Hackney who had drawn up their own "anti-heterosexism" code, and plans for the "insidious indoctrination" of children as young as three through pro-homosexual books and materials in schools by some Labour local authorities were condemned by the Professional Association of Teachers, which called for stronger legal curbs on such practices. The 42,000 strong Association registered an almost unanimous vote when the subject was debated.[49]

Another "gay pride march" in Lambeth

As the year drew to a close, the London Borough of Lambeth financed a crude leaflet for prostitutes, advising them to use condoms in connection with anal sex, even though its own trading standards department emphasised that there is no condom strong enough for this purpose,[50] with the advice "making safer sex good fun for punters keeps them coming regularly!"[51] Councillors then attempted to undermine a D.E.S. circular on the teaching of sex education, and promoted another Lesbian and Gay Pride March.[52]

Lambeth rounded off the year with its plans to send top officers on a gay "awareness" training course, to continue provision of homosexual display stands in libraries, to provide programmes of gay and lesbian events, to finance a local gay/lesbian information sheet, and to install books promoting homosexual lifestyles in play group centres and children's homes.

"Gay literature" in play groups

Play leaders went on training courses, and afterwards one said:
"Some of the books on display were terrible. I have children as young as two years old and I don't think they should be seeing pictures of grown men in the nude in different sexual practices. I personally found it very offensive." That not every playgroup leader can be relied upon to be as conscientious was illustrated when another admitted: "Gay and lesbian literature is available to us from Lambeth and we have displayed it."[53]

As 1988 got under way, it was announced by a group of homosexual film-makers from "Ealing Gay Youth Group" that Ealing Council had given the cash to make a video including nude romps outside the home of the local MP, Harry Greenway.[54]

The House of Lords vote

The Government made a concession to the homosexual lobby when the word "intentionally" was inserted before "promote" in referring to local Councils, but allowed the courts to draw any conclusion they might wish about the intentions of a local authority.

The battle for Clause 28

The Arts Loophole, moved by Lord Falkland, was defeated by 166 votes to 111, and the whole clause was carried by 202 votes to 122. Only eight Bishops voted, and of those, only the Bishops of London and Chelmsford voted for the Clause. The Archbishop of Canterbury and the Bishop of Chichester voted for the Arts loophole whilst the Bishops of Gloucester, Rochester and Manchester voted against the Clause as a whole, as did the Archbishop of York. Other notable opponents of the Clause or supporters of the Arts Loophole were Lord Beaumont, Lord Soper, Lord Gifford, Lord Melchett, Lords Henderson, Houghton and Hutchinson, Lord Monkswell and Baronesses Blackstone and Seear.[55]

After the vote, one Peer told Graham Webster-Gardiner, Chairman of Conservative Family Campaign, that in contrast to the volume of special pleading they had received from the homosexual lobby, there had only been two items sent in favour of the Clause, one of which was the submission from Conservative Family Campaign. The Minister, Michael Howard, wrote to thank the Campaign for its efforts. It might be that the gay lobby overplayed its hand; certainly, the four lesbians invited in by Lord Monkswell only to abseil over the gallery went some way to convince the Clause's supporters of the soundness of their position.

What Section 28 means

It is probably difficult to say what Section 28, as it became, of the Local Government Act 1988 means in Law until a case is brought before the Courts and ruled on by the Court of Appeal or the House of Lords. It is absurd to think in such a case, that the Law Lords would be unable to tell the difference between "The Happy Prince" on the one hand and "Young Gay and Proud" on the other, or between a showing of the film "Death in Venice" and Hackney's "Gay Pride Week."

The Clause has already had the effect of banning the letting of some premises to student homosexual groups in the Local Authority areas of Colchester, Strathclyde, Leeds and Cambridge. Other Councils have reconsidered their employment and education policies.[56]

However, a legal opinion given to the Labour-run Association of London Authorities and the National Council for Civil Liberties set out ways in which Education Authorities may still promote homosexuality whilst staying inside Section 28 and the 1986 Education Act. The opinion relies on narrowing the definition of "promotion" so that only direct advocacy to individuals to behave homosexually or to experiment with homosexual activity would be involved. A circular based on the opinion and sent to schools notes that some home backgrounds "could include lesbian or gay parents and qualities like love and compassion," and adds cynically: "The nuclear family should be discussed and valued with due regard to disadvantages (eg possible abuse and violence to children and women, restrictions on children's freedom, dependence of women on men) and with regard to any advantages."[57]

On top of that, the London Boroughs Grant Scheme still voted to award £300,000 to gay groups in the capital in 1988,[58] and "Gay Pride" was held just the same in 1988, '89, '90 and '91 and in 1992 with a march in London and a rally in Lambeth's Brockwell Park. The left continues to support the homosexual press by advertisements for jobs. During 1991, the Boroughs of Richmond-on-Thames, Waltham Forest, Nottingham, Greenwich and Newham joined Gateshead Law Centre, MIND, the National Association of Citizens Advice Bureaux, Shelter, the Rainer Foundation and Centrepoint in advertising for homosexual staff in "Pink Paper", which has a weekly circulation of 40,000. The last three charities specifically provide hostel accommodation for young people.

Centrepoint must be singled out. Although not a local authority, it receives funds and referrals from local social services and is also funded by Government Departments, groups and churches, companies and livery companies and leading charities, most of them quite innocently. They are too many to list but GKN paid for a recent Centrepoint annual report, and the Prince's Trust has provided funding. Centrepoint is by far the most regular advertiser in the situations vacant section of Pink Paper. There is a crying need for a bona fide organisation run by decent people which would provide accommodation for the homeless young, whilst any group wishing to place disturbed or homeless young people in the care of active homosexuals surely needs investigation.

Section 28 restates public policy

Possibly the major benefit of Section 28 is to demonstrate that homosexuality per se is still against public policy. Section 28 has been of value if it can be regarded by a practising homosexual as something which "casts aspersions on my sexuality," as the actor Ian McKellen put it on Radio 4's "Midweek."[59] The same man demonstrated the necessity of the clause shortly after it was passed, by telling marchers at an anti-clause rally: "We must all be out and about, in the streets, in the classrooms, talking to our friends and our families, promoting homosexuality."[60]

The battle for Clause 28

Far from confirming that there are "rights" in law attaching to homosexual behaviour, Section 28 confirms the points made by all peers during the debate on the Sexual Offences Act 1967, that homosexual activity is "utterly wrongful" and should not be promoted. Section 28 rules that homosexual liaisons may now be described in Law as "pretended family relationships." This is the first public statement in legislation about homosexuality for two decades, and if it had been lost, or watered down by the Arts Loophole, the signal would have been sent that homosexual activists could have a field day promoting homosexuality at public expense. These are the reasons why they fought so hard to "Stop the Clause," and why the passing of it was a minor triumph.

6
How many and how promiscuous?

What proportion of the population is homosexual, and of those who define themselves in that way, do they regard themselves as exclusively so? Furthermore, how promiscuous are homosexuals? On the first point, a survey was carried out by British Market Research Bureau for the D.H.S.S. AIDS unit from February 1986 to February 1987.

How do homosexuals see themselves?
Interviewing men in "gay bars," the research found that only half of those who responded identified themselves as completely homosexual. On a scale running from 0 - exclusively heterosexual - to 10 - exclusively homosexual, very few individuals, understandably perhaps, classified themselves in the heterosexual half of the scale. However, most of the respondents claimed to score from 5 to 9, with the bias towards the top end. Although the homosexual men in the gay bar sample showed some propensity to regard themselves as less than totally homosexual, it is impossible from the question to deduce the frequency of any heterosexual activity. Nevertheless, the average of the samples of respondents was 8.5, confirming the reluctance of a good half of the men interviewed in "gay bars" to identify themselves as exclusively homosexual.[1]

Is it really 10%?
When men in the population at large were asked by BMRB about their sexual orientation, 5% said they had felt attracted to someone of their own sex but had never had sexual contact, 2% said that they had had homosexual contact but "only once or very rarely," less than 1% admitted to having sexual contact with someone of their own sex "fairly often" whilst 2% claimed to have had sexual contact "only ever" with people of their own sex.[2]

The usual figure claimed by activists for the "gay population" is of course 10%, a figure which comes from the Kinsey reports, "Sexual

How many and how promiscuous? 59

Behaviour in the Human Male" (1948) and "Sexual Behaviour in the Human Female," (1953) and had seemed unassailable. Homosexuals and sexual "progressives" rely heavily on Kinsey. Recent commentators have however criticised Kinsey both for his sampling techniques and for his methodology of scoring sexuality:

> *The U.S. Justice Department's principal investigator of pornography, Dr Judith Reisman, blew the whistle on Kinsey in a broadcast interview. The rampant sexual promiscuity today, and its subsequent contribution of AIDS and other disease epidemics, can be traced directly to Kinsey's report on human sexuality, she said, "Alfred Kinsey was an insect specialist turned human sexuality researcher," explained Reisman. "He and his co-authors favored pansexuality...that is, they believed that all sexual activities were equally pleasurable and desirable. That included homosexuality, bisexuality, adult sex with children, anal and oral copulation, sex with animals, adultery, and so forth. The homosexual movement...used the theories of Kinsey to justify their way of life."*[3]

Clearly the BMRB figures add up to Kinsey's 10%, but BMRB's 10% figure includes the 5% in their survey who have never had sexual contact, and who only admitted that they "have felt attracted" to someone of their own sex, and the 2% who had homosexual contact once or very rarely.

It is more than likely that these men do not classify themselves as homosexual or even as bisexual. The true figure for active bisexuals, that is those who had homosexual contact "fairly often" is 1%, whilst for the 2% who had only ever had sexual contact with people of their own sex, these appear to be the remaining active homosexuals, but once again, the way in which the question was worded means that we cannot estimate the frequency of their contacts, or indeed how many are still sexually active.

The Van Wyk and Geist analysis

An important investigation into "Psychosocial Development of Heterosexual, Bisexual and Homosexual Behavior" was published by Paul Van Wyk and Chrisann Geist in 1984. As its title suggests, Van Wyk & Geist are helpful in studying the origins of homosexual orientation, but they also investigated the sexual behaviour of their sample, using the Kinsey "scores" as a measurement. To do this, they "cleaned" the samples, then re-analysed the data of all the Caucasian, nondelinquent subjects from the "basic sample" and the "homosexual sample" of the Institute for Sex Research at Indiana University, the adult subjects of the original Kinsey interviews.

Amongst 6,492 American white males and females, excluding biased sources, Van Wyk & Geist actually found a similar pattern to BMRB. The vast majority, 85.7%, of men were exclusively heterosexual, with overt Kinsey scores of between .000 and .004. a further 8.4% scored .005 to 1.99. Homosexual scores, 4.01 to 6.00, were recorded in 4.7%, with bisexual scores, that is 2.00 to 4.00, accounting for only 1.2%.[4]

These figures refer to activity in the samples. It appears that the claimed figure of 10% "gays," or active homosexuals, in the population is far too high for men, let alone for women. Kinsey scores of 4.01 to 6.00 were recorded by only 1.8% of women in the Van Wyk and Geist survey, with 0.7% scoring bisexually, that is 2.00 to 4.00, 3.4% being between .005 and 1.99, and 94.1% scoring .000 to .004. Van Wyk and Geist concluded:

> *The relative sexual adventurousness of males, compared with females, seems to account in part for the fact that more males than females develop overtly expressed same-sex partner preference in adulthood.*[5]

Bisexuality is very rare

An American expert asserts that: "Although some (homosexuals) claim to be "bisexual" in that they seek sexual gratification from both sexes, most do not engage in normal sexual behavior with the opposite sex."[6] This conclusion is borne out by the Van Wyk and Geist study, to their evident surprise:

> *More bisexual than predominantly or exclusively homosexual individuals had been expected. But, whether measured for the entire span between age 18 and age 40, or measured for any single year between age 11 and age 18, the distribution was extremely bipolar, with very few individuals scoring between 2 and 4. It appears that the popular conception of heterosexuality and homosexuality as polar extremes is quite accurate.*

Kinsey's original research had concluded that very many people were bisexual, and that children were sexually active. Reisman and Eichel have suggested that Kinsey was "pushing an agenda" of "child sex and bisexuality," that up to 25% of his male sample were prison inmates and sex offenders, and that "Somewhere and some time in the course

How many and how promiscuous?

of the project, Kinsey appears to have directed experimental sex research on several hundred children aged two months to almost 15 years."[7]

The problems with Kinsey

Van Wyk and Geist partially got over the first problem of Kinsey, the problem of sample selection, by only including those from unbiased sources over 21 from Kinsey's samples. BMRB went for 1,990 men aged 18-64, but sampled at random, in line with normal polling techniques, through the population. Even when the prisoners and sex offenders are excluded, Kinsey's sample still consisted of volunteers drawn from people who in the early 1940s attended his lectures on sex research, and any of their friends who could be persuaded to join in. Such people were not indicative in the 1940s of the population at large, and Van Wyk & Geist have no choice but to perpetuate this error.

The second criticism of Kinsey is that instead of asking about sexual behaviour, he investigates "psychotic reactions and overt experience," so that merely thinking about homosexuality turns the person into a Kinsey homosexual. Van Wyk and Geist discuss behaviour only, and actually eliminate people whose arousal ratings differed from their behaviour ratings by more than 3 on the Kinsey scale. BMRB kept their questions simple, and their survey is extremely valuable, but they necessarily failed to discover information that could have come out in a more exhaustive study.

The Smith report

Professor Tom Smith of the University of Chicago manages to avoid both problems with Kinsey, in a major survey funded by the American Government, carried out in 1989 for the US General Social Survey Project and presented in February 1990 to the Conference of the American Association for the Advancement of Science. The survey involved some 1,400 adults in a national, full-probability sample, rather than a self-selected sample. It then asked what people actually do, rather than employ a vague combination of behaviour and psychosexual reactions.

Smith found 98.5% of adults to be exclusively heterosexual. He found that although 5.5% of Americans have had some overt homosexual experience since age 18, that just over a fifth of the 5.5% are still active homosexually. The 5.5% breaks down like this: 3.3% are now in a heterosexual relationship, 1.2% are in a homosexual relationship, 0.8% are not sexually active and 0.2% would not say.[8]

These results are extraordinarily consonant with the results of the British Market Research Bureau survey, and show that homosexual activists will be very lucky indeed if 1.5% of the male population is active homosexually, and 1% of the female.

A sex educator and an agony aunt talk rubbish

That bisexuality is rare offends the opinion of Suzie Hayman in "It's more than sex," a sex education book for teenagers. She has been press officer to both the Family Planning Association and Brook Advisory Centres, a campaigning position which is evidently well insulated from objective evidence. "The best way of picturing it," she claims, "is to imagine a line of 100 people. Five at one end will never experience any attraction to their own sex. Five at the other end will only feel such love. [sic] The other 90 are strung out along that line. Those in the middle happily have relationships with both sexes"[9]

Journalist and "agony aunt" Claire Rayner also makes a bad start by using the word "love" too loosely for us to know whether she means friendship, affection, commitment, or ten minutes in a public convenience. She asks us in the course notes for the BBC "Two of Us" to imagine "a hundred people across a football field." Ten of them, she says, "could not possibly relate to the opposite sex even if they were ship-wrecked on a desert island." Relate? At the other end, so she says, are 20 totally heterosexual people. The remaining bisexual 70 "and I make it quite clear, this is everybody" are once more "strung out along the line."[10]

Claire Rayner, like fellow "agony aunt" Angela Willans, is a campaigning anti-Christian and gay rights advocate, a vice-president indeed of the "Gay and Lesbian Humanist Association." She had a very unhappy childhood, and may well be carrying some unfortunate emotional baggage as a result. It is valid to ask if she knew that her advice to school-children was just invention.

Homosexual promiscuity revealed

The evidence indicates that truth is the first casualty when homosexual activists and apologists wish to present a more acceptable public face of homosexuality. The subject of promiscuity amongst homosexuals was until recently no different, with the public only able to guess at what was common knowledge within the homosexual network, but vigorously denied outside it.

The spread of AIDS changed all that. The extent of homosexual promiscuity became known, and the arguments shifted, away usually from simple denials, or from eulogising promiscuity itself, toward the

How many and how promiscuous? 63

contention that active homosexuals have reformed, and only need society's approval in order to establish permanent monogamous relationships. We shall look at the various claims and see how they have developed.

The routine rejection of the sheer scale of homosexual promiscuity is commonplace, but one correspondent to a local paper claimed: "There are some promiscuous gays, but if "straights" can sleep around so can homosexuals".[11]

That writer claims that heterosexual promiscuity comes first and that homosexuals merely mimic it. Professor Smith in the Chicago University Study found to the contrary a mean number of sex partners for heterosexuals during the previous year of 0.96 for the married (9.2% abstinent,) 0.21 for the widowed (85.9% abstinent,) 1.31 for the divorced (25.9% abstinent,) 2.41% for the separated (20.0% abstinent,) and 1.84 for those never married (24.6% abstinent,).[12]

"Homosexuals less promiscuous than heterosexuals"

Lord Falkland is president of the Liberal Democrats' "lesbian and gay association," DELGA, and a patron of the homosexual lobby group "Stonewall." He amazed the House of Lords by claiming in the Clause 28 debate that: "Homosexuals are probably less promiscuous than heterosexuals."[13] The poor man should rely less on what Stonewall and DELGA tell him. Peers were convinced more of his sincerity than of the truth of what he said. Terry Casey, past general secretary of the teaching union NAS/UWT, is a man with strong views about the example set to the young by promiscuous homosexual teachers. One writer, in a campaign manual produced to promote homosexuality - it insists in cataloguing the various ways in which its writers feel "homosexuals" to have been discriminated against - but with a "straight" readership in mind, says of him:

> The equation of homosexuality with promiscuity, the view of a simple assertion of sexuality as "flaunting," ... is hardly indicative of much understanding of those homosexuals among his union's membership.[14]

In fact it is indicative of simple observation and perception, as we shall see. Promiscuity is seen within the homosexual network as bringing benefits, for example, a sense of identity:

> "I think promiscuity is the one common experience which brings the male gay community together," as one active homosexual put it.[15]

Promiscuity not seen as shameful

In a "gay history" of the last thirty years which was recently published, Scottish activist Ian Dunn claims to have "clocked up" his thousandth sexual experience in America in 1971, just nine years after he first became sexually active at the age of nineteen.[16] It falls to German psychologist and homosexual activist Martin Dannecker to spell out the obvious:

> It is clear that homosexual relationships cannot be measured with the same standard applied to heterosexual relationships.[17]

Most ostensibly monogamous homosexual couples, particularly those involving men, indulge in promiscuous contact outside their pairing.[18] Two homosexuals in Exeter gave whisky and drugged coffee to young men whom they befriended and invited back to their flat in order for them both to have sex with them.[19] In other cases, such as that of Joe Orton and Kenneth Halliwell, one man is much more promiscuous than the other, and the jealousies that arise lead to tensions within the relationship. [qv] Joe Orton records one of his promiscuous encounters thus:

> I arrived in Leicester [for his mother's funeral] at four thirty. I had a bit of quick sex in a derelict house with a labourer I picked up.[20]

Promiscuity with children

"Couples" like Orton and Halliwell are often sexually promiscuous with children, and even a sympathetic reviewer of Joe Orton's Diaries, referring to Orton and Halliwell's trips to Tangier, complains:

> The repetitive and detailed accounts of bargained-for, purchased sex seem interminable, and after a dozen or more barely-pubescent boys - almost always named Mohammed - had been knocked-up for a knock-down price, I found myself becoming exacerbated"[21]

Another active paedophile provides an insight into the mind of the active homosexual:

> The essential affair is brief, non-possessive and an end in itself. Some affairs are more powerful and probing than others. I remember and relish brief sexual encounters with many boys. I have forgotten many boys ... A surprising number of these affairs remain strong in my mind, and I have found out years later in the minds of the boys also. This staying power does not depend on the time spent - as any gay man will know. It is not necessarily linked to any sense of strong

affection, certainly not to romantic love. Ten minutes in a toilet stall
or the back seat of a Greyhound [bus] can provide sharp insights and
refreshment to mind and body even in memory."²²

Promiscuity embedded in gay philosophy
Promiscuity is so much part of the whole philosophy of homosexual
gratification, that the Terrence Higgins Trust in one of its "safer sex"
publications illustrates a point with a cartoon depicting two men sat
at a table nursing identical drinks and eyeing up another man leaning
on a bar: "I wouldn't mind negotiating safer sex with him" one is
saying to the other.²³

It might be this process of "negotiation" that leads to homosexuals
describing their contacts as "trade" (hence "rough trade" for a
particular sort of virile young man, often somewhat unpredictable,
who is picked up for "a bit of quick sex"). The concept of "trade" is
deeply ingrained. One Christmas morning, my wife and I took our
dogs for a walk on Streatham Common. We had an acquaintance at
that time who was an effeminate homosexual, and who very well
might still be. He had a "friend" who was especially interested in
young boys, and the two of them would sit in a bar commenting on
whoever came in, on the "passing trade" in other words. Comments
on young men they fancied would be: "I wonder if 'e's gay?" "Ooh,
look at 'er" and so on, ad nauseam. However on this occasion our
acquaintance was himself accompanied by a teenage boy and girl. He
greeted us with "Ooh, 'allo" and then said, "This is my nephew and
niece" - pause - "Not trade," he concluded with a giggle.

Promiscuity admitted to homosexual readership
In the face of all this and more, Andrew Hodges and David Hutter in
"With Downcast Gays," which was written with a strictly homosexual
readership in mind, had no other course than to admit:

> Homosexual public speakers find three complaints against gay
> people cropping up with monotonous regularity. Thinly disguised
> as questions come the accusations that gay men are mannered and
> effeminate, corruptors of children, and given to a mindless animal
> promiscuity that prevents their forming lasting relationships.
> "Responsible" gay activists respond in the appropriate apologetic,
> self-oppressive manner to the first two charges ... but probably none
> claim that "only a minority of homosexuals are promiscuous."²⁴

Certainly Joe Orton wouldn't have claimed that. His diaries are full of accounts of his promiscuous exploits, one of which was written on 4th. March 1967 about an encounter in a "cottage," that is, a public convenience, in Holloway. The passage gives an idea of the sort of thing that was happening even before the 1967 Sexual Offences Act, and describes frantic manual, oral and anal contacts. The conduct Orton describes is not at all private, and would still be illegal today, but his biographer writes "Human beings are driven by unreasoning desires ... which can turn them from the respectable to the rampaging."[25] Orton says of the saturnalia when at its height:

> A seventh man came in, but by now nobody cared. The number of people in the place was so large that detection was impossible.[26]

Lesbian serial monogamy

Homosexual women are not quite so promiscuous as their male counterparts. One pattern is to change partners within households of three or four. There is of course some cruising in lesbian bars,[27] and promiscuity does exist to a certain extent,[28] but, to paraphrase Van Wyk & Geist, most women still have a far greater need than men to experience feelings of deep affection before expressing them in a sexual relationship.

Where a lesbian couple lives apart from others, according to a lesbian author, "usually, in time, the two women become emotionally involved with someone else, or they drift apart or formally break up."[29] Even though there are always examples of lesbian couples remaining together for many years, two years would by usual reckoning be a long time, and "in fact what is most typical of the lesbian community is 'serial monogamy'."[30] This could be promiscuity by another name, even though it is of a different order to the antics of male homosexuals. It still shows that the "need to be loved" remains in female as in male homosexual relationships, perpetually unfulfilled.

Promiscuity levels: Denmark and Germany

A survey of homosexual behaviour patterns in the Danish towns of Copenhagen and Aarhus reported in 1984 that the average number of homosexual partners during the last year had been 18.1 for the Aarhus sample, and 28.2 for the men in Copenhagen.[31] The authors, Ebbesen et al, explain the greater promiscuity reported in Copenhagen as a product of more liberal attitudes. They say:

How many and how promiscuous? 67

In the last decade a greater acceptance of homosexuality has developed in the Western world; and Copenhagen, in particular since 1970, has developed into a major tourist centre for HS men.[32]

Significantly, about half of each group (49% and 46% respectively) had had heterosexual relationships during their period of homosexual activity, that is during the last 11 years for the Copenhagen men, and the last 8 for those from Aarhus, but again its frequency was not recorded.

Around the median number of sexual partners, the survey found wide variations. "In Copenhagen and Aarhus respectively, 8% and 9% reported that they had been monogamous during the past year, but 5% and 2% claimed to have had at least 100 sex partners during the same 1-year period."[33]

German author Martin Dannecker reports as follows on his own survey, the results of which are clearly comparable to what was found in Denmark. Young homosexuals were asked how many sexual partners they had had since their first sexual experience:

> The homosexual men questioned by Reimut Reiche and myself gave the following picture:
> 11% up to 10; 9% 11 to 20; 80% more than 20 ...
>
> In our survey of homosexual men, one in seven turned out to have had sex with more than 50 men in the previous year, which led us to view such high numbers as normal.[34]

Promiscuity levels in America

Research in America shows a higher level of homosexual promiscuity even than that claimed by the men in the Danish and German surveys. The American homosexual activist Dr Morin, chairman of the American Psychological Association's ethics committee [sic] conducted a study of 824 homosexual men to find that fear of AIDS had lowered their claimed numbers of partners from 70 per year in 1982 to 50 per year by 1984.[35] McKusick et al reported claimed reductions from 76 to 47 over a similar period.[36] Dr Hunter Handsfield, Director of the Seattle Sexually Transmitted Disease Control Program commented that in "the context of the severity of AIDS, these changes are almost ludicrous."[37]

In addition, the claimed numbers of partners are probably underestimated, because homosexuals often do not count every person with whom they have anonymous sex as a "partner." One 1980 survey asked homosexual males to keep a diary. The men had estimated that they had 60 partners per year on average, but the diaries confirmed the real figure to be around 100.[38] Bell and Weinberg, authors of another large study, wrote:

> During the course of research on AIDS it was discovered that the average homosexual who was interviewed had had 550 different sexual partners; the AIDS victims considered by themselves averaged 1,100 different sexual partners; some reported as many as 20,000. ... For example, one homosexual reported: "I believe my estimate of 4,000 sex partners to be very accurate. I have been actively gay since I was 13 (thirty-one years ago). An average of two or three new partners per week is not excessive, especially when one considers that I will have ten to twelve partners during one night at the baths."[39]

Bath houses evoke disgust in humanist

According to the humanist homosexual activist, J Martin Stafford, it was not an uncommon experience for a man to have fifty (mainly passive) homosexual couplings a night at the San Francisco bathhouses. A caller to a Radio 4 phone-in programme admitted that many in the "gay scene" are so sated with sexual activity that it means no more to them than blowing their nose. Facts like these, admits Mr Stafford, "Must evoke in people of ordinary sensitivies the most intense and well-founded feelings of disgust." As he says, promiscuity and the extent to which prominent gay figures condone it "puts a millstone round the necks of those who would make out a plausible and responsible case for gay rights." It is scarcely denied by anyone in the homosexual lobby, as Mr Stafford reports:

> In December 1986, the Chief Constable of Greater Manchester, Mr James Anderton, hit the headlines by proclaiming that those most at risk from AIDS (promiscuous homosexuals, drug addicts and prostitutes) were "swirling around in a ... cesspit of their own making." Even those who have most reason to regret his remark were quite unable seriously to dispute it. A spokesman for the Terrence Higgins Trust said it was "uncaring and unchristian" but, significantly, he did not venture to say it was untrue.[40]

Next we shall discover where homosexual activity takes place and ask if society is to blame for homosexual promiscuity, or if the cause lies rather in the homosexual psyche itself.

7
The inner drive to make sexual contact

Where do homosexual contacts take place? The answer seems to be, in spite of the 1956 & 1967 Sexual Offences Acts, in public places.

Promiscuity "revolutionary"

An American book, about and written for homosexuals, says the following about behaviour in the USA:

> It is generally well known that male homosexuals often perform sex outside the home. John Rechy's books, especially "Numbers" and "The Sexual Outlaw," document the lives of sex hunters of city streets and parks. The use of public toilets for cruising and sex is so well known that a technical book by Cornell University entitled "The Bath Room" includes a whole section discussing the homosexual issue in the design of modern public rest-rooms ... Psychiatrists have on occasion suggested that men choose public places because they find the danger attractive. Most contemporary gay writers, however, indicate that sex in public places is chosen for its convenience or its anonymity or both, and a few have even suggested that there is something revolutionary about promiscuity and public sex.[1]

It might be thought that to identify promiscuity with revolution is at best utopianism and at worst a jump onto the left-wing bandwagon. Indeed what isn't revolutionary when you put your mind to it? One Charley Shively, prominent in American homosexual circles, wrote of bestiality as an act of revolution and of sex with children as an act of revolution in the magazine "Fag Rag."[2] Revolutionary subversives do find the disruption caused to society by "gay liberation" attractive, and we shall investigate this in due course.[3]

Sex in public places

The most frequent places mentioned in the American "Gay Report" for homosexual behaviour are:

a. Public rest rooms [Lavatories]
b. Public Parks
c. Beaches
d. Public Baths or "health clubs"
e. Gay bars
f. Street corner pick-ups
g. "Glory holes" cut in WC partitions, for anonymity.
h. Pornographic bookstores[4]

The baths, "gay" bars, and bookstores were said usually to provide private rooms for sexual activity. Contact is made initially through "cruising," that is eyeing up potential partners with whom sex acts can be committed. Cruising takes place in the UK in gay bars and clubs and on the streets, as well as in public open spaces like parks and commons. At a typical nudist beach on the continent, homosexual men drive out in order to make eye contact with one another during a short stroll, before the two of them drive back separately through a maritime pine forest to park at a picnic spot and go off together. Such "cruising" places become well known in the homosexual network. Bath Houses cannot exist as such in the UK, but gay saunas provide a similar service, as activist Bruce Galloway explains in a piece critical of police attempts to enforce the law:

> *Police have in some places sought the entire abolition of gay social venues, including one successful prosecution for "running a disorderly house" and threats of another under "licentious dancing" bye-laws. .... The clientele of gay saunas and sex shops are also harassed. "Bath-houses" have a special place in gay life across the Atlantic. Exclusively gay, they provide secure venues for social and sexual contacts. In Britain they are defined as "disorderly houses," and violate the privacy clauses of the 1967 Act.*[5]

Bar "cruising"

Gay bars and pubs are, as we have seen, very important in the homosexual network: A woman involved in this "scene" explains:

> *Going to the bars means learning bar behavior. ... Many bars have rules, often unwritten, about what is proper attire. ... And there are some unwritten rules for interactions among the customers - who you look at, buy a drink for, ask for a dance. Much of this sets the standard for cruising, especially in women's bars where it may be less open than in men's bars. That cruising is an important part of bar*

The inner drive to make sexual contact 71

behavior for both women and men cannot be over-emphasised. While in a straight bar the customers are usually sitting facing the bar, watching TV or talking to the bartender, in a gay bar customers will frequently be turned at least partly away from the bar and looking at the customers. Since gay bars have been one of the few places where gay people can meet potential lovers, this cruisiness is no surprise.[6]

The things that attract homosexual men to each other seem to be less to do with depth of personality and more to do with style, youth and looks. One particular part of the anatomy is very much more important to homosexual men than any other, as we learnt when discussing homosexual entertainment. Charley Shively explains:

Phallocentricism among faggots has its unique structure. In faggot bars, men wear pants that strategically reveal (often over-emphasise) each inch. .... Everywhere in fag country, a hard or half-hard cock serves as a come-on for other faggots.[7]

Martin Dannecker explains that despite the casual character of the sexual contacts they facilitate, the bars "do require a rather greater degree of interaction with the prospective sexual partner" than some other aspects of the sub-culture. To counter this, he writes that:

Following the American example, bars are now being established in Germany too with a murky back-room where people can get down to business right away.[8]

Cottaging

The other main place in the UK for making contact is in public lavatories. Tabulated information concerning "size" of penis, "age," "likes" and "dislikes" of sexual activities are common in public conveniences used by homosexuals. Public conveniences are called in homosexual argot "cottages." "Glory holes" may be cut in the partitions for anonymous sex. Again we shall call upon an activist to explain the attractions of sexual encounters in such places:

"Cottaging" is a term used by men to describe their sexual encounters in public lavatories. The classic form involves a ritual escalation of intimacy in total silence, entirely within the cottage, although contacts may be developed outside it. The pattern varies depending on the clientele and the location - rural or urban, in department stores or by railway stations. ... The main advantage of cottaging is

that it offers a quick and easy sexual release which does not require emotional commitment to one person, and therefore need not disrupt any primary relationship. For some, especially those who do regard themselves as being gay and are more or less integrated into the gay scene, there is an element of gambling in the attraction: if the gay scene sometimes resembles a market place, the cottage is more of a betting shop.[9]

Is society to blame for homosexual promiscuity?

So what of the claim that homosexuals would like to be monogamous, but society actually drives them into promiscuity? Norman Pittenger and the so-called "Lesbian and Gay Christian Movement" are the main advocates of this line, telling heartrending tales of pairs of homosexuals being discovered living together, whose "monogamy" has brought them worse treatment than if they had been furtively promiscuous.

The particular case with which Dr Pittenger invites us to sympathise is that of a man living with someone younger whom he describes as his "nephew" until it transpires the young man is not his nephew at all, whereupon they are ostracised from polite church-going society.[10] It leaves me with an odd feeling that there was more to it than that.

Even at face value a bit more compassion could have been shown to sinners, or some strong-minded individual could have said "Hold on, why should two gentlemen not share a home; who is spreading this scandal of homosexuality between them?" From time to time an archbishop reminds us that there is nothing wrong with two homosexuals living together as long as they do not indulge in homosexual activity, and everyone sniggers, although he is right in fact and in theology and right to give them the benefit of the doubt. But I suspect I am missing the point, for Norman Pittenger, a declared homosexual himself, is arguing more for acceptance of homosexual activity as such, than discussing sin, scandal and the common human failing to attribute the best of motives until a different story is proven.

It might be attractive to see male homosexual promiscuity as a function of society's disapproval of homosexual relationships. The founder of "Parents Enquiry," whom we shall meet later, writes as follows:

Much of the promiscuity that occurs amongst gay people has more to do with the overwhelming sense of isolation they feel from the normal world than it has to do with any desire for sex as such.[11]

Increasing tolerance leads to increasing promiscuity

If we confront the evidence, then to make the claim that it would all be different if society approved of homosexuality is to display a cynicism, or a naivety, depending on which side one is standing, almost beyond belief. There is no evidence at all that with liberal values progressing over the last twenty years, today's homosexuals are less promiscuous than was Joe Orton.

"The gays" have instead become more and more outrageous and ever more promiscuous. An increasing acceptance of homosexual behaviour has brought a greater acceptance of homosexual promiscuity. Ebbesen et al demonstrated just this point in Denmark. The American bath-houses are another indicator that homosexuals become more promiscuous as society becomes more liberal towards them.

The surveys of sexual behaviour that homosexual psychiatrist Martin Dannecker carried out amongst all groups showed:

> a far greater degree of "promiscuity" among homosexual men, a fact that is scarcely contested any longer in sexual research, and is customarily ascribed to "social stigma."
>
> Yet a comparison of number of partners between homosexual men and homosexual women casts a different light. ... Whereas only 1% of homosexual women had more than 10 different sexual partners in the year prior to our survey, this was the case with 61% of homosexual men.
>
> These results indicate that the criterion of "sexual stigma" is too crude to give a satisfactory explanation for the striking way in which homosexual men are distinguished from both heterosexual men and homosexual women.[12]

It is well to have this point well established in our minds, because we shall need to rely on it later. Martin Dannecker concludes without a shadow of doubt:

> The behaviour of homosexuals is decisively influenced by factors that *do not arise from the social discrimination against them*.[13]

Easier for homosexuals to make sexual contacts

Where gay rights activists wanted to take us before AIDS was into a discussion to challenge: "the assumption that promiscuity is necessarily a bad thing."[14] Hodges and Hutter must speak with authority on the nature of homosexual encounters, even if their understanding of heterosexuality is limited:

> A heterosexual pick-up is fraught with implications of the man conquering and the woman surrendering; it is unlikely to enjoy the sense of mutual agreement enjoyed by gay people. For this reason it is easier for homosexuals to make sexual contacts, and once made there is no tedious process of persuasion - no ritualised escalation of intimacy to be carried out before sexual pleasure is reached.
>
> When apologetic gay speakers mention and then disparage the accessibility of gay sex, they display a naive belief that non-gay people themselves pay more than lip-service to the value of monogamy. Heterosexuals would dearly like the availability of desirable bodies and the affectionate sharing of pleasure that gay people can enjoy. The heterosexual world has no equivalent of a gay sauna!
>
> Moreover our detractors betray their limited vision by their mistaken assumption that promiscuity is incompatible with lasting relationships. Homosexuals are in the happy position of being able to enjoy both at once. A gay couple in the street will be admiring the same people, probably be exchanging remarks about them; already the heterosexual model is inadequate to describe what is going on.[15]

Indeed it is. The same writers make a joke out of the way some of their number parody heterosexual family life, and manage to disparage marriage at the same time, suggesting that future anthropologists would have to turn "to the pair-bonding of discreet homosexuals as the only means left available of examining the long-defunct institution of marriage."[16] The Gay Liberation Front activists were even more disparaging of homosexuals who try to ape heterosexual conventions:

> We question ... as an ideal, the finding and settling down eternally with one "right" partner. This is the blueprint of the straight world which gay people have taken over. It is inevitably a parody, since they haven't even the justification of straight couples - the need to provide a stable environment for their children."[17]

Monogamy not relevant to homosexuality

Homosexual relationships are typically of short duration, usually less than two years. In every superficially monogamous homosexual relationship that I have known, at least one of the "partners" has been having what he calls "affairs" outside the "primary relationship" and the homosexual literature bears this out as typical as well. Monogamy

The inner drive to make sexual contact

has no relevance to homosexuality and homosexuality is according to Hodges & Hutter at its most ludicrous when it parodies marriage:

> The model of heterosexual marriage often actually discourages gay people from entering into any kind of permanent relationship, since they are unwilling to accept the exclusivity which they imagine a relationship must entail; moreover partnerships which do begin often break up because one partner thinks that he ought to feel jealous, or the other is unnecessarily secretive about "extra-marital" affairs. ... Why deny the eroticism of novelty in favour of the repressive dogma that sex is only satisfactory with one lifelong partner? Is there not a genuine ideal in the ability of gay people to gain immediate trust and sexual satisfaction from anywhere in the world?"[18]

In response to criticisms from Dr Hunter Handsfield about the inadequacy of alleged reductions in sexual promiscuity amongst homosexuals in response to AIDS, McKusick wrote:

> The recommendation that gay men limit themselves to committed monogamy was discussed and found to lack creativity ... and to reflect the simple insensitivity of an outsider approaching the gay world.[19]

J Martin Stafford quotes approvingly the London Gay Teenage Group, which reported that over 200 respondents to its survey "Said that they had, or had had, a long-term homosexual lover," but fails to say what is an appropriate level of promiscuity. It is going to be fairly liberally drawn, if "a long-term" relationship can be reported by a teenager as something he has already left, but how is it defined? Mr Stafford does not dare to say. He too claims that greater acceptance of homosexual liaisons, and "positive images" teaching, would decrease homosexual promiscuity, but he produces no evidence that homosexual promiscuity has declined with greater acceptance of homosexuality in the last thirty years.[20] This is not surprising, because the evidence in Europe and the USA all points the other way.

The gays on holiday

Writing in Gay Times, Roger Baker asks whether a "gay" holiday means going somewhere to get laid as often as possible. "Could be it's hunting boys in Bangkok," he ponders. "And how do you know it's been gay when you get back?" Well, from the three holidays which he has been on and which he claims measure up to the specification "gay," they all involved frequent sexual contact with "lots of men."

Even back in 1958, he and a friend went to Brighton to explore "all those queer pubs for which Brighton was famous. Our intention was quite simple and straightforward - we wanted to meet lots of other homosexuals and go to bed with as many as possible," he writes. They succeeded. Although, as he says, Brighton would not be exotic in today's terms and with today's package holidays, especially in the homosexual subculture, where the glossy brochures are illustrated with the sort of muscular men the gay punter expects to meet, he and his friend "scored a man a day."[21]

This is not just a homosexual version of "Club 18-30." On a heterosexual singles holiday a man and woman tend to "get off" with each other for the fortnight at least, in other words, there is an attempt at building a relationship, which may even survive the duration of the holiday romance. Homosexual psychotherapist Joe Brewer claims that promiscuity is rampant in an all-male "gay" subculture because there is "nobody to say 'no' - no moderating role like that a woman plays in the heterosexual milieu."[22]

Trying to solve the impossible

Can it be simply down to the moderating role of woman, or is it possible that a heterosexual man is not driven by the same need to make sexual contact as is a homosexual man? Certainly most psychiatrists, when confronted by a promiscuous heterosexual, would suggest that an underlying immaturity is preventing him from being satisfied with the one partner he has. If this is the case, then it could be that an emotional immaturity is driving the homosexual man to an even greater extent. Another possibility is the quest, or as Quentin Crisp has described it, the "vain search" for the masculine man who will love a homosexual. This seems to be what David Reuben is suggesting in "Everything you always wanted to know about sex":

> Homosexuals are trying the impossible; solving the problem with only half the pieces. Disappointed, stubborn, discouraged, defiant, the homosexual keeps trying .... that is the reason he must change partners endlessly. He tries each phallus in succession, then turns away remorsefully; "No, that's not the one." He is in a difficult position - condemned eternally to search after what does not exist - after what never existed.[23]

McKusick wrote: "Although most of our subjects have expressed a desire for more primary partnering in response to AIDS, there has been no significant increase in these bonds during the [3 year] period of our investigation"[24]

The inner drive to make sexual contact

Comparing studies of male and female homosexual behaviour carried out in the 1940s and in 1970, we can see an increase in promiscuity and a decrease in claimed "monogamy." The percentage of male homosexuals claiming never to have had sex "just once" with a contact fell from 7% to only 1% over this period. The percentage of male homosexuals having a "one-off" encounter with over half of their contacts rose from 42% to 70%.

Amongst lesbians, the change is even more dramatic. The proportion of lesbians claiming never to have had sex "just once" with a contact fell from 63% to 38% from the 1940s to 1970. The percentage of lesbians having had a "one-off" encounter with over half of their contacts rose from 7% to 29%.[25]

The "spoiled child" syndrome

When Bergler analysed 1000 homosexuals, he found the following traits in personality structure:[26]
- masochistic provocation and injustice collecting
- defensive malice
- flippancy covering depression and guilt
- hyper-narcissism and hyper-superciliousness
- refusal to acknowledge accepted standards in non-sexual matters
- general unreliability, of a more or less psychopathic nature

Bieber carried out an intensive study on the personalities of homosexuals and characterised them as "angry, bitter people with low feelings of responsibility." Somerset Maugham (himself homosexual) said that homosexuals had: "a narrower outlook on the world ... a lack of deep seriousness ... inane flippancy ... and cynicism."[27]

It is tempting again to blame society for all this, and yet from within the network honest voices can be heard. Dannecker we have met and will meet again. Bell and Weinberg found that around a quarter of homosexuals themselves regarded homosexuality as an emotional disorder,[28] whilst Williams and Weinberg found that 37% of homosexuals said "yes" when asked "do you think YOU are psychologically disturbed?"[29]

A difference in the brain discovered

In 1991 Simon Le Vay, a homosexual biologist at the Salk Institute for Biological Studies, San Diego, published results of his research into the size of the interstitial nuclei of the anterior hypothalamus, or INAH, which is known to help regulate male sexual behaviour.

Researchers had already reported that INAH-2 and -3 were larger in men than in women. Autopsies by Le Vay of 19 homosexual men who died of AIDS, 16 heterosexual men, 6 of whom died of AIDS, and 6 women, 1 of whom died from AIDS, revealed that the INAH-3 areas of most of the women and homosexual men were about the same size. In heterosexual men the region was on average twice as large, and as big in fact as a grain of sand.[30]

Le Vay suggested that homosexuality could therefore be programmed biologically, although he was the first to admit that the difference in the brain could result from the homosexuality rather than the other way round. Any first-year biology student knows how important it is to have cause and effect in the right order. Furthermore, Le Vay cannot be sure that all the claimed heterosexual men in the control group were in fact heterosexual. The impact of AIDS on the brain could also have affected the size of the INAH-3. It is also possible that the difference actually has nothing to do with sexual orientation. Some scientists believe that the structure governs daily rhythms rather than sexual behaviour.

Finally, if the INAH-3 does in fact regulate sexual behaviour, and given that INAH-3 is smaller in heterosexual women than in heterosexual men, then given the dramatically higher levels of promiscuity in homosexual men than in either heterosexual men or heterosexual women, why is it that INAH-3 is not much larger in homosexual men than in their heterosexual counterparts, rather than smaller as reported?

Promiscuity arises from homosexuality itself

Whatever the root cause of the psychological compulsion to be promiscuous, the evidence shows that disapproval of society has nothing to do with it. When considering whether greater liberalism results in a greater reliance on monogamous partners, and less on what he describes as the homosexual "subculture," (gay clubs and bars) homosexual psychologist Martin Dannecker is unequivocal:

> The experience of recent years in West Germany, since the modification of paragraph 175, ... did not in any way weaken the organised homosexual subculture. The very opposite was the case. ... While up to 1969 such typical institutions of the homosexual subculture as sauna clubs were absent from the homosexual subculture in West Germany, soon every town of any size came to have such an establishment. The removal of legal repression ... has nowhere led to any disorganisation or elimination of the subculture.

In periods of tolerance, this expands precisely in those spheres that seem to offer casual sexual contact. .... In periods marked by a decline in anti-homosexual repression ... the specific difference in homosexual behaviour that derives from a mental compulsion presents itself more clearly than otherwise. ... If homosexuals have difficulty in attaining what they seem to desire, i.e. "a lasting relationship with a single partner"[31] this has its decisive cause overwhelmingly in the mental aspect of homosexual existence.[32]

8
Homosexual activity

When referring to a "homosexual" in this chapter we mean a person who seeks, as psychiatrist Charles Socarides puts it:

Orgiastic satisfaction from simulated sexual behaviour with members of the same sex rather than from normal sexual behaviour with members of the opposite sex.[1]

We do not mean anyone who although suffering from a homosexual orientation, has not been involved in homosexual activity.

Reality of Homosexual Practices Disturbing

This chapter contains, frankly, a sordid and depressing catalogue of activities that the poor mothers whom Miriam Stoppard or Joanna Kaye interview when they run a programme about "gays coming out to family" would not dream that their sons and daughters are getting up to. There is an impression abroad that homosexuality is about two beautiful young men talking about aesthetics of a summer morn, and reading poetry to while away the winter hours. If the families of the "gays coming out" knew that homosexual behaviour can easily involve eight men in a public convenience jostling to commit obscenities,[2] the smiles might not come so readily.

But then none of us wants to recognise that a fellow human being is involved in degrading and humiliating activities, and we usually manage by a process of psychological denial to put such perceptions out of mind. The discovery of the reality of homosexual practices was disturbing to me, and I still find it hard to imagine that homosexuals I know and have known perform the specific sexual acts listed below. Something is needed to counteract a facile treatment of homosexuality which ignores sexual [or more properly pseudo-sexual] practices, but naturally most of us would genuinely rather not get too specific.

Nevertheless, this work would be incomplete without a reference to homosexual practice, and faced with the options of refusing to discuss the activities at all, of referring to them in vague terms, or of accurately describing them, I have adopted the latter course, in I hope as dispassionate a way as possible.

Terrance Higgins Trust Categories

One of the side effects of the AIDS crisis was that the pro-homosexual Terrence Higgins Trust was obliged to categorise homosexual acts according to "risk" and had therefore to define them.

Previously, hardly anyone knew exactly what happens in the bedrooms, and bathrooms, of homosexuals. Apologists for homosexual behaviour have always complained about people being "obsessed with an unhealthy preoccupation with the physical details of what gay people get up to in the privacy of their bedrooms"[3] but of course it is the activities themselves that are unhealthy, and what "the gays" hate is that their sexual activities should now become public knowledge.

The cataloguing follows what the Terrence Higgins Trust see as the likelihood of contracting AIDS from the various perversions.[4] The trouble is that one thing inevitably leads to another, with alcohol and drugs often being consumed before sexual activity, so lowering inhibitions. The Terrence Higgins Trust itself admits, "Drink and Drugs can make you feel good but they can affect your judgment,"[5] so the cataloguing might be regarded as spurious for the purpose for which it is intended, and valuable only as an indicator of the progressive nature of homosexual activity. It should be noted that some of the activities have subsequently been up or down-graded by Terrence Higgins Trust in terms of "risk."

"No Risk" Activities

"No Risk" activities, according to the Terrence Higgins Trust booklet, include:

> solo masturbation and fantasy, sexy talking, massage away from the genital area, sex toys used on your own and kept for your own exclusive use, enemas and douches done by yourself to yourself.[6]

It might be thought odd that it should have to be explained that obscene talking can not give a person AIDS, except when it leads to other acts, but our first observation on the "no risk" category could be that the rectum is already figuring as an "erogenous zone." We see too an early reliance on "sex toys." The homosexual press has pages of 0898 numbers encouraging fantasy and masturbation through "sexy talking."

One Terrence Higgins Trust leaflet says of "no risk" activities: "Talking fantasies can really get people HOT!" and "Porn and Videos can get you hard."[7]

Pornography in its written, pictorial and videotaped manifestations is indeed very important to homosexuals, male and female alike. The Terrence Higgins Trust itself has brought out a pornographic video promoting "safer" homosexual activity, following its sought-after porn posters [qv].

"Massage" is a very popular activity in male homosexual circles, and merits on average thirty column inches of "Gay Times," under its own heading, as a "service."

Solicitation by Masseurs

Massage columns with their telephone numbers and coded details of services provided were laying Gay Times open to the accusation of abetting solicitation, so in 1987 the monthly magazine stipulated that only advertisements accompanied by genuine certificates of qualification would be accepted. What is strange is that it is difficult to spot the difference between the advertisements in (say) August 1986 and those in more recent issues. The masseurs are still nearly always "athletic" and "attractive," often "black," "Swedish," "Mediterranean" or "Oriental," and may be "considerate," "qualified," "understanding" or "satisfying." They claim sometimes to be "firm," "hard," "skinhead" or "muscular," which are code-words indicating sadism and bondage, and it might be thought a bit optimistic to assume that they will be asked by their clients to stay away from "the genital area," especially when "complete satisfaction" with "videos" is commonly offered.[8]

It is a familiar traditional device of prostitutes to advertise as "masseurs," and it enables any magazine and its prostitute advertisers, if such they be, to claim that they are staying within the law. We saw in chapter 3 that the main shareholder and editor of the magazine "Rendezvous and Gay Amie" were convicted of conspiring to corrupt public morals for publishing homosexual contact advertisements quite recently. It is odd that Gay Times, its pin-up stable mates, and newspapers like Capital Gay and the Pink Paper have not been prosecuted. For example, an advertisement in Capital Gay placed by a "muscular professional hairdresser" offering the "benefit" of "that little extra" was almost certainly referring to sexual services.[9]

"Low Risk": Government-Funded Trust Promotes Illegal Activity

"Low Risk" activities are said by the THT to be:

Mutual masturbation, group masturbation, dry kissing, dildos, vibrators, butt plugs etc. used with a partner, as long as each item is only ever used on one person, bondage, beating, whipping and spanking as long as the skin is not broken, general body to body contact and movement, penis to body contact, except between the thighs and buttocks, dripping hot candle wax onto the skin, body kissing and nipple nibbling as long as the skin is not broken.[10]

An activity is already present in the low-risk THT list which is performed by more than two persons. When masturbation occurs in a "group," it ceases to be "in private," and is against the law. A mainstream homosexual activity is the "circle jerk" which I hope speaks for itself because I really do not propose to define it. It is the origin of the innuendo-based title of the Gay Liberation magazine and book "Come Together."

Some "sex toys" are also now defined, with the hope expressed that they will not be shared. They can include, as well as the specially designed devices listed, carrots, bottles, lightbulbs or anything else. Sadism and masochism make a specific appearance. Homosexuals have no monopoly on bizarre practices, but the homosexual's inability to perform natural sexual acts, the lowering of normal inhibitions in the first place, the homosexual's subconscious disgust at his or her sexual behaviour, and a consequent need to humiliate or be humiliated, perhaps also the need or desire to parody the imagined roles of male and female, all these lead to dominant/submissive sexual behaviour which becomes over-stated into "S & M."

Sadism and Masochism

It is important to recognise that S & M is a mainstream activity between homosexuals; we looked in chapter 4 at examples of clubs for both male and female S & M homosexuals. The Islington "Gay and Lesbian Centre" now runs regular discotheques for "SM Gays,"[11] who according to some reports have almost taken the "centre" over. They have been regularly banned and un-banned. Gay Times promoted as "Book of the month" a pornographic S & M novel offered by a leading "gay" publisher.[12] Simon Harris explained in the homosexual "Pink Paper" on 6th April 1991 the attraction of the "leather scene:"

> The men at the Block and Backstreet are clearer about what they want and less prepared to play the preliminary cruising games. ... There are clear role distinctions; those who are identifiably top or bottom [dominant/active or submissive/passive - SG]. The difference is that to be dressed in leather, rubber or uniform can indicate far

more specific sexual information to a potential partner and also, perhaps, a greater willingness for sex itself.

As journalist Roy Kerridge confirms, "'Gay clubs' often have rooms attached to the dance floor where group sodomy can take place, sometimes with whips, chains and handcuffs as handy props. In a sense, many popular 'gay clubs' are brothels."[13] We referred earlier to sadism being advertised as a "Service" to Gay Times readers, with the terms "disciplined instruction," available typically from a "skinhead" (again), "dominant guy," "ex-public-school prefect," or "PT instructor," being the coded references. Some masseurs also offer "shaving" as part of their service. Submissive homosexual men and women often have their pubic and body hair removed, and this may be done by shaving - remember the "Clit Club" in Chapter 4? - or by candle wax, hence the appearance of the latter in the list.

Solicitation by Sadists and Masochists

The "Men's Personal" columns of homosexual papers are constantly used for solicitation, for even though Gay Times stipulates that: "No advertisements intended or appearing to intend to solicit for sexual purposes will be accepted," advertisements that are clearly soliciting constantly appear in all the "gay" press. It was through this route that those involved in the "Spanner" trial of sadists and masochists made their new contacts. As examples of the sort of box-number advertisements similar to those which in the past saw "International Times," the Paedophile Information Exchange and "Rendezvous and Gay Amie" convicted of Conspiracy to Corrupt Public Morals, we could note the following:

From a 1988 edition of "Gay Times:" "dominant fifties man," "seeks passive young friend," "Schoolmaster or leather interests preferred," "Submissive 21 seeks hard-working men," "anyone out there into shaving," "masculine leather guy seeks same or novice," "Executive ... available to authoritative bloke," "Straight acting and looking 28 needs masculine denim, leather teacher to obey," or "to teach me the ropes," and "Victorian guardian has vacancy for submissive ward."[14]

"Fun" in these advertisements always means sex and "active" means sexually active. From the classified ads of a 1990 edition, interspersed with some 14 pages of advertisements for 0898 telephone contact and story lines: "Tall dark student, 22, inexperienced, needs dominant type," "Young attractive schoolmaster type seeks students 21-35, ideal for novices," "Schoolmaster ... seeks boyish lad, ...

plentiful safe fun, inexperienced welcome." "Chunky, strong minded attractive guy, 50s, seeks slim clean-shaven submissive guy," "... seeks younger friends for weekday fun times," "Docile bear type sought by dominant instructor for training," "Submissive type, inexperienced, seeks experienced active guy to teach me everything," "Two young guys 23/28 seek other young guys for fun."[15]

"Medium Risk:"

"Medium Risk" activity involves such as:

> Kissing with the exchange of saliva (wet kissing or French kissing), Coitus interfemoris (penis-body contact between the thighs or buttocks), fingering (putting one or more fingers into the anus), shared douches and enemas, fellatio (cock sucking; not coming in the mouth may be safer than coming in the mouth, but both are medium risk, because there is always some leaking of fluid before orgasm, swallowing semen may not increase the risk further), cunnilingus, urination (water sports, golden showers etc.) as long as the urine does not enter the mouth, anus or eyes.[16]

Regarding the latter pursuit, in which one or more homosexuals urinate on another man or men, American lawyer Roger Magnuson points out:

> Some homosexuals, like the famous psychiatrist and sexologist Havelock Ellis, are urolagniacs, ingesting the urine and fecal matter of their partners. Eating faeces is called "Scat." A book written by and for homosexuals reports that the closeness of genital organs and holes for the elimination of body waste make it "certainly no wonder" that some homosexuals view water sports, enemas and the eating of fecal material as "a sexual turn-on." As one homosexual reported, "Water sports - yes, yes, yes!! - my favourite thing of all is (urine)."[17]

Urination: A Contact Group

The "closeness of genital organs and holes for the elimination of body waste" does not of itself explain the homosexual predilection for ingesting urine and faeces. We are all built the same in this particular anatomical respect. Rather the roots of it might lie in what a psychologist would see as an arrest of sexual development in the childish "anal" phase. Be that as it may, it is certainly encouraged by the "non-judgmental" nature of the homosexual network. This means quite simply that nothing anybody does within the network is commented upon adversely by anyone else. The only sin is to be "judgmental." This complete reversal of moral standards has led to homosexuals setting up secret societies for the enjoyment of bizarre and degrading activity. Advertisements in homosexual newspapers lure others to engage in "water sports" or showering one another with urine. One contact group was "Rainmakers," and was the brainchild of Scottish paedophile and gay activist Ian Dunn.

Advertisements first appeared in "Gay Scotland," of which Ian Dunn was editor, late in 1984. "Rainmakers forecasts golden showers" invited those interested to reply to Mr Dunn's flat in Edinburgh's Broughton Street. He also advertised in "Gay Times," "Him Monthly" and overseas, in order to build up a list of contacts who shared this interest.

Irresponsible Scottish Group Funded by The Government

What might be thought to be even more astonishing is that three of Ian Dunn's co-directors on Gay Scotland, Derek Ogg, with whom he had coordinated Gay International, Simon Taylor and Nigel Cook, were at the same time setting up the Scottish Aids Monitor, SAM for short, as a charitable trust, and applying to the Scottish Office for funds.

In December 1985, with "Rainmakers" still going strong, Ian Dunn published in Gay Scotland a full page advertisement for "SAM" containing the advice not to take urine into the mouth. However, the majority of the SAM advice was non-judgmental to the point of irresponsibility, even by the standards of gay AIDS groups. It will probably never be known whether it was the advice that "dildoes, cock rings, tit clamps, paddles, cuffs and so on are safe" or "How many partners? - You decide .... we don't think that you need worry on that score," or even SAM's advice to homosexuals not to take any AIDS tests, that most enchanted Scottish Secretary George Younger to give SAM £ 7,000 in 1985 and £ 25,000 in 1986.[18] The Welsh Office has managed only an attempt at such lunacy: a mere £ 1,300 in 1991 to subsidise Glamorgan prostitutes by providing free condoms.[19]

"Higher Risk"

Returning to the Terrence Higgins Trust classification of sexual activity, in "Higher Risk" are listed:

> *(the sharing of) dildos, vibrators and butt plugs, anilingus (rimming or tonguing), brachio-proctic stimulation (fisting or fist-fucking), putting the hand, fist or forearm into the rectum. If the penis is*

inserted before, along-side or after the hand then this act enters the highest risk category[20]

According to the Terrence Higgins Trust, brachio-proctic stimulation always results in ruptures of the rectal wall. That the rectum could be so abused by such a practice is almost unbelievable. Licking another man's anus or penis may occur prior to or after buggery.

"Highest Risk"

"Highest Risk" practices are listed as "vaginal sex," and:

> anal sex (fucking or screwing), any sex act which draws blood (including body-piercing), enemas and douches used before or after anal sex.[21]

Again, that having an enema or giving another person an enema could provide sexual pleasure is almost beyond belief. Such practices are frequently employed of course as part of a sadistic ritual with the passive partner tied up or kitted out in some sort of harness. The culmination to such a scene would be brutal oral or anal sodomy. Indeed it has been suggested that buggery is of itself a pathological and sadistic act. Certainly the frequency with which rapists inflict this humiliating violation upon their female victims gives some credibility to that view.

The deliberately light-hearted leaflet put out by the Terrence Higgins Trust to promote "safer sex" is illustrated with cartoons depicting promiscuity, wet kissing, buggery, use of sex toys, mutual masturbation and whipping. "Yes but is it clean?" is the only question asked by the masochist depicted.[22]

Like male homosexuals, lesbians are frustrated by the impossibility of natural sexual relations, and have to bring the mouth into contact with the genitals, and with the anus. Virtually all the practices that men engage in, women can and do too, with a few obvious exceptions. "S & M" is prevalent amongst homosexual women, "fisting" is growing in popularity, and transvestism is routine. We shall examine the statistics in Chapter 9.

Drugs

Researchers Ebbesen et al found considerable usage of drugs containing isoamyl nitrite which are supposed to act as an aphrodisiac when sniffed:

> Subjects were questioned about their use of oral drugs, cocaine, nitrites, and intravenous drugs. Only nitrite inhalants were in

common use by members of either group. During the prior twelve months, 36% of the Copenhagen HS men and 16% of the Aarhus men had used them; 13% and 4%, respectively had used them in the previous week. There was a wide variety of frequency of use: 38% had used them at least 20 times, and 8% at least 100 times during the year. Frequent use of nitrites was more common in persons who were very active sexually ..(and) ..correlated with the number of partners. It was more commonly used by more experienced HS men. Use of nitrites correlated very well with number of partners for all types of HS acts expect being the recipient of anal sex.[23]

The drugs being referred to are known amongst homosexuals as "poppers" and are very widely available in large towns, which accounts for their greater use in Copenhagen, "a major tourist centre of HS men" than in Aarhus.

Nitrite Drugs on Sale in Parks and Pubs

In London nitrites are sold at the Duke of York pub in Hammersmith, which also operates a mail-order service. Advising clients that "These products should not be used by people suffering from heart, lung or circulatory problems,"[24] they are referring to the increasing worries about the short and long term health risks involved in using nitrites.

The names of the "Poppers" offered by the Duke of York pub indicate their aphrodisiac intention: "Ram" and "Jungle Juice" are the brands offered of "Pure English Poppers."[25] Similar drugs are always offered whenever male homosexuals present a suitable market, for example, at a "Stop the Clause" rally in Lambeth Council's Kennington Park on 30th April 1988 and at all Gay Pride marches and festivals.

Poppers are on sale for example at the "Gay and Lesbian March" which culminates each summer in a rally in Lambeth. A stall which I saw in Kennington Park promoted "Liquid Gold" and "High Tech." Other brands include "Hard Core," "Hit," "Bolt," and "Hardware," so the emphasis is on the supposed ability of these products to encourage and sustain an erection (and possibly also to relax the anal sphincter muscle). Homosexual men are obsessed with penile size and "strength" so it is no wonder that "poppers" are widely used.

Police action fails against Nitrites; use of "Ecstasy"

Nitrite drugs have also been on sale at the Royal Vauxhall Tavern, another well-known pub in the homosexual network. The prosecutor took proceedings against five individuals not under the misuse of drugs act, but under Section 1 of the Criminal Law Act 1977 (a rewriting of the Offences against the Person Act 1861 s. 24) for conspiracy "to unlawfully and maliciously cause to be taken a noxious substance namely isoamyl nitrite (poppers) with intent to injure, aggrieve or annoy."[26]

The case was expected to come up at the Old Bailey near the end of 1988, and for the Police case to succeed, they would have had to establish that the defendants" actions were both unlawful *and* malicious, that poppers were a "noxious substance" within the meaning of the Act, and that the defendants" intentions were that the substance should "injure, aggrieve or annoy." The case was quietly dropped, and the supply and use of these drugs continues unabated.

The use of the so-called designer drug "Ecstasy" which has caused death when taken in "normal" quantities is also widespread and growing amongst homosexual men. As activist Bill Short reported this year: "In practice E is probably now available in every major gay venue in the country and takers will be found on almost every gay disco dance floor."[27]

Bestiality

The sexual practices of homosexuals are limited only by the imaginations of the human mind. One practice apparently gaining popularity amongst homosexuals is "gerbilising" or "gerbil shooting" which is the insertion of a live rodent into the anus. The recipient derives sexual pleasure from the animal trying to find its way out. Sometimes it dies before it escapes, and has to be removed surgically. Roger Magnuson quotes from one book which reports that one-fifth of all homosexuals admitted to having sexual contact, or at least masturbating, with animals, and one prominent American homosexual, Charley Shively, considered bestiality to be an Act of Revolution.

> *"The Gay Report," a widely read and much praised book in the homosexual community, reports positive testimonials with no apparent shame and no adverse comment from those having sex with Labrador Retrievers, cows and horses: "My first sexual experience ... was ... with a cow - not bad but boys are better" Most homosexuals have had some experience with oral-anal sex, sadomasochism, group orgies, bondage, or transvestism (dressing up in women's clothes).*[28]

It might be expected that the activities considered have implications for health. Let us now see if that is so.

9
Disease and the active homosexual

The sexual practices and promiscuity of active homosexuals expose them to a number of diseases. Some practices are unhealthy with multiple partners, others are unhealthy in themselves, and still others are physically dangerous. In this chapter we shall see why.

The high level of disease inherent in a "gay lifestyle" forces books intended to show young men and women how to practice homosexuality to juxtapose or amalgamate their chapters on "gay sex" and "health." A glance at almost any homosexual manual will prove the point.[1]

Reverse socialisation

From an early age, children are taught that the waste products of the body are dirty, so they must not touch their anus, or anyone else's, and they must wash their hands after going to the toilet.[2] Panosian and Gorbach are research physicians and microbiologists, and they cite Deuteronomy 23.12,13 as early evidence that:

> From the time of Moses there has been concomitant consciousness of the benefits to the public health of careful fecal disposal.[3]

Homosexuals have to unlearn what society has learned down the ages and what they were taught as children, in a process that has been described as one of reverse socialisation. No homosexual starts off having urine sprayed in his face, or ingesting faeces as a result of alternate anal and oral sodomy:

> On average, homosexuals report having their genitals manipulated by another male around age 13. It takes another two more years before the anus is used for sex rather than for biological relief; and yet another year or two before it is licked or sucked for "sexual fun" (lesbians lag about 3 to 5 years behind in most of this biological insanity.) By age 21 most gays "have come a long way." They have

Disease and the active homosexual

learned to enjoy activities that would have sickened them as children. ..once they have arrived at the stage where they can consume faeces there are no limits. They become exemplars of the adage "you are what you eat."[4]

According to one author, the social side to this progressively degrading activity is as follows:

An older man, having persuaded a young boy to live with him, humiliates the boy by bringing ever-younger teenage boys back to the flat for tea and sympathy. Often the older man and his younger partner indulge voracious and voyeuristic sensations by going out together in pursuit of young boys. ... By the time he is 21, a homosexual has often become "the older man." Young boys, and the younger the better are the chief preoccupation of predatory homosexuals.[5]

The library of scientific studies into homosexual activity and frequency of disease is enormous. I shall cover a representative sample of the studies with which I am acquainted. They are remarkably consistent in their findings, and none of them makes any bones about the extent or reasons for the ill health of practising homosexuals. Many also draw conclusions about likely effects on the public health as a whole. I have not sifted through the medical periodicals selecting those studies antipathetic to homosexual activity and rejecting those sympathetic. On the contrary, some of the studies are carried out by homosexuals, yet draw the same conclusions as those carried out by disinterested researchers. I am not aware of one single study which concludes that the average homosexual man or woman is better balanced and less prone to disease than the average heterosexual. The only question is: how much worse off are they?

All mainstream activities commonplace

The Danish survey carried out by Ebbesen et al showed that men with more homosexual experience were more likely to swallow seminal fluid.

Although almost all persons (99%) had had oral-genital contact, only 78% had had seminal fluid in their mouth. Of this group, 26% usually spit out the fluid, and the remainder swallowed it.[6]

Typical of the distortions put about by apologists for homosexual behaviour is the claim made by one Dr Peter Davies (qv) that buggery "is not practised by all gay men nor is it necessarily a common or preferred activity amongst those who do."[7] Although this is literally true, the Danish survey found that:

> Of the 240 persons who provided information, 95% had been involved in anal intercourse, approximately one-third more active as inserters, one-third more active as insertees, and one-third equally active both ways.[8]

Ebbesen et al covered all the mainstream activities listed above, including all forms of oral-genital contact, oral-anal contact, and passive and active buggery. The authors, who clearly do not disapprove of promiscuity, observed that:

> Number of partners in the past year increased with years of HS experience. Among the more "promiscuous" all forms of HS acts were common place.[9]

Corey and Holmes found from their 1980 study where homosexual men kept a diary, that on average an active homosexual had, per year:
- fellated 106 different men
- swallowed 50 seminal discharges
- experienced 72 penile penetrations of the rectum
- ingested faecal material of 23 different men[10]

McKusick studied 655 male homosexuals allegedly responding to the AIDS crisis. Their "knowledge of health guidelines was quite high but this knowledge had no relation to sexual behaviour," he concluded. Only 24% of his sample claimed to have been monogamous during the past year, yet even of these supposedly more responsible homosexual men, 5% drank urine, 7% had had a fist up their rectum, 33% ingested faeces (coprophilia), 53% swallowed semen, and 59% received semen in their rectum during the course of the previous month.[11]

It is possible to compare studies carried out in America over the years to see if they are consistent and if they indicate increasing participation in progressively unsanitary activities in tables 1 and 2.

Government-funded diaries of under-age sex

Since AIDS, according to a recent, continuing and it must be said highly selective survey, in which those taking part keep a "Sexual Diary" detailing day-to-day sexual behaviour, buggery has halved in popularity, with only 47% to 48% of a male homosexual sample now admitting involvement in it. Of those, 17% were active as either inserters or insertees, and 66% equally active both ways. In only 15% of sessions where such activity occurred was it accompanied by the

Celebrating diversity or perversion? 25,000 homosexual men and women preparing to set off from London's Victoria Embankment on 27th June 1992 for a "Lesbian and Gay Pride" march to Hyde Park. A European flavour was given by Lesbians from Belgium and homosexual men from Lille and Paris.

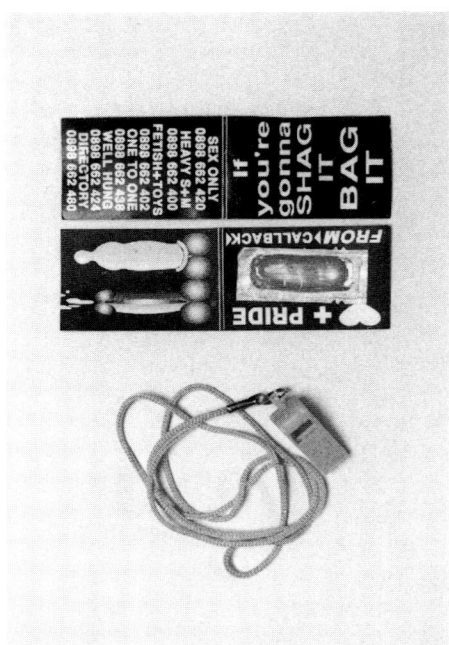 

Above: Essential equipment for a gay pride march: whistle, for drawing attention, free condoms given out by a telephone sleaze line, assorted badges. Below: Afterwards, the gay pride rally in Lambeth's Brockwell Park in South London. Organisers claimed that 100,000 attended. This stall and its travelling salesmen dispensed isoamyl nitrite drugs (poppers) that are claimed to produce an erection and relax the anal sphincter muscle.

Table 1 Participation in male homosexual activity (% of sample)

	1940s ever [12]	1970 ever [13]	1977 ever [14]	1983 ever [15]	1983 last yr [16]	1983 last mnth [17]
Activity:						
Masturbation by another	90	98		100		
Oral/genital:	83	98	99	100	99	
Oral/anal:	59	89	83	92	63	69
Penile/anal:	68	93	91	96	95	95
Sado-masochism:	22	26	37	37		
Fist in rectum:	-	-		41	34	
Urination:	10		23	29		
Coprophilia:	-	-	-	17		
Enemas:	-	-	-	12		
In Orgies:	61	-	76	88		
With minors:	37	-	>23	46		

Table 2 Participation in female homosexual activity (% of sample)

	1940s ever [12]	1970 ever [13]	1983 ever [15]
Activity:			
Masturbation by another:	81	95	100
Oral/genital:	48	92	96
Oral/anal:	18	25	53
Penile/anal:	-	-	30
Sado-masochism:	15	9	9
Fist in rectum:	-	-	8

use of a condom. Of the same sample, incidentally, only 15% claimed to be in a "closed relationship," with a further 76% equally split between "open relationships" and "no regular relationship."

The "SIGMA" researchers, Professor Tony Coxon, a declared homosexual of University College Cardiff, his fellow "gay Christian" Malcolm Macourt, who lectures in social research at Newcastle upon Tyne Polytechnic, Dr Peter Davies, (ibid) and Dr Tom McManus of St Giles Hospital, Camberwell, a contributor to the magazine of the Conservative Group for Homosexual Equality, were said to be "short

Conservative Group for Homosexual Equality, were said to be "short of volunteers under 21 and over 60."[18]

It could be seen as rather surprising that the Department of Health is funding a research project run by people with vested interests, campaigning for young men to keep a diary of under-age illegal activity. That being said, some interesting conclusions have been drawn by the researchers, and we shall consider them later when we discuss AIDS.

Frequency of sexually transmitted disease

Homosexual promiscuity when added to the reality of homosexual practice certainly puts its practitioners at enormous risk from sexually transmitted diseases, gut and bowel disorders, and blood-borne diseases such as hepatitis B and AIDS. Ebbesen et al reported thus for homosexual men in Denmark:

> Of the Copenhagen group, 40% had been treated for venereal disease during the past year, but so also had 34% of Aarhus HS males. Other treated complaints, possibly related to HS activity, included sore throat (32%) body lice (24%), anal irritation (12%), hepatitis (3%) and amoebic infections (<1%). Also noted were 10 cases described as bronchitis and 5 cases of pneumonia.[19]

The common sense view that higher promiscuity levels correlate with greater incidence of venereal disease was confirmed:

> Because some descriptions of HS practices have utilised HS men attending VD clinics, we examined the data to see in what way such men might differ from those not being treated for VD. There was no difference in age or education. Longevity of HS activity also did not differ greatly. But the number of HS partners in the past year was considerably different; 78% of those with VD in the past year had 10 or more partners, whereas only 45% of those without VD had 10 or more partners during this period.
>
> The median for persons having VD was 20 partners in Copenhagen and 12.5 in Aarhus, but for persons without VD the median number was 10 in Copenhagen and 5 in Aarhus. The sexual preference of those with VD included a higher proportion of men participating in both oral and anal sex. Use of nitrite inhalants during the past year was nearly twice as frequent among persons reporting VD (43%) as among those denying it (23%).[20]

Frequency of disease is worse in America
A similar pattern is reported in America by Roger Magnuson:

> While "gay rights" laws have been in effect for the last decade in San Francisco, the city has seen a sharp increase in the venereal disease rate to 22 times the national average; infections hepatitis A increased 100%, infections hepatitis B 300%; amoebic colon infections (gay bowel syndrome) increased 2,500%. Venereal disease clinics in the city saw 75,000 patients every year, of whom close to 80% were homosexual males; 20% of them carried rectal gonorrhoea. New York Times Magazine quotes a doctor familiar with the community as saying that the "average homosexual" is a "tropical island of exotic diseases."[21]

Both Jay and Young in "The Gay Report" and the American ISIS survey confirm high levels of disease related to homosexual activity. 78% of homosexual males had had sexually transmitted disease.[22] Jaffe found 90% illegal drug use and said that 25% of his sample carried enteric parasites.[23] Quinn put the latter figure at 39%,[24] whilst Kassler estimates that 30% to 50% of homosexual men carry the parasites.[25]

Diseases encountered by homosexual men and women fall roughly into three main categories: The first is ordinary venereal diseases, the second is "Gay Bowel Syndrome," the tropical enteric parasites referred to above, and the third group are blood-borne diseases. To these may be added immune suppression effects from sodomy, and various physical dangers arising from sodomy, "fisting" and sadism.

Venereal diseases
According to the UK Health Education Authority, homosexual men are now the main reservoir of syphilis. Over 50% of cases in the USA occur in homosexuals, with the primary chancre (ulcer) presenting, in males at least, rectally.[26] Studies have shown that homosexual males are 14 times more likely to have had syphilis than their heterosexual counterparts, whilst lesbians are 19 times more likely to have had syphilis than heterosexual women.[27] Rectal gonorrhoea is common among homosexuals and is used as a "marker disease" to indicate homosexual promiscuity. Venereal parasites such as lice (crabs) and scabies are common.[28]

Genital herpes is incurable and endemic amongst male homosexuals and lesbians. It infects the genitals, mouth and rectum, often concurrently, and has been associated with squamous [scaly] cancer of the tongue and cancer of the rectum.[29] Herpes-type viruses have been shown to act on their own as immune system depressants[30] and some patients with AIDS become especially "predisposed to more intractable and progressive forms of this (herpes) infection."[31]

Cytomegalovirus (CMV) is found in urine and particularly in semen, and is thereby passed rectally. "Intense and repeated exposure of homosexual men to infected secretions containing high titres of cytomegalovirus could contribute to immunodepression and Karposi's sarcoma (a cancer of AIDS) in this population."[32] The link between CMV and Karposi's Sarcoma is confirmed in the literature,[33] but there was debate at the time (which still continues) about whether the AIDS-virus on its own leads to AIDS. We shall come back to this.

Venereal or Genital Warts are common amongst male and female homosexuals,[34] appearing anally in males,[35] causing intense itching and producing a fetid discharge.[36] Gene Antonio researched homosexual diseases for his book on AIDS, and writes of anal warts:

They are highly resistant to treatment. These warts appear in large cauliflower-like masses in and around the anus in addition to infecting the penis. Anal coitus and elimination of the stool become excruciating and result in further rectal trauma. Various homosexual periodicals contain numerous advertisements by physicians offering specialised treatment for these and other related maladies.[37]

The "gay bowel syndrome"

This is a term thought to have been first coined in 1976 to describe a group of parasitic, viral and bacterial infections, previously regarded as "tropical" or "exotic," that became prevalent amongst homosexual men.[38] Gene Antonio describes them thus:

Amoebiasis*: a disease of the colon caused by parasites (Entamoeba histolytica). Causes dysentery and sometimes liver abscesses. Can result in diffuse inflammation and ulceration of the distal colon that can be mistaken for Crohn's colitis. Usually picked up from contaminated food.*

Giardiasis*: a parasitic (cause: Giardia lamblia) bowel disease causing diarrhoea. Can result in severe enteritis, producing symptoms ranging from acute diarrhoea to chronic malabsorption. Spread in a similar way to amoebiasis.*

Shigellosis*: a bacterial bowel disease which can cause severe dysentery. In children it can be fatal. Contaminated food is the usual cause.*

Hepatitis A*: a viral liver disease spread by faecal contamination, eg, food, water and close person to person contact.*[39]

Disease and the active homosexual

Epidemiologist Dr Oscar Felsenfeld reports that "minute amounts of faeces are able to transmit" Hepatitis A, and that in an outbreak at a boarding school, "not only were food-handlers thought to have propagated the disease, but also the water that splashed on the seats of the toilets was implicated."[40]

In tropical countries and parts of Africa, these diseases are prevalent because of poor sanitation, where water may be contaminated with sewage, and also because of inadequate food preparation. They are however increasingly observed in day care centres for small children, where toddlers mix with older, sick, children whose parents cannot afford to take time off work. Their prevalence in such centres in present day America was described in 1983 in the Journal of the American Medical Association as "reminiscent of the pre-sanitation days of the 17th century"[41]

Amongst homosexual males, and increasingly females, these tropical diseases are contracted by direct ingestion of faeces, either through the practice of "rimming" (inserting the tongue into and around the anus), or actually eating faeces or smearing them on oneself or a partner, or licking a penis, finger or "toy" that has just been inserted into the man or woman's own anus, into that of the sexual contact or into that of a previous contact of the present contact.

Such practices replicate unsanitary conditions in Africa and the tropics, and result in the high - up to 50% - occurrence of "gay bowel syndrome" in homosexual men. Dr Claire Panosian and Dr Sherwood Gorbach of the Department of Medicine, Division of Infectious Diseases at the Tuft-New England Medical Centre in Boston, Massachusetts, blame increasing multiple anonymous contacts for the "uncontrolled circulation of intestinal pathogens in male homosexuals." Although the rise in occurrence is largely due to the homosexual network, they consider that "the potential for wider dissemination also obtains."[42] They cite Dritz, who wrote in 1980, even before AIDS was recognised:

Prominent on the roster of "classic" sexually transmitted diseases are herpes genitalis, herpes proctitis, and gonorrhoeal proctitis in both men and women.

The Venereal Disease Clinic of the San Francisco Department of Public Health has 75,000 patients per year, of whom 70 to 80 per cent are homosexual men.

Since 1974 my colleagues and I have reported extensively on the sexual transmission of enteric diseases, although we realise that the sexual route is only one of the possible means of infection and we could only estimate its importance. With the expansion of the homosexual community in San Francisco, the number of cases of sexually transmitted enteric disease reported by co-operating physicians and laboratories increased by orders of magnitude: by 1979, amoebiasis had risen from 10 cases per year to 250, giardiasis had risen from 1 or 2 per year to 85, shigellosis and hepatitis A had doubled, and hepatitis B had trebled.

The incidence of acute shigellosis and hepatitis A and B in men 20 to 39 years of age was six to 10 times that in men or women in any other age group.

An average of 10 per cent of all patients and symptomatic contacts reported to the San Francisco Department of Public Health because of positive faecal samples or cultures for amoeba, giardia, and shigella infections were employed as food handlers in public establishments; almost 5 per cent of those with hepatitis A were similarly employed. Discussion with the reporting physicians or interviews with the nearly 75% of the patients and contacts whom we could reach confirmed that an estimated 60% to 70% of these food handlers were homosexual men. Sources of their infections were either food or sexual contact between male room mates, or oral and anal intercourse between partners who had no food contact. Hepatitis B, a parenteral rather than enteric infection, is considered by some investigators to be transmitted by "parenteral injection" of saliva or semen positive for B antigen through breaks in anal or rectal mucosa during analingual contact or proctogenital intercourse.

Infections in the homosexual community that are not transmitted sexually may also on occasion present a potential problem for the wider population of a city.[43]

Blood-borne diseases

Amongst the quasi-sexual practices of active male homosexuals, the act of sodomy comes closest to imitating normal sexual intercourse, but of course the rectum is not up to behaving as a sexual organ. As a study in the Journal of the American Medical Association pointed out, there are "critical structural differences between the rectum and the vagina." The authors went on:

> While the lining of the vaginal mucosa comprises a squamous multi-layer epithelium capable of protecting against any abrasive effect during intercourse, the lining of the rectum is made of a single layer of columnar epithelium. The latter, unlike the vaginal

epithelium, is not only incapable of protecting against any abrasive effect, but also promotes the absorption of an array of sperm antigens, thus enhancing their exposure to the immune apparatus in the lymphatic and blood circulation. The high immunogenicity possessed by spermatozoa, coupled with the microbiological flora of the rectum, can work in synergism to generate a state of chronic antigenic stimulation.[44]

In other words, the cells of the vaginal wall are flat, like scales, have many layers, some twenty in fact, and the structure is elastic, with glands which provide the lubrication necessary during sexual intercourse. The cells of the wall of the rectum are at right angles to the passage and are in only one layer, perfect in design for the extraction of water from faeces and for their expulsion in one direction. Sodomy forces the anal canal to expand inwards in the wrong direction and routinely tears the fragile lining as well as causing bleeding anal fissures.[45]

Spasms of the bowel wall can occur, and colitis often develops, a severe inflammation of the mucous membrane of the colon. Fever, malaise, cramps and eruptive diarrhoea containing blood or leukocytes follow. Mucosal ulceration is also common in homosexual males.[46] Colitis and rectal lesions sometimes mask the symptoms of the intestinal lesions of Karposi's Sarcoma.[47]

Also associated with sodomy is a peculiar form of inflammatory psoriasis, a skin disease marked by red patches and covered with scales, known as Kobner's phenomenon. The psoriasis covers the rectum and the pubic area, penis and scrotum. "During sexual activity, the thin silvery scales which have formed on the affected areas are rubbed off, leaving the skin raw, bleeding and exposed to infection."[48]

These various rectal traumas and lesions readily allow access to the blood stream of the passive partner of virus-infected semen and sputum. Nor are the dangers borne by the passive partner alone, as Antonio points out: "The opening of the urethra, along with penile abrasions and lesions resulting from sexual activity and disease, permit infected bloody secretions seeping out of the damaged rectal tissues to enter the bloodstream of the active partner."[49]

The major blood-borne disease affecting homosexual men is not AIDS, which we shall consider in chapter 10, but Hepatitis B. Capital Gay reported on the 19th June 1992: "Hepatitis B kills more people in one day than AIDS does in one year. And Hepatitis B is one hundred times more infectious than AIDS." In western societies according to one authority, Hepatitis B virus "infects the majority of homosexual men within three years of their becoming sexually active."[50]

However, it is not necessary for the wall of the rectum or the anal opening to be torn before the passive partner is damaged by sodomy. Sperm possess aggressive, dynamic qualities essential for the penetration of the female ovum. They will pass through an undamaged rectal canal with no difficulty, carrying any viral component with them, directly into the blood stream. Several studies have now demonstrated that after regular passive sodomy, antibodies develop to sperm which impair the immune system, without any HIV infection, and this predisposes the recipient of sodomy to infection with other opportunistic infections.[51] This suppression of the immune system has been observed in three-quarters of a sample of homosexual males claiming monogamy,[52] and also in rabbits.[53]

Immune suppression and the aids debate

In the next chapter we shall discuss AIDS on the premise of its association with the blood-borne AIDS-virus, but I promised above to consider the debate about the relationship between AIDS and the AIDS-virus, and this means a mention of the dissident view of American microbiologist Professor Peter Duesberg. Let us first agree that it is common ground that AIDS is a syndrome of many diseases that are able to attack the body because its immune system becomes impaired. It is also accepted that some individuals seem to remain healthy whilst carrying the AIDS-virus, HIV, whilst others fall ill very quickly. Most authorities write of "co-factors," which are things that must also be present with the virus, in order to get the AIDS syndrome going.

For Professor Duesberg, AIDS is caused by the co-factors alone, the damage to the immune system arising from massive medical trauma, from recreational drugs, particularly poppers, widely used as we saw by homosexual males, and by implication from the immune suppression that arises from cytomegalovirus and sperm absorbed rectally. He cites cases where immune suppression arose from the so-called co-factors in absence of the AIDS-virus.[54] Most controversially of all, he argues that the AIDS industry, particularly Wellcome, which manufactures and markets the drug AZT as "Retrovir," has a vested interest in the status quo, and claims that AZT actually causes AIDS itself. Here at least he is supported by Dr Luc Montagnier, the leading exponent of the "co-factor" theory.

I am not entirely convinced by the evidence for or against AZT. Wellcome and the Terrence Higgins Trust both claim it helps sufferers from AIDS, other reports write of people suffering from oral herpes and Karposi's as a result of taking AZT, whose symptoms became much more manageable when the drug was discontinued.[55]

These issues were raised at the symposium "AIDS - a Different View" in Amsterdam in May 1992 at the time of writing. Opinions seem to be hardening to the extent that it may not be possible to agree that AIDS may arise from the AIDS virus plus co-factors, or from another manner of immune suppression. Since discovery of the truth of the matter will depend on open-mindedness, and on the participants in the debate being neither afraid of being politically incorrect nor too concerned to defend their own corner, nor too squeamish to examine the immuno-suppressive nature of homosexual activity itself, the argument looks set in to continue for years.

Physical dangers from sodomy

The rectal sphincter of homosexuals who allow other men's penises, hands and arms into their anus gradually loses its ability to retain waste. The subject becomes rectally incontinent and dribbles at inconvenient times. The wearing of a sanitary towel becomes a necessity, and the dribbling of contaminated blood-stained stool presents dangers to others.

The practice of "fisting" which is the insertion of the fist or forearm into the rectum and colon was, like gerbilising, almost unknown in Kinsey's day, so even the famed sex investigator and pervert did not bother to ask if his homosexual samples indulged in it. "Fisting" causes, at a minimum, rectal trauma which provides a path for pathogens. It can also rip the intestine and tear the anal sphincter muscle, and if "toys" and mechanical devices such as vibrators are introduced at the same time, these can puncture the intestinal wall and allow faecal matter into the abdominal cavity. Immediate surgery may prevent death.[56]

Fisting has been known so to damage the anal sphincter that a colostomy has to be performed, and astonishingly, some individuals then have sodomy performed through the colostomy opening, causing yet more damage.[57] Dritz wrote:

> Oral and anal intercourse present physicians with surgical as well as medical problems, ranging from anal fissures and impaction of foreign bodies in the rectum to major diagnostic dilemmas. Infection in traumatized rectal mucosa and in amoebic or herpetic ulcers above the level of the anal ring may produce formations that mimic rectal carcinoma.[58]

An "anal fissure" typically involved a homosexual man needing 14 stitches after "ordinary" buggery, as recorded by a "gay" activist.[59] A "major diagnostic dilemma" is medispeak for when the surgeons stand around the patient scratching their heads. Buggery, according to the doctor above, is far from the safe and natural practice that sexual libertarians have pretended. In the case of sadism, torture and bondage, it seems that beating causing laceration, the application of lighted cigarettes to the genitals, actual cutting of the genitals, fisting and violent oral and anal sodomy involving the penis or implements are all commonly involved. Urination over the victim will allow viral agents to enter the body either through these wounds or through the mouth or eyes. The "Spanner" trial in 1991 recorded that all these things happen in the homosexual network.

Sexually-transmitted diseases are increasing amongst lesbians with their increased promiscuity and participation in more bizarre practices. This is confirmed by the opening of a "sexual health clinic" especially for lesbians at Charing Cross Hospital in April 1992 - the first of its kind in the country. The clinic, staffed partly by lesbians and NHS-funded, will be carrying out research "on sexually transmitted infections in lesbians."[60]

Unnatural acts

Gene Antonio concludes in his study of the diseases of homosexuals, as we must, that defining homosexual acts, sodomy, group masturbation, anilingus, fisting, coprophilia, urination, bestiality, torture and so on as being unnatural "is not a matter of homophobic prejudice." Overwhelming medical evidence demonstrates how well designed is the human body for sexual intercourse, and what an assault on the body and the human psyche is made by employing the rectum as a substitute sexual organ and by the reverse socialisation that delights in tasting the waste products of the body:

> From a purely biological perspective sodomy, even apart from the transmission of AIDS, is an intrinsically unsanitary and pathological act. In addition, the practice of sodomy has been a primary reason why AIDS has been so readily transmitted and fostered among homosexuals.[61]

So let us now look more closely at the virus that causes AIDS, and see whether it is "prejudiced" against homosexual men.

10
The prejudiced virus

At a superficial level, the view that the virus which leads to AIDS is not "prejudiced" is entirely accurate. The virus is quite able to infect whomsoever is exposed to it. On application to real human beings and their activities, however, the claim of those sympathetic to homosexuality that "there is no specifically gay disease"[1] is highly misleading.

AIDS stands for "Acquired Immune Deficiency Syndrome" so it is not strictly speaking a disease itself. AIDS is a syndrome of associated diseases. We shall speak loosely of AIDS as a disease, and of the HIV or "Human Immuno-deficiency Virus" as the AIDS virus. The AIDS-virus is a lentivirus [slow virus] one of the family of retroviruses. It is apparently the first one to be observed in man. There were lentiviruses previously known in sheep, horses and cattle. After becoming infected with the virus, the body develops "antibodies" to it over a period of between three and eighteen months, and these can then be detected in tests. This period is known as the AIDS "window," for although a person is infectious, it is impossible to detect the fact. The antibodies do not kill the virus.

When such a test finally indicates the presence of antibodies, the subject is said to be "HIV-positive" or "antibody-positive." He has the early stages of "AIDS" and may go on to develop, as the tabloid papers describe it, "Full-Blown-AIDS." The percentage of HIV-positive people who will die from AIDS has been variously estimated from 10% to, more recently, 100%,[2] and as some people become ill more quickly than others, onset may well depend on co-factors like lifestyle, stress, mental health, previous immune suppression or even which type of AIDS treatment is offered. We covered some of this debate earlier.

AIDS-related diseases

The HIV substitutes its own DNA for that of the host cells, and thereby compels the infected person to reproduce the virus. It is thought that the virus alters its genetic code with each new infection, so making the search for a vaccine fairly frivolous. It is also believed that stimulating antibody production with a vaccine could actually hasten the onset of AIDS anyway. That is what happens in tests on lentiviruses in animals.

The virus inhibits the body's ability to fight disease, suppressing the immune system, and so the person becomes prey to the syndrome, a group of diseases which would normally be fought and destroyed, but which in the immune-suppressed usually lead ultimately to death:

> *The most common are a particularly virulent form of pneumonia and a skin cancer called Karposi's Sarcoma. Nor is its impact purely physical. It can go straight to the brain and produces dementia among a high proportion of its victims.*[3]

But why does the virus affect so many homosexual men? The GLC, under a heading "Sexually transmitted diseases." had to admit:

> *For social and biological reasons, these are more commonly experienced by many gay men than by most heterosexuals ... two diseases of particular concern are Hepatitis, and AIDS.*[4]

What the GLC euphemistically described as "social" reasons are of course the high levels of promiscuity amongst homosexual men. The "biological" reasons we covered in Chapters 8 and 9.

How the AIDS virus is spread

HIV and Hepatitis B both behave as classic blood-borne viruses.[5] In other words, the virus is present in the blood, and is transmitted by means of infected blood from one person entering the bloodstream of another previously uninfected person. It also seems that the AIDS virus is present in other body fluids, like semen, urine and saliva. The essential route for a bodily fluid carrying the virus is through a cut, tear or abrasion in the skin, a "trauma," in medical language.

Clearly then, the most effective way of transmitting the AIDS-virus is by actually passing the blood of an infected person into an uninfected person, and before blood and blood products were screened in this country for the presence of HIV antibodies, blood transfusions in the UK carried a risk of transmitting AIDS, and some seven people had at the end of 1987 died from this source. Blood transfusions abroad are still considered to carry a risk.

Haemophiliacs regularly need a clotting agent reduced from very many pints of blood to stop them simply bleeding to death, and it is appallingly sad that these vulnerable and innocent people were among the first victims of the Syndrome.

In Italy a footballer was infected after a clash of heads with another who was HIV+, and in January 1992 it was reported that a man became infected when he tried to stop a fight involving an HIV+ gatecrasher at a party. Other innocent victims include Kimberley Bergalis, infected by her bisexual dentist in America, people who have come into regular intimate contact with an AIDS victim within their family, a number of medical and nursing staff who have contracted the disease from AIDS patients, mainly through needle-stick injuries, and of course a number of babies born to drug addict mothers.

Sharing needles and calls for "responsibility"

A devastating way to spread the AIDS virus is by sharing a hypodermic needle with someone who has the disease. As one authority makes clear, careless or absent sterilising of hypodermics used for vaccination has probably contributed to the spread of AIDS in Africa,[6] but in the UK, sharing a hypodermic usually means injecting heroin.

In passing, we should note that the schemes for issuing new needles for drug addicts and appealing to them to exercise "responsibility," both of which have been a feature of the Government's AIDS campaign, are founded on an extraordinary misunderstanding of the nature of drug addiction.

The calls for "responsibility" are doomed to failure. The heroin addict is either "high" after a fix, (the word heroin is derived from the feeling the first one or two injections give of feeling like a hero) or desperately sick to get one. As an addict makes clear,[7] if he needs heroin, he would betray his own grandmother to get some. Having "scored" from a dealer, the object is to get the "H" into the bloodstream as fast as possible.

A public lavatory might suffice, or the addict may go straight home and meet one or more addict friends. On one television programme about drug addiction, it was emphasised by a girl in Edinburgh that a new sharp needle is a prized possession. It is hard to find a good place in the skin to inject, and harder still if the needle is blunt, so if someone has "scored" some heroin for friends, the newest, sharpest needle is automatically shared as a symbol of friendship amongst the group. The girl in the film was asked if she would then share a new needle? "Yeah, yes I would" she said, after a pause. A more recent report confirms the point:

Johnny is 19 and lives with his parents in a Newmarket council house. He dropped his first acid tablets when he was 14, was injecting heroin at 16. Since then he's been injecting anything around. "We always inject, never smoke. People got a bit paranoid about AIDS but we still share needles; I suppose if you want a fix you don't care much. We do it mostly in pub toilets or round in the squats where my mates live."[8]

Futile advertising to drug injectors

The Department of Health and its Health Education Authority had to be seen to be spending money on "health education," but compared with active male homosexuals, the use of drug addicts as a target group brings the undoubted benefit that they are beyond the law, are not organised into a pressure group, and have no political clout. Features of the advertising campaign have been characterised by hopelessly bad market research or by misleading and hedged-about advice.

For example, the pale sick boy pictured on anti-heroin posters rapidly became a cult-hero amongst young people for his wistful, interesting looks, whilst the "advice" not to "take drugs at all. But if you do, never inject. And if you do, never share needles" failed to, as advertising people say, put out a clear message, or sell convincing benefits to someone who only lives to fix. The message from a more recent drugs poster seemed to be that taking drugs was above all a good way to get to be looked after by beautiful young women.

The homosexual route

The method of AIDS virus transmission that concerns us here is precisely the homosexual route that the Department of Health is keen to play down. Virtually every facet of homosexual activity carries some risk, as we saw earlier, with the highest risk being involved in practices that draw blood, primarily buggery, the introduction of the penis into the rectum. As we saw in Chapter 9, the lower intestine is simply not designed for such a use.

Whereas the vagina is fashioned correctly for sexual intercourse, twenty cells thick with an appropriate number of nerve endings, glands for the secretion of lubrication and with a strength equal to its function, the lower intestine is one cell thick, perfectly designed for the extraction of the maximum amount of water from faecal matter passing in one direction, so as to conserve the body's hydration level.[9]

Consequently, the rectum is usually torn when put to a use that nature - or God - never intended.

Infected semen, urine or saliva can easily pass from the active to the passive partner, and as the rectum is designed to absorb water, the presence of a trauma, or wound, is unnecessary. A trauma obviously assists passage of the virus from the passive to the active partner, and permits passage the other way. The Sunday Telegraph interviewed virologist Dr. John Seale:

> *"If there is a persistent viral infection around, then anal sex of a traumatic kind is a devastatingly effective way of spreading it."* That was why homosexual activity had driven the virus around the Western world. Without that and our drug addicts, we would have had only the occasional case. So much for the view that private acts between consenting adults are entirely their own affair.[10]

The astoundingly high numbers of male homosexuals with AIDS, and the statistic that they make up around eighty per cent of all UK cases of AIDS, shows that far from being "unprejudiced," the HIV could scarcely be more closely tailor-made for spread amongst participants in unnatural sexual practices.

AIDS in Africa

Homosexual activists always maintain that AIDS in Africa is "spread heterosexually" in their attempt to play down its overwhelming prevalence among homosexuals in the United Kingdom. It is a fact that AIDS afflicts mainly homosexuals in the UK and the west and all the population (which is not to say that it is spread necessarily by sexual intercourse) in Africa. There must be a reason for this fact, and it will not do to pretend that the fact itself does not exist.

It may be that heterosexual buggery and promiscuity are common in Africa. Another factor may be the use of unsterilized needles and untested blood. Also to blame could be the association with other sexually transmitted diseases that produce lesions in the private parts through which the virus can travel, lesions which may persist through lack of effective treatment.

Yet another explanation is the lack of hygiene in most of Africa which mirrors closely the unsanitary nature of homosexual practices. Many Africans live without clean water or basic sanitation, so that food and water are often contaminated with sewage. Homosexual males regularly bring the tongue or mouth into contact with another man's anus, whilst some, as we saw earlier, will ingest infected faecal matter and urine, and fall prey to the tropical diseases known collectively as "Gay Bowel Syndrome."

Neither has it been established that the mosquitoes which transmit malaria, Karposi's sarcoma and Burkitt's lymphoma (a cancer of the lymph glands) cannot transmit the AIDS virus. In fact, a number of studies have concluded that insect vectors could easily be responsible for HIV infection, perhaps even by the virus becoming incorporated into the DNA of the insect and its offspring.[11] If only one or two of the above factors were operating, it would come as no surprise that male homosexuals in the Western world are infected with a condition attacking the whole population in Africa.

Normal sexual intercourse has little AIDS risk

To suggest that it is a waste of effort to discourage by "health education" the very activity, normal sexual intercourse, that is least likely to lead to AIDS on the grounds that it might lead to AIDS is of course heresy to the HEA and to the Terrence Higgins Trust with whom they are, if the expression does not fall too awkwardly, in bed. It is heresy from the point of view of the HEA to suggest that they have participated in a "con-trick" in which £4 million of tax-payers' money has been poured down the drain, and heresy now to "the gays" to suggest that AIDS is confined, in the UK or in any part of the western world, to its high-risk groups. However, in the United States, the rate of increase of HIV positive tests has slowed markedly, and if AIDS were spreading amongst heterosexuals, this could not have happened.[12]

Department of Health breakdowns of AIDS figures into categories of sufferer are shown in the tables in Appendix 2. They display a marked reluctance on the part of the AIDS virus to "move into the heterosexual population." In response to a Parliamentary question, the Department of Health gave the figures for the numbers of deaths in the UK from 1983 to 1987 from AIDS thought to have been acquired heterosexually. The figures were respectively 4, 2, 1, 7, 6. The most recent Department of Health figures confirm that HIV is very difficult to contract unless one's partner or oneself is a member of a high risk group: homosexuals, intravenous drug users, blood recipients, and residents or visitors from Africa.

Leakage from the "high-risk" groups

In the USA, drug injectors are the group amongst whom AIDS is now spreading most rapidly. There will be some "leakage" at least from the "high-risk" groups into the rest of the population, but the bulk of the "heterosexual cases" are the partners of drug addicts. It is probably impossible to live with someone who has contracted AIDS without eventually contracting the virus oneself, sexually or socially. Paradoxically, being faithful to one drug-addict partner presents more risk than heterosexual promiscuity.

American basketball player Magic Johnson had to "accommodate," as he put it, thousands of women before contracting AIDS. Wilt Chamberlain, another basketball star, claimed sexual intercourse with 20,000 women, without contracting AIDS. AIDS can certainly enter the normal population through an occasional homosexual "fling." One homosexual barman said: "I'm so worried about AIDS, I've made up my mind I won't sleep with a man now unless he's married."[13] Once the barman catches HIV, the route is open for infection of the wives of his partners.

That being said, the AIDS figures seem to show that the disease has already reached a plateau amongst every group other than IV drug abusers, and people exposed to the virus abroad. Projections are everywhere being revised downwards, and the great heterosexual explosion has not happened. This is consistent with the blood-borne nature of the AIDS-virus. The other major blood-borne virus that affects homosexual males and drug-injectors, Hepatitis B, remains rare even amongst promiscuous heterosexuals.

AIDS simply does not behave as a "sexually-transmitted disease" in the sense that gonorrhoea does, or syphilis, for example. Cases of syphilis or gonorrhoea are not typically acquired by sharing a blood-contaminated hypodermic needle,[14] but if a man has sexual intercourse with a prostitute with gonorrhoea, he is highly likely to contract it himself. With AIDS the situation is completely reversed, so that Dr John Seale can claim:

> You are more likely to get AIDS by helping an African prostitute clean up after a nose-bleed than by having sex with her.[15]

If this is true, Dr Tom McManus, a consultant at St.Giles Hospital, Camberwell, writing in the journal of the Conservative Group for Homosexual Equality that "the way this virus is passed on is by sexual intercourse without the use of a sheath"[16] is hopelessly misleading. Dr McManus is involved in the homosexual "SIGMA" project in Cardiff, as we saw in chapter 9, so it is not surprising that he confuses buggery with sexual intercourse.

Heterosexual route may need genital lesions or buggery
We were seeing that sores arising from sexually transmitted diseases are effective at giving admission to the virus which causes AIDS in the

first place, and that this can let the virus be transmitted "heterosexually," in other words, by normal sexual intercourse even in a one-off sexual encounter. However, heterosexual couples can and do indulge in the bizarre practices of homosexuals. From February 1986 to February 1987, British Market Research Bureau (BMRB) conducted a survey of attitudes and behaviour patterns for the Department of Health. One of the findings was that 10% of men interviewed who claimed two or more women partners during the past year claimed to have "cut down on anal sex."[17]

Two or more partners in a year may be very low by the standards of homosexuality, but is still promiscuous in normal usage. Yet how many people realised that 10% of sexually active men were buggering their women-folk in the first place? The figure in fact fails to square with some other surveys. Be that as it may, as the female rectum is as certain as the male to be traumatised when treated in this way, then such an illegal and unnatural practice could well be responsible for a very high proportion of cases of AIDS amongst those who were said to have caught the virus through "heterosexual intercourse." The Health Education Authority, pressed on the sexual practices of the HIV+ women in its 1991 television advertisements, has repeatedly dodged the question.

One consultant physician said in a letter that of 17 women found to be HIV positive in his hospital in 1987, 9 were intravenous drug users, and "only 3 admitted to anal sexual intercourse"[18] That actually leaves, in his words, "only" 5 who claim to have contracted the virus by real sexual intercourse. The women who admitted to being the recipients of buggery were actually 37.5% of the non drug-users. In a study of 7 female partners of HIV+ male drug addicts,[19] one woman had developed full-blown AIDS and five others had AIDS-related complex. Four of the women had engaged in sodomy with their partners. More on this subject in chapter 11.

The worst possible advice for homosexuals

The other major finding of the BMRB survey was of "significant changes in sexual behaviour among gay men."[20] This is now an article of faith for apologists for homosexual behaviour. Dr Tom McManus maintains:

> There is continuing evidence both in the USA and here that sexual behaviour among male homosexuals has changed. They have "safer" sex and sex with fewer partners.[21]

The prejudiced virus

During the year that the survey ran, homosexual men indeed claimed to have reduced their numbers of sexual partners in the last twelve months from an average of over 10 down to an average of nearly five. This is very low, when compared to the studies in America considered in chapter 9, and the results from the SIGMA survey (qv).

Any reduction is broadly in line with the advice from the Government and its agencies. In a pamphlet issued by the Health Education Council (now incorporated into the Department of Health as the "Health Education Authority"), the following course of action is recommended under the heading "Reducing the risks for gay men:"

> *The best advice [sic] for gay men is to keep down the number of different sexual partners you have and to be as sure as you can that your partners are restricting the number of partners that they have, too.*[22]

This is of course exactly the most disastrous advice of all. After "keeping down" the sheer number of his own sexual encounters, the first problem for any homosexual man following the HEC advice is to ensure that his partners "are restricting the number of partners that they have, too." In the homosexual network the idea that a man will ask the question, let alone rely on the answer, is totally unrealistic. At the same time, about a half of active homosexuals are thought to carry the HIV virus.[23]

Even if the word of every partner could be relied upon, the exponential nature of the enterprise is frightening. Just what this means to a member of a pool in which everyone has cut his number of sexual partners down to twelve per year, or one per month, can be calculated over say a five-year period. This is a level of promiscuity higher than that claimed by the men in the BMRB survey, but more in line with other studies, including SIGMA. We need to assume that in every month everyone has their sexual experience before I, say, have mine.

The homosexual pool - an exponential curve

At the end of the first month, I have had one direct sexual partner. I have also, by the rules of the game, had one indirect sexual partner, in other words, I have also "had" the partner of my partner. At the end of the second month, I have had another direct partner, and another two indirect partners, in other words I have added both my partner's direct and his indirect partner. I have now accumulated two direct partners and three indirect partners, making a total of direct and indirect partners of five.

At the end of the third month, I have had three direct partners and three plus my partner's five equals eight indirect partners, whilst at the end of the fourth I have had four direct and eight plus three plus eight equals nineteen indirect partners. From here on, the figures show a catastrophic exponential curve, one that more than doubles at each interval.

At the end of the eighth month, I have had eight direct partners, but three hundred and seventy five indirect partners, whilst after only one year my total tally is six thousand one hundred and forty-three both direct and indirect. Eight months later, although I will have amassed only twenty direct partners, I will have "been to bed with," in the delightful phrase, over one and a half million indirect partners.

The best advice seen as judgmental

Of course some of the partners will be shared by many of the others. This does not alter the ultimate effect. It is true that it will reduce the total number of new partners, but equally true that it decreases any advantages arising from "safer sex." The "best advice" to uninfected homosexual men would have been never to become involved in another homosexual act at all.

Even from within the homosexual network, some men were saying that "sex is - quite literally - killing us ... when a terrible disease means that we purchase our freedom at the price of thousands of our lives, self-respect dictates it is time to stop until once again it is safe."[24] But this is very much a minority view amongst homosexual "opinion formers" because it may be interpreted as being "judgmental" about homosexual activity.

The SIGMA group of doctors in Cardiff, who are close to the homosexual network, found that buggery and promiscuity actually increased amongst homosexual men in England and Wales during 1988-9. The proportion of men in the cohort engaging in receptive buggery increased from 28% to 32% in the year, and those inserting increased from 28% to 29%. More men reported a regular sexual relationship, 64% as opposed to 57%, but "monogamy" did not increase, the mean numbers of partners increasing from 11.6 in 1988 to 15.6 in 1989. Their findings led Coxon, McManus, Davies et al "to predict a rise in HIV infections and marker diseases such as rectal gonorrhoea."[25]

Revenge sex

Many homosexuals are placing a reliance on "safer sex" that is simply not justified. Derek Jarman, who has AIDS, is regarded as a role model amongst homosexuals. The transvestite group who dress up as nuns and call themselves "The Sisters of Perpetual Indulgence," - a name which speaks volumes about the homosexual psyche - decided to "canonise" him. He admits freely that his mind is such that he does not tell his new sexual contacts that he has AIDS. Whether or not he uses condoms, surely basic human responsibility would demand that he refrain from sexual activity?

Homosexual activity would on the evidence be hazardous enough without revenge sex. There is growing evidence of infected men, and not just homosexual prostitutes or "rent-boys," deliberately infecting others by pretending to be free from AIDS when they are not. One newspaper's New York correspondent reported on "revenge sex" thus:

> *The term is used by some AIDS specialists and homosexuals to describe the actions of an infected individual who continues to have sexual partners after being informed he is suffering from the incurable disease.*
>
> *Doctors specialising in venereal diseases report that they encountered a similar attitude, particularly among women, during the scare a few years ago over genital herpes.*
>
> *In the case of both diseases, the attitude stems from a callous rationale that might be summarised: "Someone gave this horror to me, why shouldn't I pass it on to someone else?"*
>
> *The late Rock Hudson was said to have persisted with a homosexual affair with a new young lover even after doctors had told him he had contracted AIDS and had only months to live.*
>
> *Roy Cohn, the flamboyant New York lawyer who spear-headed Senator Joseph MacCarthy's communist witch-hunt, was similarly not impressed by the argument that he should refrain from sex after it had been established he had Karposi's Sarcoma.*[26]

The evidence is not just anecdotal. Homosexuals admitted to triple the rate of infecting "lovers" in the American "ISIS" survey compared to promiscuous heterosexuals.[27] In only one year, 1985, doctors from five different American cities went public with cases of AIDS patients deliberately infecting others.[28]

Suffering of the teenage rent boys

In Britain too, revenge sex has become evident. Two AIDS-carrying homosexuals told Robert Kilroy-Silk on television that they had no intention of either leading celibate lives or of telling future conquests about their medical condition.²⁹ However it is certainly amongst the desperately sad circuit of the teenage rent-boy that revenge sex is at its most terrifying. The National Children's Home discovered 18 boys, aged between 14 and 18, infected with the AIDS virus during a screening of 400 youngsters in 1986. According to a tabloid paper, these children:

> were seduced, sexually abused and lured into the evil world of prostitution. Some of their clients are married. They can infect their wives - and even their unborn children.³⁰

The same paper carried the heart-breaking story of just one of the boys, who it said is typical of the youngsters who hang around stations and amusement arcades in the West End:

> Alex was only nine when his father murdered his mother - and was then murdered in prison himself. Alex was taken into council care. There he was sexually abused by a residential worker who paid him with gifts. Afterwards he went to London and entered the rent boys' squalid world of drugs and degradation. The money he gets for sex pays for his heroin.³¹

David Pithers, director of child care studies for NCH, spoke about the rent boys to another national newspaper:

> "They have been given the most powerful weapon possible. They are adopting a kind of destructive bravado, but they are also terrified of dying so young.
> "They caught AIDS from having sex with members of the gay community who have the virus. There must be many more boys we have not screened who could have AIDS. It's like sitting on a time-bomb."³²

Responsibility shirked by sexual reformers

There should be a sense of shock and compassion for such children who have been "raped, tricked, emotionally and psychologically abused," as David Pithers puts it. It might indeed extend to all who have been conned into homosexual activity, with its "gay" image.

Indeed a fatalism is now creeping in to the homosexual network. As a 22-year-old regular at one of London's homosexual bars put it:

> "I don't really think about AIDS ... you just have to hope that safe sex really is safe. If I pick someone up in here, I wouldn't necessarily expect them to tell me they're HIV positive. In fact I'd probably be grateful if they didn't. I've been to bed with people who I knew were

HIV positive, but then again I've probably been to bed with people who I didn't know were positive. It doesn't really make that much difference."

Another said: "I haven't been tested for HIV, but I think I have accepted that I will die of AIDS, that most of my friends will die of AIDS. It sounds depressing but it's just easier this way."

Rupert Haselden, who reported these comments, is homosexual himself. His article admitted that homosexuals recognise that they have no future in any case. "A gay man is the end of the line," he wrote. The manager of the bar told him: "It's like a game of Russian Roulette. If that's the game they want to play, you can't stop them." Haselden concluded: "AIDS dangles like a flashing neon sign in the midst of the gay community, becoming a metaphor for the self-destructiveness and the self-indulgence that accompanies it."[33]

Even though responsibility for his actions and acceptance of the consequences ultimately rests with the individual, it is hard not to lay some measure of blame at the feet of the sexual reformers. Ordinary people knew in their hearts that sixties permissiveness was bound to end in tears, but were hard put to it to find a voice, and were treated with contempt by the anti-Christian bigots who were convinced that they knew better.

Such is human pride that those who encouraged homosexual "lifestyles" and the rest of the package of moral license most vociferously in the first place do not appear to be showing any remorse, and instead continue to campaign for greater "tolerance" for homosexual practice. They have been proved wrong but will never recant. We can look at what the leaders of American homosexuals were saying at the Boston conference which inaugurated the North American Man-Boy Love Association just over ten years ago, and marvel at the sheer blind folly of it. The reporter is Daniel Tsang, curator of the Lavender Archives in Paedophilia, no less:

> Richie McDougall (of "Fag Rag") was one of many speakers to lash out at the Judeo-Christian tradition of treating sex outside procreation as bad. Fellow Fag Rag writer Charley Shively, who had burned a Bible at a recent gay pride rally, argued that gay people are "engaged in sex for pleasure, not procreation." Sex is fun, he said, and "doesn't lead to diseases, not even skin cancer."[34]

11
The politics of AIDS

A major feature of the Government's Politically Correct education programme has been an attempt to convince us that AIDS only affected homosexual men so dramatically because they were the first group to contract it. The AIDS virus, so the argument goes, is spread by promiscuous sex, and if heterosexual people do not modify their behaviour then the virus will spread like wildfire through the heterosexual population. These arguments, although unsupported by evidence, are politically correct, since they fit the homosexual agenda.

Public sympathy for AIDS sufferers also fits the homosexual agenda, but for the public to identify AIDS with homosexuals and perhaps to blame them for spreading it does not. Put another way, gay victimhood is acceptable, gay responsibility beyond the pale. Health education has been used simply to spread anti-discrimination propaganda. The ultimate hope of the AIDS lobby is that public sympathy for AIDS sufferers, properly manipulated, may engender public sympathy for gay rights as a whole.

Princess promotes homosexual agenda

The Princess of Wales does valuable work for the homosexual lobby in this regard, minimising the connection of AIDS with homosexuality by drawing attention to children with AIDS.[1] The homosexual party line that "gays" are downtrodden innocents has also been faithfully followed by the Princess, who went so far on one occasion as to alter her script and say that AIDS was "the last straw for some people already facing discrimination." The Stonewall homosexual lobby group suggested to its members just before Christmas 1991 that they should write to the Princess to thank her "for her support for homosexual rights."

The Simon of Cyrene Sanctuary Project, an AIDS hospice based in Bournemouth, adopts the same philosophy. Its publications dwell on "families" and "children" suffering from AIDS. However, it is run by gay activists, including Neil Thomas of Bournemouth's Metropolitan Community Church (qv), has a stall now at every homosexual rally, and activists paraded under its banner in the 1992 "Gay Pride" march in London. The liberal and humanist "personalities" supporting "Sanctuary" include Paddy Ashdown MP, Simon Callow, Julia Neuberger, Claire Rayner, Simon Rattle, Lionel Blue, Shiela Hancock, Ken Livingstone MP, Joan Lestor MP and Vanessa Redgrave.

The construction that HIV was a "sexually transmitted disease," spread only by "promiscuity" was made possible because homosexual lobbyists like the Terrence Higgins Trust were the first groups to be consulted by government health departments when the desease struck. The equation of heterosexual with homosexual promiscuity in the passing of HIV was even accepted by some traditionalists. American Civil Rights lawyer Michael Fumento in his book "The Myth of Heterosexual AIDS" criticises Evangelical pro-family groups in the USA over the dishonest and self-defeating way they latched onto AIDS as something which might pull fornicating America into line when all other arguments had failed.

The early days of AIDS politics

In Britain, pro-family bodies stuck to the truth, and produced material that advised teenagers how not to get AIDS without pretending that heterosexual "screwing around," (not that they used ex-Minister Edwina Currie's less than decent turn of phrase), carries anything like the same risk. They maintained of course that promiscuity is damaging, but for reasons which are more to do with the psychological effects on subsequent capacity to enjoy a stable married life.

So far as the Government's campaign goes, Geoffrey Wheatcroft, no moralist, has observed that it "seems an odd approach to a problem of public health to begin with a flat denial of the truth."[2]

American journalist Joseph Sobran points out that as AIDS was initially confined to homosexuals, "the gay press embraced AIDS as the emblem of gay suffering."[3] When public figures like Rock Hudson died from it, and when the syndrome moved outside the homosexual circus, most notably into sufferers from haemophilia, the subject started to get out of "the gays'" control. News stories highlighted small children with AIDS, families with AIDS, who had typically become infected through transfusions of blood or of blood products, donated in the first place by active drug-using and homosexual AIDS sufferers. Talk of "gay rights" now antagonised millions who had formerly let it pass. A transformation took place. "The gay community and its media myrmidons quickly changed their tune. AIDS was no longer a "gay disease." It was "everybody's problem." The gay party line had to be adapted to retain gay victimhood while denying gay responsibility."[4]

This was done initially, according to Mr Sobran, by blaming the CIA for concocting the AIDS virus. This line was peddled by Charles Ortleb, editor-in-chief of the leading homosexual paper New York Native. In 1971, so the argument runs, the CIA tried to destroy the Cuban economy by infecting Cuban pigs with swine-fever. The plague spread to other Latin-American and Caribbean countries, and in particular to a herd next to a whore-house in Haiti. From Haiti, via a bisexual man, AIDS entered the USA. Quod Erat Demonstrandum.

Duncan Campbell praises the bath houses

It is not clear how this batty theory absolves from responsibility those who subsequently spread the virus, but let that pass, because meanwhile, over in San Francisco, fingers were pointing at activities within the gay bath-houses, "splendid 24-hours-a-day palaces of recreational sex," as journalist Duncan Campbell is said to have called them.[5] I challenged him on this observation in the Cambridge Union, and he did not trouble to deny the point. Depressingly, in his terms the description is accurate. At "the baths," as we saw earlier, it was not uncommon for a man to be involved in 20 acts of buggery or other (passive) indecency in a night. In late 1983, Public Health Director Merv Silverman's first response was health education. He unveiled a poster, and invited amongst others KCBS Radio reporter Barbara Taylor to the press launch. Questioning from Mrs Taylor showed up the poster as worthless.[6] Curiously, it seems not to have been so very different from our very own recent DHSS posters:

"Dr Silverman," she asked, "this poster says people should have fewer sexual partners. Does that mean that if somebody had ten sexual partners a week last year that they can cut down to five sexual partners a week now and they won't get AIDS?" The question embarrassed Dr Silverman. "We're trying to give a message that people will pay attention to," he replied.

"Dr Silverman, it says on this poster that people should limit their use of recreational drugs. Does that mean that if somebody was shooting up, say, three times a week, that they'd be safe from AIDS if they shot up just once a month? You're not saying not to use recreational drugs; you say limit your use of drugs."

"We're trying not to lecture people," replied Silverman. "It doesn't do any good if you give people a message they don't listen to." "I thought we were trying to tell people how not to get AIDS," said Barbara Taylor. "Why aren't we telling them that?"

Bath houses "leaders in AIDS education"

The truth was that Dr Silverman was afraid to antagonise the gay rights lobby. He would not close the bathhouses because he feared an uprising by homosexuals, and he became well-tutored by gay political leaders on the reasons for his refusal to take such a measure. "If you close the bathhouses, people will simply go elsewhere to have unsafe sex," he claimed. Six months later, following the submission of a report on the bathhouses by private detectives hired by San Francisco Department of Health, a shocked Merv Silverman gave the order to close the bathhouses. Some of the arguments used against this action[2] run uncannily like the Clause 28 protests in Britain.

The San Francisco AIDS foundation called bathhouses "leaders in AIDS education." The Gay Golden Gate Business Association said the closure was an intrusion on private enterprise. The Bay Area Lawyers for Individual Freedom, a gay lawyers group with several prominent members on retainer to bathhouse owners, said gays across the country would lose their civil rights because of Silverman's move. The Bay Area Physicians for Human Rights maintained that closure would lead to more cases of AIDS, not fewer. In the end, the only gay group to support Silverman was the Harvey Milk Gay Democratic Club.[7]

However, a rally protesting against the closure drew only 300 demonstrators, and the protest, about which Dr Silverman and San Francisco's Mayor Feinstein had been so concerned, fizzled out.

Terrence Higgins Trust enters the DHSS

AIDS started to make news in the UK at about the same time as "the gays" found an alternative scapegoat from the CIA. It was found that many AIDS sufferers in African countries were women, and this provided a convenient argument that normal sexual intercourse could transmit HIV, and that homosexuals were just unlucky to have been hit first in America and Europe. We should all soon be affected.

The Terrence Higgins Trust, having its feet under the table, was able to convince the DHSS that Terrence Higgins Trust people knew more about AIDS than anybody else. The trouble is, Terrence Higgins Trust, named after a promiscuous homosexual who was an early UK casualty of AIDS, does not exist simply to advise AIDS sufferers. It is run by homosexual activists for active homosexuals, and its output is coloured by the need to promote homosexual activity. Even the first Government AIDS publicity posters spoke of the HIV virus being contractable by "anyone - gay or straight" using language more natural to homosexuals and incidentally putting the word "gay" first. The Terrence Higgins Trust "Sex - is great!" leaflet was certainly obscene and carried the sort of non-judgmental advice that only gay activists could dream up. It was designed by Shelly Davies and Richard Green, the latter a man with the same name as he who used the pseudonym "Dominic" when he illustrated the magazines of the Paedophile Information Exchange:

"wanking - go for it - share the pleasure with a friend" [illustrated by the muscled torso of a man masturbating] "watersports - OK if piss doesn't enter your body" "yes but is it clean?" [asked by a cartoon character of another holding a whip] "Cor! I wouldn't mind negotiating safer sex with him" [said by one man to another about a hard sophisticated type propping up a bar].[8]

The leaflet contains no exhortation about "restricting partners" and is instead designed to promote promiscuity and homosexual activity, with checking for sores in the mouth and the use of the condom the only requirements. Even condoms, the leaflet admits, are not 100% safe, whilst the use of isoamyl nitrite drugs is discouraged only in the mildest of language. It is astonishing that nearly a half of the Terrence Higgins Trust's annual budget of around one million pounds is provided by the Government through the Department of Health, which is therefore financing obscene publications such as "Sex is Great" directly through the part of its grant given for "health education programmes." Also odd is the "Trust's" charitable status, because such status is not normally available to political campaigning groups.

The Terrence Higgins Trust is also a shareholder of Action Against Aids Ltd., as is its fund-raiser Jonathan Potts. HAL Nominees Ltd, a company which shared the registered office of Terrence Higgins Trust, 34 South Molton Street, is also a shareholder of Action Against Aids and is directed by solicitors George Harbottle and John Stutter. These are also directors of respectively two dozen theatre companies and twenty music, film and TV companies, as well as being partners in West End solicitors Harbottle & Lewis, late of 34 South Molton Street. 34 South Molton Street was also the registered office of the homosexual theatre group "Gay Sweatshop," and the correspondence address of the Edward Carpenter Community Trust, whose magazine "GAMUT" claims to be "a forum for discussion and expression on issues concerning us as radical/fun-loving/holistic/spiritual/nature-seeking/mingle-plobble-woozle-cuddly gay men."

Terrence Higgins Trust a gay campaigning group

It is strange that normal standards of decency and propriety have to be suspended in order to fight AIDS. One might argue that if the campaign meets homosexual activity at its own level then this will have to be so, but there is no necessity in the first place to do that. Nick Partridge of the Terrence Higgins Trust describes their material as "eye-catching," which is very true. Gay porn, or "homosexual erotica," is extremely important to homosexual men, and Terrence Higgins Trust posters are reputed to change hands for money in the homosexual milieu. It is sad that it now appears to be impossible to find a jury who will convict the Terrence Higgins Trust and its leaders under the Obscene Publications Act, or - and Terrence Higgins Volunteers admit this to have happened - for sending their obscene matter through the post.

I described the Terrence Higgins Trust as an political campaigning group. Its literature bears this out, as we have seen, and so does its personnel. The directors do include medical people, Professor Michael Adler of the Middlesex Hospital, Professor Ruth Hicks of the Middlesex and Consultant Paediatrician David Harvey, but also amongst them is Gay Times "Gay man of the decade" Tony Whitehead, who as a school biology teacher taught sex education. Its press officer Nick Partridge was like Tony Whitehead involved with the proselytising Gay Switchboard. Janet Green, another executive, came from Lesbian Line, a similar activist group.

Derek Williams of Campaign for Homosexual Equality is another director drawn from the homosexual network. Terrence Higgins Trust spokesmen are also gay activists, and are regularly quoted in the Gay press - in the case of one David Rampton, credited with comments that were, frankly, obscene.[9]

Indeed, right at the top of Terrence Higgins Trust is a man with impeccable gay activist credentials. Simon Watney, "Chair" of the shadowy Terrence Higgins Trust Policy Group, was born in 1949 and went up to Sussex University in the late 60s to read history of Art and to join CND. He was an early member of Gay Liberation Front in 1970 and set up Sussex GLF in Brighton the following year. In 1972 he became a teacher, moved to London in 1975, and in 1977 joined a group of ex-GLF Marxists and anarchists in the extremist, and pro-paedophile, Gay Left. Simon Watney contributed a recent article to a homosexual magazine entitled "Talking to the Future" about Gay Rights in Britain and the USA, in which he offered a "five point plan of resistance," spoke of "the family" as "a murderous myth" and called for a riot in Britain to match the American "Stonewall."[10]

Internal strife and incompetence at Terrence Higgins Trust

In a devastating exposure of the catastrophic policies, incompetent management and suspicious accounting of Terrence Higgins Trust, the Independent reported an astonishing turnover of senior staff, quoted a communications executive as calling the Trust a "gay cultural ghetto" where "you aren't accepted unless you wear the right kind of T-shirt" and discovered accounting irregularities.

The auditors of Action against AIDS qualified the accounts of its subsidiaries, Aids Day Ltd and Aids Day (Wembley) Ltd, because proper records were not kept and "donated income was not adequately segregated and separately identified from other income." Action against Aids and its subsidiaries owed £35,299 more than they could pay in the 1989 accounts, and at a time when Aids Day Ltd was insolvent, it continued to trade, using bucket collections and ticket donations totalling £23,972 to fund its debts.

The Independent showed that groups within the Trust for Drugs Education and heterosexual aids sufferers were so much window dressing. Liz Davies was the Trust's fund raiser until she was moved by the plight of Romanian babies with AIDS to set up a specific Romanian Baby Appeal. Within eight weeks the fund raised £200,000, the homosexuals had seen Romanian babies as a diversion from the needs of gay men, and Liz Davies had been thrown out accused of disloyalty and bringing the Trust into disrepute.

In 1989 no fewer than six professional advisors in its Drug Education Group resigned, complaining that the needs of drug users could not be met by the Trust's organisation. Radhe Bentley left in bitterness, having found antagonism to heterosexuality and deep-rooted misogyny. Ms Bentley said "I wish the Trust would have the nerve to say: "We are an organisation for gay men. Everything else, forget it."[11] At the end of 1991, yet another chief executive resigned, to be replaced by insider Nick Partridge himself. It was reported then that the THT was in such financial difficulties that it used money from its staff pension fund to pay the wages.

Health Education Authority wastes some money

It is small wonder that when the Health Education Authority decided to spend the latest £4 million advertising windfall on discouraging homosexual activities by having matchstick men doing bizarre things in odd positions, the project was rejected at "concept-testing" stage as "insulting" by Terrence Higgins Trust and by other representatives of homosexual groups.[12]

According to Dr James le Fanu, this left the HEA in the awkward position of having £4 million and nothing to spend it on, so their advertising agency dreamt up a campaign against casual heterosexual encounters. This time the target group was not given the opportunity to veto the scheme, so there were no embarrassing "concept-testing" problems. As a result, for three months of 1988, viewers were "scandalised nightly .. by actress Gabriel Mason, alluringly dressed in short skirt and matching black tights, inviting us all into her bed." Dr le Fanu's article, pointing out that the chance of acquiring HIV through such a heterosexual "one-night stand" is on a par with being struck by lightning, drew a frosty but strangely muted rebuke from the HEA.

The best the HEA could muster was a variation on "Better safe than sorry," and indeed it could go no further; the British Medical Journal had concluded the week before: "There is no evidence that HIV infection is being spread by casual vaginal intercourse."[13] However, in an attempt to fuel fears that AIDS may be contracted through heterosexual contact, a report from the AIDS monitoring team at the Communicable Disease Surveillance Centre in north London, drawing attention to a slightly higher proportion of females in the total numbers of HIV-infected cases, claimed that "some drug users categorised as being infected by sharing needles may have instead been infected through heterosexual contact."[14] No evidence was put forward for this contentious opinion.

AIDS campaign "founded on ignorance"

Writing in the Daily Telegraph, Dr Brian Evans, director of genitourinary medicine at the West London Hospital, said that warnings of an imminent heterosexual AIDS epidemic were wrong-headed and alarmist, and that "the slowness of the rate at which AIDS has been heterosexually transmitted is actually puzzling" when compared to other venereal infections.[15] John Seale argues that the AIDS virus is just as likely to be transmitted through saliva during kissing as through normal sexual intercourse, and points out that:

> *The very high prevalence of HIV infection in men who have frequent, traumatic contact with the lower intestinal tracts of many other men is not evidence that HIV is transmitted by sexual intercourse.*[16]

The massive public education campaign for people to use condoms is also, according to Dr Seale, "well and truly founded on ignorance."[17] Indeed, there is any number of charming people whose mere existence is a living witness to the tendency of condoms to break, and they will break all the more readily when forced into places nature did not intend their wearers to go. Yet 92% of homosexual men in a recent survey claimed to be placing reliance on the condom as a prophylactic.[18]

The makers of the leading contraceptive brand in the UK make the position very clear in their own leaflet:

> *Anal intercourse should be avoided. It is very risky even if a condom is used, because there are currently no condoms designed to be used in this way.*[19]

New British Standard for condoms for buggery

The Government is currently collaborating in the production of a new British Standard which will lay down a specification for thicker condoms to be used in buggery. Progress is slow because European harmonisation is being sought. Nevertheless, it might be thought odd that Dept. of Health and D.T.I. inspectors should sit on committees that are considering how to abet behaviour that in public, or between a man and a woman, is illegal, and that between two men in private remains, in British Law, immoral and accompanied by acts of gross indecency.

But to paraphrase Dr. Seale, the fact that heterosexual men and women have contracted AIDS, here and abroad, is not evidence that HIV is easily transmitted by normal sexual intercourse, except where sexually transmitted diseases have damaged the genitalia.[20] An AIDS conference in Stockholm in June 1988 was indeed told of a link between AIDS and sexually transmitted diseases. As Dr Thomas Stuttaford reported, "several diseases, including syphilis, herpes and chancroid, produce frank ulcers from which HIV-infected blood or pus can during intercourse be readily rubbed into an abrasion or cut in the skin or mucous membrane of the partner, an obvious method of transmission."[21]

Above: The Terrence Higgins Trust promoting the philosophy which earns them £1/2 million of taxpayers' money each year. Below: Two of the posters sent out by the Trust to a 17-year-old boy for display in a youth club.

Since there's **NO CURE** yet for AIDS consider adopting the following recommendations . . .

FUCKING IS very risky
because you can get or give the virus through tiny tears in the skin or body tissue.

Really Want To Fuck ?
Use Rubbers (Condoms) - they aren't 100% safe as they can tear or slip off: but they're safer than nothing.

Use plenty of water-based lubricant like KY or 121, but get the rubber on first.

SO THIS IS WHAT INTO RUBBER MEANS!

Patronising, flippant, obscene and degrading, the "Sex . . . is great" leaflet from Terrence Higgins Trust was targetted at homosexual men. Above and below are the front cover and three of the eight pages.

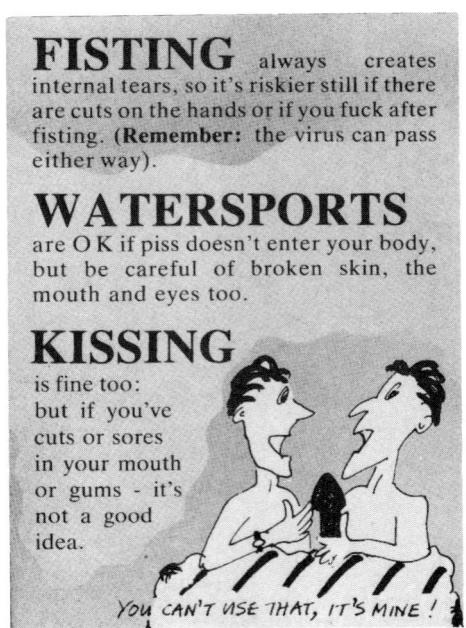

FISTING
always creates internal tears, so it's riskier still if there are cuts on the hands or if you fuck after fisting. (**Remember:** the virus can pass either way).

WATERSPORTS
are O K if piss doesn't enter your body, but be careful of broken skin, the mouth and eyes too.

KISSING
is fine too: but if you've cuts or sores in your mouth or gums - it's not a good idea.

YOU CAN'T USE THAT, IT'S MINE!

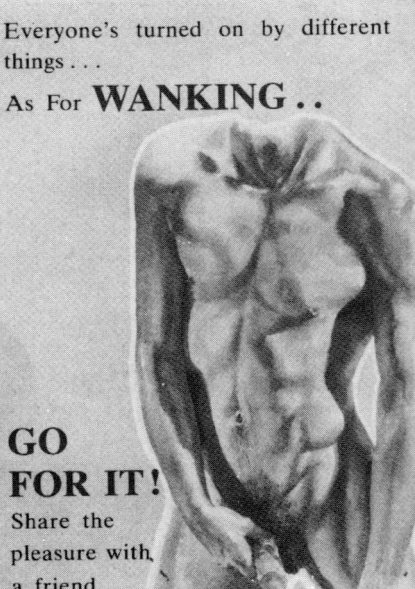

Everyone's turned on by different things . . .

As For **WANKING** . .

GO FOR IT!
Share the pleasure with a friend.

The quest for the heterosexual explosion

The treatment of AIDS in the press releases of AIDS professionals indicates a frantic search for the heterosexual epidemic, and in early 1991 they triumphantly claimed to have found it; anonymous testing revealed a four-fold increase in ante-natal mothers in London. One in 500 people in London could be infected, said Mrs Bottomley, then junior health minister, compared with the previous survey indicating one in 2000. People had to change their sexual behaviour, she said.[22] Virginia Bottomley would later describe the promiscuous homosexual musician, Freddie Mercury, who died of AIDS at the end of 1991, as "heroic."

The first thing to note is that the figures do not back up the claims made for them. Fifty-three women were found to be infected out of 36,834 in the sample. That is one in 695, not one in 500. The previous figures showed 18 infected out of 26,000, which is one in 1,444. The rate had only doubled, not quadrupled, and the real number of extra cases was thirty-five.

Then, embarrassingly, the Genito-Urinary Department of St Thomas' Hospital published information on 113 cases of heterosexuals with AIDS who attended their clinic: 52 were intravenous drug users (IDUs) and 13 were partners of IDUs, 39 had a partner from abroad, (and of those, 34 were African,) 2 were contacts of bisexual men, 2 had blood transfusions in Africa and one was haemophiliac. Only 2 were neither members of "at risk" groups nor regular partners of the same.[23]

Four other VD clinics confirmed these trends, including Charing Cross Hospital, where half of all new heterosexual cases were from Africa, and Guy's, where 7 out of 11 women being treated came from Uganda. Researchers at the Royal Berkshire Hospital in Reading concluded that results from their own and other clinics showed that:

> there is no evidence ... for major spread of HIV infection into the general heterosexual population. The results reflect the global situation of high rates of HIV infection in intravenous drug users in Western Europe and of heterosexual HIV infection in sub-Saharan Africa, with increasing rates in the Caribbean.[24]

Early in 1992 doctors Banatvala et al of St Thomas' wrote to the Lancet to report that of 4,097 women tested for HIV in 1990, only one found to be infected with HIV did not come from a high-risk group. Three out of four infected women were of African origin. The release of this information was attacked by the Royal College of Nursing for being likely to spread "alarm and prejudice," in other words, for being politically incorrect.

It is reasonable to conclude that Mrs Bottomley's 53 cases contracted the HIV by the same routes in the same sort of people, rather than from casual "unprotected" sex. Paradoxically, if Mrs Bottomley had said: "you are more likely to get AIDS from a regular IDU partner than from promiscuous normal heterosexual encounters," she would have been more accurate. Even in the case of Ray Cornes, the promiscuous haemophiliac in Birmingham who infected four women before his story broke in June 1992, those dreaming of a heterosexual explosion were disappointed: it turned out that Cornes was interested in unnatural sexual practices, and had buggered his victims.[25] The heterosexual epidemic remains on the evidence a myth.

AIDS has spoiled the homosexual party

AIDS has spoiled whatever fun there was in homosexual practice and replaced it with a curious fatalism. As the "Lesbian and Gay Youth Magazine" put it, the Terrence Higgins Trust "glossy posters and reams of leaflets" are desperately trying to put over the image that:

Safe Sex is still butch and macho, and that you can stop fucking and still be one hell of a man.[26]

The insistence that a male homosexual can decline to being little more than a masturbator and retain his masculinity does indeed seem a bit plaintive, whilst the classifying of homosexual acts into "high, medium and low risk," without which, so it seems, homosexual behaviour cannot survive if it can survive at all, already places a stigma on homosexual activity without any help from the 1988 Local Government Act. The "Lesbian and Gay Youth Magazine" was quick to point this out. Normal sexual intercourse between man and wife has never had to be classified into "risk level," whilst unnatural sex on the other hand is always "risky." Male homosexual activists have had to admit that their sexual activity is inherently unsafe, and must be made "safer" by classification and latex.

The Princess Royal described AIDS as "a classic own goal by the human race," and was predictably castigated for differentiating between "innocent" victims and the rest - who were immediately supposed to be "guilty."[27]

It is inhuman not to feel sympathy for people who have brought their suffering on themselves, whether they be AIDS sufferers, alcoholics, or lung cancer victims. Yet such is today's bizarre world that those whose illnesses can be linked to drinking or smoking receive rather less sympathy from the medical and political professions than do those suffering from AIDS. What are we to make of Sir Raymond Hoffenberg, President of the Royal College of Physicians, suggesting to a Commons Committee that smokers should pay for their hospital treatment, or of Virginia Bottomley's husband Peter boasting that he had "got a little list" of eminent people with drink-driving convictions? One can only imagine the horror of the liberal establishment if someone were to make the same suggestion about AIDS sufferers, or to boast of having "a little list" of them.[28]

AIDS used to promote homosexual activity

A fact-sheet published by Family & Youth Concern in May 1991 drew attention to the pornographic posters that Terrence Higgins Trust produces in the guise of health education. The material was described by Family & Youth Concern as "crude, explicit and degrading."

The Terrence Higgins Trust had set up a project called MESMAC ("Men who have sex with men action in the community") which according to project worker Jamie Taylor "does work with young gay and bisexual men." Taylor claims "We have been visiting some lesbian and gay youth groups," in a letter accompanying a selection of Dutch gay erotica sent in reply to a request from "a gay who is 17 years old" asking for help in spreading awareness of "gay issues" at his youth club.

Valerie Riches of Family and Youth Concern said:

> We find this deplorable, particularly as the letter comes with a selection of posters showing the naked male body in bondage poses, emphasising the genitals. The fact that the pictures come from Holland, courtesy of the Dutch Ministry of Health, does not make them less pornographic. The officers of the Terrence Higgins Trust would do well to remember that homosexual intercourse below the age of 21 is an offence.[29]

Of course the officers of the Terrence Higgins Trust could not care less that 21 is the minimum age for homosexual activity, and they have had enormous success up and down the land in promoting homosexual activity amongst the young by "taking AIDS education into schools."

When Secretary of State for Education, Kenneth Clarke adopted the same philosophy, attempting to introduce into schools compulsory sex education which promotes homosexual activity including anal and oral sexual activity by the back-door route of including study of HIV in the science curriculum for 11 - 14 year-olds. The curriculum will be taught in schools from September 1992 unless his successor, John Patten, rescinds the order.

AIDS as homosexual opportunity
Paradoxically and depressingly then, AIDS has given gay activists and liberal fellow travellers an opportunity to increase public sympathy for homosexuality and to promote homosexual activity in schools, youth clubs and colleges.

Health Authorities from Cornwall to Grampian have been told to recruit AIDS officers, in some cases to service the needs of communities with numbers of cases of the disease in single figures. The bandwagon, supported and encouraged by sex educators and local authorities, rolls on even into staid rural communities like Bedfordshire, where local MP John Carlisle was attacked by the "gays" for objecting both to "AIDS education" and to Bedfordshire Council's support for a "lesbian and gay youth group."[30]

Another example of AIDS as opportunity comes from the book Fr Bill Kirkpatrick, an Anglican, has written of his work with terminal AIDS patients. Not once does he criticise homosexual activity, nor even confront the Biblical texts. Indeed, he urges the Church to be "non-judgmental" and to promote condoms and "safer sex," maintaining that this will be a "morally correct" position.[31]

The UK Declaration of Rights of People with AIDS
A coalition of AIDS groups produced a "Declaration of Rights of People with AIDS" for launch in August 1991. It took a list of the existing human rights which apply to everyone and then repeated and amplified them to extend them to people with AIDS and HIV. So it was that they demanded the right of people with AIDS to all and any employment, to mix with other prisoners in gaols, to sexual activity, including procreation, and to much else that one might think of as totally inappropriate. The Declaration, which did not mention homosexuality by name at all, was supported by the usual run of left-wing entertainers, humanists, and churchmen. The Archbishop of Canterbury supported the Declaration without having read it, his name being listed between seasoned homosexual activists Simon Callow and Michael Cashman.

Other supporters of the "Declaration of Rights" included Paddy Ashdown MP, Professor Brian Abel-Smith, Baroness Birk, Professor Peter Campbell, Margaret Drabble, Simon Fanshawe, the Rt. Rev. Peter Hall, Michael Holroyd, Bp Trevor Huddleston, Peter Jay and his

The politics of AIDS

ex-wife Margaret (director of the National AIDS Trust), Ian Kennedy, Michael Meacher MP, Julia Neuberger, Harold Pinter, Simon Rattle, Ned Sherrin, Jimi Somerville, Janet Suzman, Victoria Wood, David Yip, Susannah York and Chris Smith MP. The latter fronted the AIDS lobby press conference in company with militant homosexual Jonathan Grimshaw, Ceri Hutton of the National AIDS Trust and an uncomfortable-looking Dr Michael Adler.

Co-incidentally, Conservative Family Campaign published a "Charter of Human Responsibility" for people with AIDS and HIV on the same day. The Campaign proposed only one piece of legislation, that it be a criminal act for a health worker with AIDS not to disclose the fact to his patients. The US Senate had just voted overwhelmingly for similar legislation after the dentist Dr Acer infected five of his patients including Kimberley Bergalis.[32]

The Charter itself suggested ways in which people with AIDS and HIV could behave responsibly, to the extent of asking them to recognise that they were carrying the virus and should refrain from sexual activity. The Campaign and its sponsor MPs received a torrent of abuse from the AIDS and homosexual lobbies, the two by then being transparently synonymous.

The position taken by pro-homosexual Ceri Hutton, defending the Declaration of Rights when she debated this issue on radio was that we were all responsible.[33] On sexual activity for example, someone with AIDS should have sex with someone who didn't, and needn't tell them, the responsibility being as much on the one who didn't have it to avoid getting it, as on the one who did have it to avoid passing it on. If this sounds like warped morality, it must owe more than a little to the morality of the homosexual world itself.

12
The myth of the gentle gay

Joe Orton and Kenneth Halliwell were friends. For fifteen years, they lived and often wrote together. They wore each other's clothes. Their wills each named the other as sole beneficiary. They shared everything except success. But on 9 August 1967, murder made them equal again. The note was found on top of the red-grained leather binder which held Orton's diary. The words, fastidiously written, had none of the horror that the scene did:

> If you read his diary all will be explained. KH
> P.S. Especially the latter part.

Halliwell lay nude on his back in the centre of the room, three feet from Orton's writing desk. The backs of his hands, the top of his chest, and his bald head were splattered with blood. Except for his arms, rigor mortis had set in. Halliwell's gory pyjama top was draped over the desk chair. On the linoleum floor near him was a glass and a can of grapefruit which had speeded the twenty-two Nembutals into his blood, killing him within thirty seconds. Halliwell had died sooner than Orton, whose sheets were still warm when the police discovered him in bed, his head cratered like a burnt candle.[1]

"Free and equal relationships"

Gay activists have been keen to present the image that "the freest [sic] and most equal relationships are likely to be between homosexuals."[2] Not content with arguing that such "relationships" are as good as those between heterosexuals,

> some militants suggest the "spiritual" or "intellectual" love of same sex partners is somehow preferable to the more pedestrian "breeding" of heterosexuals. Most of all, they want their lifestyle to be seen as "gay," free from slavery to conventional rules, exuberant, full of

The myth of the gentle gay 131

zest, and suffused with commitment to loving, caring and sharing relationships."³

Homosexuals are thought to be especially nice to women. We have seen and will see again the misogynism of homosexual men. The reader may know male homosexuals away from the "gay" scene who seem to get on well with women. But a psychiatrist tells us:

> This is so only so long as no erotic element enters into the relationship to make it dangerous. For the homosexual, women are safe only so long as they are platonic companions. Any suggestion that they might be mistresses renders them alarming.⁴

Jenny lives with Eric and Martin

The gentle image of homosexual life-styles was portrayed in the famous "Jenny lives with Eric and Martin," which was the book which ILEA and some Labour London Boroughs wanted to use with children in schools and in libraries. The book ends with cartoons that are intended to leave positive images of homosexuality, so the actual story comes first, is illustrated with photographs and goes like this:

> This is Jenny. She is five years old.
> This is Jenny's dad. He is called Martin.
> This is Eric. He lives with Jenny's dad.
> Jenny, Martin and Eric live in a little house, in Denmark.
> Living nearby is Jenny's mum, Karen. She often comes to visit them.
>   It is usually Martin who collects Jenny from school, because he is the first to come home from work. Today he collects Jenny earlier than usual. It is Eric's birthday and they are going to hurry home so they can surprise him with a birthday spread. Jenny's mum is coming too ...⁵

Eric"s birthday party

Only as many conventions are broken here as are absolutely necessary. The child is female, so as to prevent the spectre of paedophilia from spoiling the birthday party, and it is one of Jenny's parents who collects her from school, although only because of convenience. The preparations for the party proceed apace, Jenny gives Karen a hug and a great big kiss when she turns up, and then Eric, accurately to describe the picture, minces in.

The time passes much too quickly. Suddenly it is evening and Karen gets up and puts on her jacket. "I must go now," she says. "Thanks for a lovely party." "Oh, do you have to go so soon?" Jenny asks sadly. Karen lifts her up and gives her a kiss. "I am free on Monday so I will come and fetch you. Bye for now." "Oh, no ..." says Jenny. "Why aren't you coming tomorrow?" "I can't," says Karen. "I have got to work all day."

The bedroom scenes
The curtain falls on this sad little episode, and when it rises, "It is Saturday," and we are treated to the infamous pictures of half-naked Eric and Martin, at least, the halves that we can see are naked, with their drug-smoking equipment on the shelf above their bed. Before the book degenerates further from covert propaganda into the blatant positive image cartoon section, Eric and Martin have a set-to about who is to mow the lawn and who is to cook:

> Eric dries his hands on a rag, looking annoyed. He walks over to Martin. "Now look," he says angrily, "I did the cooking yesterday and the day before. It is your turn so you will have to cut the grass afterwards." And suddenly they are squabbling. They stand there, shouting all sorts of things at the tops of their voices. Jenny scratches a bit of old paint off her trike. She feels she is about to cry.

Squabbling over no mans' land
Poor Jenny. Deserted by her mother and left to witness the domestic wranglings of, not to put too fine a point on it, these two appalling queens, to borrow the late Kenneth William's description of Joe Orton and Kenneth Halliwell. Nothing could better demonstrate that the role models which Gay Liberation hates are necessary to establish real freedom.

In a normal household there would be no problem about whose job it was to mow the lawn and whose to cook. Eric and Martin on the other hand have no boundaries and no roles on which to model themselves, so they waste their time fighting over no-man's-land. Their "relationship" not only doesn't work, it cannot work.

Who wants to live with Leslie and Nigel?
The same problems exist for real "gay couples" as for fictional:

> "I suppose we ended up with a fairly neutral sitting-room," says Leslie, "for the simple reason that there was no way we were going

The myth of the gentle gay

to agree on anything else. But you've only got to look at our bedrooms (like a lot of gays, Leslie and Nigel have separate rooms) to see how different we really are. Nigel's is all spare and lean with a virtual gym in it. Mine is like the Old Curiosity shop - full of knick-knacks, pictures, odds and ends."[6]

The practice of having separate rooms hints at a separate identity that each man feels he has to retain. Most married people on the other hand will aim for a joint identity, something that reflects them as a couple. The separate rooms may also be to do with the need for homosexual couples to experience sexual encounters outside their "relationship," even though these encounters tend to take place, as we have seen, in public places. Wherever they occur, it remains, as a committed homosexual psychologist made clear, that:

> Frequent sexual contact with third parties is nothing out of the ordinary for homosexual lovers (a fifth of those who had steady relationships "often" had sexual contacts with other men, and a half did so "sometimes").[7]

The American "ISIS" survey conducted between 1983 and 1984 provided confirmation that a majority of homosexuals have started outside liaisons halfway through a primary "relationship."

Promiscuity leads to jealousies

There seems to be a need within the human psyche for stability and loyalty, so these third party contacts lead inevitably to jealousies or to feelings within at least one of the pair that he *should* be jealous. The tensions in Joe Orton's relationship with Kenneth Halliwell were a long time brewing up to Orton's murder, and Orton's professional success was probably as irritating to Halliwell as his sexual conquests. Orton's biographer puts it like this:

> Halliwell was sexually timid. Orton was brazenly promiscuous. Halliwell had to accept Orton's "trolling" but he never condoned it. In moments of anxiety his own fear of abandonment and inferiority tried to disguise itself as worry about their well-being. The danger in rough trade, the lack of intimacy in "tea room" [public lavatory] sex, were not what Halliwell craved. He wanted what J.R.Ackerley called "the sad little wish - someone to love me."[8]

Jealousy leads to violence

The jealousies may lead to physical violence. One authority explains the reasons behind it like this:

> Homosexuality is filled with destruction and self-deceit. It is a masquerade of life in which certain psychic energies are neutralised and held in a marginally quiescent state. However, the unconscious manifestations of hate, destructiveness, incest and fear always threaten to break through. Instead of union, cooperation, solace, stimulation, emotional enrichment, and a maximum opportunity for creative interpersonal maturation and realistic fulfilment, there are multiple underlying factors which constantly threaten any ongoing homosexual relationship: destruction, mutual defeat, exploitation of the partner and the self, oral-sadistic incorporation, aggressive onslaughts, and attempts to alleviate anxiety - all comprising a pseudo-solution to the aggressive and libidinal conflicts that dominate and torment the individuals involved.[9]

Violence within the homosexual network

It is a favourite pastime of the specialist homosexual press to claim that there is a large amount of violence directed against homosexual men. There is certainly some of this, for there is an element of youth that derives sick pleasure from "queer bashing." But even this phenomenon is cynically used by activists to claim that they are "oppressed."

Under the headline "Murder list grows as attacks continue," Gay Times wrote about eight murders which involved homosexual victims. One would immediately suppose that these murders had been perpetrated by nasty heterosexuals on defenceless "gays," but on closer reading, two of the murders occurred within "gay couples," three others resulted from pickups in homosexual contact clubs, pubs or cinemas, another involved a frenzied stabbing, and of the remaining two, one happened near a "cottage" or public lavatory, and the other in a 52-year-old man's home, a 20-year-old man having been charged.[10]

"Attacks on gay people" was published by the Campaign for Homosexual Equality to show that homosexuals suffer most at the hands of queer-bashers. However, violence within "couples," or in the context of casual pickups, or in defence to a homosexual advance outnumber instances of queer-bashing even allowing author Julian Meldrum to claim cases where outrageous gays wore provocative badges in pubs and were surprised to be attacked or where men wrongly thought another was propositioning them.

Homosexual murders

In the case of murders documented in "Attacks on gay people," the picture is even more stark. Of 42 murders catalogued, just 2 were the result of "queer-bashing." 4 arose from a homosexual advance being made, 5 from a mistaken advance, 4 were anonymous attackers in "cruising" areas, and 4 others had no relevance to the study. 8 murders occurred within a homosexual relationship and 15 were the result of a homosexual pick-up for sex. The conclusions of the study bore no relation to the evidence considered.

Over a period of only three months in one area of South London, in one case, in fact in one of the cases mentioned by Gay Times, a man hacked to death his "lover" who had a "penchant for black men," chopped up the body then pretended his "lover" had gone abroad for treatment for AIDS. He was subsequently found guilty and jailed for life.[11] In another, both men had had numerous affairs with other men, and the 46 year-old survivor said of his 62-year-old "lover," "I should have topped him years ago."[12] There was a sadistic twist to this case, the victim often handcuffing his "lover" to the bed.[13] In a third case, a chauffeur had a craving for teenagers and brought the boys back to his home to give them drinks and play homosexual pornographic videos to them. One of them stabbed him to death.[14]

Lesbian violence

Nor is the violence confined to homosexual men. In a lesbian "love-triangle," a teacher was convicted of "a savage attack" involving a claw hammer, which left her victim brain-damaged, after she had discovered that her lover had slept with her former girl-friend.[15] In a separate case, at one time, a woman who had killed her lover for wanting their relationship to end was Britain's longest-serving prisoner.[16]

That there is violence actually *within* lesbian relationships, and not just sado-masochistic violence in a sexual context, is again something that gay activists are anxious to deny. A 1992 edition of "Lesbian London" carried the results of a survey which found that 85% of domestic violence against lesbians had been carried out by other lesbians. A book reviewed earlier in a "Gay's the Word" publication, had the courage to "name" the violence:

"Naming the Violence" ... is not about the violence inflicted on lesbians by a misogynistic and homophobic society (although social context is certainly held to be an important contributory factor), but about the violence that lesbians inflict on each other."[17]

The reviewer admits to a large measure of denial:

> Despite the cracked ribs, blackened eyes and smashed egos that I have witnessed over the years, not to mention the scar that I myself have carried since I was fourteen, I must confess to never having given the "issues related to lesbian-battering" much serious thought before. According to the editor, Kerry Lobel, this is not at all unusual. Most lesbians, it seems, just don't want to know.
>
> Reading the contributions from lesbians who have suffered not only violence but an excruciating silence and lack of support as well, I can no longer pretend not to know, but I still don't like it. Why? Well, for one thing, I am reluctant to relinquish my vision of Utopia. As Sarah, herself a victim of lesbian violence, puts it, "Who wants to admit that anything can be wrong with lesbian relationships?"

Homosexual rape

Sadism and masochism (S & M) is such an important part of sexual life in homosexual relationships that it is inevitable that the sadism often gets out of control. Enrique Rueda, in his book "The Homosexual Network," reports that a workshop in San Francisco offered to instruct homosexuals in how to engage in sex torture without killing each other. One British gay rights activist wrote that: "Gay men rape each other, sometimes even kill each other,"[18] whilst one of the key figures in the Organisation for Lesbian and Gay Action, which was involved in demonstrations against clause 28, said: "Homosexual rape does occur; I suspect it is far more common than anyone in the gay community cares to admit."[19] Yet another admitted: "There may well be under-reporting of [violent] incidents, due to the reluctance of gays to get involved with the police in any way at all"[20]

"Outrage" and the police

Veteran homosexual activist Peter Tatchell has been campaigning through the "Outrage" group for the police to begin separate categorisation of "attacks against lesbians and gay men." Tatchell denies that such attacks are motivated by anything other than "homophobia" from outside the homosexual network, and the Police, aware of the reality, initially stood up to "Outrage."[21]

The myth of the gentle gay

Eventually, however, Chief Superintendent Peter Stevens, of the Community Relations Branch, was worn down by the pressure and wanted to be seen to be a nice man. He gave in to Tatchell's demands, and a pilot scheme will monitor any attack the victim thinks is "homophobic" in Kensington, Battersea, Holloway and Hampstead. The choice of Hampstead is interesting: homosexuals have increasingly taken over the Heath for nude sunbathing, swimming, and even for overt cruising and sexual activity. Confrontations between residents and homosexuals are increasing, with liberal tempers fraying on both sides.[22]

Chief Supt Stevens even went to the extent of asking his own personnel branch to write "homosexual orientation" into the Met's Equal Opportunities Policy, opening the doors to recruitment of homosexual police.[23] The decision was taken by the Commissioner himself, who agreed in February 1992 to another pretence that homosexuals are a sort of racial group, and recognition of their alleged separate identity. There were headlines of praise in the homosexual press, if nowhere else.

Police investigate homosexual murderer

"Gay Switchboard," the homosexual contact group, did their best to dissuade a victim of one homosexual killer from going to the police at all. At night, fashion hairdresser Michele Lupo:

> became "Rudi" the male prostitute with a taste for sado-masochism which developed into a lust for murder. He trawled the homosexual nightspots of London looking for victims. With the promise of casual sex he would lure them to a secluded place - a derelict basement, a lorry park, a disused toilet or a railway shed - and strangle them with their own scarves or a black nylon sock. Between March and May [1986] he murdered four men and attempted to kill two others."[24]

Only when his latest victim struggled free from the strangler and, after his abortive call to "Gay Switchboard," contacted the police and was promptly persuaded by a Detective Superintendent to tour known homosexual nightspots with four plain clothes officers, was Lupo spotted and held. Despite the advice of Gay Switchboard, the police took the victim's story very seriously indeed.

Homicidal homosexuals

The high level of homosexual violent crime is indicated by an American survey showing that approximately 10% of San Francisco's homicides are said to be the result of sado-masochistic sex among homosexuals,[25] and particularly gory murders are assumed to be homosexual until proved otherwise.[26] Another American study considered sexually flavoured mass murder in the years 1966 - 1983. The 23 heterosexual murderers committed a total of 168 homicides, the 16 homosexuals committed between 350 and 550. The uncertainty arises because one pair of homosexual lovers, Henry Lucas and Otis Toole, simply lost count as they travelled around America raping and killing boys, girls, men and women.[27]

Of the ten worst mass-murder sets in this study, homosexuals accounted for seven, and even taking the lower estimate of Lucas and Toole, the 1% - 2% of the population who are active male homosexuals provided 41% of the murderers and killed at least 68% of the victims.

More recent examples of homosexual serial killers simply confirm the trend. Dennis Nilson killed fifteen homeless, lonely homosexual men in Britain, whilst the victims of Thierry Paulin, the homosexual Monster of Montmartre, who has died of AIDS, and his male lover Jean-Thierry Mathurin, were 27 elderly women gruesomely tortured and killed for a few hundred francs each time during a three year reign of terror in Paris.[28]

Jeffrey Dahmer, the "Butcher of Milwaukee" went on trial in July 1991 after admitting to a series of homicides in which his mainly black victims were lured to his flat with promises of homosexual activity, then were handcuffed and dismembered before being cooked or buried. Eleven skeletons were found at his flat, and police suspect that a further 17 men were also killed for Dahmer's sexual gratification.[29]

One of the victims was a fourteen-year-old Laotian boy, who temporarily escaped naked and bleeding from Dahmer's flat, only to be caught in the street and dragged back by him, persuading the police who were called that it was just a "homosexual tiff." In fact, at the time of his arrest, Dahmer was on probation for second degree sexual assault after offering a 13 year-old boy $50 to pose for nude photos.

Early in 1992 a lesbian who became a prostitute and killed six men who picked her up on an American Highway was convicted and sentenced for what appeared to be revenge attacks for an earlier rape.[30]

Homosexual newspaper smears paedophile's victim

In 1988, a homosexual computer operator and convicted child molester who according to a newspaper less well acquainted with the ways of "gay" couples than ourselves and obviously shocked by the revelation: "even betrayed his live-in lover by taking a secret boyfriend

The myth of the gentle gay

on holiday to the Algarve,"[31] confessed to the murder of a 14-year-old newspaper boy whose naked body was found 40 miles away from his home. The boy "had been sexually assaulted and was so badly battered he could be identified only by his fingerprints."[32]

To give him whatever credit we can, the boy's killer, Victor Miller, immediately expressed remorse and pleaded guilty "to save speculation and further distress to [the boy's] family."[33] No such conventions inhibited Graham McKerrow, the aggressive homosexual editor and joint owner of the London-based homosexual "scene" newspaper "Capital Gay." He immediately alleged under an "exclusive" tag that the 14-year-old was actually a homosexual who met an older man twice a week for sex.[34]

McKerrow claimed the information came from a "penfriend," a 17-year-old soldier who could not be named. The paper added: "He also complained about his strict, narrow-minded parents with whom he could not discuss sex." But the boy's mother said that he only ever had a girl penfriend several years ago: "He was a normal teenage boy with his whole life in front of him. It's hard to imagine the sort of people who could invent a slur like this. They must be bloody mad."[35]

So why did Capital Gay run such a story? Were they mad, or bad, or just pushing homosexual propaganda? Tim Robinson, one of the paper's editorial team, explains the political motives in an extraordinary non-sequitur:

"A lot of mileage was made of the fact that his killer was gay to bring the whole paedophile label over homosexuals. If [the boy] had had gay teenage groups or a gay helpline to turn to about his sexuality problems perhaps he would still be alive."[36]

"Gay teenage groups" exist as we shall see only to give or confirm youngsters' sexuality problems, and as such have a most important recruiting role within the homosexual network. But according to the boy's parents he had no such problems in any case. He was just an ordinary teenager. His father said: "How do you find words to describe how angry this makes us. They are rubbing salt into our wounds."[37]

Violence of tolerant liberals

Although homosexuals often confine their violence to within the homosexual network, they still inflict costs on society, both financial and emotional. When the violence breaks the boundaries, heterosexual society has on the evidence more to fear from homosexuals than vice versa. There are also instances where violence is perpetrated in the name of tolerance and liberalism, in the attacks on parents in the London Borough of Haringey, for instance. The parents campaigned against a plan by the Council to introduce lessons on homosexual and lesbian lifestyles in all schools from nursery upwards. One mother was mugged, two others received death threats and a fourth person had a vehicle stolen.[38]

In San Francisco, some 9,000 people gathered to protest at the release of one Dan White, convicted only of voluntary manslaughter after shooting to death George Moscone, the Mayor, and Harvey Milk, an openly homosexual city council member. Whatever the merits of the verdict, it is evident from a glowing report in a homosexual newspaper,[39] that the crowd was stirred into a frenzy of retribution:

> The keynote speaker at the rally was "Sister Boom-Boom," one of a group of drag-queen nuns called the Sisters of Perpetual Indulgence. "Today was the last day Dan White could spend knowing that he would live through the day. Today, Dan White begins a life sentence, and I'm sorry to say I don't think it's going to be a long one," Sister Boom-Boom said. As the speeches went on, men tossed black "Dan White Hit Squad" buttons over the crowd. Buttons were quickly grabbed and pinned on dozens of shirts and jackets. Thousands in the crowd sang along with a rendition of "Oh, Danny Boy" singing "Oh Danny, where you gonna go? Someone's gonna find you, wherever you go"
>
> Another homosexual activist said: "Gay people have a right and duty to be angry over the courts kid glove treatment of Dan White. We are entitled to the life of Dan White in return for the life of Harvey Milk and we are entitled to obtain it either legally or illegally."[40]

Dan White subsequently committed suicide.

Gay consumerism

If there is a marked lack of liberal tolerance in the speeches and writings of gay activists, there is also a marked lack of care within the network for homosexuals who grow old. The homosexual network depends for its existence on the presence of youth and good looks. This is part of the explanation for the intense concentration on fitness amongst male homosexuals, and for the high turnover in "gay" taste and fashion.

> "The gay is more visually aware than a hetero; he'll see something in a shop that he wants, he'll see others running around with it and instantly he'll feel "I must have it!" ... "We're talking about an almost

psychopathic fashion-consciousness. At the end of the day it's always a search - and this is what makes it irrational and hard to please - for true love. If I have a lovely home, I'll impress someone who'll adore me. If I get a new hairstyle, or a new car, or the cassette recorder, I'll be loved as well. Much of gay consumerism boils down to a constant search for Mr. Right."[41]

The unending search

That all the searching is in vain is a point that Quentin Crisp makes. Mr Crisp is not liked by modern homosexual activists because he is a stereotypical queen, and has made a career out of being, as they would see it, "self-oppressed." He has observed that the effeminate homosexual in particular desires nothing more than the love of a real man. Yet a real man will not love a homosexual, ergo the search is unending. This "strong desire for an intense one-to-one relationship" is mentioned by activist John Shiers, who in a sad piece of writing defends his involvement in what he describes as the "gay world" with poignant honesty:

> I choose to use commercial gay facilities; I consent to the one-night stands; I also have a fairly satisfying and enjoyable social life quite independent of all this. Yet my choices are not "free": I have needs which gnaw away under the surface and which gay bars, clubs and sex do provide temporary relief for. But it is temporary; the underlying issues remain and I have no idea how to begin to go about fully understanding them, let alone sorting them out in such a way as to give me a constant feeling of personal integration.[42]

Trying to stay young

These "needs which gnaw away" do not recede with age, and if sex, even as John Shiers says "sex disconnected in any meaningful way from emotional relationships," still provides temporary relief, then it is important for the active homosexual to be able to make contacts that lead to sex. And yet, when a regular on the homosexual "scene" grows old, there becomes progressively less that "gay consumerism," or fashion, can do to help him maintain his "sex appeal":

> As we grow older we continue to slide up the line between "young" and "old." A really young faggot usually tries to look and act older because of the drinking and age of consent laws. But most of us try desperately to look younger than we are. As we age, we resort to a whole array of hair pieces, contact lenses, sprays, sun lamps, oils

and other artifices to look younger. We run after the latest fashion of the young consumer market hoping to find some magic fountain of youth. ...

Older gays just aren't happy with each other's company generally .... Or if we are willing to share our time and lives with older homosexuals, we often draw a strict line between sex and company, preferring sex with young strangers (often anonymous) and camaraderie with others our own age. Couples over thirty are an exception, and they have usually met before one or both became thirty.[43]

Youth and looks

The "gay rights" movement is very conscious of this, and is anxious to portray happy, old, homosexual couples. Unfortunately, there seems to be only one of the genre in the whole of London willing to be talked about. "Bernard with his lover of 32 years, Dudley" were pictured both in the GLC Charter for Gay and Lesbian Rights, in a call for "single sex social clubs for elderly gay men and women,"[44] and in Kennedy's "Gay Guide to London."[45] "Dudley" is in fact Dudley Cave, a homosexual rights campaigner. Nor can it be argued, as does John Hart in his book for teenagers, that:

At its worst the gay, especially male gay, world mirrors all the sexual obsessions with youth and looks - people seen as commodities - of the straight society.[46]

Leaving aside the world of film stars, models and jet setting industrialists, this simply is not most peoples' experience of normal heterosexual life. Married couples age together, and Mr Hart, who constantly blames "straight" society for all that is wrong in active homosexuality, has missed the point that successful heterosexual marriage is about growing together, and growing old together, through love and commitment, and not about "youth and looks." In any case, "gay," accordingly to its advocates, supposedly "shows the way." This slogan is revealed as just another rhyming, homosexual falsehood.

Nobody loves a fairy when she's old

The emphasis on youth and beauty in the homosexual network, on the other hand, appears to be intrinsic, and leads inevitably to the prostitution that we discussed earlier, or as an American expert puts it, "the merchandising of sex as a commodity."[47] This is confirmed by homosexuals both practising and reformed:

The myth of the gentle gay 143

Both young heterosexual males and young faggots presume that the only reason sexual relations might occur between a young and old man is for some money or other consideration.[48]

It was a sordid life. As you get older, anything good about homosexuality passes away and you are left with all of the bad things. You no longer are attractive and you cannot make contact. You have to pay for any sex you get. And then there is no involvement, there is no love. No friendship is involved; just a business transaction. So the rejection of the homosexual life is very intense. [49]

Even when ongoing sexual relationships are formed, these are rarely monogamous for very long. ... we feel the need to constantly present and preserve an image which we hope will turn on those who we want to fancy us; those of us who are still young or fairly young often fear growing old, and it seems that many who are old wish to be young.[50]

Older homosexuals valued only if they can pay

That this is a regular experience is confirmed by the Gay Liberation Front Manifesto:

Gay men are very apt to fall victim to the cult of youth - those sexual parades in the "glamorous" meat-rack bars of London and New York, those gay beaches of the South of France and Los Angeles haven't anything to do with liberation. Those are the hang-outs of the plastic gays who are obsessed with image and appearance. In love with their own bodies, these gay men dread the approach of age, because to be old is to be "ugly," and with their youth they lose also the right to love and be loved, and are valued only if they can pay.[51]

If the bleak picture these extracts paint is experienced by almost every active homosexual, what else could be honestly expected from a network based upon sexual gratification? The continued and obsessive proselytising that comes from active homosexuals,[52] together with the promotion of homosexual "lifestyles" by gay activists appear to be the saddest kind of self-deception but also a hideous confidence trick played on the susceptible youth they have to recruit. How this susceptibility arises, and what turns it into homosexual activity, are matters we shall investigate.

13
The origins of a homosexual orientation

Homosexuality was traditionally not recognised as a means by which to subdivide human beings at all, and its practices were classified along with all other forms of non-procreative, (and by implication, fornicative) sex.[1] Homosexual behaviour was looked upon purely as a matter of sinful choice. However, in the mid nineteenth century, medical science began classifying all sorts of things, and in the process, homosexuality emerged as a category, soon to be surrounded by theories.

Carl Ulrichs' theory of the third sex

Early hypotheses proposed a distinction between "innate" and "acquired" homosexuality, and this was developed by Carl Heinrich Ulrichs, who "accepted the congenital argument and went on to suggest that the male homosexual has a 'feminine soul enclosed in a male body'," a hypothesis that was repeated by Leo Abse, M.P. in debates on the 1967 Sexual Offences Act.[2] Mr Abse attributed the curse, as he put it, to a lad's growing up without a father figure with whom to identify, and not, on this occasion at least, to genetics. Ulrichs coined the term "Uranian," from Uranus, who in Greek mythology is the father of Saturn, to describe masculine homosexuals and "Dionian" from the goddess Aphrodite, for effeminates. He also elaborated a complex classification of homosexual types, which encompassed men, women, and the "third sex" in varying degrees.[3]

Ulrichs, a homosexual himself, was aware that his theories created a minority status for homosexuals. He therefore tried to justify homosexuality in terms of elitist boasting that finds echoes in positive images teaching today. Homosexuality was seen by Ulrichs as the foundation of a more rational social order, even though the search of the homosexual, as he saw it, for the ideal partner, was doomed to failure. In Ulrichs' argument the homosexual man is attracted to virility and seeks a truly masculine man to love, in the classic futile quest.

Richard von Krafft-Ebing suggests genetic predisposition

Although Richard von Krafft-Ebing viewed as perverted "any expression of the sexual impulse which fails to correspond to the purposes of nature, i.e. of procreation," [4] he continued to argue that the condition was caused by a genetic flaw in the human embryo, which resulted in a sort of hermaphrodism. In spite of writers like the French psychologist Binet, who continued to argue that homosexuality was acquired under the influence of environment, by the end of the nineteenth century, homosexuality was regarded as inborn, genetically predisposed and therefore incurable.[5]

The "third sex" hypothesis was taken on board first by socialist homosexual Edward Carpenter and then by the famous sexologist Havelock Ellis. According to homosexual activist John Marshall, who describes Ellis as "the most influential English theorist of the period":

> *Ellis was keen to show that homosexuality was inborn, harmless and non-pathological. He was deeply committed to biological theories and was provided with a convenient explanation of homosexuality when hormones were discovered at the beginning of the century.*[6]

Havelock Ellis develops Eugenics

It is interesting that Marshall quotes Ellis so glowingly. Havelock Ellis was a member of a group which included H.G.Wells, American eugenicist and racist Margaret Sanger, and Marie Stopes, the British birth controller who shared Mrs Sanger's ideals. Their private lives were, not to put too fine a point on it, a dissolute mess. We have already noted Ellis' urolagnia and coprophilia. It was he who introduced Mrs Sanger, the founder of Planned Parenthood, to eugenicist ideas and advocated a system in which prospective parents judged most capable of producing genetically superior children would be the only people permitted to breed, an identical proposal to that employed in the Nazi Lebensborn breeding houses. He used the hallucinatory drug mescaline, which helped his belief in an impersonal pantheistic deity, and started an intense sexual relationship with Margaret Sanger while his own wife was lecturing in America. Edith Ellis had a deep love for her husband that was frustrated by his sexual inadequacies towards her, and his affairs with other women often drove her to lesbian relationships.[7]

It was H G Wells who encouraged Julian Huxley in his philanderings. Like John Maynard Keymes, Wells was one of the "Bloomsbury Group" whose members held ordinary people and Christian morality in contempt.

Magnus Hirschfield maintains homosexuality innate

Ellis' proclivities are virtually ignored by homosexual activist Jeffrey Weeks in his own attempt to show Ellis as an important contributor to "personal and sexual politics."[8] Ellis evidently had good reasons for his keenness to present homosexual behaviour, not to mention other perversions, as "inborn, harmless and non-pathological."[9] The banner of Ellis and Ulrichs was meanwhile taken up by Magnus Hirschfield, who collected and edited Ulrichs' work, and published it in 1889, with a dedication to "the great champion who sacrificed himself for the liberation of lovers of their own sex from legal persecution and social contempt."[10]

In Sigmund Freud, the exponents of the theories of innate homosexuality, and the "third sex," came up against an implacable opponent. Of course there is the view that until Freud and the psychoanalysts broached the possibility of psychological causes, homosexual behaviour was treated simply as a matter of choice, and that when causes of homosexuality originating in early life were put forward, the element of choice ceased to exist. "That being the case, the argument went, it would be pointless for the state to try to deter sexual deviance; worse than pointless, unjust."[11]

Sigmund Freud opposes determinism

However, this does not really square with the history of the subject. Furthermore, according to the current evidence, the way a person makes a sexual object-choice is dependent on a great many factors, of which their early childhood, even possibly their pre-natal experiences, may be part. But Freud's arguments are a considerable advance from the "third sex," genetic disturbance, or hormonal imbalance, all of which are now unsubstantiated as theories, as a gay activists' book acknowledges:

> Reviewing the evidence for The Practitioner in 1954, Swyer concluded: "The capacity for sexual response is not primarily dependent upon the sex hormones and the direction of sexual preference is influenced mainly by psychological and environmental conditioning."[12]

No hormonal link discovered

Several studies have endeavoured to find a link between low testosterone levels and homosexual behaviour,[13] and several others have produced negative results.[14] But to return to Freud, the evidence

The origins of a homosexual orientation

suggests that he put forward his theories with the intention of helping those with the homosexual condition to reform. He believed that up to the age of seventeen young people are "still in the formative period and ought not to be exposed to perverse influences," and emphasised what he called the "latency period" from the age of six or seven until puberty when he considered it inappropriate for sexual themes to intrude into the child's experience, something that the sex education industry has been careful to overlook.[15]

It is of course possible to use Freud to see any amount of crime and delinquency as a subject for the psychiatrist's couch, rather than for the courts, but this is an absurd reduction of his position. In the following passage Freud is arguing no more than that the *roots of homosexual inclination,* rather than actual behaviour, lie for inverts in early childhood:

In all the cases we have examined we have established the fact that the future inverts, in the earliest years of their childhood, pass through a phase of very intense but short-lived fixation to a woman (usually their mother), and that, after leaving this behind, they identify themselves with a woman and take themselves as their sexual object. That is to say, they proceed from a narcissistic basis, and look for a young man who resembles themselves and whom they may love as their mother loved them.[16]

Freud finds no genetic predisposition

Freud had come to the conclusion that there was no genetic predisposition towards homosexuality, nor would hormonal imbalance be a factor. He stated categorically:

Psychoanalytic research is most decidedly opposed to any attempt at separating off homosexuals from the rest of mankind as a group of special character.[17]

This was written as a direct answer to Hirschfield, and its implications for homosexual apologists are catastrophic. For if homosexuals can gain recognition as a separate sex, or as a special group, all that remains is to educate the public as to their nature. If, on the other hand, their orientation is explainable by reference to childhood experiences, then the possibility is opened of their condition being healed. This is exactly what homosexual activists will not recognise today as even a possibility, and would not accept either at the turn of the century.

Freud's psychoanalysis rejected for political reasons

As Martin Dannecker explains: "The psychoanalytic theory of the infantile origins of homosexuality stood in sharp contradiction to Hirschfield's view, and he eventually had to oppose it in the most drastic terms. Till the end of his life, Hirschfield was unable to accept the psycho-analytic standpoint."[18] Of course Hirschfield's own homosexuality, like that of his hero Ulrichs, was influential, and Herr Dannecker admits: "One of the more superficial reasons for Hirschfield's insistence that homosexuality was an innate intermediate type may be sought in simple tactical considerations. The "Scientific Humanitarian Committee" that he founded was locked in struggle for the abolition of paragraph 175."[19] Paragraph 175 was a German statute relating to homosexual activity, and Hirschfield's campaign would have been ruined by any admission that homosexual behaviour was not inborn.

Most theorists, up to the present day, have drawn heavily from Freud. Ferenczi distinguished in 1914 between those he called "subject/object homo-erotics" and "subject homo-erotics." The former were, broadly, Freud's "inverts," who according to Ferenczi think and behave like women and are usually sexually passive. Ferenczi regarded their sexuality as fairly irreversible. The latter are masculine men who normally take an active role and have merely changed their choice of sexual object. Psychiatry, according to Ferenczi, could always help to change their sexual preference.[20]

Nevertheless the reader should not fancy that we are going to be satisfied with a psychology of homosexuality built totally on Freud. Freud was of his time and place. We have moved on from Freud, seeing large amounts of father-son hatred, Oedipus complex and penis-envy. Modern psychology has left Sigmund Freud and nineteenth-century Vienna far behind.

Homosexual behaviour stems from upbringing

West,[21] Swyer,[22] Bergler[23] and Bieber[24] all added weight to the opinion that there was no innate biological explanation for a homosexual orientation, and that psychological conditioning was the major factor, whilst Clifford Allen stressed the importance of fathers in upbringing:

One must admit that to grow normally a boy must have a suitable man from whom he can learn normal reactions. The boy normally moulds his personality on his mother during the first few years of his life but then should unconsciously and even consciously copy his

The origins of a homosexual orientation

father. If he has no father, or his father is overshadowed by his mother, he cannot do so.[25]

Activist John Marshall regards this argument as "unsophisticated and unconvincing" but dispassionate observers will recognise simple common sense. To give just two anecdotal examples: Quentin Crisp told Libby Purvis on BBC's "Midweek"[26] that his had been the classic homosexual's upbringing: "a house full of women," whilst Joe Orton's mother dominated their household, and reduced his father to a "frail, cowed presence."[27] A pattern of disrupted families runs through books of homosexual life-stories.

However, Orton's brother did not become homosexual, so siblings may react differently to the family situation around them. One twin may be homosexual, the other not, although this is more true of twins from different eggs (fraternal twins) than twins from the same egg (identical twins). Research, on a sample of 167 homosexuals, showed that where brothers were identical twins, then if one sibling became homosexual, the other was also homosexual in 52% of cases. Only 22% of the fraternal twins of a homosexual were homosexual themselves.[28]

Genetically identical people seem then to be as likely as not to react identically to damaging dynamics within the family. It has been claimed inevitably by homosexual activists that the results, published by scientists at Northwestern and Boston Universities in December 1991, show that homosexuality is genetically determined. That conclusion simply does not square with the results. Rather does the study reinforce the understanding that a homosexual orientation arises from abnormal development.

If homosexuality was predisposed by a normal gene variation, like appendicitis for example, or blue eyes, it would obviously be bred out (so to speak) in a couple of generations. Were it to be a gene abnormality, like cystic fibrosis, or in some other way congenital (born-with-it) then it would hardly be a Darwinian advance, for again it would immediately disappear. If such a gene abnormality could be detected in the womb, there would be a demand for elimination of the baby by therapeutic abortion. It might be amusing for the cynic to watch the two most sacred cows of libertarianism, fondness for homosexuality and defence of a woman's right to choose, collide in such a spectacular fashion, but no such genetic abnormality has been discovered, in spite of the determination of every homosexual geneticist to find it. I believe them to be barking up the wrong tree: it is not there to find.

Claim that normal sexuality starts in the womb

The following account comes closest to "born like it" and is reported in a book by Mary Whitehouse. It has a happy ending:

> F.J. Kallmann, the famous American psychiatrist, who did so much research into the genetic factor and could find no evidence that this was a cause of homosexuality, did observe another factor which is now being very much stressed by consultants working in this field. Namely, that the origin of homosexuality lies in parental emotional states during the patient's foetal and very early life. Scientific research shows that the human brain is formed at the age of three months of foetal life and that from that time on there is a continuous learning process at work - everything heard from them then on will be stored in the memory and will have its effect.
>
> Kallmann maintains that the primary homosexual is entirely precipitated by abnormal (in terms of moral as well as physical norms) sexual behaviour of parents during pregnancy or just after. Such behaviour, he claims, produces in the normal woman a sense of shame and anxiety. And it is this anxiety, related to sexuality, which has such a profound effect upon the foetus.
>
> This understanding is gradually revolutionising the treatment of homosexuals. One British consultant psychiatrist has documented this case history:
>
> "Male. Aged 25. Depressive, neurotic, homosexual. Schoolmaster. Unable to attend school assemblies or go to Church although a Christian. Father home on leave, from armed services, at time of conception. During consultations with mother, it transpired that she was at that time a night nurse in a male ward. She repeatedly had intercourse with patients during pregnancy. Nevertheless she felt a sense of shame and anxiety. Patient also suffered from deep anxiety and shame in relation to sex. This precipitated his condition. Mother felt constrained to tell her son about her behaviour and express regret to him. This realisation of the source of his problem completely liberated him from it. Now happily married with children and completely normal."[29]

Orthodox psychiatry voted down

It would be wrong to suggest that there were no medical voices dissenting from the view that homosexual orientation originates in abnormal development, is treatable and should be treated. Two studies in the 1950s had subjectively concluded that homosexuals are "on the whole successful and valuable members of society,"[30] whilst

The origins of a homosexual orientation 151

C.A. Tripp has maintained that "all sexual attraction is based on *positive* motives and positive sexual feelings. Unless this is recognised, no theory can ever account for the enormous variety of human sexual response."[31]

The passing of the Sexual Offences Act in 1967, and the occurrence of the Stonewall riot in America, led to a challenge to orthodox psychiatric opinion, which was seen by "gay activists" as "oppressive":

> *Clearly, once male homosexuality had been partially decriminalised in 1967, the main requirement was a fundamental challenge to the subtle forms of oppression which inevitably resulted from medical control. In Britain and America, this challenge arose in the late 1960s and early 1970s with the dramatic emergence of the modern gay movement.*"[32]

In the USA the "National Gay Task Force" orchestrated a year of demonstrations and disruptions until the American Psychiatric Association voted to delete homosexuality from the official listing of pathologies. It is crucial to note that this was not as a result of new research. The Association merely bowed to political pressure and decided medical truth by a vote. We noted in Chapter 6 that a homosexual activist, one Dr Morin, became chairman of the ethics committee of the American Psychological Society. The following account of events in America reveals the staggering ability of homosexual activists to rewrite medical textbooks:

> *In America, from 1969, gay groups began to demonstrate at psychiatric conferences and they disrupted annual conventions of the American Psychiatric Association (APA). Largely as a result of these protests, a debate occurred within the profession which culminated, in December 1973, in an official decision of the APA to cease classifying homosexuality as a psychiatric disorder ... In the 1967 edition of Freedman and Kaplan's textbook on clinical psychiatry, for example, the chapter on homosexuality was written by Irving Bieber, one of the leading advocates of the sickness theory. But in the revised edition of 1975 the chapter was written by Judd Marmor, a leading exponent of the "alternative life-style" viewpoint.*[33]

The gay counter-psychiatry group

In Britain, gay rights advocates achieved similar "successes." A "Counter-Psychiatry Group" was formed in London by the Gay Liberation Front in 1971, and demonstrated in Harley Street, campaigning about the lack of positive references to homosexual activity in a popular sex manual of the time, "Everything you always wanted to know about sex" by David Reuben. Dr Reuben has consistently rejected the genetic theory of homosexuality and his explanation of why homosexuals are promiscuous was quoted in chapter 7.

It is not surprising that Dr Reuben, being an orthodox psychiatrist, was hated by the GLF. The counter-psychiatry group published a pamphlet, "Psychiatry and the Homosexual," in which was demanded the deletion of homosexuality as a psychiatric condition:

> We are not in this pamphlet asking the medical profession for help. The sympathetic "help" of liberal-minded psychiatrists can be as dangerous to our standing as human beings as was pre-Freudian condemnation. In fact we do not want a reformed medical attitude to homosexuality. We want there to be no medical attitude at all. ... In the same way, we do not want psychiatrists to correct their chapters on homosexuality, but to omit them.[34]

A note of desperation creeps in when the "gay" liberationists explain that the very notion of a homosexual becoming heterosexual is "undermining the validity of every homosexual emotion and threatening the sense of identity of countless gay people."[35] The possibility of change from homo- to hetero- sexual is denied by them not because it is false, but because it is too challenging.

Aversion therapy challenged in sequins

Gay activists also engaged in vociferous lobbying at medical and psychiatric conferences. A symposium on aversion therapy held by the London Medical Group in November 1972, for example, was disrupted by militant organiser Peter Tatchell, who managed to gain entry even though the meeting was not open to the public. He continued to interrupt speeches from Professor Hans Eysenck and Dr Isaac Marks and had to be ejected from the meeting.[36] The pressure was kept up with other protests during 1974 including one at a conference in Bradford organised by the BMA. According to one activist:

> About 50 members of the Gay Liberation Front and the Campaign for Homosexual Equality disrupted the meeting for an hour, complaining bitterly about negative medical responses to homosexuality. Reflecting the fashion for "radical drag," Don Milligan, a member of Bradford GLF, wore a long blue velvet dress embroidered with sequins.[37]

Difference between "disorder" and "disease"

Sex therapists Masters and Johnson joined in, "insisting that homosexuality cannot be classified as a psychiatric disease."[38] Activist John Marshall, writing in a homosexual campaigning book, claims "a number of other writers," but fails to name them, and it should be noted that the Masters and Johnson work was, like Kinsey's before them, based on a self-selected and statistically weighted sample. Nevertheless, many traditional psychologists would agree with them, referring to the homosexual condition as a pathology in the sense of a developmental disorder, rather than as a "disease."

Currently, the World Health Organisation has revised its own position of classifying homosexuality as a disorder in its code F66. A conference in Utrecht in December 1987 organised by people close to the WHO was addressed by leading activists from Britain and the USA, now dressed not in sequins but in academic robes, like Dr Kenneth Plummer of Essex University and Dr Diana Richardson of Sheffield. Professor Rob Tielman of Utrecht and Virginia Apuzzo, Lesbian and Gay liaison officer to Governor Mario Cuomo of New York also attended.[39]

The new classifications of the WHO have already been published and will be adopted in January 1993. The main sexual disorders under section F65 are named as fetishism, exhibitionism, voyeurism, paedophilia and sado-masochism. It is true that under section F66 there appears "sexual maturation crisis," but this is followed by "ego-dystonic sexual orientation" associated with heterosexuality, homosexuality or bisexuality, and "sexual relationship problem." In other words, homosexuality, bisexuality and heterosexuality are placed on a par. Homosexuality will only be regarded as a disorder should the patient wish to change; as an objective behavioural dysfunction, it will cease to exist. A homosexual will only need other psychiatric help if he complains of a sexual problem of some sort. If neither of these happen, there is nothing objectively wrong with him (or her). In reality, this is simply the view only of the Politically Correct "alternative lifestyle" school, who in the politics of psychiatry are currently in the ascendant. In the UK, the PC view is supported by mental health charity MIND, vigorously so by its current national director Judi Clements.

I spent some time researching the processes of the WHO, reading its papers and corresponding with its director, Dr Sartorius. Psychiatric evidence brought before the WHO in its deliberations is conspicuous by its absence. Dr Sartorius could not name a single study that disproved homosexuality as an objective disorder. Political pressure is all too evident.

Psychiatrists still say homosexual behaviour acquired

Although defeated world-wide on a vote by the application of crude political pressure, individual psychoanalysts continue to regard homosexuality as pathological and treatable. Charles Socarides, a professor at the Albert Einstein College of Medicine in the USA, and a leading expert on homosexuality, wrote in the "Journal of Psychiatry":

> *Homosexuality, the choice of a partner of the same sex for orgiastic satisfaction, is not innate. There is no connection between sexual instinct and the choice of sexual object. Such an object choice is learned, acquired behavior: there is no inevitable genetically inborn propensity towards the choice of a partner of either the same or opposite sex.*[40]

Not all of his colleagues remain so forthright. Most professionals in the field of psychiatry and psychology have chosen to keep their heads down, whilst maintaining a public face of confirming the "alternative lifestyle" view. Again, if the typical symptoms of homosexual existence were present in a heterosexual, these psychiatrists would have no similar reluctance to pronounce the patient as suffering from a psychiatric disorder.

Common sense and traditional psychiatric opinion must surely coincide. We investigated the reality of homosexual activity in chapter 8. It is fair to say that no man or woman engaging in such practices can possibly be paddling with both oars in the water.

Deficit in parent/child relationship to blame

To sum up, the evidence strongly indicates a psychological rather than a physiological explanation for a homosexual condition, with the parents of the homosexual usually bearing the bulk of responsibility. Clearly one must be open to the possibility that there is something psychologically wrong with homosexuals in the first place. If this is simply denied, then all psychological work in this area is irrelevant.

Recent work by clinical psychologist Elizabeth Moberly has narrowed down many difficulties in the parent-child relationship to the father of the male, and the mother of the lesbian. We need to be careful that other factors are not ignored, but this is what she says:

> *From amidst a welter of details, one constant underlying principle suggests itself: that the homosexual - whether man or woman - has*

The origins of a homosexual orientation

suffered from some deficit in the relationship with the parent of the same sex; and that there is a corresponding drive to make good this deficit - through the medium of same-sex, "homosexual" relationships.[41]

Dr Moberly regards the homosexual condition as "a deficit in the child's ability to relate to the parent of the same sex which is carried over to members of the same sex in general."[42] The need to make good the earlier deficit in the parent-child relationship is what drives the homosexual to seek reparation in same sex relationships, but because he (or she) is responding in an adult body to the needs of a child, he may erroneously eroticise the need, and respond sexually to a need that should be met non-sexually:

> *The central factor in all cases is that needs that should have been met through the parent-child attachment, remain yet to be met. What the homosexual seeks is the fulfilment of these normal attachment needs, which have abnormally been left unmet in the process of growth. At the same time, it should be remembered that we are still speaking of the homosexual condition, and not its translation into sexual activity. The psychological needs of the homosexual are often expressed sexually, but these needs exist independently of sexual expression. A good non-sexual relationship with a member of the same sex is another means of fulfilling such needs.*[43]

Homosexual behaviour an attempt to repair deficit

Treating the homosexual condition as one of emotional deficiency squares overwhelmingly with the evidence of the homosexual psyche, lifestyle and activities, and with the success of programmes of healing, which we shall consider in later chapters.

Although homosexual activity indicates to orthodox psychologists an underlying pathology (in the sense of abnormality, of course, not disease) it is not itself pathological, but is rather an attempt, the wrong one, but an attempt none the less, to heal or to resolve the underlying pathology:

> *From the present evidence it would seem clear that the homosexual condition does not involve abnormal needs, but normal needs that have, abnormally, been left unmet in the ordinary process of growth. The needs as such are normal; their lack of fulfilment, and the barrier to their fulfilment, is abnormal.*[44]

Such conclusions have gone largely unchallenged in the homosexual output, but this may be because "the gays" refuse to discuss causes of homosexuality at all, preferring to stick at the facile observation that homosexuality simply exists. Most of them have recognised that the more they can persuade good-natured people to approve of homosexuality, the more difficult it will become dispassionately to agree on its cause, and vice versa.

One exception is homosexual psychoanalyst Martin Dannecker, who is happy to look at theories of homosexuality, "though in no way with the perspective that homosexuality is a disease to be cured."[45] Martin Dannecker even maintains: "Nor can I see anything negative even when the average homosexual is or seems less well adapted than the average heterosexual."[46]

Professor Anthony Flew gets befogged

In the Journal of Moral Education, J Martin Stafford tried to take on the developmental theory, with a distinct lack of success, by quoting the late Professor C D Broad (who was an early campaigner for decriminalisation of homosexual activity). He missed the mark because Professor Broad's warnings on speculations about infantile mental processes are set explicitly in the context of *babies*, whilst psychologists are writing usually about children and adolescents. Nor did Mr Stafford hit the target when he brought on fellow humanist Anthony Flew. Professor Flew ridiculed regarding homosexuality as a "physical disease."[47] Unfortunately for this argument, regarding the homosexual condition as a pathology is not the same as regarding it as a disease, physical or otherwise, or even as a "mental illness." Psychiatric professionals are careful to make this distinction:

> *Arrested development is no more a "disease" than being, say, a three-year-old or a nine-year-old is a "disease." It is simply a point at which normal growth has not yet been completed. What is pathological is that there should be barriers to such growth which have resulted in pre-adult needs persisting unmet into adult years.*[48]

The gays invent a new illness

As gay activists have scrubbed out one pathological condition by the use of intimidation rather than evidence, so they have played a huge joke by inventing another. In one debate, an activist told the audience that one of the speakers "is suffering from a psychological illness called homophobia."[49] "Homophobia" might be thought from the

The origins of a homosexual orientation

Greek to involve a morbid dread of sameness, but according to the old GLC, it is supposedly:

> the fear and resulting contempt for homosexuals. For many people, this involves the fear of being homosexual themselves, or of being thought by others to be. For some individuals, their heterosexism is a result of this fear - though for others it can be the result simply of ignorance and conditioning.[50]

For Martin Stafford, a homophobe is similarly someone "who fears or hates anything concerning homosexuals or homosexuality." The most extreme of such persons will be one "whose prejudices are sustained by an unshakeable commitment to a system of religious or superstitious beliefs," which rather reveals poor Mr Stafford's own prejudices.

Bill Kirkpatrick works with AIDS patients and homosexuals in Earl's Court and started "Streetwise Youth" (qv) with the homosexual ex-rent boy Richie McMullen to care for, non-judgmentally of course, the rent boys of the West End. He maintains that we can only accept the homosexuality of others "if we have come to terms with our own sexuality," a rather neat if evidence-free twist of the orthodox position that homosexuals are psychologically incomplete. Now you and I are in sexual turmoil, until we buckle down and agree with Fr Bill.[51]

The assumption that anyone who challenges homosexuality as a lifestyle must have an unreasoning fear or hatred within him, or be "uncomfortable" in his own sexual nature might be fashionable around the dinner tables of Hampstead. Nevertheless, it is abuse not argument. None of it applies to me, and to go further, I do not think that the reader will find homophobia as explained by the GLC, J Martin Stafford or indeed Fr Bill Kirkpatrick in any medical textbook, at least not yet. Ignorance about homosexuality, together with the sort of prejudice that accepts the promotion of homosexuality without knowledge of what is really involved, is of course what this book aims to dispel. Something written almost thirty years ago is still true:

> A few unusually well-balanced homosexuals neither deny nor advertise the tendency of their emotions, and appear to accept their own nature philosophically. All, however, have a vested interest in affirming that their condition is an inborn abnormality rather than the result of circumstances; for any other explanation is bound to imply a criticism either of themselves or of their families, and usually of both.[52]

Now let us see how homosexual inclinations are turned into practice.

14
Recruitment into the homosexual lifestyle

In the last chapter we came to the conclusion that a psychological explanation for a homosexual orientation best fits the evidence. We saw no evidence that homosexuals are "born like it" except where emotional trauma occurred pre-natally. Lord Hutchinson of Lullington, in the House of Lords Clause 28 debate,[1] claimed that homosexuality "is genetically determined," illustrating how widely this particular myth is held. That no geneticist has discovered a gene or a genetic flaw responsible for homosexual orientation is confirmed in a recent analysis of current evidence,[2] whilst McCary (writing before Le Vay, whose results, considered in chapter 7, are contentious in any case) points out that:

> Neither present day endocrinological tests nor microscopic or clinical examinations have revealed any physiological differences between a heterosexual and a homosexual individual.[3]

(Endocrinology is the study of hormone-producing glands.)

Why do people go gay?

Rejecting, in a paper published in 1985, congenital and endocrinological factors as causes of homosexuality, two clinical psychologists working at St Mary's Hospital Paddington rejected most early psychoanalytic studies as well. The behavioural influences that we shall consider in this chapter were likewise rejected for "lack of hard evidence." We shall see about that. One of them, Dr David Miller, moved to the Middlesex, complained about the "slow allocation" of Government funds for AIDS and signed the advertisement in the Independent against Clause 28. "At the moment the cause of homosexuality remains a mystery," he and his colleague John Green concluded.[4]

This might adhere to the "gay rights" line, but it is simply not good enough even for homosexual author and activist John Hart:

Even if one acknowledges [which we don't] that genetic factors play a part in influencing who it is who goes gay, then such influences must be seen in terms of the way that resultant behaviour interacts with the individual's environmental experiences.[5]

The same writer also dismisses "a line of direct causality which links hormonal differences with becoming and being homosexual"[6] observing that not all male homosexuals act like women, and not all lesbians are "butch." He criticises the author of a survey in which:

> most of the American male gays stated that there was no reason why they were gay or that they were born that way.[7]

John Hart observes that neither of these answers can be correct, drawing on his experience in the homosexual network itself:

> There must be some reasons why people are gay and being "born that way" does not account for how you live fifteen, thirty, forty-five years later. The clue given and taken up by gay people in explaining their felt difference has been, I think, that they had problems with the opposite sex, liked dreaming/acting in cross-gender roles, were too close/too distant to mother or father, were isolated in single-sex schools or seduced or were psychologically immature or disturbed.[8]

We have considered some of the factors mentioned there by John Hart, and we shall now pick up on a few others. Indeed what is the route into a homosexual lifestyle? Why do some individuals, with their various emotional and developmental backgrounds, become established in a homosexual behaviour pattern whilst others do not?

"Something to tell you" is a book that was published by the "London Gay Teenage Group," financed to the tune of £35,000 by the GLC between 1981 and 1984,[9] and by the ILEA London Youth Committee.[10] The book surveyed attitudes of young persons considering themselves to be homosexual who were known to members of the London Gay Teenage Group, which is run by adult homosexuals. It recommended a number of measures designed to make it easier for young people to become involved with homosexuals.

First homosexual experience is with someone older

When it came to asking the respondents about their first sexual experience, the book draws conclusions from the results that are simply not justified. The age of the women at first sexual experience averages out at just over 16, and the age of their first homosexual partner at nearly 21. For the men, the average age at first homosexual experience is just over 15, and the average age of first homosexual partner is 21.[11]

From this it is concluded that:

> the majority must have had their first homosexual experience with someone in a similar age range. The traditional concept of young people being seduced and "led astray" by homosexuals far older than themselves is not supported by these findings.[12]

This conclusion seems to be at variance with their evidence, which shows that these young people were introduced to homosexual practices by someone quite a bit older than themselves. Even a young writer regarding himself as homosexual agrees that: "Most people in Gay Youth don't have relationships with each other. Their relationships are outside. And generally it is with someone older."[13] Another radical lesbian activist agrees, and shows the importance of an older person in gaining recruits for the homosexual network:

> As Beth Kelly has pointed out in her autobiographical article "Speaking Out on Woman/Girl Love," relationships between young girls and women do exist. (p140) .... Boy-lovers and the lesbians who have young lovers are the only people offering a hand to help young women and men cross the difficult terrain between straight society and the gay community.[14]

In a stark display of honesty, the same writer confirms:

> Nobody is fooled when we proclaim that the gay movement has nothing to do with kids and their sexuality.... Many of us - both women and men - had our first homosexual experience with partners who were older than ourselves.[15]

Gay youth workers

It is a familiar pattern that boys are seduced into the homosexual network by an older man, and then do the recruiting themselves as they grow older. The Scottish Homosexual Rights Group in its "Gay Kids" leaflet admits this in a roundabout way: "If you phone one of the numbers in this leaflet, you will be able to talk to ... someone who has grown up experiencing the same sort of feelings you have."

The "Gay Teenage Group" survey found that "When a young person did know other homosexuals, this often included a lesbian or gay youth worker - 44% of the cases."[16] A picture shows "Gregg Blachford, a youth worker at the London Gay Teenage Group, talking with Group members." Mr Blachford contributed an article on pornography for the book "Pink Triangles - Radical Aspects on Gay Liberation," which first saw the light of day in "Gay Left." In developing "an evolution of a socialist morality,"[17] he discusses pornography aimed at male homosexuals:

> I remember the very exciting feeling I got when I first saw one of these magazines before I came out. There I saw men kissing and holding and loving [sic] each other; ... It was proof of a homosexual community and it was through porn that I learned of its existence.[18]

The seduction route

Other young people learn of the existence of homosexuality through that very seduction that gay activists are anxious to deny. The study published by Paul Van Wyk and Chrisann Geist in 1984 attempted to establish if there is a correlation between homosexual orientation or behaviour and childhood experiences. As we saw earlier, they used the Kinsey "scores" to measure sexual response, and this is their summary of results:

> Elevated K (more homosexual scores) was found for females who had few girl companions at age 10 and few male companions at 16, had learned to masturbate by being masturbated by a female, had intense pre-pubertal sexual contact with boys or men, found thought or sight of females, but not males, arousing by age 18, had homosexual contact by age 18, higher K at 17, and higher first-year homosexual behaviour frequency.
>
> Elevated K (more homosexual scores) was found for males who reported poorer teenage relationships with their fathers, had more girl companions at age 10, fewer male companions at 10 and 16, avoided sports participation, learned of homosexuality by experience, learned to masturbate by being masturbated by a male, had intense pre-pubertal sexual contact with boys or men, had neither heterosexual contact nor petting to orgasm by age 18, found thought or sight of males, but not females, arousing by age 18, had homosexual contact by age 18, higher K at ages 16 and 17, and had higher first-year homosexual behaviour frequency.[19]

This is broadly in line with what one would expect. Many of the factors are indicative of certain kinds of social and personal development, or of exposure to sexual abuse.

Spare rib communal masturbation classes

Some of the findings of Van Wyk and Geist become rather worrying when placed alongside popular material used in sex education. For example, the first edition of "Make it Happy" urged girls to practice coming to orgasm in one of "Spare Rib's" communal masturbation classes.[20]

Van Wyk and Geist stated:

> *For both males and females, those who leaned about masturbation by being masturbated by a person of the same sex had a higher proportion of homosexual behaviour as adults than did others.*[21]

Where the young girls were below the age of puberty, on the other hand, the same study found a different precursor to adult homosexual behaviour. They observed firstly that:

> *Sexual contact between adult females and pre-pubertal subjects was rare, and did not account for any meaningful outcome variance.*[22]

Young girls' trust abused

Van Wyk & Geist went on to demonstrate in the case of pre-pubertal girls, that abuse of a sexual nature carried out on a little girl by a man, particularly one whom she knows and trusts, was likely to result in her choosing to behave homosexually in adulthood:

> *The pattern seems clearer when adult males, rather than pre-pubertal males, are involved with pre-adolescent females. Merely being approached, seeing an exhibitionist, or having an experience involving non-genital touching had no significant effect. But when the experience included masturbation, oral-genital activity, or coitus, when the girls' first sight of a man's penis occurred in an experience that also involved physical contact with an adult male, when the male was much older than the subject, when he was a friend, and thus more capable of violating the girl's trust and less capable of being written off as an aberrant exception, and the contact was intense enough to be sexually arousing to the girl, she was more likely to choose to engage in sexual activity with other females as a result.*[23]

The implications here for a society in which female children may suffer incestuous abuse, involving sexual intercourse or some other form, and in which a depressingly high divorce rate results in a growing number of step-fathers and particularly live-in boy-friends being placed in just such a position of trust as the study describes, are

Recruitment into the homosexual lifestyle

worrying, unless, like gay rights activists, we regard "a homosexual choice as equally valid as a heterosexual one."[24]

Boys sexually more adventurous

In the case of boys, the study validates the common understanding that boys are more interested in sexual activity than are girls. Some boys discover masturbation, and share this knowledge with their peers, but the devastating effects of involvement with an older male are described thus:

> If an adult male is involved, he would be expected to be even more interested in and skilled at producing arousal in his young partner.
> Those males who learn of masturbation by being masturbated by another male, or to a lesser extent by observing masturbation, are more likely to prefer male partners in adulthood than are those who learn about masturbation in other ways.[25]

A pattern of abuse may easily be set up. Psychologists and criminologists agree that a homosexual is drawn to boys aged within two years of the age that he was himself first interfered with. When the Paedophile Information Exchange carried out a survey of their membership, this was exactly what they found. The men were in the main interested in boys from 10 to 13, and their own first sexual experience confirmed the two-year band with a high degree of accuracy.[26]

Corruption theory validated

It is clearly not true that: "No independent evidence has ever been presented to support the corruption theory and we as homosexuals strongly deny that our sexual orientation has been determined by some childhood association with homosexuals."[27] Despite the denials, the truth remains both that boys may be seduced into homosexual activity, and that the earlier a child learns about homosexual behaviour, the more likely is homosexual activity to become established as an adult behaviour pattern. This latter has serious implications for sex education programmes, indicating that discussion of homosexuality in class is inappropriate:

> Females who learned about homosexuality at later ages were more likely to engage in predominantly heterosexual behaviour as adults. The mean age of learning about homosexuality for those females who were predominantly homosexual as adults was 13.9 years, while that for those who were exclusively heterosexual as adults was 19.4 years.

> As with females, [males] who learned about homosexuality at later ages were more likely to engage in predominantly heterosexual behaviour as adults. Those who as adults were exclusively heterosexual learned of homosexuality at a mean age of 16.4 years, while those who were predominantly homosexual learned at a mean age of 12.0 years.[28]

Scottish homosexuals active in sex education

The Scottish Homosexual Rights Group is very heavily involved in promoting "progressive" sex education in schools, which would present "positive information about homosexuality" and "a gradual introduction of non-sexist reading material." More tractor-driving grandmothers and bossy sisters. But interesting from the point of view of encouraging contacts for the paedophiles in SHRG, a leaflet states the group's belief that: "Sex education must begin in the primary school," and "children must never be advised that homosexuality is 'just a passing phase' or 'something they will grow out of.'"[29]

We should also note the enthusiasm of SHRG for "Gay Switchboards" and for "Lesbian Line" and "Parents' Enquiry." The importance of "gay switchboards" is illustrated by figures quoted by SHRG, that in a two week period: "6,500 gays aged 14-20 telephoned phone services to help gay people (gay switchboards) and a quarter of these were under 16." Claiming one person in ten be homosexual, SHRG asks: "Think of how many other people there are in your school who feel like you do!"[30]

Establishing a sexual preference

If adolescent homosexual feelings are for some individuals part of a continuum of normal sexual development, it would seem to be inappropriate to give children with such feelings the idea that these might be indicators of adult orientation, since this might well fix the orientation at that stage. Discussion of homosexuality in a class context is therefore probably not as helpful to adolescents as the knowledge that they can talk to a teacher in private, and preferably not to a sympathiser of the "Gay Teachers' Group."

Michael Cashman is only one of many homosexual activists who deny the threat of "gay rights" to society on the "what are you afraid of?" basis. "Is heterosexuality that fragile?" he asked when I debated with him at the London School of Economics in April 1991. But it is just at the personal level when the adolescent is trying to make sense of his or her developing sexuality that heterosexuality *is* fragile. Normally, guilt will attend an adolescent homosexual experience, but if homosexuality is being presented in a positive light in the classroom, the guilt may be labelled irrational, and a homosexual pattern may be set up.

According to the findings of Van Wyk and Geist, once sexual relations with the same sex are initiated with any intensity, it does not take long for homosexual activity to become a preferred pattern of behaviour:

> *Once a particular sexual preference becomes established (which seems to occur within a short period of time, although often more than a year after beginning intense sexual activity), it does tend to become fixed and quite resistant to change. In males this process seems typically to be well on its way to completion by age 18, and in females by age 21.*[31]

The homosexual contact network

Activist Jeffrey Weeks writes:

> *Building up relationships was very much like collecting little islands - you jumped from one to another to another - and if you were lucky you eventually had a network.*[32]

The network was what helped start the "gay movement" in 1970, for Jeffrey Weeks admits that the gay friends he had were simply people he had picked up or had met through a pick-up.[33] Outside the network, however, there still remain those men whose lives are predominantly heterosexual, yet who have, from time to time, a homosexual "fling." They are usually claimed by gay rights activists to be "closet gays," and one writer deplores the way in which: "The married have, after all, successfully established a heterosexual relationship. Many of them have children."[34]

On the other hand, they may be those whom the homosexual youth worker we encountered earlier describes as "'straight rough trade dudes,' the sweaty hard-hats on the construction site, the nice hunky married Italian guy from down the street."[35] They would certainly not term themselves "homosexual" or even "bisexual." They simply, from time to time, choose to act out a fantasy or indulge a passing interest.

Choice combines with disillusion

Evidence to back up the findings of Van Wyk and Geist, together with an indication of how human beings are able to choose their sexual "orientation" are both found in the life of Joe Orton. Orton was

166 THE SEXUAL DEAD-END

molested in a local cinema at an early age,[36] and thereafter behaved in a normal if outrageous heterosexual fashion. At a family wedding, "Orton sneaked a bridesmaid upstairs to his mother's bedroom,"[37] and continued to date women regularly. He was stood up on a couple of occasions, and on one of them recorded in his diary:

> My opinion of women is going down. At present it is zero. Dot never turned up at all. Am completely fed up with girls in general." (2 Apr 1949)[38]

Men just seemed to Orton to be more available and more reliable as sex partners. Another homosexual writer says this of one of his fellows:

> Richi Macdougall of "Fag Rag" ... said that women had never found him attractive and that when he discovered that faggots liked his looks he was himself transformed into a faggot. Such a statement might be read in many ways, but I would suggest that it is essentially true at face value.[39]

Van Wyk & Geist showed that certain stimuli affect the base from which we make our future object-choice. However it is that homosexual desires become implanted in the first place, some individuals choose to act on them. They are quite wrong who claim as did the Albany Trust (qv) that: "Homosexuality is not acquired by choice."[40]

We have learnt of a number of activists who deny that homosexuality arises from seduction or corruption, and in a later chapter we shall read the words of activists who readily admit the link, whilst putting the words "seduction" and "corruption" in inverted commas to indicate that they do not recognise the usual meanings of these words. That seduction is an important route towards a future homosexual pattern of behaviour was established by Van Wyk and Geist, among others:

> Learning through experience seems to be an important pathway to later sexual preference. Those who learn to masturbate by being masturbated by a person of the same sex, those whose first orgasm is in homosexual contact, and those who have arousing or uncomfortable early sexual experiences seem to develop differently from those who do not have such experiences.[41] ... It seems quite clear that intense sexual experiences, and feelings of arousal, pleasure, or discomfort associated with those experiences, are the strongest precursors of adult sexual orientation.[42]

Tolerance creates opportunity for homosexuality

American author Roger Magnuson explains that homosexual behaviour leads "from casual thoughts and impulses to discrete acts, from acts to habits, from habits to an entrenched life-style," and that some kind of inclination, however small, must come together with the opportunity, otherwise "such tendencies may remain latent and never crystallize into behavior." It is a theme in homosexual literature, for example in the American "Gay Report" that apparent "straights" can be recruited into homosexual behaviour, and that this is easier to achieve in an atmosphere of tolerance to such behaviour. It could be observed that as homosexuals cannot procreate new "gays," so they must recruit them.

> The social acceptance that "gay rights" laws give to homosexual behavior creates a climate in which opportunities for homosexual behavior multiply. As the restraints of law and morality dissolve, and homosexuality becomes publicly celebrated as a valid lifestyle, it is logical to expect more people to explore it. More latent homosexuals will find opportunities for overt behavior. And with that overt behavior will go the undeniable consequences of that conduct. [43]

Proliferation of "gay switchboards"

This increased tolerance of homosexuality has resulted in the springing up in every major city of "Gay Switchboard" and "Friend" telephone counselling groups. There is a feeling in the media and the liberal establishment that "gay switchboard" is respectable, so that Thomson Local Directories list "Gay Switchboard" in their "community advice" pages, and many switchboard and "Friend" groups have been granted charitable status. Left-Liberal local authorities invariably support these groups with funds.

Homosexual counselling groups are however not like Alcoholics Anonymous, where people recognise the wrongfulness of what they are doing and try with each other's mutual support to shake free. Quite the contrary. Gay Switchboard arose from Gay Liberation Front, and like Lesbian Line is militantly supportive of the homosexual lifestyle. Its volunteers advise callers on the extent of the local "scene," of the location and timetable of homosexual pubs and clubs. "Friend" was started by the Campaign for Homosexual Equality, and promotes homosexual activity through its "counselling" activities. The "counsellors" at all three groups are mainstream homosexual activists, involved themselves in the homosexual network.

Malcolm Macourt, company secretary of National Friend Ltd, in his book about counselling for homosexuals, writes of what he sees as the "pressures" in society, and of the desires of callers for sexual activity with others of their own sex. He says:

> Either the pressures are to be ignored, or the desires are to be submerged. ... By thinking of the emotional and spiritual dimensions of identifying with one's own sex, the pressures can be acknowledged and put into some perspective, and the desires can be acknowledged and accepted. Volunteers concerned to empower callers will want them to recognise those feelings as good.[44]

Many callers ask "Am I gay?" and are rarely told that they are not:

> Most gay helpline volunteers assume that all, or almost all, of those who ask the question "Am I gay?" are gay, and consequently the volunteer seeks to involve the caller in the gay/lesbian community.[45]

Gay helplines promote homosexuality

"Friend" counsellors start from a preconception that there is nothing wrong with homosexual activity. Malcolm Macourt writes that "gay helplines" provide "a focus for campaigning for equal rights" as well as introducing callers to the subculture. He freely admits:

> It can be argued that the mere existence of a gay helpline is directive. It directs the caller to the view that a gay alternative exists and there are circumstances in which it is acceptable.[46]

Going further he says:

> To give direction one must start from somewhere. ... To be non-directive, in a sense one must also start from somewhere. In this context there is no reason why that starting point cannot be full acceptance of gay and lesbian equality.[47]

And further still:

> The idea of "recruiting" people to a gay lifestyle may seem unusual. However, "recruitment" is only viewed with suspicion when we view the cause which is doing the recruiting with suspicion. When the cause is a good one, recruiting people to it must also be good.[48]

Some "gay helplines," when "integrating" callers, merely give out the names and addresses of pubs and clubs the caller can visit. Others take their recruiting function more seriously to the point of procuring:

particularly those of the FRIEND tradition feel more of a sense of direct responsibility for their callers and so the volunteer will usually offer to take the caller to social venues and introduce him or her to them.[49]

Icebreakers, another Gay Liberation Front offshoot, operated in the seventies, and got a reputation for having sex with everyone who contacted them. Glenn McKee, who has an unfortunate spinal condition, says:

> I went to Icebreakers meetings which were in people's flats and houses ... They were highly political ... They wanted full gay rights, everything, no compromises. They ridiculed the family. ... I had my first sexual contact with people I met through Icebreakers. ... One of the problems I had dealing with Icebreakers was that, although there was all this theory, they only went to bed with the pretty ones.[50]

The recruiting drive among young children at school

Malcolm Macourt describes the setting up of a "gay teenage" group in Newcastle, where he works at the Poly, and which received grants from the local Education Authority. "Gay Teenage" groups have been set up by homosexual activists in every large town and are associated with "Switchboard" or "Friend." The media persist in believing that "gay teenage" groups can "help" mixed-up young people. It is clear from the existence of "Gay Teenage" groups that the main homosexual recruiting drive is amongst teenagers and even children. An activist explains the importance of such groups:

> Through membership of such societies young gay people can learn more about being gay, develop positive attitudes about themselves and their sexuality, and learn to accept themselves as being gay.[51]

Obviously it is to the advantage of a future homosexual object-choice if children as young as possible can be taught that such a choice would be perfectly valid, but the main thrust of the gay movement has been towards contact groups for teenagers. If a teenager can be persuaded that a homosexual crush or transient experience depicts their "real" sexuality, then a recruit is made who might otherwise be lost.

Gay youth clubs

A field of determined promotion for homosexual rights groups is therefore that of "gay" youth clubs. "Gay Youth" and "Gay Teenage" groups are the big growth area in homosexual contact or "befriending" organisations. The people behind gay youth groups tend of course to be active campaigning adults, sometimes perpetuating a cycle of sexual abuse.

For example, Jeff Vernon, who runs the British "Gay Youth" Movement from the offices of the Campaign for Homosexual Equality, had his first homosexual experience at the age of 13. He claims to have been sexually attracted to older males from the age of four. Mr Vernon is now a leading Executive Committee member of CHE, and a contributor to homosexual publications, including the revealing Betrayal of Youth, whose roll-call of authors and acknowledgements reads like a who's who of the paedophile movement and the libertarian left. Betrayal of Youth adopted the line that sexual relations between children and adults were perfectly acceptable, and that ages of consent were unnecessary. Mr Vernon explained in his article that such laws "oppressed" children. He is hardly likely to explain to teenagers that occasional homosexual feelings are indicative of anything other than a firm homosexual orientation.

Gay teenager groups

The Joint Council for Gay Teenagers is a paper body which claims two dozen affiliated organisations. Mrs Rose Robertson of Parents' Enquiry is involved along with several gay luminaries. We shall investigate its role in the paedophile movement in chapter 16. Michael Burbidge, involved earlier with Icebreakers, did the drafting and planning for its 1980 submission on the age of consent to the Home Office Policy Advisory Committee. The submission's conclusions had, it claimed, already been put forward by the National Council for Civil Liberties and the Sexual Law Reform Society in general terms:

> The only civilised answer to the question put to the Policy Advisory Committee would be to remove consensual sexual acts altogether from the realm of the criminal law. Only then can hundreds of thousands of young gay people freely seek and receive the best help and advice.[52]

Michael Burbidge has also been involved with the London Gay Teenage Group, along with Jonathan Walters (qv), and Peter Bradley of the Gay Teachers' Group. London Gay Teenage Group is affiliated to the "Joint Council for Gay Teenagers." It would not be stretching the imagination to expect these men to consider that "the best help and advice" would consist of encouraging teenagers away from any perception of adolescent homosexuality as a passing phase and thus recruiting new active homosexuals from among the teenagers who would come along to the London Gay Teenage Group.

Gays re-define "child"

The political needs of the homosexual movement preclude any admission that homosexuals can "corrupt" children. It is important then to understand what is meant by the expressions "corruption" and "children" when used by gay activists. Homosexual activists do not mean that they are unable to influence children into making a homosexual object-choice, for that would be against all the evidence. So what *do* they mean? Firstly, their definition of "child" is slightly different from the normal understanding. By way of illustration, we can look at the response of the Scottish Minorities Group following the first spot of media attention given in 1977 to the Paedophile Information Exchange. PIE was set up by men from SMG, later renamed Scottish Homosexual Rights Group, in the first place.

A report was prepared by Andrew Wyllie and National Secretary Malcolm Crowe for discussion within the SMG National Executive. It came out against sex between adults and children "on the whole" and "in the present circumstances" and was then roundly condemned in subsequent correspondence in the SMG journal for its "closeted," and "apologetic" approach. But what is notable is that before adopting the line it did, the SMG report made it clear that the children it was discussing were pre-pubertal. Adolescents, or boys passing through puberty, were, as I understand it, not children at all. The report simply assumed that sex with the latter group was perfectly acceptable.[53] A "child" to the gays means therefore a person under the age of puberty.

Gays re-define "corruption"

Secondly, when advocates of homosexuality claim that they do not corrupt children, they mean, as Labour Party activists Mike McNair and Jamie Gough put it, that "children cannot be 'corrupted' by gay people, since gay sexuality is itself in no way corrupt."[54] This might take some getting used to, but John Hart in his homosexual manual for teenagers gave the game away when he advised his readers:

> I am not saying that knowing someone gay will not affect you. If, after hearing all the negative things about same-sex attraction from people at school, the media and other "authorities," a young person meets someone who is gay, and is not a child-molester, spy, or pervert but a positive happy person, and they think they wouldn't mind being like them - we could hardly call this corruption, could we?[55]

15

Deceiving the young

As homosexuality cannot be passed on genetically, the "gay community" cannot procreate. And if homosexuals cannot reproduce, they must recruit. Positive images are vital, and children are receptive, as John Hart explains:

> Children are influenced by a wide range of "models" for behaviour ... Children can understand same- as well as opposite-sex attraction - they experience both. Again, it is the quality which counts, and it's important to give children positive ways of seeing gay relationships.[1]

Disgust at homosexual activity kept quiet

Activists and apologists for homosexual behaviour are always careful not to specify the details of homosexual acts, preferring young people to get involved, or to be initiated, in greater perversions as they go along, once they have overcome their initial reluctance. Even a first (relatively mild) homosexual experience is nearly always deeply disgusting. Bob Crossman, the flagrantly homosexual ex-mayor of Islington Council, once joked about this "first-time trauma."[2]

A number of homosexuals have written of the feelings of disgust that accompanied their first homosexual experience, and of the paradoxical draw back to exactly that activity. Mark Sreeves, in a written discussion with "gay teacher" Peter Bradley's house-mate Bill Thorneycroft and activist Jeffrey Weeks, said that he never fantasised about particular sexual activities until after he had had them, whilst Jeffrey Weeks bears out everything we have been finding. He had a sexual experience with someone at school, who subsequently got married and strongly denied being "gay;" another man with whom Mr Weeks was close went off with a woman: "It was not just that he had gone off with someone else but he had actually gone off with a woman and it seemed to me like a betrayal of my identity."[3]

From the other side, it seems that Stephen Spender, who was interviewed recently on "Desert Island Discs," experienced considerable antagonism when he left his homosexual contacts in order to get married. W H Auden was apparently quite put out, and these two cases show how tender are the feelings involved in maintaining a homosexual identity and why any criticism of it is not allowed. The singer Tom Robinson, after delighting homosexual audiences in the early 80s with his song "(Sing if you're) Glad to be Gay" decided he would be gladder still to be hetero- or at least bisexual, and he now lives with a woman, by whom he has had a child. Feelings of betrayal swept through the homosexual network. Jeffrey Weeks says that his first casual sexual encounter was in a park in South Wales and that afterwards "I felt a tremendous nausea for what I had done. I can remember walking away, swearing that I would never do this again, feeling physically sick." But sadly and inevitably the poor man found himself drawn back to it:

> Of course by that evening I couldn't think of anything else and it set up a pattern of repetition which I followed once I got back to London.[4]

Progressive nature of homosexual activity

If a potential recruit, a young man or young woman, knew in advance the progressive nature of homosexual activity into more and more degrading activities, and if they were aware of exactly what they would end up doing, they might choose to stay well away.

Examples of the way in which the natural distaste for homosexual activity is played down can easily be found in books sympathetic to homosexuality aimed specifically at teenagers. For example, the parity that activists claim to exist between heterosexuality and homosexuality is cynically and dishonestly assumed by John Hart:

> What can two gay people do in bed? ... Do I have to take a certain role (active or passive) in bed? The fears and anxieties are probably not radically different from those of people who are approaching heterosexual sex for the first time ... The likelihood is that the first time is going to be a bit fraught, but this is not necessarily because it is a homosexual experience. First-time experiences are not necessarily so hot for heterosexual people either.[5]

Initiation

The reason why "the first time" is "a bit fraught" could be that homosexual activities are deeply unnatural, not because of "what people say," but because of how people are. Newly-weds are not generally sickened by what goes on in the honeymoon bed. However, if the threshold between natural and unnatural behaviour is crossed, once the initial disgust is overcome or the conscience sufficiently calloused, a whole world of perversion opens up, with all that is necessary for the crossing of a new frontier being the appropriate initiation from someone who has done it before. John Hart:

> Paul's attitude is instructive: "If people say that any gay sex is wrong we might respond by thinking that if you break that initial taboo - why not do anything and everything. ... You don't have to play the all-knowing man, you can ask other people to initiate you."[6]

Research certainly shows that greater involvement in more and more degrading activity correlates with the length of time of homosexual activity.[7] It is therefore most important for the recruiters to keep the dark side very quiet, and to play up the debonair, "gay" side as much as possible. A young boy will not respond positively if asked outright by a man to lick his anus, he has to be progressively initiated, as we saw in chapter 9. Where an adult homosexual tries to go too fast, or the young man becomes simply revolted by the very idea, then violence leading to murder of one or the other is, as we saw in chapter 12, a real possibility.

Normality

Even when they allow the perverted practices of homosexuals to be known, its apologists try to say that these are really quite normal. For example, Jane Cousins, in her sex education book "Make it Happy," told teenagers that homosexuals "give and get sexual pleasure and satisfaction by kissing, cuddling, feeling and stimulating each others' sex organs with their hands and mouths just like non-gays. Some, but not all, male gays have anal intercourse (which means putting the penis into the anus) just as some heterosexual couples do."[8] She pretends that normal people regularly have dirty sex so that homosexuals are no worse. If only one homosexual man does not practice buggery her contention that "not all" are doing it is true, and she plays up a rare,[9] un-natural and illegal heterosexual practice.

Robin Squire MP claims that: "for the minority who are naturally homosexual, it is as normal and natural for them as heterosexual behaviour is for the majority"[10] We shall learn more of Robin Squire later. Here he simply begs the question, for the argument could be extended to any behaviour pattern, antisocial or not. Hooliganism, joy-riding, shop-lifting, alcoholism, all can seem the natural and normal thing to do for certain people in appropriate circumstances and company. The real question is, are they natural modes of behaviour in themselves? Do they add to the sum of human dignity? Both the psychological evidence, and the construction of the parts of the body involved, seem to answer "no" to both questions when asked in relation to homosexual activity. Robin Squire, again, maintains that "Respected studies here and abroad have demonstrated that, for the overwhelming majority of people, sexual orientation is fixed early in life."[11] I have yet to hear him name one of these "studies."

Many apologists invoke medical research without naming it, for example: "homosexuals believe that their sexual orientation is natural and that this belief is endorsed by research."[12] They could believe the Earth to be flat but the weight of evidence would defeat them.

"Natural" sexual feelings

The sexual reformers wish to create a society in which "archaic sex laws and irrational fears of sex and sex exploitation are nonexistent"[13] The word "natural" they re-define to include any feeling that might occur, however bizarre, so that sexual reformer Jane Cousins, for example, can tell children from the strange position of having no supporting evidence at all: "Holding back a natural sexual feeling can make people feel bewildered and very unhappy."[14]

However, in the stark world of today, giving in to a "natural" sexual feeling can kill people, and Dr. John Gallwey, a consultant at the Radcliffe Infirmary in Oxford, now tells bisexuals that, if homosexuality is not an important part of their lives, this is the time to ditch it. "Ten years ago," he recalled, "I'd have said, 'If you give it up, you may be repressing a very important part of yourself'."[15] Quite apart from that, it can never be wrong to suppress an urge to do wrong. Holding back a natural sexual feeling to take part in a rape would usually be seen as a good thing, and the use of rape as an example is not such a parody of the position of Miss Cousins as might be thought. Advising teenagers to masturbate using sexual fantasy, she suggests in "Make it Happy" that teenagers might care to fantasise "about having sex with someone you know well - a friend, someone in your family, a teacher - with someone of the same or opposite sex, about going with or being a prostitute or about raping someone or being raped."[16]

"Old-fashioned" morality attacked

Most of the comments of Jane Cousins about homosexuality can most charitably be described as contentious, such as the advice: "If we have sexual experiences with the same sex it isn't going to harm us any more than if we have sexual experiences with the opposite sex." Miss

Cousins says that homosexual men "have been treated very inhumanely" whatever that means, and complains about the laws of the Isle of Man, Jersey and Eire, where homosexual activity was illegal at her time of writing. She is disappointed that homosexuals are not allowed "to marry" and appears pleased that homosexual women can now in certain local authority areas adopt children and can "have babies by artificial insemination." This has happened "only very recently" however. But, she complains, homosexual men "still have to fight for the right to adopt children" and this is because public perceptions are wrong about the stability and propriety of their lives:

> Many people believe that gay men tend to sleep around a lot and change their partners as often as the weather. This could be one reason why society frowns on the idea of allowing gays to get married to adopt children. But as the divorce laws make it easier for unhappy heterosexuals to split up and as homosexuals find it easier to be open about their relationships this belief is becoming exposed for the myth that it is. There are plenty of female and male homosexual relationships which last either a lifetime or for many years. Some are shorter, but these variations exist in heterosexual relationships as well.[17]

In the 1988 edition of the same book, she rewrote the passage; as the public now knew about male homosexual promiscuity, she could not now deny it, but she still left in her claim of parity between homosexual and heterosexual promiscuity. She also claims:

> A sexually transmitted disease is not caught by being dirty or by having sex with a great number of different people. You get it by having sex with one person who is infected with the disease.[18]

This of course is strictly true, but it denies a much greater truth, which is that every new sexual liaison increases the statistical risk of contracting a sexually-transmitted disease. Ebbesen et al demonstrated that disease correlated with promiscuity, as we saw in Chapter 9.

In reality, as a past secretary of the Sexual (formerly Homosexual) Law Reform Society, Jane Cousins should have known that she was not telling teenagers the whole truth whenever she wrote about homosexuality and its practices. Indeed many sex educators seem to have an over-riding need to campaign against Christian sexual morality. Jane Cousins writes: "The law does occasionally interfere in people's sex lives, discouraging them from enjoying sex in the way they want to enjoy it and making them feel guilty, even when no-one is going to be harmed"[19] and describes prostitution just as a "job."[20]

Getting pregnant is to Jane Cousins the only sin, and any law against any sort of sex is "old-fashioned." She appears to approve of the bizarre catalogue of perversion we considered in chapter 8, even down to the bestiality:

> Some people feel sexually attracted to animals. It's not against the law to kiss, masturbate or be masturbated by an animal. But it is illegal for a woman or a man to have intercourse or buggery with an animal. It's totally impossible for a woman to get pregnant by having sex with an animal - or for a animal to get pregnant by having sex with a man.[21]

So that's all right. Her book received the approval of the Health Education Authority, Joan Bakewell and the BMJ and won "The Times Educational Supplement Senior Information Book Award."[22]

The BMA in bondage

Even the British Medical Association has managed to get into the act, with a book published for teenagers entitled "Sex for Beginners. This offering in the sex education marketplace was written by Eric Trimmer. One section purported to give the youngsters advice on bondage: not to tie people up round the neck, not to go off and leave them for hours, only to practise bondage sober, that sort of thing. It was argued by Sir Bernard Braine MP in the House of Commons that it would probably not occur to teenagers to indulge in such activity if the BMA did not promote it in the first place.

"Anal sex" was also commended to teenagers by the BMA in "Sex for Beginners," along with a catalogue of other fringe practices. The BMA's involvement was pernicious; parents would in all likelihood regard its imprint as an indication that the book could safely be given to their young adolescents to read. They could scarcely be expected to know that the BMA is actually interested in advertising bizarre sexual perversion.

BMA book re-printed and re-titled, but just the same!

It is worth considering the exchange between Sir Bernard Braine and the then Minister for Health, Barney Hayhoe, in the House of Commons. Sir Bernard asked Mr Hayhoe to take immediate action on the "irresponsible" and "offensive" BMA booklet. The Minister agreed with Sir Bernard, adding that the BMA would be re-printing the booklet "shortly." That was in 1986.[23] What the BMA did was indeed to reprint the booklet, in the same year, and to give it the coy title

"Knowing about sex." But astonishingly, and dishonestly, bearing in mind the impression they had helped the Minister to give in the House of Commons, only the advice about buggery was changed, because of the threat from AIDS. The sections about bondage, sex toys, bestiality, leather goods and so on read just the same, in Dr Trimmer's chatty, man-of-the-world style.

Right at the start of "Knowing about sex," Eric Trimmer complains about those who believe "that sex education is bad and leads only to sexual permissiveness.."[24] In addition, within the glossy covers of the 32 page stapled booklet which devotes two and a half pages to sex toys and bondage, we don't "find any questions about sexual morality dealt with." Dr Trimmer explains why this is so:

> *These matters are of course very important but unfortunately there is not enough space to discuss them.*[25]

No morals from Eric Trimmer

By a strange coincidence, the very same Eric Trimmer put his pen to paper ten years previously in support of paedophile Tom O'Carroll in the journal "Medical News." The British Psychological Society had invited Mr O'Carroll to tell it all about paedophilia at its Swansea conference in 1977. Tom O'Carroll was eventually barred, but Father Michael Ingram of Scottish Homosexual Rights Group, a paedophilia advocate who was heavily involved with Paedophile Information Exchange at its start, was present and spoke. Eric Trimmer managed to describe Fr Ingram as "a well-known child counsellor from Leicester" and proceeded to report his view that paedophile cases are "usually of insignificance to the children involved and don't leave 'psychic scars.'" As "the large majority" of the children apparently "come from families in which there is an unsatisfactory father or a rejecting mother," it is probably a bit difficult to tell, I would have thought, even giving Fr Ingram and Dr Trimmer the benefit of the doubt about their sincerity. Nevertheless, Dr Trimmer continued in a light-hearted, knowing way to present the paedophiles' case to the exclusion of all else.[26] Nor is Eric Trimmer alone in refusing to discuss morality in the context of sex education. There is seldom enough space in books written by sexual liberals to discuss the moral setting of sex.

Framed Youth

An example of the promotion of homosexuality in the classroom is a sex-education video produced by a body called the "Lesbian and Gay

Youth Video Project."[27] "Framed Youth - Revenge of the Teenage Perverts" was recommended by the quango Health Education Council,[28] and that body's incorporation into the DHSS as the Health Education Authority has not dimmed its enthusiasm for the video,[29] for use in schools. Rachel Tingle, writing in her book "Gay Lessons," was not convinced that this was an entirely good idea:

> Although this is a clever and well-made film, designed through its use of music and its informal style to appeal instantly to young people, there is little doubt that many parents would find it objectionable. It includes interviews with young homosexuals who describe their first sexual experiences and why they are so much happier being gay than "straight" and how they find gay sex so much more fulfilling. There are shots of pairs of girls and pairs of men kissing each other, and photographs in the background of girls in bed with one another. Throughout the video, heterosexuals are portrayed as being old-fashioned and rather stupid and, by the clever inter-linking of scenes of boxing matches, missiles, nuclear explosions and Mrs Thatcher, normal family life is shown as aggressive, violent, and ultra-Conservative. The video is a clever piece of propaganda designed to leave strong positive visual images of the homosexual life-style amongst the young.[30]

Even the humanist homosexual activist J Martin Stafford wrote:

> To advocate, or even to condone, promiscuity and decadence under the alluring banner of liberality and emancipation would be not only a wicked and calculating imposture on the credulity of the young, but a policy pregnant with catastrophic social consequences.[31]

Families seen by "gays" as problems or as enemies

Children are encouraged by homosexuals with whom they become involved to regard transient activity as indicative of future sexual orientation and to insist upon this point in family discussions. Parents, or their expectations of and hopes for their children, are seen variously in gay literature as a problem to be overcome, as in this advice to teenage girls:

> "So if you are a lesbian or think you might be, at some stage you will have to think about talking to members of your family about it. ... What the young lesbians did find quite often was that their parents hadn't thought about lesbianism before, and didn't know much about it. They [the girls] found that they had a lot of educating to do,

that it wasn't just a phase, etc."[32]

Or as an occupying enemy, as in this disturbed contribution from a group of young people who want to cut "gay teenagers" off from their parents and are more typical of the revolutionary left:

> Parents can be really inquisitive about what you do, where you go, who you see, what you keep in your room. After all, you're supposed to grow into them one day, so they've got to make sure that nothing interferes with your brainwashing."[33]

Parents given Hobson's choice

This failure to accept any opinion that parents might express concerning homosexual behaviour, other than the one homosexual activists regard as correct, is inherent in the philosophy of gay liberation. Parents are presented as irrelevant, as oppressors, or as people to be convinced of the rightness of homosexual activity.

A recent "Family Matters" on BBC1 illustrated this with three families, two of which had "accepted" their son's homosexuality, and the third of which had not, whereupon their son had committed suicide. The programme, which was presented by John Humphries and Joanna Kaye, ended astonishingly with suggestions to telephone Parents' Enquiry or Gay Switchboard, rather than a developmental psychiatrist.[34] The lesson to be drawn was obvious; as Wendy Cope wrote in the Spectator,[35] it is far better to accept your children's homosexuality as fact than to throw them out or let them kill themselves.

Inevitably, this is Claire Rayner's line as well. On Radio 2 on 13th May 1991 she devoted an hour and a half to promoting perversion and persuading parents to accept homosexual behaviour in their children. Thames Television in its "Helpline" programme offered material written by "Acceptance," a group of sad and misguided parents of homosexuals close to the Albert Kennedy Trust [qv].

Parents of children who have grown up homosexual are only ever offered two choices, through a common media acceptance of the erroneous view that homosexuality is inborn. The even better way, that is, to free the children from the homosexuality itself, is never considered to be worth discussing, because healing is contrary to the tenets of the homosexual agenda, and would confront parents with their guilt at failing their children.

Gay hostels and "safe houses"

Deceiving the young

Children can leave home for reasons unconnected with homosexuality. A row over something or nothing can result in a young person walking a lonely country road, or ending up at a railway station. Homosexuals are on the lookout for such young people, especially for boys; girls are normally prey to pimps and may become involved in prostitution, although boys can just as easily end up on the "meat-racks" of the overt rent-boy network. On other occasions a homosexual picks up a boy who looks lost, and offers to take care of him. The aim is slowly to integrate the boy into the homosexual network.

This can of course be described as "helping a young gay man to get away from his repressive parents," which is how the homosexuals who run the Albert Kennedy Trust put it. Hugh Fell and Christopher Payne run this group from Manchester, where they are well known in the homosexual scene - Fell as a trustee of the Manchester Gay Centre, Payne as a member of "Outrage" - but they have "safe houses" all over the country. Hugh Fell is in his forties, and has, or had, a boy of seventeen living with him. Neighbours report a succession of young callers at his house. He claimed that the Albert Kennedy Trust was a charity at a time when the Charity Commission said that a formal application for charitable status had not even been made. According to recent reports in the homosexual press, charitable status has now been granted to the "Albert Kennedy Trust."

Boys sent to homosexuals by social services and Centrepoint

Young boys have astonishingly been referred to the Albert Kennedy Trust by local authority social services departments, and by Centrepoint in central London, which as we saw in chapter 5, actively recruits homosexual staff.

Any boy falling by whatever route into the care of the homosexual network will be taken round the homosexual nightspots and shown what a jolly time can be had. Even if he has no homosexual inclination at all, he can quickly become traumatised into acceptance of homosexuality, and may be persuaded to try homosexual activity. If the activity becomes persistent, as Van Wyk & Geist showed, it can become established as a behaviour pattern and then as an orientation.

Meanwhile, the young person's parents are contacted and are strongly encouraged to accept homosexuality as a fact in the boy (or girl), being put in touch with "Parents' Enquiry" (qv) "Acceptance," or other "parents' support" groups. That in Manchester is run by Catherine Hall and Joyce Layland, who are very closely connected with the Albert Kennedy Trust. The parents of runaways find that it is always easier to speak with and see their children if they follow the guidance given by the "parents' support" group.

Metropolitan Community Church and Streetwise Youth

The homosexual front "Metropolitan Community Church" (formerly known as the "Sodomy Church") is now in a similar business. Currently involved in providing soup kitchens for destitutes and runaways, it aims to set up a nation-wide network of hostels for young "gay" people. Bournemouth and Bristol have been mentioned, and London, with so many main-line railway stations, is an obvious target.

"Streetwise Youth" is another charity supported by business trusts, primarily Mobil Oil, although British Airways, Campo Holdings, three of the Big Four banks and Norwich Union have joined Islington and Haringey Gay Group with financial support. Streetwise has links with Centrepoint, Barnado's and Childline. Started by Father Bill Kirkpatrick and Richie McMullen, Streetwise claims to care for rent boys in the West End. It ran into controversy because McMullen was a rent-boy himself. I think the point was missed. It is not that the boys are encouraged to be rent boys, but that, because Streetwise is non-judgmental, they are not discouraged. They are fed and housed, but also given advice on condoms and "safe" prostitution, so as to become "streetwise." Father Kirkpatrick does not oppose homosexual activity, even for under-age boys.

Many people behind "Streetwise Youth" are sympathetic to homosexuality or even to homosexual activity with teenagers. Professor Donald West (qv) is its current Chairman, Tony Whitehead its deputy Director. Michael Schofield (qv) as well as many leading homosexuals support it with funds. Patrons include homosexuals Rabbi Lionel Blue and Canon Eric James, and also Claire Rayner, Julia Neuberger, Lil Butler (qv), and Chris Smith MP.

Into the moral vacuum of "Streetwise" step boys like Mark, who is 18: "They give you condoms and other safe forms of protection so you are safe [sic] whilst on the game," and Nigel, 21: "Streetwise [was] a place to go for lads who were on the rent scene, a safe [sic] environment where people under 21 could get advice and support, and to introduce them to people of the same age in similar situations."[36]

Such boys desperately need to be looked after, but not in this way. It is most surprising that Esther Rantzen, Judge Steven Tumim, Anthony Scrivener QC, Rosie Barnes, Frank Field MP, Sir Charles Irving, Baroness Ewart-Biggs and Joan Lestor MP (Labour's

"Spokesperson for Children") have also allowed their names to be listed as patrons of "Streetwise Youth."

The Mother's Union's strange bed-fellow
Many parents do not know that if their son or daughter disappears and turns up staying with an organisation such as we have described, and is under eighteen, they can quickly have him or her made a Ward of Court, usually with legal aid. A "seek and find" order can be made the same day, enabling the High Court Tipstaff to bring those running the secret house or hostel to court and compel them to disclose where the child is being kept. Social Services Departments are unlikely to be helpful in such a case, and it is better to spend an hour on the telephone finding out which local solicitor is the most positive and experienced in child care.

The Social Concern Department of the Mothers' Union recently produced a permissive and pessimistic leaflet entitled "Understanding Homosexuality" which included suspect medical statements suggesting that homosexuality cannot be "cured," as they put it, and which urged parents to "accept" and "learn to live" with a son's or daughter's alleged homosexual orientation.[37]

The leaflet was largely written by Rose Robertson, who runs the London-based "Parents Enquiry." Mrs Robertson is a widow whose son became homosexual. She has denied that her son's homosexual condition arose from anything in his childhood or adolescence, and is engaged in a campaign of proselytising self-justification. She sees nothing wrong in the activities of homosexuals who allow runaway adolescents to stay with them. It would be fair to say that she sees nothing wrong in homosexuality at all. Her organisation has produced papers bearing the most surprising claims, such as: "The weight of evidence increasingly suggests [the cause of homosexuality] is genetic"[38] (when of course it actually suggests that it is not).

Another claim of Parents Enquiry is that for children who decide to be homosexual, "The love, happiness, trust and affection that your parents hoped you would find in marriage, will still happen, but with someone of your own sex."[39] This too is contrary to the evidence. Homosexual relationships are inherently extremely unstable, as we have seen.

It is surprising that the Mothers' Union has allied itself to a group whose statements owe more to desperation than truth. We must charitably assume that their choice of ally was prompted by ignorance or stupidity rather than by a wish to push a gay rights agenda. Perhaps the most bizarre activity of Parents Enquiry was explained by its founder to an audience at the Royal Court Theatre:

What we do at Parents' Enquiry is to discuss sex with them. Because there's no book they can read where they can find out what happens between two gay people, it can be quite a frightening experience for a young person. They don't know what's going to happen to them. We teach them how to take care for themselves if they're propositioned; what to do, what to say. Imagine a young person in a gay pub or club for the first time - a mixture of feelings. They're flattered that they are noticed, they're frightened at what is going to happen to them. That's why we arrange for them to go in a group, with an older person in charge.[40]

Just a passing phase usually the truth

Some degree of homosexual behaviour may sometimes be part of development from puberty through into adult life, and may be expressed verbally, in comments, language and comparisons. It should not be condoned if expressed physically, in touching, or holding hands, or indeed sexually. Nevertheless, as child psychiatrist Dr Martyn Gay put it in the "teachers' notes" for the BBC programme "Two of Us" (a television play produced to promote homosexuality amongst school-children) "it [homosexual activity] may well be a passing phase for both parties and be an important precursor of further heterosexual activity."[41] Venturing a shade more liberal, and being castigated by "The Sun" for his pains, Dr Gay wrote that after the development of normal heterosexual behaviour has been established, "it is possible for adults to take up patterns of homosexual behaviour under certain social or emotional circumstances, and then to return quite successfully to a pattern of heterosexual behaviour again." Martyn Gay had this advice for teachers:

It is important for adults to help adolescents feel reassured that if they are having any awareness of homosexual feelings within themselves, that this is not a sign of abnormality, of illness nor of perversion or of long-standing instability.[42]

The "gays" in charge of "gay youth" groups would say that this is because homosexuality itself is not abnormal, pathological, perverted or unstable, but we are gradually reviewing the evidence and seeing that their claims are false. It is quite clear what Dr Gay was saying to those responsible for young people, that a young person who experiences homosexual feelings can be reassured that these will normally be grown out of. That is something that "the gays" can not countenance.

I was surprised when I read the "Two of Us" teachers' notes. A typical piece of misrepresentation by Claire Rayner pretended there to be nothing wrong with homosexuality. That I expected. But Dr Gay's contribution simply did not follow on in the same vein. Given the effort that must have been put in by the BBC to find a psychiatrist who would present a pro-homosexual point of view, the fact that they had to put up with Martyn Gay, and his largely traditional advice, speaks volumes about the way homosexual activity is still viewed by psychiatric professionals.

16
Paedophilia

We were hailed with "Hello" from a very beautiful 16 year-old boy whom I knew (but had never had) from last year. Kenneth wanted him. We talked for about five minutes and finally I said, "Come to our apartment for tea this afternoon."
We had tea and Ken and Lhabi went into the bedroom... When Ken came out they had had sex. "I've arranged for you to have him tomorrow," Kenneth said in a confidential tone when the boy was out of the room. "I've already arranged to have Mohammed tomorrow," I said. "I really wish you wouldn't play the procuress quite so much. I'm quite capable of managing my own sex![1]

Homosexual apologists are never able specifically to deny that paedophilia and homosexuality are linked. Instead the arguments talk up heterosexual molestation, or speak of hurt feelings. The Gay Liberation Front Manifesto, for example, complained that active homosexuals are not "allowed the job of teaching children because we are all reckoned to be compulsive child-molesting maniacs,"[2] whilst in the GLC's "Changing the World":

One of the greatest areas of difficulty in overcoming prejudice is that of the relationship of children to gay men and lesbians. .... Society has an irrational sense that such exploitation and abuse is more likely to come from homosexual people. This belief is not only mistaken - as the figures for child-abuse clearly show - but is also deeply wounding to gay men and lesbians and must be rejected.[3]

NCCL fails to check its facts

This is also the collective wisdom of the National Council for Civil Liberties, which claims to be "effective because we always check our facts." In 1980 it decided that in the absence of facts, it would do just as well simply to declare that "heterosexuals are as likely to interfere with children as homosexuals."[4] Not quite so far to the left, the journal of the Conservative Group for Homosexual Equality, which always carries a piece by its chairman "explaining" that sexual orientation, "like left-handedness," is "fixed very early in life" and is not a matter "of seduction or corruption," ran a piece by its "Social Services Correspondent," Sussex gay activist Peter Radcliffe-Ludlam, in which he wrote of laws forbidding homosexual acts:

> Many of the advocates of such laws believed that children are safe within the family, that they are endangered only by child molesters from outside, and that homosexual assaults on boys are the chief form of sexual abuse of children. In fact, sexual abuse of children is overwhelmingly heterosexual and over 90 percent of sexual assaults on children are committed by heterosexuals and take place within the family.[5]

We shall take a look at the figures for criminal assaults in a moment, but even if he means that 90% of *unproven cases of child sexual abuse* occur within the family one has to ask where the statistic comes from. I suspect it is just invented to slander families and marriage, which is also something that activist Malcolm Macourt does in his book about "gay help-lines."[6] A lot depends also on the definition of "family." Abuse of children, both physical and sexual, is far more likely to come from live-in boyfriends and stepfathers, although to be fair, the latter come out rather better than the former. Natural fathers are rarely involved. The evidence suggests that child abuse increases in a society which encourages casual family relationships and allows families and marriages to fracture with equanimity.

"Gay Left" lets the cat out of the bag

The following view of the "gay left collective" on the statistics of sexual relationships between adults and children is merely a standard, and of course untrue, feminist line, though with a surprising sting in the tail:

> In fact the majority of such relationships are heterosexual, and in practice, between heterosexual men and young girls, usually in the context of the family. But it is also true that the (relatively tiny) number of people who have identified themselves as paedophiles are usually male and boy lovers.[7]

This is the first admission we have seen of a link between paedophilia and homosexuality, significantly in a book written for a homosexual readership. It is still speaking only of paedophile activists, but in another such book, American homosexual writer Tom Reeves goes further, and ridicules those homosexual apologists who deny the link:

> Gay spokespersons solemnly denounce child molesting, equating it with sex with "chicken" and intone the statistic myth: "95% of all child molesters are heterosexual ..."[8]

The "statistic myth" repeated

In spite of this, another activist, Malcolm Dobson, also writing in a "gay" campaigning book but one which is aimed additionally at liberal heterosexuals, still claims:

> The "sensitivity" of employing lesbians and gay men in jobs involving contact with the young arises from the belief that the young people will be seduced or corrupted, either physically or ideologically. The fear of physical assault arises from the belief that lesbians and gay men are predatory by nature, and the identification of homosexuality with paedophilia. Both ideas are without foundation: in fact Home Office statistics show that the vast majority of "assaults" on young people below the age of consent are by heterosexual men on girls. The other fear, that of ideological corruption, seduction to the homosexual way of life, is more basic, and lies, for example, behind Mary Whitehouse's objections to homosexual "proselytising" in schools.[9]

So what are the figures for sexual assaults that Mr Dobson invokes in support of his argument? Is the link between child molestation and homosexuality "irrational" or is it rather the carefully cultivated belief that active homosexuals are not interested in children that is the myth, as Professor Reeves maintains?

Home Office statistics reveal the truth

The Home Office carried out research that gave some answers to that very question for the year 1973, and has subsequently published a number of other studies:[10]

In 1973, there were 1,627 convictions for gross indecency between males, and 3% of these were for indecencies with boys under 16, which technically should have been charged as indecent assaults. There were a further 392 convictions under the Indecency with Children Act, in which the age of the victim is by definition under 14. Of those cases tried at Crown Court level, a staggering 55% were offences against boys, and 45% against girls.

Comparing convictions for buggery and attempted buggery with under age boys (and in the same year there were 21 convictions for buggery offences with females, and 4 with animals) with figures for unlawful sexual intercourse, that is, sexual intercourse with under-age girls, the convictions for buggery offences were 170 compared with 768 convictions for unlawful sexual intercourse. There were in fact 135 offences against boys under 16, and 35 against boys between 16 and 20. The offences against young males are disproportionate, being some 18% of the total, a high figure when it is considered that the offences have been perpetrated by the 1-2% of the male population who are active homosexuals.

For indecent assault in the year in question, there were 802 convictions for assaults on males, and 3,006 for assaults on females. Ignoring for a moment the age of the victim, the assaults on males represent 21% of all convictions. If we distinguish between ages of victim for the homosexual offences, we find the following:

Age of victim:	0-4	5-9	10-11	12-13	14-15	16-17	18-20	21+
% of cases:	3.1	32.5	18.6	15.8	18.1	4.9	2.8	4.2

And for the female victims:

Age of victim:	0-4	5-9	10-12	13-15	16-17	18-20	21+
% of cases:	3.2	24.8	15.4	26.2	7.1	7.8	15.5

In other words, offences against boys under 16 were 88.1% of the homosexual offences and those against girls under 16 were 69.6% of the heterosexual offences. So we might calculate that a homosexual man is $(21/79) \times (98.5/1.5) \times (88.1/69.6) = 23$ times more likely to interfere with someone under 16 than is a heterosexual. But this is not the whole picture. If heterosexuality is the ability to enter into a complete loving and sexual relationship exclusively with an adult of the opposite sex, then the men convicted of the offences on girls under 16 were not up to the mark either.

Offences against boys in 1980s disproportionately high

The Home Office subdivided the classifications for sexual offences for even numbered years in the 1980s. The statistics show similar results to the 1973 study: In the four years considered, there was a total of 4,000 indecent assaults on males and females aged 16 and older. Of these, 9% were on males. However, the total for indecent assaults on males and females under the age of 16 was 12,000, and in these offences against children, 21% were committed against boys.

Comparing buggery and attempted buggery with boys under the age of sixteen with unlawful sexual intercourse with girls under the age of sixteen, the homosexual offences are 9% of the total, and increasing. In the case of gross indecency with children, that is, with children under 14, 46% of all offences were committed against boys. A recent parliamentary question revealed the suggestion of a new upward trend in convictions and cautions for offences against girls, but even in the two years in which this has occurred, the offences against girls are, at 61%, still a long way short of the 90% to 95% that "the gays" have claimed.[11]

Relationship of abuser to victim

Another Home Office study gathered information from several sources to come up with figures for the relationship of child molesters to their victims. The author of the study points out that this relationship varies with the type of offence, with offences of indecent exposure, for example, more usually involving strangers that (by definition) offences of incest. The results are markedly different from what has been claimed by anti-family campaigners:

> The Nash and West research[12] which involved indecent exposure offences nevertheless suggested that more than half of all sexual abuse experiences were perpetrated by people known to the victim. Where the offender was known to the victim, about a third were relatives (18% of total sample). Walmsley and White, in their study of reported offences, found that, for those offences leading to conviction, about 70% of molesters who indecently assaulted girls were known to the victim (10% relatives) and about 55% of those who indecently assaulted boys (5% relatives).[13]

Definitely don't go with strangers

The homosexual apologists have been misleading us. Close relatives, let alone parents, turn out to be the least likely people of all to commit offences against children. The most likely person to commit a sexual offence against a boy, and especially a girl, is certainly known to the child, and therefore able to gain his or her trust, but then nearly half of the men who assaulted boys were complete strangers. The Home Office statistics show that there was a disproportionate incidence of homosexual paedophile offences, compared with the numbers of practising homosexual men in the population, and far from involving only a "relatively tiny number," paedophilia is, amongst males at least, a mainstream activity, if Tom Reeves may be believed:

Paedophilia

Sex between women and girls may or may not be widespread, but little has been written about it. Sex between men and boys, on the other hand, is widely practised to the joys and benefits of those involved. It has become a centre of attention in the straight media where it is associated with molestation, abuse, runaways and hustling. It is all of these things at times, but it is more often quiet, enduring, reciprocal and certainly voluntary. Such sex is a central feature of gay life ... gay men fuck and suck teenage boys regularly.[14]

Paedophiles blame the parents

Once normal taboos, that is, restraints on anti-social behaviour, are broken down, anything becomes possible. A familiar theme amongst sexual "liberators" is that it is the "repression" of sexual feelings that causes problems, and that guilt is a silly reaction to a sexual experience, however bizarre. The "Gay Left" group saw nothing wrong with sex with children as such, and laid the blame for any psychological disturbance on the shoulders of parents:

We see a homosexual choice as equally valid as a heterosexual one. .... We should argue for sex as pleasure, not sacrament. If it is pleasurable, on what grounds can we deny it? We must also recognise that it is often the young person who initiates sexual activity. It is the intrusion of the law or panic-stricken parents which often causes misery and guilt in the child in a caring paedophile relationship rather than the relationship itself.[15]

Psychiatrist John Bancroft agrees that the child should be excepted from any guilt involved in a paedophile experience, but does not accept that this excuses the paedophile. He holds that the central failure of the paedophile is that he sees not the person, but just the child. When the child grows up, another child takes his place. The paedophile lusts after the *image* of the child, and although Dr Bancroft does not go so far, he did after all support gay rights in Scotland, and opposed Clause 28, the evidence suggests that if this regard for another simply as a sex object is true of paedophilia then it is true of homosexuality as a whole.

Homosexual bookshops promote paedophile books

Paedophile material and books on paedophilia are widely available from all "gay book" stockists. The Gay Liberation Front Information Service publications list at one time included eleven books and pamphlets on paedophilia, most of them under that specific heading, and including three published by the Paedophile Information Exchange itself.

The popular homosexual bookshop, "Gay's the Word," carried a glowing report in its bi-monthly review of a book of paedophile memoirs, where sexual acts were described in intimate detail,[16] sold "Understanding Paedophilia" published by the Paedophile Information Exchange, and made the extraordinary paedophile book "Betrayal of Youth" briefly available on its shelves. Richie McMullen's autobiography about his experiences as a rent boy was second in the gay best-seller lists, and the paedophile books by Michael Davidson and others are hugely popular.

The so-called "Lesbian and Gay Christian Movement" promotes a bizarre book on paedophilia by one Parker Rossman.[17] "Sexual Experience between Men and Boys" chronicles tales from various parts of the world and has sections which seem to consist entirely of stories in which a male stranger walks off with a brown-skinned boy with the parents' consent, although Rossman's informers are usually very coy about what physically takes place in such cases.

Essex University don praises paedophile books

Mr Rossman deals with paedophilia from, so it is stated by L&GCM, a totally non-judgmental point of view. A strong libertarian streak is indeed highly visible for over two hundred pages of input from pederasts and their boys. Those of his conclusions which concern counselling boys through early homosexual phases and into heterosexuality are nearly sensible, and seem strangely unconnected with what went before, but it is clear early on that Rossman is arguing against "repression" of sexual feelings and against what he calls "stringent laws" in sexuality. I do not think I have done him an injustice, for he says at one point: "It may be that nature intended older males to tutor adolescent boys in sex, and unconscious or repressed pederast or homosexual tendencies are intended to stimulate an interest in such tutoring."[18] This latter statement of Mr Rossman's is unsupported in his book by any evidence whatsoever. "Sexual Experience between Men and Boys" received the following praise from Ken Plummer in Gay News:

> *Any study that can take adult-child sexuality out of the zone of shrieking horror and place it in the demystified zone of everyday experience must be welcomed.*[19]

The same reviewer, who is sociologist Dr Kenneth Plummer of Essex University, sent a "warm message of support" for "Betrayal of Youth," and, in company with Nettie Pollard (qv) and Professor Donald West (qv), also read, made suggestions and then praised "Paedophilia the Radical Case" receiving "heartfelt thanks" from its author, Paedophile Information Exchange Chairman Tom O'Carroll. Malcolm Macourt of the helplines, involved as he was with the Tyneside Gay Teenagers' Group, also finds Rossman, O'Carroll, and "The Age Taboo" edited by American paedophile Daniel Tsang "useful."[20]

When another sociologist, Dr Brian Taylor of Sussex University, edited his book "Perspectives on Paedophilia," Dr Plummer contributed an article detailing the history of PIE "from below." Brian Taylor adopted the pseudonym "Humphrey Barton" when he was research director of the PIE magazine "Understanding Paedophilia," being co-opted to its executive committee. Another contributor to his book was a PIE EC member from 1976-77: Peter Righton, who was Director of Education at the National Institute for Social Work. He contributed a chapter entitled "the adult." He too is quoted in praise of Tom O'Carroll's book.

Peter Righton was arrested in May 1992 for allegedly possessing indecent material but at the time of writing had not been charged with an offence. He told the Daily Mail that he was openly homosexual and lived with a headmaster of a school for disturbed children. Mr Righton, whose past membership of PIE is a matter of public record, was described in the Daily Mail article as "the leading authority on council residential care of children."

Ancient Greece romanticised

Many paedophiles try to invoke the alleged involvement of other societies in homosexuality, and argue that paedophilia is no more than a teaching relationship, in which a man "takes an interest" in a boy. Ancient Greece is a particular favourite.

Even Parker Rossman, who is fond of the "tutoring" angle, admits that there is a distinct lack of objective evidence about the actual extent of paedophilia in ancient Greece. The relationship between a young man and a boy could indeed have been simply tutorial, or it could be that active paedophilia was a popular pastime, particularly amongst the rich. It is difficult to tell what is the truth of the matter, because contemporary accounts vary in tone according to whether the writer is in favour of or in opposition to pederasty. Even then it is difficult to determine whether sexual relationships as such are being written about. In an aggressively-titled but well-researched and articulate booklet, writer Noel Halifax of the Socialist Workers' Party suggests that the thinking behind much Greek homosexual verse was that:

> Women had such a low status that men thought it almost impossible for a man and a woman to have an equal loving relationship - women were for children, love was with boys. It was a horrible oppressive society.[21]

This highlights at once the extraordinarily misogynist nature of male homosexuality and the impossibility of constructing a utopian system by picking and mixing from other societies.

Homosexuality in a primitive society

One Paedophile Information Exchange publication draws on the practices of the Kiwai of New Guinea - very well documented since the 1920s - to support the view that there are cultures in the world where paedophilia is acceptable today, and by implication that we ought to accept it in just the same way. The argument is that sex in these primitive societies is a much more free, relaxed and open business than in the "repressive" developed world. The choice of the Kiwai is extraordinarily revealing. Homosexual practices are indeed widespread throughout the Papuan Gulf, and are involved in male initiation rites, as an anthropologist explains:

> Institutionalised homosexuality is rooted in a belief that the attributes of masculinity are not innate in male biology but acquired through strict adherence to a ritualised regimen. This is in contradistinction to femininity which is acquired naturally by women without such effort. ... The essence and focus of maleness invariably is semen. Once this premise is accepted, the logical conclusion is clear; males must acquire semen in order to become real men. Basically, this is what ritualised homosexuality is all about; promoting masculine development by transferring semen from the haves to the have nots.[22]

Transference of seminal life-force

A similar view is held by some paedophiles, oddly enough, that sexual activity with boys will "make men of them." Getting back to the primitive tribes of New Guinea, a boy is initiated in a typical area at the "bull-roarer" ceremony at the age of 13, introduced to sexual activity and made available to whoever wishes to use him that night. He is then turned over to an older partner to be routinely anally and orally sodomised. The tribesmen believe that the boy has no semen of his own, and that the more sodomy that can be performed on him, the "stronger" he will grow. Lime is at one stage poured down his throat, and the severe burns that result are supposed to prevent the boy becoming pregnant.[23]

After some time in this role and as puberty advances, the appearance of male physical traits, particularly the growth of a beard, is taken as proof that the boy has ingested enough semen. The boy is promoted to the position of active rather than passive partner and he is put in charge of, and sodomises, a new, younger boy. This period leads eventually into renunciation of homosexuality and to marriage with a very much younger girl, who performs fellatio on her husband until her menarche. The whole philosophy is bound up with magical ideas of the power of semen; in the case of sodomy, the seminal "life-force" is transferred from the active male to the neophyte, and in heterosexual intercourse from the male to the unborn child on mixing with the mother's blood.[24]

An institutionalised confidence trick

The homosexual initiation rites, starting with the strange and frightening noise made by the "bull-roarer," are intended to instil fear into women and children, who are kept at some distance, and thus to maintain an oppressive form of male domination over women and youths. To use Noel Halifax's words, this society cited as an example by paedophiles is horrible and oppressive.

Of course initiation into manhood is important, and of course masculinity does not just happen, any more than femininity just happens. Manhood however is a quality not acquired as a result of having semen pumped up the backside. Whatever the cultural background, the result is tribesmen making sexual use of adolescent boys in the same age-group as those viewed as attractive to homosexual men in the western world. But there is more:

Practitioners themselves actually view homosexual activity as a statement of male superiority over females. Van Baal (1966) says that Marind male pride and superiority find their fullest expression in homosexual rites. These rites stress the absolute superiority of the male sex. ... The conflict between the fiction of all-powerful masculinity and the reality of female reproductive power gives rise to masculine ritual and dogma that reinforces the former in face of the latter. ... Men may try to demonstrate in many ways their ability to live without women, but male homosexuality is particularly effective in this regard since it denies the need for women in the area where women are most powerful - sexuality.[25]

Here too is a parallel with the West, in this case with male drag artists on the "gay" circuit who scorn women, and with male homosexual misogyny in general.

Robbery of childhood.

Paedophile writers commonly mock the age of innocence in childhood as a Victorian romanticisation. And yet paedophiles themselves display at least as sentimental a view of childhood, probably drawn from Rousseau and the image of the child as noble savage. One wrote: "I celebrate with them their act of rebellion." The American activist Professor Tom Reeves boasted in "The Age Taboo" of indecencies with several of a class of teenagers whom he taught in Baltimore:

> *the New Right is right: we are after the sons of straight America. We are on the lookout for them at all times and ever ready to support their first attempts to get free, their need for love and their potential for courage and self-expression. We stand ready to be seduced, and we catch that "please-seduce-me" look in boys' eyes on street corners, in movie-houses, parks and pinball arcades - yes, even on playgrounds and in classrooms. We assist their jailbreaks from the plastic and poisonous family webs in slums or suburbia, and we let them live with us when possible.*[26]

The early age at which boys are often initiated into homosexual activity is confirmed by a British writer:

> *Many boys have been sexually active through casual contacts in public lavatories or in relationships with friends or relatives since the age of 10 or 11,*[27]

whilst an American survey carried out by two homosexual authors revealed that 73% of homosexuals had at some time had sex with boys 16-19 or younger.[28] One reported "My lover and I are into many young boys 13-18 years old ..."[29] A speaker at a rally in Minneapolis held by NAMBLA, the North American Man-Boy Love [sic] Association, said:

> *There's not a boy out here ... who does not need oral sex right now. I have never met a boy who did not enjoy being given oral sex*[30]

Whether paedophile activity is as much a part of regular lesbian experience is a matter of some contention amongst its writers:

In general, women are given more freedom than men within patriarchy to love across generations. But I don't see the correlative of the man/boy relationship existing in lesbian culture as I know it. There's a lot of cross-generational contact among lesbians ... but they're mainly as friendships or as mentor relationships.[31]

When we investigated the recruitment of young people into homosexual behaviour, we saw that girls, like boys, typically had their first homosexual experience with someone older. Early in 1992 the charity Kidscape brought the possibility of sexual abuse by women generally into the public view for perhaps the first time. Even if the lesbian quoted above is right, there are still inquisitive young girls, and women ready to exploit them. The following girl claims to have been sexually active from a very early age:

I have had fully consensual sexual relationships with women (who happened to be over 21) since the age of 13.[32]

Reality of child molestation by homosexuals

I think we can say that male paedophilia is more prevalent than female, and that any discussion of homosexuality which does not involve an analysis of paedophilia is lacking in depth. According to a member of the editorial board of the "children's liberation" magazine "Minor Problems," (a PIE offshoot) a refusal to discuss paedophilia:

involved - and still involves - a wholesale denial of the reality of many gay men's (and some lesbians') relationships ... The main Dutch gay liberation organisation, COC, vehemently protested its members' imperviousness to the attractions of young boys - at the same time it was publishing boy-love poetry, stories, and erotic portraits of pre-adolescent males.[33]

Homosexual activity was legalised in New Zealand in 1986. A number of radio shows promoting homosexuality now goes out, that on Access Radio being hosted by one Neil McKenzie. In March 1991 McKenzie sympathetically interviewed on air, for the second time in a year, two men claiming to represent the "Aotearoa Man-Boy Love Association" (AMBLA). [Aotearoa is the politically correct name for New Zealand.] "Jack" said that the men made contact with boys in "very public places, shopping malls, large supermarket-type shops, bus stops," whilst "Alexander" added "Some of us are more successful than others."[34]

Denying that there were any "boy molesters" in AMBLA, Jack said: "A boy lover is a man who loves a boy." Alexander differentiated between two groups within the organisation, those "who are attracted to post-pubescent boys, say from the age of 13 to 18," and a group of "paedophiles interested or attracted to boys pre-pubescent." The local paper reported: "McKenzie rounded off the radio show by telling anyone who was interested that they could make contact with AMBLA through a post office box in Auckland."[35]

Male homosexuality inseparable from paedophilia

Prominent homosexuals have indulged in paedophile activity through history. Secret Security boss Sir Maurice Oldfield even joined P.I.E. and then left his papers on a bus. As an American expert observed:

> *Since the decadent Roman wrote two millennia ago about the attractions of man-boy love, observers have noted linkages between homosexuality and pedophilia.*[36] *The most prominent - and presumably most responsible - homosexuals, like economist John Maynard Keynes, have sought out excursions to places where, as he put it, he could enjoy "bed and boy."*[37]

It seems that among the nineteenth century homosexual group, the "Uranians," it was recognised that male homosexuality was inseparable from paedophilia.[38] In Germany, during the 1930s, the atmosphere of decadence in which homosexual behaviour was tolerated led to Berlin becoming the centre of a gay sub-culture. "People who could afford it, such as the English writers Christopher Isherwood and W H Auden (both 'fellow-travellers' of the Communist Party in the 30s), went to Berlin, as today many go to San Francisco or Amsterdam. As Isherwood put it, 'To us Berlin meant boys.'"[39] Today many male homosexual couples follow in the steps of Orton and Halliwell to Morocco, Tunisia, Thailand, India and Africa. There can scarcely be a part of the "third world" which is free from adult western homosexuals on the lookout for exotic pubertal partners. Now that the Dutch have decided to allow sexual activity at the age of 12, British homosexuals will not have to travel further than Amsterdam, where there are already numerous bar/brothels providing homosexuals with boys lured there from Britain and kept in virtual captivity. [40]

There emerged recently from the trial of a 21-year-old man convicted of living off immoral earnings, an account of various parties between May 1985 and July 1987 at which paedophile sex and drugs figured very highly. Stephen Hardy, also known as Graham X, recruited and escorted young boys to sex parties at a country mansion, according to prosecutor Patrick Bucknell. In the trial report:

> Some of the rent boys, as young as 15, were flown by helicopter to the house in Finchamstead, Berkshire, where they were introduced to celebrities and the wealthy. Hardy identified some of the guests in his statement to police, but their names were not revealed in open court.
> Some of the people at the parties were well known and rich. "The thing to do, it seems, was to sniff cocaine through banknotes," Mr Bucknell said. After snorting the drug the boys would take part in orgies lasting up to four days.
> It appears the guests didn't want the same boys twice. "What I think they were trying to achieve was to have sex with every boy in the West End," Mr Bucknell added.[41]

High recidivism rate amongst paedophiles

Home Office statistics show that the peak age for paedophile offenders lies between early twenties and early thirties and that these offenders are likely to re-offend. Paedophiles who have a preference for boys under the age of puberty can be rather specialised and are very likely to re-offend:

> Such incidents are more likely to involve strangers, offenders are likely to have an exclusive preference for young boys, ... and they are more likely to be recidivists. American research, for example, suggests that offenders against boys (35% recidivism rate) are more than twice as likely to re-offend than other child molesters.[42]

Homosexual activity involving boys of around puberty and older, does seem to be on the increase, although this may be from increased reporting, or from greater police activity in the light of the dangers to these boys of contracting AIDS. During 1984, 100 police officers investigated an organised male prostitution racket in the West End. "Operation Circus" took five months, during which 250 boys and youths were interviewed. Many of the boys, like Alex in our "AIDS" chapter, were destitute runaways, and were displayed in the Wimpy Bar at Piccadilly, which became known as the "meat rack," making hundreds of pounds a week for the pimps who "introduced" them to clients.It was reported:

> Sentences on those involved in the racket have ranged from five years to 12 months. Among the men in the dock were an Islington

council social worker, two schoolmasters, a scoutmaster, postman, street trader and the head of a Lewisham council children's home.[43]

Pornographic child poses in paedophile ring

There were 15 Old Bailey trials in all, and during one of them, Judge John Hazan said that London had become the prostitution centre of Europe. During another unconnected trial, Southwark Crown Court heard that boys as young as eleven were photographed in pornographic poses with each other and with older men.[44]

During investigations into a paedophile ring in Hackney, a number of men were charged with buggery, gross indecency and other sex offences with children aged between five and 15. Police established a link between the ring and the murder both of a 15-year old casual "rent-boy" from Hackney, who was homosexually abused before his death, and that of a little boy of six.[45]

Another paedophile ring operating from a flat in Peckham and involving up to 150 black homosexual boy prostitutes was cracked after an eight-month investigation imaginatively codenamed by police "Operation Babe." The racket was said to be one of the largest ever discovered operating in Europe, and involved "scores" of celebrities who were willing to pay £150 per night for sessions in hotels a far apart as Amsterdam and New York.

Yet a sixth child sex ring involving up to 140 boys aged between 10 and 15 resulted in dozens of arrests in North-West London. Many of the children were from deprived homes, some had been in care, and the ring was only smashed when one little boy told his foster parents what had been happening.[46] In another "gay" paedophile pornography ring in Thornton Heath, children were systematically tortured whilst being photographed and their screams were tape recorded. Pornographic videos, with sound, recording appalling real acts of sadism against children, are increasingly circulating in paedophile rings, as investigator Tim Tate has reported.[47]

Local Authority children's homes

Even more recently, and as if to show that London has no monopoly on homosexual paedophile rings, the involvement of politicians and senior civil servants in a scandal concerning the Kincora boys' home in Belfast, was mentioned in a Dublin newspaper. A group of men including Anthony Blunt and other members of the secret security services made use of the large number of adolescent, and disturbed, boys available through a certain Orange lodge in the 1970s. Going to Northern Ireland became quite a treat for highly-placed homosexuals.

Questions were asked in Parliament concerning this particular case, surprisingly enough by the man who thought that children in council homes should believe that homosexual activity was a valid option. When he was leader of the GLC, Mr Ken Livingstone was keen for choice to be exercised in sexuality. The GLC Charter for Lesbian and Gay Rights went so far as to advocate that:

> in nurseries, children's homes and services for adolescents ... young people have a right to be informed about their scope of sexual choices.[48]

Throughout the late 1980s and early 1990s there were cases of sexual abuse in council-run children's homes in Southwark, Lewisham and Leicester amongst others. The ring-leader in Leicester was Frank Beck who ran three children's homes. He was able to recruit boys who became abusers themselves as they entered their broken adulthood.[49] Work in children's homes sadly tends to attract those sexually interested in children.

There were of course Orangemen involved in the Kincora case, and Mr Livingstone has made no secret of his friendship with Sinn Fein politicians and his desire to see a united, Marxist, Ireland. Members of Parliament are of course entitled to ask whatever questions they wish, and I may have missed whatever newspaper reports there were of Mr Livingstone asking equivalent questions about sexual abuse in children's homes on the mainland.

Spartacus guide promoted by "Capital Gay"

A large child sex network was run by John Stamford from his mansion in Holland. Stamford set up the Spartacus organisation which promoted paedophile publications, including "The Age Taboo" and "Perspectives on Paedophilia." His main activity was the publication of the "Spartacus International Gay Guide." This handbook became the authority on where active homosexual men should take their holidays, and listed the current prices for sexual activity with boys in third world countries, for example in Madras, where they were "available" for 20 cents. The Spartacus Guide is still quoted and promoted by homosexual papers like "Capital Gay" as a vast authority on where to go for holidays,[50] and is available at all homosexual bookshops.

Stamford had in his research spent some considerable time touring the world in his motorised caravan, registration number "BOY 1."[51] According to a national tabloid, Stamford also published and traded in pornography, and Dutch police removed his computer mailing list of 25,000 contacts, together with a film showing him with a 12-year-old coloured boy, when they raided his home.[52]

"The moral right is correct"

There does appear to be a spectrum of sexual behaviour ranging from what anyone would call "consenting adult" homosexuality to what nobody could avoid calling "paedophilia." Where one becomes the other on this spectrum is solely determined by the age at which we draw the line. The old joke on gay switchboard was that a paedophile is someone who fancies boys younger than you do.

It is worth repeating that when homosexuals maintain that they do not corrupt children, they do not mean that they are unable to influence children into homosexuality, but rather that in their opinion homosexuality is in itself not corrupt, and that childhood is certainly over at puberty if not before. As the Gay Left Collective put it, in response to claims made by those whom they identify as "the moral right":

> *Childhood is a battlefield that gay militants have to be concerned with. And to that degree, the moral Right is correct. Homosexuals are a threat; we can, in their language, "corrupt." Gay socialists cannot afford to avoid these issues.*[53]

The same point is confirmed by an American woman writer:

> *As a sacrilegious, defiant deviant bent on corrupting anyone who's susceptible, I am angered by the sight of another lesbian, vehemently waving American-flag-and-apple-pie slogans ... Young lesbians and gay men don't need to be protected from "corruption" - they need protection from their repressive families ...*[54]

Another lesbian disagrees, aware of the way in which children can be manipulated:

> *In these circumstances the child, ... is emotionally as well as physically immature. Such a man/boy relationship or encounter can hardly be between equals. Rather a huge potential exists for physical or economic coercion of the boy, that is, rape. The ultimate resolution of this issue would be the legalisation of the rape of young boys ...*[55]

Euphemisms running riot

The connection between the abolition of ages of consent and the legalisation of the rape of young boys is terribly valid. Statutory rape laws, which in the United States are used against paedophile acts, were described by the American equivalent of PIE, the North American Man-Boy Love Association, as "the current equivalent of 19th.century legal punishments for masturbation."[56] NAMBLA is campaigning against them, and for legalisation of sex with children. The group, which is affiliated to the International Lesbian & Gay Association, attempts to gain sympathy for cases like the following:

> *This gent was found guilty of four acts of blowing [fellating] a 15-year-old hustler; he got probation. Another man, a NAMBLA member, went to trial in 1980, and was found guilty of one sex act with a 15-year-old boy. He got two years in prison. Another case NAMBLA has taken up, that of Richard Peluso, has a man doing life in prison after he pleaded guilty to blowing a 13-year-old boy on four different occasions. ... NAMBLA hears of cases every week in which extreme penalties are handed out for simple affectionate sex acts.*[57]

When an article in a gay-lib paper refers to "not being able to see my 7-year old lover any more, and not being able to go for walks in the countryside together, or wank each other off,"[58] we have another indication of the sort of activity that can be described as a "simple affectionate sex act."

17
Paedophile groups and their supporters

In 1975 the delegates at the second annual conference of the Campaign for Homosexual Equality held in Sheffield were challenged by Keith Hose of the Paedophile Information Exchange to stand if they could honestly say they had no sexual interest in children. According to the local paper, *one third* of the 1,000 delegates remained in their seats. A figure of 33% of adult homosexuals being sexually interested in children - as PIE defined them - is broadly consistent with most studies. On the last day of the conference, CHE executive member Trevor Locke resigned from both the EC and from CHE itself in protest at the defeat of his proposal to set up a separate branch for teenagers. He withdrew his resignation from CHE later when the conference voted not to impose a lower age limit for membership.[1]

Nevertheless, despite strong support for paedophiles or for abolition of the age of consent in CHE conferences regularly during the seventies, it took the election in 1980 of a new "chairperson" of CHE, Michael Jarrett, Professor of Architecture at University College Cardiff, for the abolition of all ages of consent to become CHE policy. Professor Jarrett identifies paedophiles, in a foreword to a 1983 homosexual campaigning book , as a group "oppressed" by:

> *prejudice, violence, ignorance, biased lawmaking and the denial of basic civil rights.*[2]

Campaign for Homosexual Equality supports paedophiles

Condemnation of paedophilia from "ordinary" homosexual activists is rare. The Campaign for Homosexual Equality elected Leo Adamson, a past executive member of PIE, to its own executive, and he was last found working - on matters relating to consent law - in its office. To CHE was affiliated the paedophile magazine Minor Problems, of which Adamson was a member of the editorial collective certainly until it ceased open publication in 1986.

Paedophile groups and their supporters

Going back to 1975, the CHE conference was quick to support PIE Chairman Keith Hose by "a healthy majority"[3] when he immediately moved a motion of censure on the conference organising committee, for "relegating paedophilia to ancillary status in conference." "An awareness and acceptance of the sexuality of children is an essential part of the liberation of the young homosexual, and therefore, essential for the success of the young gays campaign," the motion concluded, demanding CHE also to develop "an informed perspective" on paedophilia. Glenys Parry, vice-president of CHE, was on hand afterwards to support the way things had gone. She was also quoted earlier in the same year in support of the paedophiles themselves. As a mental hospital psychologist she was treating two paedophiles at Oakwood Hospital, Maidstone. To help them counter their paedophile desires? Not at all. The non-judgmental Miss Parry said: "I aim to get them to understand themselves and allow them to make a free choice about their sex attitudes."[4]

Scottish homosexuals set up paedophile group

The Paedophile Information Exchange itself was set up in 1974 by Ian Dunn, Michael Hanson and another, all three of whom were activists from the Scottish Minorities Group which was later renamed the Scottish Homosexual Rights Group, and which initially identified the boys in whom the majority of paedophiles are interested as being aged between 8 and 16.[5] The assumption was made that boys older than 16 are adults, but there was some discussion in the SMG newsletter, qv. We should remember that these homosexual paedophiles are typically perpetuating a cycle of abuse, looking for boys within a two-year band of the age at which they were first molested themselves, not that they recognise "abuse" or "molestation" as accurate terms to describe the sexual interaction of adults with children.

Both PIE and SHRG were initially run from premises in Broughton Street Edinburgh, above which Ian Dunn, for many years the editor of "Gay Scotland" magazine, had his flat. PIE, as an offshoot of the SHRG, was only saying what every practising homosexual man in the network knew already, that paedophiles and ordinary gays are the same people.

It all hinges on whether a boy in adolescence or puberty is a child. Most parents believe he is, but homosexuals think he isn't. The average homosexual will progressively part company with the paedophile as the development of the child dips below puberty, but will still defend the paedophile, and the "right" of the paedophile and the "gay young person" to carry out "consensual sexual acts." We shall see how this non-judgmental train of thought developed during the seventies. To demonstrate their point, a PIE publication quoted a German survey which:

> suggested that among 200 cases of men sentenced for indecent assault on children "there was not even a single one preferring children to adult partners."[6]

Paedophile Information Exchange based at Iona Community

Michael Hanson was the first PIE Chairman (they only became "chairperson" when feminist language was introduced into left-wing politics generally and PIE decided to identify with it) and PIE was initially based within the Scottish Minorities Group at the headquarters of the Glasgow Iona Community, a Scottish religious foundation set up by socialist preacher the late Lord MacLeod. The Scottish connection is significant, for many of the gay activist initiatives originated from there; Donald Busby, who according to the PIE magazine contact section used to distribute homosexual erotica from a studio in South London's Railton Road, was for many years the art editor for Gay Scotland Magazine. Mr Hanson stated in his resignation letter in February 1975:

> I have tried not to restrict pie to any one form of paedophilia; I would not like to see it run by a number of people whose interests (eg in 8/9 year-old boys) over-shadowed the interests of other paedophiles.

PIE moves postbox to Release drugs agency

When Keith Hose became chairman of PIE in July 1975, the centre of PIE's operations moved from Edinburgh to London. PIE soon lost its secure address at British Monomarks - the "BM" postbox used by groups who wish their real address to be secret - and moved care of "Release," a organisation which exists in part to explain legal rights to people caught for drugs offences, and today campaigns for "needle-swap" centres for drug-injectors and legalisation of cannabis.[7]

Release started in 1971, and its funding arm the Princedale Trust was set up three years later. One of the founding trustees of both trusts was National Council for Civil Liberties sociologist Michael Schofield, qv. A fellow founding trustee at the Princedale Trust was Lord Melchett, although even his presence has not been sufficient to encourage the two trusts to comply totally with Charities law: when I last checked, Release had filed its accounts in 1972, 73, 74 and 1985-87, and Princedale in 1975 and 1987 only.

Release joins Joint Council for Gay Teenagers

Curiously, Release became in 1980 part of an umbrella group called the Joint Council for Gay Teenagers, which we have already met. Other affiliated organisations were CHE, Parents Enquiry, London Gay Switchboard and other contact groups, various local "Gay" groups and "Gay Youth" groups, the Family Planning Association's "Grapevine," and significantly, London Gay Teenage Group and "Icebreakers," the gay "befriending" organisation which grew out of the Gay Liberation Front counter-psychiatry group.[8]

The steering committee of London Gay Teenage Group included both Jonathan Walters and Michael Burbidge. Walters was on the editorial collective of "Minor Problems" and was involved "on the periphery" of the case in which ultra-left activist and paedophile Roger Moody was tried for and acquitted of indecent assault on a ten year-old boy. Moody was placed in the position, according to a contemporary, of denying that he had done it, but of saying that he did not think it would have been wrong if he had. Both Walters and Jeffrey Weeks (qv) were thanked by Roger Moody in his book "Indecent Assault," and both of them praised it when it saw the light of day.

Michael Burbidge edited "I know what I am" and "Breaking the Silence," two publications of the Joint Council for Gay Teenagers. He was also involved, with Keith Hose, in "Icebreakers." In one of his letters to the PIE newsletter, he speaks of the reactions of normal adults to PIE as "bigoted."[9]

Prominent homosexuals hosted paedophile meetings

PIE meetings, at which Keith Hose and Warren Middleton (alias John Parratt - and not the snooker player) were usually in attendance, were held in Mr Hose's Balham home, which he shared with a succession of adult "boyfriends," and also in a house in Camden, the home of three, varying at times to four, adult homosexuals. One of these was Jeffrey Weeks. He was a member of the early Gay Liberation Front and of its pro-paedophile successor Gay Left, and a contributor to a number of books on mainstream homosexual politics. Another member of the household was homosexual ceramicist Angus Suttie, and the third regular resident was Michael Burbidge.

A typical edition of the PIE magazine "Magpie" of the late 70s concentrates mainly on pictures of boys of 9 to 11, and, very occasionally, little girls rather younger, in what is said to be "Het [heterosexual] corner." It was important for PIE to be seen as heterosexual as well as homosexual, but in reality, PIE had to appeal for more pictures of little girls to keep up appearances. The abolition of corporal punishment in schools is said to be a good thing, as is the National Union of School Students, an extreme libertarian-left organisation and supporter of Gay Youth and PIE. The NUSS magazine "Blot" offended the then Education Secretary, Shirley Williams, with its use of expletives and descriptions of masturbation and promiscuity, its demands for the abolition of the age of consent, freely available contraception, better sex advice, and to demonstrate its degree of faith in the previous two, free abortion on demand.

"The People" exposes another paedophile group

Groups like PIE were always filled both with political activists who wanted sex with children and were prepared to try to justify it within a libertarian-left context, and plain unalloyed hedonists. When "The People" in 1975 exposed five "ringleaders" of another paedophile ring, Paedophile Action for Liberation, these were just the hedonists, one of whom was reported as saying "If you want sex with children don't bottle it up - do it." The "politicos" like secretary "Jonathan" who "works in conjunction with the National Council for Civil Liberties," and convener Tony Hughes kept in the shadows, negotiating their way out with the help of a senior journalist from Gay News, and a current member of the Labour front bench who was representing NCCL. The latter told the astonished journalists that they were persecuting paedophiles on account of their sexual orientation.

PIE Chairman Keith Hose was a member both of PIE and PAL. The short-lived PAL was based initially at the Gay Liberation Front's Gay Community Centre at 78 Railton Road, Brixton, then in an old barber's shop opposite Herne Hill station, and then in a squatted house and a disused ironmongers' in Vauxhall, all within five miles of each other in the London Borough of Lambeth. PAL produced a newsletter called "Palaver," illustrated with drawings of children copulating, and had in 1976 a mailing address with the bookshop Rising Free at the offices of the Independent Labour Party, which was affiliated to and opposite the National Council for Civil Liberties at the top of King's Cross Road in London.

PAL wanted to "promote understanding" of paedophile problems, to "counter images" of child molestation, to give legal advice, and to exist as a contact group for paedophiles. However, PAL existed as an overt contact group also between adults and children - for "younger people" who "wish to extend their field of relationships to include those older than themselves."[10] and as far as the age of consent went, "to press for complete abolition of legal interference in the sexual lives of everyone."

PIE collaborated with Albany Trust

PIE absorbed the remnant of PAL in 1977, but became so well integrated with the mainstream "gays" that it went too far. In 1978, PIE published a pamphlet - "Paedophilia, some questions and answers" - containing a revised edition of its attitude to age of consent law. It was sent to all members of the House of Commons and the House of Lords, and to the media. There was an outcry.

"Questions and answers" was written with the help of the Albany Trust, which as we saw in chapter 2, was initially the charitable arm of the Homosexual Law Reform Society. During the production Albany Trust was exposed as linked to PIE by Mary Whitehouse and to PIE's dismay, had to dive out of sight.[11] Albany Trust chairman Rodney Bennett-England claimed "there has never been any connection whatsoever between Albany Trust and PIE"[12] Mr Bennett-England still holds to his claim. He told me also that Claire Rayner and Angela Willans were both involved with Albany Trust in its early days. Both women are now vice-presidents of the Gay & Lesbian Humanist Association. Albany Trust managing trustee Antony Grey, a homosexual who was also involved with Gay Liberation Front and the Sexual Law Reform Society, attended the inaugural conference of the Scottish Minorities Group, whose personnel formed PIE. These three seem to have been odd company for Mr Bennett-England who is today director of the traditionalist "Church in Danger" group which fights against homosexuality and women priests in the Church of England.

Returning to the relationship, if any, between Albany Trust and PIE, the PIE "Questions and Answers" booklet bears a striking resemblance to an earlier Albany Trust publication, "Homosexuality - some questions and answers," with identical cover material, binding, and style. And as for there never being "any connection whatsoever" between them, Tom O'Carroll explains in "Paedophilia the Radical Case" that Keith Hose first developed a contact in Albany Trust as a result of a MIND sexual minorities workshop.

In 1976 (says O'Carroll) both PIE and PAL were invited by the Albany Trust to help write the booklet, and Hose and O'Carroll wrote it with a nominee of the Trust before revising the detailed text in a series of meetings with some of the Trust's senior personnel. It was only when Mrs Whitehouse raised the connection between Albany Trust and PIE that the Trustees of Albany Trust decided not to go ahead with the booklet, which must by now have been typeset, and presumably PIE then printed it themselves. If Tom O'Carroll is correct, and his account seems reasonable, then it is hard to believe that all this went on without the knowledge of the Chairman of Albany Trust.

Confirmation of links between Albany Trust and PAL (Paedophile Action for Liberation), is found in the PAL newsletter:

> Recent talks with the Albany Trust have proved very useful in a number of ways ... the Trust is in a position to provide useful contacts with other groups and organisations.[13]

The Albany Trust also hosted two meetings to discuss "teenagers at risk in central London" in 1975. At the second, Albany Trust was duly represented, as were Campaign for Homosexual Equality, Icebreakers, Friend, Gay Switchboard, Scottish Minorities Group and the Paedophile Information Exchange.

Youth Service becomes pro-homosexual

Furthermore, in spite of a flat denial from Mr Bennett-England that Albany Trust subscribed to paedophile literature, PIE newsletters and "Magpie" magazines that I have seen were stamped with the Albany Trust imprint when it was Government supported at offices in Sutton Ground, near London's Victoria Station.

However, the dates of these coincide with the period in office of the previous chairman of Albany Trust, Harold Haywood. Haywood was instrumental in the appointment as Albany Trust youth officer of Ric Rogers, who has more recently been editor of "Scene," the pro-homosexual newspaper of the National Youth Bureau in Leicester. Rogers used Haywood's flat in Marylebone as a London pied-a-terre, as did David Howie, then director of the National Youth Bureau.

Tension arose in the Albany trust between Antony Grey and trustee Mrs Lil Butler over her support for Haywood and his friends. These tensions led to the resignation in 1977 of the outsider Grey, and of the local Chairman of MIND in Peterborough, after a curious piece of politics involving Tony Smythe, the director of MIND.

Not long afterwards, according to Rachel Tingle in "Gay Lessons," Haywood became Education and Training Officer of the National Association of Youth Clubs, which invited Denis Lemon, editor of Gay News, to address its 1978 conference. Another trustee of Albany Trust, Sidney Bunt, edited "Youth Clubs," the newspaper of the National Council for Voluntary Youth Services, which shares the address of the National Youth Bureau in Leicester. Bunt then succeeded Haywood in his post at the National Association.

Even the umbrella group of UK Youth Associations, the British Youth Council, which today claims an "affiliated membership" of "more than six million young people" and says it "represents youth nationally and internationally," has a policy, of which it is proud, embracing the full gay rights agenda. Its honorary presidents are currently John Bowis MP, Hilary Armstrong MP and Lord Tordoff.

The blatant, and continuing, pro-homosexual stance of the above youth work bodies should perhaps give cause for concern.

Government money for supporters of paedophilia

The Department of Education and Science actually funded the Albany Trust project "Youth and Sexuality," which was prepared to consider paedophilia as one shade of the spectrum of human sexuality. The eight-strong steering committee for the project included such doyens of sex education as Fay Hutchinson of the contraceptives-for-children Brook Advisory Centres, Mrs Lil Butler of the National Association of Youth Clubs and an ex-trustee of Albany Trust, and Alec Oxford, Deputy Director and Training Services Officer of the National Youth Bureau.

It is hardly surprising when a conference was set up in Loughborough in 1977 with the aim of integrating sex education by compulsion into the school curriculum, that early Gay Liberation Front member and CHE and Gay Youth organiser Trevor Locke was appointed organiser by the four man steering committee, and that the conference was sponsored by the National Youth Bureau, (which had appointed Trevor Locke as assistant information officer) the Family Planning Association, the Campaign for Homosexual Equality and Albany Trust.

It was Albany Trust who supplied PIE with a copy of the Dutch "Speijer Report," which advocated the abolition of existing legislation against homosexual activity with minors and was translated by the Sexual Law Reform Society. Lord Beaumont of Whitley, a sponsor of NCCL charity the Cobden Trust, was on the Sexual Law Reform Society's own working party on the age of consent. Originally the Rev Timothy Beaumont, he has been since the sixties, Chairman of Albany Trust for two years, an active Vice President of the Campaign for Homosexual Equality, and a supporter of the International Gay Association, the pro-abortion Birth Control Campaign and the Voluntary Euthanasia Society.

Albany Trust itself apparently ceased operating in 1979, but a relaunched Albany Trust has been heavily involved in non-judgmental counselling for homosexuals and in producing sex education videos promoting homosexuality to school children, many of which are astonishingly recommended to teachers in the Health Education Authority list of the Government of the United Kingdom.[14]

Paedophile Information Exchange exposed

In 1981 Tom O'Carroll, by then chairman of PIE, was jailed for two years for publishing a list of paedophile contacts for PIE members and thus "conspiring to corrupt public morals."[15]

A single issue campaigning group, the Campaign [or Conspiracy - I am not sure which] Against Public Morals, was specifically set up at the time by barrister Adrian Fulford and three others from Gay Liberation Front. This group published a booklet, "Paedophilia and Public Morals," the main purpose of which was to: "bugger up the nuclear family altogether - A most desirable solution." The front inside cover of the booklet carries a photograph of a child of perhaps six years of age with a banner supporting "Gay Pride '80" which was originally published, so the booklet says, in "Gay News." The caption runs "never too young to be proud."

A Christian headmaster, Charles Oxley, then managed to infiltrate PIE and got himself voted on to the committee. Declaring an interest in computers he volunteered to put the membership on data processor. He was keeping a national newspaper aware of what he was up to just in case anything went wrong.

And of course it did, but from an unexpected direction. The night before Oxley was to be given the list of members to "put on computer," a subeditor at the newspaper decided to run the story. The next morning Oxley's cover was blown and the list was seen no more. That was in 1982. In 1984 three members of PIE, chairman Steven Smith, newsletter editor Peter Bremner and a member of the editorial collective, David Joy, were remanded on bail on four counts, under the 1956 Sexual Offences Act, the Indecency with Children Act, the Obscene Publications Act 1969 and the Post Office Act 1953. Finally, in November 1984, Joy and Bremner were jailed for six months for sending indecent articles through the post, whilst Smith fled to Holland, from where the Dutch refused to extradite him.[16] He was only recently deported, and sentenced to 18 months by the Central Criminal Court in December 1991.[17]

Liberal attitudes increase paedophilia

When we considered promiscuity in the "gay" network, a homosexual activist who is also a psychologist showed that promiscuity was a fundamental psychological trait among active homosexuals, and that a more liberal attitude heightens the profile of all aspects of the gay sub-culture. The argument that if society were to be more accepting, the unpleasant aspects of homosexuality would disappear, was disproved.

Paedophile groups and their supporters

Inevitably the same arguments are employed in connection with paedophilia, like this: If society were to be more accepting of paedophile relationships, paedophile rings, so it is said, would not have to go underground and there would be less violence against the children involved. The men who practice sex with children, so the argument runs, would be less likely to kill their victims if paedophilia was legal, for there would be no crime to have to cover up. A letter sent by a paedophile activist in Holland to Ian Dunn contained the following quotation from a Professor Frenken:

> There was a man playing sexual, non-violent games. Knowing that this was prohibited, conscious of the big taboo, the man then commits a murder. I think the risk of murder would have been much lesser when paedophilia was an accepted phenomenon.

Readers will doubtless draw their own conclusions as to the value of this argument, which denies any psychopathic tendencies among paedophiles, and instead blames the law itself for a child's murder. It is certain that an increased tolerance of paedophilia, culminating in a reduction of the minimum age for homosexual activity, would increase the practice of paedophilia as surely as night follows day.

Labour MPs support Scottish paedophile

The dangers to the gays and their libertarian-left supporters of a public identification of child molestation with male homosexuality are of course obvious, as activist Roy Burns explains:

> .. we must educate public opinion that homosexuality is not corrupting, yet this is the one issue that we have tended to shy away from, for fear that any public discussion of paedophilia would benefit the conservative lobby.[18]

In spite of this danger, the homosexual network was quick to come to the defence of PIE founder Ian Dunn when he was standing for election as a labour councillor in 1984. He was exposed as a paedophile by the Sunday Mail and sued the paper for libel.[19] An Ian Dunn Defence Appeal was set up, assisted by the Scottish Council for Civil Liberties and sponsored, amongst others, by the then Labour Member for Leith, Ronald Brown. Ian Dunn had always denied that he was a paedophile himself, but evidence including a tape recording on which he boasts of a sexual liaison in adulthood with a fourteen-year-old boy persuaded him to drop his libel action against the Sunday Mail.

It was Ian Dunn and Derek Ogg of Scottish Homosexual Rights Group who convened the first International Gay Rights Congress in December 1974, with support from Gore Vidal, Christopher Isherwood, The Bishop of Edinburgh, MPs David Steel and Robin Cook. They set up the International Gay Association four years later. By 1983, IGA could boast 73 member organisations, including the American paedophile group NAMBLA, the Dutch COC, GRED from France, and PIE. In December 1982 the European Regional Conference of IGA was addressed by Robin Cook MP, by now vice-president of the Scottish Homosexual Rights Group. IGA now acts as a collator of information on what it regards as reactionary Christian churches and organisations, and says it has worked to neutralise "the Christian right-wing" through the World Council of Churches. In 1985 it changed its name to International Lesbian and Gay Association, and appointed Miriam Shapira of New Zealand as joint Secretary-General.

Such investigations are routine for "the gays". Bob Crossman, Julian Hows and Peter Bradley had set up a CHE "Information Commission" on moral groups like the National Festival of Light in 1978.[20] I also have evidence that Antony Grey worked with one Richard Savage of Kingston-upon-Thames to try to infiltrate Christian lobby groups in 1980. Again the Festival of Light (now CARE Trust) was targetted, as was the National Viewers and Listeners Association, the Responsible Society (now Family and Youth Concern), the Community Standards Association and the Order of Christian Unity.

Cooperating with the Scottish Minorities Group, and the Scottish Council for Civil Liberties, Labour MP Robin Cook had been active in gay rights a couple of years earlier. It was he who tabled the amendment to the 1980 Criminal Justice (Scotland) Bill, which extended the provisions of the 1967 Sexual Offences Act to Scotland,[21] whilst supporting the SMG "Towards a Charter for Homosexual Rights."

Paedophile motions at CHE conferences

Seconders of the PIE motion proposed by Keith Hose at the 1975 Sheffield Conference of the Campaign for Homosexual Equality included Michael Burbidge, Trevor Locke then of the CHE "Young Gays Campaign" and also an Executive Council member of the National Council for Civil Liberties, Nettie Pollard and Anna Duhig of NCCL, Dr Jonathan Cutbill, David Grove, secretary of PIE, and Bernard Greaves of the Liberal Gay Group.[22]

Paedophile groups and their supporters

In Nottingham in 1977, with The Rev Lord Beaumont in the Chair, the CHE conference "expressed its support for objective and rational discussion and exchange of views on paedophilia and child sexuality in general" and felt so strongly about holding a workshop on paedophilia that when their conference hotel objected to the workshop they moved the venue to accommodate it.[23]

In 1978, when CHE held its conference in Coventry, NCCL in the shape of Nettie Pollard and Roland Jeffrey popped up again in support of a motion proposed by gay teacher Peter Bradley calling on Gay News to give paedophilia more coverage.[24]

By 1979 NCCL had Roland Jeffrey, Ross Thomson and Richard McCance all of CHE on its executive committee and a motion proposed by lawyer Terry Munyard and others deplored "the retention of criminal penalties for any kind of consensual sexual act."[25] In Brighton CHE voted to affiliate to the group "Conspiracy to Corrupt Public Morals", and to re-affiliate to the National Abortion Campaign.[26]

Over sixty prominent personalities were listed as supporting the aims of CHE by 1980,[27] and in 1981, Nick Billingham, (CHE treasurer) and ten others saw their motion "decriminalising consensual sexual acts" involving "young people who have reached the age of puberty" carried by the CHE conference.[28]

Next year, 1982, the Campaign for Homosexual Equality adopted its Gay Charter, in Sheffield once again, of which key demands were "the promotion of gay pride," "the right to have, raise and care for children" and now "the decriminalisation of consensual sexual acts."[29] A charter for Gay Youth, even more extreme, if such a thing is possible, was also adopted.

Paedophile groups affiliate to NCCL

In 1974 the National Council for Civil Liberties had set up a Gay Rights sub-committee, and Nettie Pollard, the NCCL Gay Rights organiser, wrote a letter inviting the Paedophile Information Exchange to affiliate to NCCL in 1975. PIE and Paedophile Action for Liberation both affiliated officially during that year.

By 1975, one Patricia Hewitt had been the General Secretary of NCCL for just one year, having been women's rights officer the previous year. She also joined the Campaign for Homosexual Equality (as a "straight"). Lambeth resident Jonathan Walters had been on the NCCL executive, as was Roland Jeffrey. In the following year, 1976, Tom O'Carroll was invited by NCCL to address its conference on the issue of chemical castration treatments for paedophiles. The conference voted to "deplore" such practice.

Whatever the merits of chemical castration as a form of treatment, the NCCL conference was acting logically in its own terms. If there is nothing psychologically wrong with homosexuals, as they believe, and if paedophilia is an extension of mainstream homosexuality, or even just another sexual minority, then there is nothing psychologically wrong with paedophiles, nor any reason to treat them with drugs.

When the Sunday People ran its article exposing the hedonist ringleaders of Paedophile Action for Liberation, the article prompted the National Council for Civil Liberties to make representations to the Press Council and to come out in support of PAL's "work."[30] Patricia Hewitt was quoted in a local paper as saying that PAL was "just a counselling group." Even the arrival of Harriet Harman as NCCL legal officer in 1978 did little to dampen NCCL support for paedophiles; PIE remained affiliated to NCCL up to its demise in 1982, the year Miss Harman left the post.[31]

The Executive Committee of NCCL during the period when PIE was affiliated included, at various times, Anna Coote, Bill Birtles (barrister and future husband of Patricia Hewitt), Harriet Harman's husband-to-be Jack Dromey (a TGWU official), Martin Ennals, Tess Gill, Larry Grant, Malcolm Hurwitt, Jo Richardson MP, Michael Schofield, Sue Slipman, Catherine Scorer, MIND's Tony Smythe, humanist David Tribe, John Tuchfeld and Ben Whitaker, a signatory to Charter 88 who now helps allocate the money distributed by the Gulbenkian Foundation.

Yet it would be wrong to assume that these people actively promoted the activities of PIE and PAL. They certainly defended their "civil rights," and promoted homosexuality, but my conclusion, after looking at the records of NCCL at its offices and elsewhere, is that Nettie Pollard and the NCCL Gay Rights Sub-Committee gained lives of their own, and that the officers and EC of NCCL itself lacked the will to contain them.

On the sub-committee, some people approved of paedophilia as such, and others who did not were still prepared to serve alongside known paedophiles. The sub-committee contained at various times PIE's Peter Bremner (alias Roger Nash), Michael Burbidge, Anna Coote, Adrian Fulford, Bernard Greaves, Antony Grey, Keith Hose, Roland Jeffrey, Tom O'Carroll and Geoffrey Robertson (who has since become a QC). I doubt if at any time it would have mustered a majority prepared to condemn sexual contact between adults and children.

18
The invention of children's rights

We shall now look at the debate over what "age of consent" there should be, and whether there should be an age of consent at all.

The age of consent
Twenty-one is constantly referred to, wrongly, as "the age of consent" in a homosexual context. The word "consent" is only used in the 1956 Sexual Offences Act in connection with indecent assault. Under section 14, a girl under the age of sixteen cannot in law "give any consent" to prevent a sexual act being an assault. The expression derives from the standard defence against indecent assault and rape, that "the woman consented." If the woman is under the age of sixteen, the fact that she consented, if she did, is no defence in law.

The other place in the 1956 Act in which the word "consent" is used is in Section 15. In exactly the same way as a girl under the age of sixteen cannot give consent to prevent an act being an assault, neither can a boy under the age of sixteen. If he does give his consent, the mutual act then becomes, in most circumstances, one of gross indecency under Section 13, but this, being consensual, does not attract on indictment such a severe penalty as that for indecent assault. The offence of buggery under Section 12, which may be consensual, can however be punished by life imprisonment, or by ten years for attempted buggery.

Protection from corruption
The age of 21 in the 1967 Sexual Offences Act is not strictly an "age of consent," but a minimum age for consensual homosexual activity. The law is saying that if two men are going to corrupt each other with unlawful and immoral acts of buggery or gross indecency then such acts are not illegal so long as both men are 21 and the acts are strictly in private. But why are heterosexual acts permitted when the participants are only 16, whereas if the act is homosexual, both men must be 21?

It may be enough to say that one act is real sex and the other is "simulated," as psychologist Charles Socarides maintains, in order to point us the right direction. Sexual intercourse may well be immoral or unlawful according to the circumstances, but it is not of itself unnatural. Homosexual acts are always immoral, unlawful (in the strict sense of the word) and unnatural.

Janet Daley had this to say in The Times of 3rd December 1991:

> Throughout childhood and adolescence, girls are far ahead of boys in emotional maturity. ... They go on to reach puberty three to five years earlier than boys. Their capacity for accepting responsibility and for self-reliance comes to men only much later (sometimes never).
>
> But even without this extra helping of maturity and social skill, girls who submit to sex at 16 are not being put in the same psychological danger as boys who are drawn into homosexual relations. If a girl has sex at 16, she may or may not be too young to cope with the consequences; she may or not be exploited or traumatised, depending on her state of mind and the quality of the relationship. But one thing she will not be is initiated into a lifestyle which will separate her from the mainstream of society and preclude some of the major satisfactions of adult family life.
>
> She is not (and nor is a boy who commits a heterosexual act) being forced to make a fundamental decision which commits her to a particular circumscribed way of life: a commitment which in the present politicised climate of gay activism is likely to be irrevocable.

Recreational vs reproductive sex

The function of the sexual act is relevant to the difference between sexual intercourse and homosexual activity. One homosexual author puts it like this:

> Over the last 100 years for people of whatever sexual orientation, sexual expression has moved from the reproductive to the relationship to the recreational. We can all at different times see our sexual acts at differing points in this continuum. Perhaps gays are free to see, and at the same time are constrained to see, their sexuality in terms of recreational acts. So they have sex.[1]

Having said that "we can all" see sex in different ways, he admits that "gays" see sex in only one way, the recreational. Some homosexuals might vainly attempt "relationship-building" sex, but the reproductive element is never open to a homosexual sexual act.

The invention of childhood rights

The basis of sexual intercourse in marriage on the other hand remains reproductive, and confirmative of the marital union, a point which is underlined in every major world religion.

The argument frequently put up to challenge the reproductive function of sexual intercourse, that there are couples who are childless, is little more than a red herring. The human race reproduces itself by sexual intercourse, and MP David Wilshire, the sponsor of Clause 28, was forthright enough to say: "Homosexual activity is not open to the possibility of procreation, ergo, it is unnatural."[2]

Television campaigns for homosexual equality

Perhaps if the 1967 Sexual Offences Act had been discussed at a time when the age of majority had been 18, then 18 rather than 21 might now be the minimum age for homosexual activity. That is not to say that 21 is a bad minimum age of itself. The higher age for homosexual activity serves to protect younger men from sexual exploitation and in some cases from themselves. There seems too to be a "grey band" of a couple of years below any minimum age. An age of 16 for homosexual activity would mean in effect that prosecutions would rarely be brought for incidents involving boys over 14, and even an age of 18 would in effect give adult males access to boys of 16. Even the present Acts are not always rigorously enforced.

There has been some keen propaganda for a lowering of the minimum age on the media, particularly on BBC Television's "Eastenders." Expressions like "it's legal now" as the young man had his twenty-first birthday party, and "why can't we do this legally at sixteen?" were targeted towards softening up opinion in exactly the same way as the film "Victim" was used thirty years before.

The higher "homosexual age of consent" is seen as an injustice by homosexual activists and libertarians. In a climate where "rights" were accorded to people on account of their homosexual activity, or where homosexual activity was afforded the same status as sexual intercourse, then the same age would be agreed. Society has however given homosexual acts no status in law, and their participants are afforded no rights or for that matter, duties. Homosexual activity is partially legal on sufferance, and the arguments used by members of Parliament to arrive at this position were rehearsed in Chapter 2. The question of equalising "ages of consent" does not even arise, for that would imply an equality of status and of purpose between sexual intercourse and homosexual activity that in British Law, and also in natural law, simply does not exist.

Abolition of age of consent

Consideration of "rights" of homosexuals is the province of another chapter, but alongside the "age of consent," it leads into another area of discussion, namely the so-called "rights" of children. The thinking in the mainstream homosexual and left-libertarian movement has moved a stage further from arguing about specific ages, and now wants outright abolition of the concept that there is any "age" below which "consent" cannot in law be given.

How did "the gays" and the left come to agree that ages of consent should be abolished, and that "consent" on its own, at any age, should take its place? In the first few years of the Paedophile Information Exchange, discussion ranged over the age of children in which paedophiles were interested. It was agreed that some paedophiles were interested in pre-pubertal boys, whereas others preferred their children in puberty or adolescence. Some activists distinguished between the two by the descriptive nouns "paedophile" and "pederast" respectively. A member of the PIE executive revealed the group's early thinking on consent law in a homosexual paper:

> *adults should be prohibited under CIVIL law from having relationships with children under 4, and in the case of children over 3 and under 10 a similar civil injunction could also be made by those close to the child .... For children between 10 and 18 there should be no legal restriction in cases which did not involve proven physical/ psychological harm. Ten is the legal age of responsibility and if a child is deemed responsible for its criminal acts then it should be responsible for its own sex life.*[3]

What a weasel word is "relationships." This passage dates from 1978, but even at this time, PIE had revised its policy under its new London-based chairmen, Gay Liberation Front's Keith Hose and Tom O'Carroll, and had drawn personnel from PAL, which was founded by John Lloyd and Anthony Hughes of Peace News. Anthony Hughes was also a Gay Liberation Front man, and GLF and Peace News were very close.

The influence of "Peace News"

Gay Liberation Front, Gay Activists Alliance and Gay Liberation Front Information Service were until very recently based at Housman's bookshop in Caledonian Road, near Kings Cross, as indeed are the National Association of Teachers in Further and Higher Education (NATFHE) Gay Group and Greenpeace today. Housman's is a

Versions of the "clone" look, usually typified by moustache, short hair, leather clothing and misogynism. Above, San Francisco Police uniform, right, full leather kit, below, harness and boots.

Above: Homosexuals practising sadism and masochism (S&M or SM) paraded in the 1992 gay pride march and then set out their stall next to Gay Switchboard in Brockwell Park. Below: it is only in the last five or six years that stalls like that of SM gays, and this one selling bondage equipment have appeared openly at gay pride rallies. Right: Shops for such equipment have been going for rather longer. This advertisement appeared in Kennedy's Gay Guide to London in 1987.

The invention of childhood rights

subsidiary of the pacifist anti-nuclear group Peace News Trustees Ltd, which also owns Peace News itself. The whole stable operates out of the bookshop premises, with the exception of a typesetting subsidiary in Finsbury Park, used also by NCCL to print its journals. Peace News had its origin in the pacifist movement of the 1930s, with luminaries such as Arthur Wragg, Dick Sheppard, the renowned homosexual Laurence Housman, Donald, now Lord, Soper and the Mumfords. By the mid seventies it had embraced every "alternative" idea and lifestyle going, and was firmly aligned with the libertarian left.

Articles in Peace News were against capitalism, "patriarchy," Christianity, - whenever a verse from the Bible appeared it was in a box labelled "advert" - sexual law, and the British presence in Northern Ireland. Peace News writers were in favour of the legalisation of cannabis, for solstice celebrations, communes, earth-mother religions, feminism, Buddhism, abortion, vegetarianism, animal liberation and alternative adventure playgrounds. The principal Peace News advocate of the latter was paedophile Roger Moody, a frequent contributor and a former co-editor.

There were Peace News campaigns to destroy laws forbidding criminal trespass, for inciting soldiers to desert and for blasphemy. At the time of the Gay News blasphemy trial, after reporting that a former secretary of the National Secular Society was convicted of sending an obscene article - the Gay News poem - through the post, Peace News offered the poem to its readers at 25p including postage.[4]

Peace News supports paedophile groups

Not surprisingly, many articles, letters and notices about homosexuality also appeared in Peace News. The progress of PAL and PIE were recorded and the organisations defended. Gay Teachers and Gay Workers groups were supported by articles, but the accent remained on youth. The glowing Peace News report on the Merseyside Gay Youth Group, which it was said exists for 16 to 19 year-olds, who "have one thing in common - they are gay and proud of it"[5] turns out to be written by one Steve Smith, which curiously enough was the name of the last chairman of PIE

Again, two of the recent editorial collective of Peace News, Miss Kathy Challis and Miss Elizabeth Holtom, the latter a Quaker and director of Peace News Ltd., contributed an article to "Betrayal of Youth." In it they ventured an opinion that would have been viewed with astonishment by Josephine Butler 100 years earlier:

Ages of consent are useless. They are completely unrealistic, and they don't give children protection from exploitation in any case.[6]

Sexual "rights" swopped round

The contribution of a number of activists involved variously with Peace News, Gay Liberation Front, Paedophile Action for Liberation, Icebreakers and Paedophile Information Exchange was to alter the terms of reference of paedophilia and so to bring it under the umbrella of the mainstream libertarian left. The GLF people in PAL saw PIE's early apologia - mere reduction of the age of consent, civil remedies available to parents and so on - as a form of "self-oppression." The same ends could be arrived at sooner by ceasing all discussion of the "rights" of adults to have sex with children, and to start talking instead of the "rights" of children to have sex with adults. Roger Moody, now something of a paedophile intellectual, set out a political stratagem, the key to which was "a revolutionary perspective on social change." Roger Moody explains:

Specifically, this means we don't work to lower the age of consent, but to abolish it, and we don't argue that rights over kids be transferred from courts to parents, but that the only people who have the right to kid's rights - are the kids themselves.[7]

Paedophiles gain support from humanists

Keith Hose and Michael Burbidge had already jointly produced a PIE booklet for the Home Office Criminal Law Revision Committee late in 1975. The very first line stated: "This paper proposes the abolition of ages of consent, and the removal of consensual sexual activity at all ages from the criminal law."[8]

In the same year PIE secretary David Grove, a south-east London pensioner, produced the first of three broadsheets on "Childhood Rights." NCCL advertised in it. So did Housman's bookshop, an anarcho-left magazine titled "The Leveller" and a paper called "The Libertine" published by Arabella Melville and Colin Johnson. These days the pair co-write slimming and diet books.

One of the campaigns run in "Childhood Rights" was against corporal punishment in schools, and issue number 3 printed some letters of support. Alongside seasoned paedophilia advocates like Dutch Senator Edward Brongersma, psychiatrist Frits Bernard (also from Holland), and Father Michael Ingram of the Scottish Minorities

Group, appeared cheerful messages to PIE from Professor Freddie Ayer ("I very much welcome your cooperation") the late Baroness Wooton ("I am delighted to hear you are opening a campaign") and parliamentary gay rights advocate Jo Richardson MP ("Of course I'll support the campaign.")[9]

"Childhood Rights" was still promoting the image of the paedophile as a kind of beneficial avuncular figure, "particularly and unusually devoted," as if the idea that a teacher, for example, could be "devoted" to his tasks and to the children without touching them up had never occurred to its ageing editor. In considering the question "should the age of consent be abolished altogether," PIE now said: "Yes. Consent is important, age is not."[10]

Children's Rights made respectable

By the late seventies, under its chairman Tom O'Carroll, PIE activists had identified themselves with permissive and libertarian politics, and all their utterances were couched in the language of childhood rights. Sexuality had now become merely one of the things that paedophiles were concerned about, and sexuality could now be seen as just one aspect of the way in which children were exploited by patriarchal capitalism. Messrs Moody and O'Carroll made themselves appear radical-left and high-minded, claiming that "kids are oppressed by conventional schooling,"[11] writing about "those of us who work with the victims of schooling,"[12] and suggesting, in a review of a book about child labour in the third world, "The radical solution is to encourage and sponsor child trade unions, giving children workers' rights."[13]

Very soon, as we have seen, Campaign for Homosexual Equality chairman Michael Jarrett was identifying paedophiles as an oppressed group, and the CHE list of "demands" included the complete abolition of minimum ages for sexual activity. Children's "rights" had now been fully taken on board, made respectable even by the sensible-sounding Children's Legal Centre.[14] This last body tries to have it both ways. It claims to have no policy on age of consent, but its 1984 conference was addressed by Steve Lunniss of the London Gay Teenage Group, and the March issue of its magazine "Childright" carried an article by Steve Lunniss and two other LGTG members, David Joad and Camden lesbian activist Jane Skeates, calling for positive images of homosexuality in youth clubs. The Centre is militantly opposed to parents who teach their children a religious faith, and is linked by personnel to EPOCH, which is campaigning against the right of parents to smack children. It is chilling to find paedophiles and anti-smackers constantly allied in their desire to break the authority of parents over their children.

Joint Council for Gay Teenagers explains

The "Joint Council for Gay Teenagers" repeated anonymously in 1981 in "The Age Taboo" what Michael Burbidge told the Home Office Policy Advisory Committee on its behalf in 1980:

> The only humane and logical step would be to abolish the concept of a minimum age altogether for homosexuals of both sexes and to rely instead on the laws dealing with common assault where there is evidence that a sexual act was not consensual ... this view has already been put forward in general terms by the Sexual Law Reform Society and the National Council for Civil Liberties ... More recently a Joint Working Party (of the National Council for One Parent Families) on Pregnant Schoolgirls and Schoolgirl Mothers has recommended the repeal of the law relating to the heterosexual age of consent.[15]

The report "Pregnant at School" published by the National Council for One Parent Families in 1979 was sent to me in 1988. The report does indeed recommend that "the law relating to the Age of Consent should be repealed." The suspicion that this would be a good way to increase the size of their "client group" is deepened by a written comment from Deborah Derrick, in the NCOPF information office, that "Our policies in this area are primarily concerned with the creation of one-parent families."

NCCL supports abolition of age of consent

The National Council for Civil Liberties was rather erratic in taking up the abolition of the age of consent. In 1974 Anna Coote and Tees Gill published a book on "women's rights" illustrated by Posy Simmons, in which they complained about the age of consent.[16] NCCL also published a report in 1975, "Homosexuality and the Teaching Profession," in which was recommended the equalisation of "age of consent" for heterosexual and homosexual acts.[17] The Campaign for Homosexual Equality was still prepared at its Southampton conference in 1976 to recommend the retention of a minimum age for homosexual activity. The opening speech of that conference was given by the Member for Southampton Test.

A photograph of this local MP in Gay News, in fact in the very issue of Gay News into which editor Denis Lemon had run both an article

The invention of childhood rights

by a paedophile about his activities with children, and the blasphemously libelous poem that moved Mrs Whitehouse to bring her prosecution, identifies him as Bryan Gould, MP. As a result of his speech, PIE wrote to him to ask him to become an "Honorary Vice-President." A typescript of his refusal was printed in "Magpie."

Things were now moving quickly; in 1976, inevitably during Patricia Hewitt's reign as General Secretary, NCCL published a paper entitled "Sexual Offences; Evidence to the Criminal Law Revision Committee." NCCL's Nettie Pollard told me that this paper was written by Dr Michael Schofield, a trustee of NCCL's Cobden Trust, and also of the drugs agency Release, where PIE had its mailbox. Through a charity called the Lyndhurst Settlement, he had also supported Cobden and Release financially.

A sometime advisor to Brook Advisory Centres, Michael Schofield had made a favourable case for the subject of his book "Promiscuity," published the previous year. Indeed Dr Schofield referred to his book in the NCCL paper, which proposed the abolition of both laws against incest and of ages of consent as soon as public opinion allowed.[18] The latter proposal, that consensual sexual activity should be removed from the criminal law, is identical to the proposal to the same Committee of the Paedophile Information Exchange itself.

Dr Schofield opens by quoting "Anthony [sic] Grey of the Sexual Law Reform Society." Antony Grey was also "of" Albany Trust, which provided assistance to PIE, but Dr Schofield does not mention this. He quotes the Dutch Speijer Report: "homosexual experiences might benefit boys who later would live heterosexual lives," and states "that the children often take the initiative" in "the sexual relationship." Paedophiles are "as a rule ... gentle, fond of children and benevolent," and "childhood sexual experiences, willingly engaged in, with an adult result in no recognisable damage." Similar arguments were used by PIE in "Paedophilia, some questions and answers," and by Tom O'Carroll in "Paedophilia the Radical Case," quoting Professor Donald West. We should remember that it would not be seen as "damage" by a civil libertarian if a boy were to grow up homosexual.

Gay Teachers Group joins the fray

During the PIE trial in 1981, the Gay Teachers' Group, which has very close links with the London Gay Teenage Group, came out in favour of children's sexual rights in an article in "Gaynoise," a paper run by drag artist Julian Hows from his home in Railton Road in Herne Hill. Defending the publication of obscene paedophile contact material the teachers stated:

All people have a right to sexual self-expression. We believe too that all have a right to the information necessary for a joyful expression of their sexuality freed from false guilt.

Arguing that "we are all sexual from our earliest years," the article went on:

Children can be lovers of children. They can also be lovers of adults; the debate is should they be let be ... we accept that children do have their own sexuality and subject to the qualification of not harming others, they have the right to express that sexuality.[19]

Helpful suggestions from Director of "MIND"

The thinking behind the move away from advocacy of paedophilia and towards the promotion of children's rights was well expressed by a speaker at the famous PIE conference at the Conway Hall in 1977, no less indeed than Tony Smythe, a trustee of Albany Trust, soon to be an executive council member of NCCL, but then director of the National Association for Mental Health (MIND). MIND had earlier given a platform to Keith Hose at its own conference on "Sexual Minorities," where paedophile publications had been on sale,[20] and had listed PIE as one of the "organisations to write to" in its journal "Mind Out." According to the PIE journal "Magpie," Mr Smythe, who claims not to have agreed with the stated aims of PIE, was helpful enough to suggest that "he didn't think PIE was the ideal group to champion the cause of children's sexual rights." So who should take the initiative? Magpie Editor Warren Middleton supplied the answer:

It must come from enlightened progressives, scientific research bodies and professional pressure groups; adults whose arguments cannot be damaged or destroyed by an opposition able to claim that they're guided by self-interest. People with the courage to face the wrath of a nation poisoned by Christian attitudes to sex. But it must also come from youngsters themselves.[21]

A group of North American paedophiles freely admitted that:

It's more than a little ironic that it is the pro-gay pedo-advocates who are upfront about demanding legal equality between adults and minors ...[22]

More than a little indeed. According to a profile of the contributors to Betrayal of Youth, the former chairman of the Paedophile Information Exchange, Steve Smith, of whom the biographical notes say coyly

The invention of childhood rights

"now resides in Holland" - we saw what that meant in chapter 17 - "now hopes to become active in the Dutch crusade for children's rights."²³ Presumably he did just that, until even the Dutch lost patience.

Peter Tatchell wants children's rights

Peter Tatchell, who was allowed to appear on the Jimmy Young TV programme which considered the Cleveland child sex abuse scandal, and promptly advocated "rights" for children,²⁴ also contributed to Betrayal of Youth a chapter entitled "Questioning ages of majority and ages of consent." Mr Tatchell, "an avid supporter of socialism," tries to make the legal molestation of little children an ingredient of democracy:

> In a fully democratic and egalitarian society, there can be no question of adults usurping the rights of young people by keeping them in a state of ignorance, fear and guilt, or by resort to arbitrary and autocratic laws which deny them responsibility for decisions affecting their lives.²⁵

When I pressed him on this point at the Oxford Union it turned out that this applied to children of twelve and perhaps even as young as ten. Peter Tatchell is a leader of the media stunt group "Outrage" and is a mainstream "gay rights" Labour activist, as is Eric Presland, playwright and leading light in the Organisation for Lesbian and Gay Action (OLGA), which led the campaigning against Clause 28. Eric Presland also contributed to Betrayal of Youth. His article was a routine denunciation of the "power" that adult society has over children, prefaced by a first-person account of sexual activity with children. Mr Presland relates his first paedophile experience with a Asian boy of thirteen, and boasts of interfering with a little boy of six.

Children's rights an invention of paedophiles

Children would not dream up sexual rights on their own. The idea that children need "sexual rights" is simply an invention of those who want to use children for orgiastic satisfaction, and who have campaigned for just that for almost twenty years. We need not refer to "paedophiles" any more, but to the whole homosexual and civil liberties movement. Whenever children's rights are written about by those who belong to this movement, all sorts of "rights" are ostensibly argued for, but "sexual rights" are never far behind. Kate Millett writing in "The Age Taboo":

228   THE SEXUAL DEAD-END

> Children have virtually no rights guaranteed by law in our society and besides, they have no money which, in a money economy, is one of the most important sources of their oppression. Certainly, one of children's essential rights is to express themselves sexually, probably primarily with each other but with adults as well.[26]

The "liberation" of children can be put in socialist terms. Jamie Gough, a member of the Labour Campaign for Lesbian & Gay Rights, and another contributor to "The Age Taboo," wrote in the mainstream "gay" book "Pink Triangles:"

> The liberation of children is thus inseparable from the achievement of socialism. ... Children would not be tied, whether legally or socially, to their biological parents, and parents would no longer have the responsibility for the economic maintenance and social care of their children. Rather, this would be the responsibility of the whole community. This does not mean that children would be in nurseries twenty-four hours a day. Children could be integrated into communal households where they could develop stable relationships with a variety of adults, and where they could choose which adults they wanted to be with.[27]

Labour gays support teenage homosexuality & "child rights"

Members of the Labour Campaign for Lesbian & Gay Rights have supported both lowering or abolishing the homosexual minimum age and the existence of paedophile groups themselves. Bob Cant, who runs the "gay group" of NATFHE, and Peter Kent-Baguley have both written articles supporting teenage homosexual activity. Peter Kent-Baguley is features and reviews editor for "Lesbian and Gay Socialist," and is senior lecturer in youth and community work at Crewe and Alsager College of Higher Education. He was the author of an article in the National Youth Bureau magazine "Scene" in which he suggested that youth workers should help teenagers who "are questioning their sexuality" to see themselves as "gay" and should introduce homosexuality as a topic into youth club discussions.[28]

Bob Cant is also a member of Haringey Council's "Lesbian and Gay Unit" and is a key figure in Positive Images, based at the "Reading Matters" bookshop, which was set up in 1986 by Labour Campaign activists together with a rag-bag of the ultra left. Mr Cant's contribution to one "gay" book included a reference to "a campaign around child sexuality." "This campaign," wrote Bob Cant and his co-author, teacher Nigel Young, "strikes hard at bourgeois ideology and should be of concern to all socialists." They went on to ridicule childhood as a state of innocence, to write of "the struggle around childhood sexuality," and to describe PIE as a "sexual minority" whose "rights" were under attack.[29]

The author of the Labour Gay Rights Manifesto, Mike McNair, writing with Jamie Gough, demonstrates the link between feminist hatred of the family, children's rights, homosexuality and socialism in a book entitled "Gay Liberation in the Eighties":

> Children grow up under the power of their parents. As children, any behaviour which is obviously sexual in adult terms is repressed [sic] ... A socialist society would supersede the family household, ... gay people and children should have the right to live together. ... Children and young people should have the right to determine their own sexual lives... marriage should be disestablished ... Women need access to free contraception and abortion facilities; this applies just as much to young women as to "adults." ... Children .. should have the right to work. ... Children should be able to "divorce" their parents ... It follows from what we have already said that we favour the abolition of the age of consent.[30]

Child rights magazine relaunched at homosexual rally

The magazine "Minor Problems" took the same line. The PIE executive committee set it up in 1983 to look socialist. It ran for two years and was then briefly relaunched in 1986 at the London Gay Pride March in Lambeth. It tried to appear terribly concerned with children's problems, smoking for example.

Apart from Jonathan Walters and PIE EC member Leo Adamson, I know that Peter Bremner and Richard Travell of PIE, Jeff Vernon of Gay Youth and paedophiles Daniel Tsang and Roger Moody were also members of the editorial collective or of the "advisory board" of "Minor Problems." A letter circulated amongst the PIE executive makes no bones about its real purpose. Its last editor, Mick Licarpa, who has since died of AIDS, bemoans that changes under capitalism:

> would not bring any real individual freedoms, sexual or otherwise, to child or paedophile. Because, there will still be the present form of family control over the child, which would mean various amounts of control over an adult/child relationship outside the family circle coming from parents and guardians.[31]

There follows, in the letter, a list of full "rights" designed to mirror those of adults, indistinguishable from the proposals of

McNair & Gough and other members of the Labour Campaign for Gay Rights. Once again, the non-sexual rights begin the list, and the demands of the anti-smackers get a mention. According to Licarpa, the child:

> must be free to choose who he/she lives with, to be protected against any forms of physical punishment, in school, at home or elsewhere, to have the right to work as well as not to, the right to choose his/her own friends, whether they be child or adult, and many other rights too numerous to mention here, these are all rights Children must have as of right to their personal freedom, besides just the one right to have sexual and loving relationships with whomever he/she wishes, regardless of age or sex.[32]

"Minor Problems" welcomed in gay press

The first issue of "Minor Problems" gained glowing reviews in "Capital Gay," "Gay Community News" and "City Limits." Roger Moody, writing in the latter, concluded: "After all, most radicals give token recognition to children's sexuality. Few dare to discuss what we propose to let kids do with it."[33] But then Mr Moody, writing in "The Age Taboo," the North American paedophile book, observes:

> Within the Netherlands ... The "old style" Pedophile Workgroups campaign for abolition of age of consent laws and public acceptance of adult/child sex, while the newer youth freedom groups try to root their demands in the concept of children's liberation ... (in Britain) the ground ... would have to shift away from debate as to the "rights" of adults to love children who are not physiologically "their own" to the right of children to define their own sensual relationships with adults.[34]

Campaigns for paedophilia by the back door of "children's rights" show that the principle of a minimum age for both sexual intercourse and homosexual activity is in today's moral climate very necessary indeed. In the absence of any equality of purpose between the two, it would be inappropriate to establish an equality of "ages of consent." The hidden agenda behind "children's rights" needs constantly to be kept in mind whilst we investigate the parallel campaign, hinted at in some of the quotations above, of destabilising or abolishing the family.

19
Assault on the family

We, along with the women's movement, must fight for something more than reform. We must aim at the abolition of the family, so that the sexist, male supremacist system can no longer be nurtured there.[1]

It would be tempting to think that because the Gay Liberation Front allied itself from the start to revolutionary politics, that its anti-family stance was already established. However, there is an intrinsic rejection of the values of family and normal heterosexual marriage within "ordinary" homosexual life which the revolutionaries just happen to articulate a little better.

"Capitalist society must oppose homosexual rights"

What are homosexual activists saying about the family as an institution? In the classic gay revolutionary view, the family is seen as a tool whereby, in a capitalist society: "the ruling class (has) systematically and permanently oppressed lesbians and gays."[2]

John Molyneux, quoted above, goes on to argue that the reason for society as a whole rejecting homosexual behaviour, or as he sees it, "oppressing lesbians and gays," can not be laid at the door of "irrational prejudice and ignorance," as liberal commentators insist.

In this he is surely right. Irrational prejudice and ignorance is what this book hopes to dispel, but its conclusions are still going to be very different from those expressed in liberal opinion. The reason why stable, capitalist societies must oppose homosexual practice, according to Mr Molyneux:

> is the threat which homosexuality poses to that most hallowed of bourgeois institutions - the family.
>
> For capital the family performs the inestimable service of producing cheap privatised reproduction of the labour force, largely on the basis of the unpaid labour of women.

> In addition to its low cost, the privatisation of reproduction in the family has the advantage (for the system) of fragmenting the working class into tiny almost self-contained units with narrow conservative horizons which inhibit class consciousness and class solidarity.[3]

And finally:

> All workers are victims of the economic, legal and ideological bonds that pressure us to live in nuclear families. All workers are victims of the repressive sexual codes imposed by our rulers.
>
> Two very simple conclusions come out of this: all class conscious workers and socialists must fight for lesbian and gay rights, and all lesbians and gays should link the struggle for their own liberation to the struggle of the working class for socialism.[4]

Maybe he would say that. The great problem for the revolutionary left has always been to persuade "the workers" that they are actually oppressed. On the other hand, there are few signs that Western Governments have yet understood the importance of supporting the family as an institution.

Incompatibility between family and homosexuality

I find myself in agreement with John Molyneux's two conclusions. Paraphrased, firstly, there exists an incompatibility between the family and its values on the one hand, and homosexual lifestyles and their values on the other, and secondly, homosexual behaviour of its nature undermines a liberal capitalist society. A liberal democracy tends to appease groups within it who feel wronged, and so homosexual activists will demand more and more from it, and what they ask will steadily be given. This must mean that a liberal democracy, once it casts away objective morality, carries within it the seeds of its own destruction, a theme to which I shall return in later chapters.

Homosexual apologists usually fail to address the real argument when attempting to defend homosexuality against charges of being anti-social or anti-family, relying instead on the undisputed wish amongst all people, including homosexuals, to love and care for their own close family:

> "We're not anti-family. The average gay person has a family and wants to look after them whether children, sisters and brothers or parents ... I would never want to see gays cut off from their families."
> "I'm a lesbian and I have a daughter who has a normal family life ... we're not out to wreck anyone's families least of all our own."[5]

The end of the family proposed

But these completely miss the point. The evidence shows that society is not big enough for the institution of the normal family, "sexist" and "patriarchal" as it may be seen, and the wholesale acceptance of "gay" homosexuality. The incompatibility goes both ways. Accepting homosexual lifestyles to be as valid as heterosexual marriage challenges any system based on the normal family. Equally, normal decency and morality are deeply challenging to homosexuality. This is the reason for the attacks by homosexual activists on St Patrick's Cathedral, when consecrated Holy Communion wafers were trampled underfoot, for similar attacks on the Rev David Holloway's church in Newcastle, for the demonstrations in front of the Archbishop of Canterbury by the "Sisters of Perpetual Indulgence" and for the attacks by "Outrage" on St Michael's Belgravia, where sexual healing is part of the ministry. Homosexuality cannot live and let live. It must bring everything down to its own level. Labour politicians McNair and Gough write:

> Inequality and oppression start at home. ... Family life oppresses gay people in a myriad of ways. ... The extent of the gay scene, and the number of people living as gay is a sign that the family system is obsolescent. Gay sexual activity will not overthrow the family system. But the family's obsolescence means that it can be superseded [sic] and the growth of open gay sexuality is an advertisement that this is so.[6]

As the Gay Liberation Front put it in the Manifesto: "We are already outside the family and we have already, in part at least, rejected the "masculine" or "feminine" roles society has designed for us." Their attack on the family was not concealed at all:

> The oppression of gay people starts in the most basic unit of society, the family, consisting of the man in charge, a slave as his wife, and their children on whom they force themselves as the ideal models. ... The sexist culture gives straight men privileges which, like those of any privileged class, will not be surrendered without a struggle, so that all of us who are oppressed by this culture (women and gay people), must band together to fight it. The end of the sexist culture and of the family will benefit all women, and gay people. ... If this involves violence, it will not be we who initiate this, but those who attempt to stand in our way to freedom.[7]

Long-term influence of acid-dropping GLF

It is tempting to say that this is simply crackers, so let us look at the state of mind of those who wrote it. According to the Gay Liberation Front historian and author of "Coming Out," Aubrey Walter, the use of marijuana was "fairly general" in Gay Liberation Front, and when it came to questioning such things as gender identity, "a more powerful solvent was required, and this was found above all in LSD." It will come as no surprise to learn that communal experimentation with this dangerous hallucinogenic drug led to many GLF people "making and maintaining basic changes in their personalities and lifestyles." Group sex was one of these "basic changes." LSD was, according to Mr Walter, "one of the secret dimensions of GLF" and "an integral part of the GLF experience."[8]

None of this would be of any consequence if GLF had been an isolated cult with no influence. The reality is that the Gay Liberation Front Manifesto sold 10,000 copies, that direct splinter groups of GLF became variously the Icebreakers "counselling" service, "Gay Switchboard," the "Gay News" homosexual newspaper, and Paedophile Action for Liberation, and spawned groups like "Gay Activists Alliance" and "Gay Left" which spread the message into the mainstream left. The women in GLF split after the initial gender-freeing and manifesto-producing period, and formed the vanguard of the feminist lesbian "women's movement."[9] Individuals from GLF are now spread through the homosexual, libertarian-left and academic worlds. They have influenced the whole spectrum of the left through the National Council for Civil Liberties to the Labour Party. The LSD-shaped philosophies of GLF are now pretty well integrated into feminist and left-wing thought, not to say the whole liberal establishment.

Rather than the "gay hedonism" of the men, it is just this feminist-lesbian dimension which could have the more damaging long-term effects. The way in which both philosophies distrust normal family life may be what gay activist David Fernbach had in mind when he wrote that the women's liberation movement is "a much stronger force" than the male homosexual world when it comes to working to change what he describes as the "oppressive family structure."[10] The same writer also showed quite chillingly the direction in which the gay movement ought to move to abolish the traditional family and so end "oppression." It involves sex education:

The Gay Liberation Front attempted to combine the mass organisation of gay people with a struggle against the structures of the family that it correctly perceived as the basis for gay oppression. It failed, because the possibility for gay people, by definition outside the family, to participate in the struggle to transform it, is very limited. One of the few fields in which this is perhaps possible is sex education work directed at schools, etc., i.e., a cultural field that closely surrounds the family and aids in its reproduction, and the education group of Birmingham GLF has done some pioneering work here.[11]

A feminist plan to disparage the normal family

There is then an incompatibility between a system which approves overt "gay" homosexuality and one which celebrates normal family life, so that within feminist ideology family life is seen as "oppressive" and men are thought to "own" their wives and children. Men are believed to have invented the family on their own.[12] Clearly, the feminist movement, the "much stronger force," shares an interest with homosexuals in overturning the family as a "sexist" institution. If one were a feminist, one would always be looking out for ways to run down the family and to increase tensions between men, women, and their children. One would seize upon any issue that presented families in a bad light. One would never fail to say that families are not necessarily the best place for children to be brought up. One might even go so far as to say that normal heterosexual families are *never* the best place to bring up children. One would ensure that all one said was backed up by partisan academics, doctors, sociologists and psychologists. These latter in their turn would talk up the "problem" of families in order to justify the spending of money on their particular "research" project.

Next, one would set up a "charity" ostensibly to "help the victims" brought to light by the "research" and the victims would be used to make a public case for more and continuing "research." Protagonists would be very careful to employ the statistics thrown up by the research in a way that would disparage normal families. So committed would the charity workers be that if the statistics did not support them, they would bend them in order to substantiate their case against families. When caught out on the statistics, they would retreat into emphasising "the scale of the problem." The "charity" would create more jobs dependent on the continuation of "the problem," and its effect would be an increase in the scale of "the problem" as ordinary people began to be drawn into "copycat" behaviour, and as other "potential" victims came to identify more and more completely normal behaviour as threatening.

The plan put into action
In case this seems far fetched, let us consider the way in which all these principles have been employed in the matter of child sexual abuse. This issue presents simply the best chance the feminist lobby has ever had to denigrate families. It is probably small wonder that the activists in their enthusiasm went too far. Sexual abuse of children has been with us for a long time. All societies have known of the inadequate soul who feels sexually drawn to little children. Children have been consequently enjoined, by their parents, not to accept sweets, favours or invitations from "strangers."

Feminist and "gay" philosophy demands that children are most at risk from their own families. Sexual abuse of children within families is claimed by mainstream liberals to be a widespread practice, so much so that every child coming into hospital ought to be tested for any signs of it. This was what happened in Cleveland in 1987. Two partisan doctors, Marietta Higgs and Geoffrey Wyatt, found so much "sexual abuse" that the local Social Services department ran out of foster homes in which to rehome children on "place of safety" orders. Soon the paediatric ward was the only "place of safety" left, and it was eventually overrun with cases of "child sexual abuse."

Salem comes to the Borough
Parents rarely talk to one another when they are staying with their children on a paediatric ward. It must have taken some courage for a parent to ask another, perhaps in the "parents' kitchen," what their child was in for. "Oh," will have come the reply, "they say she been's sexually abused, but she hasn't, I know it." "That's funny," would reply the first parent, "but they say my little boy has too." And then asking around the ward, another forty parents were discovered in the same boat. These parents had been told on no account to discuss their child with other parents, on pain of losing them altogether, but now this spell was broken. The parents called their local MP, Stuart Bell, and he was drawn incredulously to the conclusion that a massive miscarriage of justice was being done.[13]

It was thanks to Mr Bell's persistence that the Cleveland Enquiry was set up, although under the chairmanship of liberal judge Butler-Schloss it whitewashed Higgs and Wyatt and smeared the police surgeon Dr Raine Roberts. Many parents were however able to start legal actions to have their children returned, and to bring charges of assault and actions for damages against the doctors and social workers involved. This is not the place to rehearse the dreadful effects of the allegations of child abuse on both parents and children. In many cases, it was assumed that the father was the only person who could have done what had never been done at all, and children were badgered into denouncing their fathers, and fathers browbeaten into admitting guilt on the fictional basis that the children would then be returned. The pied pipers of Social Services simply walked off with children whose parents had no immediate legal redress.

Doctors put philosophy before medicine

The doctors whose diagnoses had provided the medical "evidence," Marietta Higgs and Geoffrey Wyatt, had used the presence of "reflex anal dilation" - RAD - to determine the presence of past sexual abuse in the Cleveland children. One factor that was constantly overlooked during comment on the Cleveland scandal was that a diagnosis of sexual abuse based on such a diagnostic technique meant that every child diagnosed had been buggered. It is incomprehensible that non-partisan social workers could have allowed themselves to be convinced that over one hundred children had been buggered in a three-month period, whilst no other forms of sexual abuse had increased at all. Marietta Higgs now admits that in the whole of 1989, when she was not on hand, doctors in Cleveland only found 2 cases of child sexual abuse.[14] To Dr Higgs however, this means not that she was wrong, but that hundreds of cases of child sexual abuse have been missed.

Reflex Anal Dilation had been pioneered in the UK by Jayne Wynne and Christopher Hobbs of Leeds General Infirmary. As a diagnostic technique, it is controversial to say the least. Dr Raine Roberts, who opposed Higgs and Wyatt in Cleveland, criticised Wynne and Hobbs and RAD in "Archives of Disease in Childhood." Their subsequent reply was less concerned with medical evidence than with the exposition of a contentious - but to us now familiar - world-view:

> In the current controversy, it is interesting to find some paediatricians in alliance with the powerless and the abused - that is the child - and some police surgeons in alliance with the more traditional authorities in the form of the parents and the police. The New Statesman, (July 31, 1987) in a well researched analysis of the issues involved in the Cleveland controversy, underlines this point well.

It is as much these differences in philosophy that prevent us moving closer to Dr Robert's view, than merely the interpretation of the scientific material.[15]

Lustful lesbian supports feminist doctors

This is a scandalous admission, that in the minds of Jane Wynne and Christopher Hobbs, medical evidence is subservient to "philosophy." And what of the article in New Statesman, summoned up to bolster their "philosophy?" This was written by left-wing feminist Beatrix Campbell, and was a polemic attacking Stuart Bell for taking up the Cleveland parents' cases. "Bell has endorsed not the experience of the powerless, that is the children, but has invoked the rights of the police surgeon and of 'the parent.' These are the traditional authorities," she writes, in the phrases subsequently borrowed by Wynne and Hobbs.

The Leeds doctors built their case on the arguments, or more properly on the polemic, of a committed communist and lesbian activist, who is a contributor to "Marxism Today" and a journalist with the left-wing magazine "City Limits," who supports Haringey's "Positive Images," who left her husband because of her "desire for women" and whose lesbianism "is about lust."[16]

"Childline" statistics challenged

The same feminist philosophy was promptly incorporated into the BBC "Childline" initiative, fronted by Esther Rantzen of "That's Life." Childline starts from the conclusion that millions of children are being sexually abused by their own fathers and then tries to find evidence to fit. "About one in ten children - from that you can work out that 1.5 million children are suffering now," said Miss Rantzen's fellow presenter Sue Cook,[17] whilst according to Childline "it is the natural father, not the stepfather or live-in-lover, who is chiefly responsible for the abuse."[18]

Sue Cook and Childline are wrong on both counts. Dr Raine Roberts, whose experience is greater than that of Sue Cook, told a medical conference that stepfathers are five times more likely to abuse little girls than natural fathers.[19] Live in boyfriends have been responsible for even more appalling crimes against their mistresses' children. NSPCC statistics bear this out vividly, and show that proportionately very little abuse of any kind occurs in families where both natural parents are together. "Child abuse, or reports of child abuse, are much more likely to occur in alternative rather than traditional families," an NSPCC spokesman has admitted.

If we differentiate between those "traditional" families where the parents are married and those where they are not, the picture becomes even clearer. Not that the NSPCC actually do this, nor for that matter are there any centrally-held statistics at all. The cynic might say that this is because such statistics would show that the liberal establishment's view that marriage does not matter is hopelessly wrong. Zelda West-Meades of the Marriage Guidance Council, explains that it decided to change its name to "Relate" and now, failing to spot the difference in commitment involved, treats cohabiting couples, and even homosexual pairs, equally with married couples.[20] Even the Government, in the shape of the DHSS, when organising a national return of child abuse statistics, under its then Minister Edwina Currie, quite failed to appreciate the significance of marriage. So we must be grateful to an individual who wrote to Dr Digby Anderson of the Social Affairs Unit.

Abuse rare in traditional homes

The two-year survey this reader conducted of press reports and correspondence with child-care agencies and experts showed that in case after case of children who had been beaten, strangled, locked up, starved, tortured, thrown to their death, sexually abused, electrocuted, raped, the home "was anything but traditional," and tended to consist of a mother and a live-in boyfriend, or was torn by divorce, or consistent with some other alternative grouping. Such homes are in a minority, but account for the overwhelming majority of child abuse cases. For example, in homes where a single mother is living with an unrelated male, some 77% of abuse on children aged on average four occurs in such "families," which account for only 16% of homes. Digby Anderson concludes:

> *Not only is it untrue that the family in any traditional sense is to blame; it is precisely in those homes where traditional family norms are broken that abuse is disproportionately frequent and likely.*[21]

When Dr Anderson's reader consulted "the experts," most were keen to submerge the link in waffle. It was too "complicated" a subject, or abuse occurred "also" in traditional homes. "Many" non-traditional homes were "warm" and "loving." And yet as Dr Anderson points out, research "has shown unmarried couples to be less secure in their status as well as less committed. Marriage is a public and ceremonial commitment and sociologically it is highly plausible that married families will prove different from unmarried families."[22]

240   THE SEXUAL DEAD-END

Dishonest and cynical campaign exposed

For Digby Anderson, it is clear that feminists and socialists, and their media allies, used child sexual abuse as a campaign tool in their war against marriage and family life. In Cleveland, children from traditional decent working class families were picked on, torn from their families and saw their parents accused of abominable crimes. In the vast majority of cases, the families have been eventually exonerated and the now emotionally traumatised children have been returned. Marietta Higgs was banned from paediatric practice. And yet in comment columns in the press journalists have been "drawing the lesson" from Cleveland that there is a great deal of unreported child sexual abuse occurring in families, the opposite conclusion from the truth. As Digby Anderson writes:

> *Currently there is an absurd situation in which abuse is being used to discredit the traditional family and marriage at a time when such information as there is shows it to be related to non-traditional associations, especially single, young mothers with unrelated males.*[23]

The true abuse statistics

As for the number of children "being abused now," the BBC poll from which Sue Cook claimed "1 in 10" had actually asked 2,041 adults to recall if they had suffered any kind of abuse - physical, emotional, neglect, or sexual. 9% (1 in 11) had answered yes, of whom 3% (1 in 33) claimed to have been sexually abused. Of the 3%, nearly two-thirds (1 in 50) had defined sexual abuse as being "kissed or touched in a sexual way" and only one tenth had suffered sexual intercourse. One tenth of three per cent is one in 330, which is bad enough, but even 1 in 33 is not such good television as "1 in 10."[24]

The MORI poll conducted for Channel 4 had come up with similar results on a similar sample; seven people in a thousand (1 in 160) reported that they had been interfered with as a child. Even Childline's internal statistics have come under fire. Stuart Bell MP revealed that out of Childline's claimed 3,395 calls from children in its first month, only 19 cases were referred to the police, 76 to social services, and 31 to the NSPCC and to other agencies. Esther Rantzen says that this low referral rate is because very few children will give their names. The reason for this, according to a teacher of some 40 years' experience who worked as a volunteer with childline, is that most of the calls are hoaxes. Only two out of the hundreds of calls he received were genuine cases of abuse, and neither of them was sexual.[25]

EOC's Joanna Foster misleads Conservative women

As journalist Barbara Amiel has observed, "the use of misleading statistics to prove a point is a parlour game of feminists." The head of the "Equal Opportunities Commission" is Mrs Joanna Foster, and she spoke at the annual conference which Conservative Central Office organises for women executive "high-fliers." Mrs Foster tried to whip up a feeling of resentment amongst the "high-fliers" by denigrating those old-fashioned male executives who still believe that the majority of women "live in traditional groupings of two parents and two children." "Only 5% do," she told the women, according to Barbara Amiel "enjoying the slight intake of breath at this proof of the family's extinction."

What Joanna Foster had done was to speak only of traditional families consisting of a man with a non-employed wife and with exactly two children. Their wives are indeed 5% of women. But if we add in families with one child, with three or more children, or those intending to start such a family, or those who had such a family but the children have now become independent, these are nearly 66% of all households, and 80% of all people.[26] Douglas Hurd's appointee was simply misleading the women high fliers at a Conservative conference in order to marginalise traditional family life. Barbara Amiel ponders her motives:

> Later on, I wondered if the feminists have not simply taken their private psychological problems and projected them on to the rest of us.[27]

Feminist-based "abuse prevention"

Feminist activists have not failed to exploit every turn of child sexual abuse in order to disrupt families. According to an American study, child abuse prevention programmes, based on the idea that some touching is "good" and some "bad," grew out of a conference held in 1971 sponsored by the New York Radical Feminists. Many of the programmes overemphasise incest, some of them use a "child's bill of safety rights" which includes "the right to lie" and "the right to be rude," and most of the teaching tells children that parents may not always be trusted.

It has been demonstrated that such teaching does not enable the child to carry its learning into real-life situations, that in other areas of health education, improvement of knowledge has not changed behaviour, and that the child abuse programmes have never been tested, evaluated, or backed up by research.[28] This is what we would expect; the programmes are no more than feminist philosophy with any interest in the well-being of children faked.

There are some good child abuse prevention programmes about, and they are very necessary, but the most successful have managed to strip out the radical feminism, and stress the danger from strangers and those outside the family.

The information that adults whom they love and trust can do "bad touch" leaves children confused and suffering internal conflict, which can break out in irritability, anxiety, sadness, nightmares, disobedience, rudeness, and reluctance to be touched.[29] It can also lead the children to report "sexual abuse" where none has occurred.

One father reported that when he patted his child's bottom, the child told him not to touch his "private zone." Other parents have been told that "It's my body and no-one else is allowed to touch it" when they start to wash a five-year-old's hair. Such parents could be reported to a teacher, or even denounced anonymously to a social worker, and "in a day or two dad is out of the home with an allegation of sexual abuse that may destroy the family, damage the child, and, even if there is no finding of abuse ... generate terror and chaos for everyone in the family."[30]

Add a pinch of the macabre or sinister, like Satanism, mix it with the dramatic, say dawn raids accompanied by Police Officers, and it is not hard to visualise social workers being motivated into dragging screaming children of innocent parents from their homes in the early hours. As the parents in Cleveland, Rochdale and Orkney found, it then takes weeks to bring matters before a judge or sheriff to have children returned and social workers denounced as incompetent, partisan wreckers.

Gay Liberation Front revisited

Social workers constantly receive dangerous instruction based on the same feminist philosophy of Wynne and Hobbs, Higgs and Wyatt and lustful Beatrix Campbell. A book, "Child Sexual Abuse," written as a social workers' handbook by child psychiatrist Dr Danya Glaser and psychology lecturer Dr Stephen Frosch, claims that every man is a potential child abuser, that families where abuse takes place may only be "dramatising an aspect of family life inherent in all families." Did any recent research, any interviews or "field work" lead the authors to these distinctly odd conclusions? No. Their book was only theory, and Dr Frosch's previous published work, "The Politics of Psychoanalysis" and "The politics of Mental Health" showed that the

Assault on the family

presupposition of the book "Child Sexual Abuse" was that the family is an institution founded on patriarchy and the ownership of women and children by men. "There are elements in all families that are potentially abusive - that is something inherent in families themselves." In other words, Frosch & Glaser, Wynne & Hobbs, Higgs & Wyatt, and a whole host of trusted supporters in the media and the liberal establishment are little more than Gay Liberation Front revisited - early GLF feminist dogma dressed up to look like real science and real concern for children.

Children the battleground
It may be that Frosch and Glaser's contribution to the debate on child sexual abuse will have reduced the anti-family arguments to the logical absurdity they always were. By writing a book around little more than the slogan "all men are rapists," Frosch and Glaser could well have done everyone who cares for family life a service. I doubt it, however. Social workers complained after Cleveland, Rochdale and Orkney that they are criticised when they take children away, and criticised when they leave them to be murdered. That is true, so there should be a reason for it.

The reason must be that social workers are inclined to take the children of normal families, and to leave children in abnormal arrangements. They are determined that abuse is happening more in normal families than in households containing live-in boyfriends, so the children of the former are taken away wrongly to be emotionally scarred by their experience, and the children of the girlfriends of the latter are left to be beaten, molested or murdered.

Because social workers and child protection agencies have swallowed what is essentially the Gay Liberation Front argument, the children inevitably suffer. The concerted attack by feminists and homosexuals on normal family life proceeds apace, and the most vulnerable members of our society are at once the feminist left's sacrificial victims, and its potential prize.

20
Lesbianism

Because homosexuality is rarer amongst women than amongst men, and because male homosexuality, even before AIDS, has had a higher visibility than female homosexuality, it is easy to dismiss lesbianism as of lesser importance. Yet it is lesbianism which has in recent years built an anti-Christian philosophical, political and religious structure around itself, and this we shall investigate. Lesbian philosophy occupies much common ground with feminism, and much of its hatred of normal families, examined in our last chapter, can be traced back to a feminist-lesbian hatred of western Christianity and the Judeo-Christian tradition, mixed with rejection of the childbearing that is (usually) not part of lesbian life.

Male versus female homosexual promiscuity

Promiscuity occurs to a lesser extent amongst homosexual women than amongst homosexual men, with health advantages to the women. Homosexual psychologists are amongst those who have noted that a characteristic of the sexes is that men are more promiscuous than women. Research, even Kinsey's, has borne this out:

> The Kinsey findings about lesbianism were that lesbians followed the patterns of women in general, rather than those of homosexual men, in that fewer women had homosexual experiences than men, and those who did have them were less active than men.[1]

We should observe that lesbians, with their serial monogamy, are more promiscuous than a faithful heterosexual wife. Putting that on one side for the moment, Van Wyk & Geist found the same pattern as Kinsey in their 1984 analysis, and so did Dannecker & Reiche in 1977, as we saw in Chapter 14.

Even activist John Hart agrees, although he quite wrongly equates hetero- and homo-sexual male promiscuity:

the argument might be that the gay male couple follow a pattern common to all men when their lives are split between home, work, friendship, sex and love, and they have always been promiscuous. Gay women, like all women, are on the other hand home-centred, and want their sex and love and affection tied together in one person.[2]

Lesbian sexual effectiveness

Predatory masculine lesbians certainly exist, and we saw earlier that lesbian promiscuity is increasing, with greater emphasis on bizarre behaviour and sexual practices.[3] However, the predominant type of lesbian relationship has usually attempted to be more stable, aching for the role of woman as homemaker within ordinary marriage. Sex will take a lower priority than within a male homosexual pair, for similar reasons, and some lesbian relationships are characterised by an absence of sexual activity altogether. Lesbian philosophy, as American lesbian activist Deborah Goleman Wolf explains, still leans heavily on what is seen as the higher level of sexual arousal that can be achieved in homosexual contact:

> Indeed, according to Masters and Johnson, the most effective orgasmic technique is automanipulation, the second highest level of erotic intensity results from partner manipulation, and the third highest is orgasm during coitus, though there were those who argued that sexual effectiveness by itself would be rather lonely. However, to lesbians and to some feminists, these findings sustained their view that both sexual and emotional pleasure were most effectively experienced with someone who understood female arousal patterns as well as the need for nurturance and tenderness. The logical choice, based on one line of reasoning, was another female as a partner.[4]

Lesbian relationships are short-lived

Whether or not lesbian women are more skilled sexually, their relationships still tend to be short-lived. Deborah Wolf again:

> Though most women in the community say that they are looking for a long-term love relationship with a woman who is emotionally, intellectually, and sexually a partner in the fullest sense, in fact what is most typical of the lesbian community is "serial monogamy." A general pattern is being attracted to and getting to know a woman

and, since there is no fear of pregnancy, making love early in the development of the relationship - this is known as "making the move" - and gradually getting into a "primary relationship." Sometimes there is a tension for a woman when she wants to be in a close relationship with the woman to whom she is most attracted, and also wants the freedom to be open to other women.

However, as the emotional momentum increases, the two women can become a couple and are recognized as such by the community. They may move in together or they may simply appear socially together and let it be known that they are "with each other." Partly because of their own needs for the relationship to succeed and partly because of the community's definition of them as a couple, they see themselves in a viable relationship and work to keep it going.

As has been pointed out, the ideal relationship is defined as an egalitarian one in which each partner has emotional support from the other and yet each partner has the opportunity to develop her own fullest potential. In reality, most pair relationships do not reach this ideal, and usually, in time, the two women become emotionally involved with someone else, or they drift apart or formally break up.[5]

Primary and secondary relationships

In a discussion of monogamy in an issue of a periodical called "Lesbian Ethics," many women illustrate the generalisations that Deborah Wolf makes. One woman said "I am now with my fourth lover and know only two lesbians (one 78 and the other 83) who did mate [sic] for life. Yet each of them had several lovers before settling down for the long haul."[6] Another woman wrote: "I can even make a case for one night stands, on the adventure-seeking side of things ... [but] ... to be sexually active with many women in order to feel good about myself has not worked for me,"[7] whilst a third woman claimed to "belong to the group of us who can deeply, wholeheartedly commit ourselves emotionally to one ("primary") lover while on occasion sharing sexual affection with a friend or acquaintance just to be sexual, no strings attached."[8] One woman described the mechanics of a lesbian relationship breaking up:

> Once I was in a monogamous relationship and having a whole lot of painful relationship difficulties. Suddenly one week my lover believed in and was non-monogamous. We did not discuss why she

no longer wanted to be in a monogamous relationship with me. We instead discussed how monogamy was possession and could not be politically acceptable to her any longer. This we discussed at length over many painful teary conversations that were devastating to me ... We continued being lovers in a non-monogamous and not exactly primary way for over a year. Suddenly she had a new lover and pretty suddenly she and I weren't lovers any longer and also pretty suddenly she was in a monogamous relationship with her new lover.[9]

A lesbian ponders male homosexuality

Pam Mitchell, Editor of the book "Pink Triangles," a collection of essays under the sub-title "Radical Perspectives on Gay Liberation" is guilty of the same sort of politicisation of her emotions, although she makes some interesting observations along the way:

caring and sex are intertwined for women in a way that isn't as true for men ... lesbian feminists have been evolving definitions of the erotic that celebrate the connection. ... These definitions denounce sex without emotion and caring as "pornographic," as the opposite of erotic and a travesty.

But where does that leave gay men, who often participate in casual sex? ... There are aspects of gay male sexuality that I find alien and some that I consider politically reactionary. But on the other hand, I sometimes see myself and some of my sisters attaching a lot of emotional baggage to a physical act that doesn't necessarily belong there. Our expectations change and our dependencies crawl out of every corner the minute a "relationship" becomes sexual, dividing our sisters into "friends" and "lovers" as though this were a difference in quality rather than quantity; we give our power over to sex rather than deriving power from it. Ironically, while claiming that we're putting less stress on sex than men do and that we put it in its proper context, we sometimes seem to attach more importance to it and make it a symbol for *love rather than one - possibly fleeting - expression of it.*[10]

Lesbian antagonism to normal sex

Miss Mitchell's observations of male homosexual activities confirm what we have already seen, but she remains obsessed with the idea that sex is to do with power, and that it is sex which gives men power over women, rather than vice versa, as the anthropologist suggested in chapter 16. This is a fundamental plank of radical feminism, and writers such as Miss Mitchell fail to acknowledge that sex between husband and wife is a positive affirmation of love. Many lesbians have however had bad experiences of sex with men before turning homosexual, as in this example:

> "Men?" There was a very depressing experience of sexual intercourse when she was 18 and drunk. "I hated it; he didn't ask me what I wanted out of it. It was just a case of fucking me and that was it." She had to have an abortion; "I was very depressed before and afterwards."[11]

Those homosexual women who think along the same lines as Miss Mitchell may have been badly treated or even abused by men, or have never known a man of warmth and integrity, and the result is that they detest even the thought of sexual union between man and woman. This is by no means the only causative factor leading to lesbianism, but it is certainly borne out by research as *one* possible factor. Van Wyk and Geist make the point that adolescent males can seem boorish and inconsiderate both socially and sexually. Usually a young woman can learn to work out satisfactory social, romantic and even sexual relationships with young men, but if she has had concerns about her femininity, or has had sexual thoughts or fantasies about other women, this natural progression may be blocked;

> She might find, after trying intense heterosexual activity a few (or many) times and finding it less satisfying than she had hoped, that some females know more about what other females enjoy (and are more interested in providing it) than many males do. In any case, once a satisfying pattern is experienced, whether heterosexual or homosexual, it tends to be self-perpetuating, and other patterns tend to be neglected or to suffer from invidious comparison.[12]

Pam Mitchell certainly makes exactly these comparisons, and in the following passage she is expressing her revulsion from normal sexual intercourse rather than any desire not to witness buggery as such performed upon women:

> I remembered the bikini disco contest at a gay men's bar a few evenings earlier... When I'd heard about the contest I couldn't relate - to the competition, the "looks-ism," the impersonality of it. I think the response I had - a mixture of amused contempt and slightly curious, slightly annoyed envy - is a common lesbian response to the sexual exploits of our gay brothers. Let them have their fun, I

thought. *In a way I was glad to see them doing it to each other rather than to women."*[13]

Lesbian motherhood

It is far from unreasonable to detect inconsistency in the activities of lesbians who become pregnant. Some incredulity was expressed on one television programme when a young woman claimed to be a "black lesbian mother," and several participants demanded to know how this could be. They were told to mind their own business,[14] an inconsistent reaction from someone making a political point out of her private life.

On another talk programme, two lesbians were brought on and presented by the so-called "Lesbian and Gay Christian Movement" as a monogamous lesbian couple of twenty-five years standing. Viewers were invited to sympathise with this display of longevity, and to draw the conclusion that all "gay relationships" could be like this if only society was more tolerant. We have already disposed of those arguments, so there is no need to rehearse them here. Imagine the surprise of the real Christians in the studio audience when after the recording one of the women was greeted by her twelve-year-old daughter.[15]

Lesbian pregnancy

There are four main ways in which a woman in a lesbian relationship can become pregnant and not one of them brings a child into existence both naturally and as the expression of a loving permanent union between man and woman. She can sleep with a man because she likes to keep bisexual options open, she can sleep with a man simply in order to become pregnant, she can persuade a man to masturbate and then artificially inseminate herself, or she can make use of modern technology. The GLC thought that: "lesbian women have an equal right to artificial insemination if they request it."[16]

The idea is cultivated that it is quite simply the right of a woman, any and every woman, to have a child, and the child becomes as a result an extension of the woman alone, and in feminist thought, actually the property of the woman, or "part of" her body, to dispose of pre-natally if she wishes. We shall return to this.

Public perceptions led by scientists

Other lesbians are apparently hoping to clone themselves or other women into test-tube offspring,[17] and the technology for this has already been developed. Scientists can if they wish fertilise an egg with a man's sperm on a petri dish and then to replace the nucleus of the egg, which contains all its genetic information, with the nucleus from a cell, say from the lining of the mouth, from another person.[18] Only, as they see it, stuffy public perceptions are currently delaying further research into the application of this aspect of Huxley's Brave New World on human subjects.

The speed with which public opinion is pushed along by partisan scientists, doctors, journalists and politicians is illustrated by the fact that the 1985 dream of the GLC is in the 1990s a reality. Professor Colin Campbell of the Human Fertilisation and Embryology Authority has made it clear that any woman may present at a clinic for artificial insemination by donor (or vendor) and as long as the "counsellor" at the clinic just "takes into account" the well-being of a resultant child, then AID may be provided.[19]

There is no question that a "non-judgmental" clinic like British Pregnancy Advisory Service, praised by Conservative Health Minister Virginia Bottomley in the so-called "virgin births" scandal for the quality of its counselling, will have not the slightest problem with providing AID to a lesbian.[20] In fact BPAS soon dropped the service, not for any moral reason, but because it did not pay.

Extra-uterine procreation

The Gay Liberation Front in its Manifesto went further than this, maintaining that homosexuality was better than heterosexuality, because it "showed the way out of the gender trap," and a "gender-free" society would "represent a genuine qualitative leap forward in our social evolution." And eventually, when medical science had made it "possible for women to be completely liberated from their biology by means of the development of artificial wombs,"[21] human beings would be able to overcome their biological division into two sexes, and would be completely free and equal:

> When human procreation becomes extra-uterine within a gender-free society of full equality between females and males, it will be possible to reproduce ourselves as beings with no particularly determinant sex, beings who will transcend the male-female divide altogether. The jump out of the womb into the test-tube will be our next major biological leap forward as a species.[22]

The drug-crazed GLF often looks ridiculous in isolation, and yet only recently AID for lesbians was greeted with the same disdain. Researchers are working on the development of the artificial womb at the moment. A substantial section of bien-pensant society meanwhile attempts to achieve the same result without the test-tube, eliminating "sexist" attitudes amongst children. The Equal Opportunities Commission has stated itself to be in favour of state-run day nurseries precisely because it can thereby gain very early access to children. Its spokesman, Bronwen Cohen, believes that parents harm their children by transmitting sexist attitudes to them. She complained in an European Commission discussion document on behalf of the Equal Opportunities Commission that children were irredeemably "damaged" in this way by the time they start school:

> Sex stereotyping in preschool children has serious implications for subsequent educational attainment and for the personal development of an individual child. By the time they enter primary school, many children have already formed a clear view of the roles of men and women in society and about their own role in relation to other children.[23]

Lesbian pairs adopt male/female roles

The GLF and the EOC cannot abide the sexes having different roles, and "gay" supposedly "shows the way" in this matter. Nevertheless, one lesbian partner invariably gains dominance over the other. Within a lesbian pair there will usually be one woman adopting the masculine or dominant role, and the other a feminine or submissive role. This distresses activists:

> the choices available to her seem to be either a relationship with a younger or less forceful person - Liz has a very dominant personality - or a meeting of equals. She has tried both; the former she had little interest in because after a while the round of discos and parties was less important than Liz's clinical work. With an equal, Liz recognises that they compete, and rows develop as each tries to struggle for control. She simply doesn't have that much energy left at the end of a hard day's work to maintain such a situation. "I can't cope with stroppy relationships after a hard day at the hospital and I'm not much interested in having someone around with nothing but a pretty face." ... She is unsure about what her thirties may bring.[24]

Yet again the conclusion must be that human beings just cannot cast off the adoption and acting out of male/female roles, even in homosexual relationships. If expecting homosexual relationships to last is utopian, if heterosexual relationships depend on the acceptance of male/female roles, if homosexual couples should reject masculine/

feminine roles, and if these roles are going to be adopted anyway, perhaps poor Liz would be happier if she forgot about lesbianism, and tried to work through what is blocking her development to heterosexuality.

A large turnover in living arrangements

Most lesbian writers seem to view the breaking up of lesbian relationships after a short period as fairly inevitable. In the words of one of them, this leads to:

> a large turnover in living arrangements in the community. ... Aside from financial considerations, one reason for a fairly large turnover in living arrangements is that women who are lovers often live together. When they break up, one or both of them may want to move away from a place that has unhappy associations.[25]

Another pattern emerges amongst lesbians which runs parallel to "serial monogamy" and this is the tendency of three or four lesbians to set up house or flat together.[26] Anyone who has known lesbian women living under such an arrangement will confirm that they are continually falling out and swapping partners; there is a cycle of confined promiscuity within the group. In one such group of three known to me, two girls were in a "primary" relationship, and as it happens their appearance was typically "lesbian," for each was slim, below average height, pretty in a small-featured way, and with hair cut short. Jeans were usually worn, skirts never, and the house was shared with four cats and a mongrel bitch. This last confirms activist Deborah Wolf's assertion that:

> It seems to be a pattern for lesbians without children to have an unusually high number of pets - cats, dogs, mice, birds - soft creatures who respond when a woman comes home, something to cuddle and talk to, particularly when other people are unavailable. This may be a widespread pattern with single urban-dwellers in general, but it is very prevalent in the lesbian community.[27]

There are of course many women who regard themselves as lesbian who bear absolutely no relation to this modern stereotype, and this is in any case not the sort of text that discloses "ten ways to spot one." One of the girls I describe was quite happy to have sexual encounters with men, whereas the other had occasional liaisons with the third girl, who was bisexual and had been her lover previously. The previous lover of the first girl was a typically nasty butch lesbian,

Above: lesbians from Hull on the 1992 gay pride march. Below: lesbian mothers took their children on the march and to the rally in Brockwell Park.

Sadism and masochism are growing amongst lesbians. Above, this stall selling bondage equipment is, like the Simon of Cyrene Sanctuary alongside, a recent addition to such rallies. Below left, trying on a harness. Below right, one emotionally scarred young woman towing another on a collar and dog lead.

Lesbianism

whose visit was dreaded because it would be accompanied by violence. In the end the three moved away, and one of them married the brother of one of the others.

Lesbianism an acquired pattern of behaviour

This story demonstrates homosexuality as an acquired pattern of behaviour. Lesbianism seems sometimes to be taken up after many years of heterosexuality, the underlying psychological hurts having remained quiescent for all that time. There are many male homosexuals who have never had sexual contact with a woman, but the equivalent seems not to be as true for lesbians. John Hart quotes two women who are or have been heterosexual. One says: "If I gave up Michael I would probably go gay."[28] and the other, a 37-year-old mother says she would "become gay" - "that means I would be seen openly as the partner of a woman," "if I had an intimate relationship with a woman in the future."[29] The lesbian literature indicates that few women claiming to be lesbian have not had sexual intercourse with a man and that some could easily return to heterosexuality. For example, an essay in "The Furies" which is a lesbian-feminist newspaper, makes a political point:

> The base of our ideological thought is: Sexism is the root of all other oppression, and Lesbian and women oppression will not end by smashing capitalism, racism, and imperialism. Lesbianism is not a matter of sexual preference, but rather one of political choice which every woman must make if she is to become woman-identified and thereby end male supremacy.[30]

Mrs Linda Bellos, the former Labour leader of Lambeth Borough Council, who has two children, now tells anyone who will listen that she is a lesbian, or a "Black Lesbian" in terms that make it quite clear that she is making a political point. Like Anne Matthews, the "lesbian" leader of Southwark Council, she is a "socialist feminist-lesbian" by choice.[31]

The editor of the activist book "Pink Triangles" stated: "Most lesbians were once practising heterosexuals, although practice didn't make it perfect."[32] This seems to refer more to women who have chosen lesbian activity other than to make a political statement, and might be seen as an indictment of contemporary manhood. Miss Mitchell appears to be telling us that these lesbians were in such an unsatisfactory relationship with a man that they were able to be seduced by a woman. Not for nothing it seems was the video

"A Different Story" subtitled "How to be a lesbian in 35 minutes."[33] Mrs. Bellos told a rally of gay activists that: "Most of us were heterosexuals,"[34] whilst the Gay Liberation Front sells a badge which claims: "Every woman can be a Lesbian!"[35] Not actually true, and we shall look at the psychology of a lesbian orientation in a moment.

Lesbian seduction

There is evidence that lesbianism may be acquired as a behaviour pattern through seduction. Just as in male homosexuality, a girl with emotional problems may be drawn into homosexual behaviour through involvement with a older woman, a teacher perhaps, who seems to provide the warmth and love that she is lacking at home.[36] Even when there is minimal predisposition, lesbian seduction can occur and can cause subsequent emotional problems that take a long time to heal.

I know of one case history: Amanda (as we shall call her) first knew Carol when the former was a sixth-former and the latter a young teacher. Mandy left school at seventeen and not long afterwards met Carol socially. They started to move in the same circle and one night Mandy had had so much to drink that Carol had to run her home. Actually she took Mandy back to her flat and in the morning Mandy was horrified to wake up in bed with a woman.

She has no recollection of the actual events of that night but she knew that "something happened," that she had been "interfered with." She imagined all sorts of things that might have taken place, and spent months thinking that she must be a lesbian, "a dyke," because she had slept with another woman. The story has a better ending than it might have had. Mandy is now married with children whilst she finds it hard to express normal affection towards women. And Carol is married too, after a brief flirtation with a homosexual behaviour pattern in which she took advantage of a naive young girl, and nearly destroyed her chance of a normal life.

The psychological origins of lesbianism

Homosexuality is a complex subject, with many different factors leading to the establishment of a homosexual lifestyle, but Christian healer Leanne Payne writes:

> *As a sexual neurosis, lesbian behaviour (except when manifested in an hysterical personality) is not nearly so complicated as male homosexual behaviour. Most that I have seen and worked with is*

rooted in a need for a mother's arms, a need that was never or only insufficiently met.[37]

Until the polarisation of the psychological debate that we investigated in chapter 13, this was only standard psychology. It is nevertheless confirmed by modern programmes of healing; it works, in other words. Anthony Storr wrote that lesbians usually exhibit "evidence of a deep sense of insecurity in general," together with "a failure to realise their own femininity." He observed a "stronger element of dependency" in lesbian attachments than is usually seen in heterosexual couples. The reason is:

The homosexual woman is generally looking for a mother as well as a sexual partner; and in many instances the mutual dependence of the couple upon each other is more important than the sexual satisfaction which each may obtain from the other. Indeed the intense jealousy which often springs up if one partner becomes involved with an outside companion seems more like the rivalry of children competing for a parent's attention than the result of damaged adult pride.[38]

Where a girl was deprived of her mother in infancy, Dr Storr explains that she clings to her partners, making demands upon them that an infant would make. These demands are not tolerated for any length of time, and even where cases are less extreme, we have an indication of why lesbian relationships are transient. Each of the pair may be seeking both a mother upon whom to depend and a feminine role model in the other, and each may feel some maternal instinct to the other, but these relationships are only "partially satisfactory."

It may be that abuse of some kind from a male in childhood drove the girl into lesbianism. Some argue that this can only be present or can only have such an effect in default of the strong emotional presence of a mother, and there may be something in that. In a curious way, those whose route into lesbianism was via abuse or denigration, or those who simply wish to emphasise their existence in a "women-only" environment, often pass through a process where they identify with the men whom they rightly or wrongly see as the aggressor. They "tend both to express contempt for men, and yet also to behave in some ways like the very sex they affect to despise."[39] We shall return to "identification with the aggressor" later.

If we regard heterosexual maturity as the ability to form a stable emotional and sexual relationship with an adult of the opposite sex, then the homosexual woman is denied the support that might be given to her by a man, and her lesbian partner cannot fulfil the function of an adult who can give as well as receive such love. The frustrations involved can boil over into hostility, and we see another reason why lesbian relationships are short-lived. It is all very sad, and yet there is evidence that passage into emotional adulthood is possible if the childhood deficiencies are made good. Denial that an emotional disorder exists obviously blocks the process, and even where the woman actively seeks healing, Leanne Payne writes that a lesbian "may or may not recognise why she is compulsively drawn toward women for the affection she craves. It is my experience that she usually does not."[40] Anthony Storr also has sympathy for lesbians, and this is not incompatible with wanting something better for them than their intrinsically second-best relationships:

> *those lesbians who protest that, for them, this kind of relationship is better than any possible intimacy with a man do not know what they are really missing. ... For women who for whatever reason have been unable to get married, a homosexual partnership may be a happier way of life than a frustrated loneliness; but this is not to say that it can ever be fully satisfying.*[41]

We have had a brief look at lesbian lifestyles and philosophy and at some of the psychology behind them. We shall now look more closely at the political philosophy of feminist lesbianism and at its religious expression.

21
Lesbian religion

Lesbian religion arises from its political philosophy of rejecting maleness in all its forms. This can be developed in strange ways. Nuns often take a saint's name with their vows, and some lesbians who see patriarchy everywhere also change their names, investing the change with a religious significance:

> The assumption of a new name reflects the desire of the woman to divest herself of every aspect of male domination. Since family names in our culture are derived from the father's line, many women who are feminists, whether or not they are lesbians, change their family names as a symbolic gesture of separation from a male-orientated social identification. Often women take the first name of their own mothers and incorporate it in a new last name. Thus one of the most articulate members of the early feminist group, Redstockings, was known as Kathie Sarachild. Jewish women sometimes use the Hebrew form of "daughter of" - thus Deborah Bat Ruth: Deborah, daughter of Ruth. In this way, they are acknowledging matrilineal descent as the legitimate line. This attitude was made clear in a letter to the editor of the San Francisco Chronicle, October 28, 1976:
>
> "There are many of us across the country who take seriously the connotation of 'son' or 'man' in our surnames and have chosen to modify or change them. My own case is an example. In 1974, I legally changed my name from P.E.Johnson to P.E.Lauradaughter. I view it as a declaration of independence - for myself - refusing to identify myself in the traditional patriarchal manner and terms. I am no one's 'son' and I don't know who John is anyway. I do know Laura, my mother, and I credit her with much of my strength to celebrate my woman-ness in a society where woman-hating is part of the basic fabric." P.E.Lauradaughter
>
> Other feminists take the name of the city in which they were born. Judy Chicago, for example, is a well-known feminist artist and

author, one of the guiding spirits behind Womanhouse in Los Angeles. Other women take names from nature, such as Sage, Dawnspirit, Amber. In doing so, they are reasserting their identification with the precivilization aspects of life.[1]

Lesbian language and clothing

Although we are trying to avoid stereotyping lesbian women, it is not always easily avoidable. One of the illustrations used for the "Wimmin" column in Private Eye depicted the "wimmin" with straggly hair and glasses and wearing loose chunky-knit pullovers, woolly hats and dungarees. "Wimmin" or "womyn" are, incidentally, only feminist ways of writing "women" without including the hated word "men." This can get silly; an article in the British pacifist journal "Peace News" was signed by "Theresa McWomynus."[2] But the clothing that Private Eye's cartoonist drew was uncannily accurate, if an account by lesbian feminist Deborah Wolf is to be believed:

> *Feminist and lesbian-feminist clothing is virtually indistinguishable except for subtle indications in dress or accoutrements. The dress for both groups begins with a body that is clean, healthy, unshaven, unbleached, and without makeup. Feminists may wear no underclothing at all, except possibly panties.*
>
> *Most women, unless they have uncomfortably large breasts, do not wear bras, which they say artificially distort and enhance the natural shape of the breast. The women who cultivate such a natural appearance are refusing to conform to the "degrading artifice" which the male-oriented culture dictates as appropriate, but which these women feel makes them into unwilling sex objects.*
>
> *The outer garments that the women wear tend to become almost a uniform of utilitarian clothing. The women feel that in their choice of clothing they are striking a blow against the consumerism of a capitalist society as well as levelling class distinctions that might exist in the community.*[3]

Lesbianism adopts Marxist philosophy

The political philosophy hints at what lesbianism intends for society. To quote Eisenstein:

> *Lesbianism is revolutionary because it challenges the basic organization of the family, the sexual division of labor, and the heterosexual world.*

The lesbian alternative challenges those dimensions of power which are sexually based. Two of the major positions that have been developed are: (1) that the ultimate goal of feminism is to collapse all sex-role stereotypes such that the normal sexual orientation is bi-sexual and that unless sexual relations with men can be entered on an equal footing, feminists at this time must be lesbians; and (2) that to be a true feminist one must be a lesbian and the only way to avoid oppression by men is to remove all women from contact with men through the creation of self-sufficient communities of lesbians.[4]

Lesbianism needs a golden age

The belief that there can exist "self-sufficient communities of lesbians" is bolstered by various feminist studies of mythical communities, of Amazons, or followers of Sappho on the isle of Lesbos. In discussing how a centre for lesbian women in San Francisco got its name, Deborah Wolf gives us a glimpse of something lying deeper than mere political utopianism:

The name, Demeter's Daughters, was chosen because the five women who made up the original collective had wanted a name that was mythical and that had connotations of a matriarchal place. The moon has always been identified as a symbol of women; to the Greeks and Romans the moon was governed by a goddess - Diana, Artemis, Cybele - and these connotations have remained in Western symbolism. The moon goddess has been identified, as well, with women's monthly cycles, and has a regenerative quality. As one of the founders described the process of naming the coffeehouse: "We were kicking around names and we wanted one that was mythic and represented women. Phyllis Chesler's book (Women and Madness) was lying on the table and we flipped through it and came to a passage about the moon:

"Artemis, the youngest of Demeter's daughters, returned to her mother's house. First, she had Demeter consecrate her to the moon, so that no matter how far she'd have to wander, she would never forget, never betray her origins. That done, Artemis quickly perfected the arts of hunting and riding and warfare, of plant healing and midwifery. Then, with the moon for a guide, she left to found a city - no, it was a tribe - no, it was a culture, the likes of which the world had never known. Every woman in it was a soldier and mother, tears were as common as physical bravery, marriage was scorned, rape unthinkable, and the love of young girls was praised in poems

written by even the most hardened veterans. Artemis herself had many female lovers, and many daughters, each of whom founded other Amazon cities in Africa, in South America and elsewhere in Asia.

"So we kept thinking of moon names, and of sisterhood, and finally I said: "What about Demeter's Daughters?" Everybody liked it and we also asked other women in the community and they all liked it, so that's what the name was."[5]

What to do with the male children?

Artemis seems to have been very busy. I wonder who fathered her children? And what happened to the sons she must have had? On this last question, feminism has an answer:

> Some women who are ideologically committed to separatism say that they will take the responsibility for raising a girl child, but will relinquish the care of a boy to an appropriate male adult to bring up. ...
>
> In practice, to my knowledge, few women actually turn over their male children to these men to bring up; however, they do make attempts to be sure that nonsexist men are frequently in contact with their children, perhaps as members of their communes. Jill Johnston, in a speech, reported that she had arranged for her twelve-year-old son to move to a collective of men who had developed a Men's Liberation group and were dedicated to working through incipient sexism in their own lives.
>
> The practice of keeping female children and turning males over to be raised elsewhere has precedent in how the Amazons were thought to live.[6]

As Deborah Wolf explains, some lesbian mothers have ideological problems with male offspring:

> Part of a mother's reluctance to raise a son seems to be based on a theory of innate dominance of the male, that any person with a penis is imbued from birth with a sense of his superiority over all females, no matter what his upbringing. A few women feel that if they had a son they would give him up, simply because they would not want to be intimidated by "the enemy" in their own homes.[7]

Most lesbian and feminist writers are so steeped in pantheistic mysticism that they wrongly see external manifestations, in their case the male member (with the Kiwai tribesmen it was semen), as the

Lesbian religion

essence of maleness, rather than the hormone testosterone and the Y chromosome.

Promotion of lesbian "family" reaction to unhappy childhood

Of course lesbians and their feminist and liberal travelling companions reject inherent roles in any case, and see growing up in a lesbian "family" as an advantage for their children. Much of this attitude stems from unhappy experiences in their own childhood:

> Many women report being raised by parents who felt it was wrong to show too much affection. The scars of these emotional dishonesties linger, and they are determined that their own children will not be so deprived. They do their best to show affection readily, to listen attentively to how their children feel, and to take these feelings into consideration in their actions. They want their daughters and sons to allow themselves to be tender and nurturing, strong and self-confident, without regard to their sex. They want their children to allow themselves the full range of emotion available to them - to be, in fact, the "first generation of human beings."[8]

There is absolutely no reason why such admirable qualities should not be present in an ordinary family. And it must be that seeing two (or more) women in their home one (or more) of whom is acting out a parody of the male role is an unsettling experience for a child. A strange letter which appeared in a thing called "Growing up Gay" illustrates this. It is written by "a young lesbian called Sky, who left home at 15 to come and work with the American organisation, Youth Liberation," and is extracted here from "Paedophilia and Public Morals:"

> Although my best friend called me a "lesbian" at age 9 when I tried to sit very close to her, I didn't consider myself a lesbian until I was 11. That year I moved in with my wild "liberal" mother, and I met some of her lesbian friends. I finally saw that women loving women were real, and not a myth.[9]

That child, with her fractured background, for we read that she moves *back in* with her mother at the age of 11, has had the seeds of sexual perversion sown frighteningly early. Broken homes can have the same effect on a child as overtly homosexual homes. With no man to model himself on, a male child is at a disadvantage, which may or may not be compensated for outside the home. A female child developing normally models herself on her mother, and gains her recognition of male behaviour from her father, who in turn affirms her in her femininity.

Fathers who desert their families as well as men who seduce their lover's daughters bear an awesome responsibility. Van Wyk and Geist showed that sexual contact between a preadolescent girl and an adult male is likely to result in the girl choosing female sexual partners. This was found to be particularly so when the man was known to or close to the girl.[10]

Returning to the female child in a lesbian household, she sees male behaviour only outside the home. And given the circle in which the "lesbian mum" moves, roles of men and women outside the home are likely to be as perverted as those within. It should not be terribly surprising that most lesbian mothers when pressed told a "Daughters of Bilitis" meeting that they would prefer their sons not to be homosexual, because of the promiscuous and extremely unstable life that this involves, although many of the mothers said they would not mind if their daughters grew up lesbian.[11]

The summit of feminism

Lesbianism is seen in feminist philosophy as the summit of feminism.[12] Feminism promised to liberate women and in feminist thought a woman realises her true potential in lesbianism:

> *There is a kind of contamination theory implicit in the structuring of lesbian-feminist relationships when it is felt that the more contact one has with men, the more one's inner strength and resourcefulness are sapped, since men, even inadvertently, try to dominate any situation and to cannibalize the strength of women. Therefore, the lowest category of people is the sexist male. Next are heterosexual and bisexual women who associate with men. They are conceived as sometimes well intentioned, but not basically trustworthy because, it is believed, their real commitment is to men. Next are nonpolitical lesbians, with whom certain kinds of social activities are appropriate but with whom the deepest kind of bonding is not. Finally, politically oriented lesbian-feminists are seen as the most trustworthy and affirming, a vanguard of feminism in its purest form.*[13]

I am not making the following up, although I cannot find the reference. It is thought desirable for a lesbian not to have anything male or masculine around her, not a neutered tom-cat, not a book by a man, nothing male at all. That much is routine. One young woman who became a feminist lesbian rejected male influences even to the extent that she became a vegetarian, not on pseudo-religious grounds, not because she disliked meat, or could not bear to think of animals being killed for her, but because she could never be sure that the meat she was eating did not come from a male animal.

Whilst lesbianism is seen as the highest form of feminism, abortion is seen as the greatest experience of the feminist. In her book "Understanding Abortion," feminist Mary Pipes quotes women finding fulfilment ("making positive changes to their lifestyle") in abortion: "At the age of 18 I killed a baby girl, became a feminist and never trusted orthodox medicine again," said one of her sources.[14]

Abortion and lesbianism might have more in common than meets the eye. Abortion perverts woman from caring, loving and nurturing her children into rejecting and killing them, with the prostaglandin and R236 abortion, in which labour is brought on prematurely with the object of delivering a dead child, a perversion of childbirth itself. Lesbianism perverts woman from homemaking, childbearing and loving, which are all things that lesbians say they want, into a sterile, transient, serially-monogamous existence.

Woman as midwife, abortionist and healer

What has helped abortion remain a cornerstone of feminism is paradoxically the feminist belief that women are the true healers and that men have usurped this function.

One feminist book suggests that the reason why the Hippocratic Oath forbids a doctor to procure a miscarriage is that this was the province of midwives. The Hippocratic Oath by this argument merely contains a restrictive covenant.[15] Polly Toynbee reviewed a children's book called "Lots of Mommies," which was apparently purchased and installed in the children's section of a Lambeth library, where it sits on the shelves, awaiting its first date-stamp:

> It is about Emily, whose mother Jill is studying to be an electrician. The other mommies she lives with are Annie Jo, a carpenter, Vicki, driver of a school bus and Shadowoman, an osteopath and healer. Emily has her first day at school, and is asked about her family. "Emily thought about her family. Was there a word for what she had?"

(I can think of a few), puts in Polly Toynbee, and continues:

> "She thought about the way everyone in her family took care of her. 'I have lots of mommies,' she said. All the other children laugh at

her. But then she falls off the climbing frame at school, and all her mommies rush to the rescue. Jill the electrician, Vicki the bus driver, Annie Jo the carpenter, and Shadowoman the loony osteopath who heals her on the spot.[16]

Certainly this book has impeccable feminist credentials to set against the fact that no child wants to read it. The woman as healer applying her gifts to another female, the inclusion of what the 1988 Local Government Act calls a "pretended family relationship," all is there save the application of the gifts of Shadowoman to the procuring of someone's miscarriage.

The ancient role of the sorceress

Many readers will not be able to understand why women's rights have to encompass abortion. Surely, they will ask, do not feminists ignore the rights of the little women in the womb? The feminist answers no, for two reasons. Firstly, a child is not considered by the feminist to have a human existence until very late in its gestational period. This echoes mediaeval theology, in which the foetus was thought to be vegetable for three months, animal for three months and human only for the last trimester, and astrology, in which the state of the stars at birth is considered to impose a "fortune," and pre-natal existence is irrelevant. Feminist philosophy demands psychological denial of its adherents, in this case, an inability to look at an ultrasound screen and see a child. Secondly, one of the functions of witches or sorcerers - wisewomen - in the middle ages was indeed to supply potions to bring on a miscarriage.

The role of women in sorcery is certainly confirmed in history. One famous fortune-teller and suspected abortionist had catered to ladies of very high rank at the court of Louis XIV in the middle of the 17th century. Catherine Deshayes, known as "La Voisin" (the neighbour,) acted as a supplier of poisons, charms and black magical ceremonies. Investigations into her activities were carried out by the Police Commissioner of Paris:

> When her house was searched a curious chapel was discovered. Its walls were draped in black and behind the altar was a black curtain with a white cross embroidered on it. A mattress rested on the altar, covered by a black cloth, and on top of this were black candles. A furnace was found in which, apparently, the bodies of children sacrificed in the Black Mass had been destroyed.[17]

The mediaeval wisewoman

The offering of unbaptised children to Satan was an essential part of a Black Mass, or of similar magical ceremonies. The dramatic accusations of one Henry Boguet, writing in 1590, are said by feminist author Ann Oakley to contain "a germ of truth" about the role of the mediaeval wisewoman as abortionist and witch:

> Those midwives and wisewomen who are witches are in the habit of offering to Satan the little children which they deliver, and then killing them, before they have been baptised, by thrusting a large pin into their brains. There have been those who have confessed to having killed more than forty children in this way. They do worse; for they kill them while they are still in their mother's wombs.[18]

Although we know that there are many hundreds of covens of witches in Britain today, with the practice of witchcraft growing steadily, and although it is true that the killing of children "while they are still in their mother's wombs" is now institutionalised, it is still difficult to make a link between the two, and to say that the modern feminist approves both abortionist and witch. And yet, a view of the witch as a benign healer and of an unwanted pregnancy as a problem resolves the difficulty, as Ann Oakley explains:

> The mediaeval wisewoman in her role as lay healer and obstetrician almost certainly tried to help [sic] women carrying unwanted babies. Midwives in small-scale societies perform the same role today, and in our modern industrialised culture, it is still common for women to offer other women advice on how to bring about the miscarriage of an unwanted baby. The illegal backstreet abortionist, operating with her knitting needles or soap-and-water, can be seen as the direct descendant of the mediaeval midwife-witch.[19]

We saw that lesbianism is viewed in feminist thought as the crowning glory of feminism. The lesbian connection is more tenuous in the historical context of witchcraft, despite desperate attempts to link it. Modern lesbians do however regard the witches, the women healers, with veneration simply because of their following of pagan religion:

> The period of about 1300 - 1700 in Europe was looked upon by some as a time of martyrdom for women healers who were secret followers of the Mother cult and who were burned as witches by the church. Many of the estimated nine million women who were burned were said to be lesbians, and it was this difference from the norm which led to their being accused of witchcraft.[20]

Feminist religion

The spiritual life of many feminists has indeed gone back to the pre-Christian "old religions" of magic and idolatry, but in a modern form:

> As a body of knowledge and new practices have been developed by cultural feminists, particularly in the area of women's spirituality, many lesbians have evolved a more personalized awareness of a religious-spiritual identification with their conception of the Mother Goddess. They see the Mother Goddess as the true life force, rudely displaced by the male Godhead, whose worship has caused war, pestilence, inhumanity, and the rape of the planet. By getting in touch with the Mother Goddess, they reinforce their strength as women, as part of a history and a future in which both the force and the nurturing elements of women are the foundation. With this in mind, members of the community who worship the Mother Goddess have turned to witchcraft, or have developed rituals that encompass a kind of pantheism and draw strongly on the moon and the earth as symbols of the goddess and the intuition and sisterhood of all women.[21]

This regard for pantheism (God in everything) and polytheism (many Gods) is evident in the feminist following of eastern religions like Hinduism, with its female demons and goddesses, whilst the lunar cycles find an additional outlet in astrology, to which lesbian feminists seem to be as addicted as they are to the tarot. In the San Francisco lesbian "community" parties would be held for all women born under a certain star-sign.[22]

Patriarchal godhead scorned

There is certainly a loathing within feminist thought for Christianity with its male God and Redeemer and its elevation of the Virgin and Mother to be the apotheosis of womanhood. According to feminist cosmology:

> The patriarchal godhead, symbolic of the heterosexual, male-dominated cultural milieu, has been interpreted as a source of repression of natural instincts and dominance by the powerful over the oppressed. As the entire world of linear thinking and hierarchies has been reflected, so has the godhead that exemplifies this view. The male godhead, finally, is seen as anti life. [sic]
>
> Women are thought to be inherently deeply involved with the rhythms of the natural world. This involvement is personified by the concept of the Mother Goddess as a source of healing, intuitive

Lesbian religion

thinking, and the unity of all sentient beings. The contemporary concept of the Mother Goddess is perhaps not historically "correct," but it has intuitive components of the resurgence of the female principle, the deep strength and caring of women.

An awareness of whatever aspects of the concept of the Mother Goddess are appropriate to the individual woman provides a new source of resilience and insight about her "true" nature. This process can be intensified in a group context. Thus, group rituals have developed within the community which celebrate the Mother Goddess, while a resurgence of Wicca is part of this revived awareness of a strong female symbol.[23]

Worship of the mother earth goddess

The concept of "group rituals" will be well-known to anyone who has studied witchcraft, as will the belief that they are more effective on certain days of the year, for example the eves of May Day, All Saints and Midsummer, together with Lammas in August. A witches' celebration of one of these days is described thus, with an indication of how fast such practices are growing:

> There has been a burgeoning of activity and knowledge in the spiritual realm. There are now several all-women's covens in the Bay Area, and there has been an increase of serious practitioners learning about alternative forms of healing, and a decrease in dilettantism. One interesting development is the participation of older women, who feel they exemplify the wisdom of the crone aspect of the Mother Goddess.
>
> One major event in the spiritual community was a dawn ritual involving several covens in the area as well as many women who are concerned with spirituality but who do not belong to a coven. The ritual was held on November 1, 1979, a significant holiday in practitioners' calendars. It took place on Twin Peaks in San Francisco, its purpose was a reclaiming and purification of the city by women. Held in concord with similar rituals across the country and in Greece, it involved invocations, the sharing of gifts, chanting, anointing, and a reaffirmation of the spiritual aspects of women's power.[24]

British practitioners of Wicca

Even though an American feminist has been quoted here at some length, it would be wrong to see pantheistic spirituality as an exclusively American phenomenon. Routledge Kegan Paul have published in the UK a number of books on pantheistic feminist spirituality, qv Chapter 23, of which a recent example is written by a man. "The Horned God - feminism and men as wounding and healing" by John Rowan, explores, according to Peace News reviewer Chris Booth, ways in which men may be integrated or "healed" into feminism.

> Rowan's third channel of healing is through spirituality; specifically, that of the Great Goddess in the western witchcraft religion called WICCA. With its strong images of women, WICCA has been an important source of inspiration to many feminists, Starhawk being one. The male counterpart to the Goddess is the Horned God, a powerful, positive model of masculinity, sexual, untamed, but with his power always directed toward the service of life.[25]

It is difficult to see how the phallocentricism of the Horned God would get along with lesbian antipathy towards men and the male organ, unless the feminist practitioners of WICCA concentrate on the regenerative force (artificially inseminated, of course) rather than on the copulatory nature of the beast. However, the entire spiritual dimension is missing from the literature on the male homosexual life even though pantheism is a logical concomitant to the beliefs of feminism and homosexuality. I mean that sexual license is a central feature of witchcraft, but that the male writers prefer to adapt the atheistic beliefs of Marxism to homosexual practice.

Of course in many ways, the following of witchcraft or of atheism is a more honest approach for those trying to justify homosexual behaviour than is attempting to modify Christianity. The attempts by feminist "Christians" to attribute motherhood to God and to claim an androgynous nature for Jesus are surely less intellectually coherent than pantheism. Even though the pantheist starts from what Christians would regard as the wrong premise, acceptance of homosexual activity is then logical. The same applies to humanists; to deny the spiritual altogether is a wrong premise, but accepting homosexuality is a logical conclusion from the premise. Feminist and "gay" Christians, on the other hand, lurch from one logical inconsistency to another, and we shall now watch them try to fit homosexuality into the Christian tradition and fail.

22
The myth of a Christian homosexual theology

Is it possible to fit homosexual activity into Christianity, or is a combination of ignorance, sophistry and wishful thinking based on psychological denial engaged in a vast pretence? An indication of the answer should be contained within the Biblical texts. I shall quote from three versions of the Bible; the Authorised (AV), the Revised Standard (RSV) and the New International (NIV). I only choose between versions for euphony and clarity; they all agree in meaning. Where I disagree with those who try to build a homosexual theology, I invite the reader to look up the passages mentioned in whatever version comes to hand to see who is more faithful to scripture.

The Biblical texts

The modern liberal position is to say that where homosexual activity is mentioned in the Bible, that the Biblical injunctions do not actually refer to homosexual acts, or that they do, but that these are specific types of homosexual acts, or homosexual acts between heterosexuals, and that there were some obvious homosexual relationships in the Bible which God seems to have favoured.

There are some places in the Bible, so the argument runs, where certain practices are forbidden, but in none of these is a stable, loving union between homosexuals mentioned or condemned. The Bible was in any case written for a nomadic bronze age people, especially those parts of it we do not like. These people neither had the benefit of our enlightened ways of looking at things, nor did they understand the ways of God like we do today. I do not think that to be much of a parody of the liberal position.

Anyone who wishes to make homosexuality compatible with Christianity must start from the Word of God in the books that make up the Bible. The Bible must be read in the context of the whole, and it is possible to follow a thread about human sexuality through various specific passages that refer to this aspect of our existence.

Sodom and Gibeah: Gen 13.13, 19.1-13; Judges 19

The story of Sodom and Gomorrah is where most considerations of God's attitude to homosexuality start; it is not the first place in the Bible to indicate God's plan for His people's sexuality, but we shall come to that later. The story of Gibeah in Judges is similar. In the account of Sodom, two angels are sent by God to see if the men of Sodom are indeed "wicked, great sinners against the Lord" (Gen 13.13 RSV). Lot takes them under his roof, and feeds them. Later that night, the men of Sodom demand that the newcomers are brought out "that we may know them." (Gen 19.5 AV/RSV) Lot goes out and implores the men of Sodom, "do not act so wickedly." He has two daughters, who "have not known man; let me bring them out to you, and do to them as you please; only do nothing to these men, for they have come under the shelter of my roof." The men of Sodom, all of them, "to the last man" as the story puts it, tell Lot that he is only a visitor himself, and should not be judgmental. Things then start to turn really ugly, and the angels pull Lot indoors, slam the door, and strike the nearest men blind. Lot's family is evacuated, and Sodom and Gomorrah destroyed.

As long ago as 1955 Canon D.S. Bailey ventured, in "Homosexuality and the Western Christian Tradition," that the sin of Sodom was not homosexuality but violation of ancient laws of hospitality. He argued that to translate the Hebrew word "yada" literally "know" as "have sex with" is an erroneous assumption. A better interpretation of a word which in over 900 Old Testament occurrences means "have (heterosexual) intercourse" in only ten of them is "get acquainted with."[1] The men of Sodom were not sure, says Bailey, of the credentials of these visitors to a resident alien (Lot) and wanted to interrogate them. They went so far though as to violate the privacy of Lot's house. Bailey claimed passages in the rest of the Old Testament to support him: Isaiah, Jeremiah and Ezekiel do not mention homosexuality as one of the sins of Sodom and not until the letter of Jude does a hint of homosexuality surface.

This argument is flawed. Firstly Isaiah and Jeremiah hold Sodom and Gomorrah up only as examples of how God deals with those who depart from His law and Ezekiel, in a fair description of present-day San Francisco, says that the people of Sodom were "arrogant, overfed and unconcerned, they did not help the poor and needy," and then "They were haughty and did detestable things (AV abominations) before me. Therefore I did away with them" (Ez 16.49,50 NIV) Secondly the verb "yada" is used to mean "have sex with" in the

The myth of a Christian homosexual theology

Sodom story itself, when Lot offers his daughters who have "never known (yada) a man" to the men of Sodom. Even Robert Arthur, an American liberal pastor, says of Bailey's argument "When the same word is used twice in the same passage, we have no choice but to understand it in the same way."[2] Mr Arthur, however, still draws Canon Bailey's ultimate conclusion that routine homosexuality was not involved. For Robert Arthur, the sin has become not homosexuality but attempted gang rape. This is surely nit-picking and yet having said that, homosexual gang-rape of innocent passers-by has reportedly begun in Britain. It is arguably a logical progression of the effects of liberal attitudes.

The letter of Jude (vs.7) tells us that "Sodom and Gomorrah and the surrounding towns gave themselves up to sexual immorality and perversion." This New Testament observation cannot be ignored. Taken with Ezekiel it makes it clear that homosexual activity was a major part of the reason for the destruction of Sodom. Mr Arthur, drawing upon the Authorised Version of Jude, in which it is said that the sin of Sodom was "going after strange flesh," eventually announces that the men of Sodom did wrong only to want to bugger angels! The men of Sodom had no idea that Lot's visitors were angels, and the passage is universally agreed to refer to "unnatural lust" as the RSV puts it, in other words to homosexual practice.

The parallel story of Gibeah in Judges concerns a Levite and his concubine. Here an "old man" took them under his roof, but "some of the wicked men of the city surrounded the house. Pounding on the door they shouted to the old man who owned the house: 'Bring out the man who came to your house so we can have sex with him.'" (Judges 19.22 NIV; AV has "know him") Again women are offered to the men and the poor concubine is raped and left for dead. The adjectives used in the text for what the men proposed, "wicked, vile, disgraceful," leave no doubt that there is more than a breach of hospitality involved in the two stories and that the adjectives are applied because of something inherent in the homosexual act. Rape was against the Jewish Law. That Lot and the Levite considered heterosexual rape to be a lesser evil than enforced buggery may seem repugnant to us today, but it shows why the additional element of homosexuality invoked the adjectives used.

Leviticus: Lev 18.22; 20.13

The whole of Leviticus, as its name implies, concerns the priestly function of the Israelite nation and of its Levites, the priest tribe. It is a challenge to the people of God to obey His law and not to follow the practices of Egypt whence they escaped nor of Canaan whither they are headed. This is the context in which we read the two verses which refer to homosexual acts. The first says: "Thou shalt not lie with mankind, as with womankind; it is abomination." (Lev 18.22 AV) The second speaks of the penalty: as with many of the offences, it is death by stoning.

Norman Pittenger in "Time for Consent" takes the argument of context further. "The Leviticus passages in the Old Testament," he says, "are found in contexts which make it clear that the primary concern is with prohibitions of acts which would violate the so-called 'holiness code.'"[3] Robert Arthur makes the same point, that practices such as bestiality, child sacrifice, idolatry, weird haircutting, tattooing, sorcery and menstrual intercourse were all involved in the worship of the Canaanite god Molech and that homosexual activity must be seen in the same way.

Both verses are however set in chapters concerning a complete blueprint of sexual morality, and Chapter 19 broadens the injunction to encompass moral behaviour of all kinds, from paying the labourer at the end of his day's work, to loving the stranger "as yourself," and also lays down rules of culinary hygiene and indeed bans the practices of pantheistic magic. Within Chapter 18 itself, whilst the prohibition on homosexual acts is side-by-side with the other rules on sexuality mentioned by Dr Pittenger and Mr Arthur, these are outnumbered by the incest and adultery rules. To be specific, Lev 18 leads with a 5 verse reminder to the Israelites not to be like Egypt or Canaan. Verses 6 to 17 concern incest of various kinds, verse 19 abstinence during menstrual period, verses 18 and 20 adultery, verse 21 child sacrifice, verse 22 homosexuality and verse 23 bestiality. The remainder of the chapter, 24 - 30 exhorts the Israelites not to "follow any of the detestable customs" and not to "defile yourselves with them."

Leviticus chapter 20 concerns the punishments to be dealt to those who defile themselves with practices in the previous two chapters. I do not read that God will make an exception if instead of doing these things out of worship for Molech or Baal, we do them through following WICCA, or liberal humanism, or middle-class tolerance.

Finally, I do hope we can take it that Norman Pittenger and Robert Arthur are against child sacrifice, incest, adultery and bestiality, and if so, in spite of seemingly high-minded warnings against "biblical literalism," it seems to quote Norman Pittenger himself "preposterous

The myth of a Christian homosexual theology 273

to single out one set of texts, dealing with sexual contacts between males" and to say that these are the only verses in these chapters that God did *not* really mean.

The Pauline texts: Rom 1.24-27; 1 Cor 6.9,10; 1 Tim 1.9,10

In Romans 1, Paul is describing the contemporary idolatrous pagan Graeco-Roman world. Their Godlessness manifested itself in homosexual activity:

> *Therefore God gave them up in the lusts of their hearts to impurity, to the dishonouring of their bodies among themselves, because they exchanged the truth about God for a lie and worshipped and served the creature rather than the Creator, who is blessed for ever! Amen.*
>
> *For this reason God gave them up to dishonourable passions. Their women exchanged natural relations for unnatural, and the men likewise gave up natural relations with women and were consumed with passion for one another, men committing shameless acts with men and receiving in their own persons the due penalty for their error. (Rom 1.24-27 RSV)*

The arguments made are inevitably that Paul could not be referring to those whose homosexuality comes "naturally" to them, that he could not know what he meant by "natural" in any case, and that the involvement of idolatry - "worshipped ... the creature" - excludes Christian gays in loving relationships in particular. Neither can a God who has "given them up" possibly be the Christian God. We shall come to all that. In the other two texts, Paul lists those involved in certain sinful practices as being outside the kingdom, and in this follows the example of Jesus, who warned his hearers to beware of the day when men "will see the Son of Man coming in a cloud with power and great glory." It will come "like a snare," he says, to those whose hearts are "weighed down with dissipation" - some translations have "debauchery" - "drunkenness and cares of this life." (Luke 21.27,34 RSV) This is what St Paul says:

> *Do you not know that the wicked will not inherit the kingdom of God? Do not be deceived: neither the sexually immoral nor idolaters nor adulterers nor male prostitutes nor homosexual offenders nor thieves nor the greedy nor drunkards nor slanderers nor swindlers will inherit the kingdom of God. (1 Cor 6.9,10 NIV)*
>
> *We also know that the law is made not for the righteous but for law-breakers and rebels, the ungodly and sinful, the unholy and*

irreligious; for those who kill their fathers or mothers, for murderers, for adulterers and perverts, for slave traders and liars and perjurers - and for whatever else is contrary to the sound doctrine that conforms to the glorious gospel of the blessed God, which He entrusted to me. (1 Tim 1.9,10 NIV)

In 1 Corinthians, two Greek words are used: malakoi and arsenokoitai, in 1 Timothy only arsenokoitai appears. The Revised Standard Version lumps the two words together as "homosexuals," whilst the Jerusalem Bible uses the accurate if unpleasant terms "catamites' and "sodomites' respectively. The New International Version, quoted above, translates malakoi - literally "soft to the touch" - as "male prostitutes" and arsenokoitai - literally "male in bed" - as "homosexual offenders" and then as "perverts." It is impossible to ascribe to malakoi the meaning "people who will not stand up for what is right," as Robert Arthur does, nor is it possible, with Letha Scanzoni and Virginia Mollenkott in "Is the homosexual my neighbour" - to which the answer, by the way, is "yes, but not in the way you mean" - to say that Paul is referring only to prostitution, and to child prostitution in particular.

As the Rev Dr John Stott points out, arsenokoitai was used by the Greeks to refer to men who took the active role in homosexual activity. The word refers to mainstream homosexual activity. Again, Dr Stott explains that malakoi is a Greek slang term for males, and not necessarily boys, who took the passive role in buggery. It is analogous then to our own words "fairy" or "pansy" and refers to effeminate sexually-active homosexuals. The word "dogs" used by John in Revelation 22.15 in a list of people to be excluded from the New Jerusalem is usually regarded as similar slang usage.

What of the arguments that Paul did not understand natural law, homosexual inverts and monogamous homosexual relationships? The first two points we shall put on one side and come back to, but the monogamous homosexual is quite honestly a fiction. At best, as we saw earlier, serial monogamy is what is meant, and even within this, the homosexual psyche drives constant "affairs" or "cruising" which happen outside the relationship. Male homosexuals in addition really do worship the image, in the shape of handsome young men, and their organs, rather than God, and are thus guilty of idolatry as well. When a young man came up to a friend of mine and whispered: "I'm a gay Christian," he was doing two things, firstly soliciting and secondly saying that his homosexuality meant more to him than his Christianity.

The search for homosexual relationships in the Bible

These specific passages in Scripture are far from the end, or the beginning, of God's word on sexuality. Traditionalists will be looking to what Jesus had to say about love and marriage, and linking His words, and those of Paul, right back to Creation. We shall, as I said, come to that. The "gay rights" side will in contrast be searching for homosexual relationships in the Bible. John Boswell seems to claim a lesbian affair between Ruth and Naomi her mother-in-law that has no warrant in Scripture at all. If he is not claiming such a relationship, then I fail to see what point he is making when he writes:

> It would be wrong to think of the ideals of the Old Testament as exclusively heterosexual; indeed the famous line "Whither thou goest" is in fact addressed by one woman to another, [Ruth to Naomi] and there are many other ideals of non-heterosexual love in the Old Testament - David and Jonathan, for instance.[4]

The story of David and Jonathan is also interpreted in this extraordinary way by one Dr Lambert in the journal of the Conservative Group for Homosexual Equality:

> Much the most explicit reference in the Old Testament is the story of David and Jonathan: a homosexual relationship if ever there was one. "The soul of Jonathan was knit with the soul of David, and Jonathan loved him as his own soul" [1 Sam 18:1 AV]. We are given absolutely no evidence of divine displeasure, and the only person who objected was Saul, who reacted in just the same way as some modern parents and told his son "Do not I know that thou hast chosen the son of Jesse to thine own confusion, and unto the confusion of thy mother's nakedness. For as long as the son of Jesse liveth upon the ground, thou shalt not be established nor thy kingdom." [I Sam 20.30-31 AV] David was clearly bisexual, as subsequent events demonstrate, though his heterosexual adventures were not always entirely successful.[5]

No evidence that David was "bisexual"

This is spectacularly wrong! We are given in the texts not the slightest evidence of homosexuality, and it is far from clear to me, reading the story of David from his dispatching of Goliath in 1 Samuel 17 through to his lament for Saul and Jonathan in 2 Samuel 1, and his death in 1 Kings 2, that David was bisexual. One of the first acts of Saul after the pledge of David and Jonathan that Dr Lambert mentions is to offer

David his younger daughter in marriage, (David declined the elder) in order to set him a task to win her hand that Saul hopes will lead to David's death (1 Sam 18:25). David has to kill 100 Philistines, and sets about the task with such vigour that, much to Saul's annoyance, 200 Philistines are slain and Saul has to give Michal to David to be wed as promised.

Dr Lambert's description of David's adulterous and murderous affair with Bathsheba (2 Sam 11:12), and his lack of interest in Abishag the Shunammite girl provided by David's servants off their own bats to keep the old king "warm," (1 Kings 1:4) as "not entirely successful heterosexual adventures" are respectively a hopeless understatement and a bit of idle tittle-tattle.

Homosexuality of David and Jonathan invented

It is when lack of objective scholarship is combined with lack of understanding of how men can love each other without feeling homosexual inclinations, that bizarre conclusions can be drawn. It is surprising that Dr Lambert does not quote the end of the lament as do most other apologists for homosexuality:

> *I am distressed for thee, my brother Jonathan: very pleasant hast thou been unto me: thy love to me was wonderful, passing the love of women. (2 Sam 1.26 AV)*

It is not enough to invoke a nod and a wink and claim "a homosexual relationship if ever there was one," in the absence of actual Biblical support. Saul is also described as "lovely and pleasant" in the lament, notwithstanding trying consistently to spear David to various parts of the Royal Palace earlier in the story. Saul's hatred of David was actually nothing to do with the homosexual relationship that exists in the mind of Dr Lambert, but rather because Saul had reached a conclusion that David was trying to take the kingdom from him by plot. That is why Saul believes Jonathan will not inherit his kingdom, and why he goes to the lengths he does, attempting to blackmail Jonathan by invoking the name of his mother.

I have little trouble in imagining a love between two warriors so deep and trusting that it "passes the love of women," and causes them to call upon God as a witness "between my descendants and your descendants, for ever" (1 Sam 20.42 RSV), without any thought that a sexual dimension could exist. In other words, those writers who claim David and Jonathan, or Jesus and St. John (the subject of the Gay News poem) as pairs of homosexuals say more about themselves than about the biblical persons they discuss.

What St Paul meant by "nature"

I promised to return to a discussion of what St Paul meant by "nature" and to what Jesus understood to be the relationship between love and marriage.

Robert Arthur claims that "natural" is what is usually observed, and others have said that Paul could not have known about sexual inversion or about individuals with homosexual tendencies. On another tack, Norman Pittenger speaks for many apologists who claim that heterosexual people act naturally when they act heterosexually, and that homosexual people act naturally when they act homosexually. But this ignores modern knowledge of the roots of homosexual orientation and homosexual activity, and is in any case disingenuous. I have as yet failed to catch any gay rights advocate condemning those with broadly heterosexual feelings who go cottaging as a pastime.

Returning to inversion, we might have more dysfunctional upbringing and hence more individuals with homosexual tendencies today than St Paul observed in his day, but I find it difficult to believe that we invented the condition. As for the other argument, that the more people bugger each other, the more natural it becomes, that is not what St Paul means by "natural" in the context of Romans 1. When Paul uses the word "nature" he refers to the divine nature of God, and things that are against "nature" are against God. He is not "condemning people who are acting against their own truth" a claim drawing on humanism and situation ethics and made by Robin Green of the Campaign for Homosexual Equality,[6] but people who act against God's truth, the objective truth, in other words. This is abundantly clear from Romans 1.20:

> Ever since the creation of the world his invisible nature, namely, his eternal power and deity, has been clearly perceived in the things that have been made. (Rom 1.20 RSV)

When St Paul tells us in Romans 1 that God gave homosexuals up to their perversions, he is not immediately concerned with how they got the inclination in the first place. They are certainly part of an evil society that condones such debauchery, but it is their own behaviour, giving in to temptation and stepping outside God's plan, that requires God, who has allowed his creatures free will, in sadness to "give them up." As evangelist Gavin Reid puts it, God seems to be saying "If you do not want any relationship with me, I will keep right out of the way and allow you to experience the totality of your request."[7]

Paul goes on to write of the "due penalty" that men involved in homosexual activity will receive "in their own bodies." This again sounds unchristian, until we realise that it is not God who puts the penalty there, but the actions of the men themselves. Gavin Reid suggests an analogy with a pottery manufacturer who says that his products are not suitable for a dishwasher. If I overstress the potter's creation by putting it in a dishwasher, the "wrath" of the company is "revealed" in the cracks that occur in the pot. Gavin Reid continues:

> Paul's specific charge was that God did not design men and women to be promiscuous or homosexually active. Once such activities take place the physical, emotional (yes, and spiritual) tolerances are exceeded and obvious damage takes place.[8]

Both theologically and practically, as ex-Lesbian Jeanette Howard points out,[9] a homosexual orientation cannot be given to anyone at conception. God would not create someone homosexual and then proscribe homosexual activity. God is just. He does not take the Mickey.

Complementary nature of male and female

The Christian believes that what God has designed us for is "natural," and that any behaviour outside God's plan is "un-natural." This accords far better with the words of Jesus than any alternative explanation, and Dr John Stott is surely right to remind us that any consideration of sexuality does not begin in the Bible with the story of Sodom. The negative prohibitions on homosexual practices only make sense in the light of the positive teachings about human sexuality and heterosexual marriage, which are found at the beginning of Genesis, and which are part of God's created order.

In Genesis 1, God said: "Let us make man in our image, in our likeness." "So God created man in his own image, in the image of God he created him; male and female he created them." Genesis 2 goes further: God made Eve out of Adam, to be a reflection of him, a complement to him, and as John Stott says, "indeed a very part of himself." Heterosexual intercourse within marriage becomes then more than union, metaphysically it "is a kind of reunion." Two persons who were originally one, in the central and sexual act of marriage, in "the profound mystery of heterosexual intimacy," become one again:

> Heterosexual intercourse is much more than a union of bodies; it is a blending of complementary personalities through which, in the

midst of prevailing alienation, the rich created oneness of human being is experienced again. And the complementarity of male and female sexual organs is only a symbol at the physical level of a much deeper spiritual complementarity.[10]

This reunion is something so profound as to need a book of its own. It involves both the reproductive nature of the sexual act and its metaphysical significance. The bonding of man and woman in sexual intercourse is not just a physical romp; something spiritual is going on. They become one, and together achieve the full image of God. Jews believe that a man is only half of what he may be, and is made whole when he takes a wife. When St Paul advises his readers not to go with prostitutes, it is not because they will start a pregnancy or catch something if they do not wear a condom (they had been invented by then) but because "you become one flesh with her."

Jesus affirms heterosexual marriage

The Lesbian & Gay Christian Movement claims that Jesus said "nothing" about homosexuality. This illustrates how something may be true yet still deceitful, for God's created order of sexuality was affirmed by Jesus whenever He spoke of marriage. Repeating Genesis, Jesus indicates that an exclusive union between two individuals is what is intended, accompanied by a public ceremony - the leaving of parents - and that in the lifelong heterosexual partnership which follows, sex_al intercourse becomes a sign of the marriage covenant:

> But at the beginning of creation, God "made them male and female." "For this reason a man will leave his father and mother and be united to his wife, and the two will become one flesh." So they are no longer two, but one. Therefore what God has joined together, let man not separate. (Mark 10.6-9 NIV)

Heterosexual monogamy, which was instituted by God thousands of years before the birth of Christ, is said by Jesus Christ Himself to be just as relevant in His day, and if we take the words of Jesus seriously, it remains God's will getting on for two thousand years after that, for the reason that it is founded, not on a culture, but on a created order. Its validity is thus permanent and universal, and "there can be no 'liberation' from God's created norms; true liberation is found only in accepting them."[11] This does not put a prohibition on homosexual practice alone, for any and every sexual relationship which deviates from this created order distances us from God. As John Stott writes:

This includes polygamy and polyandry (which infringe the "one man - one woman" principle), clandestine unions (since these have involved no decisive leaving of parents), casual encounters and temporary liaisons, adultery and many divorces (which are incompatible with "cleaving" and with Jesus' prohibition "let man not separate"), and homosexual partnerships (which violate the statement that "a man" shall be joined to "his wife").[12]

It is perfectly clear that homosexual practice of any kind is prohibited by the Bible, and for that matter by two thousand years of Christian tradition. Both celebrate and affirm heterosexual monogamous marriage. Furthermore, we cannot find evidence of Biblical homosexual relationships unless we suspend common sense.

23
The Lesbian & Gay Christian Movement

The Bishop of Kingston, the Rt Rev Peter Selby, who is a leading Church of England liberal, writes in his book "BeLonging" (1991) that when a group of people say that their homosexuality is God-given and to be celebrated, then we should at once examine our reaction to them. If we accept what they are saying after our navel-searching then we are "Christian." If not, he describes us for some reason as "tribal." I believe it to be intellectually more courageous to examine their claims, to look at their works, and to see if these measure up to the Gospel.

What sort of people *are* asking the Christian Church to accept homosexual activity? Are they just ordinary Christians? Or are they part of the mainstream "gay" culture, with all that this implies? In a moment we shall find out.

Nothing theological to say

The homosexual campaign manual "Prejudice and Pride" devoted a whole chapter to the way in which, so it claimed, homosexuals were "oppressed" by the Church. The chapter turned on a few hard cases of individuals who had had to give up their clerical positions because of their latent homosexuality or their homosexual activity, and it invited the reader to sympathise with these cases in which intolerance and discrimination was argued to have been shown. One might have thought that the author, activist Robin Green, would address the Biblical position, but he had very little theologically to say at all. It was assumed that if the Church said anything contrary to the views of gay rights activists, this was just because of "homophobia."[1]

At the same time the position taken by some Christians that homosexual activity is in some way the "unforgivable sin" finds no warrant in Scripture. The Rev Dr John Scott puts this point well, arguing against a "holier-than-thou attitude of moral superiority" that heterosexual Christians can have about homosexual Christians, although he makes it clear that he does not recognise "homosexual" and "heterosexual" as being valid categories in which to put people:

> Being all of us sinners, we stand under the judgment of God and we are in urgent need of the grace of God. Besides, sexual sins are not the only sins, nor even necessarily the most sinful; pride and hypocrisy are surely worse.[2]

Pride, hypocrisy & idolatry within gay liberation

However, one of the reasons why the "gay liberation" mind-set is spiritually so damaging to its participants is that pride, hypocrisy and idolatry are invariably part of it. As John Stott argues, and most Christians agree, these sins of the spirit are greater and more insidious than simple sins of the flesh. They are still forgivable, of course.

The Christian truth of forgiveness needs to be made consistently in the Church in connection with homosexual activity. It is tempting to feel that although forgiveness and reconciliation work for everyone else, that although the cross and the precious blood take away the sins of the whole world, that *my* sins are so vast and unforgivable, that it won't work for me. It is a statement revealing pride mixed with unbelief, that my sins are the only ones that in their enormity cannot be forgiven. The theology of forgiveness is central.

Gay theology arises from "Just as I am"

Homosexual activists have built their theology not on a passage of Scripture, but on the first line of a hymn, which they have elevated to the level of scripture.

The hymn is "Just as I am," and the theology based upon it, as I understand it, is that God created me as a homosexual and that this is how he wants me to express my sexuality. I am to take pride in it (which is itself sinful) and offer it up to him for his glory. The leaders of the Lesbian & Gay Christian Movement are incomprehensibly "proud of our homosexual ancestors."

However, a shortsighted resignation to something viewed as an unchangeable spiritual state is not what Charlotte Elliott had in mind. Her middle verses speak of spiritual development, and again I invite the reader to look up the hymn. "Just as I am" says that God "bidst me come" to Him for "healing of the mind." The only reason "that thy Blood was shed for me," was to "welcome, pardon, cleanse, relieve." To be "thine, yea, thine alone," means subjecting my will to the will of God, who has "broken every barrier down," and we have demonstrated that neither homosexual activity, nor orientation, is part of God's plan for His people.

Guilt inherent in homosexual lifestyle

Another way in which the Church is thought to "oppress lesbians and gay men" is by making them feel guilty. However, in the same way as promiscuity is inherent in the homosexual lifestyle, so is guilt. It is not the church that makes people feel guilty, as some "gay" commentators maintain, but that, as St. Paul says, God's law is written on our hearts, in the form of our conscience. Active homosexuals, especially those trying to reconcile homosexual activity with Christianity, can never shake off their deep feeling of guilt, however calloused their conscience becomes.

A common statement from "gay Christians" is that "Jesus never condemned loving relationships, but he had a lot to say about love and forgiveness." This is sophistry. Jesus did not ask the woman caught in adultery if she was expressing a loving relationship. Now those condemning her were trying to catch Jesus out. The Jews were not allowed under the Roman occupation to stone the woman, so Jesus suggests that someone "without sin" cast the first stone. When they have all gone the mood changes. Jesus tells the woman that He will not condemn her, then tells her to "sin no more." (John 8.11 AV) (I heard a minister on the BBC "Morning Service" quote the story and omit that uncomfortable last half-verse. Somehow I knew he would.)

As for forgiveness, homosexual activists may not both have their cake and eat it. It is not only unrealistic but unscriptural to expect to be forgiven when you consider that you have done no wrong. "We have sinned," we say in the general confession, "in thought and word and deed." These are specific sins, not our general sinfulness as part of mankind. If some particular action, taking a company pen home, an act of adultery or homosexual activity, slandering the vicar, a spiteful thought, is not a sin, then we need not repent of it. No repentance, no possibility of forgiveness. How can it possibly be otherwise? The only valid course for the homosexual Christian is either a refusal to accept homosexual acts as sinful, or a recognition that one's homosexual acts are sinful *and* forgivable.

Liberals show false compassion

A similar argument is put forward by liberals, that the church is or should be based on forgiveness and compassion, and that these are lacking in a church which does not accept homosexuals "as people."

But it is a false compassion that lets the sinner keep on sinning, because it denies the joy of finding Christ's love in repentance. The commandment to "sin no more" is in the Gospel, so it is Good News. And as God's design for His creatures is realised away from the sphere of homosexual activity, then those who claim otherwise, leading their fellows astray, are false prophets.

One such is John Yates, who when Bishop of Gloucester was quoted in a newspaper article as saying: "a homosexual act of intercourse performed with love is preferable to a heterosexual one performed with lust," which is a rather curious piece of utilitarianism. If he is talking about sexual intercourse in the context of marriage, which is all he logically can be doing as a Christian minister, he seems to have a view of human sexuality in which a man is not allowed to have desire for his wife, or her for him, a view contrary to scripture. That homosexual activity of its nature blends lust with despair cannot have entered his mind. An act of buggery is not an act of love, it is an act of exploitation, a pathological act. I would go so far as to challenge the Bishop to say which of the homosexual practices revealed in chapter 8 could be an act of love. This argument deriving from a "good" intention of helping homosexuals into stable loving homosexual partnerships, in ignorance of the evidence that these are neither the will of God nor psychologically possible, has the effect of paving the pilgrim's road to hell by encouraging all homosexual activity.

The origins of the Gay Christian Movement

The Lesbian and Gay Christian Movement itself was started by an ordained deacon, the Rev Richard Kirker, and for many years had its headquarters (illegally) at St Botolph, Aldgate, in the City of London, where the Rev Malcolm Johnson is vicar. It was the sending round of lobby papers to the General Synod of the Church of England by the "Lesbian and Gay Christian Movement" and the Rev Tony Higton's exposure of that body as purveyors of pornography which led eventually to its being evicted from St Botolph's.

The briefing papers which the L&GCM prepared leant heavily on the presumption that if the Synod only accepted homosexual activity within a monogamous relationship, then homosexuals would give up their promiscuous lifestyles. "There is no reason to suppose that homosexuals are by nature any more promiscuous than heterosexuals," said L&GCM "Briefing 1," in stark opposition to the evidence. Their promiscuity is, as we saw in chapter 7, rooted in the depths of the homosexual personality and has nothing to do with the Church's or society's well-founded lack of recognition of homosexuality as morally equivalent to heterosexuality.

The conclusion that all homosexual activity is outside the will of God was indeed adopted by the General Synod of the Church of England, in 1987 in a resolution originally tabled by Tony Higton and after amendment containing only one weasel passage, where "homosexual genital acts" were said to "fall short of the ideal" rather than to be "sinful," as were adultery and fornication. They were nevertheless to be met by a similar call to repentance.

Bishops' report and statement on sexuality

In 1986, before the Church of England General Synod debate on homosexuality, the Bench of Bishops commissioned a report. The committee that considered the subject was chaired by leading feminist June Osborne and included the pro-homosexual Bishop of Gloucester, the Rt Rev Peter Coleman, and Malcolm Johnson. It reported back to the Bishops early in 1990. It was promptly leaked to Granada TV by a bishop that the report was rather uncritical of homosexual practice, and the Bench of Bishops, fearing controversy, have to date not released the "Osborne Report."

Instead, they sat down themselves with a copy of the Bible, and published, in 1991, their own booklet, "Issues in Human Sexuality." Their Chapter 2, on "Scripture and Human Sexuality" reads especially well. One possible weakness is that the only references are Biblical, so the Bishops can state that "damage to sexuality, sometimes irreversible, can be done very early in life," and provide no supporting evidence. However, they recognise the possibility of healing for the homosexual (and for us all), are clear that those who are homosexual are as valued by God as are heterosexual people, and state that "the clergy cannot claim the liberty to enter into sexually active homophile relationships,"[3] although they are a little hazy about whether the same discipline applies to the laity. Nevertheless, the Bishops' "statement" is a more prayerful and Godly offering than the Osborne "report" and was worth waiting for.

Homosexual ethic does not exist

The L&GCM argument presupposes a homosexual ethic equivalent to that applying to heterosexual marriage, but as homosexual theologian John Boswell admits, no such ethic exists. The homosexual world has to be "non-judgmental" and ethics of any sort, not to mention what St Paul calls "shame," cannot find a place within it. But perhaps the most disturbing aspect of the cynical L&GCM argument for acceptance of monogamous homosexual relationships is that its philosophy, gathered from that of its leaders, does not advocate monogamy in the first place. Malcolm Johnson has in a number of places reassured homosexuals that when he writes of "gay couples' he does not consider that way of life to be superior to community living or having a number of lovers.[4] Tony Higton, in a discussion with Richard Kirker, could get him to go no further than that the L&GCM "prefers' such a relationship.[5]

Bishop John Spong out of his depth

In November 1989 the Rt Rev John Spong, Episcopalian (Anglican) Bishop of Newark, New Jersey, contributed an article to the journal of the L&GCM, as did Monica Furlong, ex-"Moderator" of the Movement for the Ordination of Women. Monica Furlong wrote about American Episcopalian "Bishop" Barbara Harris and that woman's campaigning for homosexual rights. She found space to draw a parallel between "Women and gays, both groups silenced, marginalised, and insulted in a church deadened by patriarchal power."[6] Bishop Spong, like a warmed-up version of Gay Liberation Front, wrote "Peer relationships will replace the dominant-submissive, male-female models of the past. From a woman bishop to a polygamous marriage is an enormous stretch, but both are steps along the path to a full humanity ... ultimately for all people, self-definition will replace anyone else's definition of a human being and when it does a new day for all humanity will dawn."[7]

The readers of the L&GCM Journal will have liked that vision of a humanist new dawn, but in another part of the Journal, John Cullen of the so-called Institute of Christian Studies was puzzled by the Bishop's book, "Living in Sin?" John Spong claims to base his views on "new medical and scientific insights," but has tangibly failed to consider the evidence from psychology or the lack of evidence from genetics at all. He has concluded that homosexuality is both "a condition resulting from chemical or biological 'malfunction'" and "a normal variation serving a purpose in the evolutionary process that has not yet been identified." Even the sympathetic L&GCM reviewer concluded charitably that John Spong was "somewhat out of his depth."[8]

On December 16, 1989, Bishop Spong ordained as priest one Robert Williams, a man openly living with his gay lover James Skelly, who also took part in the service.[9] Any hopes of Bishop Spong that Mr Williams would be a model of "holiness, fidelity and monogamy"

The Lesbian & Gay Christian Movement

were soon dashed. Williams was put in charge of a special ministry to the lesbian and gay community and immediately claimed that monogamy was as crazy an idea as celibacy, and that Mother Teresa "would be better off if she got laid." Bishop Spong was widely ridiculed over his appointee and even he was left with no option but to sack Robert Williams from the Diocese, and ultimately to defrock him.[10]

Just to keep his liberal credentials alive, John Spong waded out of his depth again, trotting out the old chestnut that St Paul was a misogynist, attributing this imagined fault to equally imagined repressed homosexuality on the part of the apostle.

The desecration of St Patrick's Cathedral

On Sunday December 10, 1990, at the 10.15 am mass, there was a demonstration at St Patrick's Roman Catholic Cathedral in New York. Thousands of homosexuals and feminists gathered to voice their hatred of the Catholic Church, its teachings on homosexuality and abortion, and its Bishop, John O'Connor. They shook placards:

> Keep your rosaries off my ovaries. Eternal life to John O'Connor NOW! Keep your church out of my crotch. Know your scumbags. Curb your dogma. Papal Bull.

Dozens worked their way inside, and as the Cardinal's sermon began, they stood on the pews, screaming and waving their fists, throwing condoms in the air. One, taking Holy Communion, broke the consecrated host in half, and did what every satanist yearns to do, threw it to the floor and trampled on it. Others outside hoisted a large portrait of a naked Jesus "drawn in such a way as to appeal to the prurient interest of homosexual males," according to Bill Reel of the Daily News. Why did such a manifestation of evil take place? Patrick Buchanan explains:

> Cardinal O'Connor has done nothing but assert Catholic doctrine on homosexuality and abortion, i.e. both are intrinsically wrong. That doctrine is found in the Old and New Testaments, revered as revelation by all Christians. The Cardinal has no more authority to alter that teaching than does the Governor of New York; indeed, as Archbishop, he is under moral obligation to witness to the truth.
>
> Considering that no U.S. bishop has power to stop the sale of condoms, or to interfere with acts of homosexuality, or to shut

down even one of the human butcher shops where 1.5 million children are yearly done to death, what were the fanatics screaming about?

The answer is at hand. Paganism is a jealous devouring god that abides no other. Militant converts to this all-consuming heresy were witnessing to their faith. Unable to shut their ears and eyes to what Cardinal O'Connor has to say, they want him to shut up; they want the Catholic Church to shut up; they want all men of God to cease bearing witness against the devils that possess them.And, their frustration is all the greater because they know the church cannot do what they want it desperately to do: Bless a lifestyle that is carrying them away in numbers reminiscent of the Black Death.[11]

A similar sacrilege occurred in Britain in September 1991 at the parish church of Jesmond. ACT-UP and militant lesbians entered the church during Holy Communion and demonstrated against the stance of the vicar, the Rev David Holloway, on adoption by lesbians and homosexual males. St Michael's, Chester Square in London has been on the receiving end of such behaviour, (qv) which seems to be spreading. What would the Lesbian & Gay Christian Movement say to this?

Gay Christians promote pornography

Richard Kirker admitted to me that L&GCM is simply part of the mainstream homosexual movement. Literature available from L&GCM bears this out. It was astonishing, when I wanted to find out more about the GCM as it then was, in the early stages of this research to receive from the organisation a leaflet promoting Haringey's positive images campaign and describing parents as "bigots," another leaflet describing the events which led up to the murder of PC Blakelock as "the Broadwater Farm Rebellion," other leaflets on "gay rights' legislation, "Gay Pride" festivals, and fliers for various books advocating "sexual freedom," including some by homosexual publishers Pluto Press Ltd, and also including the paedophile book "Sexual Experience between men and boys."

When Tony Higton visited the L&GCM offices he was astounded to see gay pin-ups, some of the more obscene examples of Terrence Higgins Trust publications, Kennedy's "Gay Guide to London," which lists homosexual bars, clubs and discos, and the book "The Joy of Gay Sex."[12] "The Joy of Lesbian Sex" and "Lesbian Nuns," were also on sale.

L&GCM is affiliated[13] to the European Forum of Lesbian and Gay Christian Groups, the International Lesbian and Gay Association, the

The Lesbian & Gay Christian Movement   289

British Association for Counselling, the Organisation for Lesbian and Gay Action, the National Council for Civil Liberties, and COSPEC, qv.

Gay Christians promote pantheism

On another occasion I asked Richard Kirker to send me L&GCM's current thinking on the age of consent, and this turned out to be extraordinarily muddled. At various points in a wordy submission to the Criminal Law Revision Committee, GCM suggested abolishing the category of sexual offences, fixing the heterosexual age higher than the homosexual, setting the heterosexual age at 13, and setting them equally at 16. On this occasion L&GCM sent out a flier for the Campaign for Homosexual Equality book "Prejudice and Pride," which we have already met, and for a book edited by Linda Hurcombe called "Sex and God" subtitled "some varieties of women's religious experience."

This book is entirely feminist with contributions from such luminaries of the women's ordination movement as Una Kroll and Sara Maitland, and essays from "Starhawk" and "Jenjoy Silverbirch Strongbody Clevermind." [sic] The latter two are exponents of pantheistic witchcraft, the "old religion" of the earth-mother goddess, WICCA, as they call it, which is central to lesbianism. This religion, with its cycle of birth, death and rebirth, binds spirituality to this world only, within the reproductive cycle, and locks religion thereby into sexuality. It is precisely from this erroneous religion that the Israelites were set apart in the lands of Egypt and Canaan, and from which Mohammed later set the Arab peoples free. The whole point of what St Paul is saying in Romans 1 is a reminder to Christians that some of them once were followers of paganism, with all its God-less practices, including those of homosexuality, but that Christ could and did release them.

Of course it is strange for a body calling itself "Christian" to promote a book that attempts to turn the clock back to paganism, but there again, it is consistent with the L&GCM approach generally, which has a circle, one of the symbols of pantheism, as part of its logo, with the Greek "lambda" letter, signifying homosexuality, at the very centre, and the cross present only peripherally, and fractured.The symbol must be a metaphor for the whole approach of the Lesbian and Gay Christian Movement.

Gay Christians involved with Soviet "peace" front

Another strange thing about the L&GCM is its relationship with the pseudo-Christian Soviet-bloc front that is - or was - COSPEC.

Christian Organisations for Social, Political and Economic Change is a federation, as it describes itself, "of Christian groups committed to the struggle for a just, participatory and sustainable society." Any doubts that this involves a Marxist analysis are dispelled by the explanation: "This will of necessity involve a break with the existing social, political and economic order."[14] COSPEC claims that "a society which is based on gross inequalities between the rich and the poor and is maintained by the City, the Banks and the Transnationals ... has got to go root and branch." According to its manifesto, COSPEC was founded to campaign against "gross inequality in the national and international economic order" and to encourage "critical Christian support of and participation in the Labour movement."

COSPEC grant from World Council of Churches

COSPEC's initial funding in 1980 was apparently provided by "a generous donation grant from the World Council of Churches." During its first three years COSPEC started up a number of "projects," which included "Feminist Theology Project," "Peace Project," "Peace Theology Project" and "Theology of Sexuality."

The latter "project" is of course the justification of homosexual activity, and naturally "Peace" in the context meant unilateral nuclear disarmament, and eulogising about the Soviet Union. Member organisations, which COSPEC-inclined people are invited to join, included the notorious Soviet-controlled front organisation set up in Prague in 1958, Christian Peace Council. CPC is run by Canon Edward Charles, Scottish Episcopalian Bishop and exponent of "gay theology," Michael Hare-Duke, and Brian Cooper, who is also a member of the international CPC working committee. Other COSPEC organisations include Mr Cooper's own "Mainstream" group, an alliance of "Christian Feminist Groups," the Quaker Socialist Society, Christian CND, the Anglican Pacifist Fellowship, the Iona Community, whose Glasgow office acted as mailbox and office accommodation for the Scottish Minorities Group and the Paedophile Information Exchange in the 1970s, the Urban Theology Unit, One for Christian Renewal and the One World Movement. Christians for Socialism and the Christian Socialist Movement, the homosexual Canon Eric James' Christian Action, the Fellowship for Reconciliation, which advertises its meetings in Peace News and is based at Lambeth Mission, which also houses the Urban Ministry Project run by Michael Fielding, COSPEC's convener, complete the roll call, along with the intensely pro-gay hard-left Student Christian Movement.

The Lesbian & Gay Christian Movement 291

Most of the groups are members also of NACCAN, the National Centre for Christian Communities and Networks which expounds liberation theology, and the people behind them, with the addition of Paul Oestreicher, Donald Reeves of St James' Piccadilly - the New Age Church - and Bruce Kent, are almost without exception on the committee of European Nuclear Disarmament. END and Pax Christi personnel took part in the organisation of an international conference held in 1984 in Budapest.[15] The Gay Christian Movement itself is a "basic Christian community" listed by NACCAN, and appears alongside "End loans to South Africa" as a "Sympathetic Organisation" to COSPEC, being represented by extreme-left racist agitator and lesbian activist Savitri Hensman, a frequent contributor to Gay Christian publications.

Gay Christians support positive images education

As a member of the Haringey Lesbian and Gay Sub-Committee, Savi Hensman was involved in the promotion of "positive images' in the borough, and in the adoption of books like "Jenny lives with Eric and Martin" and "Young Gay and Proud." The latter was recommended for 13 year-olds, and contains language and advice that most parents would blanch to read themselves. Masturbation is "just making love with yourself," according to the authors, and so far as AIDS is concerned, "If you're having sex with another boy and neither of you has had sex before, then you don't have much to worry about."[16]

Nor is Miss Hensman going out on a limb. The Lesbian & Gay Christian Movement itself advocates "Jenny lives with Eric & Martin" and "Something to tell you" published by the London Gay Teenage Group, and the latter, together with the Gay Youth Movement, the Gay Teachers Group and Parents Enquiry, are listed as contact groups for pupils and teachers in an L&GCM "Statement on the Treatment of Homosexuality in Education." The "Statement" carries the information that:

> L&GCM fully supports those Education Authorities who have already made such [policy] resolutions to encourage teachers to provide "positive images' of homosexuality in the curriculum. From primary to secondary age, there are opportunities for providing accurate [sic] information.

Young children to be taught about homosexuality

The L&GCM statement provides an example of the kind of dishonesty inherent in such a curriculum: Homosexuality should be seen not as a "freak issue" nor as a problem. Nor should it be seen simply as a physical act, but as "part of a relationship between people." These arguments, no matter how much the reader may disagree with them, are standard gay-lib stuff. But then: "The need to hold and touch friends and family is a feeling that children can relate to at an early age." The idea that a child in a primary school should be taught that homosexual activity is acceptable because mummy or daddy give him a cuddle is surely nauseating to a particularly high degree.

The L&GCM attempts to justify the teaching of homosexuality in its education statement by a single sentence, namely that: "Christian education has always sought the fullest development of each individual, its aim being that all children should grow up to a greater awareness and acceptance of themselves and of others." Of course Christian education, like any proper education, wishes the child to develop and learn, but the claimed "aim" is not "Christian." The aim of Christian education is for every child to grow into a greater awareness and acceptance of God. L&GCM are describing the classic humanist man-centred position, to which of course they adhere.

New front organisation set up using AIDS

"Christian Action on AIDS" is the latest and most visible example of the way in which a front organisation can be set up to use AIDS to promote homosexuality, in this case pushing a "pro-gay" theological party line. The group grew out of the "AIDS Faith Alliance," whose credentials for leading a pro-homosexual response to AIDS were first class: Richard Kirker of L&GCM and Peter Harris of Quest, a pressure group of Roman Catholic homosexuals, set up AFA in 1985 with financial support from Terrence Higgins Trust. Declared homosexual Barnaby Miln, a General Synod member who made a speech against Tony Higton's 1987 motion in Synod was co-opted. Barnaby Miln and Richard Kirker went on a junket to San Francisco - where else? - in March 1986 where was held the National Episcopal Church Conference on AIDS, and the advice they received was to broaden their base immediately.

On their return, a London conference was promptly set up for July 1986 with the support, so it is claimed, of "British Church Leaders," and especially that of the Archbishops of Canterbury and York. Christian Action on AIDS was duly formed. The next eighteen months were concerned with making sure that British denominations were involved with AIDS and that churches had "caring and compassionate statements and guidelines for their members." No-one was allowed to condemn homosexual acts. The "Christian Council on AIDS" is now involved with the British Council of Churches, the World Council of Churches and the Anglican Consultative Council, and keeps in close contact with the World Health Organisation, whose ex-director, Jonathan Mann, participated in CAA's activities.

A CAA paper boasts that following Barnaby Miln's speech at General Synod, it is not surprising "that he is regularly invited to the World Council of Churches, to speak and discuss and encourage action at an international level." Not surprising in the least. What may be surprising is that he was commissioned by the then Archbishop of Canterbury to prepare the discussion papers on AIDS for the 1988 Lambeth Conference of Bishops. Cynics may, of course, not be surprised by that either.

The difficulties of a Christian AIDS hospice

This lack of objectivity has sadly been absorbed by some Christian Hospices working with people with AIDS. Of course they all do wonderful work caring for the sick out of Christian love, but it worries me that love may not be totally present in a hospice such as Mildmay which disowned its Chairman Eddy Stride when he condemned homosexual activity.

Mildmay went out of its way in the homosexual press to explain that its approach would be truly "non-judgmental," in response to an orchestrated campaign of hatred from homosexual activists. They do have a dilemma, of how to care for homosexual AIDS patients without tacitly or vocally condoning homosexual activity. On the one hand, Jesus healed the ten lepers even though only one would come back to thank Him. On the other, Jesus saw his role in forgiving sins as much as healing the sick, and sometimes did the two together and equated sin with sickness. He told us to preach the Gospel, and if we fail to do that, we fail to extend totally the love of Jesus to those we meet.

Richard Kirker of the L&GCM wrote at the time Mildmay was being persecuted that Christians were the last people who should care for people with AIDS.[17] That was of course an odd statement from someone who claims to be a Christian himself, but perhaps the evidence vindicates him. If so, it may be less because Christians will pollute the non-judgmental atmosphere in which homosexuals with AIDS must live, which is his point, than because this atmosphere seems to corrode objective Christian faith in the carers. It might just be that by facing up to his sin, and repenting of it and receiving God's forgiveness, that a homosexual with AIDS will be saved and thereby done a service.

The "non-judgmental" approach, as recommended by Christian Action on AIDS, is based on false theology and so is bound to fail, but saddest of all, by failing even to criticise homosexual practice it will condemn many more young men to death from AIDS. It will also deny, to young men and women who are homosexually oriented, God's healing grace from the homosexual condition. This is a tragedy, because, as we shall see, this potential for healing is very real indeed.

24
Homosexual marriages and emotional orphans

Michael Baughn, the Bishop of Chester, appeared on television after the General Synod vote in 1987.[1] In a saintly and sensible way he explained how the "Gay Christian Movement" had done a disservice to priests with homosexual tendencies by claiming them as part of their client group. He would not discipline anyone who kept such tendencies a matter between himself and his confessor, but someone who insisted that he be recognised as "a gay priest" left his bishop with no choice. This was not "hypocritical" as his interviewer tried to suggest, but the only possible response to being put in an impossible situation. The Bishop of Southwark put it like this:

> Most of us have always recognised that a clear distinction must be made between homosexual orientation and practice. Homosexual clergy are among those who have made a valuable contribution to the life of this diocese and I want them to know that their ministry will continue to be welcomed and upheld, but I shall not be able to support those whose way of life wilfully contradicts the clear intention of the General Synod's decision.[2]

Although this does not go so far as to offer healing, it is clear that open co-habitation in the sexual sense is not something which the Bishops as a body hold to be compatible with a priestly calling. I am sure that this applies equally to all believers, but the Bishops are, as we saw earlier, not yet ready to confirm this point. It is absolutely certain that they would not allow homosexual "marriages" which is a key demand of gay rights.

Homosexual "Holy Union"

It is exactly the solemnisation of homosexual partnerships that has been advocated by the Lesbian and Gay "Christian" Movement and which reaches dizzy heights of absurdity in the Rev Tony Crowe's church in Charlton, South London, and in the openly homosexual Metropolitan Community Church of America and the UK. Formerly known as "The Sodomy Church," this organisation has branches meeting in Bournemouth, in Balham, South London (at its own premises), and every Sunday evening at Bloomsbury Baptist Church in Shaftesbury Avenue. The latter venue, founded as a bastion of Biblical Christianity, has also hosted meetings of the L&GCM.

In "The two of us," Larry Uhrig of the Metropolitan Community Church in Washington DC puts forward his idea of "Holy Union." He places the "order of service" for this ceremony in an appendix, but it would honestly not be out of place in Private Eye's "Rocky Horror Alternative Service Book." He spends most of his book, and much of his time, so it appears, explaining to homosexual couples that they have not known each other long enough, or have too great a difference in age, or income, to make a successful life together or to warrant "Holy Union."

Mr Uhrig obviously wants the "Holy Unions" that do come off to last for a respectable period, so as not to make him look an utter fool, though the background to his warnings appears to be the tacit recognition that "Holy Union" is undertaken, as often as not, frivolously, or in the words of the prayer book, "wantonly, like brute beasts that hath no understanding."

On one occasion, for instance, he claims to have a good laugh at the expense of two men who have just interrupted their one-night stand of homosexual revelry to call him and ask if he can solemnise their relationship. It occurred to me that in all his strictures he was describing the reasons for the inevitable breakdown of homosexual relationships which arise from inherent psychological characteristics of the participants. This impression was reinforced by the numerous occasions where a homosexual man or woman was seeking "Holy Union" in order to tie down or "capture" another. Many of Larry Uhrig's "couples" are told to go away and live together first. Cohabitation will sort out whether they are "compatible" and "is also a time of marvellous discovery of each other."[3] Mr Uhrig himself writes that "I discovered only after many months with my spouse that I was responding to him with anger and hurt which were really directed at my first lover. ... three years were required to conclude the grieving and healing process."[4] As most homosexual "relationships" are staggering to a close within two years, the angers and hurts must simply pile up on top of each other.

Absurdity of gays copying wedding traditions

Larry Uhrig's use of the word "spouse" is so twee and ridiculous that if the reader kept a straight face above I confess that to be more than I did. The truth is that there is no euphonic word to describe the participants in such a liaison. Mr Uhrig talks of "gay couples" saying: "This is my other half," or "This is my spouse" for all the world as if they were a man and wife, and he promptly does it himself. He says that homosexual couples are today beginning to reject modelling their roles on heterosexual marriage, but he still maintains that "when challenged, a couple is often adamant that one is the husband and the other the wife."[5] This carries over into his "Holy Unions" and he is uncomfortable with it, but unable to do much, on pain of the new "sin" of being judgmental:

> In the early seventies, I observed many occasions in which lesbian and gay couples participated in Holy Unions which looked for all the world like traditional heterosexual marriages. The painstaking measures adopted by these couples even included such extremes as one of the male partners wearing a long white wedding gown and the other a tuxedo. These extravaganzas were attended by bridesmaids, flower girls, ring-bearers and the throwing of rice. It made no difference whether the couple was two men or two women, the outward symbols would be the same.

This is confirmed by a picture in Gay Times. At a homosexual weekend at a holiday camp in March 1991, two lesbians "got married." Sure enough, the photograph of them shows one in a dress, the other in a suit.[6] The same pattern was repeated at the "queer weddings" in Trafalgar Square later the same year. Even Larry Uhrig writes:

> I am always amazed at our inability to question these symbols. For example, the tradition of throwing rice originated as a fertility rite to express the hope that the couple would bear many children. This is, of course, grossly out of place in a gay union.[7]

Different sexual configurations suggested

The whole thing seems to be a gross, macabre parody of marriage, a dead end for humanity as a whole and for these individuals in particular. They are not even mandated to be sexually loyal to each other. They might agree to be, or might not, in these "Holy Unions."

Any combination is acceptable, as long as it is "successful," whatever that means in the context:

> It is true that couples occasionally share sexual experiences with a third person, or even with several others. Couples also have close intimate relationships with others. These may involve love, sex, and significant bonding, but they are not often long-term relationships.
>
> I have known people who have formed three-party bonding. My experience indicates that this is not in the long term a "successful configuration."[8]

These different "configurations" are surely what Malcolm Johnson had in mind when he wrote that "I feel we need today to re-think and re-examine *all* our relationships in their diversity and richness."[9] These two words "diversity" and "richness" carry the meaning that they are Good Things To Have, but we should bear in mind that they are just words, chosen for their purpose of putting a pleasant face on the unacceptable. Another supporter of L&GCM, Malcolm Macourt, has a vision of "a wide variety of life patterns" each of which is held "in equal esteem in society"[10] that owes more to the pages of Peace News than to those of the Bible. These Malcolms must be advocating sex as recreation, going even further than the argument usually advanced that sex is not just about procreation, but about relationships.

Which relationships may involve sex?

In heterosexual monogamous lifelong marriage, sex is indeed "about relationships" as much as it is about procreation. This is beautifully expressed in Genesis, and Biblical characters understood it. The father of Samuel says to Samuel's mother, when thought to be barren: "Am I not more to you than ten sons?" (1 Sam 1.8 RSV) Furthermore, sex is appropriate in that setting, and Scripture makes it quite clear that that is indeed the only setting in which sex is appropriate. In the relationship between a man and his son or daughter, or in the relationship between siblings, or for that matter between casual acquaintances, it is not appropriate. If in addition we draw upon the psychological explanation of the roots of homosexual orientation, we may be able to discern the problem with homosexual "marriages" and to see why sex may not be part of a same-sex relationship.

It is not that a homosexual man or woman may not love another man or another woman, indeed quite the opposite, but by "love" we cannot mean sexual expression. The marital relationship certainly involves sexual intercourse, but as psychologist Elizabeth Moberly says, homosexuals have legitimate needs for love, within the parent/ child relationship where sexual activity plays no part:

> The complementarity of male and female is certainly in God's plan, but it is in God's plan for adulthood. Men and women are not born adult. Rather, we are designed to undergo a long period of physiological and psychological development before reaching maturity.
>
> Homosexual acts are prohibited, not because they repudiate the man-woman relationship, but because sexual expression is not appropriate to pre-adult relationships.[11]

Orientation not identical to activity

St Paul would probably maintain that it is for both reasons, if the psychoanalytical position were to be presented to him. This is a complex subject, and there is a fine line between the "orientational" homosexual and the "hedonist". Psychologists used to differentiate between "essential" and "acquired" homosexuality, but this is not a distinction that finds much favour with psychologists today, and indeed the one can blend into the other. The consensus is that in a homosexual of whatever sex or type normal development has become stuck.

Arrested development usually arises from deficiencies in the relationship with the parent of the same sex, and yet from my reading of the subject, other factors are sometimes involved. For the male homosexual, some happening probably involving his mother may have implanted a fear of women, whilst for the female, a lack of positive affirmation by her father may have caused her to doubt her femininity. For both sexes, sexual abuse by someone in a position of trust, or persistent sexual bullying by a contemporary, can place a block in the way of normal development. We need to write "can" and "may" a lot because different individuals react differently. We saw this earlier when looking at the development of brothers and twins in a dysfunctional family. Two or more factors may also be present simultaneously. In some cases regular homosexual activity seems to bring on, and then establish, a homosexual orientation, but in these cases there is nearly always a hurt or emotional trauma underneath the surface which has allowed the homosexual activity to become established.

This could provide an explanation for the constant attraction of homosexuals to younger partners. They may be trying through this narcissism to relive, or to justify, or even to heal, their experiences as a boy or girl, or as an adolescent. This would be consistent with the cycle of abuse found by researchers, where (particularly male) homosexuals tend to interfere with children at or around the same age and sex at which they were themselves abused.

It is nevertheless right to maintain the distinction between the homosexual condition and homosexual acts, and Dr Moberly reminds conservative theologians who speak of "homosexuality" as a unit and as "the most extreme form rebellion can take because it is acting in exact opposition to the way God created us," as Kent Philpott puts it, that:

> *Such statements are both true and false. They are true in asserting the impropriety of homosexual activity, which is the eroticisation of pre-adult psychological needs. But they are incorrect and utterly misleading if taken to imply that no legitimate needs are involved in the homosexual condition. The homosexual urge as such is entirely in accordance with the will of God and the divine intention in creation. It is neither unrealistic nor rebellious, since it belongs to the maturational process that is the will of God for human development.*[12]

Homosexual activity akin to incest

The homosexual John Boswell has written of the "romantic love poetry" that issued from monasteries in the eleventh century, and in some cases it is interesting to read of the fantasies - we have to be open to the possibility that they are no more than that - that arise from the libido fastening on to the nearest available object. But surely the point is that monastic life is organised to reflect a love of fraternity, or family, illustrated by the terminology applied to individuals in a monastery. The word "abbot" means "father" and he is the father of a family of "brothers" - or "friars," from the French "freres." In a convent, the same imagery is used, with a "mother" guiding and directing the "sisters."

Curiously, this is what those within the homosexual network have taken to calling each other, especially but not exclusively in lesbian circles. "Our gay brothers" and "lesbian sisters" are expressions intended to draw upon the depths of the familial relationship, establishing a sexual and political "fraternity," but the use of these words inadvertently displays the inappropriateness of sex between the "sisters" or the "brothers." Depressingly, the exponents of homosexual sexual activity are also those who would legalise incest, but we must assume incest to be quite out of the question, and contrary to the intention of God.

What John Boswell thinks of incest is not clear, and he admits that he simply does not know whether the "romantic" love of certain of these religious was expressed sexually or not. Nevertheless he sees "romantic love" as an archetype of love for "gay people." I think he is guilty of a spectacular sleight of hand. I certainly agree with him that "romantic passions are distinguishable from other kinds, but not necessarily tied to physical acts."[13]

However, between brothers or between sisters, romantic passions must be suppressed if we accept that incest is inadmissible. In other words the libido has, with God's grace, to be brought under control. No-one ever suggested that monastic life was easy, but chastity in mind has clearly to follow chastity in body. Between practising homosexuals on the other hand, who accept a validity for homosexual activity in the first place, then "romantic love," if the term does not seem too pretty to describe the reality of homosexual encounters, would be allowed full rein to find its ultimate expression in sexual acts, and John Boswell is surely not naive enough to miss this.

Legitimate psychological needs must be met

Elizabeth Moberly explains that because the homosexual has not attained an adult gender identity, he or she is unable to find companionship in someone who, being of the opposite sex, is complementary. We all need to grow to psychological maturity, where we shall find community in the opposite sex, but the maturation process cannot be hurried, and if it has been interrupted, it still needs to be fulfilled. We cannot then say without qualification that man's desire for community is found in the opposite sex and leave it like that:

> Such a statement is true only of psychological maturity, and not of the pre-adult state. A man does, properly, fulfil a man's desire for community in the father-son relationship. And a woman does, properly, fulfil a woman's desire for community in the mother-daughter relationship. Relationships such as these are within the purposes of God, and their significance must not be overlooked.[14]

The avoidance of sexual activity is an important question, but one that should not neglect "the underlying personality structure." The issue is one of what is necessary for growth and development to psychological maturity, and what one is to do to make up for any deficits therein:

> The solution to the problem of the homosexual condition is not sexual activity. Unfortunately, mere abstinence from sexual activity has often been mistaken for the solution, without the realisation that there are certain legitimate psychological needs involved, which ought not to be left unmet. One should neither ignore unmet needs (the "conservative" mistake), nor eroticise them (the "liberal" mistake). It is the failure to understand this that has led to the polarisation of the debate on homosexuality.[15]

The difference of opinion with both "conservatives" and "liberals" does not imply a classic British finding of a "middle way." In denying that emotional fulfilment should be merely sexual, and in regarding healing as more than the mere suppression of sexual activity, we reach "the main point at stake," which is that "there are legitimate needs involved in the homosexual condition. These ought not to be met sexually, but they ought to be met."[16]

Psychology and theology are often thought to be in opposition, but this is only another myth. We have found both a psychological and theological basis for maintaining that sexual or emotional maturity is "the ability to form a stable relationship with the opposite sex which is both physically and emotionally satisfying, and in which sexual intercourse forms the main, though not the only, mode of expression of love."[17]

Heterosexuality is the goal of homosexuality

Elizabeth Moberly puts the case that whichever way we look at it, a homosexual man or woman is always abnormally detached from the parent of the same sex, and carries this detachment over to all members of the same sex. For her this is true even in the case where maybe a younger son has not cast his mother aside to bond with his father. The homosexual condition is still one of emotional immaturity, with the homosexual locked into the parent-child phase of development, but she argues that homosexuals are relating to both their own and the opposite sex "as incomplete members of their own sex." Maturity is then "the ability to relate to both sexes, not just to the opposite sex, as a psychologically complete member of one's own sex."[18]

We then have a paradox that "it is homosexual love that is itself the striving for heterosexuality, understood as same-sex psychological completeness."[19] The solution is for homosexuals to become "complete members of their own sex," in which they will be "truly heteros, truly other (complementary) to the opposite sex."

We can rarely speak of "reversing" a homosexual orientation, because homosexuals have rarely been heterosexual in the first place. Normality is where we get over the "homosexual" phase in early childhood, progressing in adolescence to heterosexuality:

> Homosexual relationships must therefore be regarded as inherently self-limiting, since they belong to the process of maturation, and cease if they have fulfilled their purpose. Homosexuality (same-sex incompletion) has a goal beyond itself, and that goal is heterosexuality (same-sex completion). By contrast, heterosexuality has no goal beyond itself. This is not to imply that all heterosexual relationships are stable and successful - many are not - but it is to state that there is nothing inherently self-limiting about heterosexuality.[20]

A bit of process theology

If indeed a homosexual orientation involves arrested emotional development, with heterosexuality as the goal, then it is far from being "a gift of God gladly to be accepted, honoured and enjoyed," as the statement of conviction of the Lesbian & Gay "Christian" Movement has it.

God did not create homosexuals as homosexuals, but "as men and women who are intended to attain psychological maturity in their gender identity."[21] Norman Pittenger, as one would expect of a homosexual activist, takes a different view, writing that all people are "in process," and urging an acceptance of homosexual sexual expression:

> The important thing is that the person shall be on the way, moving towards the goal and open to the possibilities which conspire to promote such actualisation. He is not yet fulfilled; he is being fulfilled. Man, like the rest of creation, is "in process" towards the greatest good; he has not yet arrived there.[22]

One could say that this is what we are arguing, that the constitutional homosexual is not yet fulfilled, and that it is through healing of his deficiencies that he is being fulfilled. Poor Norman Pittenger has missed the point, as Dr Moberly is quick to point out:

> It is perhaps ironical that a study of homosexuality based on "process theology" has not grasped the special sense in which homosexuals, as homosexuals, may truly be said to be "in process" - striving for the psychological completion of gender identity that has not yet been attained.[23]

How should a Christian treat a homosexual?

The psychological rationalisation of the Biblical position that sex is appropriate within marriage alone brings the considerable benefit of showing the Christian how to treat the homosexual. For if a homosexual is suffering from a deficiency in the parent/child relationship, then such a person must be regarded as a sort of emotional orphan. Then we can draw upon the strong theme in Scripture which is the care of orphans:

> The duty of care for orphans and the denunciation of their oppression is a theme to be found throughout the Old Testament. Ill-treatment of the orphan is condemned, as in Isaiah 1:23, Jeremiah 5:28 and Ezekiel 22:7. There is a reiterated prohibition of such oppression:
> You shall not ill-treat any ... fatherless child (Exodus 22:22). You shall not deprive ... orphans of justice (Deuteronomy 24:17). A curse upon him who withholds justice from ... the orphan (Deuteronomy 27:19). Do not ill-treat or do violence to ... the orphan (Jeremiah 22:3). Do not oppress the orphan (Zechariah 7:10).
>
> It is God who protects and helps orphans (Deuteronomy 10:18, Psalms 10:18, 146:9), for he is himself the "father of the fatherless" (Psalm 68:5). "In thee the fatherless find a father's love" (Hosea 14:3).[24]

Jesus tempted like us

The fatherless have to find the Father's love through Christians in the churches as well, and there is no place in this analysis for fellow penitents to be banished or excluded or frozen out of the church community. Where I do think Dr Moberly is wrong is to suggest that Jesus did not experience homosexual temptation. This is an important point, because during the healing process that the penitent is to pass through, temptation is going to arise, and it is no good at all denying the solace of the knowledge that the Lord felt this temptation, fought it and won. This is what she writes:

> It is not plausible that Jesus Christ in his incarnate life experienced homosexual temptation, as some Christian writers have suggested. The homosexual urge arises where there has been a deficit in the relationship with the parent of the same sex. However, the scriptures testify to Jesus' close and deep communion with his heavenly Father - a relationship such that there could be no possible

basis for speaking of a deficit and a drive to make good this deficit, i.e. the homosexual urge.[25]

It is surely possible that Jesus went through the same adolescent phases as other boys, and that a quasi-homosexual phase may have been part of this growing up process. Indeed, that we all pass through the homosexual phase of our development at some time is at the core of psychology of sexuality. Furthermore, sexual temptations cannot be ruled as the exclusive property of the constitutional homosexual. If Jesus was not tempted in every way as we are, yet without sin, then Scripture is a lie.

Homosexuals must refrain from sexual activity

Until full healing is achieved, the homosexually oriented individual must refrain from the sexual expression of homosexual needs. Some might say that I am asking people to make sacrifices that I myself could not make, but I think I should reply that they do not know me well enough to say that I am not tempted in all kinds of ways.

Norman Pittenger goes further to say that the control of sexual urges does not bear considering. "So near to an impossibility that it's hardly worth talking about."[26] One answer to this might be that it is strange that it is only ever sexual urges that get included in this pessimistic analysis. What about urges to steal, to murder, to lie or slander? However, a better response is to recognise in his statement the terrible compulsion that drives the homosexual to new sexual contacts.

Sexual license is of course always singled out for special dispensation, rather in the way libertarians apply the "old civil libertarian principle" of "no crimes without victims" only to sexual law. They usually make clear that this is to undermine Christianity, and in this present examination, we find poor Norman Pittenger and the "Gay Christians" doing precisely the same.

As John Stott points out, St Paul told the Corinthians that some of them had been involved in sexual immorality, idolatry, adultery and homosexual activity. Others were thieves, slanderers and swindlers. (I Cor 6.9-10) But they were delivered from all these activities: "You were washed, you were sanctified, you were justified in the name of the Lord Jesus Christ and by the Spirit of our God." (I Cor 6.11 NIV) For Dr Stott, "To deny this is to portray Christians as the helpless victims of the world, the flesh and the devil, and to contradict the gospel of God's grace."[27]

Christian sustained by faith

Making sacrifices for the Gospel is what being a Christian is all about in any case, otherwise we belittle the efforts being made by orientational homosexuals to reject homosexual activity while they are becoming freed from their orientation. We do have to face the possibility that some people may never be freed from homosexual temptation, even though they are delivered from the sexual expression of homosexual needs. But at the same time none of us is ever fully healed of the vagaries of our human condition. The Christian is sustained by faith and by the hope that a day will come when the soul will be freed from the limitations of its earthly body. We can all identify, I think, with homosexual writer Alex Davidson, when he writes of his own drive to rebellion and of his despair of ever being freed from his homosexuality: "That's why I find a comfort, when I feel desperate, or rebellious, or both, to remind myself of God's promise that one day it will be finished." [28]

Love does not only mean sex

An insidious aspect of homosexual equality is its belief that spiritual closeness and physical contact cannot exist independently of sexual expression. Homosexuality refuses to allow men to be tender or loving towards each other without assuming that homosexual activity will follow. In a society where love is equated with sex, it becomes impossible for a man to lay a hand on the arm of another without being looked at suspiciously. If two clergymen take a holiday together, they are assumed to be homosexual. Two men shopping together are immediately under suspicion of being consenting adults. John is lying at Jesus' breast, ergo, "there is a physical aspect to the relationship."

The belief that "love" has to mean sex seems to be held by most writers of a homosexual apologetic or gay activist disposition, not to mention the current batch of sex educators. Sex, so far as the sexual libertarian is aware, is merely "the friendliest thing two people can do," to quote the song. Aubrey Walter of the Gay Liberation Front thought it odd for the Festival of Light to condemn homosexual activity whilst gathering together to proclaim their love for Jesus, a man. It is staggering that a man of reasonable intelligence could be blind to something so obvious:

> Love is important, but not all love is intended to be sexual. Indeed, even for the heterosexual only the marital relationship is intended to be sexual. All other relationships - with relatives, friends, and

colleagues - are meant to be non-sexual. Love is far wider than its manifestation in sexual expression.[29]

Role of the churches in Christian healing

It is in helping the individual to achieve the goal of heterosexuality that there is a role for Christian counselling and healing. Most churches wishing to offer such a service will already be clear that "healing" is different from "curing." It is important that churches know the difference. The condition of homosexuality is channelled into its heterosexual destination when the spirit is healed of the underlying pathology that prevents normal relationships.

Any church or Christian fellowship involved has also to be absolutely sure of the validity of God's refusal to accept homosexual activity as part of His Divine plan, and neither liberal angst about having to be "tolerant" or "non-judgmental" of different lifestyles, nor "Bible-bending" to smooth away the prohibitions on homosexual activity, have any place in a healing ministry for homosexuals.

In dealing with the overt sexual sins, rather than with the underlying orientational condition, there is little room for anyone to feel sanctimonious about his own life. To say "Thank you God that I am not like that homosexual" is perhaps human and understandable in considering the underlying wounds that need healing. Where the illicit sexual activity is concerned however, it is too close to the sin of the Pharisee in Luke 18:9-14 for comfort.

Keeping our spiritual nerve

Any church that believes it is called to exercise God's true mission to homosexuals should be equally sure that it is God's intention that any homosexual who comes for healing is indeed to be healed. Of course it is difficult when the gay rights agenda is being pushed to exercise compassion for homosexuals, or to agree upon programmes of healing, but there is no place in a Christian understanding of the homosexual condition for antipathy towards its sufferers. Christian counselling agencies already offer a real service of healing to homosexuals through the combination of a reliance on and trust in the healing power of God, and the application of modern psychological understanding and technique. More are needed, and if they are associated with a particular church, so much the better.

Proper pastoral care and love in which the homosexual may be healed and brought into fulfilment in heterosexuality is only possible in a church which has not lost its spiritual nerve. Leanne Payne, whose approach to healing draws upon both Evangelical and Catholic traditions, puts it like this:

> *To cry out for pastoral answers is to cry out for the power to heal the lame in spirit and soul. Homosexual behaviour is at once sinful and immature. The sinful aspect has to do with the lameness of the human spirit and is healed through confession and absolution of personal sin. The immature aspect is part of the lameness of the soul - that which is to be set straight so that both spirit and soul can grow into freedom.*[30]

So let us now look at the process of healing, and at the challenge it presents both to the individual homosexual man or woman and to the gay rights movement.

25
Changes of scenes: healing the homosexual

Healing for the homosexual is entirely possible - but it has not yet genuinely been tried! - Elizabeth Moberly "Homosexuality: a New Christian Ethic."

The challenge of healing

Any attempts to be freed from homosexuality can be regarded by a practising homosexual activist in the same light as Section 28, as something which "casts aspersions on my sexuality."[1] When one writer proclaims that: "It should also be stressed that most attempts to "cure" homosexuality have a poor record and are usually unsuccessful"[2] and a homosexual psychiatrist on television "drones on" in the words of a "gay" reviewer "about the 'obscure origins of homosexuality' and the 'largely unsuccessful' cures for it,"[3] we should be suspicious enough to examine the evidence to see if a homosexual orientation is "incurable," to use their language.

Gay activists try to apply the word "cure" to sexual healing in order to disparage it. Homosexuality, they then say, is not a disease. Being emotionally a nine-year-old and physically a twenty-six-year-old may not be a disease to be cured but it remains a pathology which needs to be healed. We have covered this earlier, but it is as well to be sure. Homosexual activists can be exceedingly dense over the point. Others, like Ben Summerskill, the editor of "Pink Paper" tell me that they've "tried heterosexuality but didn't like it," when of course all they have done is to try heterosexual activity whilst remaining in a homosexual persona. That is not what becoming heterosexual means.

So we should recognise the challenge that healing of whatever sort presents to gay rights, and conversely the obstacle that gay rights presents to the full emotional development of homosexuals as people.

I may understand the psychology of homosexuality and the processes of healing imperfectly, but it would be better for homosexual men and women for there to be a discussion of where those imperfections lie, rather than that we continue to pretend that sexual healing is impossible on the one hand or unnecessary on the other.

Homosexual subculture supportive to participants

It might be tempting from all that has gone before to conclude that there is no support within the homosexual network for those caught up in it. Such a conclusion would be wrong. Even though a few urban areas, mainly in the United States, have a homosexual ghetto, a homosexual "community" is generally a fiction if we ascribe to the word its usual meaning, replete with corner shop, village hall, church, school, local Bobby and the neighbourhood watch. And yet, as we saw earlier, there certainly is a homosexual network revolving around the sub-culture, its bars, shops, newspapers and "gay scene."

Within the network active homosexuals find safety and identity by conforming to type. They gain support by surrounding themselves with the protective environment of a culture alien to those outside.

In itself this is as understandable as the existence of the criminal sub-culture. In the same way as criminals manage through the support network that operates via their pubs and clubs and telephone lines to know when certain activities are attracting higher than normal police activity, so the homosexual network does the same. For example, the weekly Capital Gay free newspaper, which circulates in "gay" pubs and clubs, prints intelligence whenever arrests have recently taken place at public conveniences. This information about which "cottages" to avoid is a service performed by the homosexual "community" for its own.

Promiscuity helps the support network

It is the promiscuity of homosexuality which builds the support network, and which helps in political campaigning. The active campaigning homosexual is obsessed by his homosexuality, and the absence of a family to support or with whom to spend time enables him to devote his whole life to convincing others of his point of view. His promiscuity gives him a vast telephone book of people to call on. One active homosexual, diagnosed as suffering from Hepatitis B, spent two whole evenings telephoning contacts, so the network is very real, highly intertwined, and in its way supportive. Although this does not prove the existence of a political or media "homosexual mafia," it strongly suggests that it might exist. Homosexual writer John Hart advises the use of the network:

You can be monogamous, live with or without your lover. Perhaps "serial monogamy" - relating to one person at a time - whether that be days or weeks or longer - is for you, or you may decide to have a number of casual "relationships" which perhaps should not even be called such.[4]

Hart's conception of "serial monogamy" - "relating" for "days or weeks or longer" would certainly be another man's promiscuity, and he goes on from the passage quoted to give the advice "to make friends with some of those lovers on the way, because you will need them as social supports."

Suspension of all morality

The supportive nature is of course non-judgmental. The only way in which the homosexual network can survive is by refusing to adopt a moral line, and this is why the sexual behaviour of its participants becomes ever more disgusting and degrading, why paedophilia is supported even by those homosexuals who do not practice it, and why one man spoke to me of the "complete suspension of morality" in the headquarters of the Scottish Homosexual Rights Group in Edinburgh.

The effect of the suspension of morality extends far beyond sexual activity. With no absolute standard of right and wrong, in fact with no standards at all, save that of "tolerance," it is open to active homosexuals to lie to themselves and to those close to them, and for homosexual apologists to lie to the rest of us. The condition of "denial," well-known to psychiatrists, is very evident. This is where people, in this case those active in homosexuality, refuse to believe anything which challenges their preconceptions.

Investment made in homosexual lifestyle

Let us consider a young man or woman who has been drawn into homosexual activity, initially as an experiment, perhaps through contacting a so-called "gay help-line," but now with more regularity. At some stage he - or she - will begin to identify as homosexually oriented. This may well be the occasion of perverse pride:

> *Paul .. began to see his sexual orientation as a preference. ... Despite the horrendous disadvantages it became almost a delight to be what society saw as sexually deviant.*[5]

Having made the decision to behave homosexually, the initiate is, according to John Hart, established in a homosexual lifestyle more by a refusal to admit that the decision was a bad one, than by anything else:

> I am suggesting that potentially sexual orientation is not necessarily confined, life-long, to the same or the opposite sex, but such categories as homosexual or heterosexual do become important to people. .... Once a person faces up to such an identity crisis, if you like, s/he will invest a lot in the new identity of homosexual or gay, enjoying and accepting the difference. And to return to the question of reasons for the apparent fixity of identity - having gone through all that, few people will easily give up something hard won.[6]

Replacement support network needed

Once the habit of homosexual activity becomes established to the point of being persistent, then it is extremely difficult to change, and the sense of guilt at participation in homosexual activity is gradually smothered. The eventual depth of involvement in the homosexual sub-culture makes it very difficult to escape. It is this investment in lifestyle rather than any shortcomings in treatment techniques, that militates against the renunciation by active homosexuals of their activities. If such a person is going to be freed from homosexual practice and ultimately from the accompanying tendencies, a support system is required in the heterosexual world to replace the one given up in the homosexual. The matter is akin to that of religious conversion, for example where Muslims convert to Christianity. Unless those with whom they are in contact are prepared to spend a great deal of time with and even offer accommodation to the convert, the experience can be quite miserable. John Hart seems to agree, before going on, rather simplistically, to involve bisexuality:

> For the people involved, becoming gay or straight means living in social worlds which are at present divided. This separateness is in my view what makes change (of heterosexual or homosexual identities) so difficult, rather than it being a simple task of assuring people that, with practice and relaxation, they might relate sexually to either sex.[7]

Homosexual man "could be straight"

Hart quotes one young man who speaks of his "mental attraction to girls." The man says that he could imagine himself falling in love with a woman. The reader will remember the British Market Research Bureau investigation into "gay lifestyles" quoted in chapter 6 which discovered that very few men using gay bars saw themselves as 100% homosexual. That survey did not ask how many of the respondents had had sexual experiences with women in the past, and certainly a previous heterosexual existence is much more common in homosexually active women than men. Be that as it may, this is what "Tony" says:

> I haven't any experience of sexual relationships with girls. I suppose I'm more scared than anything. But I do feel some kind of attraction towards girls although it doesn't override my gay feelings. I suppose it might be like being scared the first couple of times I went with men but then I got right into it. Various people have told me I've got it in me to be straight as well. I don't know.[8]

A parallel with alcoholism

American lawyer Roger Magnuson draws a parallel between homosexuality and alcoholism. Fifty years ago, drunkards were pessimistically regarded as beyond redemption, but today no-one doubts that they can regain their place in society. Groups like Alcoholics Anonymous emphasise the importance of taking responsibility for one's own life:

> What alcoholics learned is that an honest "coming out," without excuses or rationalisations but with a sincere desire to change, is a powerful tool for success. They found that a humble declaration of need provokes not just compassion but respect from others. ... Just as it would have been ludicrous to call for "alcoholics' rights," or to have a day celebrating drunkenness, it is equally ludicrous to call for "gay rights" legislation, or to have a day celebrating perversion. The alcoholic discovers in AA that the fault is not with others (society, wife, boss) but with himself; likewise, the responsibility for change lies not with others, but with himself.[9]

Many heterosexual men and women who indulge in a homosexual act more or less infrequently can probably have their energies more properly directed by the general attitudes prevailing in society, by fear of disease, or by positive application of the laws forbidding homosexual activity in public. A more compulsive pattern of behaviour may respond to treatment of a behaviourist nature.

Behaviourism - hated by gay activists

Behaviourist therapy is regarded by gay activists as particularly "oppressive," since it views homosexuality as a pattern of behaviour rather than as an identity, and can therefore help people who are unwillingly homosexually active and who wish to change. It is contrary to gay ideology that any person should have such a desire, so any psychiatric help to be offered should be targeted instead at helping the patient accept his homosexuality. He must be mad, the "gays" say, not to want to be homosexual. Even amongst general practitioners, according to the homosexual campaigner and present editor of Gay Times John Marshall, a small but worrying minority exists who would refer a homosexual who "has difficulty in accepting his or her own homosexuality" to "a gay self-help group."[10]

Indeed the classic forms of behaviour therapy, aversion and electric shock treatment, are certainly unpleasant enough to have provided gay activists with an easy target to parody and vilify. Behaviourism has nevertheless escaped the clutches of "gay anti-psychiatry groups" by simply and relentlessly providing a service for those who wish to take advantage of it. One of its exponents is psychiatrist John Bancroft, who is actually fairly liberal towards "gay rights" (see p191). Dr Bancroft acknowledges in his book "Deviant Sexual Behaviour" that it is currently unfashionable to offer psychiatric treatment to homosexuals who wish to change. Nevertheless, he argues, there will continue to be a number of individuals who are distressed by their homosexuality and doctors and clinical psychologists can help these persons to modify their behaviour.

Behaviour therapy is only useful when a person's homosexuality can be seen, in the words of one text book, as "a maladaptive behaviour pattern acquired through traumatic or inappropriate learning."[11] Much homosexual activity is exactly that. Behaviourists have accordingly had some success, but it should be observed that successful treatment depends on the subject wanting it to work.

The approach of psychoanalysis

The treatment and reversal of underlying homosexual tendencies, in those individuals suffering from them, is often seen as indicating conventional psychoanalysis rather than behavioural therapy as a method of treatment. Psychoanalysis attempts, according to Freudian Eric Berne, to "untangle the personality," and the classic form follows a pattern of three or more hourly sessions per week for a period of a year or more, during which the analyst attempts to discover a pattern of ungratified tensions originating from early childhood. The analyst then evaluates the point at which normal development became sidetracked, and attempts to correct the anomaly and to channel the patient into sexual normality. Again, if this treatment is going to work,

Change of scenes: healing the homosexual

it requires considerable perseverance on the part of the patient, who continues to be subject to social pressures to maintain a homosexual identity in between his visits.

There has nevertheless been some success achieved by psychoanalysts amongst people with homosexual personalities. Irving Bieber published as long ago as 1962 the results of a study in which the theory that the roots of homosexual development lay in early childhood, with dominant mothers and emotionally absent fathers, was vindicated. Christian healing often uses psychoanalytical principles and methods, but brings God into the equation as well. One psychiatric survey suggested that "psychotherapy appears to be unsuccessful in only a small number of patients of any age in whom a long habit is combined with ... lack of desire to change."[12]

Well, up to a point. A friend of mine who is a priest is working with a young homosexual whose mother tried to abort him as a baby. To him, women equal death. What a difficult place to start.

The Brisby appendix

Although a homosexual can become heterosexual, it is clear that this is only possible with adequate support, encouragement and motivation. The most effective motivation seems to be through the channel that also offers the most encouragement, and carries the promise of the most dedicated support. The BMA report "Homosexuality and Prostitution" to the Wolfenden Committee carried an appendix which homosexual activists have always been careful to ignore, because it detailed the release from homosexual activity and orientation of 14 homosexuals both men and women, through the experience of Christian conversion.[13]

Another appendix was contributed to the BMA report, by F H Brisby, the prison psychiatrist at Liverpool Prison, and visiting psychiatrist at Liverpool Psychiatric Clinic. Writing from a standpoint that had not yet been assailed by "gay counter-psychiatry groups," Dr Brisby described the different types of homosexual tendency and behaviour, ranging from "the constitutional homosexual or true invert, with all the graduations due to the development of the libido up to the heterosexual who may have transient deviationary tendencies towards homosexuality." He sets himself against the "sexual liberators" with his description of "erroneous doctrines that have received wide assent but which I think are utterly untenable. First and foremost is the doctrine that conscious control of any instinct is injurious. On the contrary, it is helpful." But referring to the categories of homosexual personality, Dr Brisby writes:

No matter in which of the foregoing types one puts a homosexual, there is one basic trait of personality common to all and that is an innate sense of inadequacy, and one is forced time and again to assessment of the integration of his personality and his view on his behaviour, first of all qua Society and or the victim or accomplice and secondly as to himself and his conception of right and wrong.[14]

Hope and confidence coming from God

Warning against the belief that "some magic nostrum or potion or gland therapy" will remove temptation, Dr Brisby maintains that the hope and confidence necessary to sustain a programme of release can only come from God:

> A belief in a personal helper is essential. A merely intellectual conception of God will have all the shortcomings of the intelligence of the disciples of such a Deity. When I speak of God in this respect I mean the God as propounded in the New Testament and the One Mediator.
>
> Above all, in cases of homosexuality of no matter what grade or type, cure is "a goal only reached after striving and fighting oneself, with victory probably the greatest satisfaction one can experience," as one of my patients put it, but it is a fight which one cannot undertake alone, and if there is any other solution than belief in Christian doctrine and principles and faith then I do not know it, nor do I find myself able to conceive of one.[15]

Fourteen people freed from homosexuality

In Appendix E of the BMA report, 14 case histories were described in which persons obtained release from homosexual actions and desires through belief in God brought about by Christian conversion. The four women were equally represented by "acquired" and "essential" behaviour, and the ten men split six "essential," four "acquired." Perhaps the most beautiful and dramatic story concerns a homosexual described as "essential" whose occupation was as a window dresser. He reports that from the earliest age he could remember being attracted to his own sex:

> Brought up by his mother, he played mostly with his older sister and her friends. He commenced to masturbate at 13; this became a frequent habit. He always played girls' parts in school plays and loved dressing up in his sister's clothes. At 18 he went into the drapery trade. At his work he was seduced by another, was first

repelled and then enjoyed the experience and imagined it with other men.[16]

Total loving support essential

Fortunately he met some Christians whose lives exhibited "sincerity, reality and effectiveness," and he decided to give his life to God. One of them only told him later that he too had been a homosexual but that "When he gave his life to God for him to direct, God gave him the victory and he began to be different." During the war he maintained his Christian discipline, even as a prisoner of war. His witness seems to have led others to faith at that time. It was not all plain sailing, however:

> After return to England he had lapses, but his friends stuck to him and he later had the conviction he should marry. He then met a childhood friend, courtship went well and they married. Even then there were occasional lapses, but eventually he told his wife everything about the past and since then victory has been complete and intercourse normal.[17]

One significant boost that this man received was the total loving support of his friends and his wife. It seems that her forgiveness and their commitment to him, added to his Christian recognition that homosexuality was outside God's plan, was what enabled him finally to be free of it. He writes, in a letter included with the report, of homosexual vice as "soul-destroying" and of his release from it as "a miracle and one which can happen to others."

> You can hardly imagine [he writes] the relief to be freed from the physical weight and the fearful oppression, and deceit, of an indulgence which had become an affliction, and from which I could see no escape. ... My shame at my abnormality created a resentment against society and I developed an urgent need to compensate for the sense of inferiority I felt (usually by showing off.)
>
> I do see a great need for forgiveness, not for being abnormal so much, but for being so slow and difficult and unconsciously, I suspect, unwilling to give it up. ...
>
> I have a very real sense of God's forgiveness and of salvation, and I would like to take this chance of saying how much the love and understanding and challenging friendship of people ... and the uplifting and purifying influence of my loving and forgiving wife coupled with a completely satisfying purpose in life, have all

brought me to a place where I am today, completely victorious and different in "the whole armour of God."[18]

Person of same sex needed to assist healing

Where the nature of the homosexual's problem is a deficiency in the relationship with the parent of the same sex, its solution lies through one or more good relationships with members of the same sex. The male homosexual in other words needs a male to assist his healing, and the female homosexual likewise a female. There is a problem here, and for once it really is not the homosexual's problem but that of others. Out of fear for their reputation, men are often very wary of offering friendship to a male homosexual of the depth necessary for healing. In default of such a relationship, the homosexual converted to Christianity, although he may have ceased sexual activity, remains homosexual, as "David" writes:

> I can praise God that I do not go out seeking homosexual relationships. At the time of writing I can testify to over three years of freedom from homosexual activity. I have not changed to a heterosexual in that time. Homosexual temptation is still a very real thing. But through Jesus - "who in every respect has been tempted as we are, yet without sin" (Hebrews 4:15) - I know the victory.[19]

This is not to deny the real achievement made by this man through his faith, which in some ways is the greater for the continued existence of temptation, and is supported by the knowledge that Jesus did indeed experience the same sort of temptations. However, the sort of Christian healing that we are discussing goes a great deal further. The goal is for the homosexual "to meet his or her psychological needs deeply and completely without sexual activity." As Elizabeth Moberly puts it:

> It is the provision of good same-sex relationships that helps to meet unmet same-sex needs, heal defects in the relational capacity, and in this way forward the healing process. ...
>
> It may be difficult at first for some Christians to accept that same-sex needs should be fulfilled, but this is necessary and it does not imply sexual activity. One will do well to remember that the capacity for same-sex love is essentially the love-need of the child for the parent, even if not consciously experienced as such.[20]

Christian healer Leanne Payne writes the following in connection with lesbianism:

Change of scenes: healing the homosexual

The loss of a mother's love is perhaps the greatest deprivation, humanly speaking, a person can know. ... Not all lesbian behaviour is primarily connected with this early failure to be in a trusting and loving relationship to the mother. But when it is, ... this has left an awful deficit - one that she simply cannot make up for until healed of the old deprivations ... Healing (wholeness) has to do with mended relationships.[21]

Prayer is essence of Christian healing

Christian healing arises out of love, and although a conventional psychotherapeutic input may be involved, it is not always essential. What is important is firstly the recognition that we can all be used in the healing process, and secondly the involvement of prayer, both to support such a ministry of healing and in prevention, supporting children at known periods of vulnerability, or when strain is being placed on a child's attachment to the parent:

All can pray, and prayer is of the essence of healing. And the need for healing - of homosexuality and of other conditions - is so great that all should pray.[22]

What must not be denied is the ability of God to work miracles, in the sense that it is surely possible for the constitutional homosexual to be healed miraculously in the course of an extensive healing programme. Although neither Dr Moberly nor Leanne Payne mention it, a male homosexual may well establish in prayer the deep personal relationship which is necessary for healing with the Saviour Himself.

Healing of memories

Leanne Payne's approach to the fractured relationship between child and parent is to attempt to heal the subconscious memory rather than to substitute a new child/parent relationship. This is a psychotherapeutic technique as well. When it works, the therapist, or the Holy Spirit, brings the memory up from the subconscious into the open, and healing can be quick and dramatic. Often the initial healing after intense prayer is but a first step. It can, for example, be:

The basic healing that would enable him to look upward freely and begin the breathtaking uphill climb from immaturity to maturity with its proper humility and self-acceptance, which is the antithesis to self-centredness, the wrong kind of self-consciousness and self-love. With this healing he could press on into the freedom to act from the centre of his being, that centre where Christ dwells and forms the new man, rather than from the locus of the unloved and hurting little boy under the authority of unloving parents and an enigmatic world.[23]

Parents need to be forgiven

What unites the various Christian healing therapies is that the homosexual is brought to a point where he or she can, and must, forgive the parent or other person for the hurt, trauma or desertion that brought about the homosexual condition. Without this conscious decision to forgive, healing of the homosexual condition is impossible. This is only basic Christianity, of course. "Forgive us our trespasses, as we forgive those who trespass against us."

Time and again, the response of the groups involved in promoting homosexuality is to tell parents whose child has announced his or her homosexuality that they have done nothing wrong and they must just "accept" the child's homosexuality. They get away with it because the parents are glad to be reassured that they are in the right, and that an accident of nature is to blame. The truth, that often they have indeed let their children down, is hurtful, but if the child is to reach the goal of heterosexuality, it needs to be faced.

Christian healing agencies are putting into practice the injunction of Christ that we are all called to heal. They give the Christian Church a better alternative than simply arguing over whether homosexual *acts* are justified, and whether homosexual relationships are valid. The answer to each question is of course "no," but healing is the positive and intellectually secure way forward.

In effect, Christian healers ask a more challenging question: "Do we love the homosexual so much that we can offer Christ's saving and healing power?"

Heterosexuality *can* be achieved

Reports of Christian agencies involved in both release from homosexual activity and in healing detail countless statements from people, both men and women, who have been freed from homosexual activity and have channelled such an orientation into normal heterosexual love and marriage. One such testimony says:

> *I came to crisis as I realised that a homosexual lifestyle was not what God had planned for anyone's life. Jesus made it clear through His example and teaching that people should remain single without sexual attachments or be faithful within marriage. I knew I had to*

Change of scenes: healing the homosexual 321

change my life and go God's way. As a gay person that meant I was prepared to be single for the rest of my life. I found that, through His Spirit, God gave me the power to overcome temptation. AND He has done what I thought impossible - God has so changed my life that I am now married with a family!

Don't get me wrong, the Christian life isn't all plain sailing. At times it can be very hard, but believe me, following Jesus is the best life there is! It's worth giving up relationships and exciting experiences that are wrong, because the experience of God's love, forgiveness and power is far more exciting - and it lasts for ever! [24]

Elizabeth Moberly concludes:

Love is the basic problem, the great need, and the only true solution. If we are willing to seek and to mediate the healing and redeeming love of Christ, then healing for the homosexual will become a great and glorious reality.[25]

In the next chapter we shall look at recognitions from outside the Christian Faith that an absence of parental love leads to emotional problems, and also at real attempts to heal the pathologies involved. We shall relate these to homosexuality. But psychotherapy, wild men in the woods, or Christian conversion, which heals the broken best and why? Who is missing from modern man, and especially from the homosexual, Iron John or Jesus Christ? Are the hurts of women, especially where these lead to lesbianism, being recognised? Are there any wild women in the woods? Let us see.

26
Iron John
or Jesus Christ?

Although we see accounts of homosexuals healed in the appendices of the Wolfenden report, and psychiatrists like Irving Bieber, Eric Berne and Anthony Storr have been writing since the sixties, secular sexual healing as practised by their colleagues has been sent underground by "gay counter-psychiatry groups." Sexual healing has re-emerged in the Christian form that we were looking at in the previous chapter only recently. Elizabeth Moberly only began writing up her work on the psychology of homosexuality in the mid 1980s and the books of Leanne Payne, dealing with the healing of the broken images of men and women, and with a crisis in masculinity, also only date from the 1980s. The first accounts of the work of active healing ministries to homosexual men and to lesbians were written in 1989 and 1991 respectively. American poet Robert Bly, also concerning himself with the passage from boyhood into manhood, published his book Iron John at the end of 1990 in America and in September 1991 in the United Kingdom.

All this new work has been accelerating more or less over the last ten years. Although the emotional absence of a mother may lead to lesbianism, and her dominance to male homosexuality, running through the Christian texts is concern over the way fathers too are today failing to affirm their children in their gender roles. The way in which modern man has forgotten his role as father and mentor is also the theme of Robert Bly. Iron John, who provides the title to his book, is a Wild Man, who acts as mentor to a young prince. The prince in the story passes through many stages of initiation under the tutorship of Iron John, who is a paradigm of true and wild masculinity. The prince treads his path to manhood, whilst the Wild Man himself becomes a King. The Grimm Brothers recorded the story, which Bly believes to be many centuries older. It is worth reading, as is Robert Bly's book, which is a work of great insight and beauty.

Iron John or Jesus Christ?

I must say before going any further that Robert Bly does not state as openly as the Christians that a homosexual is the un-fathered, un-mentored man with whom he is concerned writ large. Two reasons for this occur to me. Robert Bly has been difficult enough for the liberal media to understand and his thesis is already awkward for commentators to accept. Application of his work to the psychological deficiencies of homosexuals would tip him immediately into political incorrectness and obscurity. Secondly, Bly is a poet, storyteller and mythologist. The psychological evidence for treating homosexual men, and women, as emotional orphans may simply be of lesser importance to him. This is what he says, in passing, about homosexuality:

> *Most of the language in [Iron John] speaks to heterosexual men but does not exclude homosexual men. It wasn't until the eighteenth century that people ever used the term homosexual; before that gay men were understood simply as a part of the large community of men. The mythology as I see it does not make a big distinction between homosexual and heterosexual men.*[1]

Well he is right that healing must not exclude homosexual men, and that it is not useful to distinguish homosexuals as a separate group. He is right too that homosexuality was only recently categorised, we covered all that in Chapter 13. But before that time, in our culture at least, homosexual activity was regarded as simple sinful behaviour, nor were there such persons as "gay men" at all. The mythology, as I understand it, and I admit I am not on my home ground, does not entertain the possibility that a homosexual persona, or homosexual activity, is appropriate in adulthood, whereas heterosexual attraction, love, and activity are the very stuff of mythical stories (which is not to say that the sex always has good consequences).

There are countless stories where as culmination the prince and princess live happily ever after, finally cleaving to each other as psychologically complete members of their own sex. The final scene of the story of Iron John itself is the wedding breakfast of the prince, now fully grown, physically and emotionally, Bly carefully explains, as a result of his initiation by Iron John into manhood.

The absence of the father and mentor

According to Robert Bly, there has been no coherent masculine response to feminism, which recognises only two types of man, its favourite hated Aunt Sally of macho-man, and the approved vulnerable new man. Bly asserts that the hard-drinking, womanising bully is most certainly not a valid role model for a man, but then neither is the wimpish - or "soft" - new man, who throws out the baby of masculinity with the bath water of macho-man.

In rejecting both of these modern stereotypes, Bly claims that no man modelling himself on either is going to be good for himself, his wife, children or society. A man must feel comfortable with his masculinity, and neither suppress it nor feel the need constantly to prove it. Robert Bly observes that in pre-industrial times men had time to be with their children, and grandfathers, elders, were able to become involved in the mentor role as well, passing on their wisdom to the young.

Nowadays this is no longer the case and in flat contradiction of the views of feminists who blame everything on "patriarchy," Robert Bly scathingly remarks that patriarchy has been in retreat for two hundred years, and is now virtually non-existent in the western world.

In the absence of real fathering, there is no one to act as mentor to the male child. Fathers of today are emotionally or physically absent from their children. For a start they work away from home. Sons do not see their father at work, and when they do see him, if he comes home early enough, he is too often impatient, uncommunicative, and tired from the energy he has expended away from the family. Grandparents retire to the seaside, or go into an old peoples' home.

In the case of men raised by single women, Robert Bly observes that they are in tune with women's values at the expense of those of the male, emerging as "life preserving" rather than "life giving." Try as she might, the lone mother cannot tell her son what it means to be a man. When the woman who denies men raises a son, then rather than the warmth and nurturing of woman being implanted in the son, what is sown is confusion and resentment. No loved and admired man has affirmed the boy in his manhood. His "hunger for the father and mentor" remains unsatisfied.

And then what happens? Some young men - and women - reject all authority. Others seek and find the mentor, or worship some kind of hero. Such a relationship may well be non-sexual, and will fulfil a need. Anthony Storr showed that the need of the girls in these cases is for a mother,[2] in the same way as the boys are seeking a father:

> *In such instances the boy will often feel a powerful attraction to older men who show an interest in him; for they may be providing him with something which he needs but which has been missing from his home."*[3]

However, we noted earlier that the adult homosexual is constantly on the look out for younger partners, frequenting places, jobs, part-time activities and even marriages which offer access to them. A girl missing her mother or a boy whose father is indifferent, absent or hostile is easy prey for the lesbian or homosexual male respectively.

Still other young people, in particular boys, turn to their peer group. They try to learn how to be loyal and disciplined and just plain masculine from each other, in a pair, or more, perhaps in a gang. It works for some, says Bly, "but for most it doesn't."

The crisis in masculinity

In effect, Robert Bly notes the same crisis in masculinity as do Christian healers like Leanne Payne and for that matter conventional psychologists. He is emphatically opposed to the feminist notion that in the raising of children men are at best superfluous and at worst a hindrance. He clearly does not agree that men brought up to a feminist world-view become "better people." He quotes the police chief of Detroit, who said that the young men he arrests not only don't have any responsible older man in the house, they have never met one.[4] Research has indeed confounded the notion that men are "nothing more than mobile sperm-banks, their role over as soon as they roll over:"

> *The importance of paternal involvement in the development of adult empathy was underlined in a recently completed 26-year study by psychologist Richard Koestner of Montreal's McGill University, in which 379 people were interviewed when they were five and again when they were 31.*
>
> *It showed that out of a combination of maternal factors (warmth, strictness, toleration of dependency and satisfaction with maternal role) and three paternal dimensions (firmness, warmth and active involvement), the father's involvement was the most critical by a significant enough margin to confound researchers. What is needed is more and better fathering.*[5]

Certainly, Robert Bly's work, steeped as it is in symbolism, mythology and psychology, has touched a chord in America. A television programme on Bly's 10 years' of work with men "brought a flood of calls attesting to the confusion, pain and impotence that many men are experiencing."[6]

The tales told by these men and others who have felt the need of "wild man" weekends are harrowing. One spoke of the success in his medical career being no more than "proving himself to the father who left him when he was eight."[7] Another told of "his inability to feel strongly, his over-attachment to his mother and his fear that he felt more female than male."[8] Some had fathers whose brutality makes one shudder: One man remembers "being beaten till I cried then beaten till I stopped crying. I learnt to feel no pain."[9] Another remembers beatings and humiliations, from a father so unsure of his own masculinity that he had to grind down his son: "You'll never amount to anything, Norman." His mother would join in, describing her son as "a worthless piece of s—t."[10]

Wild men in the woods
Bly's solution to the problem of this anguish is to set aside weekends where men can together "celebrate their manhood" and get in touch with the wild man. He and his colleague Michael Meade take the men who turn up through the stages experienced by the young pupil of Iron John, by means of a well-structured pattern of stories, music and group therapies.

It is Bly's disciple Marvin Allen, a psychotherapist from Austin, Texas, who has added Bly's work and the ingredient of American Indian mythology to his own practise with men's groups and set up Wild Man Gatherings first in Texas and then in Colorado and in the woods of the Catskill mountains of New York State.

There have been reports of Wild Man Gatherings in the press. Briefly, the weekends provide an opportunity for men, away from women, to exorcise the hurts of their childhood, and undergo initiation into manhood. The men described above speak of having "unfinished business" with their parents, and fairly soon after arrival each man is advised to go away into the wood, draw a circle around a tree and invite his father inside. The woods ring to the sound of trees being struck, to cries of "I hate you," and "Look what you did to me." There is real anger and anguish being drawn out. Later the men will hug each other and tell each other what they should have heard in childhood, that they are loved and valued, not rejected and despised. It should all have happened to them thirty or forty years ago, but it is at least happening now.

There follow basic ceremonies of initiation into manhood, simple rites of passage. It is this emphasis on ritual and initiation which sets such healing weekends apart so powerfully from the twice-a-week sessions on the psychiatrist's couch. During the wild man gathering a change comes over everyone, trepidation and brokenness being replaced by assurance and reverence. Men seem to emerge from Bly's and Allen's gatherings simply more masculine. Psychiatrist Robin Skynner visited one of Bly's weekends, and on the second day noticed "a powerful yet quiet energy and attentiveness in the room that had not been there the night before."[11]

No reader should imagine that a magic wand has been waved, for these weekends are acknowledged to be just a start, trying, if not to heal completely the hurts of childhood, at least to recognise them and begin the healing process, and to be put in touch with the masculinity embodied in the Wild Man.

Living Waters

Christian ministries involved in sexual healing start from the same premise as Bly and Allen, "A man, to be whole, must find affirmation of his true masculinity; a woman, affirmation of her true femininity."[12] Ex-homosexual Andy Comiskey writes of discovering "a newly secured sense of my maleness" as a result of entrusting his sexuality to Jesus and being, and continuing to be, healed.

The same unfinished business with parents is spoken of. "Men with homosexual tendencies have often experienced rejection by fathers to whom they never measured up."[13] ("You'll never be half the man I am.") The parents have to be forgiven before the sufferer can go any further. There is agreement with Bly and Allen that the need for affirmation of true masculinity (and for the Christians, femininity) exists in the majority of today's heterosexual people as well, as Leanne Payne writes, in a foreword to Andy Comiskey's book "Pursuing sexual wholeness":

> Few heterosexuals emerge from adolescence having secured this affirmation of themselves as persons. Although it's seldom understood or dealt with as such, most of the need for therapy and counselling today is directly related to an imbalance of some sort in one's masculine or feminine identity. The need for the heterosexual, though much the same, is simply not so evident as the need Andy expressed.[14]

But how is it done? Bly seeks to put men in touch with Iron John, the Wild Man, whilst Andy Comiskey and the men he knows first find, then embark on a journey with, Jesus Christ. Is this Jesus, today represented by some of the most gentle, "feminine" men on earth, men who comfort and conduct away tensions, men made as Bly puts it of copper not of iron,[15] able to affirm masculinity in the same way as Iron John?

I believe so. There has been a tendency to concentrate on the "feminine" meekness of Jesus at the expense of his "masculine" anger. We forget that He promised to "bring a sword," to set brother against brother for the Faith, that He told the pharisees that they were a "brood of vipers," and that He drove the money changers out of the temple with a whip. When we read that He simply told Simon and Andrew to follow Him, we may forget that these were fishermen like those we see on holiday in Padstow or Roscoff. The Archbishop of Canterbury in all his robes would not get the captain of a Cornish trawler simply to put down his filleting knife and follow him, and yet when Jesus asked, up they got and left their nets and followed. Jesus was just as masculine as Iron John, and perhaps a bit more, in His own way. The prince in the myth takes a risk when he goes away to the forest with Iron John. Like Iron John in the story, Jesus too demands that we take a risk and go with Him. He is not a safety first figure. Jesus took the biggest risk of all, going to the cross, a risk so great that He thought for one despairing moment that He had been abandoned.

Jesus today works through ministries such as Comiskey's Living Waters, using Christians as healers and ministers. This again is a parallel with the Wild Man Gatherings, where men are affirmed by other men. In both cases, agents are stepping in to perform a function that should have been carried out by a man's father.

Wild women and fathering of girls

Are there any wild women in the woods? Jeanette Howard, who runs a ministry in Sussex to homosexual women, writes about a woodland retreat for recovering lesbians, but in general the answer is no, and there certainly is no feminine secular equivalent to the work that Robert Bly has done. It seems that what is usually termed "the women's movement" has gone down a different path, marked feminism. If Bly is right that fathering has been and is being done poorly if at all in our industrialised, liberal, capitalist society, then it is, as he says himself, being done poorly for girls as well as boys. Girls too will have unfinished business with their parents, and anger against distant fathers who never affirmed their femininity or others who abused it or belittled it with sneers. The result is damage, as Bly puts it, to "the daughter's ability to participate good-heartedly in later relationships with men."[16]

It seems then that men, referring mainly but not exclusively to heterosexual men, nursed this anger against their fathers in silence until Bly touched the chord. Then some could confront the anger, and seeing it, would try to deal with it, that is, try to forgive the father and discover masculinity, with or without support from God. Other men still nurse the anger, unaware. Perhaps a louder chord will be struck, that more will hear.

Women, on the other hand, brought out the anger sure enough, in a flood of books and touched chords, yet instead of confronting it and trying to forgive the father responsible, they instead extended the anger to all men, none of whom would be forgiven. They blamed men and paradoxically "patriarchy" for the anger, yet because their femininity was unaffirmed, and this was what they were angry about, they could only try to be like the very men they rejected and despised. They did not and still do not yell "give me my femininity" as the men in the woods cry "give me my masculinity!" Rather they shout at men "give me the trappings of your masculinity," and they demand men's jobs, to the extent of leaving their children and going to the front line to kill.

When we looked at the assault on the family, Barbara Amiel suggested that feminists were foisting their own psychological problems on the rest of us, and I expect the reader thought that she was going too far. Nevertheless, psychologists have recognised just the phenomenon we have described above as "identification with the aggressor."[17] It became known more recently as the Stockholm syndrome after the hostage-taking incident there; the hostages came out pressing the terrorists' demands. Perhaps a study should be carried out to see if there is a correlation between a feminist personality and a lack of proper fathering.

Jeanette Howard in her book "Out of Egypt: leaving lesbianism behind," writes that women often see God literally as their father. Men do this as well, of course. If the father was weak, then God must be ineffectual, if the father was abusive, a spoiler, unsure of himself, God is mean-spirited too. If her father is emotionally or physically absent, then so is God uninvolved with her, unaffectionate, or if her father is harsh and unforgiving, his love conditional, then that is what God is like. Or suppose the father controls and manipulates, is over-protective, then God is mushy and wants to run her life.[18]

The philosophy of Desert Stream

If there are similarities between the imagery used by Andy Comiskey and Jeanette Howard in their books, then that is only to be expected. The umbrella group for ministries to homosexual men and women draws on the book of Exodus and is called "Exodus Ministries," whilst

Comiskey's own project is "Desert Stream." The book of Exodus is the account of how the Israelites were brought by God out of slavery in Egypt and dwelt in the desert until the time was right for them to enter the promised land across the river Jordan.

In the "Living Waters" programme, the desert is a metaphor for the barrenness and spiritual starvation of the homosexual life, and the "desert streams" which satisfy the thirsty are the "living waters" of Jesus Christ (one of His descriptions of Himself).

For Jeanette Howard, the lesbian life is a form of slavery akin to that faced in Egypt by the Israelites. Coming "Out of Egypt," she and others are "leaving lesbianism behind," and enter into the "desert," which is for her (as it was for the Israelites) a time of growth, spiritual healing and learning about God. It is only after this time spent in the desert that the promised land of sexual and spiritual wholeness is entered into.

What baffles some observers of these ministries is that they are not heterosexuality shops. We might imagine that people join them as homosexuals, and come out after some weeks as perfect heterosexuals, and say "Thank you and good-bye, I'll be off now and get married."

In the first place the healing process can take very much longer, and some individuals are so hurt before they join that they will never be "normal." Like Moses, they can see the promised land, but not enter it. But secondly, heterosexuality is not the goal of those involved in these ministries. They have their sights fixed on Jesus Christ, who is to a Christian both the path and the goal. They follow Him, trying to get closer to Him and with His Grace to do His will. As it is God's will that all should be healed, then healing arises out of trust in God, and heterosexuality is almost a by-product.

This is not to deny that homosexuality, or dissatisfaction with it, brings people to Living Waters, for a homosexual condition, pace Robert Bly, is an obvious manifestation of deep emotional hurts which need healing. However, recognition of the hurts, and of the power of God to heal them whilst drawing His children closer to Him, is the real starting point. Going further, although homosexuality is an obvious and evident indication for sexual healing, a need for healing at this deep emotional level is not the property of people locked into homosexuality alone. Many of us need healing for wounds that were inflicted long ago. Because the scars are not so visible as those of the homosexual, few of us turn up for it. As I am a Christian, I must lean towards Living Waters rather than to Wild Man Gatherings, and yet I sense good in the latter, too. There is a certain spiritual power that human beings draw upon when they confront wrongs and repent of them or forgive them. Spiritually speaking, we wound the Devil every time we forgive a fellow creature or repent of the harm done to one, and God's creation must be fractionally restored every time a psychotherapist or a Wild Man Gathering helps restore our brother or sister to wholeness. Following this line of thought, it is good that there is a way of healing that does not involve the Christian Church, for it will be open to more people, even at the expense of leading some away from the Christian path. Time will tell which works better, in the sense of which helps men (for the secular ministries do not yet exist on any scale for women) heal the hurts of childhood and become properly masculine (or feminine). In the meantime, it is better that hurts and the need for healing are being recognised, that forgiveness is being attempted, and healing begun somewhere, than nowhere.

Although both ministries are clearly applicable to heterosexual and homosexual men and women, we have the curious state of affairs that Christian ministries for sexual healing are used almost exclusively by homosexual men and women, and Wild Man gatherings almost exclusively by heterosexual men, Christians amongst them. There is nothing for heterosexual women to parallel Wild Man gatherings that I know of.

I should like to see that change. I should like heterosexual Christian men and women to explore the ways in which their sexuality and emotional hurts can be healed within the church, and I should like to see Bly and Allen recognise the special way in which their work applies to homosexual men and to women. If they take my advice, however, they will become politically incorrect and will be attacked by homosexual activists, as we shall now see.

Healing ministries attacked

It will come as no surprise that homosexual activists deny their need of healing and seek to prevent other homosexuals from taking advantage of it. Let us remember that "gay rights" demands that there is nothing wrong with homosexuality and that anyone not happy being "gay" must be mad. Counselling for the homosexual, by this argument, should comfort and reinforce the homosexual lifestyle and that is all. The Living Waters ministry does not do that, and in asking men and women to confront their homosexuality and decide whether they wish to continue to live in that sinful way or not, and then to help and support those who do not, it is much more like Alcoholics Anonymous, a true self-help ministry which has people released and being released involved in it.

So it is natural that some will ask themselves this huge question and will conclude that the risk of being let down is too great. They will say that they do not wish to leave the gay life. And now the superficial wellbeing of their homosexual life will have been disturbed and rippled. These people will rush back to "gay switchboard" or "lesbian line" for reassurance that homosexuality is still valid. Let us see if that is what happens.

Two Christian groups, Pilot and True Freedom Trust, have a well-established but very quiet ministry to homosexual men and women in Britain. The majority of homosexuals probably do not even know of their existence. "Capital Gay," which circulates amongst homosexuals, claimed that the activities of these two ministries "led to an increased workload for counselling organisations like Friend which helped people over the experiences they suffered at the hands of the evangelists."[19] And about Living Waters: " A west London art teacher said that people who were not "cured" were made to feel guilty that they were persisting in sin. One man was made to relive his experience of being raped as a six year old."[20]

Those who encounter goodness and compare it with their own persistent sinfulness are going to feel guilty. They will need reassurance from others persisting in the same sin. They are those who count up the cost of continuing to follow Christ, as Jesus said people should do, and decide that the costs of leaving their homosexual friends and the "gay" lifestyle behind are too great compared with the risky and nebulous benefits that they can only dimly see. No-one can force them into sexual wholeness.

And what of the claim that a man was "made to relive" an experience of sexual abuse? The "Capital Gay" article appeared at about the same time as the National Society for the Prevention of Cruelty to Children ran a poster campaign based on a man of fifty who, after failure as a husband, had finally discovered, with the help of psychotherapy, the memory that he was raped as a child. He was able to confront the memory, forgive the abuser, and become whole, so very late. "Capital Gay" is only describing a therapeutic technique used by medical practitioners and Christian healers alike, the drawing out and healing of memories. The man in the advert had trouble with his sexual identity and could not relate from a position of wholeness to his wife. Revealingly, the homosexual man or another attending the Living Waters Sexual Redemption programme had a similar appalling experience in childhood. The "Capital Gay" reporter simply could not see that in this episode of child abuse lay the root of the homosexuality of the complainant. How sad.

Intimidation by militant gays

It is notable that in spite of their personal testimonies, which any interested reader should get hold of, Andy Comiskey and Jeanette Howard are not accepted by "the gays" as having been homosexual at all. They were bisexual according to the activists, and have just decided not to have same-sex partners. I have read their books, and met those involved in their ministries, and the "gay" activists are wrong. The reader should, as I say, buy the books from Monarch or through CARE Trust in London, and decide.

It is now no secret in the homosexual activist world that one Living Waters ministry is based at St Michael's Church in Chester Square, Belgravia in London. The militant "Outrage" first tried to browbeat the vicar and his team into discontinuing the ministry, and when that failed, they demonstrated outside and inside, intimidating worshippers, men, women and children.

Such intimidatory methods against Christians have been imported from America. California's "Traditional Values Coalition" is headed by the Rev Louis Sheldon, and his meetings are regularly picketed and invaded by "gay rights" activists, who call Sheldon "hatemonger", "religious bigot" and "Nazi". The media have taken to using these labels too, calling the "Coalition" a "fundamentalist hate group." The activists and the media seek to prevent Sheldon from speaking, and wish to obstruct his message, which is no more than routine psychology, and traditional Christianity. He says:

> *Homosexuality is not something you are born with. Homosexuality is a developmental disorder; it's a traumatised condition, arising out of a dysfunctional family. We love homosexuals, and we want to help them. Homosexuality is recoverable. There is a reparative process, and there are thousands of recovered homosexuals.*[21]

What a challenge to the homosexual rights movement! No wonder they dare not let him speak, and no wonder they seek to spoil the Living Waters ministry. No wonder that they would rather every homosexual stayed that way than that just one might accept the positive choice offered. How bigoted are the non-judgmental.

We have now considered the homosexual lifestyle and its implications, religion and healing. Over the next few chapters, we ought finally to look at politics before getting back to normality.

27
Homosexuality and the parties of the left

What were the 1992 manifesto positions of left-wing political parties on the subject of homosexuality? Were their policies directed towards recognising the psychological reality of the homosexual condition, and helping healing of the pathologies? Or would they rather consider a homosexual orientation as predetermined, or more libertarian still, regard the choice of a homosexual lifestyle as equally valid as conventional heterosexual family life? Would they have used the law to discourage homosexual expression and activity, or to enshrine in the law measures for homosexual rights? And how did they arrive at their positions? We shall try to answer these questions.

The Green Party

The Green Party, the political New Age, combines a pantheistic world-view with mistrust of humanity. A belief that mankind is not only sinful but irredeemable leads the Green Party into large measures of coercion. However, a rosy-eyed picture of homosexuality is entirely consistent with the "green" mind set. Being sympathetic to homosexual activity and being an environmentalist are both politically correct things to be, but there is more to it than that.

That the world is overpopulated is an article of faith for greens. It is a waste of breath to suggest to them that the area taken up on the surface of "the planet" by people is only that of the Isle of Wight, or that food production is at an all time high, or that most of Africa is so underpopulated that there is no infrastructure, or that fertility decreases in any country as prosperity increases, or even that poverty is too often brought about by third world despotic government. These are all true, but they cut no ice with the greens. The while homosexuals do not breed, the more homosexuals are helping "the planet."

Of all the parties, Green Party supporters are the most tolerant of homosexual activity by a long way, being largely in favour of "gay rights." In this respect the Green Party Manifesto reflected its supporters' views, something that could only also be said in 1992 of the Conservatives.[1]

The Social and Liberal Democrats

It was a 1992 manifesto commitment of the Social and Liberal Democrats to

> Guarantee equal rights for gay men and lesbians through changes to criminal law, anti-discrimination legislation and police practice. We will repeal Section 28 of the 1988 Local Government Act. We will create a common age of consent [sic] regardless of gender or sexual orientation.[2]

Social and Liberal Democrats believe then that homosexuals are akin to a racial group. An earlier policy document admits that "the European Convention of Human Rights does not itself make reference to discrimination on the grounds of sexual orientation," but, unabashed, Liberal Democrats relentlessly use the language of gay rights activists. The central plank of what amounted to a charter for homosexual rights stated:

> We would legislate to make discrimination on the grounds of sexual orientation unlawful in all fields both legal and social. In particular there are many areas of the criminal law which are discriminatory in their effect and should be changed. ... We would also introduce the offence of incitement to hatred on the grounds of sexual orientation.[3]

The Social and Liberal Democrats believe that "legitimate and proper activities of local government" are to give sex education which includes "the teaching of an awareness of different sexual orientations" and to provide "support for organisations giving information, advice and counselling." The use of public funding for proselytising homosexual "help-lines" and contact groups would then have been encouraged by the Liberal Democrats, and parents who object on moral grounds to their children being taught about homosexual activity would at best have been marginalised and at worst could have been prosecuted under Liberal Democrat "incitement to hatred" legislation.

Robert MacLennan promises "gay equality"

To hammer these points home, Liberal Democrat Home Affairs Spokesman Robert "Bob" MacLennan MP went out of his way to attend a meeting of "Liberal Democrats for Lesbian and Gay Action" (DELGA) at the London Lesbian and Gay Centre in Cowcross Street to "make clear the commitments a Liberal Democrat government would make to law reform."[4]

He explained also that Liberal Democrats would "make the un-collaborated testimony of the police insufficient as grounds for prosecution." His Party's policy document claimed that the police do not treat "gay men and lesbians as equal citizens," but as "criminal by the nature of their sexuality."[5] This is flawed. Firstly, the law categorises actions, not nature, and secondly, in no other sphere would we respond to the existence of a pathology by legalising the criminal actions of its sufferers, especially where these harm the public health and cause public offence.

Robert MacLennan has a long interest in "gay rights." In 1983 when in the SDP, he met some men who claimed to represent the Gay Youth Movement at a meeting organised by Jo Richardson MP in the House of Commons. Frank Allaun, Tom Cox, Alf Dubs, Clement Freud, Joan Lestor (now a patron of Streetwise Youth) and Clive Soley were also courteous enough to turn up. Four unmarried MPs also attended, but I do not propose to name them. Robert MacLennan proposed a reduction of the minimum age for homosexual activity at that meeting, as did Jo Richardson, proposals which I fear did not go far enough for Jeff Vernon of Campaign for Homosexual Equality and Gay Youth, or for Chris Perry and Leo Adamson of the Paedophile Information Exchange who made up the "Gay Youth" delegation.

One Bernard Greaves was heavily involved with DELGA's predecessor the Liberal Gay Group for many years. He was named by Paedophile Information Exchange as one of the seconders of their motion at the Campaign for Homosexual Equality Conference at Southampton in 1975. DELGA can actually be contacted at the Liberal Democrat Party Headquarters at 4 Cowley Street, SW1, according to Gay Times. The President of DELGA is Viscount Falkland, its vice-presidents are Julia Neuberger and veteran homosexual campaigner Michael Steed.

Support for gay rights in Labour Party and TUC

There is no question about where the Labour Party stands. In 1985 the Trades Union Congress and Labour Party Conferences passed, for the first time, resolutions supporting lesbian and gay rights.[6] The TUC resolution was put forward by the National Association of Probation Officers (NAPO), affiliated to the Campaign for Homosexual Equality, and seconded by NALGO,[7] whilst that of the Labour Party was proposed by militant lesbian Sarah Roeloffs, a member both of Haringey's Lesbian & Gay sub-committee, and of the London Labour Party L & G working party. This criticised Nick Raynsford for appearing with his family in posters for the Fulham by-election in 1986 in which he beat Matthew Carrington (only to lose to him in 1987). Labour's conference resolution called for legislation which would:

> a) declare that lesbian and gay relationships and acts are not contrary to the public policy of the law and that judges must not use their discretion under common law to create new crimes.
> b) repeal all criminal laws which discriminate against lesbians and gay men, and clarify and codify those sections of the common law which deal with "public morality"
> c) In this clarification they should be guided by the maxim that "there should be no crimes without victims"
> d) prohibit discrimination and unfair dismissal on grounds in any way connected with lesbian and gay sexuality or life-style
> e) prevent police harassment of lesbians and gay men.[8]

NCCL uncovers minimal discrimination at work

The pro-gay stance of the unions was as a result of pressure from the National Council for Civil Liberties, which had since the mid seventies had its very own well-established Lesbian & Gay Group. One Barry Prothero was appointed to be its full time gay rights officer in 1980, again inevitably during the tenure of Patricia Hewitt and Harriet Harman. Mr Prothero's qualifications for this post included being a member of Gay Activists Alliance and having shared a home with Paul Crane, the "gay" lawyer, Stephen Gee of the pro-paedophile Gay Left and John Lloyd, co-founder of Paedophile Action for Liberation.

Mr Prothero and his NCCL colleague, Gay Left founder-member and far-left Hackney infants' teacher Nigel Young, soon prepared a report on "discrimination" experienced by homosexuals at work. This led in turn to an organisation called "Lesbian and Gay Employment Rights," which produced a report in 1986 with financial help initially from the GLC and then from the London Boroughs Grants Committee.

Two hundred predominantly white, middle-class, young people were recruited through "gay" retail outlets, homosexual venues and "gay pride" days and were asked if they had experienced "trouble" at work arising from their homosexuality. Only 25% had, and many of them, so it seems, had gone out of their way to offend the feelings of others. Had they actually been sacked for being homosexual? Only 12 had. The report calls this a "very high number," although it seems that many of the 12 were either dismissed from the services for homosexual conduct, or removed from posts involving proximity to children. In time-honoured fashion for homosexual apologia, the report complained that "gay men" are considered to be promiscuous and to be sexually interested in children without attempting to deny either point, and this imparted a whinging feel to the whole expensive project.

Homosexual influence in trades unions

Perhaps the most revealing part of the report concerned the way in which "the gays" say they have manipulated Trades Union policies in their favour, by becoming active and then by taking on the posts of shop stewards and officers of their union. As we saw earlier, the absence of family ties leaves plenty of time for such activities, and the total concern with their homosexuality, that being "gay" involves, provides the motivation:

> *The trade unions which have developed policies or passed motions against the discrimination of lesbians and gay men have done so almost invariably because of the efforts of lesbian and gay members active in their union. It has often been a small group of lesbians and gay men who have put forward demands to their union.*[9]

The report makes it quite clear that "lesbians and gay men" must go away and formulate their demands "without the interference of heterosexual members." However, once the demands have been set down, the LAGER report was explicit that the heterosexual infantry are expected to muck in with the gay campaign. Such campaigns have indeed been successful in a large number of unions, including most of the big ones. This after all secured the vote at the 1986 Labour Party conference, as we shall see in a moment.

The unions who supported gay rights

An article in the house magazine of the Labour Campaign for Lesbian and Gay Rights, "Lesbian & Gay Socialist," records the Trades Unions who voted for "lesbian & gay rights" in 1985 and 1986, oddly omitting NALGO, the National Association of Local Government Officers, which was the first union ever to add "sexual orientation" to its non-discrimination clause.

> *Firm support had been secured in 1985 from a number of unions, notably the Transport and General Workers (T&GWU), National Union of public Employees (NUPE), which has been affiliated to*

Homosexuality and the Left

LCL&GR since 1985, the National Union of Railwaymen (NUR), AUEW-TASS, builders union UCATT, and of course the miners of the NUM. Healthworkers' union COHSE, along with a number of smaller trade unions, such as the cine-technicians of ACTT, made up the final roll call of some 2.8 million block votes.

The most important breakthrough in 1986 was the switch of the General and Municipal, GMBATU. Almost as significant was the move to our support of the shopworkers of USDAW, while the effect of the prolonged Wapping struggle shifted the traditional printworkers' unions SOGAT and NGA onto the right [sic] side.

The only opposition worth noting came from the electricians of the EETPU and the engineers of the AEU. To these were added the postal workers (UCW), who had voted for lesbian and gay rights in 1985 but have now moved to the right. A similar attempt to move the telecoms union NCU against us was defeated in their delegation. A sad note was sounded by ASTMS, which supported us in 1985, but on this occasion Clive Jenkins railroaded through the delegation, with no opportunity for discussion, a decision to abstain.[10]

Labour Conference decision becomes party policy

In 1986 the Labour Campaign for Lesbian and Gay Rights published its "Manifesto," intended to put the flesh on the bones of the 1985 conference decisions, and two months later the 1986 Labour Party conference actually reaffirmed Labour's policy by a majority of four-to-one. Voting on a resolution proposed by Manifesto author Mike McNair himself, 4.8 million votes were cast for and only 1.26 million against, and Labour's National Executive Committee was instructed to mount a public campaign to "further and defend the rights of gays and lesbians," and to institute a witch-hunt of Labour local authorities which had not yet included "lesbians and gay men" in their "equal opportunities policies." So embarrassed was the Labour leadership over this motion that the conference organisers made sure that the 15 minute debate would coincide with Play School, the only time when the BBC broke its live coverage of the conference.[11]

Any resolution gaining more than two thirds majority becomes official Labour Party policy and in theory goes into the Labour Party Manifesto. At the 1986 conference, the same Jo Richardson MP who addressed the annual conference of the Campaign for Homosexual Equality, and who twice came to the support of the Paedophile Information Exchange, pledged that a working party would be set up. The party's hierarchy at Walworth Road, staring a general election in the face, had other ideas, and managed to prevaricate. By passing the buck from one Walworth Road dignitary to another, the leadership made sure that "gay rights" would not figure in the 1987 general election manifesto.

The Labour Party Manifesto 1992

The Labour Party is constantly torn between the demands of socialism, or at least of socialist activists, and the desire to be electable. In 1982 a proposal to lower the minimum age to 16 for homosexual activity was opposed by Neil Kinnock and Robin Cook, who had earlier worked so very closely with paedophile activist Ian Dunn in applying the 1967 Act to Scotland. This stirred up Gay Scotland, and Neil Kinnock felt obliged to write to Ian Dunn in person to say that he was himself in favour of 16 as the age for homosexual activity.[12]

It was surprising that it took Labour ten years from the date of this letter finally to include gay rights measures in its manifesto. Patricia Hewitt was during this time a leading light in the Labour leader's office. At the NCCL she defended what she saw as the rights of homosexual and even paedophile groups, then Mr Kinnock opposed "gay sex" at sixteen, then he supported it, then denied he ever wrote his letter to Ian Dunn, then Miss Hewitt wrote her own famous letter explaining how gay rights was proving an electoral liability for the Labour Party, next Mr Kinnock supported Clause 28, and then he opposed it, then sent a message of support to the North West Lesbian and Gay coalition for their march in April 1991 to "oppose Clause 28" and to "celebrate gay sexuality."

On the 2nd May 1991, a "pink plaque" was unveiled at the London School of Economics on the occasion of the 21st anniversary of the first meeting of Gay Liberation Front. The usual homosexual activists sent messages supporting this commemoration of the LSD-dropping, anti-family, anti-Christian, pro-paedophile, promiscuous Marxists.

Messages of support came also from Tony Banks, Tony Benn, Ron Brown, Harry Cohen, John Fraser, Bernie Grant, Ken Livingstone, Joan Ruddock, Clare Short, Chris Smith, Daffyd Ellis Thomas and Keith Vaz, all but one of them Labour Members of Parliament.

Finally, Labour's Election Manifesto in April 1992 promised to repeal "the unjust Clause 28" and "introduce a new law dealing with discrimination on grounds of sexuality." The Manifesto gave no recognition to the view that strong stable traditional families are important, not even in its "Ministry for Women" section, the usual relegation zone of Labour family policy.

Labour abandons the family

In September 1990 the Rt Hon Neil Kinnock MP told social services directors in London that unprecedented levels of divorce and illegitimacy, rather than giving cause for concern, created "opportunities," not least for women. In his reaction to the concern of Margaret Thatcher at the erosion of family life, Mr Kinnock, instead of suggesting ways to bolster the traditional family, was content to view the evidence of its erosion. Government policies had to "respond to the growing shifts away from the conventional family structure and not try to turn back the clock."[13]

A few days later, The Institute for Public Policy Research, a registered charity, but in fact a left-wing humanist pressure group, published a paper entitled "The Family Way" on exactly the same subject, drawing exactly the same conclusions. The paper was written by old NCCL friends Anna Coote, Patricia Hewitt and Harriet Harman after deliberations chaired by feminist writer Juliet Mitchell. They cheerfully accepted rising divorce and illegitimacy as a reaction to "the service economy, information technology, declining birthrate, expansion of higher education and modern expectations of women." Fathers were irresponsible people who would only fritter away money from family tax cuts on themselves, but who should nevertheless spend more time with their children to ensure "better prospects of a child maintaining a good relationship with both parents after a divorce." Marriage was changing "from social institution to private relationship," "fewer people will marry and a greater proportion will divorce," and the authors were not the slightest bit concerned, calling for more contraceptives for teenagers and even quicker divorce.[14]

In September 1990 the morally crippled Labour Party gave up its last pretence of being a Party which supports the Judeo-Christian ethic. There are of course many decent Christian pro-family Labour Members of Parliament. But amongst the ideologues of the Labour party, humanism has supplanted Methodism to the extent that Labour cannot bring itself to recognise the importance of the values of traditional family life. It prefers to support illegitimacy and homosexual equality. Labour has changed support for abortion, as another example, away from being a conscience issue, to become party policy. There is indeed a battle raging in the Conservative Party between traditionalists and humanists, but in the Labour Party, the battle is over. Any pro-life, pro-family MP was elected long ago and faces regular attempts by local party members at deselection. No new candidate can be adopted who is pro-life.

Opinion polls reject gay rights

Homosexual rights was never tested as a general election issue itself, although the Labour and LibDem manifestos were decisively rejected as a whole by the electorate. It may be that if the Tory campaign had focussed on "gay rights" that the Conservatives would have been returned with an even larger majority. Despite increasing media promotion of permissiveness, and in the face of AIDS "tolerance education," the British public relentlessly maintains a sanguine view of homosexuality. Anxious to be fair, people tend to side with "the gays" when asked general questions, especially when the questions are biased to achieve a favourable response. However, we still react strongly when challenged to apply these generalities to specifics.

Over the period from 1983 to 1987, British Social Attitudes found the proportion of the British population agreeing that "homosexual relationships are almost always or always wrong" rose as follows: 1983: 62%, 1984: 67%, 1985: 69%, 1987: 74%.[15]

Asked whether homosexuals should be employed as teachers, 50% said "no" and 43% "yes" and when asked in 1985 and again in 1987 whether female or male homosexual couples should be allowed to adopt a baby, it was reported "There was always massive resistance to this idea and, if anything, opinion has hardened: 86% would forbid lesbians and a decisive 93% would forbid gay men. It is rare in the British Social Attitudes Series to find such near unanimity."[16]

Gallop in 1991 asked whether "Homosexuality should be considered as an accepted alternative lifestyle or not?" 53% said "yes" and 36% said "no." But then 35% of the sample held to the view that "homosexuality" was "something a person is born with," with 33% identifying "upbringing" as the main causative factor and 19% saying "both." [17]

Asked whether homosexual relations between consenting adults should or should not be legal, 66% said "should, and 24% "should not." Considering the sort of profession in which homosexuals should or should not be hired, people were happiest with homosexuals as sales staff (77% "should," 16% "should not"), and progressively less happy to hire them to be soldiers (55% / 36%), clergy (49% / 41%), doctors (49% / 42%), teachers (39% / 50%) and prison officers (40% / 52%). In line with BSA, attitudes had hardened through the eighties, but had then softened in 1991.

However, when asked whether homosexuals should or should not adopt children, one of the key "gay rights" demands, only 20% said "should" against 67% "should not." On the homosexual minimum age, opinion hardened further, with 16% in favour of reducing the age from 21 to 16, and 74% against.[18]

The Stonewall homosexual rights group asked Harris to conduct a survey in early 1992. The survey results were reported as showing a massive swing towards support for "gay rights." On the "age of consent" for instance, compared with Gallop in 1991, public opinion seemed to have moved from 3 to 1 against equalisation to 3 to 1 in favour.

The question asked by Harris was:

"Should the age of consent - that is the age at which people can legally have sex together in private - be the same for everyone irrespective of their gender or sexual orientation, or not?"

Not surprisingly, 74% said it should, and only 22% "should not." "Gay men and lesbians should have the same rights under the law as everyone else" found 71% agreeing and 23% disagreeing.[19]

Pollsters generally accept that asking questions in a less than neutral form distorts the results. One famous survey asked on one page if a woman in consultation with her doctor should be able to choose to have an abortion, and a majority said "yes." On another page in the same questionnaire it was asked if the right to life of an unborn child should be protected, and a majority answered "yes" to that as well.

Anyway, respondents were finally asked by Harris to agree that "gay men or lesbians who are suitably qualified in every other way should be allowed to foster or adopt children." Tolerance here deserted the sample, of whom 72% disagreed (2/3 of them "strongly") and only 17% agreed.[20] That is a hardening of attitudes from Gallop 1991, casting doubt on the usefulness of the rest of the Stonewall/Harris survey.

So let us now look at what successive Labour Party Conferences voted for, at what the Liberal Democrats proposed, and what the "gay rights" Stonewall lobby group are currently demanding of the 1992 Parliament, as we examine the reality of homosexual rights.

28
Gay rights and the victimless crime

It might seem odd to leave the examination of "gay rights" to such a late stage in our discussions, but it was necessary to build a thorough picture of the homosexual network and of its real aims, before considering what is being demanded exclusively for the practitioners of unnatural practices. This will lead to an examination of the claim that a wrong-doing needs a specific victim before it can be a crime.

The argument has moved on from Wolfenden, so that "the gays" do not now ask for the right to keep themselves to themselves in private. They now want, as we saw in chapter 1, full recognition in law and in the public mind that homosexual activity is morally equivalent to heterosexual love and marriage. Of course, even if they succeed in law, and this chapter explains the detail of their demands, they will never achieve parity in the normal mind. Their search for approval is like their search for a partner, a futile quest.

The legal mess in America
"Gay rights" have made more progress in the United States than here, possibly because American gay rights protagonists gained a five-year head start, and also because American activists were very quick to appropriate the arguments of black civil rights, a phenomenon which did not exist in the UK to any great extent.

As American Lawyer Roger Magnuson has pointed out, the law in America concerning homosexual activity itself is hopelessly ambiguous, with the US Supreme Court upholding state anti-sodomy laws in one judgment, and then refusing in another to review the New York state court decision that struck down the New York criminal sodomy law.[1] Gay Rights activists have had more success in the US by repealing state anti-sodomy laws through state legislature than by asking courts to void them as unconstitutional.

In approximately half the American states, laws against sodomy have been repealed, whilst actual gay rights legislation has been passed in some 50 towns, villages, municipalities and the states of Wisconsin and New York, the latter in March 1986.[2]

The New York measure empowers the city's Human Rights Commission to investigate complaints of discrimination in housing, employment, public accommodation, ownership of land and the leasing of commercial space, on grounds of sexual orientation. The Commission can impose maximum penalties of a $500 fine or a year in prison.[3]

What 'gay rights' involves

In practice, according to Roger Magnuson, legislation of this form has the following effects:[4]

1. A motel or hotel owner can be investigated for refusing to let a room to a homosexual couple or to an unmarried couple for the purposes of fornication, adultery or prostitution. This would amount to discrimination in the use of public accommodation on grounds of sexual orientation, in the cases mentioned, for orientation towards one's own sex, towards unmarried partners, people married to someone else, or to prostitutes.

2. A convicted child molester can complain about a day-care centre that refuses to hire him to look after children, because they would be discriminating against him on grounds of his sexual orientation. Such an ordinance in effect sanctions criminal behaviour.

3. A church will be unable to refuse to hire a homosexual minister or lay worker, and will have to let a function room to a homosexual activist group, even if homosexual activity is contrary to the teachings of that faith. A commercial enterprise could similarly be unable to refuse to lease premises to someone who wished to use them as a "gay" bar.

4. The owner of a rooming house would be forced to act against her conscience if she viewed homosexual behaviour as morally repugnant.

Mrs Murphy's rooming house

In his consideration of the latter point, Roger Magnuson invites us to consider this admittedly fanciful case: a student applies for a room in Mrs Murphy's house. She asks him various questions, ending with the strange request to know if he likes the music of Bach. "Yes," he says. "Then you'll never rent a room from me!" she replies. Then a man wearing makeup and high heels applies, accompanied by another man in leather jacket and menacing chains. Mrs Murphy does not like the look of them at all, and retreats in haste back into her rooming house, slamming the door.

Without a gay rights ordinance, the rights of the parties turned away are the same, to whit: none at all. Mrs Murphy's dislike of baroque music might well be opinionated or perverse, but the student cannot claim the protection of the law for his preferences, be they for Bach, Buick automobiles or backgammon.

Before the passage of a gay rights law, "the gays" come out the same way, and Mrs Murphy seems on much firmer ground. Hers is not now a whimsical and unreasoning hatred of counterpoint, but a choice based on the moral fibre of people she wants in her rooming house. However, after the passing of a gay rights law, her irrational decision is backed up in law, whilst her moral repugnance towards homosexual behaviour is vetoed. As Roger Magnuson puts it:

> *Laws that protect "sexual preferences" create a new and privileged class. From all the now unprotected preferences there are in the world - for clothes, cars, special sleeping habits, gourmet food, pets, music, poetry - the "gay rights" laws carve out a special set of preferences related to perverted sexual behaviour and give it a special protection available to no one else.*[5]

The story of Mrs Murphy's rooming house illustrates that all rights have corresponding duties imposed on others. Mrs Murphy loses her right to determine what sort of person should stay in her house, and has a duty imposed upon her to contradict her own conscience. If a homosexual teacher has a right to teach children that homosexuality is normal, the school authorities and the children's parents lose their right to have a say in the moral character of people who teach their children. This is why "the gays" are in favour of compulsory HIV and AIDS education in the UK.

Homosexual conference ends in shambles

The position in the UK is akin to that of an American state which has abolished its anti-sodomy law, but has not passed a gay rights ordinance. Implementation of a "gay rights" bill such as proposed by Stonewall would change that.

After the success of the gay rights lobby at the Labour Party's 1985 and 1986 conferences, an activists' conference to discuss how to advance the cause of "lesbian & gay rights" was held at the Camden Centre in Bidborough Street at the end of May 1987. This two-day event was called jointly by the Labour Campaign for Lesbian and Gay

Rights, the Campaign for Homosexual Equality and the National Council for Civil Liberties. In one weekend, the conference plumbed new depths in internecine warfare between far-left groups, and finally, a right of veto was granted to seven groups set up just for the purpose: lesbians, lesbian mothers, black lesbians and gay men, older lesbians and gay men, lesbians and gay men with disabilities, young lesbians and gay men and lesbians and gay men in care. Nothing was decided in the ensuing confusion.

The conference was organised out of CHE's offices by its offshoot, the Legislation for Lesbian & Gay Rights Campaign, set up for the purpose and run by Eric Presland (qv). After the conference, this group gained a life of its own as the Organisation for Lesbian & Gay Action (OLGA). After the failure of the conference, OLGA got the blame, and so great did antipathy become that OLGA was condemned by the Labour Campaign for ineptitude during the Clause 28 protests.

Labour gay rights manifesto published

The Manifesto of the Labour Campaign for Lesbian and Gay Rights had already been published at the time of the gays' conference. The front cover depicts justice as two lesbians hand-in-hand, one holding the scales of justice, the other holding the sword. The production of a "Manifesto" itself was the idea of the Campaign Group of hard-left Labour MPs,[6] which had a membership in the last parliament of about forty-five, so it was hardly the idea of a tiny minority.

According to Gay Scotland, Jeremy Corbyn MP was sent to approach LCL&GR for a draft Bill to be used by a private member or under the ten-minute rule procedure in the House of Commons, as "a focus for demands for changes in the law."[7] The job of drafting the Manifesto fell to Mike McNair, a lecturer in law at Leeds University, although it is ultimately anonymous. Much of it is based on the GLC's "Changing the World - A London Charter for Lesbian and Gay Rights" which was published to coincide with the conference season in 1985, and was subsequently adopted by many Labour local authorities.

The Labour Campaign "Manifesto" boiled the 142 recommendations of the GLC's 'London Charter for Lesbian and Gay Rights' down to 28 clauses, whilst being more detailed in its lawmaking, even if the absence of ratepayers' money makes it far less lavish a production than "Changing the World."

Ken Livingstone MP, architect of "Changing the World," is said in "Minor Problems" to be in favour of the complete abolition of the age of consent, an authentic civil libertarian position. The Labour MP for Brent East has committed himself to bringing forward the draft legislation, or something similar, as a Private Member's Bill, although the Manifesto makes it clear that a future Labour Government, should one ever happen, would be expected to legislate along the general lines of the Manifesto for Lesbian and Gay Rights anyway.

Stonewall

The Stonewall Group aims to present a moderate face of homosexual law liberalisation. It is of course named after the June 1969 Stonewall riot in America. It gained credibility in the last Parliament amongst Conservative Ministers, even being described by one as "totally responsible," although party politically there is only one Conservative on the Stonewall board of trustees, Matthew Parris. The other trustees, including Ian McKellen, "Chair" Michael Cashman and Simon Fanshawe are all left of centre. The last director, Tim Barnett, was a Labour Councillor, his lesbian assistant Anya Palmer squatted in Paris, lived on a women's commune in Denmark and worked for the left-wing Charter 88 before joining Stonewall. Tim Barnett left in November 1991, to be replaced by Ann Bond, the leader of the Labour Group on Kensington and Chelsea council. Miss Bond lasted seven months before resigning in June 1992, after "a clash of management styles."

Stonewall runs a "postal action scheme" in which prominent figures are targeted for co-ordinated mailings. Targets have included local authorities, Amnesty International, the Chief Rabbi and the Bishop of London. The postal action scheme is run by militant homosexual humanist teacher Austin Allen from Bradford. Stonewall's mailing envelopes have usually been franked by Bradford University's post room. Its patrons include Lord Falkland, Glenys Kinnock, Claire Rayner and Robin Squire MP.

The Stonewall Group has published a "Homosexual Equality Bill" based on a manifesto agreed by the Campaign for Homosexual Equality and the National Council for Civil Liberties. We shall consider it as we go along. The measures are thought by "responsible" Stonewall to be better thought-out than Liberal Democrat policy and more achievable than the Labour Manifesto's utopianism. The architect of the Stonewall Bill was "gay" lawyer Peter Ashman of "Justice," now Director of the European Human Rights Foundation in Brussels, which advises Jaques Delors at the European Commission.[8]

The Manifestos

The central aim of all three manifestos is the overturning of "the idea that lesbian and gay sexuality is 'unlawful'" and "the basic general

Above, the banner of the Metropolitan Community Church says: "The Lord Is Our Shepherd And He Knows We're Gay." They are marching behind the "Backstreet," a leather S&M club. Below, the Sisters of Perpetual Indulgence are a group of militant anti-Christian homosexual men who dress up as nuns. In a deliberate parody of Christian practice they are "hearing confessions."

PIE MAGAZINE:
MAGPIE (No 1)
MARCH 1977

PIE Notes & News (continued)

Thorne Trial -- P I E's Response

You may have read remarks in the Press in connection with the judge's summing up at the end of the Andre Thorne trial; the report of his remarks varies according to which paper you buy, but all of them indicated his obvious distaste for PIE, and his ignorance of the way we conduct our affairs.

The Executive Committee of PIE of course takes great exception to his comments and it has been considering the best way of repudiating them in order to establish our position and to make clear for once and for all our undoubted legality as an organisation.

We have consulted the NCCL on this matter, and they feel as strongly as us about it. On our behalf they are going to write to the Lord Chancellors Department to register a complaint about the comments of the judge. For our part, we are investigating the possibility of putting a Parliamentary question in the House -- this is not as far fetched as it seems for at least one M.P. -- Jo Richardson -- has expressed an interest in acting for us in the matter.

Ideas, please

You may remember that at the last AGM it was decided that we should invite one or more prominent people to become 'Honorary Vice-President' of PIE. A number of names have been put forward and some of these have been written to, although as yet no one has taken us up on our offer!

One of the people written to was Bryan Gould MP -- chosen largely because of the speech he gave to the CHE Conference in Southampton last year. Although he declined to accept, his reply is worth reporting. It reads:-

> "Thank you for your letter and for your invitation to become an honorary Vice-President. I am afraid that I have so much on my plate at the moment that it would be unwise of me to take on any further respociblities for the time being. I should be less than honest with you however if I were to give you the impression that lack of time is my only difficulty. As you say, yours is an unpopular cause, and whilst I have a good deal of sympathy for your objectives, I do not think it would be fair to my wife and family for me to take a public stand on it. They suffered somewhat as a result of my speech to CHE and while I am robust enough to take the comments, correspondence etc., my wife in particular reacts badly to it. I am sorry to have to send you such a disappointing reply."

Now, if an MP, who depends upon votes and public good-will, can give us such a considerate reception, there must be someone, somewhere who would be prepared to help us in this way. Any ideas please?

QUOTE ...

And that is why I cannot give pederasty anything like a first place among the evils of the school. There is much hypocrisy on this theme. People commonly talk as if every other evil were more tolerable than this. But why? Because those of us who do not share the vice feel for it a certain nausea, as we do say, for necrophily? I think that of very little relevance to moral judgement. Because it produces permanent perversion? But there is very little evidence that it does.

C.S.LEWIS
"Surprised by Joy"

Only the later magazines of the Paedophile Information Exchange were well-produced but they always thought that they were part of a sexually-liberated new dawn. A measure of their confidence is their invitation to the young Brian Gould and others to be vice-presidents of their organisation.

crimes of 'immorality' used against lesbians and gay men."[9] The Labour draft legislation for example begins by declaring:

> that homosexual sex acts, whether between women or between men, are in no way inferior from the standpoint of public morality or policy or the public interest to heterosexual sex acts.[10]

The homosexuals who have drawn up the various manifestos thereby claim authority to decide morality. All three Manifestos, the Labour, the Liberal Democrat and the Stonewall, would repeal the Conservative's Section 28, and they all believe that children should be taught in the classroom that homosexuality is equally as valid as heterosexuality, against the provisions of the 1986 Education No2 Act.

They all include a new offence of "incitement to hatred (or violence) on the grounds of sexual orientation." This would proscribe the ability of the Christian Church, or of other Religious Faiths, to preach against homosexual activity. We shall see what the authors of one of these Manifestos think of the Christian Church in a moment.

They all abolish offences of homosexual activity in the armed forces, and would criminalise "discrimination" in the fields of employment, immigration, accommodation, and inheritance. The latter would mean that a homosexual or any unmarried couple could inherit each other's property in the case of intestacy.

Clauses would extend the laws of unfair dismissal to cover grounds of "lesbian or gay sexuality," prevent courts from taking a parent's homosexual lifestyle into account in custody cases, and forbid the defence of provocation to be used to a charge of murder where homosexual advances have been made.

Sexual immorality given legal protection

Stonewall proposes to facilitate these measures by allowing pairs of homosexuals to appear before a solicitor to make a "public declaration" of their "relationship," which could as easily be dissolved.[11] The Labour Campaign gives an automatic recognition to cohabitees who have lived together for two years, a long time in homosexual circles, and its Manifesto claims that these are commonly called "stable relationships." Effectively, both manifestos would jettison the remnants of public policy in favour of marriage, legalising all forms of sexual liaison outside marriage. Interestingly, the Labour Manifesto does not call for equal treatment by the tax system for homosexuals and for married couples, stating that the tax system already discriminates against marriage.

The Labour Manifesto also explains that damages could be claimed for "discrimination", so not only would Mrs Murphy be unable to refuse to let her rooms to whomsoever she wishes, but she could be sued, as could churches who refuse lettings to homosexual groups or preach against homosexual or fornicative sexual acts. They and other employers would be bound, if the expression does not fall too awkwardly, to employ homosexuals in any and every capacity including work with children. The Manifesto boasts that it would be possible to be able to sue for "being thrown out of a club or pub."

Brothel keeping, importuning and public sex legalised

So far as activities now regarded as street offences and brothel-keeping are concerned, none of them would by the Labour Campaign Manifesto be prohibited by law. The Manifesto aims to encourage "prostitutes forming lesbian relationships and cohabiting," abolishes the offence of keeping a disorderly house and the offences of soliciting and importuning for an immoral purpose, and permits "a person whether male or female to approach another person whether male or female to invite or request them to engage in sexual relations."[12] The only exception is put in "harassment" terms, where a woman is "intimidated" or put "in fear of sexual assault" or if the solicitation causes "a nuisance." Furthermore, a police officer could not bring anyone to book under this new offence without corroborating evidence from the woman "harassed." According to the manifesto, "This is to prevent abuse by the police."

Stonewall also abolishes the offence of soliciting, and the restrictions on privacy. Any problems created by this could, they claim, be dealt with under laws relating to public order. The Labour Manifesto states that: "dramatic sex acts in the street" might be prosecuted only if they were to obstruct the highway.

Common law crimes abolished

The Labour Manifesto at this point goes much further. It proposes the abolition of the common-law offences of conspiracy to corrupt public morals and outraging (and conspiracy to outrage) public decency. The courts, according to the Manifesto, would be forbidden to act as guardians of public morality (custos morum) and all common law crimes against nature and similar crimes in canon law would be abolished.

The present law bans the publication of material (and stage performances) which are 'obscene,' that is, which have a tendency to

Gay rights and the victimless crime

deprave and corrupt. The Labour draft legislation does not abolish in law the concepts of obscenity or immorality in themselves. Instead it allows "the publication, importation or sending through the mails of any obscene or indecent matter" and "the presentation of an obscene performance." The offences of obscene libel and blasphemy are abolished and the whole corpus of the law on obscenity is replaced by a crime of "incitement to violence against women", which is intended to retain the concept of "obscenity" within it. The Manifesto bans all pornography, except homosexual pornography, for the interesting reason that "sexually explicit material is more important to homosexuals than to heterosexuals."[13]

No arts loophole permitted
The crime of incitement to violence is drawn so as to include:

> much sexist advertising, a good deal of crime and horror fiction, many pulp romantic novels and stories, much of the political output of the right wing and of patriarchal religious groups on sex-roles; and a good deal of literature and fine art (eg The Taming of the Shrew, parts of DH Lawrence etc.) Unlike the existing law, we have not put in an escape clause for "public good" so that all of this would in principle be prosecutable.[14]

There is no "arts loophole" either, and someone convicted of staging "The Taming of the Shrew" would under the draft Labour Lesbian and Gay Legislation be made criminally bankrupt, any company involved would be compulsorily wound up, and the state would pocket the proceeds. The Manifesto leaves nothing to chance, and includes draft legislation to abolish retrospectively any "anti-gay" local authority bye-laws. The authors have in mind Manchester's "licentious dancing" bye-laws. Councils would in addition be stripped of powers to create:

> a) any sexual offence or offence against sexual morality
> b) any offence of licentious, indecent or immoral conduct
> c) any offence relating to the publication, distribution, or display for sale of obscene, indecent, immoral or profane publications, or to the presentation of an obscene or indecent performance.[15]

The law on homosexual activity itself
In relation to sexual activity, the Liberal Democrats would "create a common age of consent,"[16] oblivious to the fact that there is a common age of consent at present. As we saw in Chapter 18, the ages of consent for heterosexual and homosexual activity for both boys and

girls are set at 16 in the 1956 Sexual Offences Act. However, there are then Clauses which prohibit all homosexual activity, under which consensual gross indecency is punished less severely than indecent assault which is by definition non-consensual. These sanctions are then modified by the 1967 Sexual Offences Act, which says that two men may commit an act of buggery or gross indecency in private if they have both reached the age of 21.

Stonewall and Labour propose what the Liberal Democrats meant. Both abolish the offences of buggery and gross indecency from the 1956 Act, so there is no need for the 1967 Act which sets out conditions (including the separate minimum age) for exceptions. The simple age of consent for boys set already at 16 would apply without the sanctions which now forbid homosexual activity. Homosexuals would then be able to give free reign to both group sex and (as we saw above) public sex. The Labour Manifesto observes that abolition of the offence of buggery has the side effect of legalising "anal intercourse" between men and women, and sexual relations with animals. Bestiality, so the Manifesto claims, is properly covered by legislation banning cruelty to animals.

How does lowering the minimum age benefit homosexuals?

Whenever someone asks for something, it is a good idea to see how they would benefit from it before agreeing. How would lowering the age from 21 to 16 benefit homosexuals? Homosexuals say that it helps "young gays," but this begs the real question of how best to help a young person of that age through a homosexual phase, or how best to offer healing for a developmental disorder.

The Stonewall demand to abolish the offences of buggery and gross indecency between males from the 1956 Sexual Offences Act altogether would mean that homosexuals could tell the rest of us that the law treats their sexual behaviour in exactly the same way as it treats ours and they would be right.

So we come to the first benefit: Homosexuals desperately want to "feel good" about themselves, mainly because of the inner turmoil they are in. The approval of the law would give them an enormous fillip. But there is another way in which "equality" at 16 could be achieved.

The "compromise" that is sometimes talked about of amending the 1967 Sexual Offences Act so that a minimum age of 16 or 18 would apply does not go technically so far in the direction of removing the "aspersions" cast on their "sexuality." The descriptions of homosexual activity (of "gay sex" as "the gays" put it) as "buggery" and "gross indecency" would remain in law. However, an amendment of the age in the 1967 Act to 16 might leave the disapproval of the law intact, but whatever was said by their Parliamentary friends during passage of such a Bill, it would nevertheless be presented afterwards by the "gays" as "equalising" homosexual and heterosexual lifestyles.

The second benefit is rather more practical. A minimum age of 18 for homosexual activity would make it borderline whether men would be prosecuted for sexual activity with boys of 16 or 17. An age of 16, however achieved, would make prosecutions unlikely for acts with 14 and 15 year-olds. But even should the law if amended to 18 be strictly enforced, it would still allow adult homosexuals legal access to teenagers, in other words to precisely those adolescent boys and youths who are most impressionable and to whom the active adult homosexual male is most attracted.

The old civil libertarian principle is anti-Christian

The framers of the Bills base their proposals on the belief, or as the authors of the Labour Manifesto put it, the "old civil-libertarian principle", that there is "no crime without a victim." As they explain, this means "essentially that conduct should not be criminal unless it can be shown that somebody suffers by it."[17]

This "principle" is applied somewhat selectively, to say the least. "We are not arguing," say the authors of the Labour Manifesto, "that nothing should be criminal unless some individual can be shown to be directly and immediately affected." For example:

> Incitement to racial hatred may not directly result in any individual black person being attacked, but it still makes it more likely that black people as a group will be subjected to racial attacks. It is therefore quite right that it is a crime.[18]

Of course the Manifesto accepts this in any case with its "incitement to violence against women" clause. But it gives further examples of other areas in which "any state would have laws making these activities criminal," even though the activities described "hurt others only in the most indirect way." Examples of such things range from tax evasion and smuggling, to "parking on double yellow lines."

As it turns out, the Labour Campaign for Lesbian and Gay Rights intends to apply the "old civil-libertarian principle" to "the laws relating to sexual morality" and to nothing else at all. So for that matter does Stonewall. Why this selectivity? "because we don't think that the state should uphold Christian sexual morality."[19]

The cat is out of the bag and it is a queen on heat. The principle of "no crimes without victims" is simply an excuse to have a bash at Christianity in general and "any system of sexual morality" in particular.

Does a crime need a named victim?

The authors of the draft Bills blithely accept or reject the principle of "no crimes without victims" as and when it suits them. But then other libertarians, who tend to be those on the far right, accept the principle in its entirety, as part of a package that extols the material welfare of "the individual" above all else. We must therefore challenge the "old civil libertarian principle" in order to see whether that principle is right in itself. This will be useful when in subsequent chapters we ask why a liberal capitalist democracy must oppose homosexual lifestyles and activities.

Firstly it would be good to see if there is such a thing as "private" behaviour.

It was and is a tenet of permissiveness that so long as all are consenting, permissiveness never does anyone any harm. But as Canon Ian Dunlop has explained, this rather hinges on what we regard as harm. "Do you regard a spoilt child as having been harmed?" he asks. "Do you regard it as 'harming' a person to make it easy for them to be satisfied with something less than the highest of which they are capable?"[20]

Libertarians opt out of mutual responsibility

Canon Dunlop clearly does, and he uses the example of marriage and divorce to illustrate his point further. A life-long partnership based on mutual love is the best that marriage can offer, but many people content themselves with something much less than this, including cohabitation and "serial monogamy" often resulting from, and in, divorce. He says of these people:

> *Insofar as it is the general climate of opinion about marriage and divorce which makes them content with second best, I would claim that the climate of opinion has harmed them. It has made the door to the high tops difficult to penetrate. It may make it easier to reach this door if alternative doors are kept shut.*[21]

The "climate of opinion" is of course created bit by bit by everyone. All those who work at a happy and successful partnership contribute to the example of what *can* be done, and those who make a mess of it also contribute, by making it easier for others to proceed from marriage to divorce, the more so if they are highly visible in public life. He concludes:

> It is therefore utter nonsense to claim that what you do "in private" is no concern of anyone else - it is their concern as part of their creative environment. ... I think that permissiveness can be seen as harmful if you see it as a readiness to allow other people to go down hill as fast as they like and to opt out of mutual responsibility. But I suspect that permissiveness implies that there is no hill to go down. If that is true of sexual morality, it may be true of morality as a whole.[22]

Private immorality has public consequences

Canon Dunlop clearly cares about his fellow human beings, and it is this readiness to adopt the sufferings of others, which Christians call "compassion", that so irritates the libertarians of the left and of the right. The true libertarian regards such concern for others as Canon Dunlop demonstrates as an unwarranted interference in the rights of others to go to the Devil in their own way. Their private behaviour, so the argument runs, is entirely their own affair. But this just will not do. The law intrudes into the bedroom already, as it were, in cases of unlawful sexual intercourse, incest, polygamy, evaluation of paternity, and prostitution. Sexual "reformers" have inevitably argued against its intrusion in most if not all of these cases, but the Christian view has prevailed so far.

It is necessary to point to a few instances in which private morality, or its lack, has public consequences. Even the Labour Campaign Manifesto recognised the insidious effects of the cause majeure of the libertarian, pornography. Images of sex and violence whether photographic, cinematographic or written, have in the very recent past led to a large increase in rape, and to the Hungerford massacre.[23] Police have found pornographic hordes of the most appalling material in which children are sexually abused and tortured. By depraving the viewer, they blur his whole conception of morality, his distinction between right and wrong, and this spills over into the rest of his life. None of us is so self-sufficient as to be untouched by what Canon Dunlop calls our "cultural environment." If the police of the Vice-squad need special help and support when wading through pornographic material, then what must be the effect on the regular user?

The law does affect behaviour

If the simplistic civil libertarian slogans of "victimless crime" seem better chanted than analysed in this one example, doubt must also be cast on the sloganising about homosexual activity. With an increased tolerance of homosexual activity, and in the face of its more visible and open manifestations, more men and women, at lower and more impressionable ages, will be drawn into such behaviour. We saw earlier that those with homosexual tendencies are able to exercise a choice of whether to allow their inclinations to spill over into actions, and also that many practitioners of homosexual activity do not and would not classify themselves as homosexual, let alone "gay." There is a continuum, or if you like a slippery slope, to do with homosexuality, and Roger Magnuson puts it better than I could:

> *It reaches from casual thoughts and impulses to temptations, from temptations to discrete acts, from acts to habits, from habits to an entrenched life-style. ... Not everyone with homosexual tendencies acts out his behaviour, just as not everyone with temptations to steal, steals. Unless the inclination comes together with the opportunity, such tendencies may remain latent and never crystallise into behaviour.*[24]

The existence of the victims

The activists in Stonewall or the Labour Campaign would see it as a pity if the tendencies remained latent. The opposite view, that harm will accrue within the individual who becomes involved in homosexual activity, is not only borne out by the psychological and behavioural problems of active homosexuals, but also by disease.

We have covered all of this earlier, and we also looked at the impact of AIDS. If anything will nail the idea that what we do in our own home is only our own business, it must be AIDS. People who have been infected range from the drug-injector and the promiscuous active homosexual, through the man having "a bit of quick sex," to the haemophiliac and the newborn child. It was through the sexual activities of homosexuals and the injecting of drug users and their subsequent blood donations that haemophiliacs and other recipients of infected blood became affected.

Getting away from AIDS, the young boy or girl recruited into homosexual behaviour who would not have been if the 1967 Sexual Offences Act had not been passed is still a victim of that Act unless homosexual behaviour is good in itself. And moving away from homosexuality, the victims of divorce and abortion are likewise denied by the civil libertarian. Against all the evidence, the libertarian persists in a denial-based belief that children must be better off if the parents divorce, and that there cannot possibly be a human being in the womb.

The victims are always there, invisible to the blind civil libertarian. Furthermore, the old civil libertarian principle which demands that a victim stand up in court before a crime can be said to have been committed will not allow the understanding that the death of any AIDS victim has affected or diminished us all, no matter whether he was innocent or culpable of an action which led to AIDS. By extension, we are all involved in the activities of those of our fellows recruited into homosexual activity. John Donne recognised this, three hundred and fifty years ago:

No man is an Iland, intire of it selfe; every man is a peece of the Continent, a part of the maine; if a Clod bee washed away by the Sea, Europe is the lesse, as well as if a Mannor of thy friends or of thine owne were; any mans death diminishes me, because I am involved in Mankinde; And therefore never send to know for whom the bell tolls; It tolls for thee.

29
Homosexuality and Conservatism

Is the Conservative Party most at ease with traditional morality, or with a morality which includes liberal views on homosexuality? Since 1979, Conservatives like Norman Tebbit and especially Margaret Thatcher have espoused "Victorian Values" and individual responsibility. Has this rhetoric been put into action by a reversal of the permissive society, driving back the immoral tide of the sixties and seventies? Anti-Christian, anti-family legislation from the late sixties liberalising abortion, homosexuality, divorce and obscenity, and abolishing capital punishment, is heavily associated with the Labour party, and was there to be repealed. Martin Durham, a senior lecturer in politics, has investigated this area. This is what he says:

> *Commentators have taken the anti-abortion movement to be the same as the organisations campaigning for "family values," have drawn an equals sign between both movements and Thatcherism and, above all, have argued that the Thatcher government and the British New Right is engaged in a campaign to enforce traditional moral values.*[1]

Arguing that "none of these is the case," Durham concludes that in its dealings with pro-life and pro-family groups the Thatcher government was less than consistent:

> *On key issues the government proved to be a disappointment or even an antagonist rather than an ally.*[2]

Conservative Christians had some successes, over sex education, Section 28, the re-introduction of Christian assemblies in schools and the voting down of Sunday trading, but these were small if worthwhile victories, and generally, Mrs Thatcher, whilst economically dry, was morally wet.

The confusion that Martin Durham notes amongst "commentators" is understandable. Senior Conservative politicians, from Mrs Thatcher and Keith Joseph in the 70s to senior ministers today, constantly affirm that the presence of strong, independent and self-sufficient families is essential for stability in both the economic and social spheres.

In October 1990 Angela Rumbold was the platform speaker in a scheduled debate on "The Family" at the Conservative Party Conference in Bournemouth. Those of the party faithful who spoke before her lamented the continuing demise of the traditional family and the rise in teenage pregnancies, abortions, divorce, the visibility of homosexuality, immoral sex education, and indeed all of the anti-Christian, anti-family paraphernalia of the permissive society.

Mrs Rumbold agreed. The family as understood in its traditional form was the building brick of society. When families broke down they placed a burden on the state. We needed strong families both as a defence against socialism and to act as the foundation of a strong happy society. The Government would continue to support the family.[3]

Virginia Bottomley said these same things in the debate on the family at the 1991 Tory Party conference in Blackpool. This was the balloted motion, which says something about the strength of feeling of ordinary Conservative Party workers about the lack of Government action supporting the traditional family. The family for Mrs Bottomley was "the basic building brick of society." "Crime, degeneracy, violence and horror break to the surface of our society" when "the basic cohesiveness of the family unit breaks down."[4] Indeed, the evidence is all around us. How very perceptive these Conservative lady ministers are on the essential role of the traditional family in a capitalist democracy, and how observant of the ill effects of neglecting the institution of the family.

Curiously, such affirmation never results in positive supportive action. The 1992 Tory Manifesto said that it would "tackle crime at its roots" and then failed to list a root, let alone a measure to pull up a root. As the evidence supports Mrs Bottomley's analysis, we should suppose that the Conservatives would support marriage and the institution of the family in every way possible. The Conservative Party has long thought of itself as the prime defender of the family, and has traditionally regarded such a stance as being incompatible with a liberal attitude towards homosexuality. There are good reasons both for the support for the family and for the dichotomy between the values nurtured by the family and those espoused by gay rights, which we shall come to. Well it is true that the Government removed the double mortgage tax relief for cohabiting couples, and put the taxation of wives onto the same footing as single women, but these measures only removed two of the more glaring *dis*incentives to marriage and were targeted at the childless. There was no positive support of marriage and traditional stable family life in public policy from Mrs Thatcher at all. Not one positive measure. Nothing. In the 1991 Budget for example, and again in 1992, every tax allowance was uprated in line with inflation except the married couple's allowance.

When asked how the Conservative Party has specifically supported the family since it came to power in 1979, ministers these days can only say that the Government is to make absconding fathers support their families, and will make parents responsible for their children's criminal acts. These are both very necessary, but rather negative. Moreover, they are still only proposals.

With the greatest of respect to Mrs Rumbold and Mrs Bottomley, "the family" is just as much only a "women's issue" for Tories as it is for Labour. Two years in succession it was sadly not even worth asking a male minister to conclude a debate.

The record of the Conservative Party

Let us look at the record of the Conservative Party on homosexuality. Leaving aside Section 28, it is overwhelmingly liberal.

The Department of Health as we have seen promotes homosexuality through fortunes paid out in grants to proselytising homosexual AIDS "charities." A Grant was given to the SIGMA researchers in Cardiff to encourage under-age homosexual activity and there has been collusion over a new British Standard condom for buggery.

Any single woman or lesbian may since 1991 apply for AID, and the Chairman of the Human Fertilisation and Embryology Authority, Professor Colin Campbell, admitted that under the rules laid down by the Government, the final decision would rest with specialists and counsellors. The welfare of the child need only be given "attention."[5] The homosexual press joyfully reported Flora Goldhill, chief executive of the HFEA who said "No category of women will be precluded from treatment on the basis of sexuality. It will be up to the centre to decide whether a single mother is able to meet the needs of the child."[6]

A combination of pressure from militant lesbian groups like "Rights of Women," which is funded by the London Boroughs Grants Group, and non-judgmental counselling from organisations like the amoral British Pregnancy Advisory Service will ensure that no lesbian who wants a baby is turned away. The "Women's Reproductive Rights Centre," an offshoot of the National Abortion Campaign, already organises "self-insemination groups" quite independently of clinics or the NHS.[7]

Gay and lesbian adoption

Within weeks of the insemination guidelines, militant homosexuals claimed an even bigger success over guidelines on fostering and adoption.[8] The draft wording of Paragraph 16 of the guidelines to the Children Act 1989 had stated that "gay rights and equal rights have no place in fostering or adoption policies."

The "Stonewall" lobby group objected to this wording, and its then director Tim Barnett and Michael Brown, MP for Brigg and Cleethorpes, went to see Virginia Bottomley in February 1991 to explain that "lesbians and gay men" would be "offended" by the guidelines.[9] Virginia Bottomley agreed with them that the wording could cause offence, and when the full guidelines appeared in April 1991, the offending words had gone. In the meantime there were demonstrations outside the Department of Health by lesbians, members of Outrage and at least one former member of Gay Liberation Front. The lie that "The vast majority of abuse of children occurs in heterosexual family groups" came out again, and the Haldane Society of Socialist Lawyers supported the action.[10]

The latter body, working with "Rights of Women" has been achieving success very quietly also in the field of gaining custody of children in divorce cases for lesbian mothers over their normal fathers.

Health Minister Mrs Bottomley herself praised the promiscuous homosexual musician Freddie Mercury as "heroic" after he died from AIDS. None of this was what party workers who heard her speech on the family had expected.

Liberal establishment

"Politically Correct" views about homosexuality appear to be endemic in Government. On whether this demonstrates the existence of a "gay mafia" I have no evidence.[11] But certainly the cause of homosexual activists is assiduously championed by every Government Department, not just by the Department of Health.

The Department of Education and Science has provided youth service grants to organisations known to promote homosexuality, all the way back to the Albany Trust of the 70s. In 1988, the Home Office was funding a publication of the National Youth Bureau entitled "Sparetime, Sharetime," which listed six "gay voluntary organisations."[12] More recently, under Education Secretary Kenneth Clarke, orders were laid to introduce compulsory amoral sex education for 11-14 year olds into the syllabus by the back-door route of writing knowledge of the HIV virus into the science curriculum.

Of course at the DHSS Kenneth Clarke opposed Victoria Gillick, who wished to be responsible for whether or not her under age daughter should be given hormonal contraception. Having said that he would abide by whatever decision the Appeal Court handed down, when his Department lost, Mr Clarke appealed to the House of Lords, and won. The irony of a Conservative Minister undermining parental responsibilities was not lost on Mrs Gillick. More recently it was Kenneth Clarke who forced abortion on demand up to birth through the House of Commons. He is now Home Secretary.

The Home Office brought relentless pressure to bear on the Isle of Man until its House of Keys caved in and voted to decriminalise homosexual acts, and encouraged the inclusion of "sexual orientation" in the equal opportunities statement of the Metropolitan Police.

The Ministry of Defence has now announced that homosexual activity in the forces will no longer constitute an offence, although persons involved in such activity will continue to be dismissed from the services. Legislation will be brought before Parliament soon.

In November 1991, the Lord Advocate for Scotland, a Government minister, tried unilaterally to reduce the homosexual "age of consent" in Scotland from 21 to 16 without reference to Parliament at all. Only swift action by the president of Conservative Family Campaign, Bill Walker, MP for Tayside North, in setting down an Early Day Motion with the support of leading parliamentarians, stopped this move. In addition, the Scottish Office has regularly poured money into the most irresponsible and obscene Aids group yet, Scottish AIDS Monitor.

The Welsh office provided money to subsidise Glamorgan housewives with free condoms if they decide to supplement their incomes by prostitution, as we saw in chapter 8. There can scarcely be a Government Department involved in decisions about morality that has not acquiesced to every demand made by permissive lobbyists.

Paradoxically, the Government gains no credit for its weakness. The liberal media and especially "the gays" are only momentarily pleased by these results. They regard every concession as a sign of weakness and promptly demand more. The only way was to say "no" at the start, and mean it.

Which side is John Major on?

There was a report in the Londoner's Diary pages of the early edition of the Evening Standard on Tuesday 11th December 1990 which repeated the claim made by Capital Gay that John Major himself was in favour of a lowering of the homosexual "age of consent." So embarrassed was No10 by this report, the telephone lines fizzed and the report was pulled by the late edition.

It seems that the Prime Minister was collared by gay rights activists in his constituency surgery some years ago, and declared his support for a reduction. Indeed he voted to extend the 1967 Sexual Offences Act both to Scotland and to Northern Ireland.[12] There again he voted for Section 28 as a member of Mrs Thatcher's Cabinet. Be all that as it may, letters asking him to clarify his position went unanswered until No 10 wrote to the Chairman of Conservative Family Campaign to deny the story in the Standard and to say that John Major was not in favour of lowering the minimum age.

Only two weeks later, John Major announced in the House of Commons that homosexuals would no longer be regarded as a security risk in the secret and diplomatic services because of "changing public attitudes." Next, he asked the homosexual actor and activist Sir Ian McKellen to visit No 10 and discuss an agenda for "gay rights." Just before the election, he indicated support for the "Tory Campaign for Homosexual Equality" (TORCHE).

John Major himself is known to be passionately pro-family and opposed to gay rights. Everyone to whom I have spoken says that he is a genuinely nice man with a willingness to listen. But the conflicting signals from him and from his Government make things very confusing for the outside world.

Tory moves on liberalisation of homosexuality

So where does the pro-homosexual pressure come from? Members of a small cabal within the Party, whilst not necessarily homosexual themselves, are sympathetic to homosexuality and further liberalisation. It is almost certain that it is their ignorance of homosexuality which is colouring their judgment, although one or two of them certainly seem to devote an untoward amount of energy to the issue. They are in the main decent people anxious to be kind to unfortunates, or concerned about what they see as injustice. Being reasonable people, when the evidence in these pages is brought to their attention, they will certainly change their minds on these matters.

The group includes MPs Andrew Rowe, Matthew Carrington, Emma Nicholson, Michael Brown and Steven Norris MP, who was Parliamentary Private Secretary to Kenneth Baker, and is now a junior minister. It is led by Sir John Wheeler MP, who in the last Parliament was Chairman of the Home Affairs Select Committee, and Robin Squire MP, who was PPS to the Party Chairman before the election and is also now a junior minister. They have since the election been joined by Edwina Currie and John Bowis.

In spite of the fact that, unlike that of all the other parties, the Conservative Party Manifesto remained a gay rights-free zone, Sir John Wheeler in particular was hoping to remain as Chairman of his committee in order to use it to promote further liberalisation of homosexuality, if not measures for "gay rights." This was initially complicated by the problems in the Labour Party, which has only recently been able to put forward its own names to the select committees. Then Sir John was caught by the new rule that MPs may not sit on a select committee for more than three parliaments, which was invented by the whips to push Nicholas Winterton off the Health Select Committee. The new elected chairman of the Home Affairs Select Committee is Sir Ivan Lawrence, who is thought to incline more towards the status quo. The pressure for liberalisation will not abate, however. Those pushing homosexuality went so far as to try to organise a debate before the summer recess. The special pleading will continue.

I believe that the reason why liberalisation of the law is taken seriously at all in Conservative circles is firstly ignorance of homosexuality, but secondly the same reason why various pro-gay, anti-family measures have advanced as Government policy. Conservatism simply lacks a political philosophy. The Party does not know what being pro-family means, and is not even too sure if it should be pro-family at all "in the modern world," with its "changing mores." The David Mellor affair illustrated this perfectly. But the Conservative Party is in power now and for the next four years, maybe also to the turn of the century. Its policies, and the political philosophy upon which they are founded, are those necessarily of the United Kingdom itself. So whether the Conservative Party can do without supporting traditional family life and forget about being "the Party of the Family" is a question I shall now address.

30
Gay rights v liberal democracy

In the last chapter but one, we saw the myth that homosexual acts are "victimless crimes" exploded by simply considering the effects of homosexual behaviour on individuals and on society at large. We could leave the matter there, and yet in chapter 19 we came across conflict between the values of gay rights and the values of the family. It is on the values of the family that our society is founded, that and the Christian faith. Most parents will put their opposition to homosexuality in the terms of not wanting their children to be corrupted into a lifestyle characterised by disease, degradation and death. But supposing society itself was so corrupted, what then? It is the function of the political philosopher to tell us the answer.

The reader will forgive first dragging religion into a discussion of homosexuality and now introducing political philosophy. Politics and religion may hold the most important questions we ever consider, and seeing how demands for homosexual rights fit into one worldview or another is a worthwhile exercise. It should be obvious by now that no-one could be an expert on every one of the areas of study that we have considered in this book, and that is why I have drawn on the evidence of others throughout and will do so again here.

The need for a conservative political philosophy

The political question is simply put: Why should a liberal capitalist democracy like ours oppose the range of permissive social policies of which one example is homosexual rights? Upon what foundation should it build its political philosophy? Until recently that foundation in the UK was unspoken but indeed Christian, broadly following the Bible in which the author of the book of Proverbs says that any society which follows the laws of God will be successful: "Righteousness exalteth the nation." But that principle needs testing and explaining in today's world, where Christian values are used one moment to attack the capitalist system, and the next moment are attacked themselves for not being permissive enough. Little work has been done to show why righteousness exalted the nation and whether abandoning the Christian and family base to our capitalist, democratic system is a good idea. We shall have to feel our way carefully, standing on the shoulders of many men greater than ourselves in order to see a little further than they could individually.

The first problem is that Conservatives seem to have no articulated political philosophy. By "conservatives" I mean those political parties of the right and centre throughout the developed world, such as the Conservative Party in Britain, the Republicans in the United States and their counterparts in Australasia and elsewhere. Norman Barry of the Institute for Economic Affairs believes that Conservatives have never seen the need to build a coherent political ideology:

Conservatives have tended to retreat from abstract, ideological debate: hunch, instinct, faith in immanent wisdom of an inarticulated tradition have always been preferred to the dissolving powers of human reason.[1]

David Willetts, late director of the Centre for Policy Studies, now Tory MP for Havant, agrees. Conservatives distrust "ideologies" and prefer tradition. Willetts himself traces a line of free-market, one-nation Toryism from the eighteenth-century philosophers William Burke, David Hume and Adam Smith through to John Major.[2] He suggests also that when Conservatives have put forward new ideas, such as free trade, or social reforms, Conservatism has thrived, and when it has simply reacted, as to turn-of-the-century Liberalism, or to the Fabians, or to post-war socialism, that it has floundered.

Professor Barry argues in his overview of the "New Right" that the MacMillan/Heath years in Britain, together with the Labour governments that alternated with them, formed a "consensus" characterised by market intervention, nationalisation, the extension of the welfare state, and a "permissive" social policy. Margaret Thatcher can be seen as "anti-consensus" in that she went some way towards returning to a more traditional Conservatism which the consensus had threatened totally to submerge. But her's was still "hunch" Conservatism, driven by little more than good housekeeping and rolling back the state. Of course those things are a necessary part of what a conservative political ideology would be, but they are not sufficient.

A clue to what is missing lies in the one important area in which Mrs Thatcher left the "consensus" intact to this day. Her Government allowed the liberal establishment to thrive and it continued to enact permissive legislation, relaxing the rules on divorce and abortion, for instance. Existing permissive legislation was consolidated, whilst liberal attitudes became, as we have seen, firmly established in government departments.

Let us not be too hard on the Conservatives; in the absence of a coherent ideology, and in the face of feminist humanist pressure, they have no alternative to caving in to the liberal establishment, the single parent lobby, homosexual pressure groups and all the rest of the permissives. Whilst periodically eulogising the family, they see no need to defend it.

In a report about the way single parenthood and fractured households are advancing, Malcolm Wicks of the Family Policy Studies Centre said:

All the key indicators have moved away from the traditional family model. There are fewer marriages, more cohabitation, more children born out of wedlock, high divorce rates and more one-parent families.

These are powerful forces and, faced with them, governments are relatively powerless. The trends in the last 12 years were not for turning.[3]

On the face of it, this is not the undisguised glee at the demise of the traditional family that issued from Neil Kinnock or from the Labour think tank the Institute for Public Policy Research. But Wicks' conclusion of the powerlessness of government is false. Although laws cannot make people good, some laws permit them to do bad. Permissive legislation does not just allow the few hard cases through, but creates a whole new market in the behaviour that was previously the province only of the hard cases. Martin Luther King once said:

Morality cannot be legislated, but behaviour can be regulated. Judicial decrees may not change the heart, but they can restrain the heartless.

If government found the will, born of a coherent ideology, it could reverse the trends. Obliging couples to open their minds to reconciliation would result in fewer divorces. Weighting the tax system strongly in favour of marriage and children, instead of, as at present, single parenthood and dual-income-no-kids, would surely have some effect. Abolishing single-parent benefit and the right of single mothers to jump the council housing queue, and increasing benefits for couples who are married, by removing the fiscal deterrent to having a man about the house, whether we might like such measures or not, might encourage marriage and its stability amongst those on benefit.

None of these would be impossible for government to do, given the will. In 13 years, with three landslide majorities, Mrs Thatcher could have done them all. So where does that leave the Family Policies Study Centre? For all the hands-wringing, Malcolm Wicks, who stood as the Labour Parliamentary candidate for Croydon North West in 1987, winning it in 1992, is not saying that governments *can not* reverse the trend, but saying that in his opinion they *should not*.

As a result of consensus approval for alternative lifestyles, the family as traditionally understood has in the last twenty-five years declined, and the various alternative and permissive groups have advanced. Visible and vocal homosexuality is only one example of a society going badly wrong. The Austrian then naturalised British economist and philosopher Frederick von Hayek who died in March 1992 held that this was bound to happen; the lack of an ideological anchor for conservatism allows it to be swept away by pragmatism and political opportunism, adopting policies ultimately destructive of a free society.[4]

Over thirteen years the Conservatives have watched illegitimate births soar by 250%, from one in ten to one in four, and have done nothing to arrest let alone turn the trend. It cannot be a source of pride to Conservatives that out of every three children conceived by women in the younger age groups, one is now killed by abortion, one is brought up by an unmarried mother, and only one is able to live and grow up in a stable traditional family. To look at another area of policy, the decline in standards in schools is almost solely the result of consensus egalitarian teaching methods and philosophy, and has only now been addressed by the Party.

It has been said that some of these disasters are the result of Thatcherism not going far enough in the economic sphere. The "New Right" about which Professor Barry writes would have introduced education vouchers at once, and would have increased the marginal benefits of work at the expense of welfare. He says of Mrs Thatcher that "her failure to tackle effectively the vast elements of statism in education, housing and welfare dismayed some of her supporters."[5] But at the same time, "new right" Conservatives can advance no more than pragmatic reasons why these measures should have been introduced: that education vouchers would have increased "choice" for example.

Indeed, the extension of "choice" is in danger of passing for the ideology of Conservatism. Chris Patten, as Conservative Party

Chairman, said at the Party's 1991 conference in Blackpool that it was important for Conservatives to reassert their principles and to set out a clear and precise view of what they wanted victory at the election for. This is all he came up with:

> Tories want sound money, the encouragement of enterprise, the enlargement of opportunity and choice and the improvement of public services within a country secure at home and able to place its mark on international affairs abroad.[6]

The problem is, Neil Kinnock and Paddy Ashdown said much the same in their party's 1992 election manifestos. The bald adoption of "opportunity and choice" as an ideology, whilst superficially attractive, is unsatisfactory. It begs the question: what may I exercise choice about? What have I an opportunity to do?

I can validly choose which vegetables or what car to buy. But I can now choose, if I am a mother, to kill the child in my womb or let it live to be born. Is that right? We may be asked to legislate to allow euthanasia. Homosexual activity is seen by radicals simply as a matter of "choice." And do we just tell the small boy whose safe little world is being blown to pieces by his parents' divorce: "Tough luck son, grown-ups are making their choices?" A society must decide where to draw the line on what is a valid choice, and we are back once again to asking what is the ideological base from which it makes that decision.

Again, we can say, with Chris Patten, that Conservatism aims for "opportunity;" material advancement, the increase of wealth and the building of a prosperous society, and so it does, but these are all economic means to what end? A materialistic consumerism is the aim of both atheistic Marxism and the humanist New Right and has not been demonstrated to bring contentment. Additionally, do we really mean to give adult homosexual males the "opportunity" to bugger teenagers? Entrepreneurs (such as Richard Branson with his "Heaven" homosexual nightclub) can make a lot of money from "gay" consumerism, others (such as Richard Branson with his Virgin stores and now W H Smith as well) can sell the Terrence Higgins Trust gay pornographic video to teenagers - it has an "18" certificate - or to take a "green" example, men may operate a factory which kills a river with unscrubbed waste. Presumably people of good will wish the pursuit of prosperity or recreation to have some morality, and do not wish to poison either the natural or the spiritual environment, but if Conservatism does not accept unrestrained hedonism, it must give a reason.

To complete this line of thinking, the problem of present-day Conservatism is that because it lacks a coherent political philosophy, it does not always know why it does what it does. Certainly it responds to pressure, and it always desires to be re-elected. But all that and making the trains run on time really is not good enough. The 1992 general election was characterised by a lack of issues and the Tory manifesto by a lack of substance. The Party was returned more because voters knew what Labour would do to their wallet or purse and didn't like it than because they were fired up by a Conservative vision. All the trumpeting of "opportunity" and "choice" still did not tell us "what we wanted victory at the election for." In the language of today, where is the big idea, where's the beef? The voters have a right to ask, and Conservatives have a duty to tell them: What is Conservatism for?

The failure of socialism

Let us look firstly at the democratic capitalist system which Conservatives defend. Conservatives are constantly pushed onto the back foot when asked how their capitalist vision of society measures up to that of the socialist, or that of the Christian. There is no reason for such defensiveness. Firstly, socialism is hopelessly utopian and flawed for the Christian because, like humanism, it denies the doctrine of original sin. It denies the complete creation narrative, come to that. For the socialist, men are born good and are corrupted by the institutions of their society: crime, violence, riot are indicative of poverty, not wickedness, and deprivation is only material, never spiritual. It is inequality, not the devil, who finds work for idle hands. But Luke tells us in Acts 5 that voluntary collectivism failed even in the early church. Men must be like angels for socialism to work.

Intellectually, Hayek showed that to understand let alone control an organism, a market, for example, one must be more complex than the organism under study. A human mind will therefore never understand the human mind. A board of trade can never know enough to fix the correct prices, and no local authority can know enough to manage its schools. For Hayek, decisions must be taken as far down the line as possible, and socialism's state control ends in failure every time.

That being said, socialism where it works at all, works in the family. Our children do not give bonds redeemable on their future economic performance in return for pocket money. We on the other hand do not charge them for board and lodging. A man and his wife pool their resources, of time, ability and money. The family is a fundamental unit of loyalty. Sin has not been abolished in it, but the ties that bind the members of a family together are strong enough to take the strain that temporary discontentments put upon them, before bringing all together again. If it is argued that some families do not work as well as I describe, then how do these critics expect the wider socialist "family" to work?

The American theologian and economist Michael Novak has for the first time explained how democracy, capitalism and the Christian ethic interconnect. In "The Spirit of Democratic Capitalism," he observes that socialism has failed to deliver prosperity wherever it has been tried. There is no country in the world where socialism has enriched, or even properly fed, the population. Socialists are undaunted by failure, and do not preach the superiority of the works of socialism, preferring to concentrate on its values:

> Although some try to place the best face they can upon existing socialist experiments elsewhere, and continue to greet new ones with fresh hope, most insist upon distinguishing what they mean by socialism from what occurs within existing socialist states. In this sense, socialism has lost its grip on concrete reality.[7]

Socialism cannot stand comparison with capitalism as a means of delivering the goods upon which populations depend, and it is for this reason, Novak contends, that its adherents have raised socialism instead to the status of a religion, and stress its vision, and "the moral worth of its ideals." They rest the case for socialism not on its results but on "its supposed moral superiority over capitalism."

The success of "Democratic Capitalism"

The failure of socialism is however at its most complete on its own ground. It fails to bear the moral fruit it promises. Socialist countries are not free, happy and moral. On the other hand, although what Novak calls "democratic capitalism" never promised to be a moral system, nevertheless, certainly up to the present, virtues of loyalty and thrift somehow thrive within it. Even selflessness grows under democratic capitalism to the extent that democratic socialists may appeal to the altruism of the electorate in their campaigns to extend the welfare state.

So this is the second point, that capitalism and Christianity are perfectly compatible. "Democratic capitalism" does not claim high moral ideals, but rests its case on what it has achieved. It was built upon a divergence of property-owning interests, a market economy and the application of hard work. The vast majority of people came to own their homes and land, and they built and worked for tomorrow. They created wealth, stability and community. It is no coincidence that capitalism and democracy are found together, for they flourish symbiotically, with the one nourishing the other. This thesis provides the title of Novak's book, with the "spirit" of the moral-cultural system supporting a democratic polity and a capitalist economy. These three are to Novak the very pillars of democratic capitalism.[8]

Importance of the moral-cultural system

Novak is confident that the rules or "logic" of the democratic process and of the market economy support each other. However, these two are still dependent upon the moral-cultural system:

> Without certain moral and cultural presuppositions about the nature of individuals and their communities, about liberty and sin, about the changeability of history, about work and savings, about self-restraint and mutual co-operation, neither democracy nor capitalism can be made to work. Under some moral-cultural conditions, they are simply unachievable.[9]

Perhaps working too much from an American standpoint - he clearly admires the American constitution, which separates church from state - Novak puts the case that the moral-cultural values of democratic capitalism derive from its Jewish, Christian and humanist inheritance. At the same time he observes that the Church, in developing a theological understanding of democratic capitalism, has lagged behind its practical expression. After two hundred years of the material and, Novak argues, the spiritual success of the democratic capitalist system, his own Roman Catholic Church is only now dimly understanding that capitalism can exist in something other than the traditional peasant economy version which Southern Europe exported to South and Central America. It is interesting in David Alton's visionary book "Faith in Britain," that examples of exploitative capitalism are invariably taken from Latin America. As Novak points out in some detail, Latin America is not an example of the democratic capitalism he is writing about.

But to cross swords with Novak, it is open to question whether the humanist inheritance that he cites has done much good at all. The only good values of humanism seem to be those about the worth of the individual and treatment of neighbour which it shares with Christianity and Judaism. It might be, and we shall come to this, that it is this humanistic pluralism of democratic capitalism that is its Achilles heel. Novak does not accept that, but still goes so far with some who predict the fall of democracy paradoxically through material success as to concede that the flaw in democratic capitalism is that "its successes in the political order and in the economic order undermine it in the cultural order."[10]

Michael Novak makes the point that intellectuals, "poets, philosophers and priests," have not sought to love their own culture. He believes that this is for many reasons, amongst which are: that their status is lower than in traditional societies, where they were feted by aristocrats and bowed down to by the peasantry, that they are rewarded less for their efforts than are the captains of industry and politics, and that they cannot abide the lack of taste, the vulgarity and prejudice of an affluent bourgeoisie. Socialism for the intellectual elite seems to offer the ability to put the citizenry back in its place. Novak asks of democratic capitalism: "Can any political system or economic system long survive whose moral-cultural guardians loathe it so?" [11]

Many of the people whom Novak regards as the "guardians of the moral-cultural system," teachers, academics, and so on, are largely the constituency in the United States of the Democratic Party and in Britain of the Labour Party.[12] They refuse to allow the good faith of those who defend democratic capitalism, displaying all the prejudices, the intolerance even, of the "pathologically tolerant." Being politically leftist and humanist in thinking, they cannot see either that morality could possibly justify capitalism, or that democracy could depend on Christian morality.

Strangely enough, these two propositions are difficult for some conservatives, particularly for the "new right" economic liberals, whose ideology we shall now consider.

31

The sexual marketplace

In classic liberal economic theory, the state has little to do. Virtually all economic activity depends upon the market, in which the price of everything from labour to property is subject to market forces. If a commodity is priced too high, its demand falls until the price is what the market will accept. Conversely, a commodity priced too low will rise in demand and in price until its price is what the market will bear. This process theoretically is in constant operation if free competition is allowed, and Adam Smith maintained that the price of every commodity so determined by the market was guided by what he termed an "invisible hand." Anyone wandering around a wholesale food market will soon see that prices seem to stabilise within limits without the aid of cartel meetings or outside interference. This shows the invisible hand at work, and Hayek demonstrates that it works better than any controlling committee "hand" ever could.

Those economists who advocate that more or less unrestrained market forces should fix the supply and demand of every tangible and intangible commodity claim that their system has never actually been given a chance to prove itself. Because the left always wants to limit the effect of the market by state regulation, it was easy to identify what was a fresh wave of classical liberals as the New, or Radical, Right. Professor Norman Barry wryly notes that classical liberal ideas "are not associated with any political party in Britain (certainly not the Liberal Party) though their influence has in contemporary times been felt most strongly in Conservative ranks."[1]

There is some suspicion of the classical liberalism of the "new right" amongst Conservatives. Traditionalists are sceptical about the benefits of the individualism of such unfettered market philosophies. Roger Scruton has shown that social relationships in particular cannot be reduced to "choice." No-one "decides" to act homosexually or "chooses" to have an affair in quite the same way as he chooses between the relative merits of two CD players, or decides to have fish

The sexual marketplace

and chips for dinner. The former decisions are of course of much more import, affect more people, and are considered less rationally, than the latter.

Nevertheless, as we saw in chapter 1, radical gay activists claim that it is, or should be, possible to "choose" to be homosexual. We saw in chapter 20 that some political lesbians say that they have chosen homosexuality in order to be fully feminist. The psychology of homosexuality indicates that some emotional hurt must have been there in the first place, so that it is not true that "any woman can be a lesbian," although we saw in chapter 14 that homosexual activity itself is chosen behaviour. So although "choosing" a homosexual lifestyle is not as simple as "choosing" this car over that car, the use of the language of the marketplace is a shrewd move by radical gays, allying them with the libertarians of the right.

Yet although the libertarian right assumes the sovereignty of the market in all spheres, it has yet to prove that free market forces are beneficial anywhere other than literally in a market. In other words although we might agree that if no-one wants to buy 78rpm records any more, such a commodity may with impunity disappear from the shelves, can the same be said in the social and sexual sphere, in particular, in relation to marriage and childbearing? In the case of the latter, the radical right simply assumes that the "market" can operate, having its cake and eating it. In Britain at least, marriage, having children and bringing them up in the traditional manner (where father provides and mother cares) are all firmly discouraged in the tax and benefit systems, and libertarians then proceed fraudulently to say that rising illegitimacy and falling birth-rates demonstrate that marriage, birth and motherhood are unpopular.

If we were to meet the new right on its own ground, we should agree that people will make their own moral decisions in numerous areas of personal conduct, "choosing" between different "products" in the "market," between divorce and staying together, for example. We should then say that the job of Government is to make those "products" which are beneficial to a stable society relatively more attractive than those conducive to disorder. At present our society does the opposite, and the invisible hand, if there is one in this social, sexual "marketplace," is tied behind its back.

Conservatives however traditionally hold a scepticism concerning the ability of direct policy initiatives to bring about desirable ends. This is not to say that no policy initiative will ever bring about a desirable end, but it can be argued that those that work with human nature will have more success than those which try to work against. In economic activity this is accepted by classical liberalism:

> Politics should be limited to preserving social order and not extended to the promotion of substantive equality or social justice. This will only raise expectations that cannot be fulfilled and will result in a threat to the fabric of the social order.[2]

Noting that Conservatives see a central function for the state in upholding order, Professor Barry overstates by naming conservatism "pessimistic" and accusing it of a belief in "the ultimate depravity of man."[3] Novak reminds us that the concept of original sin (with which Barry is uncomfortable) "does not entail that each person is in all ways depraved, only that each person sometimes sins."[4] Barry accepts original sin in other realms, for example when he writes that governments tend to be deflected by the necessity to secure their re-election from the policies that they know they should pursue for the public good. They might go so far as to offer bribes to the electorate.[5] He even writes of "certain contingent (but scarcely alterable) features of the human condition,"[6] an acceptance of the sinfulness of humanity if ever there was one. He explains also that at the heart of socialist economic theory is the problem of the altruism of the public sector:

> If public officials are treated as utility-maximisers, then even though they are not motivated by profit, their actions can still be explained in terms of the individualistic calculus. They are just as likely to maximise the size of their bureaux as they are the public interest.[7]

That, we must agree, is original sin at work. It is the foundation of what is known as "public choice theory," which Barry is there quoting. We have to operate realistically acknowledging our sinful condition. We can not formulate any coherent philosophy if we first deny its existence.

Extending liberalism into the social sphere

All shades of opinion on the centre and right accept the need for private property, the market, and economic and personal liberty subject to the rule of law. The radical, or libertarian right would extend this personal liberty into the social sphere, as we have been seeing. They see traditionalist and Christian Conservatives as patronising and authoritarian for opposing them. On the other hand, it is as much a source of irritation to the radical right that left-wing, consensus conservatives, liberals and above all socialists constantly advocate sexual, civil or moral liberalism whilst denying any real economic freedom. In addition, according to Novak:

> The guardians of the moral-cultural system are typically less concerned about liberty in the economic system than about their own liberty. Intellectuals insist upon a free market for their own work, but easily endorse infringements upon the liberty of economic activists.[8]

Advocates of the new right contend that both economic and personal freedom must be unrestrained, and they thereby run into accusations of "economism," that is, of basing their social policy on economic theory alone. In their "rationalistic" liberalism, there are few social problems that cannot be resolved, as Norman Barry puts it, "by the application of the basic principles of market economics." In the extreme, they believe "that market mechanisms are always superior to the state."[9] They attack those conservatives who defend the economic free market but who cannot accept a free market, as they put it, in personal morality.[10] But as we saw earlier, they have produced no evidence that market forces work beneficially in the field of personal morality. This is hardly surprising. The evidence from the last twenty-five years is rather to the contrary.

The Utilitarians

Modern economic liberalism traces its roots back to the "Enlightenment" and its two principle Scottish exponents, David Hume and Adam Smith (although seeds were sown earlier by Hobbes and Locke).[11] Smith (1723 - 1790) was appointed professor of Moral Philosophy at Glasgow University in 1751 and published his "Theory of the Moral Sentiments" eight years later. Turning to economics, he published in 1776 "The Wealth of Nations," which laid the foundations of modern democratic capitalism. Democratic Capitalism is just over two hundred years old.

Smith's friend Hume (1711 - 1776) first put forward the doctrine of free trade which Smith took up, but he was also an early Utilitarian. The latter doctrine was developed in turn by Jeremy Bentham (1748 - 1832) and John Stuart Mill (1806 - 1873). Bentham is the source of the famous utilitarian maxim that "the greatest happiness of the greatest number is the foundation of morals and legislation." Thomas Paine (1737 - 1809) contributed to the "enlightenment" with his "Rights of Man" (1791) and "Age of Reason" (1793). It may be pertinent to ask whether the utilitarians ever expected pleas from sexual special interest groups to arise. Did Bentham really mean that no-one has any responsibility for anyone else? Given that sexual license as a social phenomenon only took off in the sixties, could the phenomenon of demands for "homosexual equality" have occurred to them?

If homosexual activist Jeffrey Weeks is right, then it did. He claims that Bentham "classed homosexuality as an 'imaginary offence,' dependent on changing concepts of taste and morality."[12] Norman Barry draws the conclusion that libertarian philosophers are content for anyone to go, if they believe that such a place exists, to hell in his own way:

> From Bentham onwards, liberals have made it an act of faith that the individual is the best judge of his own interests. They have asserted that however foolish a persons's choices might be, to deny him the right to make them cannot possibly "liberate" him from self-destructive desires, but will serve only to subordinate his personal ends to those of some paternal authority.[13]

The economist Samuel Brittan has been a friend of the "permissive society" and of the belief that personal or sexual freedom belongs to Conservative philosophy along with economic freedom. In Brittan's liberal utilitarianism, according to Barry, "happiness is maximised if individual choice is widened across all areas, subject to the necessary constraints imposed by the rule of law."[14] Bentham's maxim was contentious and anti-Christian, but Brittan's is merely false. He cannot possibly guarantee what he promises, with or without the get-out clause invoking "the rule of law." With choice comes decision-making, and many of us are at our most unhappy when confronted with decisions or at least with the ill effects of bad ones. We may even be asked to make decisions in areas in which we have no competence. It is argued by pro-lifers, for example, that a mother is not competent to decide whether or not to kill the baby in her womb. They argue further that she will be ultimately and bitterly unhappy if she chooses death for the child. How does a liberal agreeing with Brittan cope with the problems of competence and unforeseen effects?

Indeed Jeremy Bentham is not really in the same tradition as Hume, Smith and Mill, who all accepted or assumed that there was a God-given rule of law outside the control of man. This in their day was the common law, and they would be appalled at the way in which we today interfere with it by legislation.

We have to be even more careful when wheeling out the utilitarians in support of the contention that a crime must have a tangible identifiable victim. It was John Stuart Mill, after all, who said: "The liberty of the individual must be thus far limited; he must not make himself a nuisance to other people."

I am sure that the parents who cannot take their children onto Epsom Common or Hampstead Heath because of the activities of homosexuals would agree with that. The discarded sexual detritus and no-go areas give a new meaning to David Hume's "tragedy of the commons." However, we must now begin to put the case that the liberty of the individual must be limited further; his behaviour must not prejudice the very existence of liberty itself.

The humanist convergence

Norman Barry wrote of the Heath-Wilson "consensus" that it was typified in its approach to sexual morality by "permissive" social policy. Those who supported permissiveness then and now were mainly campaigning humanists. Today a broad spectrum from the right through the centre and ending up at the hard left supports libertarian sexual policy. Why do the hard left and the humanist "consensus" converge over issues involving sexuality? This is a problem which has exercised moral campaigners. Valerie Riches of Family and Youth Concern has analysed this area. She demonstrates the humanist involvement of the "family planners" in the sort of sex education which will depress the birth-rate by every means possible, including the promotion of homosexuality as a valid lifestyle.[15] But where are the permissives coming from? Is there a communist plot, or a humanist plot, or a big money plot, or a world domination plot, or what plot? Is it coordinated, and if so, by whom?

A conspiracy to destroy capitalist society cannot be the whole answer. The far left are clearly working towards destabilising society to bring about revolution, but right-wing humanists would not feel totally at ease in a socialist state. Yet there they all are, whittling away at Christian decency and morality as if their lives depended upon it.

Do humanists such as Professor Anthony Flew believe that the socialists are simply wrong to say that capitalism is supported by strong families, that homosexuality and feminism fragment and disrupt families, and that in the end the destruction of the family base will prepare the ground for socialism? Socialist John Molyneux had no doubt, as we saw in chapter 19: the family is a privatised reproduction system, and it passes on its bourgeois values from one generation to the next. Feminism and homosexuality upset this pattern and divert the energies released into the destruction of capitalism itself.

Violent revolution is not necessary. In "The Road to Serfdom" Hayek argued that when social reforms go against the grain of human nature they will fail and the unintended consequences will demand further interventions until the whole of society is controlled in a totalitarian manner. Society is subverted by stealth rather than by revolution. Christians would say that legislation which opposes the laws of God opposes human nature, and is bound to fail in this way.

Socialists characteristically resent the allegiance that people owe their families, because the family provides an alternative focus of loyalty to the state. At a basic level, deserted wives and children depend on the state rather than on a man for their income, and they will then tend to support socialist policy which increases their dependence on the state. Any proper socialist tract confirms that undermining the traditional family by any means possible is the socialist aim, and yet Tory libertarians contend that a liberal society can tolerate any amount of family failure, pornography, debasement and perversion with impunity. Are the socialists wrong and the liberal humanists right? Whom do we believe, Molyneux or Flew? What drives the two of them down the same path of means, and why does one of them think he can turn off before he reaches the ultimate destination of the other? Which one of them has the map?

A hatred of Christianity

Is it too simplistic to venture that on the face of it the only unifying factor is a hatred of God and of Christian morality? Libertarians on the Right agree with Socialists that Christianity is an impediment to their aims. But where are the right-wing libertarians going? It seems to me that they make an end out of the means, namely the destruction of religious faith, and that they can see no further. They really do think that they can turn off before the socialist destination heaves into view, at the point where sexual behaviour is another market commodity, and where men, women and children are all liberated and blissfully happy in their sexual abandon.

Are these right-wingers not guilty of vast utopianism? Where has such a dissolute immoral society worked before? Has rigorous evaluation of historical evidence become subservient to subjective belief? The scorn of any liberal feminist for the Judeo-Christian ethic knows no bounds of reason. Humanists are united with Green Party activists that human beings should have very few children, and the early advocates of feminism, Sanger, de Beauvoir, Friedan, et al, all supported birth control of the coercive type and hoped that feminism

Above and below, just four of the twenty pages of advertisements for obscene telephone numbers in Gay Times August 1992. TV is transvestite, TS trans-sexual, CP corporal punishment, S+M sadism and masochism, yellow & brown is urination and coprophilia. Such advertisements appear in every UK homosexual magazine.

The drive to make anonymous open-air contacts is part of the male homosexual psyche. This "cruising" area is on Wimbledon Common in South London. The bad news for gay rights and the good news for the individual homosexual is that the evidence shows that healing can resolve the underlying pathologies and that the homosexual life can be left behind.

would depress the birth rate.[16] They were all humanists, as was Gloria Steinam:

> We have to abolish and reform the institution of marriage ... by the year 2000 we will, I hope, raise our children to believe in human potential, not God ... it is humanism that is the goal.[17]

Margaret Sanger, the racist who founded the Planned Parenthood Federation of America in 1916, stated, "Our objective is unlimited sexual gratification without the burden of unwanted children."[18]

Teresa Gorman and Germaine Greer, like Simone de Beauvoir and Gloria Steinam before them, will die childless. Every one of them approves women who work or who abort their babies and scorns women who become full-time non-earning mothers. Mrs Gorman spoke in a more virulently anti-Christian manner in the House of Commons during the embryology debate than anyone could remember. Miss Greer writes of the menopause with a scarcely concealed bitterness now that her own is upon her.[19] Does this contain a clue? Are these humanists so mixed-up themselves that they wish to mess everyone else up out of self-justification?

There is another possibility. It must be asked, are these anti-Christian men and women simply fatheads? Has the hatred of religion that drives humanists on the right and in the centre emasculated their intellect? Socialists know where they are going, but for other humanists, is it better to travel the anti-Christian road than to arrive?

Drawing lines with "the rule of law"

Central to the libertarian "faith," for that it what it comes down to, of the radical right, is the view "that individuals must not be prevented by a paternalist state from harming themselves." Barry admits that this is "a radical view which is in many respects at odds with conventional morality."[20] It is anti-Christian, not to put too fine a point on it. Barry himself is on the side of the radicals:

> Given the fact that liberalism denies the right of the state or society to impose collective ends on individual choosers, it is necessary that it should recommend a considerable loosening of the bonds that coercive law has confined individual conduct involving private choices in moral matters. Hence, liberals actively supported the repeal of oppressive [sic] legislation in the field of personal morality, in homosexuality, abortion and in political, literary and artistic expression, which was such an important feature of consensus social policy.[21]

Some conservative philosophers have concluded, and not necessarily from any Christian starting point, that the liberal capitalist order is not self-sustaining. Barry names American neo-conservative Irving Kristol and the German Democrat William Ropke, Novak names Joseph Schumpeter and Daniel Bell. I sense an unease within Barry of the new right and Novak, the defender of pluralism, that they may be right.

Still the new right claims not to see the intellectual rationale for, for example, legal controls on pornography, besides "that kind of paternalism that seems to accompany almost any conservative disposition."[22] Norman Barry feels that the existence of pornography, to continue with the example, and presumably of whatever pornography can be produced for whatever market, is only to be ruled by "the outcomes of an exchange process." His qualification that the market in filth should be "subject to the rule of law" again begs the question. Whose rule of law if not God's? Based on what, and why? Barry fears that "all sorts of ad hoc interventions in the (exchange) process can be justified" if pornography is restricted.[23] It is just the removal of the present "ad hoc" system of controls, and their replacement by a coherent philosophy, that western democratic capitalism so badly needs.

Once the libertarian accepts the need for a law which regulates or in his language "oppresses" any personal behaviour, incest for example, or pornography, he has to explain where his rule of law is drawing the line and why. If there are no lines, or permissive lines, he has to explain where he thinks such a society will go and why. Perhaps that is why "new right" economists, amongst many others, are loathe to enter the discussion. As this final part of the story unfolds, we shall not be nearly so coy.

32
Gay materialism or family values?

So far in this final section we have seen that economic theory is based upon the principle that each individual in the economic system takes decisions that maximise his own self-interest. At the most basic level, for one to sell and another to buy, each must believe that the transaction will benefit him. The new right makes the principle an act of faith in economics and they and other permissives apply it to social policy, to "personal morality."

When we looked at the assault on the family in chapter 19, we heard from gays saying that they valued their families, but we saw also a deep conflict between the values of "the family" and the values of "gay rights," with its consumerism, its hedonistic fatalism, and its individualism. "The gays" claimed not to understand that "family" involves not just ancestors and siblings, but descendants, and furthermore that the institution of the family encapsulates a particular value system.

So why does democratic capitalism need the family and its values, and why must we oppose, amongst other anti-family, anti-Christian lobbyists, those advocating homosexual rights?

Individualism loses touch with reality

Michael Novak believes that the tradition of the British utilitarians "has many noble features." Its aim of "genial tolerance" makes it "of all intellectual traditions one of the least morally pretentious."[1] However, where it becomes distorted into radical individualism it parts company with reality. "In freeing individuals from too much dependency, individualism plays an important role. Taken too far, it is plainly wrong about human life."[2]

In fact, the popular socialist criticism of modern democratic capitalism, that it is all about individual climbing upon individual scrabbling greedily to do one another down, is exposed by Novak as a caricature. Certainly, during the last twenty-five years, consumerism and hedonistic individualism have increased whilst the traditional family and its values have declined. But to observe this is more to criticise the secular humanism that modern socialists love, than the capitalism they hate.

Novak suggests that normally the real interests of individuals are rarely concerned just with the self. "To most persons," he writes, "their families mean more than their own interests; they frequently subordinate the latter to the former. Their communities are also important to them."[3]

Because families look after their own, and because they strive to improve themselves through economic activity, learning from each other across generations, each family network is of immense benefit to the society of which it is a part. That is not to say that families do not go downhill, but then other families, working harder, or having more luck, continually rise up. Parents and grandparents look to their children and see the future in them, and this gives them something to work for, and to make sacrifices for. It gives them a long-term view. Self-regarding, self-interested people, concerned for today and its instant gratification, unused to self-restraint, are more readily found in alternative lifestyles and above all in the homosexual network, so that the values of sexual liberation are the exact opposite of what a thriving nation requires. Novak writes:

> *For those men and women who have chosen to establish families of their own, there can be no doubt whatever that much of their economic conduct makes no sense apart from the benefits they are trying to accrue for their children. The fundamental motive of all economic activity seems clearly to be, far more than economists commonly suggest, family-regarding.*[4]

The importance of strong families

The new right frankly dithers about the importance of the family, torn between individualist idealism and the rigours of reality. Norman Barry explains that:

> *For a conservative, the family has value not merely because it is a natural phenomenon but also because if it is undermined, it transforms an integrated society into a mere 'collection' of anomic and alienated individuals without secure values.*[5]

Quite so, and the radical right is happy to use the institution of the family to resist the growth of its bugbear, welfare. Welfare to the radical right "encourages the break-up of the family and the presence

Gay materialism or family values? 385

of unmarried mothers and makes vast numbers of people dependent upon the state."[6] This effect is particularly strong amongst younger people who have been denied the acquisition of a traditional work-ethic. American sociologist Charles Murray has described the young women in this underclass as being "married to the state." The radical right do not criticise too harshly those who actively choose state welfare, for such people are only behaving logically in the presence of the welfare rules. In theological terms of course the system itself should not be an occasion of sin.

Another practical reason for strong families which increase or at least replace the population, lies in the future ability of the economy to pay for pensions. The radical right sees in one of the last acts of the consensus, the 1975 state earnings-related pension scheme, the ultimate example of a government promising something that will only be delivered a generation hence. There is no pension fund to be built up in SERPS, or in any state pension for that matter, for money is simply transferred from the taxpayer to the pensioner on a pay-as-you-go basis. Workers in their youth now will have to honour a commitment made almost twenty years ago with massive taxes twenty years hence to support an aging population.[7] It could well be argued at that time that as successive governments did not offer, in the late 70s, the 80s and 90s, any more financial help than £7.25 per week child benefit to parents to bring up their children, then the state has no call upon the earnings of the children to pay the pensions of any persons other than their own parents. That would be very hard, not least upon those who dearly wanted children and could not have them, but it could easily happen where a society forgets that children are a communal resource and so discourages their birth.

Even without this long term economic benefit of the family, the savings of families are the capital of capitalism, for strong united families pay the taxes that enable governments to govern whilst broken families put a strain on the state benefit system. For Michael Novak and for most conservatives, there are other values nurtured by the family:

> Between the omnipotent state and the naked individual looms the first line of resistance against totalitarianism: the economically and politically independent family, protecting the space within which free and independent individuals may receive the necessary years of nurture.
>
> For those who seek totalitarian state control, it is always evident that the independent bourgeois family must be destroyed. This is

so because the individual bound by responsibilities and loyalties to spouse and children is bound, as well, to traditions welling up from the past and extending into the future.*8*

Novak writes of the "ordinary heroism" of parenthood. A father or mother would willingly die, in a fire for example, to save one of his or her children, an act which seems heroic, but for parents is only ordinary. Below that, there are countless acts of self-denial that parents willingly perform for their children. This all indicates how God uses family life "to teach as a matter of course the role of virtue." The values held by the traditional stable family unit are indispensable for stable government:

> Self-government is not possible without self-discipline. It is not possible, either, men and women being what they are, without the whip of the law. The childrearing practices of the citizenry of our republic either strengthen or undermine in its some sixty million families the habits of mind and soul, the moral skills, so to speak, of the republic itself.*9*

Self-discipline in liberal democracy

Self-discipline is not a fashionable quality to possess in the 1990s. Novak, as we saw earlier, considers that its nurture or lack of nurture in the family is an indicator of whether a whole society will accept it or not. He argues that the traditional family had an inbuilt tendency to self-discipline and self-denial in its desire to pass on savings and investment to future generations:

> Insofar as democratic capitalism depends for its economic vitality upon deferred gratification, savings, and long-term investment, no motive for such behaviour is the equivalent of regard for the future welfare of one's own progeny.*10*

Once again, we cannot resist wondering what will drive any interest in the longer term amongst those who have opted out of child-rearing and into a life characterised by short-term hedonism. "If it feels good, do it," is the cry of that "gay" man who is the end of the line. If you want to, then "Why Not?" as a "boy escort" bar in Amsterdam is called. But the evidence shows that this is not a good long-term value system:

> Where self-government is not possible in personal life, it remains to be seen whether it is possible in the republic. Every prognosis based upon history would suggest that lack of self-government in the

Gay materialism or family values?

individual citizenry will lead to lack of restraint in the government of the republic.

As individuals liberate themselves from costs, responsibilities, and a prudent concern for the future, so will their political leaders.[11]

Bearing the costs of decisions

Central to liberal economics is the understanding that a man is responsible for the effects of his market decisions. Because of this, a market transaction is not made unless both parties can see a benefit to them. They have to live with the results of what they have done. But bluntly, if people do well, work hard and make the right decisions, they and their families live well, but if they do not, they and their families starve. The problem with welfare, according to this analysis, is that "the knowledge that suffering will be alleviated anyway will increase the incentives for people not to provide privately for their own welfare."[12] To be fair to the radical right, there is also their argument that welfare benefits are a public good in the sense that, putting it crudely, we all feel better if persons are not visibly in distress, particularly the deserving poor, and "especially in an economic environment of general prosperity."[13]

The strange thing about the radical right is that they fail to make the same connections before demanding "personal freedom." Right-wing libertarians, often tinged with a feminist streak, are happy to campaign for "personal freedoms," in the sure knowledge that those taking advantage of them will never bear the cost. Democratic socialists and liberals are the humanist allies of the radical right in this process, to the extent that they always expect the rest of us to pay for the personal freedoms of others in our taxes.

It is quite apparent that there are costs to the Exchequer arising from the lifestyles encouraged by the permissive society. Divorce fractures one household into two, increases the demand on housing and usually puts a woman and children on public support. Teenage sexual intercourse usually means contraception which costs money, and irrespective of that, the inevitable illegitimate births and abortions which follow cost respectively welfare and housing, again, or the cost of the abortion and psychological treatment afterwards. The freedom to indulge in homosexual practice costs in health education, in public health measures, in the treatment of personal and mental problems and in research and the treatment of venereal disease; spectacularly in the case of AIDS. Lack of full-time mothering and paternal discipline cost in a higher crime rate. Insurance premiums have risen according to the Association of British Insurers as a result of increasing theft and fraudulent claims. In the case of the latter, people "add a bit on" and it is useless of the ABI appealing to the fraudulent to keep their claims factual in order to keep down premiums (as their representative did on radio).[14] The individual has no incentive to do that in a Godless society. The marginal benefit of lower premiums spread across all policy holders is lower than the immediate benefit of the fraudulent claim.

If the recipients of these various welfare payments argue that they are public goods, then to put it crudely again, supporting the ill effects of crime, illegitimacy, homosexuality, dishonesty, disease and divorce does not benefit the public at large or the stability of our society at all. One of these days somebody will calculate the percentage of the gross national product being used to fund the permissive society, and I believe that we all might have a shock when we see how much we are paying, and consider what we are getting for our money.

Where governments are concerned, they too will rarely bear the costs of their decisions, because these are set farther into the future than is the next election. What this means is explained by Professor Barry:

> *Conventional majority-rule democracy fails because it gives each individual no incentive to reverse this ultimately socially destructive process, for the voter will inevitably vote for a party that maximises his sectional interests, since he can be sure that others will do likewise. The public interest is defined by classical liberals as zero inflation, the strict enforcement of the rule of law and the absence of group privilege; but no person has any incentive to vote for it since the benefits of these policies are all long-term and thinly spread across the whole population.*[15]

Barry notes that in the European collective systems, the absence of the price mechanism had an effect that was more than just economic. "The destruction of personal responsibility for action that collectivism entailed also generated a certain kind of moral deformity."[16] If this is true in economic activity, how much greater must be the moral deformity that results from destruction of personal responsibility in the social sphere.

33
Pressure groups, AIDS, and the myth of pluralism

American theologian and economist Michael Novak is so keen on the place of pluralism in the moral-cultural system of democratic capitalism that he strongly defends the presence and activities of "interest groups." It is perfectly clear why he takes this stance; he cannot stand know-all left-wing political idealists sneering at the capitalist system: "Interest-group politics, they say, is always narrow, selfish and expedient. They are rather more certain that they know what is good."[1] But is the pluralism he defends real, is genuine pluralism possible, and do we need "pluralism" at all?

Interest groups and "rent-seekers"

Novak and others contend that the pleadings of special interest groups cancel each other out. However, James Buchanan and Gordon Tullock of Virginia, Mancur Olson and Hayek have all demonstrated "that the traditional political scientists' view that the activity of special interest groups is a benign, and indeed necessary, adjunct to the formal political process is false."[2] Olson shows that the democratic process allows groups, or even coalitions of groups, to gain advantages which will eventually work against the public interest. In the economic system, the power of these groups destabilises the market, preventing the effective operation of its usual self-adjusting processes.[3] It is usually the trades unions who are cited as prime examples of the sort of pressure groups complained about. However, Norman Barry identifies farmers as consistently successful lobbyists:

> *Throughout British history the ability of farmers, through price-support schemes, tariffs and other impediments to the free importation of cheap foreign food, to exempt themselves from market forces has been a familiar source of frustration to classical liberals. The success of farmers' groups is entirely due to their curious capacity to influence government: indeed, in Britain, the Ministry of Agriculture is virtually a spokesman for the National Farmer's Union.*[4]

It is possible to identify other rent-seeking groups whose successes have distorted economic activity. In Britain the single parent lobby is especially strong, and has managed to gain benefits and tax concessions for its client group that have weighted both the benefit and tax systems and council housing allocation policy strongly against the traditional family. No government dare stand up against it, out of fear of being labelled "uncaring." Professor William Mitchell writes of this process:

> Whenever the gains of tiny minorities mean more to them than do the losses to a majority, we may expect that minorities will coalesce and win.[5]

Resisting the rent-seekers

One would have to live in a hermitage not to notice the constant rent-seeking to which the political process is subject, mainly from trades unions, demanding more "resources," or money, to you and me, whether for nurses, doctors, ancillary staff or the NHS generally, teaching, local government, railways, the probation service, and so on and so on. Then there are the employers' groups, the roads lobby, the farmers' union, the merchant fleet, fishermen, large builders. Some have good cases, some poor cases, but all put pressure on governments of all parties. Jo Grimond wrote of the ultimate result, addressing his remarks to the unions:

> If every interest extorts higher and higher wages each union leapfrogging over each other, jostling for a bigger share from the trough of public resources, scornful of exhortations to make their business more efficient, then wages will be inflated beyond what industry can support. Inflation generates unemployment. The cry goes up for more taxes and subsidies, more jobs unjustified by results, until Liberal Democracy may collapse.[6]

Norman Barry points out that the underpinning motivation of rational self-interest will cause the citizen "to vote for his immediate group interests rather than for the public interest."[7] What is more, "there will always be more interest groups demanding political action that culminates in government expansions than those demanding financial probity. The liberal asks the question: "Who is to speak for the 'public,' the main beneficiaries of financial rectitude, when people are organised into groups considerably smaller, but more effectively organised, than the public?"[8] The same question can be posed about social or sexual rectitude. Answer comes there none.

Both Barry and Hayek before him have emphasised that although individual or family self-interest seems to work to the benefit of liberal capitalist democracy, pressure group self-interest never can. It is argued that the analysis of "pressure-group politics" is "perhaps the most significant of the innovations that have taken place in traditional individualist thought in the post-war years" and that it questions one of the fundamental tenets of political thought in the 50s, 60s and 70s "consensus," namely, "that politics is a benign activity and that social stability is secured by permitting a plurality of groups to operate in an almost unconstrained manner in the political system."[9] The architects of the consensus failed to appreciate that pluralism will produce a "new tyranny of minorities."[10]

One way to prevent Jo Grimond's nightmare of the collapse of our society through successful financial rent-seeking could be to stand up to the minorities and tell them that there is no more money, or to explain to the electorate that they will have to pay for it. However, with an adversarial party political system, and a liberal media, which characterise Western democracy, these two arguments are not easily made to stick. Only Margaret Thatcher did it, in spite of the media, and only because she held firmly to her economic philosophy.

The culture of the national media is critical. Novak suggests that it will always be simply the culture of those who work in it, artists, entertainers, directors, producers, make-up artists, script writers, and the rest, and that it has traditionally been sympathetic to the left. "It nurtures few conservatives, and few with comprehension of or respect for the economic system."[11]

Social rent-seekers

Professor Mitchell's dictum can be seen to apply also to the social sphere, to the detriment of the moral-cultural system. We are concerned principally with the demands of homosexual rights activists, but there are other examples of individuals organised into groups operating out of self-interest, campaigning for relief from the operation of what to everyone else might be a perfectly impartial law.

Part of the homosexual campaign is ideological, and like so much other social rent-seeking, humanist-driven. Indeed, humanists need only one or two hard cases to mount an effective social rent-seeking exercise, and their hatred of Christian morality seems to provide sufficient motivation. All the permissive legislation from the 60s to the present is the result of humanist lobbying, whether on divorce, pornography, abortion, sex education, illegitimacy rules or homosexuality.

There may be some agreement here with the liberals of the new right. It seems that the common law did a better job of keeping these social rent-seekings at bay than has Parliament. Liberals maintain that legislatures often display caprice, arising from "shifting and transient coalitions of interests."[12] The humanist coalition is so powerful because it is neither shifting nor transient, but well-organised and consistent. Even without such determined activity, the enactment of legislation, as opposed to "law," "is likely to advance the interests of particular groups rather than those of the general public."[13]

A further point is that social rent-seekers are usually overt or incidental economic rent-seekers as well. Lobbyists for easier divorce are assuming that there will be access to the legal process, whose judges and clerks will have to be paid for by the majority. Lobbyists for sex education, mainly the ill-named "Family Planning Association" and "Brook Advisory Centres" are the producers and providers of sex education and contraception, the former providing a market for the latter.

According to Suzie Hayman in "Say Yes, Say No, Say Maybe", Brook Advisory Centres will provide contraceptive drugs in secret even to under 13's. In reality, Brook has no lower age limit at all. Its dangerous policy of providing contraceptives and arranging abortions for under-age girls without the knowledge or consent of their parents or GPs makes it worrying that Brook Advisory has been supported specifically by Paddy Ashdown MP, Dr. Michael Adler, Margaret Becket MP, Katie Boyle, Will Carling, Gill Cox, Baroness Ewart-Biggs, Simon Fanshawe, Michael Foot MP, Lords Henderson and Houghton, Virginia Ironside, Mr & Mrs Neil Kinnock MP, Ken Livingstone MP, Baroness Llewelyn-Davies, Joanna Lumley, Julia Neuberger, Marjorie Proops, Anna Raeburn, Claire Rayner, Baroness Seear, Sir David Steel MP, Miriam Stoppard, Janet Suzman, Terry Wogan, Angela Willans, Lord Winstanley, Victoria Wood and Susannah York, amongst over one hundred fashionable names, in the recently published Brook Advisory Centres 89/90 Annual Report.

The abortion lobby, which started as a social rent-seeking exercise, is now a multi-million pound economic rent-seeker. Whilst pretending to care for "women in trouble," it works hard to increase, or at least to maintain, its market and thereby its access to the public and private purse. In general terms, it is always useful for a lobby to win government money to promote its own position, and groups like the Family Planning Association and the Terrence Higgins Trust are very good at this technique.

Pressure groups, AIDS, and the myth of pluralism 393

The economist Robert Whelan demonstrated a spectacular example of the fusion of social and economic rent-seeking when he exposed the workings of the AIDS lobby. We saw in chapter 11 that AIDS and homosexual pressure groups have directed all their efforts to minimising the stigma attached to AIDS, rather than adopting appropriate public health measures. Hysteria control, not disease control, was the order of the day. The special interest group promoted homosexuality as a legitimate lifestyle (the social rent-seeking) and demanded a cure for AIDS at almost any cost (the economic rent-seeking). The Department of Health itself came in the process to have a similar relation to the homosexual lobby as Norman Barry said the Department of Agriculture has to the Farmers' Union.

Whelan discovered that the AIDS lobby persuaded the Government to spend a total of £160,235,000 on "health education" and research into AIDS in the year 1989/90. In 1989 there were 553 deaths from AIDS in the UK. Over the same period, the Government spent £9,900,000 on health education and research into heart disease. The nation's biggest killer claimed 197,721 victims. Translated into expenditure per death, the Government spent £50 in relation to each death from heart disease, and £289,756 in relation to each death from AIDS, in 1989. It was easy, claims Whelan, for the Government to accede to the demands by simply re-arranging the NHS budget. Sufferers from other diseases could never be expected to form themselves into a coalition to stop the AIDS rent-seekers, even though:

> The allocation of huge sums of money to AIDS programmes means that less is available for other illnesses. People will die from cancer and from heart disease who would not have died if additional funds had been available. Their names will never be embroidered in a quilt, and they will never be celebrated at gala entertainments. But they will die just the same.[14]

Furthermore, the health education money that the Government provided went directly into the production of pornography. The Terrence Higgins Trust has been the largest supplier to the young of posters and now videos extolling homosexual activity and depicting it in an erotic manner, and we investigated the THT earlier. However, even Community Health Councils and teachers have seen AIDS as an excuse to promote homosexual activity to schoolchildren whilst pretending to offer health education. This shows yet again why AIDS was such a paradoxical boon to the homosexual lobby; "the gays" have been able to promote homosexuality as never before, and never before have they been able to do so using my money and yours.

What happens when there is private money at stake is markedly different. The Department of Health found this out when trying unsuccessfully to bully the Association of British Insurers out of questions relating to the lifestyle of people applying for life assurance who take AIDS tests even where they test negative. The D of H does not like the Insurers asking these "responsible" people why they thought they were at risk. Underwriters do not care to be exposed to "responsible" homosexuals like Freddie Mercury who take yearly AIDS tests, and they insist that the questions remain. Nor, it must be said, do they offer their most favourable terms to smokers or those with a history of heart disease. It is of course always open to AIDS or homosexual groups to start up a life company that regards those who take regular AIDS tests as a particularly good risk. To date they have not done so. Risking one's own money concentrates the mind in a way that applying for government money to support an ideological principle does not.

Standing up to the social rent-seekers

If it is difficult to stand up to the economic rent-seekers without a coherent political philosophy, it is next to impossible to resist the claims of social rent-seekers, especially as they too are supported by a media which overwhelmingly agrees with them, and presents its own prejudices as "public opinion." Political philosophers are not even sure that we should stand up to social rent-seekers at all.

The "New Right" are clear about the danger from economic group interests, but they react with incomprehension when the analogy is made between economic and social rent-seekers. And yet the latter may be much more damaging to the long-term success of democratic capitalism. Novak quotes Joseph Schumpeter, expressing the fear that our society faces its "most mortal danger" from the so-called guardians of the moral-cultural system:

> *Democratic capitalism is more likely to perish through the loss of its indispensable ideas and morals than through weaknesses in its political system or its economic system. In its moral-cultural system lies its weakest link. ... many participate in the "adversarial culture" which plays so large a role in debunking institutions and values which stand in the way of their own new morality, new culture, and new politics.*[15]

Relentlessly, Novak persists in relying on "pluralism" to defeat social group-interests. He echoes the founders of democratic capitalism, who were more afraid of absolutism than pluralism. "In a genuinely pluralistic society, there is no one sacred canopy. By intention there is not. At its spiritual core, there is an empty shrine," he writes, approvingly.[16] He sets down all the fears of the feudalist and socialist critics of liberal democratic capitalism:

> Thus, democratic capitalism is an affront both to traditional and to socialist conceptions of unitary order. If the system genuinely permits pluralism, does it not, in effect, lack unitary vision? Does it not set humans at cross-purposes? Does it not permit some to engage in what to others seems to be evil behaviour? Is not its moral laissez-faire, howsoever dignified by the name of tolerance, an impermissible concession to errant consciences?[17]

Solzhenitsyn is one of those who hold this view which Novak dismisses, that we are over-drawing our spiritual bank account, and that it is as likely that liberal democracy may collapse from the pressure of social group interests, as from economic ones.

When Solzhenitsyn looks at liberal western society with fresh eyes viewing its sexual perversions and rotten excesses for the first time and concluding that it will fail, Novak is not bothered in the slightest:

> Outsiders like Solzhenitsyn are often shocked by such a nation's public immoralities: massage parlours, pornography shops, pickpockets, winos, prostitutes, pushers, punk rock, chambers for group sex - you name it, democratic capitalism tolerates it and someone makes a living from it.[18]

Coming close to erecting an altar to tolerance, he continues:

> A free society can tolerate the public display of vice because it has confidence in the basic decency of human beings, even under the burden of sin. ... Belief in original sin is consistent with guarded trust in the better side of human nature.[19]

Well yes, but if the better side is constantly assaulted by the seamier side of permissive life, the basic decency is worn away. Users of pornography need more and more explicit images as they go on, so inured do they become to it. Something in them and indeed in society is progressively corrupted. Who can deny that our society has become progressively morally more decadent over the last twenty-five years? Added to that, I do not want my children exposed to public displays of vice; but I am racing ahead; we shall come to that.

Novak admits that it would be possible for a democratic capitalist society to put the breaks on public vice. However, in the United States, "the heart of most citizens is clearly not in the wholesale legal repression of all sinful behavior." I suspect that this is because those who run the moral-cultural system prefer public exhibitions of vice to continue. As Novak says: "The present ethos is still in an anti-bourgeois phase, in which some forms of decadence are not only not ridiculed, but are admired as "liberation". The wheel may turn again, more than once."[20]

For the wheel to turn, it must be agreed first that immorality and permissiveness are harming society, which Novak admits, then disputes, according to whether he is criticising liberal intellectuals, or defending pluralism. "Interest-group pluralism, in this scheme of things, serves the search for realism by assembling the many different angles from which the reality of things is perceived," he writes. He can not or will not see that the social special interest groups are today all coming in from the same politically correct, humanist, permissive, anti-Christian angle. To this extent it can be argued that there is no pluralism in our social policy at all. Novak writes: "When a majority of groups agree upon a policy or program, there must be *some* reality to it; it can scarcely be completely wrong."[21]

Really? Then what about Germany in the thirties or the Soviet Union in the fifties? What about the House of Commons allowing abortion up to birth? Novak is sound when he draws on hard evidence, but here, like the socialists whom he accuses of letting their preconceptions run away with them, he loses touch with reality, and retreats to the high ground of pluralist idealism.

Novak misses the point that the founding fathers set up the pluralism of the American constitution as a break on the contemporary European version of organised Christianity, never imagining that the Christian base itself, and its Protestant work-ethic, would ever be challenged. Abraham Lincoln, in the Gettysburg address, spoke of "This nation under God."

Once permissive legislation is granted to the social rent-seekers it is next to impossible to reverse. Its victims invest so much emotional energy into the new lax way of life, that they defend it with an energy that those seeking to overturn it are unable to match. This again is only the standard theory of the rent-seekers, born out of course by the evidence. There arises a kind of public desensitisation to the reality, almost a denial, as if we refuse to believe that we are part of a society going wrong. Psychologist and broadcaster Roy Masters explains:

Pressure groups, AIDS, and the myth of pluralism 397

When the government legitimses and coddles immorality, human weakness, and perversity, it is letting the proverbial genie out of the bottle. ... One can hardly imagine the effect of making drugs legal, and then changing back that policy - there would be riots. The immoral mentality, once legitimised, is a stubborn mind-set.[22]

Masters reminds us that the victims of con men are unwilling to recognise that they have been had, and that not even the hypnotist can bring his subject to realise that a compulsion was deliberately implanted. In the same way, the average abortion activist will never accept that her - or his - slogans and arguments are empty of content. Bernard Nathanson was one of three people who invented the dishonest slogans that paved the way for legal abortion in America. "A woman's right to choose!" "Our bodies our right to decide!" and so on, Nathanson and his friends made them up knowing that they were specious, but chantable. Thousands of abortions later, Nathanson stepped back and saw that he was killing human beings. He knew already, but he had not seen. He came clean, exposed the dishonest way the National Abortion Rights Action League had gone about its business and explained how they invented the slogans. He told what happened in abortion. It was all to no avail:

After years of promoting abortion, and helping to make it acceptable in the minds of the media and the public, he could not undo his manipulations. Once he sold them on the idea, he could not un-sell them - even by explaining the mechanics of behind-the-scenes manipulation, or by producing films showing frighteningly clear video footage of the horrors of abortion. To many pro-abortion activists, Nathanson is a fanatic, a heretic, and a liar who has lost all reason. [23]

The genie will not easily go back into the bottle. Like the abortionists, so the homosexual activist minority, unless we can articulate why we oppose them, will simply coalesce and win.

34
Homosexuality, decline and fall

It was during the 1970s reaction to the consensus that government spending was first appreciated by the electorate to be largely wasteful, and manipulated too often by economic special interest groups like the unions. Because it was recognised to pose a threat to the political stability of liberal democracy itself, and the rights of individuals,[1] the political will was found by Margaret Thatcher to stand up to the groups concerned.

The will was rarely found to oppose any group that had a social rent-seeking function either alone or in tandem with its economic pleading. This lack of will was in spite of the traditional feeling amongst conservatives that extending individualist values into the social sphere of personal morals and social welfare is destructive of an ordered society.[2] But by grafting a thirst for material advancement onto sixties and seventies hedonism, Thatcherism laid itself open to the accusations of selfishness and greed that are made against Conservatism today by socialists. If it had possessed an ideology that empowered it to push back the consensus permissive society, Thatcherism would have been able to refute the socialist charges from the moral high ground.

Threats to stability

We have seen that homosexuals in particular will fight much harder for that which will benefit them, namely legal acceptance of their lifestyle, and access to teenagers, than the rest of us will to stop them. Furthermore, they will not be grateful for minor concessions. These they will see, like a spoilt child, and quite correctly, as weakness, and after each concession they will come back for more. Their demands, which culminate in requiring that society recognise homosexual activity as morally and socially equivalent to heterosexual marriage, are literally insatiable. It is better in the long run to say no to the spoilt child at once, and mean it.

Homosexuality, decline and fall 399

American economist and neo-conservative Irving Kristol recognised that social liberalism, like democratic socialism, can only exist where sin is abolished, and brilliantly sent up the evidence-free position of the radical right, coining the aphorism: "A neo-conservative is a liberal who has been mugged by reality."

The capitalist crisis for Kristol is that the danger to democracy arises not from socialism, but paradoxically from the success of capitalism itself. It has produced tremendous, proven material success. Even though the American constitution is pluralist, it was underpinned by the Protestant ethic. Personal excess was constrained by the moral base, there was a higher aim than simple consumption, and the reward of virtue and hard work was wealth. The Protestant foundation, or the "bourgeois ethic" of modern capitalism has since been eroded. A "modern nihilism" stalks the earth, materialism and consumption, sexual consumption even, have become ends in themselves, there are no values beyond consumption and intellectuals see the freedom of the market as encompassing "the freedom to destroy the market."[3]

So for Kristol, democratic capitalism is internally self-destructive. The "invisible hand" was as we saw earlier Adam Smith's expression of the strange way in which the market seemed to come to an agreement about the fair price of a commodity, with no external pressure or secret meetings. Kristol suggests that it is foolish to expect the same to happen in an invented market in social values:

> That selfishness which powers the exchange system in goods and services is potentially fatal to social values. There is, then, no invisible hand at work to produce equilibrium in the moral world as there is in the economic world.[4]

Indeed with the so-called guardians of the moral-cultural system chipping away at morality, it is obvious why Schumpeter regards their workings as presenting democratic capitalism with "its most mortal danger."[5]

The evidence of the last twenty-five years shows that the immoral mindset, once it gains a foothold in a society, is progressively more and more difficult to dislodge, so that we make a mistake in raising "tolerance" of immorality to the status of a religious benchmark. Tolerance can be an excuse for moral cowardice. It was William Burke who said that there is a limit "at which forbearance ceases to be a virtue."

Original sin means that there is a fundamental weakness in mankind, so that in the absence of controls we will take whatever is going, whether that is a jump to the top of the housing queue, a bit of quick sex, or some cash from a fraudulent insurance claim. Norman Barry puts it well, when refuting yet another vision of a new man who can cope disinterestedly with the seductions of the modern world:

> *man is a maximiser who responds to signals, whether they are of a kind favourable to the market or conductive to its ultimate destruction.*[6]

Professor Barry also agrees with the German, William Ropke, who articulates one of the problems which now confront contemporary liberal democracy: "material success is not enough and, paradoxically, too much prosperity may be harmful to its long-term prospects."[7]

Prosperity would surely not be harmful if we could keep our moral nerve in the face of the immorality that is constantly promoted by the liberal establishment. In addition, we should have to be sure of the real difference between "moral" behaviour and "immoral." Many centrist and leftist politicians and their supporters redefine "morality" so that it loses all meaning. It becomes "immoral" to reduce income tax, or to restructure the health service, or to refuse to indoctrinate children with "safe sex" values. For some bishops, it is "immoral" for Church schools to opt out of local authority control.[8]

Failure of liberal democracy unthinkable

A man who denies that our books, films and videos today are less decent and more violent than those of only ten, or five, years ago has surely lost all reason. The fact that someone makes money from sex and violence does not make such material a beneficial or proper commodity to have on sale. "See this film," said one reviewer of "Basic Instinct," "and a little bit of your humanity will be chipped away." Ropke tells us that we make a mistake when we suppose "that an unending supply of consumer goods can be sufficient to create independent individuals, morally self-sufficient and therefore able to resist modern mass ideologies."[9]

It is difficult to find positive support for the positive values of our culture. Michael Novak relentlessly refuses to imagine the failure of democratic capitalism, denying that rent-seekers have anything but benign effects, whilst the new right acknowledge the existence and ill effects of economic rent-seekers, see the possible failure of democracy in acceding to their requests, but their humanism makes it difficult for them to extend their vision to include social rent-seekers. Both vouch for the importance of the family in keeping the state at bay, neither consistently stresses the importance of concrete action to support the family economically and philosophically.

To be fair, Novak is worse in this regard than is Barry of the New Right. They both say things which taken together, indicate that without action, liberal democracy will die if it does not tend the good ground in which it flourishes, and when they say these things, it is as a result of confronting reality. When they forget the evidence, they are left with their preconceptions, which in Novak's case, lead to conclusions which are rather too complacent.

The spiritual vacuum

Michael Novak wrote approvingly that there is an "empty shrine" at the spiritual core of democratic capitalism. A better simile is perhaps that the shrine was filled with respect for the God-given rule of law, and the familial structure of society. Then it emptied. Again coming close to agreeing with William Ropke, Norman Barry suggests that the capitalist spiritual vacuum has now been filled "by socialist ethics."[10] He allows too that positivism and ethical non-cognitivism, those humanist arguments that there are no ultimate moral values, and that "ethics is a matter of subjective choice," did much "to create that spiritual vacuum."[11]

Irving Kristol travels much the same route, but is harder on conservatives for their failure to produce a philosophy which would oppose the left. He argues that although "the new Left's morality is little short of a return to barbarism, the philosophy of capitalism (or its lack of a philosophy) is as much to blame for the moral nihilism of our times."[12]

Ropke, ruling out pluralism, points out that our society must base its morality on something: "If it is denied that there are values that are to some extent 'natural' and universally shared, then even a market economy can have no permanence and stability."[13]

In a chilling example of the way in which those universal values which remain may be used to undermine the morality from which they spring, homosexual pressure groups appeal to our sense of fair play in order to press their case for equalisation of "age of consent" and so on. When that fails they try to intimidate us through violence, outrageous demonstrations or public displays of pornography. In America, "Queer Nation" activists converge on any entertainment establishment considered to be exclusively heterosexual and "educate" the customers by dancing and embracing. The organiser, Matt Nagle, a writer with Gay News in Seattle, says:

> "At one bar we went to all the customers left and by the end of the evening we were the only ones there. The manager came out and

berated us but about a month later he began having a Gay Night once a week."[14]

Ordinary people can then become so emotionally traumatised by this process that, like the manager of that bar, we come to agree with our violators and identify with their values. Lest this sound too silly, let us remember again that this is what happened in the Stockholm siege. The terrorists bullied and cajoled their hostages to the extent that when the hostages were liberated, they came out pressing the terrorists' demands. As we saw earlier, some psychologists now refer to this tendency to identify with the viewpoint of the oppressor, long known to them as "identification with the aggressor," as the "Stockholm Syndrome".

The self-destruction of liberal democracy

So far, we have spoken airily of "problems," "harm," even "destruction" arising to liberal democratic capitalism when it abandons its moral base. What do we mean? How shall we tell? Can we not carry on giving in to the social rent-seekers, even up to the point where every child is illegitimate, every mother is out at work, homosexual brothels are established and legalised, sex education sexualises primary school children, whilst disease and crime touch every household? Liberal democracy is fertile soil, and the seeds for its own destruction have already germinated and are sprouting merrily. At what point do the plants of dishonesty, corruption and immorality grow so big as to exhaust the soil?

There may be lessons in history, from the decline and fall of the Roman Empire, for example, but they are unlikely to impress anyone today. We ought to bear in mind firstly that we are ourselves literally living in history, and secondly that the progress of own society, like that of own lives is the real thing, and not a rehearsal. These are platitudes but we must recognise that this moment is unique and precious. Never before have mass communications, capitalist economy, permissive humanist values, rising social problems and indeed nuclear weapons, coincided.

No political economist is keen to indulge his apocalyptic vision of the ultimate end of our democratic system. Novak doesn't, nor does Norman Barry nor Jo Grimond. The "destruction" of which they write is inarticulated, at least in print. But during those dark winter evenings, what do they imagine?

Is it that the financial base of western democracy collapses? Can we not fund our old age pensioners or the economic effects of unemployment and the permissive society, so that the welfare system simply breaks down and we are all left on our own resources, at subsistence level? J G de Beus, former Dutch Ambassador to Moscow, predicts a revolt before that stage is reached. Noting the increase of welfarism and the aging population of Europe, he predicts on current demographic trends that in West Germany (he wrote pre-unification) at the turn of the century a non-working 53% of the population would be supported by a working 47%. By the year 2030, today's ratio of workers to non-workers would be reversed from 2:1 to 1:2. De Beus asks:

> How long will a working minority in any country be prepared to support a non-working majority? Will a labourer or a peasant be prepared to set off to work early every morning to gain a nominal income, knowing that the major part of it will not be paid out to him but will be used to support his neighbour who is still enjoying a comfortable sleep when he leaves and a good beer when he comes home?
> At the beginning of our century the have nots rose in revolt against the have gots. In the future we may see on the horizon of social relations a new revolt, that of the workers against the non-workers, or, as they will probably say, of the worker bees against the parasites.[15]

Or is it that before it reaches that stage, immoralists like the "gays" and militant feminists of New York and London become tired of waiting for full acceptance and take to the streets? Such frustration is likely because they will never gain full acceptance from the majority heterosexual population, no matter how much "gay rights" legislation is passed. I suggested earlier that the quest for approval from the majority mirrors the quest for the perfect partner. Each quest will remain perennially unsuccessful because each is working against the grain of human nature. Well, being non-judgmental, "the gays" just cannot tolerate intolerance. I have been threatened by homosexual activists in the past, so I can personally refute the myth of the gentle gay. But perhaps "the gays" attack and assault ordinary folk with whatever weapons come to hand, including blood terrorism, donating HIV-infected blood and leaving infected needles in public places. ACT-UP, the "AIDS Coalition To Unleash Power," has threatened to do this and California is seeing just such militance growing daily.

Homosexuality works against human nature in the many ways that we have considered through this book. One error which we touched on when considering healing was the gay activists' denial of guilt.

Those caught up in a homosexual lifestyle, for example, are wracked with guilt. So for that matter is the man who abandons his wife to commit adultery, the woman who allows a doctor to kill her baby by abortion and indeed the doctor himself. In all these cases, the guilt can be submerged, and the conscience hardened. Any conscience remaining drives the residual guilt, so that an absence of guilt after sinful behaviour indicates an absence of conscience. Guilt can be relieved but usually only by a God-based process, as for example in post-abortion counselling and homosexual healing.

It must be the same with collective guilt and collective conscience, so that a society which denies the role of guilt, or fights against its conscience, is fighting the losing battle which will end in the breakdown of peace and order. Roy Masters puts the problem most graphically:

Most people have trouble grasping man's individual capacity for hate and violence. It boggles the mind. But not only can human beings do heinous things, they can also make laws that do heinous things by institutionalising the perverse mentality of the law-makers. Once that happens, society is on a fast slide to national self-destruction because hateful laws can make relatively civilised people do hateful things. Not only are they tempted by this new negative law to succumb to their darker fears and hates, but they are actually pressured by law to succumb to those urgings.[16]

Masters sees such a process ending like this:

If things continue to go the way they have, with one outrageous "freedom" leading to another, all in the name of tolerance, we may one day be hiding in cellars behind locked doors, ... and injustice will rule in the place of justice.[17]

Just before the 1992 general election the "One-Nation" group of traditionalist Conservatives published a document observing "less self-discipline" in the family and "more broken marriages." The One-Nation group worries that "the very concept of established society, orderly and respected without being repressive, is under threat." They are right to be concerned: It is only in the last two hundred years that it has become possible to walk down an average high street without being robbed, and those two hundred years are contemporaneous with the rise of democratic capitalism, supported up till now by its Christian moral-cultural system. The One-Nation group sees the implications for law and order as bleak:

The steps from here to anarchic violence to widespread drug-taking, to destructive gangs of purposeless youths who neither support nor understand any higher form of social order, are all too short.[18]

Earlier, in chapter 26, we encountered the work of Robert Bly. He devotes some space in his book "Iron John" to explaining how those gangs of youths are suffering from hunger for the father and mentor.

The One-Nation group have correctly identified family breakdown as one cause of teenage crime. Other factors, besides those mentioned by Bly, could be the anti-authority elements of the media and schooling, the growing lack of a common morality as once taught by the church, consumerism and envy, and the drift of jobs from men to women. The whole package could of course be inter-related in a way we have not yet begun to consider.[19]

Another doomsday scenario could be the opposite of one earlier. Ordinary people, even those who could not be troubled to oppose the social rent seekers, might suddenly find themselves beleaguered. They cannot take their children out without seeing homosexual couples kissing in the street. Their children are taught increasingly revolting perversions at school in the name of "AIDS education." They cannot turn on the television or walk into the street without encountering some repellent imagery. Churches have either lost the will or have been forbidden by law to criticise the immorality around them. Ordinary people are now afraid to venture out for fear of criminals, for increased crime is but one symptom of a collapsing moral order. The police cannot cope. Moreover, ordinary people know in their hearts that there are things being permitted by law which are completely wrong. Even when criminals are brought to court the punishment rarely fits the crime. God's law is written on people's hearts and they look around and recognise that an assault is being made on all that they love and hold dear.

Perhaps they will not stand for this, and decide that permissive laws are bad laws and that they must take the law into their own hands. Most ordinary people are decent and easy-going up to the point where they perceive that they are being taken advantage of. Do they suddenly recognise tolerance not as virtue but as weakness? Do decent mothers rebel, ordinary fathers rise up, and oppose those who are the source of the corruption all about them? This process has started in America already, where pro-life Christians are peacefully obstructing access to the slaughterhouses, as they see them, of the abortionists. It is ironic that the police and the courts then crack down - in great severity - on Christian people whose values made western democracy great in the first place, and shelter the abortionist. Such a process, where law is used to uphold murder and evil and to oppress decency, might well end in full civil war. Some people felt provoked enough in New York in 1991 and again in Boston in 1992 to throw bottles at militant homosexuals participating in St Patrick's day marches.

That could not happen here, in the United Kingdom, and yet the Home Office and the Police are now increasingly worried by the growth of vigilante groups, particularly but not exclusively on council estates. On Anglesey a boy believed to be responsible for a spate of burglaries and other offences constantly taunted the law-abiding residents of Newborough with their ineffectiveness and that of the police against him. The villagers formed a mob one evening, surrounded the house, and the boy was taken off the island by the police for his own safety. On other occasions, such vigilante action ends less happily, with men being wrongly identified, or killed for minor offences. Psychologists and sociologists have warned for some time that once a few people take the law into their own hands the habit can spread.[20]

It seems to me both that the police cannot cope with rising crime and that no police force of reasonable and affordable size *could* cope when common morality breaks down, and that sentencing has become either inconsistent or too lenient or both.

In a famous case in early 1992, a boy was killed by a lorry driver in a hit-and-run accident. The driver, who was driving without insurance, was let off with a light sentence, expressed no remorse and even desecrated the son's grave. The boy's father, Mr Stephen Owen, sought the lorry driver out. He shot him with both barrels of a shot gun, despite the lorry driver's brave attempt to shield himself with his girl friend. The father was charged with malicious wounding and admitted it in court. The jury found him not guilty. That is gun law in action, upheld as a principle by twelve good men and true, because the statutory law was too lax. The jury had seen some justice done outside the law, and they liked it.

So is our doom-mongering too fanciful? Is not one nor a mixture of these scenarios what economists and political philosophers mean by "the failure of democratic capitalism"? But the question remains: If none of these scenarios has got it right, then in what manner will our society fail, and when?

35
Filling the spiritual vacuum

In the last few chapters we have been seeing that in the absence of a moral foundation, liberal capitalist democracy becomes self-destructive. How it destroys itself is open to speculation. That it will is scarcely doubted by political philosophers looking at the evidence. It is not going to destroy itself because of homosexuality, but the values of "the gays" are typical of the values that a stable society does not need. It short, they are corrupting.

Making the decision

"Pluralism" we have seen cannot help. Inasmuch as pluralism exists, it leads in economics to domination, leapfrogging and eventual collapse, and in social policy to a dangerous laissez-faire attitude towards morality. However, pluralism in social policy is a mirage, because every social special interest group is pulling in the same secular humanist direction.

Permissive social attitudes and laws become embedded into society, and are not easily, if at all, reversed. We are asked to bear the costs of our decisions (or choices) in a capitalist democracy, but the humanist new right exempts social rent-seekers from the costs of their decisions, and for democratic socialists, we all pay for the social rent-seekers anyway. The sexual market-place has no "invisible hand."

Although the architects of our liberal capitalist democracy took for granted shared values nurtured by the family and a God-given rule of law, Conservatives have been shy of articulating this fact, and have watched these values evaporate to leave an empty spiritual core at the heart of democratic capitalism. The vacuum has been filled by socialist secular humanism. Our liberal society consequently tolerates and even encourages the growth of permissiveness which corrupts the liberal democratic capitalist system itself. Because liberal democracy does not know what it believes, it cannot say "No" to special interest groups. So the seeds of its own destruction, which it carried within it, have germinated, sprouted, and are already choking it to death. Put less graphically, political philosophers recognise that because of the incompatibility between "moral" values and "permissive" values, a financial or emotional tension is already building up which could ultimately destroy our society.

At some stage, a decision has to be made by society between the ideology of those who would safeguard the foundations of our political and economic system, and that of those who would undermine it. This decision will "define right and wrong and transform that distinction into law."

We might at that time re-adopt the values of self-respect, self-restraint and self-denial, values of decency, thrift and attention to the future, values indeed nurtured by and in the family and the Christian faith. Or we could continue to accept the values of permissiveness, exemplified by homosexuality, values of short-term hedonism, degradation, individualism, consumerism, childlessness and lack of concern for the future. What I do not think we can do is have it both ways. Nor do I think we can continue to pretend to support the values of the family whilst in reality promoting permissiveness.

The source of absolutes

Professor Norman Barry observed the secular nature of modern conservatism, its suspicion of religion and its lack of a coherent political ideology. These three go together. Nature abhors a vacuum, and socialist humanism rushed in to occupy the vacant space where a conservative ideology ought to be. If conservatives acknowledge the sociological requisite for a stable society, then they can only conclude that democratic capitalism must be founded on a natural law that ultimately derives from God.

For a humanist, with no faith in God, there is no source of ultimate goodness, righteousness or justice. There are, as one might say, absolutely no absolutes.

This is so self-contradictory, that there must be a source of absolute right and wrong. Even if we do not like this source, we must still believe that it exists, and we might as well call it God. Unless the whole nation of Israelite people were engaged in a vast confidence trick when the books of the Old Testament were written, then this God gave them laws for their own good, setting out the boundaries of what would lead to a stable society. Cornwall County Council were criticised when three boys drowned off Land's End because they failed to put up warning signs. God has put up plenty, recognising, as

Michael Novak puts it, that: "Every community first of all needs social peace and order, even at the price of some freedom."[1]

Liberty and equality may well be twin principles of justice, but we have to place them in the real world. They are not gods themselves. Novak concludes:

> A society is not under a suicide pact, and therefore makes claims against liberty in the name of security, order, and social justice. Similarly, a society cannot function on one identical plane, and therefore makes claims against equality in the name of a hierarchy of social function and the integration of its daily life and work.[2]

Imposing morality

Michael Novak suggests that our current indecision is the worst decision of all:

> It does not follow from the fact that persons (and groups) stand in radical moral disagreement that "anything goes," "to each his own," etc. It may well be that when persons or groups stand in radical moral disagreement, only one is correct. The problem for a free society is to discern which.[3]

If we are not to surrender to moral relativism then a decision has to be made about which way we wish society to go. However, at this point, Novak, drawing on Bonhoeffer and still clinging to pluralism, articulates what many faint-hearted people believe, that "we cannot impose our morality on everyone else:"

> The political system of democratic capitalism cannot, in principle, be a Christian system. Clearly, it cannot be a confessional system. But it cannot even be presumed to be, in an obligatory way, suffused with Christian values and purposes.
>
> On the question of abortion, for example, no one is likely ever to be satisfied with the law, but all might be well advised not to demand in law all that their own conscience commands.[4]

Novak used the greater part of his book to explain that conservative democratic capitalism is perfectly compatible with Christianity, and yet he persists in conceding unnecessarily that "Christian values" mean in economics the further extension of the left-wing understanding of welfare. I do not know what he means on abortion, for he surely recognises that the womb contains a baby who is a child of God and a party to the cross-generational contract that family-based democratic capitalism involves. At other times Novak has encouraged his Roman Catholic Bishops when they stand up for Christian values against homosexuality and abortion.[5]

Probably voicing the fears of many Christians, and recognising that even Christians break the legal and moral code, Novak says:

> *Prematurely, before the endtime, to attempt to treat any society of this world as "a Christian society" is to confound precious hope with a sad reality. Human beings, even the most devout and serious Christians, cannot be expected to act always and in all ways as Christians ought to act, under the sway and impulse of God's grace. A political system based upon such expectations must necessarily end in disaster.*[6]

Although I acknowledge that American fear of the left, of socialist hijacking of Christian values to promote welfarism is driving his observations, I do not agree with his last sentence. We have a political system which is going to end in disaster already. Novak knows well that the whole corpus of God-given law recognises the problem of original sin, calling us back when our actions work against the stability of society. There is a shortfall between the strength of the spirit and the weakness of the flesh which it will be prudent of society to recognise and mitigate rather than encourage. It is ridiculous to abolish the legal force of the moral code on the grounds that we sometimes fail to live up to it.

Objective right and wrong

Again it is psychologist and broadcaster Roy Masters who says the uncomfortable:

> *It is obvious that* someone *must define right and wrong, and transform that distinction into law. Someone has to draw the line and say, you shall not commit adultery, polygamy, murder, robbery, and so forth. Of course, you can hear those immoral citizens cry out in vehement protest, "you can't impose your morality on us." But surely, to be blunt, if we do not impose our just way on them, they will impose their unjust way on us.*[7]

This assumes two valuable propositions. Firstly that the "someone" who draws the line is the source of absolute right and wrong whom we call God, and secondly, that ordinary people are in touch with that "someone" and with his line-drawing already. It never seems to be with the utmost confidence when someone proclaims that a form of immoral behaviour "is right for me" or that it is "in line with my own truth." There is an objective right and wrong, an objective truth, or we shall build morality and law on quicksand.

The Archbishop of Canterbury, George Carey, accepts much of what we have observed. He told charity directors in June 1992 that "a wishy-washy secular liberalism, with God privatised, is not a promising basis for tackling the world's problems." The general election campaign, he said, had given the impression that the purpose of life was shopping. The campaign had "dramatised our society's weak sense of moral purpose." The collapse of world communism had exposed deep problems in western society. These included materialism and consumerism:

> They also include the spread of relativism in moral questions, as if morals were simply a matter of individual opinion and there was no other source of spiritual or moral authority. They include a fragmentation of spiritual beliefs to the point where a sense of society's shared values has partly collapsed. It is widely regarded as embarrassing to talk about God, spirituality or even ethical values in polite society. The purpose of life, in many circles, is a topic banished to a purely private domain.[8]

Not my job

It is marvellous to have an Archbishop of Canterbury who believes in the fundamental values of God and who is not afraid to say that their absence is affecting society badly. Dr Carey has evidently thought hard since October 1991, when he told an audience at Kent University that it was simply not his job to proclaim that these values should in fact permeate society. Defending the Church of England against charges that it fails to give an adequate moral lead, he said that the church could only teach morality when people felt called to follow the Christian faith and to base their lives on Christ's teaching. "To insist that the church first teaches morality is to put the cart before the horse," he said.[9]

Going on, he told politicians and the "secular authorities" that they should recognise that each person is "essentially a spiritual being" with "an absolute worth" in the eyes of God. If this is ignored or forgotten, he went on, "the community becomes potentially demonic."

Now, as a statement that there is a Christian foundation to morality which our democracy cannot ignore, this was valuable. However, it followed logically not that the Church can only teach that foundation to Christians, but rather that the Church must proclaim it to everyone. God's law is after all written on all our hearts, but that quality, which we call "conscience," regularly needs reminding. Moreover, the moral imperatives that underpin society are not there only to be observed by those who happen to agree with them, still less just by the minority washed clean by the Blood of the Lamb, as the evangelical in Dr Carey would put it.

That would mean that everyone else had permission to murder, rape, cheat, pillage, promote pornography, have sex in the street and brawl as it took their fancy so to do. Some Christians really do believe this in the case of homosexuality, euthanasia and abortion: that they would not do these things, but why should others not be allowed to? I fancy that they have forgotten John Donne. That principle (or lack of principle) is bad enough, but if we extend it, then those of us who are Christians or indeed just decent or concerned for the moral growth of our children would have placed upon us the increasing and bizarre duty of avoiding such public manifestations of evil in our daily lives. We are doing this already to a certain extent, in the newsagent, the video shop, in parks used by homosexuals for "cruising," when we pass an abortion clinic, when we watch television. Such a society - demonic is a good description - can not last long.

Whose job then?

There are three Conservative responses to the lack of Clerical support for the fundamental values of our society. One is simply to ignore it. Another is to take the fight to them, as Margaret Thatcher did with the Church of Scotland, and John Patten in The Spectator.[10] Mrs Thatcher set out the Christian base for a property-owning democracy, which the Kirk did not care for. Mr Patten spoke of right and wrong, and the fear of God. Both were criticised by the liberal media, which I am sure buoyed them up a great deal. The third response is to criticise the bishops for their lack of a moral lead.

Unfortunately, the impression given by bishops blaming politicians, and politicians blaming bishops in the third response is of Tweedledum and Tweedledee. The Bishops have the safer jobs, so one supposes that they should be more fearless in saying the unthinkable, and yet some of them believe that they are fulfilling this function by scorning democratic capitalism itself, or by questioning the tenets of their faith, rather than proclaiming the Gospel.

As for the politicians, when in office they are naturally cautious, and try not to lead public opinion in support of politically incorrect propositions. And yet, if those who wish capitalist democracy to survive agree that claims against complete liberty have to made and

Filling the spiritual vacuum

that society cannot afford to let a kind of death wish suffuse it, then the measures that ensure peace and order must surely be founded on something other than the current prejudices of media people masquerading as "public opinion."

Certainly there must be public acceptance even of a system of law and morality founded on the absolutes of God, but there is really no problem with this once we leave behind those in the media and the various pressure groups rooted in or dependent upon immorality. The ordinary voter can discern right from wrong.

It worries politicians that they might get a back-lash from the media, and they worry unnecessarily. Television is not the real world. For the majority, that conscience which is implanted by God is still very real amidst all the pressures of modern life. We know when we have done wrong because we feel guilty. Sin and guilt have not been abolished, in spite of all the humanist pressure of the last thirty years. John Gummer strikes a better chord amongst ordinary people when he criticises liberal bishops for failing to condemn the permissive society than they do when they debate the legalisation of brothels.

The only reasonable choice

The only possible conclusion which agrees with the evidence is that those who believe in the worth of liberty, democracy and capitalism must accept that the moral-cultural system that underpins the political and economic order can only be God-given, and in our society that means Christian. Our law must be based again on the laws of God which Smith, Burke and Hume took for granted, and every policy must be examined to see if it is Godly, and if it advances the Christian Faith and the institution of the family in its traditional form. The spiritual nature of mankind must be acknowledged, and every policy must advance mankind and not debase it, which is to say that every policy must go along with God's created order, and not try to push against it.

In case such a moral-cultural system seems fanciful, let us remember that the Queen at her coronation took a series of binding oaths. One of these oaths is important for our argument. She swore:

> To maintain the laws of God and the profession of the Gospel.

It would be difficult to be more categoric than that. What is binding on Her Majesty is binding on her Government, so that it may be that every piece of permissive legislation ever passed is actually illegal under the British constitution. Our laws must be founded on the laws of God, and the Christian Faith - the Gospel - must be professed. It may be argued that in a multi-cultural, multi-faith Britain Her Majesty's oath is unrealistic, and yet less than 3% of the population profess other faiths or cultures.[11] Another 4% are professed atheists, who must all be employed in the media, in academia or in Government Departments. Britain is not on the evidence "multi-cultural" or "multi-faith" at all. Nor would it matter if we were. We are discussing measures to preserve our democratic way of life, and people of other faiths are likely to support a Godly, even a Christian framework. It was Lord Jakobovits, the previous Chief Rabbi, who argued most strongly in the House of Lords that religious education and assemblies in Britain's schools should be Christian. Ultimately, Her Majesty's coronation oaths are not up for debate.

A Christian-based programme

When we begin to consider the policies which a government following a Christian political philosophy would adopt in practice, then naturally we come up literally with an anachronistic programme. It simply does not fit today's politically correct agenda. Thirty years ago, the various measures would have looked simply ordinary, and twenty years from now, if we react in time, they will seem merely sensible. If it is to survive at all, surely our society will need to recover its moral nerve, and with a permissive media, cautious politicians and a liberal established church the atmosphere conducive to change may not arise in time at all. On the other hand, America is showing the first signs of waking up, or at least of bringing these matters to a head, and the emerging democracies of eastern Europe are amazed that we discourage marriage and traditional child-rearing and subsidise family breakdown, immorality and irresponsibility.

Let us then consider how a Christian political philosophy might work in practice. It would give a lead to prudence in private affairs because its government would state clearly that the only money it had was tax-payers' money, and it would not spend money it had not got. It would balance the budget, and might even put in a leaflet with our income tax return showing its own sources of income and where it was spent, as does the local authority. It would be open and honest.

Tax allowances and social security would probably be weighted in favour of marriage, children, family and motherhood and consequently against single parenthood and neglect. The poll tax, which encouraged parents to throw their adult children out, and which taxed non-wage-earning wives as individuals but forced husbands to be responsible for their bills would never have seen the light of day.

Filling the spiritual vacuum

Divorce is anti-family and would only happen after every possible attempt to keep a couple together had failed. A sensible society would recognise at once that parental neglect leads to crime, and would strike at the roots of such problems rather than tinker with symptoms. It would be highly suspicious of "sex education," "personal and social education" (PSE) and "teaching the whole child," recognising that it is the role of parents to implant moral values and indeed prejudices in their children.

Pornography is corrupting and destructive of the human spirit and would not be allowed in a Christian society. Nor would blasphemy, even if artistic. Public broadcasting would be wholesome and decent, echoing the words of the original BBC charter, now ignored. Abortion, which denies the humanity of the child in the womb and as Dr Carey puts it, his "absolute worth," and does this against all the medical evidence, would again be illegal, except where the life (not the lifestyle or livelihood) of the mother was in danger. Such a society would recognise the value of innocent human life, and would be more gentle, relaxed and compassionate as a result. For the same reasons it would in all likelihood restore the death penalty for murder.

This society would set great store by its spiritual dimension, and would acknowledge the centrality of God, the meaning of sin and guilt, and the worth of virtue and decency. It would probably recognise the need for one day off out of seven, because that is what God says and it is sensible to rest and spend time with friends and family. Indeed it would work with the grain of human nature and not across it all the time, being realistic and not indulging in wishful thinking. It would accept objective evidence on social matters, as humanists and permissives so signally fail to do. Accepting Hayek's conclusions on the inability of the state to take decisions effectively, it would allow matters like schooling and health to be decided at the lowest possible level. Politicians would accept their limitations.

This democratic capitalist society founded on Christian ethics would above all be just, and justice would extend not just to domestic matters but to all dealings with "neighbours" in the Biblical sense. It would be generous with overseas aid, but would grant money for specific small low-technology projects rather than give despots cash to improve their status or with which to buy arms. In this way it would please, or enrage, right and left alike. On the matter of debt, it is quite ridiculous that the poorer countries of the world are paying back more money in interest on existing loans than they receive in aid.

Homosexuality

As to homosexuality, homosexual activity would be forbidden by a Christian society on every ground. It debases those human beings who are its practitioners, and corrupts others directly, especially the young. It denies God's created order, has a corrosive effect on society and destroys its own practitioners. At the deepest level, it is anti-family and anti-Christian. A report prepared for the Tasmanian legislature concluded:

> Instead of being a bonding force in the service of society, gay sexuality becomes a mechanism to assault the body, debase the mind and rend civilisation.[12]

Add to that the public health problems and public offence that visible expressions of homosexuality bring, and even without our sense that the stability of society itself is in opposition to the values exemplified by gay rights, any sensible society would discourage homosexual activity and expression. From a recognition that homosexual practice is wrong, and that homosexual orientation is a developmental anomaly, would flow a willingness to provide relevant treatment and to engender an atmosphere in which homosexuals could come forward for it. In other words the reaction to someone claiming to be "gay" would be of compassion rather than either acceptance or horror. This would be what its friends thought the Sexual Offences Act 1967 would do, but without the Act itself, which was unnecessary, and corrupting because of the veneer of legality it gave to homosexuality generally. The required atmosphere did not come about after 1967, but that was because the Act sent out the wrong signals. The Sexual Offences Act 1967 was in every sense a failure.

It is certain that the liberal, feminist establishment is too firmly in place for it to be possible in the near future to repeal the 1967 Sexual Offences Act and to offer proper treatment to help orientational homosexuals achieve heterosexuality in the light of modern knowledge. There is also the matter of those who have invested time and emotional energy in an overt homosexual identity and the "gay industry" dependent upon them. But if we cannot repeal the Sexual Offences Act 1967 for a generation, in the meantime the suggestion by Edwina Currie (of all people) that homosexuality should not be promoted indicates a sensible way forward. It should be possible even today to outlaw the promotion of homosexuality and homosexual activity in the written, visual or spoken media.

Filling the spiritual vacuum

Yet at the same time, much more effort should be put into providing healing for the homosexual, and indeed for heterosexuals as well. We are not starting at the right place for any of this, and I shall try to say what can be done in the meantime in my final chapter. What we are doing here is setting out some of the policies that would be put into effect by a government following the only political philosophy under which our democratic capitalist way of life can survive.

Christian political philosophy not "statist"

It may be objected that a Christian, pro-family political philosophy is "statist," the criticism levelled at Roger Scruton for his traditionalism. However, the Common Law and those statutes like the 1956 Sexual Offences Act which are restatements of it are founded in the developed world on Christianity. The Common Law, as Professor Barry admits, is generally sound and consistent. It is the "state" and its permissive legislation which has so emasculated the Common Law that the traditional morality necessary for the survival of democratic capitalism has been undermined. To continue the metaphor, the "democratic" state has dug out the foundations of democracy by listening to social rent-seekers rather than to its heritage and indeed to its electorate.

The state should do literally as little as possible, and take as small a proportion of gross national product as possible. But so far as we need a central state for the delivery of common goods like road-mending, defence, welfare and education, it has to be funded and so there must be taxation. Taxation favours some groups above others. There is no reason why weighting it in favour of the family, which must be done if the family is not to wither from permissive social pressure, should be any more "statist" than weighting it against. Indeed, with a Christian political philosophy in place, the burden of paying for permissiveness would wither and the demands of the state on taxation and on the allegiance of its client welfare-receivers would reduce. For this reason alone, the New Right should be supporting a Christian moral framework in every word and deed.

Nor is it to be "paternalist," the criticism made against old-style traditional conservatives. Rather the re-adoption of a Christian moral-cultural base is a hard-headed recognition that the common law, based on the law of God, is there to safeguard the very stability and continuation of society itself. One man is put in authority over another in every society, although permissiveness and "new rightism" are antipathetic to "authority." St Paul tells us that all authority is from God, and of course a Christian moral framework accepts that God is an authority higher than any earth-bound authority, and that all law is from God. God tells us that his law is given "for your good" and so "that all will go well with you," and in context this seems to be addressed to the individual and to his society.

Of course anyone who accepts John Donne's conclusion that "no man is an island" will be pleased that as a consequence of a Christian political ideology some people are protected from themselves or from the consequences of actions to which they are tempted (or encouraged, by permissive law) but which it is good for them and even better for society as a whole that they should resist. Of course, this unintended consequence will be reason enough for libertarians, who deny that we are all responsible for each other, to oppose a Christian political ideology.

Christianity not left-wing

Still less is a Christian political system inherently left-wing, which is what worries Novak and others on the right. The Christian duty to care for the poor and for widows and orphans is a personal duty in the first place. The welfare state is an admission that personal charity is ineffective, because not everyone can be relied upon to discharge his Christian duty. Not everyone in a Christian political society is in fact Christian. Those who are Christian are equally prey to sin, and may not always act with perfect altruism. For these reasons, a Christian society may ask the state to discharge collectively the duty to the deserving poor that it cannot discharge individually. Whether this means a state bureaucracy or support to welfare charities would be debated. Whichever way it went about it, its Christian base would ensure that welfare neither undermines society, nor discourages enterprise, and its success in achieving these ends would be a measure of its success as a Christian society. To put that in theological terms, the welfare system would not be an occasion of sin to anyone; it would not encourage anyone into wrongful behaviour if democratic capitalism is to survive.

A Christian political philosophy would however be "patriarchal," immediately because the Christian God is "Our Father," despite the vote of the Methodist Conference, and then because the created nature with which He has endowed human beings contains gender differences which demand different gender roles. It might become patriarchal enough that fathers would spend more time with their children, but that cannot be legislated; such attitudes are part of the feeling which brings a society to insist on a moral basis in the first place.

Filling the spiritual vacuum

Feminists will oppose a Christian political foundation if only because of its inbuilt patriarchal bias. Humanists will oppose it because it is Christian and because Christianity is a Faith which maintains that there is a created order and a spiritual dimension to life. To all those who cannot accept the principle of a Christian political ideology, we shall have to fall back on practicalities, and explain patiently that the secular humanist permissives have had their chance for twenty-five years and that we can see that their ideology does not work.

In concluding that only a Christian foundation can support a modern democratic capitalist superstructure we looked at the evidence of social stress and disintegration over the last twenty-five years. Even without the detailed costing of the effects of permissiveness that needs to be done, the evidence demands a conclusion agreeing the practicality of a system which is founded on Christian moral standards over one founded on permissiveness. The downfall of democracy was argued by Ropke to lie in its own success. In the absence of a strong Christian foundation to democracy he will surely be proved right.

36
Back to normality

As individuals we need a response to the proselytisation of gay rights, and we need a proper understanding of the homosexual condition. People who have grown up homosexual need to find healing, and those of us who are parents will be concerned to do all in our power to ensure that our children grow up normally. So this final chapter is intended for individual men and women of goodwill. Let us firstly look at an inappropriate response to homosexuals and homosexuality.

Violence against homosexuals

"Queerbashing" has long been a pastime of a certain type of young man, and we looked at violence towards and within the homosexual network in chapter 12. The gays make rather too much of "queerbashing," and occasionally invite it, and we saw that society has more to fear from homosexuals than vice versa. There is a standard defence to an allegation of assault on a homosexual man, that the victim initially made an indecent assault upon the perpetrator. Where that is true, reasonable defensive action has often been supplanted by an unreasoning if understandable lashing-out, but at other times it is simply not true at all. I wish to make it quite clear that no-one should take anything in this book as legitimising attacks on homosexuals for reason of their homosexuality. For what good any denunciation of mine will do, I believe that "queerbashing" is a wholly inappropriate response to the presence of homosexuals in society. We would not treat orphans like that, and we should not treat emotional orphans any differently. American Lawyer Roger Magnuson puts this point well, in a new edition of his book "Are Gay Rights Right?:"

> Homosexuals are made, not born. They are responsible for their conduct. But no person of good will should use this as a justification for personal acts of cruelty, violence or insult. On a personal as well as legal basis, homosexuals are entitled to respect as human beings, as persons with immortal souls. But this respect does not require the

provision of special privileges that would infringe on the rights or liberties of others. A concern for homosexuals as people will lead, paradoxically, to withholding social acceptance of their behavior.[1]

Public promotion and flaunting of homosexuality does bring its own backlash, and is probably encouraged by the left simply for the antagonism it arouses. They know well that in a society with liberal or permissive laws, where the intolerable in conscience is tolerated in law, people take the law into their own hands, outraged at the inability of law to uphold a decent standard. We saw this in chapter 34. It is easy to see how public flaunting of homosexuality, by "kiss-ins" or hand-holding, incite ordinary members of the public to violence. This is one reason why those outraging public decency in this way are usually charged with conduct likely to cause a breach of the peace.

Where parents throw their children out

It is desperately sad that parents have beaten or thrown out children found to be homosexual. There may be guilt or self-blame involved on the parent's side in many cases, and of disappointment that the child has turned out wrong. Again the gays and permissives contribute to the misery.

The problem this time is that healing for the homosexual is being withheld as an option from the parents, leaving them to choose between two equally bad extremes. The answer is neither eviction from the home nor an unreasoning acceptance of the homosexual nature of the child, and yet these are the only options presented by the intellectually bereft and self-justificatory "Parents Enquiry," "Support" and "Acceptance" groups. Such groups get away with it because most parents, including their founders, cannot confront their own guilt. It is so very tempting to say that nobody was at fault, and indeed liberal society hates to apportion blame.

When a child turns out homosexual, something certainly *has* gone wrong, probably in the parent-child relationship. In many cases parents bear a direct responsibility for the breach of the duty of love and trust involved in normal upbringing, and at other times, abuse has occurred outside the parents' control. Whatever the initial cause, parent and child must start from where they are, without recriminations, and seek through forgiveness to overcome the shortcomings that have arisen. Christian faith will obviously help, but parents and friends have a duty to support a child making the healing journey, and if they believe in prayer, to support the child and the whole process of healing in prayer, and most certainly to pray incessantly for a change of heart if the child initially refuses to be involved in the healing process.

I hope that this book will also help such parents to be aware of the reality of the homosexual condition, in order to be able to dismiss the usual arguments a homosexually active child is encouraged to put forward by the "gay self-help groups" with whom he or she might have been in contact.

Normal development starts in the home

Every parent can help his or her child to develop into a normal happy heterosexually-oriented individual in the first place. Other benefits will accrue from such an approach, but this is after all a book about homosexuality. The first and most important matter is to safeguard and build a successful marriage. This would make a book on its own, as several authors have found, but the keys seem to be a refusal to countenance even the possibility of the marriage breaking up, in other words, commitment, and a simple self-giving love in which all wrongs are forgiven. It is only by building love and commitment between each other within marriage that a couple can offer their love to their children.

From the security of a loving and committed marriage, a couple must give time, love and commitment to their children. If this is done properly there will be no favouritism shown because none will be felt. It follows that a child is not to be neglected and that a deep and loving relationship must be forged. I hope it is needless to say that love involves guidance and discipline; just letting a child learn its own standards as it goes along is a form of neglect. So, it might be said, is sending the children downstairs in the morning to watch whatever is on television - perhaps there might be a video lying around - because we are too idle or too tired to get up ourselves.

Fathers have a special duty to spend time with their children, to hug them, read them stories, go out with them and just be with them. It is useless to work late earning money for the family if there is no time left for the family itself. Such a father is classically emotionally absent. It seems to be almost a mantra of our time that "we gave them everything money could buy." Time is also vital, ordinary time, not just "prime time." Mothers too have a duty to spend time with their children, especially when they are very young. This may seem obvious, but it has escaped the advocates of creches at the workplace.

A crisis in masculinity

Just as the mother is undeniably important to the development of the child in infancy, so is the father as the child grows through puberty into adolescence. Leanne Payne writes that we are listening at that stage of development for the "masculine voice."

> It is the strong masculine love and affirmation coming through that voice that convinces us that we are truly and finally separate from our mothers.[2]

We touched earlier on the need for the father to affirm his children in their gender identity. If he fails, or never bothers, a daughter will remain unaffirmed as a woman, and a son will suffer from low self-esteem, a prime characteristic of male homosexuals. It should be apparent that a father can only carry out his duty in this sphere if he is affirmed himself in his own masculinity, and the apparent emasculation of men today, their failure to exercise "the power to act as father, husband and leader," is the subject of Leanne Payne's book "Crisis in Masculinity."

Robert Bly, after ten years of work with men experiencing "confusion, pain and impotence" believes that these symptoms stem "not from female anger, scorn or inadequate mothering," but from "hunger for the father and mentor." We covered all this in chapter 26. Bly believes that where a father spends time with his son, fishing, mending the car, whatever it is, then "something tangible, something almost like food" passes from the father to the son.

Divorce leaves father-sized hole in child's life

It almost goes without saying that parents should divorce only in the most extreme circumstances. Most children involved in divorce end up living with their mother. Except where the mother has become lesbian, this is often the least bad way out of an impossible conundrum, particularly when children are young, but as both boys and girls grow up, the father-sized hole in their lives becomes more and more apparent. As Leanne Payne puts it, in the context of emotional healing for the homosexual:

> The finest and most capable mother, try as she may, cannot repair the gap an absent or emotionally remote father leaves on the young teenager. She simply cannot affirm a son or daughter in the way a whole father can. This is one of the awful tragedies of divorce and broken homes. There is seldom a father substitute who is both capable and willing to affirm the struggling adolescent boy or girl.[3]

Boys affected worst by divorce

A divorce or separation very frequently leaves a child with a sense of betrayal and is highly likely to have a lasting effect on the child's ability to forge relationships. In this way are the sins of the fathers visited on the sons, even to the third or fourth generation. In particular, the child may well enter a period of melancholy and emptiness as a result of a divorce, indistinguishable in form or substance from mourning. Again, this particularly applies to boys, who bear the scars of even the most carefully-arranged divorce very badly. Other external factors can fracture the parent-child relationship; it is going to be no surprise at all if some of the children involved in the Cleveland, Rochdale and Orkney scandals, torn from their parents in the way they were, do not demonstrate exactly these emotional symptoms, and exhibit a corresponding need for healing. Again, we can draw on a sound psychological explanation:

> *Any incident that disrupts the child's attachment to the parent of the same sex may result in the homosexual condition, but it may be most clearly illustrated in the case of early separation. ...*
>
> *Mourning as a psychological process can take place not only when a parent dies, but when the child is temporarily separated from the parent; or when parental behaviour hurts the child to such an extent that he or she represses the capacity for attachment to the parent. It is the absence of, and defence against, attachment to the parent that constitutes the psychological orphan.*[4]

The dramatic representation of homosexuals as psychological or emotional orphans is one we encountered in chapter 24. The effects on children of what their parents probably regarded as a sensible thing to do in the circumstances has been far beyond what anyone might have predicted when divorce was liberalised over twenty years ago. Since then, the initiation of divorce has been made easier and easier, and a law commission report recently suggested, astonishingly, that divorce should become quicker still.

It is my conclusion that the liberalisation of divorce bears as much blame for homosexual behaviour as does the "do as thou wilt" sexual philosophy, although in some degree it is part of the same parcel. This is not a conclusion that I expect to go down well with the divorced reader, whether or not their child has turned out homosexual. I am sorry for them, for often the divorce has not been the path to happiness that friends and "counsellors" indicated it would be. Human nature will not allow such a commitment as marriage to be so easily broken.

Better to stay together for the sake of the children

A study published by the Social Affairs Unit shows that although parents squabbling and fighting but staying together *may* damage children emotionally, a divorce on the other hand *always* does.[5] These two - divorce or squabbling - are often presented as the only options. There is, once more, a third way, and that is for the parents to work at getting on and simply loving each other. If more energy went into this avenue, there would certainly be fewer broken homes and fewer damaged children.

If we are genuinely concerned with the wellbeing of our children, we will make sure that proper attempts are made at reconciliation, for the good of both parents and children. Reconciliation is not to be confused with procedures of "conciliation" at present being advocated from libertarian quarters. Conciliation means agreeing at an early stage of divorce on who-gets-what, and it is just another polite term for facilitating marital breakup. It matters little to a child whose parents are in the process of destroying his world that it is all being done amicably and in a grown-up fashion. Divorce must not be a "choice" nor an "opportunity" but a last resort when all attempts to find common ground and to convince parents of their mutual responsibility to their children have failed.

One-parent families

The mother left on her own has many problems, not least of which is how to mitigate the absence of the children's father. If she does not remarry, she incurs financial hardship, and if she does, she brings a tension into the home. Her children may resent the step-father and their mother's marrying him. Studies show that where the mother is widowed, the children paradoxically adjust better than where the mother is divorced, at least if the mother does not remarry. The father who has died is in some way still emotionally present. Some divorced mothers try to blacken the father's name in front of the children, or indulge in emotional war through them. Divorced fathers can do this too. It is wicked, selfish, short-term behaviour. Wicked and selfish because it scars the children emotionally, regularly ruining their own chances for a stable married life, just to satisfy some spirit of vengeance in the parent. Short-term because children grow up, and may well then see things as they are, and blame the parent who orchestrated the feuds.

It is possible that where children have never known their father, that there might not necessarily be a higher incidence of homosexuality at least in boys. A notable study by Irving Bieber of male homosexuals indicated that "only a small group had no father."[6] This rather surprising result does tie in fairly well. If such a one-parent family is headed by a mother, there is no father by whom a boy can be deserted.

However, Robert Bly disagrees, drawing attention to the need for the father in all children. Additionally, single parents find that without a father as a role model and as a token of authority and discipline, children and especially boys turn to the peer-group and copy detrimental group behaviour, so in neither way are we saying that these children will always grow up to be model citizens, entirely free from unruly behaviour.

The divorcee and stepfather

The man who is separated from his children by divorce still has a duty towards them. Many fathers recognise this, and try their best to maintain contact with their children. Sadly, others do not, and the majority of divorced fathers have lost contact with their children after two years. And yet I have had a father tell me that it is only by insisting on taking his maintenance cheque round in person that his wife permits him to see his children. We touched on the way feuding parents use children above. Fathers of goodwill know that they simply have to keep up contact with their children, and try to be as much a father to them as they can. Eventually, as the children grow up, they may get their children back. Mothers who wish the best for their children will give all possible access to their father, and encourage his visits, unless there is some over-riding reason why not.

The man who marries into another man's family has a different problem. He has to be a father to the children even though there is a father already. He has to be emotionally involved, and yet aware of the risks that this brings with step-daughters. He has to impose discipline without alienating already emotionally scared children. I wish him well, and know that associations of step-parents are doing the best they can to advise men, and women, in this situation.

Active homosexuals must be denied recruits

People of goodwill will wish to starve active homosexuals of new blood. This can be done in schools, through the youth service and in law. One of the criticisms of "positive images" sex education about homosexuality is that it bathes homosexuality in a "positive" light, without any of the negative information that most people feel exists, but that has not previously been set down in any systematic way. However I am not advocating that this "whole story" approach is appropriate for young people, for two reasons, firstly because it is likely to encourage experimentation in a "dangerous" and "anti-social" activity, coated with glamour, as the young would see it, and secondly because children simply do not need to be exposed to such a seamy side of life. Section 46 of the Education (No2) Act 1986, which was put down after intense pressure from parents worried about immoral sex education, is a step in the right direction:

> The local education authority by whom any county, voluntary or special school is maintained, and the governing body and head teacher of the school, shall take such steps as are reasonably practicable to secure that where sex education is given to any registered pupils at the school it is given in such a manner as to encourage those pupils to have due regard to moral considerations and the value of family life.[7]

Sex education of doubtful worth

The 1986 Act allows school governors to decide not to have a sex education programme at all. One should be conscious of Van Wyck & Geist's findings that homosexual behaviour correlates with early *knowledge* of homosexuality and for this reason I suggest that homosexuality should not feature in any school sex-education programme at all. I know this begs the question of whether sex education is advisable in the first place, and my view, after looking at what leading child psychiatrists have to say, is that it should never be given before all the children in a class achieve puberty and never to a mixed class. My real sympathy lies with those who say that it is the job of parents to give children sex education, and that there was never very much wrong with behind-the-bike-sheds in any case. It certainly is undeniable that there was a lot less anguish in society over sex and its after-effects, and it must be said, fewer teenage pregnancies, abortions, suicides and sexually transmitted diseases, when children learnt about sex from those of their peers whose parents *had* told them.

What does sex education actually comprise? School biology courses have included human reproduction for some years, although the human race has managed to reproduce itself for thousands of years without this valuable assistance. So is it sexual technique, consideration as a lover, that is intended? It is hard to see how a "karma sutra" approach would get past the fifth form without ribald laughter and embarrassment. So we are left with morality or its absence. Indeed both sides of the argument take for granted that sex education is not just "about the plumbing."

The problem seems to be that those who are interested in giving sex education are often those to whom "morality" means little more than risk prevention. Wearing a condom is to them a moral act. It becomes "immoral" to be judgmental, or to dissuade two people whether married or not, of the opposite or the same sex, to express their affection sexually. In this way are children "empowered" to "make their informed life-choices."

This sort of value-free "personal and social education" is being promoted hard by the National Curriculum Council itself. Where it can lead was demonstrated in chapter 15. The government might be happy with it, but as Katie Ivens of the Campaign for Real Education has pointed out, it is not what parents of goodwill expect their children to be taught when they send them to school.[8] We are not in "partnership" with a school, we have delegated part of our children's education to them. They are literally our servants, because we not they are responsible for our children's education. Teachers should teach traditional subjects, and indeed Christian-based RE, but if their opinions on the moral and personal side do not coincide with ours, they can leave that area to us.

Questions parents must ask all sex educators

I suppose some "experts" and "counsellors" who feel they cannot give up their sex education, are driven by missionary zeal or their own domestic finances. Others may have been involved in extra-marital sex, or in fringe sexual practices or downright perversion. Rather than simply get on with these quietly, or better still, recognise them as wrong and turn round and stop, their guilt actually pushes them to tell others that the practices themselves are correct. Many sex educators must suffer from the psychological condition known as "denial" where the truth about sex education - that it is "a mass of misinformation, misrepresentation, and outright fraud," as child psychiatrist Thomas Szasz put it[9] - is denied because it fails to support their own preconceptions.

Either way, they must be amazed and delighted that ordinary people are fool enough to allow them access to teach these things to their children. Parents should try to pluck up the courage to question anyone proposing to give sex education or PSE to their child to find out if they are involved in extra-marital sex, or in fringe practices, or perversion. If the answer is "yes," or worse, that the sex educator does not acknowledge that there is such as thing as perversion, or that all fringe practices are normal, then the parents must demand the right to withdraw their children from being taught by that person.

Parents must demand that *if* sex education is given, homosexuality should not appear in it, and if the subject arises, that it should be made clear that young people with homosexual inclinations which persist into adulthood should seek psychiatric help.

Sex education should not mention homosexuality

The Department of Education and Science did in fact issue a circular in November 1987, drawing attention to the 1986 Act, and telling teachers:

> *There is no place in any school in any circumstances for teaching which advocates homosexual behaviour, which presents it as the "norm" or which encourages homosexual experimentation by pupils. Indeed, encouraging or procuring homosexual acts by pupils who are under the age of consent is a criminal offence. It must also be recognised that for many people, including members of various religious faiths, homosexual practice is not morally acceptable, and deep offence may be caused to them if the subject is not handled with sensitivity by teachers if discussed in the classroom.*[10]

Left-wing boroughs and education authorities were very swift to circulate teachers and school governors with the advice that a DES circular has no status in law. They were quite right, it does not, and it is time to incorporate it into the next Education Bill so that it does.

Youth service needs watching

The youth service has a similar duty to be prepared to offer a sympathetic ear and appropriate information to young people who admit to homosexual tendencies. It should be explained to them that there is no fault or blame attached to someone with such tendencies, not that "many" boys or girls have them, but that when they do, it is due to an underlying problem which can be helped. Again, one would hope that youth clubs and other organisations for young people would be attached to a church or be run by adults of Christian sympathy or at least goodwill.

It is the duty of parents to find out if this is the case in any youth club or other group to which their children belong, and if it is not the case, to remove them and to send them to one which does. A mere physical connection with a church is not always a cast-iron indication of goodwill, unfortunately. A youth club known to me attached to a church in South London showed homosexual propaganda videos to its children. The responsibility is on parents to make very sure indeed that a correct attitude prevails.

Parents must be on their guard

Homosexuals who are sexually interested in young boys and adolescents try to obtain positions where they can be involved with them. Parents have to be vigilant and children sadly have to be warned against paedophile approaches, lest the cycle of abuse widen its network. Homosexuals may try to gain access to children through the youth service, voluntary organisations, schools, babysitting or even through marriage to a divorcee or widow.

Parents will take pains in the ways suggested above to prevent their children from acquiring homosexual tendencies in the first place, but they must also take care that such tendencies are not implanted by allowing a homosexual the opportunity to involve their child in homosexual activity. As we saw in chapter 14, this can become learned and established as a behaviour pattern within a very short time, once the initial distaste has been overcome, and a homosexual orientation can then be established. If there is a homosexual inclination already in the child, it is still important that it does not progress to homosexual activity, or the child may be drawn into the full homosexual lifestyle and its subculture.

Courage needed to admit mistakes

The homosexual man or woman reading this book will already have seen, principally in chapter 25, that healing is a reality which simply depends on a positive attitude towards it. The homosexual who has never "come out" is better placed to accept healing than he who has decided that he should announce his homosexual behaviour to all and sundry. In this sense if in no other, "gay pride" has been counter-productive to homosexuals, who were better off in so many ways in the "closet." We rejected "opportunity and choice" as a political philosophy earlier, but here those words come into their own; the opportunity for healing is there, and all it needs is a positive choice to take advantage of it.

It is true that it requires courage of a degree that can normally only be supported by religious faith to admit one's past mistakes and to express a desire to change. There will be very many people sadly trapped in homosexual lifestyles for lack of this courage and for political and attitudinal reasons. If we accept that homosexual behaviour is corrupting to individuals and to society at large, which is the conclusion reached in these pages, then it becomes important to dissuade those contemplating homosexual activity and to provide an alternative. The latter is quite frankly the responsibility of the Christian church in this country and of psychoanalytic practitioners of goodwill, but I shall come to that in a moment.

Anyone needing sexual or emotional healing can find the various addresses for Pilot, True Freedom Trust and St Michael's in the text or the references.

Church ministry for healing and marriage

Previous chapters attempted to describe the psychiatric healing of homosexuals, but we saw that the spiritual content involved means that it is probable that the best place for such healing is in the various Christian churches. Every church should have a healing ministry, extending the love of God to those in need. The Church need not hold a monopoly of healing, but attitudes towards those suffering from a homosexual orientation probably need to be spirit-led to enable this vital ministry to succeed. In such an atmosphere, homosexuals will find not the tolerance they do not need, but the compassion they do. In addition, Government grants to such healing groups within churches as do become established would go some way to redress the damage that has been wrought by torrents of public money tumbling into the various "gay" youth groups in the past.

The churches have a better role to play in marriage. Ministers and priests spend what they would regard as a considerable period of time talking with couples preparing for marriage, but it often seems that as soon as the newlyweds have passed through the wedding ceremony, they are left to get on with it as best they may. It is as if lengthy instruction were to be given in the art of swimming in a side room away from the pool, and that on the great day, the instructor took his pupils to the water's edge, blessed them, pushed them in and walked off.

Every church should have a ministry to young married couples, and it is failing in its Christian duty if it does not. The priest or minister should expect to be supported with prayer and time by other couples within his church as the whole church fulfils this task.

The churches need a better ministry to their young as well. Nearly one-third of the members of church youth groups believe it morally acceptable to have sex before marriage, according to a report on young peoples' relationships. More than one in twenty of those under 16, the age of consent, claimed to have had sexual intercourse. Researchers were particularly concerned because most of these people were regular churchgoers. They are calling for churches to give more guidance to young people on sexual issues.

The teenager least likely to be sexually involved lived in a home where both parents were active Christians and where there was a good relationship with the father. The average father only spent three minutes a day talking to his son or daughter, who watched three hours of television a day. One in four of those aged 13, and more than half of those aged 14-15, had watched 18-rated films and videos.

The report's author, Boyd Myers, of the Marc Europe research organisation, said: "I found this quite shocking." More than half the members of 150 church youth groups took part in the survey, by Agape, an evangelical missionary organisation.[11]

Compassion better than tolerance

It is said that when Saint John of Patmos was very old he used to be brought to worship by his disciples and invited to give a sermon. Often he would say, with a brevity that other priests might emulate: "Little children," - as he always called them - "love one another."

If we love one another we shall invest a lot of time in our marriages and in our children, and we shall devote time and money to helping those of our fellows who have been damaged to find healing. But if parents are not to be undermined by what happens outside the home there will have to be a major change of attitudes to isolate the advocates of homosexuality, self-fulfilment, feminism and sexual license. Now that those of us who are sufficiently open-minded know the truth about homosexuality we shall never again feel tempted to accord its practitioners rights and privileges. Those things belong in the past along with the promotion of homosexuality as a lifestyle; as a society, we have tried it once and didn't like it. The way forward lies not in tolerance of what is intolerable, but in genuine compassion based on the true reality of human existence, and in a proper understanding of natural law. I have only limited hope that Government will find the necessary confidence to adopt the political philosophy in which these qualities will thrive, but the rest of us had better start now.

Appendix 1:

The following list of signatories appeared in The Independent newspaper on 1st February 1988 expressing "A sense of alarm" over Clause 28, which sought to ban the promotion of homosexuality by local authorities. The story of Clause 28 is told in chapter 5. The descriptions given of the signatories typically concealed left-wing, homosexual, permissive or anti-Christian credentials. I have added some of those known to me.

Brian Abel-Smith: described as "Professor of Social Administration, University of London." But: On the advisory council of the strongly pro-abortion Birth Control Campaign. Also see text.

Ron Aitken: described as "Conservative School Governor, Haringey." But sadly: Homosexual. Involved with Heley qv in FACTS.

Martin Amis: described as "Author." Signatory to fashionable left-wing "Charter 88," champagne socialist.

Bill Ash: described as "Board. Soho Poly Theatre"

Paddy Ashdown MP (Liberal Democrat). See text.

Sir Alfred Ayer: described as "Former Wykeham Professor of Logic, University of Oxford." Vice-president of the hard-line pro-abortion Abortion Law Reform Association (As is his wife, Dee Wells). Campaign for Homosexual Equality Vice-president. Rationalist Press Association (a humanist publishing group): Honorary associate. Member of Advisory Council British Humanist Association. Prominent supporter of Voluntary Euthanasia Society. Signatory to "Charter 88." Also see text.

Dr John Bancroft. See text.

A L Barker: described as "Author" (Audrey Barker). Writes novels about outcasts. Won Maugham award in 1947.

David Barker: described as " Emeritus Professor of Zoology, University of Durham.

Chris Barlas: described as "Author"

Stephen Barlow: described as "Conductor"

Alan Bennett: described as "Playwright."

Michael Berkeley: described as "Composer"

Baroness Birk. On the Birth Control Campaign Advisory Council. Voted against clause 28. Also see text.

Benedict Birnberg: described as "Benedict Burnburg [sic] Lawyer." On the Executive Committee of National Council for Civil Liberties in early 70s, Hon Secretary then committee member of the Haldane Society of Socialist lawyers, qv text. Inevitably defends left-wing causes.

Sheila Black: described as "Writer." Wife of Lee Howard who was editor of the Daily Mirror. Close friend of homosexual journalist Andrew Lumsden qv.

Peter Blake: described as "Painter"

Sir Herman Bondi: described as "Master Churchill College Cambridge." But also: Member Rationalist Press Association. Chairman British Humanist Association. Contributor to magazine of the extreme anti-Christian National Secular Society "The Freethinker." Vice-president "Gay & Lesbian Humanist Association." Supports legalisation of cannabis.

Appendix 1   435

Guy Borchgraef: described as "Psychotherapist"

Katie Boyle. See text

Billy Bragg: described as "Singer." Militant far-left. Concert Sept 1987 raised £2000 for the Mark Ashton AIDS Trust; recent single entitled "Sex." Signatory to "Charter 88". Supports legalisation of cannabis.

Melvyn Bragg: described as "Broadcaster." Labour Party supporter, signatory to "Charter 88."

Howard Brenton: described as "Dramatist." 1981 Play "The Romans in Britain" produced by Michael Bogdanov had a scene involving simulated buggery. (prosecution against it ulimately failed) Recently translated 2 plays by socialist intellectual libertine Bertolt Brecht. Married to Jane Fry.

Hugh Brogan: described as "Historian"

Eleanor Bron: described as "Actress"

Brigid Brophy: described as "Author." But also: Involved in 1960s with Homosexual Law Reform Society. Campaign for Homosexual Equality Vice-president. Member of Advisory Council British Humanist Association. Wife of Sir Michael Levey. Famous member of National Secular Society. Vice-president "Gay & Lesbian Humanist Association."

Michael Brown MP. (Conservative) Defended Labour Councillor Steven Bayes (Homosexual Vice-Chair of Humberside under five's committee) against calls for his resignation from Tory members. See text.

Richard K Brown: described as "Professor of Sociology, University of Durham."

Malcolm Bruce MP (Liberal/SLD)

Stephen Burn: described as "Journalist"

Dr Stephen Burton: described as "Psychiatrist." See p309.

A S Byatt: described as "Writer." Antonia Byatt is the sister of Margaret Drabble (qv) and is married (2) to Peter Duffy.

Simon Callow: described as "Actor." But also: Patron of London Lighthouse homosexual AIDS hospice. Homosexual activist. Signatory to "Charter 88". Also see text.

Duncan Campbell: described as "Investigative Journalist" Defendant in 1970s ABC secrets trial: Convicted under Official Secrets Act. Conditionally discharged, had to pay costs. Signatory to "Charter 88". Homosexual activist, member of Stonewall Group. Involved in "Gay media group" during Clause 28.

Menzies Campbell MP, QC (Liberal/SLD)

Peter Campbell: described as "Professor of Politics, University of Reading, Chairman, Conservative Group for Homosexual Equality." All quite true! Also a member of "Gay & Lesbian Humanist Association." See text.

Gordon Canning: described as "Counsellor"

Angela Carter: described as "Writer." Labour Party supporter. "Writes of the sixties with unfailing affection" (says Elizabeth Wilson). Observes "concealed matriarchy" behind "prostitute society." Satirises Western patriarchy and capitalism. There!

Anna Carteret: described as "Actress"

436 THE SEXUAL DEAD-END

Michael Cashman: described as "Actor." But also: Performed with McKellen in Martin Sherman activist play "Bent" to raise £25,000 for "Stonewall," of which "Chair of Board." Homosexual activist. Labour party member. Patron of homosexual AIDS group Frontliners (which collapsed in 1991). Attended unveiling of pink plaque 02/05/91 at LSE to commemorate founding of the Gay Liberation Front. Supports legalisation of cannabis. Also see text.

Robin Chambers: described as "Head Teacher, Stoke Newington School."

Glenn Chandler: described as "Writer"

Graham Chapman: described as "Actor." But also: Funded Gay News & the first London Gay Pride March.

Richard Chapman: described as "Professor of Politics, University of Durham."

Julie Christie: described as "Actress." Signatory to "Charter 88." Supports legalisation of cannabis.

Sir George Christie: described as "Chairman, Glyndebourne Productions"

Professor Anthony Clare

Margi Clark: described as "Actress." Champagne socialist. Supports legalisation of cannabis.

Michael Clark: described as "Choreographer, Dancer." But also: homosexual "lover" of dancer Stephen Petronio, with whom he has reportedly had "actual sex together" on stage.

Billy Connolly: described as "Entertainer." Champagne socialist.

Robin Cook MP. (Labour) See text.

Philip Core: described as "Artist." His "sexually explicit paintings" are popular in poster form with homosexual men.

Jane Cousins Mills: described as "Writer." See text under "Jane Cousins." Also: Signatory to "Charter 88."

Gill Cox: described as "Problem Page Editor, Woman's Realm." But also: Birth Control Campaign: on the Management Committee. Recommends women to "Lesbian Line." See text.

Anthony P M Coxon: described as "Professor & Director: Social Research Unit, University College, Cardiff." See text.

Edward Cullinan CBE: described as "Architect."

Jonathan Cutbill: described as "Curator." See text. Also director of "Gays the Word" bookshop.

Anna Joy David: No description.

Nicholas De Jongh: described as "Journalist." Homosexual: wrote in the Guardian about the 1974 Campaign for Homosexual Equality Malvern Conference as a "new vocal confidence - a 'gay breakthrough'" for homosexuals. In 1985 described Geoffrey Dickens MP as "porcine" and like "Hitler" for wanting to close gay clubs & pubs to stop the spread of AIDS.

Brian Deer: described as "Journalist"

Jane Dibblin: described as "Journalist." Also: left-wing author.

Alec Dickson CBE: described as "President Community Service Volunteers"

Joan Dickson: described as "Counsellor"

Appendix 1

Peter Diggory: described as "Gynaecologist FRCA." But also: Abortion Law Reform Association Advisory Council. Birth Control Campaign Advisory Council. Supports Pro-Choice Alliance (ALRA offshoot) which wants a "more liberal abortion law" and "easier access to free abortion."

Frank Dobson MP (Labour)

Revd Graham Dowell

Margaret Drabble CBE: described as "Author." But also: Campaign for Homosexual Equality Vice-President. Member of the socialist June 20 Group which meets at Campden Hill Square. Married to Michael Holroyd. Signatory to "Charter 88". An authors' guide writes: "Obsessed with 'equality and egalitarianism,' scrutinises & condemns 'patriarchy.'" Also see text.

Douglas Dunn: described as "Poet"

Ian Dunn: described as "Publisher." See text.

Ronald Dworkin FBA: described as "Professor of Jurisprudence, Oxford." But also: Leading US Democrat supporter and author of "Taking Rights Seriously." Civil Liberatarian.

A E Dyson: described as "Academic." See text.

David Edgar: described as "Dramatist." But also: Contributor to Marxism Today. Signatory to "Charter 88." Very left-wing.

Tony Elliott: described as "Publisher"

Martin Ennals: described as "General Secretary International Alert." But also: Contributor in the 60s to Albany Trust magazine "Man & Society." On the Executive Committee in the 70s of the National Council for Civil Liberties. In 1976 General Secretary Amnesty International (British Section). 1982-85 1st head of the GLC police committee support unit. Previously to that information officer of National Committee for Commonwealth Immigrants. Now deceased.

Erasure: described as "Musicians." Large homosexual following.

Matthew Evans: described as "Chairman, Faber & Faber." See text.

Baroness Ewart-Biggs. Voted both for arts amendment and then against Clause 28. Signatory to "Charter 88". Supports Pro-Choice Alliance. See text.

Viscount Falkland: described as "Lord Falkland." See text.

Simon Fanshawe: described as "Entertainer." In fact: Campaigning homosexual: member of Stonewall Group: "Chairs the sub-group on Fundraising." Previously "Chair" of War on Want. Also see text.

Lynn Farley: described as "Actress"

Charles Farthing: described as "Registrar, St. Stephen's Hospital, London." Patron of homosexual hospice London Lighthouse.

Christopher Fettes

Penelope Fitzgerald: described as "Author." Feminist.

Ken Follett: described as "Author." Champagne socialist.

Lord Foot. Voted both for arts amendment and then against Clause 28. Member of Advisory Council British Humanist Association

Rt.Hon. Michael Foot MP (Labour) Famous member of National Secular Society. See text.

Lady Antonia Fraser: described as "Writer." But also: Married to playwright Harold Pinter (qv). Socialist June 20 Group meets at their home. Signatory to "Charter 88."

Michael Frayn: described as "Writer." But also: Signatory to "Charter 88." Extremely left-wing. Married to Gillian Palmer. Received Maugham Award 1966.

Sir Clement Freud. See text. Also supported the principle of girls under 16 having contraception and abortion in secret from their parents during Gillick case. Signatory to "Charter 88."

Dr John Gallwey: described as "Consultant Physician, Radcliffe Infirmary." See text.

Paul Gambaccini: described as "Broadcaster." But also: Homosexual: Subject of "Out" column in Pink Paper and also featured in Gay Times. Disc Jockey. Champagne socialist.

Harriet Gilbert: described as "Novelist." Article by her in New Statesman wrote about "enormous contribution" made by "lesbian & gay artists." Clause 28 would mean "Cultural dark ages."

W. Stephen Gilbert: described as "Journalist." In 1979 for BBC Pebble Mill produced Ian McEwan's "Solid Geometry." It was banned. BBC complained of "grotesque & bizarre sexual elements in the play." Still at Pebble Mill, produced Drew Griffiths & Noel Grieg play: "Only Connect," about socialist homosexual Edward Carpenter. New book "Spiked" (publ: Gay Mens Press) is about closet homosexuality. Set in the "Gay London" of 1982. Scenes in gay pubs and clubs.

Junior Giscombe: described as "Singer"

Dr Jane Glover: described as "Conductor"

Alexander Goehr: described as "Professor, Composer"

Bryan Gould MP (Labour). See text. Currently involved with Institute for Public Policy Research Environment Policy Group.

Dr Harry Gray: described as "Lecturer"

Antony Grey: described as "Writer." In fact: Veteran homosexual campaigner: As A E G Wright was on the executive committee then secretary of the Homosexual Law Reform Society, was director of Albany Trust. Article in New Society 1969 "New Law But no new deal" called for further reforms and was written with D J West (qv). Joined Gay Liberation Front. Supported Paedophile Information Exchange in 1977 over remarks by Old Bailey judge in blackmail trial. Thanked by Jane Cousins (qv) for help & support with "Make it Happy." Addressed first meeting in Manchester of N. Western Homosexual Law Reform Committee which became the Campaign for Homosexual Equality. Humanist.

J A G Griffith: described as "Emeritus Professor of Public Law, University of London." But also: On the Executive Committee of National Council for Civil Liberties in early 70s, sponsor of NCCL charity the Cobden Trust in early 80s.

Rt.Revd. Peter Hall: described as "Bishop of Woolwich." See text.

Sheila Hancock: described as "Actress." (Mrs John Thaw). See text.

Gillian Hanscombe: described as "Poet." But also: Writer for Gay News. In 1990 "Flesh and Paper," a book of lesbian poetry produced with Suniti Namjoshi (qv)

Appendix 1 439

H L A Hart: described as " Emeritus Professor of Jurisprudence, University of Oxford." Writer of numerous books on utilitarian philosopher Jeremy Bentham, qv text.

Rt Hon Roy Hattersley MP (Labour) In 1990 met with Stonewall and agreed that homosexual men should have access to 16 year-olds.

Rt Hon Denis Healey MP (Labour)

Dr Andrew Heley: described as "General Practitioner." But also: GP "at the centre and the principle medical officer of FACTS" (Foundation for AIDS Counselling Treatment & Support) which he runs with Aitken qv.

Dr James Hemming: described as "Psychologist." Advisor 1970s-80s to Brook Advisory, qv text. President British Humanist Association 1977-1980. In 1980 wrote that it is "accepted that students in university and colleges are sexually active, but equal acceptance is denied to young people still at school." Member Editorial Board: Journal of Moral [sic] Education. Vice-president "Gay & Lesbian Humanist Association."

Alison Hennegan: described as "Writer." But also: Early contributor and worker with Gay News, then "literary editor." 1975-1977 Elected to executive committee then became vice-chair of Campaign for Homosexual Equality. 'Friend' national organiser. In 1980 book "Homosexuality Power & Politics", article: 'Thoughts on Lesbians in literature.'

Lenny Henry: described as "Entertainer." Champagne socialist.

Andrew Hodges: described as "Author." But really: co-author with Hutter of Gay Liberation book "With Downcast Gays." See text.

Philip Hodson: described as "Broadcaster." Resident sex doctor on LBC radio in London. But also: former editor of pornographic Forum Magazine qv text.

Rt Revd Richard Holloway: described as "Bishop of Edinburgh" which he is. But also: Patron of Crusaid: "the leading national fund-raiser for AIDS". Patron of Streetwise Youth.

Michael Holroyd: described as "Author." But also: Married to Margaret Drabble. Member of June 20 Group. Signatory to Charter 88. Also see text.

Anne Hooper: described as " Author and Counsellor." Author: "The Body Electric" Virago 1980 and "Divorce and Children" 1983.

Revd Oliver Horrocks

Sir Michael Howard: described as " Regius Professor of Modern History, Oxford." Countless books on war.

Bob Hughes MP (Labour) And also: Founder member CND

Simon Hughes MP (Liberal/S.Dem) Moved amendment in the 1988 Education Bill to allow in sex education the teaching of "an awareness of different sexual orientations."

Lord Hutchinson of Lullington: described as " "Lord Hutchinson QC". Voted both for arts amendment and then against Clause 28. Signatory to "Charter 88". Sponsor of British Defence and Aid Fund for Southern Africa. Critised Police for alleged "entrapment" in debate on "Clause 25" of 1991 Criminal Justice Bill. Formerly married to the late leading humanist and actress Peggy Ashcroft.

Jean Hutton: described as "Social Researcher"

Virginia Ironside: described as "Problem Page Editor for 'Woman'." See text.

Kazuo Ishiguro: described as "Author." Friend of Harold Pinter who has turned his

1989 Booker prize-winning book "The Remains of the Day" into a screenplay.

Clare Jacobs

Canon Eric James: described as "Director, Christian Action" See text. Resigned from BBC "thought for the day" slot over alleged BBC "bias." Chaplain to H M the Queen. Homosexual.

Michael Jarrett: described as "Professor of Architecture, University College, Cardiff." See text.

Peter Jay. See text.

Baroness Jeger. Voted both for arts amendment and then against Clause 28. Formerly Lena Jeger (m Dr Santo Jeger 1948). Abortion Law Reform Association Vice-President. 1970-1985 Birth Control Campaign Vice-president. Member of Advisory Council British Humanist Association.

Lord Jenkins of Putney. Was Hugh Jenkins. Past chairman of CND and sponsor of British Defence and Aid Fund for Southern Africa. Member of the "Progressive League" (affiliated to NCCL, BHA, ALRA), supporter of Voluntary Euthanasia Society.

Peter Jonas: described as "Managing Director. English National Opera." See text.

Terry Jones: described as "Writer and Actor." Signatory to "Charter 88."

Wilfred Josephs: described as "Composer"

Rt Hon Gerald Kaufman MP (Labour). In Parliament has said that homosexual men should not be convicted for importuning on the sole evidence of a policeman or in gay clubs. Wanted a "change in the law." Attacked legal assumptions which kept homosexual activity unacceptable.

Judith Kazantzis. Feminist poet: "anti-militarist, anti-establishment." God is a "rich myth figure" who inspires "patriachal arrogance."

Ian Kennedy: described as "Professor of Medical Law & Ethics, Univ. of London." Took part in 1982 BBC programme "Doctor's Dilemmas." Talked "earnestly in favour of school girl contraception." DHSS engaged Professor Kennedy as its Leading Counsel for the defence in Gillick trial. Also see text.

Ludovic Kennedy. Member of Advisory Council British Humanist Association. Prominent supporter of Voluntary Euthanasia Society. Signatory to "Charter 88." Supports legalisation of cannabis. Married to Moira Shearer.

Robert Kilroy-Silk. When a Labour MP, submitted an amendment to 1981 Criminal Justice Bill to extend 1967 Sexual Offences Act to Northern Ireland. Submitted an amendment to Criminal Justice Bill in 1982 to abolish imprisonment for male importuning.

Rt Hon Neil Kinnock MP (Labour). See text.

Revd Bill Kirkpatrick: See text. 1988 book: "AIDS Sharing the Pain." Foreword by Bp Mark Santer (also a Patron of "Streetwise Youth.")

Archie Kirkwood MP (Liberal/SLD)

Lord Kirkwood

Oliver Knussen: described as "Composer and Conductor"

Hanif Kureishi: described as "Scriptwriter and Dramatist". But also: Signatory to "Charter 88". Author of "My Beautiful Launderette" and "The Buddha of Suburbia," both of which are obscene & explore homosexuality. Supports legalisation of cannabis.

Appendix 1 441

Francis Lafitte: described as "Emeritus Professor of Social Policy, Chairman of BPAS." BPAS is the British Pregnancy Advisory Service, and Lafitte is a leading abortionist.

Dr Tony Lake: described as "Psychologist"

Mark Le Fanu: described as "Director. Society of Authors"

Revd Kenneth Leech. Is director of left-wing Runnymede Trust.

Mike Leigh: described as "Dramatist." Mainly improvisational. Left-of-centre.

Jim Lester MP (Conservative)

Sir Michael Levey: described as "Former Director, National Gallery." Married to Brigid Brophy, qv.

Dr Arnold Linken: described as "Physician."

Maureen Lipman: described as " Actress." M. to Jack Rosenthal (qv). Featured in Gay Times: Did a play with "2 gay friends."

Baroness Llewelyn-Davies of Hastoe: described as "Baroness Llewelyn-Davies." Voted both for arts amendment and then against Clause 28. See text.

Joanna Lumley: described as "Actress." See text.

Andrew Lumsden: described as "Journalist." Founder member in 1972 of original Gay News collective (collective had already changed by issue no1). Early member of Gay Liberation Front. Recently sacked from long-running column on the New Statesman.

Kate Markus: described as "Secretary, Law Centres Federation & Barrister."

Adam Mars-Jones: described as "Author". Homosexual: on production team of "Out on Tuesday," (did voice-overs.) Signatory to "Charter 88."

John Marshall: described simply as "Editor." Of Gay Times! Involved with Campaign for Homosexual Equality and university Gay Society whilst at Essex University. Thanked by Gregg Blatchford qv for help in article in "Pink Triangles." Article in CHE book "Prejudice & Pride" on: 'The Medical Profession.' See text.

Michael Mason: described as "Publisher." Editor of Gay News: Supported PIE in Mar/Apr 1977 over remarks by Old Bailey judge in blackmail trial. Then owner of "Capital Gay," along with McKerrow (qv). In 1975 over Sunday People article: "Support for PAL from Gay News & Michael Mason never waned." (PIE newsletter No6)

Robert McCrum: described as "Author & Editor."

Ian McEwan: described as "Author." See Gilbert. Signatory to "Charter 88" Latest book "The Innocent" (1991) has "long and fetid scenes which have Leonard & girlfriend sawing & chopping up her boyfriend." Labour Party supporter.

Ian McKellen: described as "Actor." See text, see Cashman above.

Graham McKerrow: described as "Editor." Of Capital Gay! See text.

Iain S McLean: described as "Fellow & Praelector in Politics, University College, Oxford."

Sheila McLeod: described as "Author"

Lord McNair: Voted for arts amendment and then against Clause 28

Michael Meacher MP. (Labour) See text.

Lord Melchett. See text.

Dame Margaret Miles: described as "Retired Headmistress." Also Chairman of Campaign for Comprehensive Education.

David Miller: described as "Principal Psychologist, Middlesex Hospital." See text.

Adrian Mitchell: described as "Author." But has described himself as "Far Left," and "outraged by the cruelty of man to man and especially by the criminal record of rich white nations. Viva Cuba, Viva Castro," in a directory of authors. Supports the Campaign for Homosexual Equality and legalisation of cannabis.

Jacqueline Morreau: described as "Artist"

Blake Morrison: described as "Poet & Journalist"

Dame Iris Murdoch: described as "Novelist and Philosopher." Authentically establishment left-wing. See text.

Michael Murname

Suniti Namjoshi: described as "Poet." In 1990 "Flesh and Paper" book of lesbian poetry produced with Gillian Hanscombe (qv).

Dr Peter Nathan: described as "Physician"

Rabbi Julia Neuberger: Patron of: London Lighthouse and Crusaid. Also see text. Signatory to "Charter 88."

Michael Neve: described as "Historian of Medicine, University of London."

Stephanie Norris: described as "Writer"

Steven Norris: described as "Former MP, Cons. Oxford East. Now an MP, see text. Involved in April - July 1991 with setting up Conservative Parliamentary Group for Homosexual Law Reform

Trevor Nunn: described as "Theatre Director"

Edna O'Brien: described as "Author." "Writes frankly about women's desire for, and response to, sexual attraction." Married to Ernest Gebler.

Rt Hon Dr David Owen MP (SDP): patron of London Lighthouse.

Tony Palmer: described as "Film Director"

Doris Seddon Parr: described as "Health Adviser, Middlesex Hospital"

Matthew Parris. Homosexual campaigner, ex-Tory MP.

Edward Pearce: described as "Journalist"

Dr Michael Perring: described as "Medical Psychotherapist"

Pet Shop Boys: described as "Musicians." Huge homosexual following. Never fail to support a homosexual or AIDS cause.

Edward Petherbridge: described as "Actor"

Ben Pimlott: described as "Professor of Politics & Contempory History, Univ.of London." Member of June 20 Group. Married to Jean Seaton. Member of William Morris Society. See text.

Harold Pinter: described as "Dramatist." Member of Advisory Council British Humanist Association. Married to Antonia Fraser (qv). June 20 Group meets at their home. Signatory to "Charter 88" Also see text.

Norman Pittenger: described as "King's College, Cambridge, & Faculty of Divinity," University of Cambridge. See text.

James Plaskitt: described as "Councillor, Oxfordshire County Council"

Lord Ponsonby: voted for arts amendment and then against Clause 28.

Appendix 1 443

Lisa Power: described only as "Journalist." However: Joined Gay Switchboard in 1979 and wrote its history. Now member of Stonewall Group. Joint Secretary-General of International Lesbian & Gay Association. See text.

John Prescott MP (Labour)

Jacquetta Priestley: described as "Writer." But also: Trustee of Albany Trust as Jacquetta Hawkes. Married J B Priestly 1953. Trust meeting held at their home. See text. Sponsor of British Defence and Aid Fund for Southern Africa.

Marquess of Queensberry: described as "Former Professor of Ceramics, Royal College of Art." Made his maiden speech in favour of 1967 Sexual Offences Bill.

Lord Quinton. Author of book on "Utilitarian Ethics"

Craig Raine: described as "Poet"

Adam Raphael. Signatory to "Charter 88""

Simon Rattle CBE: described as "Conductor." See text.

Claire Rayner. See text. Also: Signatory to "Charter 88." Supports Pro-Choice Alliance. Supports the Campaign for Homosexual Equality. Patron of Stonewall Group. Champagne Socialist.

Bruce Reed: described as "Social Researcher"

Revd Donald Reeves: described as "Rector of St. James, Piccadilly." See text. Something called the "International Security Information Service" is run from his Rectory.

Christopher Reid: described as "Poet"

Dr Jennifer Rich: described as "General Practitioner"

Emily Richard: described as "Actress"

Jo Richardson MP (Labour). See text.

Doctor Robert: described as "Singer"

Sadie Roberts: described as "Equality Officer, ACTT" (qv text), in which post she succeeded Diane Abbott MP, who set up the ACTT Gay and Lesbian section.

Kenneth Robinson: described as "Former Minister, Retired Chairman, Arts Council." Also: Introduced first (failed) bill into House of Commons to take "early action" over Wolfenden Report. Committee member of Homosexual Law Reform Society.

Tom Robinson: described as "Singer." See text. Also supports legalisation of cannabis.

Deborah Rogers: described as "Literary Agent"

C H Rolph: described as: "Vice-President then Chairman of the Homosexual Law Reform Society." Also involved with Albany Trust.

Margaret Rose: described as "Psychotherapist"

Jack Rosenthal: described as "Writer." Married to Maureen Lipman qv.

Lord Ross of Newport

Hon Miriam Rothschild

Michael Rubinstein. Thanked by Jane Cousins for help & support in sex education book "Make it Happy." His firm retained as solicitors to Family Planning Association.

Julian Ruddock: described as "Director, Greater London Citizens Advice Bureau"

Willy Russell: described as "Playwright"

Richard Sandell: described as "Actor"

Dr Q J Sattentau: described as "Immunologist"

Prunella Scales: described as "Actress." Also see text. Married to Timothy West. Very left-wing.

John Schlesinger: described as "Film Director." Declared homosexual: Signed letter of support defending Ian McKellen's knighthood when he was attacked by Derek Jarman for accepting it.

Michael Schofield: described as "Sociologist." See text. On committee of Albany Trust in 60s and 70s. Books include: "Sociological Aspects of Homosexuality" (Longmans 1965), "The Sexual Behaviour of Young People" (Penguin 1968) "The Sexual Behaviour of Young Adults" (Allen Lane 1973) and "Promiscuity." Also written under the name of Gordon Westwood: "A minority: a report on the life of the male homosexual in Great Britain" On the Abortion Law Reform Association Advisory Council, advisor also to Brook Advisory Centres, and on Birth Control Campaign: advisory council. Former Research Director "Council for Health Education." Executive Committee of National Council for Civil Liberties 1970-77. Said of Tom O'Carroll's book "Paedophilia the Radical Case: "No-one can claim to have an unprejudiced view about paedophilia until they have seriously considered his arguments." Wrote to Gay Times in 1991 complaining that he had supported Terrence Higgins Trust in the past with money, and they now ring him up for more donations. Both personally and through his charity "Lyndhurst Settlement" has funded a large number of permissive and anti-Christian charities. Supports legalisation of cannabis.

Dorothy Scott: described as "Health Advisor"

Baroness Seear. Voted both for arts amendment and then against Clause 28. Signatory to "Charter 88" Also see text.

Martin Sherman: described as "Playwright." Stonewall Group "Volunteer." Declared homosexual. See Cashman above.

Ned Sherrin. See text.

Chris Smith MP. Openly homosexual Labour member for Islington. See text. On executive of National Council for Civil Liberties.

Rt Hon John Smith MP (Labour)

Barbara Smoker: described as "Writer." Actually: 1970s-90s president of virulently anti-Christian National Secular Society, qv text. Recently "married" two lesbians. Renegade nun. Thinks newborn babies are not quite human. Member Executive Committee British Humanist Association. Prominent supporter of Voluntary Euthanasia Society. Vice-President Gay & Lesbian Humanist Association. Supports legalisation of cannabis.

Tony Smythe: described as "Former General Secretary, National Council for Civil Liberties." See text. Campaign for Homosexual Equality Vice-President. Trustee of Albany Trust. Has denied any close connection between PIE, Albany Trust and MIND. Supports legalisation of cannabis.

Jimi Somerville & the Communards: described as "Musicians." But Somerville is an outrageous homosexual - "non-elected spokespervert of a generation" (Gay Times) See text.

Yolanda Sonnabend: described as "Painter"

Lord Soper. Vice-President of Campaign for Homosexual Equality and Abortion Law

Appendix 1 445

Reform Association. On Birth Control Campaign Advisory Council. Sponsor NCCL charity Cobden Trust. Sponsor of British Defence and Aid Fund for Southern Africa. See text.

Liz Spencer: No description.

Tom Spencer: described as "Prospective Conservative Candidate, European Assembly."

Robin Squire MP (Conservative). See text.

Jack Straw MP (Labour). Argued in debate on Local Authorities in 1986 that sex education should be used to "end discrimination" against "gays and lesbians."

Graham Stringer: described as "Leader Manchester City Council"

Janet Suzman: described as "Actress." Patron of London Lighthouse. Entirely left-wing. See text.

Bob Swash: described as "Vice-president, Society of West End Theatres"

Tilda Swinton: described as "Actress"

Matthew Taylor MP (Liberal/SLD)

Rt Rev James Thompson: described as "Bishop of Stepney Rt Rev James Lawton Thompson." Another patron of London Lighthouse.

Cllr Jeffrey Tillet: described as "Conservative Group Leader, Derby City Council."

Sir Michael Tippet OM: described as "Composer." Sponsor of British Defence and Aid Fund for Southern Africa; Left-wing and homosexual - very sad childhood.

Claire Tomalin: described as "Writer." Also: Signatory to "Charter 88." Biographer of Mary Woolstonecraft.

Lord Tordoff. Voted for arts amendment and then against Clause 28. See text.

Wendy Toye: described as "Stage Director." Bit of a feminist.

Roy Trevelion: described as "Designer"

Clifford Tucker JP

Jim Wallace MP (Liberal/SLD). Said in Parliament that homosexual men should not be convicted for importuning on the sole evidence of a policeman. Tabled amendment to protect them.

Nicholas Walter: described as "Journalist." But also: Managing Editor of Rationalist Press Association. Member Exec Committee British Humanist Association. Humanist Lecturer. Supports legalisation of cannabis. Correspondent to Gay Times.

Michelene Wander: described as "Writer." How true: Has written on lesbian motherhood. Credited with "articulating and supprting interaction of feminism, theatre, socialism and gay liberation in Britain." Involved with women's liberation movement since 1969. Prolific feminist playwright, poet, short-story writer & critic.

Gillian Weir: described as "Concert Organist."

Colin Welland: described as "Actor, Playwright." Consistently on the political champagne left.

Paul Weller: described as "Musician." Band is called Red Wedge: virulently left-wing.

Richard Wells: described simply as "Royal College of Nursing." In fact: Patron & Nursing Consultant to Simon of Cyrene Sanctuary Project qv text.

Arnold Wesker: described as "Playwright"

Professor D J West: described as "Clinical Criminology, University of Cambridge." Donald West's 1955 book "Homosexuality" was influential in arguing that homosexuality was an unfortunate condition which should be tolerated. See Antony Grey above. Has written that paedophiles have "sincere fondness for the objects of their sexual desire .. are capable of striking acts of charity .. are interested in the child's happiness." Paedophile approaches to children can be "affectionate & gentle," their sex acts "resemble sexual behaviour between children." Author of "Children's sexual encounters with adults." Contributor to "Journal of adolescence." See text.

Hugh Whitemore: described as "Author." Recent play performed about homosexual code-breaker Alan Turning.

David Wiggins: described as "Fellow & Praelector in Philosophy, University College Oxford."

Angela Willans: described as "Problem Page Editor, "Woman's Own." Member Advisory Council British Humanist Association. See text.

Jill Williams: described as "Health Education Unit Director."

Rt Hon Shirley Williams: described as "President, Social Democratic Party."

Lord Winchelsea & Nottingham. Voted for arts amendment on Clause 28. Was Chris Hatton.

Lord Winstanley. Vice-President of the Campaign for Homosexual Equality. As Dr Michael Winstanley, president of Birth Control Campaign. See text.

Dr Enid Wistrich: described as "Principal Lecturer in Public Administration, Middlesex Polytechnic"

Audrey Wood: described as "Retired Midwife"

Cllr Robin Wood: described as "Vice-Chairman, Conservative Group for Homosexual Equality."

Victoria Wood: described as "Entertainer." See text.

Maurice Yaffe: described as "Clinical Psychologist." (At York Clinic Guys Hospital). Contributed to: "Perspectives on Paedophilia" ed Brian Taylor, qv text. His Article: "The assessment and treatment of paedophilia." Also: Expert witness brought on to defend pornography in the obscenity trials of the 60s and 70s.

Alan Yentob: described as "Controller, BBC2"

David Yip: described as "Actor." See text.

Susannah York: described as "Actress." Left-wing. See text.

Dr Michael Youle: described as "Registrar. St. Stephen's Hospital, London."

Benjamin Zephaniah: described as "Poet."

Appendix 2.

Figures for AIDS deaths, AIDS cases, HIV positive cases.
Source: Department of Health published statistics.

Key: Homo=Homosexual, Bi=Bisexual, I/V=intravenous drug user, Haem=Haemophiliac, T/F=receipient of blood transfusion, OS=believed infected overseas, UK=believed infected in United Kingdom, P/Risk=Sexual partner in another risk category, Het=Heterosexual, Child=Baby born to I/V mother, Und=Undetermined, M=male, F=female

AIDS Deaths per year:

	to 1986		1987		1988		1989		1990		1991	
	No	%	No	%	No	%	No	%	No	%	No	%
Homo / Bi	244	83.3	333	82.4	286	79.0	432	78.1	494	76.7	861	75.9
I / V all	2	0.7	9	2.2	10	2.8	17	3.1	32	5.0	71	6.3
Homo I / V	4	1.4	4	1.0	7	1.9	4	0.7	13	2.0	21	1.9
Haem	19	6.5	35	8.7	27	7.5	33	6.0	42	6.5	53	4.7
T / F OS	5	1.7	5	1.2	3	0.8	6	1.1	4	0.6	6	0.5
T / F UK	4	1.4	3	0.7	5	1.4	5	0.9	5	0.8	3	0.3
P / Risk					5	1.4	5	0.9	9	1.4	10	0.9
Het OS	9	3.1	5	1.2	8	2.2	31	5.6	40	6.2	74	6.5
Het UK	3	1.0	7	1.0	-2	-0.6	2	0.4	2	0.3	13	1.1
Child	2	0.7	4	1.0	2	0.6	5	0.9	2	0.3	7	0.6
Other	1	0.3	2	0.5	11	3.0	13	2.4	1	0.2	16	1.4
Total	293		404		362		553		644		1135	

AIDS Deaths cumulative to year end

	1986		1987		1988		1989		1990		1991	
	No	%	No	%	No	%	No	%	No	%	No	%
Homo / Bi	244	83.3	577	82.8	863	81.5	1295	80.3	1789	79.3	2650	78.1
I / V all	2	0.7	11	1.6	21	2.0	38	2.4	70	3.1	141	4.2
Homo I / V	4	1.4	8	1.1	15	1.4	19	1.2	32	1.4	53	1.6
Haem	19	6.5	54	7.7	81	7.6	114	7.1	156	6.9	209	6.2
T / F OS	5	1.7	10	1.4	13	1.2	19	1.2	23	1.0	29	0.9
T / F UK	4	1.4	7	1.0	12	1.1	17	1.1	22	1.0	25	0.7
P / Risk					5	0.5	10	0.6	19	0.8	29	0.9
Het OS	9	3.1	14	2.0	22	2.1	53	3.3	93	4.1	167	4.9
Het UK	3	1.0	7	1.0	5	0.5	7	0.4	9	0.4	22	0.6
Child	2	0.7	6	0.9	8	0.8	13	0.8	15	0.7	22	0.6
Other	1	0.3	3	0.4	14	1.3	27	1.7	28	1.2	44	1.3
Total	293		697		1059		1612		2256		3391	

AIDS Cases per year:

	to 1986		1987		1988		1989		1990		1991	
	No	%	No	%	No	%	No	%	No	%	No	%
Homo / Bi	538	88.2	494	80.1	602	79.7	654	77.1	946	74.6	963	71.2
I / V M	7	1.1	7	1.1	14	1.9	33	3.9	62	4.9	53	3.9
I / V F	2	0.3	3	0.5	6	0.8	8	0.9	19	1.5	31	2.3
Homo I / V	6	1.0	13	2.1	12	1.6	7	0.8	23	1.8	22	1.6
Haem	25	4.1	45	7.3	57	7.5	42	5.0	59	4.7	62	4.6
T / F OS	6	1.0	10	1.6	4	0.5	6	0.7	11	0.9	5	0.4
T / F UK	4	0.7	4	0.6	7	0.9	6	0.7	9	0.7	4	0.3
P / Risk M					5	0.7	2	0.2	4	0.3	5	0.4
P / Risk F					10	1.3	5	0.6	8	0.6	9	0.7
Het M OS	9	1.5	15	2.4	14	1.9	31	3.7	76	6.0	83	6.1
Het F OS	5	0.8	6	1.0	5	0.7	15	1.8	32	2.5	53	3.9
Het M UK	1	0.2	2	0.3	2	0.3	4	0.5	4	0.3	20	1.5
Het F UK	3	0.5	3	0.5	-4	-0.5	2	0.2	9	0.7	4	0.3
Child	3	0.5	10	1.6	6	0.8	4	0.5	13	1.0	13	1.0
Other	1	0.2	5	0.8	15	2.0	29	3.4	-7	-0.6	26	1.9
Total	610		617		755		848		1268		1353	

(Negative figures in categories are the result of Dept of Health adjustments)

AIDS Cases cumulative to year end

	1986		1987		1988		1989		1990		1991	
	No	%	No	%	No	%	No	%	No	%	No	%
Homo / Bi	538	88.2	1032	84.1	1634	82.4	2288	80.8	3234	78.9	4197	77.0
I / V M	7	1.1	14	1.1	28	1.4	61	2.2	123	3.0	176	3.2
I / V F	2	0.3	5	0.4	11	0.6	19	0.7	38	0.9	69	1.3
Homo I / V	6	1.0	19	1.5	31	1.6	38	1.3	61	1.5	83	1.5
Haem	25	4.1	70	5.7	127	6.4	169	6.0	228	5.6	290	5.3
T /F OS	6	1.0	16	1.3	20	1.0	26	0.9	37	0.9	42	0.8
T /F UK	4	0.7	8	0.7	15	0.8	21	0.7	30	0.7	34	0.6
P / Risk M					5	0.3	7	0.2	11	0.3	16	0.3
P /Risk F					10	0.5	15	0.5	23	0.6	32	0.6
Het M OS	9	1.5	24	2.0	38	1.9	69	2.4	145	3.5	228	4.2
Het F OS	5	0.8	11	0.9	16	0.8	31	1.1	63	1.5	116	2.1
Het M UK	1	0.2	3	0.2	5	0.3	9	0.3	13	0.3	33	0.6
Het F UK	3	0.5	6	0.5	2	0.1	4	0.1	13	0.3	17	0.3
Child	3	0.5	13	1.1	19	1.0	23	0.8	36	0.9	49	0.9
Other	1	0.2	6	0.5	21	1.1	50	1.8	43	1.0	69	1.3
Total	610		1227		1982		2830		4098		5451	

HIV positive cases per year

	to 1987		1988		1989		1990		1991	
	No	%	No	%	No	%	No	%	No	%
Homo / Bi	3435	51.8	868	62.4	1358	37.2	2936	84.1	1357	81.6
I / V all	483	7.3	159	11.4	1085	29.7	290	8.3	207	12.5
Homo I / V	52	0.8	20	1.4	20	0.5	70	2.0	31	1.9
Haem	1011	15.2	-14	-1.0	117	3.2	139	4.0	14	0.8
T / F	64	1.0	15	1.1	35	1.0	24	0.7	17	1.0
P / Risk M	5	0.1	3	0.2	7	0.2	9	0.3	17	1.0
P / Risk F	58	0.9	16	1.2	46	1.3	45	1.3	70	4.2
Het M OS	113	1.7	42	3.0	79	2.2	130	3.7	254	15.3
Het F OS	75	1.1	24	1.7	50	1.4	114	3.3	227	13.7
Het M UK	35	0.5	-18	-1.3	2	0.1	13	0.4	26	1.6
Het F UK	22	0.3	-7	-0.5	2	0.1	23	0.7	37	2.2
Het M Und			29	2.1	76	2.1	65	1.9	-22	-1.3
Het F Und			31	2.2	76	2.1	82	2.3	-35	-2.1
Child	23	0.3	12	0.9	109	3.0	57	1.6	-94	-5.7
Other	1259	19.0	210	15.1	589	16.1	-507	-14.5	-444	-26.7
Total	6635		1390		3651		3490		1662	

(Negative figures in categories are the result of Dept of Health adjustments)

HIV positive cases cumulative to year end

	1987		1988		1989		1990		1991	
	No	%	No	%	No	%	No	%	No	%
Homo / Bi	3435	51.8	4303	53.6	5661	48.5	8597	56.7	9954	59.2
I / V all	483	7.3	642	8.0	1727	14.8	2017	13.3	2224	13.2
Homo I / V	52	0.8	72	0.9	92	0.8	162	1.1	193	1.1
Haem	1011	15.2	997	12.4	1114	9.5	1253	8.3	1267	7.5
T / F	64	1.0	79	1.0	114	1.0	138	0.9	155	0.9
P / Risk M	5	0.1	8	0.1	15	0.1	24	0.2	41	0.2
P / Risk F	58	0.9	74	0.9	120	1.0	165	1.1	235	1.4
Het M OS	113	1.7	155	1.9	234	2.0	364	2.4	618	3.7
Het F OS	75	1.1	99	1.2	149	1.3	263	1.7	490	2.9
Het M UK	35	0.5	17	0.2	19	0.2	32	0.2	58	0.3
Het F UK	22	0.3	15	0.2	17	0.1	40	0.3	77	0.5
Het M Und			29	0.4	105	0.9	170	1.1	148	0.9
Het F Und			31	0.4	107	0.9	189	1.2	154	0.9
Child	23	0.3	35	0.4	144	1.2	201	1.3	107	0.6
Other	1259	19.0	1469	18.3	2058	17.6	1551	10.2	1107	6.6
Total	6635		8025		11676		15166		16828	

Appendix 3

The following article was written by one Michael Swift, a self-styled "Gay Revolutionary" of the paedophile group "BLAZE". It first appeared in the 15th-21st February 1987 edition of 'Gay Community News' in Australia.

*This essay is **outre**, madness, a tragic, cruel fantasy, an eruption of inner rage, on how the oppressed desperately dream of being the oppressor.*

We shall sodomize your sons, emblems of your feeble masculinity, of your shallow dreams and vulgar lies. We shall seduce them in your schools, in your dormitories, in your gymnasiums, in your locker rooms, in your sports arenas, in your seminaries, in your youth groups, in your movie theater bathrooms, in your army bunkhouses, in your truck stops, in your all-male clubs, in your houses of Congress, wherever men are with men together. Your sons shall become our minions and do our bidding. They will be recast in our image. They will come to crave and adore us.

Women, you cry for freedom. You say you are no longer satisfied with men; they make you unhappy. We, connoisseurs of the masculine face, the masculine physique, shall take your men from you then. We will amuse them; we will instruct them; we will embrace them when they weep. Women, you say you wish to live with each other instead of with men. Then go and be with each other. We shall give your men pleasures they have never known because we are foremost men too and only one man knows how to truly please another man; only one man can understand with depth and feeling the mind and body of another man.

All laws banning homosexual activity will be revoked. Instead, legislation shall be passed which engenders love between men.

All homosexuals must stand together as brothers; we must be united artistically, philosophically, socially, politically and financially. We will triumph only when we present a common face to the vicious heterosexual enemy.

If you dare to cry faggot, fairy, queer, at us, we will stab you in your cowardly hearts and defile your dead, puny bodies.

We shall write poems of the love between men; we shall stage plays in which man openly carresses man; we shall make films about the love between heroic men which will replace the cheap, superficial, sentimental, insipid, juvenile, heterosexual infatuations presently dominating your cinema screens. We shall sculpt statues

Appendix 3

of beautiful young men, of bold athletes which will be placed in your parks, your squares, your plazas. The museums of the world will be filled only with paintings of graceful, naked lads.

Our writers and artists will make love between men fashionable and de rigeur, and we will succeed because we are adept at setting styles. We will eliminate heterosexual liasons through usage of the devices of wit and ridicule, devices which we are skilled in employing.

We will unmask the powerful homosexuals who masquerade as heterosexuals. You will be shocked and frightened when you find that your presidents and their sons, your industrialists, your senators, your mayors, your generals, your athletes, your film stars, your television personalities, your civic leaders, your priests are not the safe, familiar, bourgeois, heterosexual figures you assumed them to be. We are everywhere; we have infiltrated your ranks. Be careful when you speak of homosexuals because we are always among you; we may be sitting across the desk from you; we may be sleeping in the same bed with you.

There will be no compromises. We are not middle-class weaklings. Highly intelligent, we are the natural aristocrats of the human race, and steely-minded aristocrats never settle for less. Those who oppose us will be exiled.

We shall raise vast, private armies, as Mishima did, to defeat you. We shall conquer the world because warriors inspired by and banded together by homosexual love and honor are invincible as were the ancient Greek soldiers.

The family unit - spawning ground of lies, betrayals, mediocrity, hypocrisy and violence - will be abolished. The family unit, which only dampens imagination and curbs free will, must be eliminated. Perfect boys will be conceived and grown in the genetic laboratory. They will be bonded together in communal setting, under the control and instruction of homosexual savants.

All churches who condemn us will be closed. Our only gods are handsome young men. We adhere to a cult of beauty, moral and aesthetic. All that is ugly and vulgar and banal will be annihilated. Since we are alienated from middle-class heterosexual conventions, we are free to live our lives according to the dictates of the pure imagination. For us too much is not enough.

The exquisite society to emerge will be governed by an elite comprised of gay poets. One of the major requirements for a position of power in the new society of homoeroticism will be indulgence in the Greek passion. Any man contaminated with heterosexual lust will be automatically barred from holding a position of influence. All males who insist on remaining stupidly heterosexual will be tried in homosexual courts of justice and will become invisible men.

We shall rewrite history, history filled and debased with your heterosexual lies and distortions. We shall portray the homosexuality of the great leaders and thinkers who have shaped the world. We will demonstrate that homosexuality and intelligence and imagination are inextricably linked, and that homosexuality is a requirement for true nobility, true beauty in a man.

We shall be victorious because we are fueled with the ferocious bitterness of the oppressed who have been forced to play seemingly bit parts in your dumb, heterosexual shows throughout the ages. We too are capable of firing guns and manning the barricades of the ultimate revolution.

Tremble, hetero swine, when we appear before you without our masks.

References and notes:

Latin abbreviations used in references and text:
ibid = the same (as before)
op cit = (literally "work cited") = same book (as before)
loc cit = (lit. "location cited") = same place (as before)
sic = "in brackets after a word or expression to guarantee that it is quoted exactly, although its incorrectness or absurdity might suggest that it was not" (OED)
qv = (lit. "which see") = more about this elsewhere
In general, editorial comments in quoted text are placed in square brackets [].

Chapter 1: An Introduction to Gay Politics

1. Roger J Magnuson "Are 'Gay Rights' Right?" Straitgate Press, Minneapolis 1985, p5
2. Andrew Hodges & David Hutter "With Downcast Gays: (Aspects of Homosexual Self Oppression)" Pink Triangle Press 1974/1977 p5
3. Magnuson op cit p3
4. Roy Burns in Bruce Galloway (ed) "Prejudice and Pride" Routledge & Kegan Paul, London 1983 p216
5. Magnuson op cit p3
6. Roy Burns in Galloway op cit p216. Gay Liberation Front was formed at a meeting in the LSE in 1970
7. Magnuson op cit p4/5
8. ibid p4/5
9. ibid
10. There are numerous examples of this Politically Correct usage
11. The term "bugger" possibly originates from the time of the Albigensian heresy of the 12th century in France, whose proponents were believed to have originated in Bulgaria and to use unnatural practices: Hence "bougre". "Sodomy" arisesfrom the Old Testament town of Sodom. See chapter 22.
12. "Gay Times" popular placard 01/1988 p13
13. Peter Campbell "Open Mind" No.3 1987
14. Lords Hansard 01/02/88 col 970
15. Socarides "Homosexuality: Basic Concepts and Psychodynamics" 1972
16. GLC Gay Working Party "Changing the World: A London Charter for Gay & Lesbian Rights" Greater London Council 1985 p8
17. ibid p11
18. Daily Telegraph 01/12/86
19. Peter Kent Baguley "Lesbian & Gay Socialist" Spring 1988 p16
20. Annual Report London Lesbian Line 1987/88
21. London Lesbian Line leaflet 1986
22. New Dimensions Magazine October 1990 P42
23. Rachel Tingle "Gay Lessons" London Pickwick Books 1986
24. Hugh Warren "Talking about School" "Teaching Staff Group Proposals" London Gay Teenage Group 1984 p47
25. Streatham Guardian 02/10/86
26. Jimmy Young TV programme
27. Australian Federation for the Family Submission to Criminal Justice Committee on the Decriminalisation of Homosexuality for the Tasmanian State Legislature 1990 p13
28. Hodges & Hutter op cit p15
29. Roy Burns loc cit p217

Chapter 2: Homosexual behaviour & the Law

1. Act of Parliament Chapter 6 1533
2. Nigel Warner in Bruce Galloway (ed) "Prejudice and Pride" Routledge & Kegan Paul, 1983 p79 (1861 in England & Ireland, 1889 in Scotland)
3. Offences against the Person Act Section 63 1861
4. see for example: Anna Coote & Tess Gill "Womens Rights, A Practical Guide" Penguin 1974 p152
5. Criminal Law Amendment Act Section 5 1885
6. Michael Jackson "The English Pub" Quarto Publishing, London 1976 p22
7. Criminal Law Amendment Act 1885 Section 11
8. Nigel Warner loc cit p79
9. Vagrancy Act 1898
10. Warner loc cit
11. Warner p81 quoting Lord Desart
12. Warner p82
13. John Hart "So you think you're attracted to the same sex" Penguin, Harmondsworth 1984 p90
14. Sexual Offences Act 1956 Section 32
15. "Open Mind" No3 Obituary CGHE 1987
16. Warner p83
17. ibid p84
18. John Marshall in Galloway (ed) p177
19. Warner p84 quoting the Wolfenden report para 22
20. Keith Howes in Galloway (ed) p199
21. The Times 07/03/58 and 19/04/58
22. Keith Howes loc cit
23. John Marshall (quoting Hansard 16/6/1966 col160) loc cit p86
24. Lords Hansard 01/02/88 col 869) 1988
25. John Marshall loc cit
26. ibid (quoting Hansard 19/12/66 col 1120)
27. Sexual Offences Act 1967 Section 1(7)
28. GLC Gay Working Party "Changing the World .. A London Charter for Gay & Lesbian Rights" Greater London Council 1985 p35
29. Quoted in Galloway (ed) "Prejudice and Pride" p92
30. Richard Cavendish "The Black Arts" Pan Books 1969 p52
31. John Trevelyan in "Forum - The journal of human relations" Forum Press Ltd London 05/72 p13
32. Professor John Taylor loc cit p19
33. Dr Robert Chartham loc cit p24
34. Rev Chad Varah loc cit p30
35. Dr Philip Cauthery loc cit p38

Chapter 3: The effects of the Sexual Offences Act 1967

1. Lords Hansard 01/02/88 col 867
2. Newsnight BBC2 01/02/88
3. "Knuller vs DPP" 1973 AC 436 p457 (Quoted in "Prejudice and Pride" ed Galloway Routledge & Kegan Paul, London 1983 p87)
4. Peace News 11/06/76
5. The Times 19/12/85
6. Betrayal of Youth CL Publications London 1986 p255
7. ibid p257
8. Nigel Warner in Galloway (ed) op cit p89
9. ibid p90

10 Lord Gifford Lords Hansard 01/02/88 col 970
11 ibid
12 Nigel Warner in Galloway (ed) op cit p90
13 Judgement Dudgeon Case Dissenting opinion of Judge Matscher European Court of Human Rights 1981 p27
14 Judgement Dudgeon Case para 54
15 ibid para 60
16 ibid: Dissenting opinion of Judge Zekia p23
17 Gay Times April 1990 p5
18 Nigel Warner in Galloway (ed) op cit p90
19 ibid
20 op cit p91
21 ibid
22 ibid
23 Hansard 22/01/88 col 1292 1988
24 see Mary Whitehouse "Whatever Happened to Sex?" Wayland Hove 1977
25 Stephen Gee in "Homosexuality Power and Politics" (ed Gay Left Collective) Allison & Busby 1980 p198
26 ibid
27 R v Goddard Court of Appeal 08/11/90
28 The Times 20/12/90
29 Sunday Telegraph 24/01/88
30 Hansard Leo Abse 05/07/66 col 262 quoted in Galloway p86
31 Lord Longford Lords Hansard 14/12/57 col 743 (loc cit p85)

Chapter 4: The homosexual subculture

1 Roy Burns in Galloway (ed) "Prejudice and Pride" p213
2 D J West "Homosexuality" Penguin 1960 quoted in John Hart "So you think you're attracted to the same sex" Penguin 1984 p88
3 Gay Times 01/1988 p25
4 ibid p95
5 Kennedy's Guide 1986 p14
6 ibid
7 ibid p15
8 ibid p13
9 ibid p17 (refering to the Royal Vauxhall tavern)
10 John Hart op cit p49
11 Kennedy's guide 1986 p19
12 Dennis Altman in "Homosexuality Power & Politics" ed by Gay Left Collective Allison & Busby Ltd, London 1980/82 p52
13 Gay Times March 1988 p24
14 John Hart op cit p45
15 Kennedy's Guide 1986 p41 & p44
16 Roy Kerridge in "The Spectator" 08/08/87 p19
17 Kennedy's Guide 1986 p14
18 John Hart op cit p92
19 Peace News 11/06/90
20 Jeffrey Weeks in: "Homosexuality Power and Politics" p9
21 Kennedy's Guide 1986 p45
22 Capital Gay 25/03/88
23 Kennedy's Guide 1986 p29
24 Gay Times 08/1987 (But any 'gay' mag will prove the point)
25 John McVicar "Body builders Men or Beasts?" in Sunday Telegraph magazine 17/01/88
26 ibid
27 ibid
28 John Shiers in "Homosexuality Power and Politics" op cit

29 Ken Livingstone Report to GLC GLC Agenda 22/05/84 Quoted by Rachel Tingle in "Gay Lessons" p7
30 The Guardian "Calculating the threat posed by AIDS" 11/09/87
31 Sunday Times 10/05/92
32 The Times 28/04/86
33 ibid
34 Hugh Warren "Talking about school" London Gay Teenage Group 1984 p28
35 Gay Times 01/1988 p47
36 ibid p43
37 Gay Times 08/1987 p41
38 The Times 28/04/86
39 Gays the Word Review Feb/Mar 1987 1987 No45 p3
40 The Spectator 07/1987
41 Evening Standard 23/07/87
42 ibid 23/07/87
43 The Times 09/04/90

Chapter 5: The battle for Clause 28

1 GLC Agenda 22/05/85
2 Streatham News 05/07/85
3 Streatham Guardian 08/08/85
4 Evening Standard & 31/01/86, South London Press 17/10/85
5 Jane Walker GLC Women's Committee Bulletin June 1985 p19
6 Daily Telegraph 11/10/85
7 ibid 30/10/85
8 Streatham Guardian 31/10/85
9 Evening Standard 10/01/86
10 Streatham & Tooting News 21/03/86
11 ILEA Contact 16/05/86
12 ibid 13/06/86
13 ibid 13/07/86
14 London Evening Standard 23/06/86
15 The Times 26/06/86
16 ibid 09/07/86
17 London Evening Standard 15/07/86
18 New Statesman 12/09/86
19 London Evening Standard 20/08/86
20 The Times 23/09/86
21 Daily Telegraph 27/09/86
22 The Times 21/08/86
23 The Universe 06/06/86
24 The Times 11/08/86
25 Rachel Tingle "Gay lessons" Pickwick books 1986 p12
26 Hansard 01/02/88 Col 865
27 Lambeth Star 10/07/86
28 The Sun 01/10/86
29 Daily Telegraph 27/10/86
30 ibid 01/11/86
31 Evening Standard 06/11/86
32 Daily Telegraph 21/11/86
33 Evening Standard 10/11/87
34 ibid 05/01/87
35 Streatham & Tooting News 09/01/87
36 Evening Standard 26/03/87
37 Gay Times 04/1987
38 South London Press 01/05/87
39 ibid 29/05/87
40 ibid
41 ibid 22/05/87
42 Evening Standard 23/06/87
43 Hornsey Journal 17/04/87
44 Hansard No93 Also Programme for Event,

References and notes

45 HOC 22/04/87 p1123
45 Evening Standard 23/06/87
46 ibid
47 ibid 05/01/87
48 ibid 07/07/87
49 Daily Telegraph 29/07/87
50 Streatham & Tooting News 13/05/87
51 ibid 14/08/87
52 Lesbian & Gay Working Party minutes 03/11/87
53 Evening Standard 25/11/87
54 "Ealing film romps" 1988
55 Hansard 01/02/88 & 02/02/88 Col 897/898 & 1021/3
56 Lesbian & Gay Socialist Spring 1989
57 The Guardian 26/07/88
58 Evening Standard 21/03/88
59 Midweek 01/06/88
60 Stephen Jeffery Poulter "Peers, Queers and Commons" (Quoting Gay Times March 1988) Routledge, London 1991 p229

Chapter 6: How many and how promiscuous?

1 Simon Orton and John Samuels "What we have learned from researching AIDS" British Market Research Bureau Ltd 1987 p325
2 ibid p323
3 New Dimensions March 1990 p48
4 Paul Van Wyk and Chrisann Geist "Psychosocial Development of Heterosexual, Bisexual and Homosexual Behavior" Archives of Sexual Behavior Vol.13 No.6 1984 p513
5 ibid p541
6 Roger J Magnuson "Are 'Gay Rights' Right?" Straitgate Press, Minneapolis 1985 p13
7 Dr Judith Reisman & Edward Eichel "Kinsey Sex and Fraud - The Indoctrination of a People" Louisiana 1990 (quoted from The Times 29/12/90)
8 Tom W Smith "Adult Sexual Behavior in 1989: Number of partners, frequency, and risk." NORC University of Chicago November 1989
9 Daily Telegraph 06/10/86
10 Claire Rayner "Two of Us" Teachers notes BBC TV Publications March 1988
11 Streatham and Tooting News 13/12/85
12 Tom W Smith op cit
13 Lords Hansard 01/02/88 col 867
14 Mike Daly in "Prejudice and Pride" ed Bruce Galloway Routledge & Kegan Paul, London 1983 p56
15 John Hart "So you think you're attracted to the same sex?" Penguin 1984 p48
16 Ian Dunn "Scotland against the odds" in "Radical Records" (ed Bob Cant & Susan Hemmings) Routledge, London 1988 p39
17 Martin Dannecker "Theories of Homosexuality" Gay men's Press London 1981 p11
18 see chapters 7 & 8
19 Daily Telegraph 22/10/86
20 quoted by John Lahr "Biography of Joe Orton" 29/12/66 p62
21 "Gay's the Word Review" No45 Feb/March 87 p14
22 Tom Reeves in "The Age Taboo" ed Daniel Tsang reprinted from "Fag Rag" Alyson Publications and Gay Mens Press 1981 p32
23 "Sex - is great" Terrence Higgins Trust 1987
24 Andrew Hodges & David Hutter "With Downcast Gays subt: Aspects of Homosexual Self Oppression" Pink Triangle Press 1974/1977 p11
25 John Lahr "Prick up your ears" p280
26 John Lahr op cit p281 quoting Orton's Diary 4/3/67
27 Lorraine Trenchard "Talking about young lesbians" London Gay Teenage Group p45 and Deborah Goleman Wolf "The Lesbian Community" Berkeley Los Angeles London University of California Press 1980 p24
28 Lesbian Ethics Vol.1, No.2 Venice California 1985
29 Deborah Goleman Wolf op cit p94
30 ibid p93
31 Ebbesen Mads Melbye and Biggar "Sex Habits, Recent Disease and Drug use in Two Groups of Danish male homosexuals" Archives of Sexual Behavior Vol.13 No.4 1984 p294
32 ibid p299
33 ibid p294
34 Dannecker & Reiche "Der gewohnliche Homosexuele" quoted by Martin Dannecker, op cit pp236 ff
35 Stewart S A "USA Today" 21/11/84
36 McKusick L et al "AIDS and sexual behaviour reported by gay men in San Francisco" American Journal of Public Health 1985 75 pp 493/496
37 Dr Hunter Handsfield: Letters to the Editor "American Journal of Public Health" Dec 1985
38 Correy L & Holmes K K "Sexual Transmission of Hepatitis A in homosexual men" New England Journal of Medecine 1980 302 p435/438
39 Bell A P & Weinberg M S: Study, US Center for disease 1982
40 J Martin Stafford in "Journal of Moral Education" Vol17 No1 Social Morality Council 01/88 p15

Chapter 7: The inner drive to make sexual contact

1 Jay and Young "The Gay Report" Summit 1979 pp500 & 563
2 Tom Reeves in "The Age Taboo" ed Daniel Tsang reprinted from "Fag Rag" Alyson Publications and Gay Mens Press 1981 p27
3 in chapters 19 & 31
4 Roger J Magnuson "Are 'Gay Rights' Right?" (quoting from the Gay Report) Straitgate Press, Minneapolis 1985 p15
5 Bruce Galloway (ed) "Prejudice and Pride" Routledge & Kegan Paul, London 1983 p113
6 Christine Riddiough in "Pink Triangles" (edited Pam Mitchell) Alyson Publications, Boston 1980 p17
7 Charley Shively in "Pink Triangles" p43
8 Martin Dannecker "Theories of Homosexuality" Gay Men's Press 1981 p115
9 Julian Meldrum in Galloway (ed) p73
10 Pittenger William Norman "Time for Consent" SCM Press 1976
11 Rose Robertson of "Parents Enquiry" Open Mind No3 Conservative Group for Homosexual Equality 1987
12 Dannecker op cit p73

13 ibid p74
14 Andrew Hodges & David Hutter "With Downcast Gays: Aspects of Homosexual Self Oppression" Pink Triangle Press 1974/1977 p11
15 ibid p12
16 ibid
17 Gay Liberation Front "Manifesto" London 1971 revd 1979 p10
18 Hodges & Hutter op cit p13
19 McKusick L Letters to the Editor "American Journal of Public Health" Dec 1985
20 J Martin Stafford in "Journal of Moral Education" Vol17 No1 Social Morality Council 01/88 p16
21 Roger Baker in "Gay Times" article "We're all off on a Summer Holiday" March 1988 p50
22 Joe Brewer in "Gay Times" article "Conflict on Castro" March 1988 p44
23 to David Reuben "Everything you always wanted to know about sex" quoted by Fraser in Ayrshire Herald 31/10/80
24 McKusick L loc cit
25 Bell A P & Weinberg M S "Homosexualities: a study of diversity among men and women" Simon & Shuster New York 1978
25 Gebhard P H & Johnson A B "The Kinsey Data: marginal tabulation of the 1938 - 1963 interviews conducted by the Institute for Sex Research" Saunder New York 1979
26 Edmund Bergler "Homosexuality, Disease or Way of Life?" Hill and Wang New York 1956
27 Irving Beiber "Homosexuality: a psychoanalytic study" Basic Books New York 1962 and Somerset Maugham: both quoted in: "Submission on Decriminalisation of Homosexuality" Australian Federation for the Family 1990 p13
28 Bell A P & Weinberg M S op cit
29 Williams C J & Weinberg M S "Homosexuals and the Military" Harper and Row New York 1971
30 Le Vay S. report in Time Magazine 09/09/91 pp54/55
31 M Hoffman "Die Welt der Homosexuellen" Frankfurt 1971 p132
32 Dannecker op cit p77

Chapter 8: Homosexual activity

1 Socarides "Homosexuality: concepts & psychodynamics" International Journal of psychiatry 118 1972 p118
2 John Lahr "Prick up your ears" Penguin 1986 p 280 Quoting from Orton's diary 04/03/67
3 For example Dr Davies in Wimbledon News 06/12/88
4 "Sex - is great" Terrence Higgins Trust 1989 p7: designed by Richard Green and Shelly Davies illustrated by John Lupton
5 ibid p8
6 "AIDS & HTLV III" 2nd. Edition Terrence Higgins Trust October 1985 p12
7 "Sex - is great" p7
8 Gay Times 1987/88 various issues
9 Capital Gay 01/04/88
10 "AIDS and HTLV III" p12
11 Progrramme for centre and Gay Times May 1992
12 Gay Times August 1987 p73
13 Roy Kerridge The Spectator 08/08/87 p19
14 Gay Times January 1988 p96-100
15 Gay Times April 1990
16 "AIDS and HTLV III" p13
17 Roger J Magnuson "Are "Gay Rights" Right?" Straitgate Press, Minneapolis 1985 p14
18 Sunday Post 07/09/86
19 Daily Telegraph 9/9/91
20 "AIDS and HTLV III" p13
21 ibid
22 "Sex - is great" p6
23 Ebbesen Mads Melbye and Biggar "Sex Habits, Recent Disease and Drug use in Two Groups of Danish male homosexuals" Archives of Sexual Behavior Vol.13 No.4 1984 pp294,298
24 Gay Times Advertisement August 1987
25 Gay Times 1987
26 ibid January 1988 p5
27 Bill Short in Gay Times March 1992
28 F.DuMas "Gay is not Good" Thomas Nelson 1979, and Jay and Young "The Gay Report" pp 553-96, 490-93, quoted by Roger Magnusson op cit p14

Chapter 9: Disease and the active homosexual

1 for instance Terry Sanderson: "How to be a Happy Homosexual" and John Hart: So you think you're attracted to the same sex"
2 Dr Louise Eickhoff "Towards Maturity" BHL 1988 p4
3 Panosian C B & Gorbach S L "Bacterial Diarrhea in Homosexual Men" in Pearl Ma and Donald Armstrong "The Acquired Immune Deficiency Syndrome and Infections of Homosexual Men" Plenum Medical Book Co, New York 1983 pp63-76
4 "Submission on the Decriminalisation of Homosexuality" Australian Federation for the Family 1990 p11
5 Roy Kerridge in The Spectator 08/08/87
6 Ebbesen Mads Melbye and Biggar "Sex Habits, Recent Disease and Drug use in Two Groups of Danish male homosexuals" Archives of Sexual Behavior Vol.13 No.4 1984 p294
7 Dr.P.M.Davies letter to Streatham & Tooting News 03/01/86
8 Ebbesen et al loc cit
9 ibid
10 Correy L & Holmes K K "Sexual Transmission of Hepatitis A in homosexual men" New England Journal of Medicine 1980 302 pp435-8
11 McKusick L et al "AIDS and sexual behaviour reported by gay men in San Francisco" American Journal of Public Health 1985: 75 pp493-496
12 Gebhard P H & Johnson A B "The Kinsey Data: marginal tabulation of the 1938 - 1963 interviews conducted by the Institute for Sex Research" Saunder New York 1979
13 Bell A P, Weinberg M S & Hammersmith S K "Sexual Preference: statistical appendix" Bloomington: Indiana University Press 1981
14 Jay & Young "The Gay Report" Summit New York 1979
15 ISIS national random sexuality survey (conducted in 5 metropolitan areas: Los Angeles, Denver, Omaha, Louisville, Washington DC) involving 4,340 adults in

1983, 842 in Dallas in 1984. A questionnaire of over 550 items was answered by each respondent anonymously. See Cameron et al, "Nebraska Medical Journal 1985 70, pp292-299
16 Jaffe H W et al "National case-control study of Karposi's sarcoma and Pneumocystis carinii pueumonia in homosexual men: part 1: epidemiological results" Ann of Int Med 1983;99 pp145-151
17 Quinn T C et al "The polymicrobial origin of intestinal infection in homosexual men" New England Medical Journal 1983 309 pp576-582
18 University College Cardiff (reported in Gay Times) 1988
19 Ebbesen et al op cit p297
20 Ebbesen et al op cit pp297/8
21 Roger J Magnuson "Are 'Gay Rights' Right?" Straitgate Press, Minneapolis 1985 p20
22 Jay & Young op cit and ISIS survey loc cit
23 Jaffe et al op cit
24 Quinn et al op cit
25 Kassler "Gay Men's Health" Harper & Row New York 1983 p52
26 Ma & Armstrong op cit p6
27 Jaffe et al op cit and ISIS survey loc cit
28 ISIS survey loc cit
29 Gottlieb M S et al "The Acquired Immunodeficiency Syndrome" Ann of Int Med 1983;99: pp151-158
30 David Ostrow, Terri Sandholzer & Yehudi Felman "Sexually Transmitted Diseases in Homosexual Men" Plenum Medical Book Co, New York 1983 p204
31 Gottlieb et al op cit p212
32 Ibid pp209-210
33 Ma & Armstrong op cit p220
34 ISIS survey loc cit
35 Ma & Armstrong op cit p7
36 Ostrow et al op cit p147
37 Gene Antonio "The AIDS Cover-up" Ignatius Press San Francisco 1987 pp55-56
38 Kazal H L et al "The Gay Bowel Syndrome. Clinico-pathologic correlation in 260 cases" Ann Clin Lab Sci 1976;6 p184
39 Antonio op cit p50 drawing on P J Buchanan & J Gordon Muir "Gay Times and Diseases" The American Spectator August 1984
40 Oscar Felsenfeld "The Epidemiology of Tropical Diseases" Charles C Thomas Illinois 1966 pp395-397
41 Maria Blum "The Day-Care Dilemma" Lexington Books 1983
42 Panosian C B & Gorbach S L loc cit
43 Selma K Dritz M.D. (San Francisco Department of Public Health) in "The New England Journal of Medicine" 21/ 2/80
44 Mavligit G M et al "Chronic Immune Stimulation by Sperm Alloantigens; Support for the Hypothesis that spermatazoa induce immune dysregulation in homosexual males" JAMA 1984;251 pp237-241
45 Ostrow et al op cit pp141-149
46 Ma & Armstrong op cit p4 and Ostrow et al op cit p144
47 A Bernal et al "Endoscopic and Pathologic Features of gastrointestinal Kaposi's Sarcoma: a report of four cases in patients with the Acquired Immune Deficiency Syndrome" Gastrointestinal Endoscopy 1985;31 pp74-77
48 Antonio op cit paraphrasing Ostrow et al op cit p192
49 Antonio op cit p36
50 John Seale MD MRCP "The Aids Epidemic and its Control" in British Medico-Chirurgical Journal Vol 102(iii) Aug 87 p66
51 for example: Mavligit et al op cit, Ma & Armstrong op cit p241, Science 27/04/84 and S Hsia et al, "Unregulated Production of virus and/or sperm specific anti-idiotypic antibodies as a cause of AIDS" Lancet 02/06/84 pp1212-1214
52 Mavligit et al op cit 9241
53 Richards J M et al "Rectal Insemination modifies immune responses in rabbits" Science 1984;224 pp390-392 and Hurtenbach U & Shearer G M "Germ cell-induced immune suppression in mice: effect of synergenic spermatazoa on cell-mediated immune responses" J Exp Med 1982;155 pp1719-1729
54 The Times 11/5/92
55 Daily Telegraph 13/05/92
56 Ostrow et al op cit pp151-156, Jaffe H W et al "The Acquired Immune Deficiency Syndrome in Gay Men" Ann of Int Med 1985;103 pp662-640
57 D J Atkinson "Homosexuals in the Christian Fellowship" W B Eerdmans Michigan 1979 p48
58 Selma K Dritz M.D. loc cit
59 Bruce Galloway "Prejudice and Pride" Routledge & Kegan Paul, London 1983 p15
60 "Lesbian London" May 1992 p1
61 Ma & Armstrong op cit p100

Chapter 10: The Prejudiced Virus

1 GLC Gay Working Party "Changing the World: A London Charter for Gay & Lesbian Rights" Greater London Council 1985 p25
2 John Seale MD MRCP "The Aids Epidemic and its Control" in British Medico-Chirurgical Journal Vol 102(iii) Aug 87 p66
3 Sunday Telegraph 23/11/86
4 GLC Gay Working Party op cit
5 Dr Shiela M Gore and Dr A Graham Bird (immunologists) in a letter to the Independent 05/05/92 confirm the blood-borne nature of both the AIDS virus and the Hepatitis B virus.
6 Dr John Seale quoted in the Sunday Telegraph 23/11/86
7 according to William Burroughs in The Naked Lunch Corgi 1981
8 Independent 31/12/87
9 Dr. John Seale loc cit and see also Chapter 9.
10 Dr John Seale loc cit
11 De Cock K M "AIDS: an old disease from Africa?" British Medical Journal 1984 289: pp306-308; Slaff & Brubaker "The AIDS epidemic" Warner Books, New York 1985 p182; A C Bayley et al "HTLV III Serology distinguishes a typical and endemic Karposi's sarcoma in Africa" The Lancet 16/02/85 pp359-361; D J Volsky et al "Antibodies to HTLV III/LAV in Venezuelan patients with acute malarial infections" N Eng J Med 1986 314: p647; Siegal & Siegal "AIDS THe medical mystery" Grove Press New York 1983 pp 119 120; R J Biggar et al "ELISA HTLV Retrovirus associated with malaria and immune complexes in healthy Africans" The Lancet

12 07/09/85 pp 520-523
13 James le Fanu in the Sunday Telegraph 21/01/88
13 Daily Telegraph 01/12/86
14 Dr John Seale in The Times 12/09/87
15 Dr John Seale in the Sunday Telegraph 23/11/86
16 Dr Tom McManus in "Open Mind" No3 Conservative Group for Homosexaul Equality 1987
17 Simon Orton and John Samuels "What we have learned from re searching AIDS" British Market Research Bureau Ltd 1987 p338
18 Dr A G Lawrence (St Stephens Fulham) The Independent 19/02/88
19 C Harris et al "Immunodeficiency in Female Partners of men with the acquired immune defficiency syndrome" N Eng J Med 1983 308:1181 1184
20 Simon Orton and John Samuels op cit pp337
21 Dr Tom McManus loc cit
22 "Some facts about A.I.D.S" Health Education Council 01/86
23 Government info. tape 01 981 7188 DHSS 03/02/88
24 Randy Shilts "And the Band Played on" p28
25 Hunt Davies Weatherburn Coxon & McManus "Changes in Sexual Behaviour in a large cohort of homosexual men in England & Wales 1988-9" British MedicalJournal 02/03/91 p505,506
26 Daily Telegraph 05/11/86
27 ISIS national random sexuality survey (conducted in 5 metropolitan areas: Los Angeles, Denver, Omaha, Louisville, Washington DC) involving 4,340 adults in 1983, 842 in Dallas in 1984. A questionnaire of over 550 items was answered by each respondent anonymously. See Cameron et al, "Nebraska Medical Journal 1985 70, pp292-299
28 Gene Antonio "The AIDS Cover Up" Ignatius Press, San Francisco 1987 pp 89-91
29 Day to day 03/87
30 Daily Mirror 24/11/86
31 ibid
32 Daily Telegraph 25/11/86
33 Rupert Haselden in The Guardian 07/09/91
34 Daniel Tsang "The Age Taboo" Alyson Publications and Gay Mens Press 1981 p3

Chapter 11: The Politics of AIDS

1 Alan Clark, who was a Cabinet Minister until leaving the House of Commons in 1992, has suggested a reason: that the Princess agreed to promote AIDS and homosexual rights in order to ingratiate herself with a Palace homosexual mafia. Sunday Telegraph 2/8/92
2 Geoffrey Wheatcroft in The Spectator 18/06/88 p28
3 Joseph Sobran in Gay Times February 1988 23/05/86
4 ibid
5 Wheatcroft loc cit quoting Duncan Campbell
6 Randy Shilts "And the Band Played On" Penguin
7 ibid
8 "Sex - is Great" Terrence Higgins Trust p9
9 Gay Times April 1987
10 Gay Times February 1988
11 The Independent 31/08/91

12 James le Fanu in Sunday Telegraph 21/01/88
13 The British Medical Journal Jan 1988
14 Guardian 09/02/88
15 see Wheatcroft loc cit
16 Dr John Seale in the Daily Telegraph 13/03/87
17 ibid
18 Simon Orton and John Samuels "What we have learned from researching AIDS" British Market Research Bureau Ltd 1987 p336
19 "AIDS and the condom" London Rubber Co Products Ltd.
20 Guardian 03/02/88
21 The Times 23/06/88
22 Daily Telegraph 18/05/91
23 Sunday Telegraph 21/06/91
24 Daily Mail 14/08/91
25 Sunday Times 28/06/92
26 Lesbian & Gay Youth Magazine Summer 86 Issue 19
27 The Times 27/01/88
28 Sunday Telegraph 31/01/88
28 The Spectator 18/06/88
29 "The facts behind the Terrence Higgins Trust" Family & Youth Concern May 1991
30 Pink Paper 30/03/91
31 Bill Kirkpatrick "AIDS sharing the pain" Darton Longman & Todd, London 1988
32 Daily Telegraph 30/07/91
33 "The Moral Maze" BBC Radio 4 September 1991

Chapter 12: The myth of the gentle gay

1 John Lahr "Prick up your ears - The Biography of Joe Orton" Penguin Harmondsworth 1980 reprinted 1986 p1
2 Gay Liberation Front "Manifesto" London 1971 revd 1979 p9
3 Roger J Magnuson "Are "Gay Rights" Right?" Straitgate Press Minneapolis 1985 p12
4 Anthony Storr "Sexual Deviation" Pelican Harmondsworth 1964 p84
5 Susanne Bosche tr Louis MacKay "Jenny lives with Eric and Martin" Gay Men's Press London 1983 (1981 in Denmark)
6 Evening Standard Magazine 08/01/88
7 Martin Dannecker "Theories of Homosexuality" Gay Men's Press London 1981 p74
8 J R Ackerley "My Father and Myself" London Bodley Head 1968 p140 quoted by John Lahr op cit p14
9 Socarides "Homosexuality Concepts & Psychodynamics" quoted by Magnusson op cit p26 p118
10 Gay Times 02/88 p18
11 South London Press 29/01/88
12 South London News 03/07/87
13 Streatham Guardian 02/07/87
14 South London Press 29/05/87
15 Times 16/08/86
16 Julian Meldrum (ed Bruce Galloway) "Prejudice and Pride" Routledge & Kegan Paul London 1983 p70 (Mary Scorse who murdered Joyce Reynolds: sentenced in 1952)
17 Lyndie Brimstone (Reviewer) Gay's the Word Review No45 02/03/87 p4 reviewing: "Naming the Violence" ed Kerry Lobel The Seal Press Seattle
18 Pam Mitchell (ed) "Pink Triangles" Alyson Publications, Boston 1980 p50
19 Eric Presland in (ed Daniel Tsang) "The Age

References and notes

Taboo" Alyson Publications and Gay Mens Press 1981 p75
20 Julian Meldrum (ed Bruce Galloway) loc cit p69
21 Evening Standard 02/10/90
22 Sunday Times 08/09/91 and Evening Std 12/09/91
23 The Times 05/08/91
24 Daily Telegraph 11/07/87
25 Associated Press "Coroner battles Sado masochistic injuries" 12/03/81 also "Blade" 11/09/81 quoted by Magnusson op cit p23
26 Karlen A "Sexuality and Homosexuality" Norton New York 1971
27 Cameron P "Report on Homosexuality and Murder" Institute for Scientific Investigation of Sexuality 1984 quoted by Magnusson op cit p23
28 Evening Standard 04/12/87
29 Daily Telegraph 26 & 29/07/91 and Evening Std 24/07/91
30 See The Sun 15/01/91. The trial was reported early 1992
31 Today 02/02/88
32 ibid
33 ibid
34 Capital Gay 05/02/88
35 The Sun 06/02/88
36 ibid
37 ibid
38 Daily Telegraph 27/10/86 and see chapter 5
39 Magnuson op cit p23 Event took place 6/1/84: Equal Time No3 25/01/84
40 Halfil and Shamback "Homophobia & Berean League Report" GMPDG 1985 Quoted by Magnusson op cit p23
41 "Jeremy" Evening Standard Magazine 08/01/88
42 John Shiers in (ed Gay Left) "Homosexuality Power and Politics" Allison & Busby London 1980 p146
43 Charley Shively in "Pink Triangles" edited Pam Mitchell Alyson Publications Boston 1980 p77
44 GLC Gay Working Party "Changing the World A London Charter for Gay & Lesbian Rights" Greater London Council 1985 p29
45 "Kennedy's Gay Guide to London" Phase Four Productions London 1987 p1
46 John Hart "So you think you're attracted to the same sex" Penguin Harmondsworth 1984 p44
47 Magnuson op cit p17
48 Charley Shively loc cit
49 Interview in Philpot "The Gay Theology" Logos 1977 p17 quoted by Magnusson op cit p23
50 John Shiers loc cit p149
51 Gay Liberation Front "Manifesto" p9
52 Obituary in The Times Oct 1986 of Sir Robert Helpman the choreographer and examined later as a pattern of recruitment

Chapter 13: The Psychological Debate

1 John Marshall in Bruce Galloway (ed) "Prejudice and Pride" Routledge & Kegan Paul, London 1983 p167
2 Hansard vol 731 col 262 quoted in Galloway op cit p178
3 Martin Dannecker "Theories of Homosexuality" Gay Mens Press, London 1981 pp33 37
4 Richard von Krafft Ebing "Psychopathia Sexualis" quoted by Dannecker op cit p3
5 Marshall loc cit p168
6 ibid
7 Elasah Drogin "Margaret Sanger: 'Father of Modern Society'" CUL, Coarsegold 1980
8 Jeffrey Weeks "Socialism and the New Life" (on Edward Carpenter and Havelock Ellis) Pluto Press, London 1977
9 Roger J Magnuson "Are 'Gay Rights' Right?" Straitgate Press, Minneapolis 1985 p14
10 Leipzig 1898 quoted by Dannecker op cit p109
11 Peregrine Worsthorne Sunday Telegraph 31/01/88
12 Gerald Swyer in The Practitioner vol 172 1954 pp374-7 (quoted by John Marshall loc cit p172)
13 R C Kolodny, W H Masters et al in New England Journal of Medicine, 1971 p285, M S Margolese "Hormones and behaviour" 1973 p285, Loraine J A et al in British Medical Journal iv, 406 1970
14 H K H Brodie et al in American Journal of Psychiatry, 1974 pp131, 82, R C Friedman et al, American Journal of Psychiatry, 1977;571 p134 14L Birk et al, Archives of General Psychiatry, 1973;314 p25
15 Mary Whitehouse (quoting) "Whatever Happened to Sex" Wayland, Hove 1977 p72
16 Sigmund Freud "3 Essays on Theory of Sexuality" 1905 quoted by John Marshall in Galloway op cit p171
17 Sigmund Freud "3 Essays on Theory of Sexuality" standard edition 1905 Vol.7, p145 quoted by Dannecker op cit p46
18 Danneker op cit p39
19 ibid p40
20 Galloway op cit p170
21 D J West "Homosexuality" London Duckworth 1955
22 G I M Swyer "Homosexuality: endocrinological aspect" in The Practitioner, vol 172 1954 pp374-7
23 Edmund Bergler "Homosexuality, Disease or Way of Life?" Hill and Wang New York 1956
24 Irving Bieber "Homosexuality: a psychoanalytic study" Basic Books New York, 1962
25 Clifford Allen "Homosexuality: Its nature causationn and treatment" Staples Press St.Albans, 1958 p47-48 quoted by John Marshall loc cit p174
26 BBC Radio 4 Midweek, in the late 1980s, but no exact date
27 John Lahr quoting from the biography of Joe Orton in "Prick up Your Ears" Penguin p48
28 Daily Telegraph 18/12/91 "Study of 167 homosexuals with twin or adoptive brothers Northwestern University and Boston Univ"
29 Mary Whitehouse op cit p67
30 Desmond Curran and Denis Parr "Homosexuality: an analysis of 100 male cases seen in private practice" BMJ 06/04/57
30 Evelyn Hooker, "Male Homosexuality" in the Rorschach Journal of Protective Techniques 1958 vol22 pp18-31
31 C A Tripp "The Homosexual Matrix" Quartet

London 1975 quoted by John Marshall loc cit p175
32 John Marshall loc cit p180
33 ibid p180/1
34 Gay Liberation Front "Psychiatry & the Homosexual" Gay Liberation Information Service 1978 p26
35 ibid p27
36 Gay News no11 1972
37 Guardian 14/09/74 quoted by John Marshall loc cit p182/3
38 Masters and Johnson "Homosexuality in Perspective" quoted by John Marshall loc cit p182/3
39 Gay Times December 1987
40 quoted by Magnuson op cit p24
41 Elizabeth Moberly "Homosexuality: a New Christian Ethic" James Clarke, Cambridge 1983 p2
42 ibid p5
43 ibid pp9/10
44 ibid p18
45 Martin Dannecker op cit p7
46 ibid p8
47 J Martin Stafford in "Journal of Moral Education" Social Morality Council 01/1988 Vol 17, No 1 p13
48 Elizabeth Moberly op cit p50
49 Said of Graham Webster-Gardiner when Chairman of Conservative Family Campaign, at the Duke of York, Kings Cross, in 1986 in a debate organised by the Socialist Party of Great Britain
50 GLC Gay Working Party "Changing the World: A London Charter for Gay & Lesbian Rights" Greater London Council 1985 p10
51 Bill Kirkpatrick "AIDS sharing the pain" Darton Longman & Todd, London 1988 p18
52 Anthony Storr "Sexual Deviation" Pelican Harmondsworth 1964 p82/3

14: Recruitment: the homosexual route

1   Lords Hansard 01/02/88 col 896
2   Money J in Marner (ed) "Homosexual Behaviour: a modern reappraisal" 1980
3   Dr James McCary "Sexual Myths and Falacies" Van Nostron Reinhold 1981 pp94,119
4   John Green & David Miller "Male Homosexuality and Sexual Problems" British Journal of Hospital Medicine June 1985
5   John Hart "So you think you're attracted to the same sex?" Penguin, Harmondsworth 1984 p66
6   ibid
7   Spada: "The Spada Report" Signet, New American Library, 1979 quoted by John Hart op cit p68
8   John Hart op cit p68
9   Rachel Tingle "Gay Lessons" Pickwick Books, London 1986 p44-5
10 "Something to tell you" London Gay Teenage Group 1984 p8
11 op cit p133
12 ibid p134
13 Mark Moffett in Daniel Tsang (ed) "The Age Taboo" Alyson Publications and Gay Mens Press 1981 p20
14 Pat Califia in Tsang op cit p144
15 Pat Califia loc cit p135
16 "Something to tell you" London Gay Teenage Group 1984 p80
17 Gregg Blachford in Pam Mitchell (ed) "Pink Triangles" Alyson Publications, Boston 1980 p70
18 Gregg Blachford loc cit p65
19 Paul Van Wyk and Chrisann Geist "Psychosocial Development of Heterosexual, Bisexual and Homosexual Behavior" in Archives of Sexual Behavior Vol.13 No.6 1984 p505
20 Jane Cousins "Make it Happy" Virago Ltd 1978
21 Paul Van Wyk and Chrisann Geist op cit p517
22 ibid p518
23 ibid p537
24 Gay Left Collective in Pam Mitchell op cit p85
25 Paul Van Wyk and Chrisann Geist op cit p536
26 "Understanding Paedophilia" PIE Vol 1 No 3 Aug/Sep 1977 pp4/5
27 Roy Burns in Bruce Galloway (ed) "Prejudice and Pride" Routledge & Kegan Paul, London 1983 p219
28 Paul Van Wyk and Chrisann Geist op cit p516
29 leaflet on education: Scottish Homosexual Rights Group 11/78
30 SHRG leaflet 'For Gay Kids' 05/80
31 Paul Van Wyk and Chrisann Geist op cit p541
32 Jeffrey Weeks in Bob Cant & Susan Hemmings (eds) "Radical Records" Routledge & Kegan Paul London 1988 p157
33 ibid
34 Anna Durell in Bruce Galloway (ed) "Prejudice and Pride" Routledge & Kegan Paul, London 1983 p8
35 Gregg Blachford loc cit p66
36 John Lahr "Prick up your ears" Penguin 1986 p52 quoting Joe Orton's diary
37 John Lahr op cit p53
38 John Lahr op cit p72 (Orton's diary 02/04/49)
39 Charley Shively in Pam Mitchell (ed) op cit p42
40 "About Homosexuality some questions and answers" The Albany Trust 1979 p8
41 Paul Van Wyk and Chrisann Geist op cit p541
42 ibid p540
43 Roger J Magnuson "Are 'Gay Rights' Right?" Straitgate Press, Minneapolis 1985 p76
44 Malcolm Macourt "How Can We Help You?" National Council for Voluntary Organisations Bedford Square Press, London 1989 p38
45 Malcolm Macourt op cit p39
46 ibid p61
47 ibid p62
48 ibid p11
49 ibid p84
50 Glenn McKee in "Walking after Midnight" Routledge 1989 p193
51 Ken Barnes in "Open Mind" No2 Conservative Group for Homosexual Equality 11/78
52 Michael Burbidge "I Know what I am" Joint Council for Gay Teenagers 1980 p14
53 "SMG News" Scottish Minorities Group 11/77
54 Jamie Gough and Mike Mcnair "Gay Liberation in the Eighties" Pluto Press Limited, London 1985 p107
55 John Hart op cit p113

Chapter 15: Deceiving the Young

1   John Hart "So you think you're attracted to the same sex" Penguin, Harmondsworth 1984 p81/82

References and notes

2 New Statesman 12/09/86 p13
3 Jeffrey Weeks in Cant & Hemmings (eds) "Radical Records" Routledge 1988 p157
4 Jeffrey Weeks loc cit p156
5 John Hart op cit pp33,37,45
6 John Hart op cit pp39,47
7 "Submission on the Decriminalisation of Homosexuality" Australian Federation for the Family 1990 p11
8 Jane Cousins 'Make it Happy' (New Edition) Penguin 1986 p25
9 Recent evidence in discussed on pages 110 & 126
10 Robin Squire MP "Open Mind" No3 Conservative Group for Homosexual Equality 1987
11 Robin Squire MP loc cit
12 Peter Campbell "Open Mind" No2
13 Valerie Riches "Sex and Social Engineering" Family and Youth Concern 1986 p20 quoting "Sex education, An FPA Statement" Family Planning Association 08/74
14 Jane Cousins op cit p24 and Jane Cousins "Make it Happy Make it Safe" (Another New Edition) Penguin 1988
15 Sunday Telegraph 23/11/86
16 Jane Cousins "Make it Happy" Penguin 1986 p37
17 Jane Cousins op cit pp25/27
18 ibid p102
19 ibid p121
20 ibid p119
21 ibid p123
22 ibid frontispiece
23 Hansard col 562-567 06/03/86
24 Dr Eric Trimmer "Knowing About Sex" BMA Family Doctor Publications 1986 p4
25 ibid p5
26 Medical News 21/09/77
27 Rachel Tingle "Gay Lessons" Pickwick Books, London 1986 p16
28 "Personal Relationships Resources List" Health Education Council 1985
29 Rachel Tingle op cit p20
30 ibid
31 J Martin Stafford in "Journal of Moral Education" Vol17 No1 Social Morality Council 01/88 p16
32 Lorraine Trenchard (ed) "Talking about young lesbians" London Gay Teenage Group 1984
33 Lesbian & Gay youth magazine Summer 1986 issue 19
34 Family Matters BBC1 04/04/90
35 The Spectator 14/04/90
36 "Streetwise Youth" Annual Report 1990
37 Social Concern Department, "Understanding Homosexuality" Mothers Union 01/84
38 Parents Enquiry Fact [sic] Sheet
39 ibid
40 "The Kids are Alrite" at the Royal Court Theatre 10/79
41 Dr Martyn Gay: Teachers' notes for "Two of Us" BBC 25/03/88
42 ibid

Chapter 16: Paedophilia

1 John Lahr "Prick up your ears - the biography of Joe Orton" Penguin 1986 p15 quoting Orton's diary 09/05/67
2 Gay Liberation Front "Manifesto" London 1971 revd 1979 p3
3 GLC Gay Working Party "Changing the World: A London Charter for Gay & Lesbian Rights" Greater London Council 1985 p9
4 motion on "discrimination" at AGM National Council for Civil Liberties 1980
5 Peter Radcliffe-Ludlam "Open Mind" Conservative Group for Homosexual Equality 1986 No2
6 Malcolm Macourt "How Can We Help You" National Council for Voluntary Orgnaisations Bedford Square Press, London 1989 pp xiii,70,99
7 Gay Left Collective in Pam Mitchell (ed) "Pink Triangles" Alyson Publications, Boston 1980 p81
8 Tom Reeves in Daniel Tsang (ed) "The Age Taboo" Alyson Publications and Gay Mens Press 1981 p26 (reprinted from "Fag Rag")
9 Malcolm Dobson in Bruce Galloway (ed) "Prejudice and Pride" Routledge & Kegan Paul, London 1983 p23
10 Roy Walmsley and Karen White "Sexual Offences, Consent and Sentencing" HMSO 1979 pp 56-62 and "Supplementary Information on Sexual Offences, Consent and Sentencing" Home Office 1980.
11 Written No223 23/05/88
12 C L Nash and D J West "Sexual molestation of young girls" in West (ed) "Sexual victimisation" Gower Aldershot 1985
13 Hilary Jackson Research Bulletin no23 "Child molestation: a research note" Home Office 1987 p35
14 Tom Reeves ibid p25
15 Gay Left Collective loc cit p85
16 Gay's the Word Review Feb/Mar 1987 no45
17 Tony Higton "Sexuality and the Church" ABWON Hockley 1987 p10 and flier sent out to Lesbian & Gay Christian prospects
18 Parker Rossman "Sexual experience between men and boys" Maurice Temple Smith, Hounslow 1985 p17
19 Ken Plummer "Gay News" from L&GCM on a flier
20 Malcolm Macourt op cit p141
21 Noel Halifax "Out Proud and Fighting" Socialist Workers' Party London 02/1988 p6&7
22 Gerald Creed "Sexual Subordination: Institutionalised homosexuality and social control in Melanesia" Ethnology Vol23 No3 07/84
23 ibid p160
24 ibid p163
25 ibid p166
26 Tom Reeves loc cit p28
27 Anna Durell in Galloway op cit p8
28 Jay and Young "The Gay Report" Summit 1979 p275
29 Roger J Magnuson "Are 'Gay Rights' Right?" Straitgate Press, Minneapolis 1985 p18
30 Magnuson op cit p18 quoting from "Twin Cities Christian" 05/07/84
31 Kate Millett in Tsang op cit p81
32 "Militant young dyke" in Tsang op cit p130
33 Roger Moody in Tsang op cit p150
34 "New Truth" (New Zealand) 05/04/91 p5
35 ibid

36 Jay and Young op cit p277
37 Magnuson op cit p17
38 Brian Reade "Sexual Heretics" London 1975
39 Noel Halifax op cit p19
40 "The London Programme" 30/11/90 Thames TV. Presenter Trevor Phillips and his team visited the "Why Not," "Boys Club 21" and "Blue Boy" bars in Amsterdam.
41 The Guardian 16/01/88
42 Hilary Jackson op cit p36
43 Daily Telegraph 18/02/87
44 South London Press 04/12/87
45 Daily Telegraph 27/06/87
46 The Times 02/12/87
47 Tim Tate "Child Pornography" Methuen London 1990
48 GLC Gay Working Party op cit p28
49 The Frank Beck trial lasted from September to November 1991
50 Capital Gay 24/02/89
51 Daniel Tsang op cit p165
52 The Star 23/03/87
53 Gay Left Collective in Mitchell op cit p79
54 Pat Califia in Tsang op cit p136
55 Lesbians Rising in Tsang op cit p125
56 NAMBLA ("North American Man Boy Love [sic] Association") in Tsang op cit p99
57 NAMBLA loc cit p103
58 "Tom" in Lesbian & Gay Youth Magazine Summer 86 no19

Chapter 17: Paedophile groups and their supporters

1 Sheffield Morning Telegraph 26/08/75
2 Michael Jarrett in "Prejudice and Pride" ed Bruce Galloway Routledge & Kegan Paul, London 1983 preface p vi
3 "Palaver" Magazine of Paedophile Action for Liberation 1976 No4 (a South London Gay Liberation Front offshoot)
4 The People 25/05/75
5 "Information about PIE" 1975
6 "Childhood Rights" Paedophile Information Exchange Vol1 No2 here quoted by Gay Left Collective in "Pink Triangles" p84
7 Guardian 04/05/88 and The Times 24/07/92
8 Aubrey Walter "Come Together" Gay Mens Press, London 1980 p38
9 PIE Newsletter no7 1975
10 Tony Hughes & John Lloyd: signed letter from Brixton Gay Community Centre 01/12/74
11 "An introduction to PIE" 1982
12 Guardian 08/02/78
13 "Palaver" Paedophile Action for Liberation 1976 no5
14 HEA booklist DHSS late 1980s
15 "Betrayal of Youth" CL Publications London 1986 p255
16 ibid p257
17 The Times 17/12/91
18 Roy Burns in "Prejudice and Pride" p223
19 Sunday Mail 25/03/84
20 "Broadsheet" Campaign for Homosexual Equality Nov 1978 p2
21 Galloway op cit p89, Gay Scotland 04/80
22 Newsletter Paedophile Information Exchange 1975
23 Broadsheet CHE Oct 1977: Conference report
24 Newsletter Paedophile Information Exchange 1978
25 Broadsheet CHE Aug 1979: Conference agenda
26 Broadsheet CHE Oct 1979 p4
27 ibid May 1980 p3
28 ibid Aug & Nov 1981 Motions & p4
29 Annual Report Campaign for Homosexual Equality 1983 p1
30 Peace News 13/06/75
31 PIE Newsletters 1975-1982, Bowker "Directory of Pressure Groups" 1979

Chapter 18: The invention of children's rights

1 John Hart "So you think you're attracted to the same sex" Penguin, Harmondsworth 1984 p47
2 Woman's Hour 02/02/88
3 Richard Auchinloss, letter in SMG NEWS January 1978 signed as PIE member no10
4 Peace News 04/11/77
5 ibid 07/03/80
6 John Parratt alias Warren Middleton (ed) "Betrayal of Youth" CL Publications London 1986
7 "Palaver" Paedophile Action for Liberation 1976 no5
8 Keith Hose and Michael Burbidge "Evidence to the Criminal Law Revision Committee on the law relating to & penalties for sexual offences involving children" Paedophile Information Exchange 11/75
9 "Childhood Rights" 1977 Vol1 No3 Paedophile Information Exchange
10 "Paedophilia, some questions and answers" Paedophile Information Exchange qn34
11 Peace News 09/01/76
12 ibid 08/02/80
13 ibid
14 Rachel Tingle "Gay Lessons" Pickwick Books quoting the Children's Legal Centre on age of consent
15 "Joint Council for Gay Teenagers" in Tsang (ed) "The Age Taboo" Alyson Publications and Gay Mens Press 1981 p90
16 Anna Coote and Tess Gill "Women's Rights a Practical Guide" Penguin, Harmondsworth 1974 p130 131
17 Peace News 29/08/75
18 Michael Schofield "Age of Consent, paper on Sexual Offences" evidence to the Criminal Law Revision Committee" NCCL 1976
19 Gay Teachers Group "Gaynoise" article by Julian Hows 15/01/81 quoted by Rachel Tingle "Gay Lessons" p25
20 "Palaver" Paedophile Action for Liberation 1976 no5
21 Magpie 1977 No 10 P.I.E.
22 NAMBLA ("North American Man Boy Love [sic] Association") in Tsang (ed) op cit p101
23 Parratt alias Middleton op cit p257
24 Jimmy Young TV programme 1987
25 Parratt alias Middleton op cit: cover
26 Kate Millett in Tsang (ed) op cit p80
27 Jamie Gough in Pam Mitchell (ed) "Pink Triangles" Alyson Publications, Boston 1980 p91
28 Rachel Tingle op cit p33 (quote)
29 Bob Cant & Nigel Young "New Politics Old Struggles" in "Homosexuality power & politics" Allison & Busby & Gay Left p116f
30 Jamie Gough and Mike Mcnair "Gay Liberation in the Eighties" Pluto Press Limited,

References and notes

London 1985 p19,68,93,108,111
31 letter to exec committee of PIE 19/04/83
32 ibid
33 Roger Moody: review of "Minor Problems" City Limits 14/06/83
34 Roger Moody in Tsang (ed) op cit p152/3

Chapter 19: Assault on the Family

1 Gay Liberation Front "Manifesto" London 1971 revd 1979 p7
2 John Molyneux in "Socialist Worker" 16/01/88
3 ibid
4 ibid
5 Streatham Guardian (both quotations) 02/10/86
6 Jamie Gough and Mike Mcnair "Gay Liberation in the Eighties" Pluto Press Limited, London 1985 pp17,21,59
7 Gay Liberation Front "Manifesto" pp1,8,12
8 Aubrey Walter "Come Together" Gay Men's Press London 1980 p23
9 ibid p38
10 David Fernbach in Pam Mitchell (ed) "Pink Triangles" Alyson Publications, Boston 1980 p154
11 ibid p157
12 Christine Kelly (ed) "Feminism v Mankind" Family Publications, Wicken, Milton Keynes 1990
13 Stuart Bell MP "When Salem came to the Boro" Pan books 1988
14 Radio 4, 6pm 24/04/90
15 Wynne & Hobbs in "Archives of Diseases in Childhood" quoted by Barbara Amiel, The Times 22/4/88
16 Beatrix Campbell "Lust and the Left" Gay Scotland Jan/Feb '87
17 Daily Mail 28/10/87
18 ibid 30/10/87
19 ibid 29/11/86
20 London Evening Standard July 1991
21 Digby Anderson "Abusing the Family" in the Times 08/06/88
22 ibid
23 ibid
24 Daily Mail 28/10/87
25 ibid 30/10/87
26 Robert Chester in Anderson & Dawson (eds) "Family Portraits" Social Affairs Unit 1986 p21
27 Barbara Amiel "Mrs Foster is a grievance monger" The Times 25/03/88
28 Wakefield & Underwager "Accusations of child sexual abuse" Chapter 6: "Prevention of child sexual abuse" p175
29 ibid p196
30 ibid p202

Chapter 20: Lesbian & Feminist Philosophy

1 Deborah Goleman Wolf "The Lesbian Community" Los Angeles & London University of California Press 1980 p16
2 John Hart "So you think you're attracted to the same sex" Penguin, Harmondsworth 1984 p102
3 S & M and other practices were examined in chapters 8 and 9 and the clubs and cruising in chapter 4.
4 Deborah Goleman Wolf op cit p15
5 ibid p93/94
6 "Lesbian Ethics" Vol1 No2 1985 p80
7 ibid p90
8 ibid p91
9 ibid p94
10 Pam Mitchell "Hetero sexualities common cause" in her (ed) "Pink Triangles" Alyson Publications, Boston 1980 pp52/3
11 John Hart op cit p22
12 Paul Van Wyk and Chrisann Geist "Psychosocial Development of Heterosexual, Bisexual and Homosexual Behavior" in Archives of Sexual Behavior Vol 13 No 6 1984 p539
13 Pam Mitchell loc cit p53
14 The Time The Place Thames TV 01/88
15 Kilroy BBC1 10/87
16 GLC Gay Working Party "Changing the World - A London Charter for Gay & Lesbian Rights" Greater London Council 1985 p25
17 Deborah Goleman Wolf op cit p139
18 Genetic engineering of this type has already been developed in the veterinary world for farming.
19 The Times 22/03/91
20 The "Virgin Births" story unfolds in: Daily Mail and Evening Standard 11/03/91, The Times 12/03/91, Birmingham Post 08/04/91, Pink Paper 13/04/91, The Times 26/04/91, Sunday Times 09/06/91
21 Gay Liberation Front "Manifesto" London 1971 revd 1979 p8
22 Aubrey Walter "Come Together" Gay Men's Press London 1980 p39
23 Bronwen Cohen in "Caring for Children - services and policies for child care and equal opportunities in the UK" - Commission of the European Communities 1988 p69
24 John Hart op cit p96
25 Deborah Goleman Wolf op cit p98
26 ibid p100
27 ibid p105
28 John Hart op cit p52
29 ibid p55
30 Deborah Goleman Wolf op cit p68
31 Gay Times 10/87 p39
32 Pam Mitchell loc cit p52
33 Flier for screening in Haringey
34 Sunday Times 21/02/88
35 Another badge (for homosexual men) depicts a zipper being pulled down, with the word "Ready?" Others have "Master" or "Slave" written on them.
36 Leanne Payne "The Broken Image" Kingsway, Eastbourne 1988 (originally published in USA 1981) pp15-29
37 ibid p29
38 Anthony Storr "Sexual Deviation" Pelican Harmondsworth 1964 pp75-6
39 ibid p78
40 Leanne Payne op cit p30
41 Anthony Storr op cit pp79-80

Chapter 21: Lesbian Religion

1 Deborah Goleman Wolf "The Lesbian Community" Los Angeles & London University of California Press 1980 p84
2 Peace News 11/09/87

3   Deborah Goleman Wolf op cit p85
4   Eisenstein 'Connections between class and sex' p15/16 quoted by Deborah Goleman Wolf op cit p68
5   Deborah Goleman Wolf op cit p109
6   ibid p156
7   ibid p157
8   ibid p152
9   Adrian Fulford et al "Paedophilia and Public Morals" Campaign (or Conspiracy) against Public Morals p28
10 Paul Van Wyk and Chrisann Geist "Psychosocial Development of Heterosexual, Bisexual and Homosexual Behavior" in Archives of Sexual Behavior Vol 13 No 6 1984 p537
11 Deborah Goleman Wolf op cit p164
12 Germaine Greer "The Female Eunuch" was originally published in 1970 by MacKinnon & Kee
13 Deborah Goleman Wolf op cit p164
14 Mary Pipes "Understanding Abortion" Womens Press 1986
15 Ann Oakley "Wisewoman and Medicine Man" in Juliet Mitchell & Oakley (eds) "The Rights and Wrongs of Women" Penguin 1976
16 The Guardian 17/12/87
17 Ian Cavendish "The Black Arts" Pan Books 1969 p371
18 Parinder "Witchcraft" Faber 1958 p51 quoted by Ann Oakley op cit p27
19 Ann Oakley op cit p27
20 Deborah Goleman Wolf op cit p25
21 ibid p82
22 ibid p104
23 ibid p17
24 ibid p183
25 Peace News 19/06/87

Chapter 22: The Myth of a Homosexual Theology

1   Derrick Sherwin Bailey "Homosexuality and the Western Christian Tradition" Longmans, Green 1955 p4
2   Robert Arthur "Homosexuality and the Conservative Christian 1982 p2
3   William Norman Pittenger "Time for Consent" SCM Press 1976 p83
4   John Boswell "Rediscovering Gay History" Gay Christian Movement 1982 p13
5   "Open Mind" Conservative Group for Homosexual Equality Autumn 1986
6   Robin Green in "Prejudice and Pride" ed Bruce Galloway Routledge & Kegan Paul, London 1983 p143
7   Gavin Reid "Beyond AIDS" Kingsway Eastbourne 1987 p33
8   ibid p34
9   Jeanette Howard "Out of Egypt: Leaving lesbianism behind" Monarch Publications Ltd, Eastbourne 1991 p59
10 John Stott "Issues facing Christians Today" Marshall, Basingstoke 1984 p311
11 ibid p313
12 ibid p312

Chapter 23: The Lesbian & Gay Christian Movement

1   Robin Green in Bruce Galloway (ed) Prejudice and Pride Routledge & Kegan Paul

London 1983 p143
2   John Stott "Issues facing Christians Today" 1984 p302
3   The House of Bishops "Issues in Human Sexuality" Church House, London 1991 para 5.11 p43
4   Malcolm Johnson "Exploring lifestyles" L&GCM p133 in "Christian" L&GCM p1 Aut/Win 1982
5   Tony Higton "Sexuality & the Church" ABWON 1987 p9
6   "Journal" Lesbian & Gay Christian Movement Nov 1989 p5
7   ibid p6
8   ibid p39
9   Gay Times Feb 1990
10 Christian News World Apr 1990
11 Patrick Buchanan writing in New Dimensions magazine March 1990 p66-67
12 Tony Higton op cit p8
13 "Journal" Lesbian & Gay Christian Movement Nov 1989 p31
14 COSPEC "Statement of intent" 1983 END churches register Autumn 1984
15 ibid
16 "Young Gay & Proud" p58
17 The "Pink Paper" 23/06/88 p19

Chapter 24: Homosexual Marriages & Emotional Orphans

1   "The Heart of the Matter" BBC2 28/02/88
2   "Southwark News" C of E Diocese of Southwark 02/88
3   Larry Uhrig "The Two of Us" Alyson Publns. Boston 1984 p30
4   ibid p40
5   ibid p68
6   Gay Times 1991 p42
7   Larry Uhrig op cit p67
8   ibid p72
9   'Christian' Aut/Win 1984 p135
10 Malcolm Macourt "Towards a theology of gay liberation" SCM Press 1977 p25
11 Elizabeth Moberly "Homosexuality: a New Christian Ethic" James Clarke, Cambridge 1983 p28
12 ibid p33
13 John Boswell "Rediscovering Gay History" Gay Christian Movement 1982 p16
14 Moberly opcit p34
15 ibid p21
16 ibid p39
17 Anthony Storr "Sexual Deviation" Pelican Harmondsworth 1964 p12
18 Moberly opcit p22
19 ibid p25
20 ibid p23
21 ibid p30
22 William Norman Pittenger "Time for Consent" SCM Press 1976 p72
23 Moberly loc cit
24 ibid p35
25 ibid p31
26 Pittenger op cit p7
27 John Stott "Issues facing Christians Today" Marshall, Basingstoke 1984 p318
28 Alex Davidson "The Returns of Love" IVP 1970 p52 quoted by John Stott op cit p320
29 Elizabeth Moberly op cit p37
30 Leanne Payne "The Broken Image" Kingsway,

References and notes

Eastbourne 1988 (USA 1981) p38

Chapter 25: Change of scenes: Healing the Homosexual

1. Ian McKellen on Radio's Midweek 01/06/88 (also quoted on p56)
2. C A Tripp "The Homosexual Matrix" London Quartet 1975 ch11 (quoted by John Marshall in Galloway (ed) "Prejudice and Pride" Routledge & Kegan Paul, London 1983 p165
3. Dr Stephen Burton, reviewed by Jonathan Sanders in Gay Times 06/88
4. John Hart "So you think you're attracted to the same sex" Penguin, Harmondsworth 1984 p107
5. ibid p25
6. ibid p13/14
7. ibid p29
8. ibid p30
9. Roger J Magnuson "Are 'Gay Rights' Right?" Straitgate Press, Minneapolis 1985 p28
10. John Marshall loc cit p189
11. Peter Fonagy & Anna Higgitt "Personality Theory & Clinical Practice" Methuen & Co, London 1984 p70
12. Socarides "Homosexuality Concepts and Psychodynamics" p75
13. "Homosexuality and Prostitution" British Medical Association 1955 Appendix E
14. F H Brisby in "Homosexuality and Prostitution" BMA 1955 Appendix C
15. F H Brisby loc cit
16. "Homosexuality and Prostitution" BMA 1955 Appendix E
17. ibid
18. ibid
19. Testimony in leaflet from True Freedom Trust
20. Elizabeth Moberly "Homosexuality: a New Christian Ethic" James Clarke, Cambridge 1983 p42
21. Leanne Payne "The Broken Image" Kingsway, Eastbourne 1988 (USA 1981) p29
22. Moberly op cit p52
23. Leanne Payne op cit p49
24. True Freedom Trust testimony
25. Elizabeth Moberly op cit p52

Chapter 26: Iron John or Jesus Christ?

1. Robert Bly "Iron John" Element Books, Shaftesbury 1991 pref
2. Anthony Storr "Sexual Deviation" Pelican 1964 p76/77
3. ibid p85/86
4. Bly op cit p32
5. Daily Telegraph 20/03/91
6. ibid
7. Independent 20/01/92
8. Guardian 09/03/91
9. Independent loc cit
10. Daily Telegraph Magazine March 1991
11. Guardian loc cit
12. Leanne Payne in Comiskey p10
13. Andrew Comiskey: "Pursuing Sexual Wholeness." Monarch Publications, Eastbourne 1990: p49
14. Leanne Payne loc cit
15. Robert Bly op cit, p171
16. ibid p97
17. Storr op cit p78
18. Jeanette Howard: "Out of Egypt - leaving lesbianism behind." Monarch Publications, Eastbourne 1991: pp38-50
19. "Capital Gay" 20/09/91
20. ibid
21. "New Dimensions" magazine July 1990 p25

Chapter 27: Homosexuality and the parties of the Left

1. Manifesto Green Party 1991 and Harris Research Centre "JN 29216" prepared for Stonewall February 1992 pp1-8
2. "Changing Britain for good:" Liberal Democrat Manifesto 1992 p41
3. "Partners for Freedom & Justice" Social & Liberal Democrats 1991 p14/15. The ages of consent are already equal, of course. As we saw in chapter 18, neither a girl under 16 nor a boy under 16 can give the consent which would prevent a sexual act from being an indecent assault. Additionally, homosexual acts between males are proscribed in law unless both parties are 21, consenting, and commit an act of buggery or gross indecency in private.
4. Liberal Democrat News April 1991 p2
5. Liberal Democrat Policy Document 1991
6. Labour Campaign for Lesbian and Gay Rights " Manifesto" 1986 back cover
7. Phil Greasley "Gay Men at Work" Campaign for Homosexual Equality (Lesbian and Gay Employment Rights) p60
8. LCLGR "Manifesto" p3
9. Phil Greasley "Gay Men at Work" Campaign for Homosexual Equality (Lesbian and Gay Employment Rights) p64
10. Lesbian & gay Socialist Winter 87 p7
11. Noel Halifax "Out Proud & Fighting" Socialist Workers' Party 1988 p34
12. Gay Scotland Nov/Dec 1982 p22
13. The Times 21/09/90
14. ibid 27/09/90
15. Stephen Harding "Trends in permissiveness" in "British Social Attitudes 5th Report 1988/89" Gower, Aldershot 1989 pp36-37
16. ibid p74
17. Gallop "Report 374" October 1991 pp35
18. ibid p36
19. Harris Research Centre "JN 29216" prepared for Stonewall February 1992 pp1-8
20. ibid

Chapter 28: Gay Rights and the Victimless Crime

1. Roger J Magnuson "Are 'Gay Rights' Right?" Straitgate Press, Minneapolis 1985 p99
2. The Times 22/03/86
3. ibid
4. Magnuson op cit p51/52
5. ibid p7
6. Labour Campaign for Lesbian and Gay Rights (LCLGR) "Manifesto" 1986 p4
7. Gay Scotland Jan/Feb 1986 p6
8. Capital Gay 05/06/92
9. LCLGR Manifesto p5
10. ibid p10: Clause 1
11. Peter Ashman of Stonewall in Gay Times July 1990 pp18-19
12. LCLGR Manifesto p20

13 Lesbian & Gay Socialist Autumn 86
14 LCLGR Manifesto p25
15 ibid p28
16 "Partners in Freedom and Justice" Liberal Democrats 1991 pp14-15
17 LCLGR Manifesto p6
18 ibid p7
19 ibid
20 Church Times 27/12/85
21 ibid
22 ibid
23 Capital Gay 05/06/92 bears the point out, but of course experts deny the link. The Hungerford killer copied his crime from one of his large library of videos of sex and violence.
24 Magnuson op cit

Chapter 29: Homosexuality and Conservatism

1 Martin Durham "Sex and Politics" ("The Family and Morality in the Thatcher Years") Macmillan Education Basingstoke 1991 p2
2 ibid p179
3 The Guardian 10/10/90
4 The Guardian 12/10/91
5 The Times 22/03/91
6 Pink Paper 30/03/91
7 Pink Paper 13/04/91
8 ibid 27/04/91
9 Lynette Burrows Sunday Telegraph Mar/Apr 91
10 Pink Paper 06/04/91
11 Although Graham Turner explored the gay mafia in the civil service, the Church, medicine and the media in the Sunday Telegraph 05/06/88. Few people to whom he spoke voiced their fears at any length.
12 Evening Standard 11/12/90

Chapter 30: Gay Rights v Liberal Democracy

1 Professor Norman Barry "The New Right" Croom Helm, Beckenham, Kent 1987 p115
2 David Willetts "Modern Conservatism" Penguin London 1992 p4
3 Daily Telegraph 11/10/91
4 Barry op cit p86
5 ibid p137
6 Daily Telegraph 09/10/91
7 Michael Novak "The Spirit of Democratic Capitalism" Institute of Economic Affairs, London 1991 p191
8 ibid p14
9 ibid p16
10 ibid p31
11 ibid p35
12 Barry op cit p127

Chapter 31 The sexual marketplace

1 Professor Norman Barry "The New Right" Croom Helm, Beckenham, Kent 1987 p116
2 ibid p8
3 ibid p59
4 Michael Novak "The Spirit of Democratic Capitalism" Institute of Economic Affairs, London 1991 p351
5 Barry op cit p71
6 ibid p68

7 ibid
8 Novak op cit p352
9 Barry op cit p31
10 ibid p99
11 Thomas Hobbes 1588-1679 author of "The Leviathan" and John Locke 1632-1704 who wrote "Essays concerning the human understanding" and "The reasonableness of Christianity"
12 Jeffrey Weeks "Coming Out" Quartet Books, London 1990 p11
13 Barry op cit p50/51
14 ibid p122
15 Valerie Riches "Sex and Social Engineering" Family and & Youth Concern, Milton Keynes: a brilliant and highly factual account of the activities and philosophy of the humanist network.
16 Cornelia Ferreira (ed Christine Kelly) "Feminism versus Mankind" Family Publications, Milton Keynes 1990 p58
17 Valerie Riches (ed Christine Kelly) op cit p36
18 New Dimensions Oct 1990 p58
19 Germaine Greer "The Change: Women, ageing and the menopause" Hamish Hamilton London 1991
20 Barry op cit p66
21 ibid p63/64
22 ibid p183
23 ibid p148

Chapter 32: Gay materialism or family values

1 Michael Novak "The Spirit of Democratic Capitalism" Institute of Economic Affairs, London 1991 p60
2 ibid p61
3 ibid p93
4 ibid p162
5 Professor Norman Barry "The New Right" Croom Helm, Beckenham, Kent 1987 p90
6 ibid p90/91
7 ibid p128
8 Novak op cit p165
9 ibid p168
10 ibid p163
11 ibid p170
12 Barry op cit p18
13 ibid p78
14 Radio 4 Today programme 24/03/92
15 Barry op cit p125
16 ibid p178

Chapter 33: Pressure groups, AIDS, and the myth of pluralism

1 Michael Novak "The Spirit of Democratic Capitalism" Institute of Economic Affairs, London 1991 p59
2 Professor Norman Barry "The New Right" Croom Helm, Beckenham, Kent 1987 p27/28
3 ibid p38,118
4 ibid p118/9
5 Professor William Mitchell "Government as it is" Institute for Economic Affairs 1988 p43

References and notes 467

6 Jo Grimond "Memoirs" Heinemann, London 1979 p261
7 Barry op cit p71
8 ibid p73
9 ibid p74
10 ibid p75
11 Novak op cit p184
12 Barry op cit p60
13 ibid p120
14 Robert Whelan in "Economic Affairs" Institute for Economic Affairs June 1991
15 Novak op cit p186
16 ibid p53
17 ibid p51
18 ibid p350
19 ibid p351
20 ibid p350
21 ibid p62
22 Roy Masters in "New Dimensions" Oregon USA Oct 1990 p63
23 ibid p41

Chapter 34: Homosexuality, decline and fall.

1 Professor Norman Barry "The New Right" Croom Helm, Beckenham, Kent 1987 p21
2 ibid p100
3 ibid p146/7
4 ibid p147
5 Michael Novak "The Spirit of Democratic Capitalism" Institute of Economic Affairs, London 1991 p185
6 Barry op cit p187
7 ibid p185
8 The Universe 08/03/92
9 Barry op cit p184
10 Barry op cit p147
11 ibid p183
12 ibid p147/8
13 ibid p184
14 Sunday Telegraph 20/10/91
15 J G de Beus "Shall We Make the Year 2000?" (Originally published in Holland in 1982) Sidgwick and Jackson, London 1985 p165
16 Roy Masters in "New Dimensions" Oregon USA Oct 1990 p53
17 Roy Masters loc cit p60
18 "One Nation 2000" (quoted in The Independent 29/02/92) Conservative Political Centre, London, March 1992
19 Conservative Family Campaign report on effects of non- maternal day-care, and see James Buchan Daily Mail 24/07/92
20 Sunday Telegraph 14/06/92

Chapter 35: Filling the spiritual vacuum

1 Michael Novak "The Spirit of Democratic Capitalism" Institute of Economic Affairs, London 1991 p324
2 ibid
3 ibid p63
4 ibid p351
5 Michael Novak in "New Dimensions" article: "Say 'Morality' and the cheering stops" Oregon USA July 1990 p24
6 Michael Novak "The Spirit of Democratic Capitalism" p68
7 Roy Masters in "New Dimensions" Oregon USA Oct 1990 p56
8 The Guardian 10/06/92
9 Daily Telegraph 26/10/91
10 The Spectator 18/04/92
11 British Social Attitudes "The eighth report" 1991 & Hart CJ "Acts to Action" CATS Trust 1991
12 "Submission on the Decriminalisation of Homosexuality" Australian Federation for the Family 1990 p33

Chapter 36: Back to normality

1 Roger Magnuson "Are Gay Rights Right?" (Updated edition) Multnomah Press 1990 pp61-62
2 Leanne Payne "Crisis in Masculinity" Kingsway, Eastbourne 1988 (Originally published in USA 1985) p13
3 Leanne Payne The Broken Image Kingsway, Eastbourne 1988 (USA 1981) p44
4 Elizabeth Moberly Homosexuality: a New Christian Ethic James Clarke, Cambridge 1983 p15
5 Social Affairs Unit
6 Elizabeth Moberly Homosexuality: a New Christian Ethic James Clarke, Cambridge 1983 p4
7 Education No2 Act 1986 Section 46
8 Freedom Today April 1992.
9 Professor Thomas Szasz 1981 quoted in "Sex education in schools" the Responsible Society.
10 DES Circular No11/87 Department of Education 09/87
11 The Times, 19 June 1991

Counselling groups:
True Freedom Trust
PO Box 3, Upton, Wirral, Merseyside
L49 6NY and PO Box 592, London SE4 1EF.
Pilot, a counselling group in Northern Ireland, is c/o Shanklin Road Mission, 116 Shanklin Road, Belfast BT13 2BD

Index of names, publications and organisations

Abbott Diane MP 443
Abel-Smith Prof Brian 128,434
Abse Leo 19,31,144
Acceptance 180-1,421
Acer Dr 129
ACT-UP See Aids Coalition To Unleash Power
ACTT 339
Adamson Leo 204,229,336
Adler Prof Dr Michael 121,129,392
Adrian Hester 18
AEU 339
African National Congress 51
Age of Reason 377
Age Taboo, The 193,196,201,224,227-30
Aids Coalition To Unleash Power 288,403
Aitken Ron 434
Albany Trust 18,209-11,225-6,361
Albemarle Diana 18
Albert Kennedy Trust 180-182
Alcoholics Anonymous 313
Alexander the Great 42
Allaun Frank MP 336
Allen Austin 348
Allen Clifford 148
Allen Marvin 326-7,331
Altman Dennis 36
Alton David MP 29,372
AMBLA See Aotearoa Man-Boy Love Association
Amiel Barbara 241,329
Amis Martin 434
Amnesty International 27
ANC See African National Congress
Anderson Dr Digby 239-40
Anderton Mr James 68
Anglican Consultative Council 293
Anglican Pacifist Fellows 290
Annan Lord 18
Antonio Gene 102
Aotearoa Man-Boy Love [sic] Association 197-8
Apuzzo Virginia 153
Aristotle 42
Armstrong Hilary MP 210
Arran Lord 19
Arrest of Oscar Wilde, The 51
Arthur Robert 271-2,274,277
Arts Council 51
Ash Bill 434
Ashcroft Peggy 439
Ashdown Paddy MP 117,128,369,392,434
Ashman Peter 348
Association of British Insurers 394
Association of London Authorities 55
ASTMS 339
Attlee Lord 18
Auden W H 42,173,198
AUEW-TASS 339
Ayer Prof Sir Alfred J 18,223,434
Bacon Francis 42
Bailey Canon D S 270-1
Baker Rt Hon Kenneth MP 49
Baker Roger 75
Bakewell Joan 177
Banatvala Dr 125
Bancroft Dr John 191,314,434
Banks Tony MP 340
Barker A L 434
Barker David 434
Barlas Chris 434
Barlow Stephen 434
Barnardos 182
Barnes Rosie 182
Barnett Tim 348,361
Barrie Dennis 45
Barry Prof Norman 366-93,400-02, 408,417
Baughn Bishop Michael 295
Beaumont Lord 55,211,215
Becket Margaret MP 392
Bedfordshire Council 128
Bell & Weinberg 68,77
Bell Daniel 382
Bell Stuart MP 236,238,240
Bellos Linda 253-4
BeLonging 281
Benn Rt Hon Tony MP 340
Bennett Alan 434
Bennett-England Rodney 209-10
Bentham Jeremy 377-8,438
Bentley Radhe 122
Bergalis Kimberley 104,129
Bergler Edmund 77,148
Berkeley Michael 434
Bernard Frits 222
Berne Eric 314,322
Betjeman John 51
Betrayal of Youth 192,221,226-7

BHA See British Humanist Association
Bieber Irving 77,148,151,322,426
Billingham Nick 214
Billy Budd 51
Birk Baroness 128,434
Birnberg Benedict 434
Birth Control Campaign 211
Birtles Bill 216
Blachford Gregg 160-1
Black Sheila 434
Blackstone Baroness 55
Blake Peter 434
Blakelock PC 288
BLAZE (Australia) 450
Block, The 36
Bloomsbury Group 145
Blot 208
Blue Rabbi Lionel 117,182
Blunt Anthony 200
Bly Robert 322-8,330-1,405,423,426
BMA See British Medical Association
BMRB See British Market Research Bureau
Bogarde Dirk 18
Bogdanov Michael 435
Boguet Henry 265
Bond Ann 348
Bondi Sir Hermann 434
Bonhoeffer 409
Booth Chris 268
Boothby Lord 18
Borchgraef Guy 435
Boswell John 275,285,300-1
Bottomley Peter MP 127
Bottomley Rt Hon Virginia MP 125-6, 250,359-61
Bowis John MP 210,364
Boyle Katie 392,435
BPAS see British Pregnancy Advisory Service
Bradley Peter 170,172,214-5
Bragg Billy 435
Bragg Melvyn 435
Braine Rt Hon Sir Bernard 177
Branson Richard 369
Bratza Nicholas 26
Breaking the Silence 207
Brecht Bertolt 435
Bremner Peter 24,212,216,229
Brent Council 53
Brenton Howard 435
Brewer Joe 76
Brisby F H 315
British Association for Counselling 289
British Council of Churches 293

British Humanist Association 28, 51, 434ff
British Market Research Bureau 58-62,110-11,312
British Medical Association 17,177, 315-6
British Pregnancy Advisory Service 250,360,441
British Psychological Society 178
British Youth Council 210
Brittan Samuel 378
Broad Prof C D 156
Brogan Hugh 435
Bron Eleanor 435
Brongersma Edward 222
Brook Advisory Centres 51,62,211,225,392
Brophy Brigid 435
Brown Lewis 23
Brown Michael MP 361,363,435
Brown Richard K 435
Brown Ronald 213,340
Bruce Malcolm MP 435
Bruinvels Peter 49
Buchanan James 389
Buchanan Patrick 287
Buckmaster Viscount 49
Bucknell Patrick 199
Bunt Sidney 210
Burbidge Michael 170,207,214,216,222,224
Burke William 366,399
Burn Stephen 435
Burns Roy 2-3,10-11,32-33
Burton Dr Stephen 435
Busby Donald 206
Butler Josephine 13,221
Butler The Hon Mrs Lil 182,210,211
Butler-Schloss Judge 236
Byatt A S 435
BYC See British Youth Council
Byron 42
Callow Simon 22,51,117,128,435
Cambridge Council 55
Camden Council 47,52-3,223
Campaign Against Public Morals See Conspiracy Against Public Morals
Campaign for Homosexual Equality 9,28,38,167-70,204-15
Campaign for Homosexual Equality 223-4,277,336,339,347
Campaign for Nuclear Disarmament 51
Campaign for Real Education 428
Campbell Beatrix 238,242
Campbell Denis 48

Index of names, publications and organisations 471

Campbell Duncan 118,435
Campbell Menzies MP 435
Campbell Prof Colin 250,360
Campbell Prof Peter 5,128,435
Canning Gordon 435
Cant Bob 228
Canterbury Archbishop Carey 128,328,411-15
Canterbury Archbishop Runcie 55, 292-3
Capital Gay 35,82,99,201,30,310,32,62
CAPM See Conspiracy Against Public Morals
CARE Trust 333 See also Festival of Light
Carling Will 392
Carlisle John MP 128
Carpenter Edward 121,145,438
Carrington Matthew MP 337,363
Carter Angela 435
Carteret Anna 435
Casey Terry 63
Cashman Michael 128,164,348,436
Catholic Lesbian Sisterhood 48
Cauthery Dr Philip 21
Cave Dudley 142
Centre for Policy Studies 366
Centrepoint 56,181-2
CGHE See Conservative Group for Homosexual Equality
Chain Reactions 35
Challis Kathy 221
Chamberlain Wilt 109
Chambers Robin 436
Chandler Glenn 436
Changing the World 186
Chapman Graham 436
Chapman Richard 436
Charles Canon Edward 290
Chartham Dr Robert 21
CHE See Campaign for Homosexual Equality
Chelmsford Bishop of 55
Chesler Phyllis 259
Chichester Bishop of 55
Child Sexual Abuse 242
Childhood Rights 222-3
Childline 182,238
Childrens Legal Centre 223
Childright 223
Christian Action 290
Christian Action on AIDS 292,294
Christian CND 290
Christian Council on AIDS 292

Christian Peace Council 290
Christian Socialist Movement 290
Christians for Socialism 290
Christie Julie 436
Christie Sir George 436
Church in Danger 209
City Limits 230,238
Clare Anthony 436
Clark John 28
Clark Margi 436
Clark Michael 436
Clarke Rt Hon Kenneth MP 127,361-2
Clay Jill 48
Clements Judi 153
Clit Club 35
Clone Zone 37
Club on the Park 39
CND See Campaign for Nuclear Disarmament
Cobden Trust 206,211,225
COC (Holland) 197,214
Cohen Bronwen 251
Cohen Harry MP 340
Cohn Roy 113
COHSE 339
Colchester Council 55
Coleman Rt.Rev. Peter 285
Comfort Dr Alex 18
Coming Out 234
Comiskey Andy 327-30,333
Community Standards Association 214
Connolly Billy 436
Conservative Family Campaign 49,52,55,363
Conservative Group for Homosexual Equality 5,16,187,275
Conservative Party 358,360,364,366,374
Conspiracy Against Public Morals 212,215,261
Cook Nigel 86
Cook Robin MP 24,214,340,436
Cook Sue 238,240
Cooper Brian 290
Coote Anna 216,224,341
Cope Wendy 180
Corbyn Jeremy MP 347
Core Philip 34,436
Corey & Holmes 92
Cornell University 69
Cornes Ray 126
COSPEC 289-90
Cousins Jane 174-77,436
Cox Gill 8,392,436
Cox Tom MP 336

Coxon Dr Anthony P M 93,112,436
Crane Paul 26,337
Crisis in Masculinity 423
Crisp Quentin 76,141,149
Crossman Bob 172,214
Crowe Malcolm 171
Crowe Rev Tony 295
Crowley Aleister 21
Cullen John 286
Cullinan Edward 436
Cunningham Dr Jack MP 50
Cuomo Governor Mario 153
Currie Edwina MP 117,239,364,416
Cutbill Dr Jonathan 214,436
D H S S AIDS Unit 58
Dahmer Jeffrey 138
Daily Mail, The 193
Daily News, The 287
Daley Janet 218
Dannecker Martin 64-7,71-8,148, 156, 244
David Anna Joy 436
Davidson Alex 306
Davies Dr Peter 91,93,112
Davies Liz 122
de Beauvoir Simone 380-1
de Beus J G 403
De Jongh Nicholas 436
Deer Brian 436
DELGA See Democrats for Lesbian & Gay Action
Delors Jaques 348
Democrats for Lesbian & Gay Action 22,63,336
Derrick Deborah 224
Desart Lord 15
Desert Stream 330
Deshayes Catherine 264
Deviant Sexual Behaviour 314
Dibblin Jane 436
Dickens Geoffrey MP 436
Dickson Alec 436
Dickson Joan 436
Different Story, A: How to be a Lesbian in 35 Minutes 53,254
Diggory Peter 437
Dobson Frank MP 437
Dobson Malcolm 188
Donne John 357,412,418
Dowell Graham 437
Drabble Margaret 128,437
Dritz Selma 97
Dromey Jack 216
Dubs Alf 336
Dudgeon Jeffrey 25-6

Duesberg Prof Peter 100
Duhig Anna 214
Dunlop Canon Ian 354-5
Dunn Douglas 437
Dunn Ian 64,86,205,213-4,340,437
Durham Martin 358
Dworkin Ronald 437
Dyson A E 18,437
Ealing Council 48,54
Ealing Gay Youth Group 54
Eastenders 218
Ebbesen et al 66,73,87,91,94
Edgar David 437
Edinburgh Bishop of See Holloway Richard
EETPU 339
Eisenstein 258
Elliott Charlotte 282
Elliott Tony 437
Ellis Edith 145
Ellis Havelock 85,145-6
Elwyn Jones Lord 48
END See European Nuclear Disarmament
End Physical Punishment Of Children 223
English Collective of Prostitutes 48
Ennals Martin 216,437
EPOCH See End Physical Punishment Of Children
Equal Opportunities Commission 241,251
Erasure 437
European Nuclear Disarmament 291
Evans Dr Brian 123
Evans Matthew 51,437
Evening Standard, The 362
Ewart-Biggs Baroness 182,392,437
Exodus Ministries 329
Eysenck Prof Hans 152
Fag Rag 166
Falkland Viscount 22,51,55,63,336,348,437
Family & Youth Concern 214,379
Family Matters 180
Family Planning Association 62,392
Family Policy Studies Centre 367-8
Fanshawe Simon 128,348,392,437
Farley Lynn 437
Farthing Charles 437
Feinstein Mayor of San Francisco 119
Fell Hugh 181
Fellowship for Reconciliation 290
Felsenfeld Dr Oscar 97
Ferenczi 148

Index of names, publications and organisations 473

Fernbach David 234
Ferrer Judge 23
Festival of Light, Nationwide 214,306
  See also CARE Trust
Fettes Christopher 437
Field Frank MP 182
Field W T 17
Fielding Michael 290
Fitzgerald Penelope 437
Flew Prof Anthony 156,379,380
Follett Ken 437
Foot Lord 437
Foot Rt Hon Michael 392,438
Forster E M 42
Foster Joanna 241
Framed Youth 178-9
Fraser John MP 340
Fraser Lady Antonia 438
Frayn Michael 438
Freedman & Kaplan 151
Frenken Prof 212
Freud Sigmund 146-8
Freud Sir Clement 336,438
Friedan Betty 380
Friend 167,170,210
Frosch Dr Stephen 242-3
Fry Jane 435
Fulford Adrian 212,216
Fumento Michael 117
Furies, The 253
Furlong Monica 286
GAA See Gay Activists Alliance
GALHA See Gay And Lesbian
  Humanist Association
Galloway Bruce 70
Gallwey Dr John 175,438
Gambaccini Paul 438
Gateshead Law Centre 56
Gay Activists Alliance 220,234,337
Gay And Lesbian Humanist Association
  62,209
Gay Christian Movement. Renamed as
  Lesbian & Gay Christian Movement
Gay Community News 230,450
Gay Dr Martyn 184-5
Gay Guide to London See Kennedy's
Gay Left Collective
  30,122,61,91,202,207,234,337
Gay Lessons 52,179,210
Gay Liberation Front 3,8,10,152,167-
  9,191,207-12
Gay Liberation Front 220-2,231-5,242-
  3,250-4
Gay Liberation Front 306,340,361
Gay Liberation Front Manifesto 186

Gay Liberation in the Eighties 229
Gay Men's Press 43
Gay News 29-30, 192,208,210,212,
  214, 221
Gay News 224,234,401
Gay Report 167
Gay Scotland 205,340
Gay Sweatshop 48,121
Gay Switchboard
  164,167, 170,180,207,210,234
Gay Teachers Group
  48,164,170,225,291
Gay Teenage Group 160,169
Gay Times 36-43,53,75,82-6,297,314
Gay Youth Movement 160-70,208-
  10,214,229,291,336
Gaynoise 225
Gays the Word 43,192
GCM See Gay Christian Movement
Gebler Ernest 442
Gee Stephen 30,337
Gifford Lord 5,24-6,55
Gilbert & George 44
Gilbert Harriet 438
Gilbert W. Stephen 438
Gill Tess 216,224
Gillick Victoria 362
Giscombe Junior 438
GKN 56
Glaser Dr Danya 242-3
GLC See Greater London Council
GLC Lesbian & Gay Charter 6
GLF See Gay Liberation Front
Gloucester Bishop of See Yates John
Glover Dr Jane 438
GMBATU 339
GMP See Gay Men's Press
Goehr Alexander 438
Goldhill Flora 360
Goodhart Sir Philip 20
Gorman Teresa MP 381
Gough Jamie 171,228,230,233
Gould Bryan MP 225,438
Grant Bernie MP 50,340
Grant Larry 216
Grapevine 207
Gray Dr Harry 438
Greater London Council 2,39-47,104,
  159,186,201,250,337
Greaves Bernard 214,216,336
GRED (France) 214
Green Janet 121
Green John 158
Green Party 334-5,380
Green Richard 120

Green Robin 277,281
Greenpeace 220
Greenway Harry MP 54
Greenwich Council 53,56
Greer Germaine 381
Grey Anthony 18,209-210, 214, 216, 225,438
Grieg Noel 438
Griffith J A G 438
Griffiths Drew 438
Grimond Lord (Jo) 390-1,402
Grimshaw Jonathan 129
Grove David 214,222
GTG See Gay Teenage Group
Gulbenkian Foundation 216
Gummer Rt Hon John MP 413
GYM See Gay Youth Movement
Habgood John See York Archbishop
Hackney Council 48,53
Haldane Society of Socialist Lawyers 31,51,361
Halifax Noel 193-5
Hall Catherine 181
Hall Rt Rev Peter 128,438
Hallidie Smith Andrew 18
Halliwell Ken 64,130,132-3,198
Halsbury Lord 50
Hamilton Archie MP 20
Hammarskjold Dag 42
Hancock Sheila 117,438
Handsfield Dr Hunter 67,75
Hanscombe Gillian 438
Hanson Michael 205-6
Harbottle George 120
Hardy Stephen 198
Hare-Duke Bp Michael 290
Haringey Council 48-53, 140, 228, 288,291,337
Harman Harriet MP 216,337,341
Harris Barbara 286
Harris Peter 292
Harris Simon 83
Hart H L A 439
Hart John 35,38,142,158-9,171-4 244,253,310-2
Hartley Betty 23
Harvey Dr David 121
Haselden Rupert 115
Hattersley Rt Hon Roy MP 439
Hatton Chris see Winchelsea Lord
Hawkes Jacquetta See Priestly
Hayek Frederick von 368,370,374, 389-91,415
Hayhoe Barney 177
Hayman Suzie 62,392

Haywood Harold 210
Hazan Judge John 200
HEA See Health Education Authority
Healey Rt Hon Denis 439
Health Education Authority 108, 111, 123,177,179,211
Heaven Discotheque 34,369
Heley Dr Andrew 439
Helpline 180
Hemming Dr James 439
Henderson Lord 19,55,392
Hennegan Alison 439
Henry Lenny 439
Hensman Savitri 291
Hewitt Patricia 216,225,337,340-1
Hicks Prof Ruth 121
Higgs Dr Marietta 236-243
Higton Rev Tony 284-5,288,292
Him 37
Hind Kenneth MP 48
Hirschfield Magnus 146,148
HLRS See Homosexual Law Reform Society
Hobbes John 377
Hobbs Jane 238,242-3
Hockney David 43,51
Hodges Andrew 65,73,75,439
Hodson Philip 439
Hoffenberg Sir Raymond 127
Holloway Rev David 233,288
Holloway Rt Rev Richard: Bp of Edinburgh 214,439
Holroyd Michael 128,439
Holtom Elizabeth 221
Home Office 188-90
Homosexual Law Reform Society 18,28,209 Renamed as: Sexual Law Reform Society qv
Hooper Anne 439
Horned God, The 268
Horrocks Oliver 439
Hose Keith 204-9,214,216,220-2,226
Houghton Lord 55,392
Housman Laurence 221
Housmans Bookshop 220,2
How to be in Lesbian in 35 Minutes See "Different Story A"
Howard Jeanette 278,328-30,333
Howard Michael MP 55
Howard Sir Michael 439
Howie David 210
Hows Julian 214,225
Huddleston, Bishop Trevor 18,128
Hudson Rock 113,117
Hughes Anthony 208,220

Index of names, publications and organisations 475

Hughes Bob MP 439
Hughes Simon MP 439
Hume David 366,378-9
Humphries John 180
Hurcombe Linda 289
Hurd Rt Hon Douglas MP 241
Hurwitt Malcolm 216
Hutchinson Fay 211
Hutchinson Lord 55,158,439
Hutter David 65,73,75,439
Hutton Ceri 129
Hutton Jean 439
Huxley Julian 18,145
I know what I am 207
Icebreakers 207,210,222,234
IGA See International Gay Association
ILEA See Inner London Education Authority
ILEA London Youth Comm. 159
ILGA See International Lesbian & Gay Association
Independent Labour Party 208
Independent, The 51
Ingram Fr Michael 178,222
Inner London Education Authority 48-9,52
Institute for Public Policy Research 341,367
International Gay Association 211,214. Renamed as:
International Lesbian & Gay Association 27,203,214,288
International Times 23,84
Iona Community 290
IPPF See Planned Parenthood Federation of America
IPPR See Institute for Public Policy Research
Ironside Virginia 392,439
Irving Sir Charles 182
Isherwood Christopher 198,214
Ishiguro Kazuo 439
Islington Council 47,52
Islington Gay & Lesbian Centre 83
Issues in Human Sexuality 285
IT See International Times
Ivens Katie 428
Jacobs Clare 440
Jakobovits Lord 414
James Canon Eric 182,290,440
James Henry 42
Jarman Derek 112,444
Jarrett Prof Michael 204,223,440
Jay & Young 95
Jay Margaret 129

Jay Peter 128,440
JCGT See Joint Council for Gay Teenagers
Jeffrey Roland 214-6
Jeger Baroness 440
Jenkins of Hillhead Lord (Roy) 20,28
Jenkins of Putney Lord (Hugh) 440
Jenny lives with Eric & Martin 48,131
Joad David 223
Johnson Colin 222
Johnson Magic 109
Johnson Rev Malcolm 284-5
Joint Council for Gay Teenagers 170, 207,224
Jonas Peter 51,440
Jones Terry 440
Joseph Sir Keith 359
Josephs Wilfred 440
Joy David 24,212
Joy of Gay Sex, The 288
Joy of Lesbian Sex, The 288
Kallmann F J 150
Kaufman Rt Hon Gerald MP 440
Kaye Joanna 80,180
Kazantzis Judith 440
Kelly Beth 160
Kennedy Ian 129,440
Kennedy Ludovic 440
Kennedy's Gay Guide to London 35, 36,38-9,288
Kent Bruce 291
Kent-Baguley Peter 7-8,228
Kerr Brian 26
Kerridge Roy 38,84
Keynes John Maynard 42,145,198
Kidscape 197
Killing of Sister George, The 18
Kilroy-Silk Robert 51,113,440
Kincora Boys Home 200
Kinnock Glenys 348,392
Kinnock Rt Hon Neil MP 51,340-1, 367,369,392,440
Kinsey 58-61,101,153,161,244
Kirker Rev Richard 9,284,288-9,292-3
Kirkpatrick Fr Bill 128,157,182,440
Kirkwood Archie MP 440
Kirkwood Lord 440
Knight Dame Jill MP 50
Knussen Oliver 440
Koestner Richard 325
Kramer Larry 41-2
Kristol Irving 399,382,401
Kroll Una 289
Kureishi Hanif 440
L&GCM See Lesbian and Gay Christian

Movement
Labouchere Henry 14
Labour Campaign for Lesbian & Gay Rights 7,228-30,339,346-356
Labour Gay Rights Manifesto 229,346-356
Labour Party 336,340-1,346,373
Lafitte Francis 441
Lake Dr Tony 441
Lambert Dr 275-6
Lambeth Council 47,52-4,208,253
Lambeth Mission 290
Lawrence Sir Ivan MP 364
Layland Joyce 181
LCL&GR See Labour Campaign for Lesbian & Gay Rights
le Fanu Dr James 123
Le Fanu Mark 441
Le Vay Simon 77-8,158
Lear Edward 43
Leech Kenneth 441
Leeds Council 55
Leicester 48,178,201,210
Leigh Mike 441
Lemon Denis 210,224
Leonardo da Vinci 42
Lesbian & Gay Employment Rights 337
Lesbian & Gay Socialist 228,338
Lesbian and Gay Christian Movement 10,72,192,249,279-98,295,303
Lesbian Herpes Sufferers 48
Lesbian Line 8,164,167
Lesbian Nuns 288
Lester Jim MP 441
Lestor Joan MP 117,182,336
Leveller, The 222
Levey Sir Michael 441
Levin Bernard 41-3
Lewis Cecil Day 18
Lewisham Council 53,201
LGTG See London Gay Teenage Group
Liberal Democrats 349,352
Liberal Party 374
Libertine, The 222
Liberty See National Council for Civil Liberties
Licarpa Mick 229-30
Lincoln Abraham 397
Linken Dr Arnold 441
Lipman Maureen 441
Living Waters 330
Livingstone Ken MP 41,53,117,201,340,347,392
Llewelyn-Davies Baroness 392,441
Lloyd John 220,337
Lobel Kerry 136
Locke Thomas 377
Locke Trevor 204,211,214
London Bishop of 55
London Gay Teenage Group 75,159-70,207,223-5,291
London Labour Party Lesbian & Gay Section 337
London Lesbian & Gay Centre 38,48
London School of Economics 3,340
Longford Lady see Packenham
Lorca 42
Lots of Mommies 263
LSE See London School of Economics
Lucas Henry 138
Lumley Joanna 392,441
Lumsden Andrew 48,434,441
Lunniss Steve 223
Lupo Michele 137
Luther King Martin 367
MacCarthy Joseph 113
Macdougall Richi 166
MacLennan Robert MP 335-6
MacLeod Lord 206
MacManus Dr Tom 109
Macourt Malcolm 93,168-9, 187, 193,298
McCance Richard 215
McCary 158
McCrum Robert 441
McDougall Richie 115
McEwan Ian 441
McGrath Tom 23
McKee Glenn 169
McKellen Sir Ian 56,348,363,441
McKenzie Neil 197-8
McKerrow Graham 139,441
McKusick et al 67,75-6,92
McLean Iain S 441
McLeod Sheila 441
McManus Dr Tom 93,110,112
McMullen Richie 157,182,192
McNair Lord 441
Mcnair Mike 171,229-30,233,339,347
McVicar John 39-40
Magnuson Roger 3-4,89,95,167,313,344-6,420
Magpie 208,210,225-6
Mainstream 290
Maitland Sara 289
Major Rt Hon John MP 362-3,366
Make it Happy 162,174-5
Man Isle of 27
Manchester Bishop of 29,55
Manchester Council 48

Manchester Gay Centre 181
Mann Jonathan 293
Mapplethorpe Robert 45
Marks Dr Isaac 152
Markus Kate 441
Marland Michael 49
Marlowe Christopher 42
Mars-Jones Adam 441
Marshall John 145,149,314,441
Marxism Today 238
Mason Gabriel 123
Mason Michael 441
Masters & Johnson 153,245
Masters Roy 397,404,410
Mathurin Jean-Thierry 138
Matthews Anne 253
Maugham Somerset 77
Meacher Michael MP 129,441
Meade Michael 326
Medical News 178
Melchett Lord 55,206,441
Mellish Lord 48
Mellor Bob 3
Mellor David MP 364
Melville Arabella 222
Melville Herman 42
Mercury Freddie 125,361,394
Metropolitan Community Church 182,296
Michelangelo 42-3
Middleton Warren 207,226
Midweek 56
Mildmay Hospice 293
Miles Dame Margaret 441
Milk Harvey 40
Milkman's On His Way, The 52
Mill John Stuart 377-8
Miller Dr David 158,442
Miller Victor 139
Millett Kate 227
Milligan Donald 152
Miln Barnaby 292-3
MIND 56,153,209,215,226
Mind Out 226
Minor Problems 197,204,207,229,230
Mister 39
Mitchell Adrian 442
Mitchell Juliet 341
Mitchell Pam 247-8,253
Mitchell Prof William 390-1
Moberly Dr Elizabeth 154-5,298-309, 318-9,321-2
Mollenkott Virginia 274
Molloy Lord 48
Molyneux John 231-2,379-380

Monkswell Lord 55
Monson Lord 48
Montagnier Dr Luc 100
Moody Roger 207-8,221-223,229-230
Morin Dr 67,151
Morreau Jacqueline 442
Morrison Blake 442
Moscone George 40
Mother Teresa 287
Mothers Union 183
Movement for the Ordination of Women 286
Mumford, Philip & Margery 221
Munyard Terry 26,215
Murdoch Dame Iris 18,442
Murname Michael 442
Murray Charles 385
Myers Boyd 432
NAC See National Abortion Campaign
NACCAN 291
Nagle Matt 401
NALGO 336,338
NAMBLA See North American Man-Boy Love Association
Namjoshi Suniti 442
NAPO 336
NARAL 397
NARAL (USA) See National Abortion Rights Action League
NAS/UWT 63
Nash C L 190
Nash Roger See Bremner Peter
NATFHE 220,228
Nathan Dr Peter 442
Nathanson Bernard 398
National Abortion Campaign 215,360
National Abortion Rights Action League 397
National Association of Citizens Advice Bureaux 56
National Association of Youth Clubs 210-211
National Council for Voluntary Youth Services 210
National Children's Homes 113-4
National Council for Civil Liberties 26-31,51-5,170,186,206-8, 211,214-6,221-6,234,289,337,340,347
National Council for One Parent Families 224
National Endowment for the Arts (USA) 45
National Friend Ltd. 168
National Health Service 390
National Organisation of Women (USA)

8
National Secular Society 29,51,221
National Union of School Students 208
National Youth Bureau 210-211,228
NAYC See National Association of Youth Clubs
NCCL See National Council for Civil Liberties
NCH See National Children's Homes
NCOPF See National Council for One Parent Families
NCU 339
NCVYS See National Council for Voluntary Youth Services
Neuberger Julia 117,129,182,336,392,442
Neve Michael 442
New Statesman, The 48 238
Newham Council 52,56
Newsnight 22
NGA 339
Nicholson Emma MP 363
NIGRA See Northern Ireland Gay Rights Associatic·ı
Nilson Dennis 138
Norris Stephanie 442
Norris Steven MP 363,442
North American Man-Boy Love [sic] Association 196,203,214
Northern Ireland Gay Rights Association 24
Norwood Graham 47
Nottingham Council 48,56
Novak Michael 371-6,82-6,389-402,409-10
NOW (USA) See National Organisation of Women (USA)
NSPCC 238-9,332
Nunn Trevor 442
NUPE 338
NUR 339
NUSS See National Union of School Students
NYB See National Youth Bureau
O'Brien Edna 442
O'Carroll Tom 24,178,193,209,212, 215-6,220-5,444
O'Connor Cardinal John 287-8
Oakley Ann 265
Observer, The 51
Oestreicher Rev Paul 291
Ogg Derek 86,214
Oldfield Sir Maurice 5,198
OLGA See Organisation for Lesbian & Gay Action

Olson Mancur 389
One for Christian Renewal 290
One World Movement 290
Order of Christian Unity 214
Organisation for Lesbian & Gay Action 227,289,347
Ortleb Charles 118
Orton Joe 64-6,73,130-3,49,65-6,198
Osborne June 285
Out of Egypt 329
Outrage 10,181,227,233,333,361
Owen Rt Hon Dr David 442
Owen Stephen 406
Oxford Alex 211
Oxley Charles 212
Packenham Elizabeth 18
Paedophile Action for Liberation 208-16,220-2,234,337
Paedophile Information Exchange 23-4,30,84,163,171,192-8, 203-216,220-229,336,339
Paedophilia the Radical Case 193,209,225
Paine Thomas 377
PAL See Paedophile Action for Liberation
Palaver 208
Palmer Tony 442
Panosian & Gorbach 90,97
Parents Enquiry 72,164-84, 207, 291, 421
Parr Doris Seddon 442
Parratt John See Middleton Warren
Parris Matthew 348,442
Parry Glenys 205
Partridge Nick 121-2
Patten Rt Hon Chris 368-9
Patten Rt Hon John MP 128,412
Paulin Thierry 138
Pax Christi 291
Payne Christopher 181
Payne Leanne 254-6,307-8,318-25,423
Peace News 23,220-2,268,290,298
Pearce Edward 442
Peluso Richard 203
People, The 208
Perring Dr Michael 442
Perry Chris 336
Perspectives on Paedophilia 193,201
Pet Shop Boys 442
Petherbridge Edward 442
Petronio Stephen 436
Philpott Kent 300
PIE See Paedophile Information Exchange

Index of names, publications and organisations 479

Pilot 332
Pimlott Ben 51,442
Pink Paper 56,82-3,309
Pink Plaque Guide 43
Pink Triangles 161,228,247,253
Pinter Harold 129,439,442
Pipes Mary 263
Pithers David 114
Pittenger Prof Norman 72,272,277, 303-5,442
Planned Parenthood Federation of America 381
Plaskitt James 442
Plato 42
Plummer Dr Kenneth 153,192
Politics of Mental Health, The 242
Politics of Psychoanalysis, The 242
Pollard Nettie 193,214-5,225
Ponsonby Lord 442
Porter Cole 42
Potts Jonathan 120
Power Lisa 28,443
Pregnant at School 224
Prejudice & Pride 281,289
Prescott John MP 443
Presland Eric 227
Priestley (nee Hawkes) Jacquetta 18,443
Priestley J B 18
Prince's Trust 56
Princedale Trust 206
Private Eye 258,296
Professional Association of Teachers 54
Proops Marjorie 8,392
Prothero Barry 337
Proust 42
Puddephat Andrew 31
Purvis Libby 149
Quaker Socialist Society 290
Queensberry Marquess of 443
Quest 292
Quinton Lord 443
Radcliffe-Ludlam Peter 187
Radice Giles MP 49
Raeburn Anna 8,392
Raine Craig 443
Rainer Foundation 56
Rampton David 121
Rank Organisation 18
Rant Judge James 31
Rantzen Esther 182,238
Raphael Adam 443
Rattle Simon 117,129,443
Ravel 43

Rayner Claire 62,117,180,2,5,209,348,92,443
Raynsford Nick MP 337
Reading Matters 228
Rechy John 69
Redgrave Vanessa 117
Reed Bruce 443
Reel Bill 287
Reeves Donald 291,443
Reeves Prof Tom 188,196
Reid Christopher 443
Reid Gavin 277-8
Reisman Judith & Eichel Edward 59,60
Relate 239
Release 206-7,225
Rendezvous & Gay Amie 82,84
Responsible Society See Family and Youth Concern
Reuben David 76,152
Rich Dr Jennifer 443
Richard Emily 443
Richardson Dr Diana 153
Richardson Jo MP 216,223,336,339,443
Riches Valerie 127,379
Richmond-on-Thames Council 56
Righton Peter 193
Rights of Man 377
Ripon Bishop of 50
Rising Free 208
Ritner Luke 51
Road to Serfdom, The 379
Robert Doctor 443
Roberts Dr Raine 237-8
Roberts Sadie 443
Robertson Geoffrey QC 216
Robertson Rose 170,183
Robinson Kenneth 443
Robinson Tim 139
Robinson Tom 173,443
Robson-Scott Markie 41
Rochester Bishop of 55
Roeloffs Sarah 337
Rogers Deborah 443
Rogers Ric 210
Rolph C H 443
Ropke William 382,400-1,419
Rose Margaret 443
Rosenthal Jack 443
Ross of Newport Lord 443
Rossman Parker 192-3
Rothschild Hon Miriam 443
Rothschild Teresa 18
Rousseau 196
Routledge Kegan Paul 268

Rowan John 268
Rowe Andrew MP 363
Royal Princess 126
Rubinstein Michael 443
Ruddock Joan MP 340
Ruddock Julian 443
Rueda Enrique 136
Rumbold Rt Hon Dame Angela MP 359-60
Russell Bertrand 18
Russell Willy 443
SAM See Scottish AIDS Monitor
Sandell Richard 444
Sanger Margaret 145,380-1
Sartorius Dr 153-4
Sattentau Dr Q J 444
Savage Richard 214
Say Yes,Say No,Say Maybe 392
Scales Prunella 444
Scanzoni Letha 274
SCCL See Scottish Council for Civil Liberties
Scene 210,228
Schlesinger John 444
Schofield Dr Michael 182,206,216,225,444
Schumpeter Joseph 382,394,399
SCM See Student Christian Movement
Scorer Catherine 216
Scott Dorothy 444
Scott Rev Dr John 281
Scottish AIDS Monitor 362
Scottish Council for Civil Liberties 213
Scottish Homosexual Rights Group 160,4,171,8,205,213,311. Was:
Scottish Minorities Group 210,222
Scrivener Anthony 182
Scruton Roger 374,417
Seale Dr John 107,109,123-4
Seaton Jean 442
Seear Baroness 55,392,444
Selby Rt Rev Peter 281
Sewell Brian 44
Sex & God 289
Sex for Beginners 177
Sexual experience between men and boys 192
Sexual Law Reform Society 28,170,176,209,211. Was Homosexual Law Reform Society qv
Sexual Minorities (MIND Conference) 226
Shapira Miriam 214
Shea Alan 27
Shearer Moira 440

Sheldon Rev Louis 333
Shelter 56
Sheppard Dick 221
Sherman Martin 444
Sherrin Ned 129,444
Shiers John 40,141
Shively Charley 69,71,89,115
Short Clare MP 340
SHRG See Scottish Homosexual Rights Group
SIGMA Project (Cardiff Univ) 109, 111-2,360
Silverman Dr Mervyn 118-9
Simon of Cyrene Sanctuary Project 116-7
Sisters of Perpetual Indulgence 10,113, 233,140
Skeates Jane 223
Skelly James 286
Skynner Robin 327
Slipman Sue 216
SLRS See Sexual Law Reform Society
SMG See Scottish Minorities Group
Smith Adam 366,374,377-8,399
Smith Chris MP 7-8,129,182,340,444
Smith Prof Tom 61,63
Smith Rt Hon John MP 444
Smith Steven 24,212,221,226
Smoker Barbara 444
Smythe Tony 210,216,226,444
Sobran Joseph 117-8
Socarides Charles 6,80,154,218
Social & Liberal Democrat 335
Social Affairs Unit 425
Socialist Workers Party 193
Socrates 42
SOGAT 339
Soley Clive MP 336
Solzhenitsyn Alexander 395
Somerville Jimi 129,444
Something to tell you 159
Sonnabend Yolanda 444
Soper Lord (Donald) 18,55,221,444-5
Southwark Bishop of 295
Southwark Council 53,201,253
Spare Rib 162
Spartacus International Gay Guide 201
Speaking Out on Woman/Girl Love 160
Spectator, The 180,412
Speijer Report 211
Spencer Liz 445
Spencer Tom 445
Spender Stephen 18,172
Spong Bishop John 286-7
Squire Robin MP 174-5,348,363,445

Index of names, publications and organisations 481

Sreeves Mark 172
St John of Fawsley Lord 19
Stafford J Martin 68,75,156-7,179
Stanbrook Ivor 49-50
Steed Michael 336
Steel Rt Hon Sir David MP 18-19, 214, 392,445
Steinam Gloria 380-1
Stevens Chief Supt Peter 137
Stonewall Bar and riot 2
Stonewall Lobby Group 63,116,343,346-354,361
Stopes Marie 145
Stoppard Miriam 5,80,392
Storr Anthony 255-6,322,324-5
Story of O, The 37
Stott Rev Dr John 274,278-9,281,305
Strathclyde Council 55
Straw Jack MP 445
Streetwise Youth 51,157,182,336
Stride Eddy 293
Stringer Graham 445
Student Christian Movement 290
Stuttaford Dr Thomas 124
Stutter John 120
Summerskill Ben 309
Sunday Mail, The 213
Sunday People, The 215
Support 421
Suttie Angus 207
Suzman Janet 129,392,445
Swash Bob 445
Swift Michael 450
Swinton Lord 48-9
Swinton Tilda 445
Switchboard See Gay Switchboard
Swyer Gerald 146,148
Szasz Thomas 428
T&GWU 338
Tatchell Peter 136-7,152,227
Tate Tim 200
Taylor Barbara 118-9
Taylor Dr Brian 193,446
Taylor Matthew MP 445
Taylor Prof John 21
Taylor Prof Laurie 40
Taylor Simon 86
Tchaikovsky 42-3
Tebbit Rt Hon Norman 358
Terrence Higgins Trust 34-5,65,68, 81-87,101,108,117,119-123, 126-7,288,292,369,392-3
Thatcher Rt Hon Margaret 50,179,341,358,360- 368,391,398,412

That's Life 238
Thomas Daffyd Ellis 340
Thomas Neil 117
Thompson Rt Rev James 445
Thomson Ross 215
Thorneycroft Bill 172
THT See Terrence Higgins Trust
Tielman Prof Rob 153
Tillet Jeffrey 445
Time for Consent 272
Tingle Rachel 50,179,210
Tippet Sir Michael 445
Tomalin Claire 445
Toole Otis 138
TORCHE See Tory Campaign for Homosexual Equality
Tordoff Lord 210,445
Tory Campaign for Homosexual Equality 363
Townsend Cyril MP 30
Toye Wendy 445
Toynbee Polly 263
Travell Richard 229
Trevelion Roy 445
Trevelyan John 21
Tribe David 216
Trimmer Eric 177-8
Tripp C A 151
Trollettes, The 38
True Freedom Trust 332
Tsang Daniel 115,193,229
TUC 336
Tuchfeld John 216
Tucker Clifford 445
Tullock Gordon 389
Tumim Judge Steven 182
Turning Alan 446
Two of Us, The 184-5,296
UCATT 339
UCW 339
Uhrig Larry 296-7
Ulrichs Carl Heinrich 144,146
Understanding Abortion 263
Understanding Paedophilia 192
Urban Theology Unit 290
USDAW 339
VALA See Viewers and Listeners Association
Van Baal 195
Van Wyk & Geist 59-61,66,161-6, 181,244 248,262,427
Varah Rev Chad 21
Vaz Keith MP 340
Vernon Jeff 170,229,336
VES See Voluntary Euthanasia Society

Victim 18
Vidal Gore 214
Viewers and Listeners Association 214
Voluntary Euthanasia Society 211
von Krafft-Eding Richard 145
Vulcan 37
Wales Princess of 116
Walker Bill MP 362
Wallace Jim MP 445
Wallace Rev Martin 53
Walmsley & White 190
Walter Aubrey 3,234,306
Walter Nicolas 445
Walters Jonathan 170,207,215,229
Waltham Forest Council 56
Wander Michelene 445
Warner Nigel 28-9
Watney Simon 121-2
WCC See World Council of Churches
Webster-Gardiner Graham 55
Weeks Jeffrey 38,165,172-3,207,378
Weir Gillian 445
Welland Colin 445
Weller Paul 445
Wells Dee 434
Wells H G 145
Wells Richard 445
Wesker Arnold 445
West Prof Donald James 34,148,182,190,193,225,446
West Timothy 444
West-Meades Zelda 239
Westwood Gordon 444
Wheatcroft Geoffrey 117
Wheeler Sir John MP 363-4
Whelan Robert 393
Whitaker Ben 216
White Dan 140
White Dr Maurice 40
Whitehead Tony 121,182
Whitehouse Mary 29-30,150,188, 209-10,225
Whitemore Hugh 446
Whitman Walt 42
WHO See World Health Organisation
Wicks Malcolm MP 367-8
Wiggins David 446
Wilde Oscar 14-5,43
Willans Angela 62,209,392,446
Willetts David MP 366
Williams & Weinberg 77
Williams Derek 121
Williams Jill 446
Williams Kenneth 132
Williams Robert 286-7
Williams Rt.Hon Shirley 208,446
Williams Tennessee 42
Wilshire David MP 50,218
Winchelsea & Nottghm.Lord 446
Winstanley Lord 392
Winterton Nicholas MP 64
Wise Audrey MP 29
Wistrich Dr Enid 446
Wogan Terry 392
Wolf Deborah 245-6,252,259-60
Wolfenden Committee 17-8,315,322
Women & Madness 259
Wood Audrey 446
Wood Robin 446
Wood Victoria 129,392,446
Wooton Baroness (Barbara) 18,223
World Council of Churches 213,290,293
World Health Organisation 293
Wragg Arthur 221
Wyatt Dr Geoffrey 236-243
Wyllie Andrew 171
Wynne Geoffrey 238,242-3
Yaffe Maurice 446
Yates Rt Rev John Bp of Gloucester 50,55,284
Yentob Alan 446
Yip David 129,446
York Archbishop of (Rt Rev John Habgood) 55,292
York Susannah 129,392,446
Youle Dr Michael 446
Young Gay and Proud 53
Young Nigel 228,337
Younger George 86
Zephaniah Benjamin 446
Zipper 37,39